Monographs in Computer Science

Editors

David Gries
Fred B. Schneider

Springer
New York
Berlin
Heidelberg
Hong Kong
London
Milan
Paris
Tokyo

Monographs in Computer Science

Abadi and Cardelli, **A Theory of Objects**

Benosman and Kang [editors], **Panoramic Vision: Sensors, Theory, and Applications**

Broy and Stølen, **Specification and Development of Interactive Systems: FOCUS on Streams, Interfaces, and Refinement**

Brzozowski and Seger, **Asynchronous Circuits**

Cantone, Omodeo, and Policriti, **Set Theory for Computing: From Decision Procedures to Declarative Programming with Sets**

Castillo, Gutiérrez, and Hadi, **Expert Systems and Probabilistic Network Models**

Downey and Fellows, **Parameterized Complexity**

Feijen and van Gasteren, **On a Method of Multiprogramming**

Leiss, **Language Equations**

McIver and Morgan [editors], **Programming Methodology**

Misra, **A Discipline of Multiprogramming: Programming Theory for Distributed Applications**

Nielson [editor], **ML with Concurrency**

Paton [editor], **Active Rules in Database Systems**

Selig, **Geometrical Methods in Robotics**

Annabelle McIver
Carroll Morgan
Editors

Programming Methodology

With 68 Figures

Annabelle McIver
Department of Computing
Macquarie University
Sydney 2109, Australia
anabel@ics.mq.edu.au

Carroll Morgan
Department of Computer Science
  and Engineering
The University of New South Wales
Sydney 2052, Australia
carrollm@cse.unsw.edu.au

Series Editors:
David Gries
Department of Computer Science
The University of Georgia
415 Boyd Graduate Studies
  Research Center
Athens, GA 30602-7404, USA

Fred B. Schneider
Department of Computer Science
Cornell University
Upson Hall
Ithaca, NY 14853-7501, USA

Library of Congress Cataloging-in-Publication Data
McIver, Annabelle   1964–
    Programming methodology/Annabelle McIver, Carroll Morgan.
      p.   cm.—(Monographs in computer science)
    Includes bibliographical references and index.
    ISBN 0-387-95349-3 (alk. paper)
    1. Computer programming.   I. Morgan, Carroll, 1952–.   II. Title.   III. Series.
QA76.6 .M3235 2002
005.1—dc21   2002017377

ISBN 0-387-95349-3   Printed on acid-free paper.

© 2003 Springer-Verlag New York, Inc.
All rights reserved. This work may not be translated or copied in whole or in part without the written permission of the publisher (Springer-Verlag New York, Inc., 175 Fifth Avenue, New York, NY 10010, USA), except for brief excerpts in connection with reviews or scholarly analysis. Use in connection with any form of information storage and retrieval, electronic adaptation, computer software, or by similar or dissimilar methodology now known or hereafter developed is forbidden.
The use in this publication of trade names, trademarks, service marks, and similar terms, even if they are not identified as such, is not to be taken as an expression of opinion as to whether or not they are subject to proprietary rights.

Printed in the United States of America.

9 8 7 6 5 4 3 2 1   SPIN 10849846

Typesetting: Pages created by authors using a Springer T_EX macro package.

www.springer-ny.com

Springer-Verlag   New York Berlin Heidelberg
A member of BertelsmannSpringer Science+Business Media GmbH

Preface

The second half of the twentieth century saw an astonishing increase in computing power; today computers are unbelievably faster than they used to be, they have more memory, they can communicate routinely with remote machines all over the world — and they can fit on a desktop. But, despite this remarkable progress, the voracity of modern applications and user expectations still pushes technology right to the limit. As hardware engineers build ever-more-powerful machines, so too must software become more sophisticated to keep up.

Medium- to large-scale programming projects need teams of people to pull everything together in an acceptable timescale. The question of how programmers understand their own tasks, and how they fit together with those of their colleagues to achieve the overall goal, is a major concern. Without that understanding it would be practically impossible to realise the commercial potential of our present-day computing hardware.

That programming has been able to keep pace with the formidable advances in hardware is due to the similarly formidable advances in the principles for design, construction and organisation of programs. The efficacy of these methods and principles speaks for itself — computer technology is all-pervasive — but even more telling is that they are beginning to feed back and influence hardware design as well. The study of such methods is called *programming methodology*, whose topics range over system- and domain-modelling, concurrency, object orientation, program specification and validation.

That is the theme of this collection.

Programming Methodology

Most systems today aim to be secure, robust, easy-to-use and timely. To achieve these aims the programmer needs the right tools, which in this context are "intellectually-based", and comprise techniques to help organise complex problems and express them in a way that can be both understood by developers and interpreted by machines.

The desire to reduce complexity (or at least to hide it where possible) has been the driving force behind the invention of design methods and principles, many of which are now built in to popular programming languages and (automatic) program-development tools. Typed languages for instance help with error detection, and the object-oriented programming method and data abstraction (both present for example in Java) support program modification, programming at the interface-level and readability. Meanwhile concurrency has flourished with the introduction of concurrent languages together with formal tools, including the model-checkers and proof assistants which are used in validation.

Many of these tools have at their heart impressive theoretical credentials — "assertions" and "program invariants" rely on a theory of programming logics; and specification and refinement techniques have program semantics at their basis. The essays in this collection concentrate on new and emerging techniques for constructing modern applications; they deal with the problems that software designers face and propose practical solutions together with their theoretical foundations.

The idea of assembling papers on this theme to form a book arose in the technical meetings of the members of the Working Group 2.3 of the International Federation for Information Processing (IFIP).

Working Group 2.3

The working groups of IFIP meet regularly to discuss new ideas — their own, and others' — and to evaluate and promote trends in many aspects of computing systems. Their official output varies widely between individual groups, and depends largely on the traditions and style of the current membership, though they frequently promote special courses and host conferences.

The term "programming methodology" was coined by one of the members of WG2.3, and over the group's nearly thirty years of existence, its members have contributed to many of the topics mentioned above; and indeed many flourishing areas of research in programming methodology today are based on ideas which were once discussed and developed in WG2.3 meetings.

This Collection

The present volume represents the second official publication by the group. Our aim was to gather material which would attract both students and professionals working either in an academic or industrial environment. Indeed we hope that this collection will form a reference and guide to the front line of research activity in programming methodology.

The range of subjects reflects the interests of the current membership and addresses in particular the problems associated with contemporary demands for highly complex applications that actually work. Many of the essays contain new material, highlighting specific theoretical advances, whilst others aim to review or evaluate a particular area, or to outline suggestive problems for further investigation.

Structure

The book comprises three parts, each one devoted to a major theme in programming methodology. The parts are further divided into subsections where essays focussing on a particular topic lying within the scope of its overall section are gathered together. The short introductions at the beginning of each subsection serve to set the scene for the detailed articles to follow.

Systems may be complex because they are distributed over a network, or because they are time-critical or concurrent — the first part deals with the business of describing, modelling and analysing such systems. The second part concentrates on specific programming techniques, the "programmer's toolkit", whilst the final part elaborates on some topical applications including security and telephony.

Acknowledgments

It goes without saying that this book would have been impossible to put together without the creative work of the authors of the articles. We thank especially Natarajan Shankar (chairman of WG2.3) for the initial motivation for this project and David Gries for help in its realisation.

Annabelle McIver
Carroll Morgan
Sydney, Australia, 2002

IFIP WG2.3 dedicates this book to the fond memory of two of its founding members:

*Ole-Johan Dahl (1931–2002)
and
Edsger Wybe Dijkstra (1930–2002)*

Contents

Preface   v

Contributors   xv

Part I   Models and correctness   1

A   Concurrency and interaction   3

1   Wanted: a compositional approach to concurrency   5
C.B. Jones
- 1.1   Compositionality   5
- 1.2   The essence of concurrency is interference   7
- 1.3   Reasoning about interference   8
- 1.4   Some problems with assumption/commitment reasoning   10
- 1.5   The role of ghost variables   11
- 1.6   Granularity concerns   12
- 1.7   Atomicity as an abstraction, and its refinement   12
- 1.8   Conclusion   13
- References   13

2   Enforcing behavior with contracts   17
Ralph-Johan Back and Joakim von Wright
- 2.1   Introduction   17
- 2.2   Contracts   19
- 2.3   Achieving goals with contracts   27
- 2.4   Enforcing behavioral properties   33
- 2.5   Analyzing behavior of action systems   39
- 2.6   Verifying enforcement   43
- 2.7   Conclusions and related work   50
- References   51

B Logical approaches to asynchrony — 53

3 Asynchronous progress — 57
Ernie Cohen
- 3.1 Introduction — 57
- 3.2 Programs — 59
- 3.3 Achievement — 61
- 3.4 Decoupling — 63
- 3.5 Example — Loosely-coupled programs — 64
- 3.6 Asynchronous safety — 65
- 3.7 Caveats — 66
- 3.8 Conclusions — 67
- 3.9 Acknowledgements — 68
- References — 68

4 A reduction theorem for concurrent object-oriented programs — 69
Jayadev Misra
- 4.1 Introduction — 69
- 4.2 The Seuss programming notation — 71
- 4.3 A model of Seuss programs — 78
- 4.4 Restrictions on programs — 80
- 4.5 Compatibility — 83
- 4.6 Proof of the reduction theorem — 87
- 4.7 Concluding remarks — 91
- References — 91

C Systems and real time — 93

5 Abstractions from time — 95
Manfred Broy
- 5.1 Introduction — 95
- 5.2 Streams — 96
- 5.3 Components as functions on streams — 99
- 5.4 Time abstraction — 100
- 5.5 Conclusions — 104
- References — 106

6 A predicative semantics for real-time refinement — 109
Ian Hayes
- 6.1 Background — 109
- 6.2 Language and semantics — 111
- 6.3 An example — 124
- 6.4 Repetitions — 126
- 6.5 Timing-constraint analysis — 129

6.6	Conclusions	131
	References	132

D Specifying complex behaviour   135

7 Aspects of system description   137
Michael Jackson
- 7.1 Introduction 137
- 7.2 Symbol manipulation 138
- 7.3 The Machine and the World 140
- 7.4 Describing the World 144
- 7.5 Descriptions and models 147
- 7.6 Problem decomposition and description structures 153
- 7.7 The scope of software development 156
- 7.8 Acknowledgements 158
- References 159

8 Modelling architectures for dynamic systems   161
Peter Henderson
- 8.1 Introduction 161
- 8.2 Models of dynamic systems 163
- 8.3 Architectures for reuse 168
- 8.4 Conclusions 172
- References 173

9 "What is a method?" — an essay on some aspects of domain engineering   175
Dines Bjørner
- 9.1 Introduction 175
- 9.2 Method and Methodology 178
- 9.3 Domain Perspectives and Facets 181
- 9.4 Conclusion 199
- References 201

Part II Programming techniques   205

E Object orientation   207

10 Object-oriented programming and software development — a critical assessment   211
Manfred Broy
- 10.1 Introduction 211

	10.2	Object orientation — its claims and its limitations	212
	10.3	Object-oriented programming — a critique	214
	10.4	Object-oriented analysis and design — a critique	219
	10.5	Concluding remarks	220
	References		220

11 A trace model for pointers and objects — 223
C.A.R. Hoare and He Jifeng

	11.1	Introduction: the graph model	223
	11.2	The trace model	229
	11.3	Applications	236
	11.4	Conclusion	242
	References		243

12 Object models as heap invariants — 247
Daniel Jackson

	12.1	Snapshots and object models	249
	12.2	Object-model examples	250
	12.3	A relational logic	253
	12.4	Diagrams to logic	255
	12.5	Textual annotations	258
	12.6	Discussion	260
	References		266

13 Abstraction dependencies — 269
K. Rustan M. Leino and Greg Nelson

	13.1	Introduction	269
	13.2	On the need for data abstraction	270
	13.3	Validity as an abstract variable	272
	13.4	Definition of notation	273
	13.5	Example: Readers	278
	13.6	Related work	285
	13.7	Conclusions	286
	References		287

F Type theory — 291

14 Type systems — 293
Benjamin C. Pierce

	14.1	Type systems in computer science	293
	14.2	What are type systems good for?	295
	14.3	History	300
	References		301

15 What do types mean? — From intrinsic to extrinsic semantics   309
John C. Reynolds
- 15.1 Syntax and typing rules 310
- 15.2 An intrinsic semantics 312
- 15.3 An untyped semantics 314
- 15.4 Logical relations 315
- 15.5 Bracketing 321
- 15.6 An extrinsic PER semantics 323
- 15.7 Further work and future directions 326
- 15.8 Acknowledgements 326
- References 326

Part III   Applications and automated theories   329

G   Putting theories into practice by automation   331

16 Automated verification using deduction, exploration, and abstraction   333
Natarajan Shankar
- 16.1 Models of computation 335
- 16.2 Logics of program behavior 337
- 16.3 Verification techniques 339
- 16.4 Abstractions of programs and properties 341
- 16.5 Verification methodology 347
- 16.6 Conclusions 348
- References 348

17 An experiment in feature engineering   353
Pamela Zave
- 17.1 Feature-oriented specification 353
- 17.2 The challenge of feature engineering 354
- 17.3 A feature-oriented specification technique 356
- 17.4 A modest method for feature engineering 359
- 17.5 An application of the method 370
- 17.6 Evaluation of the method 375
- 17.7 Acknowledgments 376
- References 376

xiv   Contents

H   Programming circuits   379

18   High-level circuit design   381
Eric C.R. Hehner, Theodore S. Norvell, and Richard Paige
- 18.1   Introduction 381
- 18.2   Diagrams 383
- 18.3   Time 384
- 18.4   Flip-flops 385
- 18.5   Edge-triggering 387
- 18.6   Memory 389
- 18.7   Merge 390
- 18.8   Imperative circuits 392
- 18.9   Functional circuits 401
- 18.10   Hybrid circuits 405
- 18.11   Performance 406
- 18.12   Correctness 407
- 18.13   Synchronous and asynchronous circuits 410
- 18.14   Conclusions 410

I   Security and keeping secrets   413

19   Power analysis: attacks and countermeasures   415
Suresh Chari, Charanjit S. Jutla, Josyula R. Rao, and Pankaj Rohatgi
- 19.1   Introduction 415
- 19.2   Power analysis of a Twofish implementation 419
- 19.3   Power model and attacks 425
- 19.4   Countermeasures to power analysis 428
- 19.5   Conclusions 436
- 19.6   Acknowledgments 436
- References 436

20   A probabilistic approach to information hiding   441
Annabelle McIver and Carroll Morgan
- 20.1   Introduction 441
- 20.2   Background: multi-level security and information flow 442
- 20.3   Classical information theory, and program refinement 443
- 20.4   Information flow in imperative programs 448
- 20.5   Example: The secure file store 454
- 20.6   The Refinement Paradox 457
- References 460

Index   461

Contributors

Members of the WG2.3 working group:

Professor Dr. R.-J. Back
Dr. R.M. Balzer
Dines Bjørner
Professor Dr. M. Broy
Dr. Ernie Cohen
Dr. P. Cousot
Professor Dr. E.W. Dijkstra
Professor D. Gries
Professor I.J. Hayes
Professor E.C.R. Hehner
Professor P. Henderson
Professor C.A.R. Hoare
Dr. J.J. Horning
Professor Daniel N. Jackson
Mr. M.A. Jackson
Professor C.B. Jones
Dr. B.W. Lampson

Dr. K. Rustan M. Leino
Dr. M.D. McIlroy
Dr. Annabelle McIver
Dr. W.M. McKeeman
Dr. K. McMillan
Professor J. Misra
Dr. Carroll Morgan (vice-chairman)
Dr. Greg Nelson
Professor Benjamin Pierce
Dr. J.R. Rao
Professor J.C. Reynolds
Dr. D.T. Ross
Professor F.B. Schneider
Dr. N. Shankar (chairman)
Professor M. Sintzoff
Dr. Joakim von Wright
Dr. Pamela Zave

Members who contributed are:

Dines Bjørner
Department of Information
    Technology
Technical University of Denmark
DTU-Building 344
DK-2800 Lingby
Denmark

Ernie Cohen
ernie.cohen@home.com

Ralph Back
Abo Akademi University
Department of Computer Science
Lemminkainenkatu 14
SF-20520 Turku
Finland

Manfred Broy
Institut für Informatik
Technische Universität München
D-80290 München
Germany

Contributors

Ian Hayes
School of Information Technology and
    Electrical Engineering
The University of Queensland
Queensland, 4072
Australia

Eric C.R. Hehner
Pratt Building, Room PT398
University of Toronto
6 King's College Road
Toronto, Ontario M5S 3H5
Canada

Peter Henderson
Department of Electronics and
    Computer Science
University of Southampton
Southampton, SO17 1BJ
United Kingdom

Tony Hoare
Microsoft Research
Cambridge, CB3 0FB
United Kingdom

Daniel Jackson
Lab. for Computer Science
200 Technology Square
Cambridge, Massachusetts 02139
USA

Michael Jackson
jacksonma@acm.org

Benjamin Pierce
University of Pennsylvania
Department of Computer and
    Information Science
200 South 33rd Street
Philadelphia, Pennsylvania
19104-6389
USA

Rustan Leino
Compaq SRC
130 Lytton Avenue
Palo Alto, California 94301
USA

Annabelle McIver
The Department of Computing
Macquarie University
Sydney, 2109
Australia

Jayadev Misra
Department of Computer Sciences
University of Texas at Austin
Austin, Texas 78712-1188
USA

Carroll Morgan
Department of Computer Science and
    Engineering
The University of New South Wales
Sydney, 2052
Australia

Greg Nelson
Compaq SRC
130 Lytton Avenue
Palo Alto, California 94301
USA

C.B. Jones
Department of Computing Science
University of Newcastle
Newcastle-upon-Tyne, NE1 7RU
United Kingdom

John C. Reynolds
Computer Science Department
School of Computer Science
Carnegie Mellon University
Pittsburgh, Pennsylvania 15123-3890
USA

Josyula Rao
IBM Research
T.J. Watson Research Center
P.O. Box 218
Yorktown Heights, New York 10598
USA

Natarajan Shankar
SRI International
MS EL256
333 Ravenswood Avenue
Menlo Park, California 94025-3493
USA

Joakim von Wright
Abo Akademi University
Department of Computer Science
Lemminkainenkatu 14
SF-20520 Turku
Finland

Pamela Zave
180 Park Avenue
P.O. Box 971
Florham Park, New Jersey 07932-2971
USA

The following people also contributed:

Suresh Chari
IBM Research
T.J. Watson Research Center
P.O. Box 714
Yorktown Heights, New York 10598
USA

Charanjit S. Jutla
IBM Research
T.J. Watson Research Center
P.O. Box 714
Yorktown Heights, New York 10598
USA

Pankaj Rohatji
IBM Research
T. J. Watson Research Center
P.O. Box 714
Yorktown Heights, New York 10598
USA

He Jifeng
International Institute of
    Software Technology
United Nations University
P.O. Box 3058
Macau

Theodore Norvell
Electrical and Computer Engineering
Faculty of Engineering
Memorial University of Newfoundland
St. John's, NF A1B 3X5
Canada

Richard F. Paige
Department of Computer Science
York University
4700 Keele Street
Toronto, Ontario M5J 1P3
Canada

Part I
Models and correctness

Section A

Concurrency and interaction

1 Wanted: a compositional approach to concurrency   5
   Cliff Jones

The practical application of a formal method to the correct design of industrial-strength programs is impeded if the method does not scale. But scalability (equivalently efficiency for large problems) can be tricky. In particular a problem must be reduced to smaller subproblems, analysed in some way, and the results recomposed to produce a solution to the original problem. The litmus test for scalability in such a procedure is that the analysis of the subproblems must be both cost-effective and composable — have one without the other and the enterprise flounders. Unfortunately having both is not as easy as it might seem, because a cost-cutting analysis implies 'measuring' only the absolutely essential details, and has a tendency to encroach on composability. Methods that do compose arc called compositional.

A simple chemistry example illustates the point. An analysis of chemicals might be based on colour which, for the sake of argument, is a more obvious candidate for observation than weight. In reactions however the colour of the product cannot be deduced from the colours of the reagents, so a weight-based analysis is compositional but a colour-based analysis is not.

This paper explores this crucial idea of compositionality, focussing on its application to concurrent programs, which present special challenges to the designer.

2 Enforcing behavior with contracts   17
   Ralph-Johan Back and Joakim von Wright

Interactive systems are a generalisation of the traditional notion of concurrency in that they allow different kinds of scheduling — typically demonic and angelic — during computation. The important mathematical idea underlying both concurrency and interaction is that of multi-user games, where subsets of users can form coalitions to comply with some particular contract. The analysis of temporal properties for these systems is relatively tricky, and the aim of research on this topic is to simplify analysis, either by discovering straightforward proof rules or by simplifying the systems themselves.

This paper can be seen as contributing to both those areas. Using an operational description of the kinds of contracts and interactions involved in game playing, this work demonstrates how to develop simple verification rules in the well-known action-system framework.

Action systems enjoy impressive credentials as a formal method because of their descriptive clarity and expressivity for concurrent programs. Indeed they are a natural choice for this application, for their predicate-transformer semantics extends easily to cope with both angelic and demonic scheduling. Moreover other typical features of contract-games, such as various kinds of contract breaking, are modelled by termination, abortion and miracles in action systems. Other specialised treatments of games are unable to deal with these concepts.

1
Wanted: a compositional approach to concurrency

C. B. Jones

Abstract
A key property for a development method is *compositionality*, because it ensures that a method can scale up to cope with large applications. Unfortunately, the inherent *interference* makes it difficult to devise development methods for concurrent programs (or systems). There are a number of proposals such as rely/guarantee conditions but the overall search for a satisfactory *compositional approach to concurrency* is an open problem. This paper identifies some issues including granularity and the problems associated with ghost variables; it also discusses using atomicity as a design abstraction.

1.1 Compositionality

Formal specification languages and associated rules for proving that designs satisfy specifications are often called *formal methods*. As well as providing completely formal criteria, it is argued in [Jon00] that formal methods offer thinking tools –such as invariants– which become an integral part of professional practice. The main interest in this paper is on the contribution that formal methods can make to the design process for concurrent systems. Just as with Hoare's axioms for sequential programs, the sought after gains should come both from (the reference point of) formal rules and from the intuitions they offer to less formal developments.

The development of any large system must be decomposed into manageable steps. This is true both for the construction phase and for subsequent attempts to comprehend a design. For software, understanding after construction is important because of the inevitable maintenance and modification work. But, for the current purposes, it is sufficient to concentrate the argument on the design process.

It is easy to see that it is the design process of large systems which requires support. Regardless of the extent to which techniques for error detection of finished code can be made automatic, there is still the inherent cost of reworking the design when errors are detected and little greater certainty of correctness after modification. The only way to achieve high productivity and correctness is to aim to make designs correct by construction.

What is required therefore is to be able to make and justify one design decision before moving on to further steps of design. To take the design of sequential programs as a reference point, specification by pre- and post-conditions offers a natural way of recording what is required of any level of component. So, in facing the task of developing some C specified by its pre- and post-conditions, one might decide that a series of sub-components sc_i are required and record expectations about them by writing their pre- and post-conditions. The design step must also provide a proposed way of combining the eventual sc_i and this should be one of the constructs of the (sequential) programming language. Each such construct should have an associated proof rule like the Hoare axiom for **while** which can be used to show that any implementations satisfying the specifications of the sc_i will combine with the stated construct into an implementation satisfying the specification of C. This idealised top-down picture requires some qualification below but the essential point remains: pre- and post-conditions provide an adequate description of the functionality of a system to facilitate the separation of a multi-level design into separate steps. A method which supports such development is classed as *compositional*; one that requires details of the implementations of the sc_i to justify the decomposition is non-compositional.

The above ideal is rarely achieved. The first difficulty is that there is no guarantee against making bad design decisions which result in the need to backtrack in the design process. What a compositional method offers is a way of justifying a design step — not an automatic way of choosing good design decisions. Secondly, there was above a careful restriction to functional properties and performance considerations, in particular, are commonly excluded. There are also a number of technical points: the case for separating pre- from post-conditions and the arguments for employing post-conditions of two states (plus the consequent search for apposite proof rules) are explored in [Jon99]. It will also come as no surprise to anyone who has read this author's books on VDM that the method of data reification is considered an essential tool for program design; fortunately there is also a transitivity notion for reification which again facilitates compositional design (see [dRE99] for an excellent survey of data refinement research).

Nothing which has been written above should be seen as assuming that all design has to be undertaken in a top-down order: separate justification of design steps is necessary in whatever order they are made; a top-down structure of the final documentation might well enhance comprehensibility; and arguments based on specifications rather than on the details of the code have much to commend them however these arguments are discovered.

1.2 The essence of concurrency is interference

The easiest way to illustrate interference is with parallel processes which can read and write variables in the same state space. Simple examples can be constructed with parallel execution of assignment statements; but to avoid an obvious riposte it is necessary to resolve an issue about granularity. Some development methods assume that assignment statements are executed atomically in the sense that no parallel process can interfere with the state from the beginning of evaluation of the right hand side of the assignment until the variable on the left hand side has been updated. The rule is reciprocal in the sense that the assignment in question must not interfere with the atomic execution of one in any other process. Essentially, assignments in all processes are non-deterministically merged in all processes but never allowed to overlap. A few moments' thought makes it clear that such a notion of granularity would be extremely expensive to implement because of the setting and testing of something equivalent to semaphores. There is a suggestion to remove the need for semaphores: sometimes referred to as "Reynold's rule", the idea is to require no more than one reference (on the left or right hand sides) in any assignment to potentially shared variables. Section 1.6 argues that not even variable access or change are necessarily atomic; but even without opening this facet to investigation, one can observe that Reynold's rule is also arbitrary and prohibits many completely safe programs.

Thus, for the purposes of this section, assignment statements are not assumed to be executed in an atomic step. If then a variable x has the value 0 before two assignment statements

$$x \leftarrow x+1 \| x \leftarrow x+2$$

are executed in parallel, what can be said of the final value of x? In the simplest case, where one parallel assignment happens to complete before the other begins, the result is $x = 3$; but if both parallel assignments have their right hand sides evaluated in the same state ($x = 0$) then the resulting value of x could be 1 or 2 depending on the order of the state changes.[1]

Some computer scientists recoiled at the difficulty of such shared state concurrency and their idea of stateless communicating processes might appear to finesse the problem illustrated above. Unfortunately, escaping the general notion of interference is not so easy. In fact, since processes can be used to model variables, it is obvious that interference is still an issue. The shared variable problem above can be precisely mirrored in, for example, the π-calculus [MPW92] as follows

---

[1] Atomicity of update of scalar values is assumed – for now!

$(\bar{x}0 \quad | \quad !x(v).(\overline{r_x}v.\bar{x}v + w_x(n).\bar{x}n)) \quad | \quad r_x(v).\overline{w_x}v + 1 \quad | \quad r_x(v).\overline{w_x}v + 2$

One might argue that assertions over communication histories are easier to write and reason about than those over state evolutions but the issue of interference has clearly not been avoided. Furthermore, interference affects liveness arguments as well as safety reasoning.

1.3 Reasoning about interference

Before coming to explicit reasoning about interference, it is instructive to review some of the early attempts to prove that shared-variable concurrent programs satisfy specifications. One way of proving that two concurrent programs are correct with respect to an overall specification is to consider their respective flow diagrams and to associate an assertion with every pair of arcs (i.e. quiescent points). So with sc_1 having n steps and sc_2 having m, it is necessary to consider $n \times m$ steps of proof. This is clearly wasteful and does not scale at all to cases where there are more than two processes. There is also here an assumption about granularity which is dangerous: are the steps in the flow diagram to be whole assignments? For the current purposes, however, the more fundamental objection is that the approach is non-compositional: proofs about the two processes can only be initiated once their final code is present; nothing can be proved at the point in time where the developer chooses to split the overall task into two parallel processes; there is no separate and complete statement of what is required of each of the sc_i.

Susan Owicki's thesis [Owi75] proposes a method which offers some progress. Normally referred to as the Owicki-Gries method because of the paper she wrote [OG76] with her supervisor David Gries, the idea is to write normal pre/post condition specifications of each of the sc_i and develop their implementations separately with normal sequential proof rules. Essentially, this first step can be thought of as considering the implementation as though it is a non-deterministic choice between one of two sequential implementations: $sc_1; sc_2$ or $sc_2; sc_1$. Having completed the top level decomposition, developments of the separate sc_i can be undertaken to obtain code which satisfies their specifications. So far, so good — but then the Owicki-Gries method requires that each program step in sc_i must be shown not to interfere with any proof step in sc_j. With careful design, many of these checks will be trivial so the worrying product of $n \times m$ checks is not as daunting. It is however again clear that this method is non-compositional in that a problem located in the final proof of "interference freedom" could force a development of sc_i to be discarded because of a decision in the design of sc_j. In other words, the specification of sc_i was incomplete in that a development which satisfied its pre- and post-condition has to be reworked at the end because it fails some criteria not present in its specification.

Several authors took up the challenge of recording assumptions and commitments which include a characterisation of interference. In [FP78], an interference constraint has to be found which is common to all processes. In [Jon81], pre/post conditions specifications for such processes are extended with rely and guarantee conditions. The subsequent description here is in terms of the rely/guarantee proposal.

The basic idea is very simple. Just as a pre-condition records assumptions the developer can make about the initial state when designing an implementation, a rely condition records assumptions that can be made about interference from other processes: few programs can work in an arbitrary initial condition; only vacuous specifications can be met in the presence of arbitrary interference. Thus pre- and rely conditions record assumptions that the developer can make.

Just as post-conditions document commitments which must be (shown to be) fulfilled by the implementation, the interference which can be generated by the implementation is captured by writing a guarantee condition.

A specification of a component C then is written $\{p, r\}\ C\ \{g, q\}$ for a pre-condition p, a rely condition r, a guarantee condition g, and a post-condition q. It has always been the case in VDM that post-conditions were predicates of the initial and final states [2]:

$$q : \Sigma \times \Sigma \to \mathbb{B}$$

Since they record (potential) state changes, it is natural that rely and guarantee conditions are both relations:

$$r : \Sigma \times \Sigma \to \mathbb{B}$$

$$g : \Sigma \times \Sigma \to \mathbb{B}$$

Pre-conditions indicate whether an initial state is acceptable and are thus predicates of a single state:

$$p : \Sigma \to \mathbb{B}$$

The compositional proof rule for decomposing a component into two parallel components is presented in Fig. 1.1. It is more complicated than rules for sequential constructs but is not difficult to understand. If $S_1 \parallel S_2$ has to tolerate interference r, the component S_1 can only assume the bound on interference to be $r \vee g_2$ because steps of S_2 also interfere with S_1. The guarantee condition g of the parallel construct cannot be stronger than the disjunction of the guarantee conditions of the components. Finally, the post-condition of the overall construct can be derived from the conjunction of the individual post-conditions, conjoined with the transitive closure of the rely and guarantee conditions, and further conjoined with any information that can be brought forward from the pre-condition $\overleftarrow{p}$.

There are more degrees of freedom in the presentation of such a complex rule than those for sequential constructs, and papers listed below experiment with various presentations. It was however recognised early that there were useful generic thinking tools for reasoning about concurrent systems. "Dynamic invariants" are

---

[2] See [Jon99] for discussion.

$$\boxed{\|\|} \frac{\{p, r \vee g_2\}\ S_1\ \{g_1, q_1\}}{\{p, r\vee g_1\}\ S_2\ \{g_2, q_2\}} \\ \frac{g_1 \vee g_2 \Rightarrow g}{\overleftarrow{p}\ \wedge q_1 \wedge q_2 \wedge (r \vee g_1 \vee g_2)^* \Rightarrow q}}{\{p, r\}\ (S_1 \| S_2)\ \{g, q\}}$$

Figure 1.1. A proof rule for rely/guarantee conditions

the best example of a concept which is useful in formal and informal developments alike. A dynamic invariant is a relation which holds between the initial state and any which can arise. It is thus reflexive and composes with the guarantee conditions of all processes. It is accepted by many who have adopted methods like VDM that standard data type invariants are a valuable design aid and their discussion even in informal reviews often uncovers design errors. There is some initial evidence that similar design pay off comes from dynamic invariants. In fact, they have even been seen as beneficial in the design of sequential systems (e.g. [FJ98]).

There have been many excellent contributions to the rely/guarantee idea in the twenty years since it was first published ([Jon83] is a more accessible source than [Jon81]). Ketil Stølen tackled the problem of progress arguments in his thesis [Stø90]. Xu Quiwen [Xu92] in his Oxford thesis covers some of the same ground but also looks at the use of equivalence proofs. Pierre Collette's thesis was done under the supervision of Michel Sintzoff: [Col94] makes the crucial link to Misra and Chandy's Unity language (see [CM88]). Colin Stirling tackles the issue of Cook completeness in [Sti88], and in [Sti86] shows that the same broad form of thinking can be applied to process algebras. Recent contributions include [Din00][3] and [BB99].

Returning to the fact that there have been other assumption-commitment approaches which record interference in ways different from the specific rely-guarantee conditions used here, the reader is referred to the forthcoming book from de Roever and colleagues for a review of many approaches. As far as this author is aware, none of the recorded approaches avoids the difficulties discussed in the following sections.

1.4 Some problems with assumption/commitment reasoning

In spite of the progress with rely-guarantee specifications and development, much remains to be done. It should not be surprising that reasoning about intimate in-

---

[3] Note [Sti88, Din00] employ unary predicates and experience the problems that are familiar from unary post-conditions when wanting to state requirements such as variables not changing.

terference between two processes can be tricky. An illustration of the delicacy of placing clauses in assumptions and commitments is given in [CJ00]. Perhaps much of what is required here is experience and the classification of types of interference.

One obvious conclusion is to limit interference in a way that makes it possible to undertake much program development with sequential rules. This echoes the message that Dijkstra et al. were giving over the whole early period of writing concurrent programs. One avenue of research in this direction has been to deploy object-based techniques to provide a way of controlling interference; this work is outlined –and additional references are given– in [Jon96].

Turning to the rules for the parallel constructs, that given in Figure 1.1 is only one with which various authors who are cited above have experimented. There more degrees of freedom than with rules for sequential constructs.[4] Again, experiments should indicate the most usable rules.

There are some general developments to be looked at in combination with any form of assumption-commitment approach. One is the need to look at their use in real-time programs. Intuitively, the same idea should work, but determining the most convenient logic in which to record assumptions and commitments might take considerable experimentation. Another extension which would require careful integration is that to handle probabilistic issues. This is of particular interest to the current author because –as described in [Jon00]– of the desire to cover "faults as interference".

1.5 The role of ghost variables

A specific problem which arises in several approaches to proofs about concurrency is finding some way of referring to points in a computation. A frustratingly simple example is the parallel execution of two assignment statements which are, for this section, assumed to be atomic.

$$\langle x \leftarrow x + 1\rangle \,\|\, \langle x \leftarrow x + 2\rangle$$

The subtlety here is that because both increments are by the same amount one cannot use the value to determine which arm has been executed. A common solution to such issues is to introduce some form of "ghost variable" which can be modified so as to track execution. There are a number of unresolved questions around ghost variables including exactly when they are required; what is the increase in expressivity and their relationship to compositionality.

For the specific example above, this author has suggested that it might be better to avoid state predicates altogether and recognise that the important fact is that the assignments commute. Of course, if one branch incremented x and the other

---

[4]There is of course some flexibility with sequential constructs such as whether to fold the consequence rule into those for each programming construct.

multiplied it by some value, then they would not commute; but it would also be difficult to envisage what useful purpose such a program would have. So the proposal is that reasoning about concurrency should not rely solely on assertions about states; other –perhaps more algebraic techniques– can also be used to reason about the joint effect of actions in parallel processes.

1.6 Granularity concerns

Issues relating to granularity have figured in the discussion above and they would appear to pose serious difficulties for many methods. The problems with assuming that assignment statements can be executed atomically are reviewed in Section 1.2 but the general issue is much more difficult. For example, it is not necessarily true that variables can be read and changed without interference. This should be obvious in the case of say arrays but it is also unlikely that hardware will guarantee that long strings are accessed in an uninterrupted way. There is even the danger that scalar arithmetic value access can be interrupted.

Having ramified the problem, what can be done about it? Any approach which requires recognising the complete proof of one process to see whether another process can interfere with proof steps appears to be committed to low level details of the implementation language. To some extent, a rely-guarantee approach puts the decision about granularity in the hands of the designer. In particular, assertions carried down as relations between states can be reified later in design. This works well in the object-based approach described in [Jon96]. But granularity is a topic which deserves more research rather than the regrettable tendency to ignore the issue.

1.7 Atomicity as an abstraction, and its refinement

As well as rely and guarantee conditions, the object-based design approach put forward in [Jon96] employs equivalence transformations. The idea is that a relatively simple process could be used to develop a sequential program which can be transformed into an equivalent concurrent program. The task of providing a semantic underpinning in terms of which the claimed equivalences could be proved to preserve observational equivalence proved difficult (see for example [PW98, San99]).

The key to the equivalences is to observe that under strict conditions, islands of computation exist and interference never crosses the perimeter of the island. One of the reasons that these equivalences are interesting is that their essence – which is the decomposition of things which it is easy to see posses some property when executed atomically– occurs in several other areas. In particular, "atomicity" is a useful design abstraction in discussing database transactions and cache coherence: showing how these "atoms" can overlap is an essential part of justifying a useful implementation. There are other approaches to this problem such as [JPZ91, Coh00]; but the ubiquity of atomicity refinement as a way of reasoning about some concurrency problems suggests that there is a rich idea lurking here.

1.8 Conclusion

The general idea behind assumption/commitment specifications and proof rules would appear to be a useful way of designing concurrent systems. Much detailed research and experimentation on practical problems is still required to come up with some sort of agreed approach. Even as a proponent of one of the assumption (rely) commitment (guarantee) approaches, the current author recognises that there are also quite general problems to be faced before a satisfactory compositional approach to the development of concurrent programs can be claimed. One area of extension is to look for more expressiveness whether to merge with realtime logics or to cope with probabilities. Another issue is that of arguments which do not appear to be dealt with well by assertions about states. In all of this search for formal rules, one should continue to strive for things which can be adopted also informally as thinking tools by engineers.

Acknowledgements

I gratefully acknowledge the financial support of the UK EPSRC for the Interdisciplinary Research Collaboration "Dependability of Computer-Based Systems". Most of my research is influenced by, and has been discussed with, members of IFIP's Working Group 2.3.

References

[BB99]   Martin Buechi and Ralph Back. Compositional symmetric sharing in B. In *FM'99 – Formal Methods*, volume 1708 of *Lecture Notes in Computer Science*, pages 431–451. Springer-Verlag, 1999.

[BG91]   J. C. M. Baeten and J. F. Groote, editors. *CONCUR'91 – Proceedings of the 2nd International Conference on Concurrency Theory*, volume 527 of *Lecture Notes in Computer Science*. Springer-Verlag, 1991.

[CJ00]   Pierre Collette and Cliff B. Jones. Enhancing the tractability of rely/guarantee specifications in the development of interfering operations. In Gordon Plotkin, Colin Stirling, and Mads Tofte, editors, *Proof, Language and Interaction*, chapter 10, pages 275–305. MIT Press, 2000.

[CM88]   K. M. Chandy and J. Misra. *Parallel Program Design: A Foundation*. Addison-Wesley, 1988.

[Coh00] Ernie Cohen. Separation and reduction. In *Mathematics of Program Construction, 5th International Conference, Portugal, July 2000. Science of Computer Programming*, pages 45–59. Springer-Verlag, 2000.

[Col94] Pierre Collette. *Design of Compositional Proof Systems Based on Assumption-Commitment Specifications – Application to UNITY*. PhD Thesis, Louvain-la-Neuve, June 1994.

[Din00] Jürgen Dingel. *Systematic Parallel Programming*. PhD Thesis, Carnegie Mellon University, 2000. CMU-CS-99-172.

[dRE99] W. P. de Roever and K. Engelhardt. *Data Refinement: Model-Oriented Proof Methods and Their Comparison*. Cambridge University Press, 1999.

[FJ98] John Fitzgerald and Cliff Jones. A tracking system. In J. C. Bicarregui, editor, *Proof in VDM: Case Studies*, FACIT, pages 1–30. Springer-Verlag, 1998.

[FP78] N. Francez and A. Pnueli. A proof method for cyclic programs. *Acta Informatica*, 9:133–157, 1978.

[Jon81] C. B. Jones. *Development Methods for Computer Programs including a Notion of Interference*. PhD Thesis, Oxford University, June 1981. Printed as: Programming Research Group, Technical Monograph 25.

[Jon83] C. B. Jones. Specification and design of (parallel) programs. In *Proceedings of IFIP '83*, pages 321–332. North-Holland, 1983.

[Jon96] C. B. Jones. Accommodating interference in the formal design of concurrent object-based programs. *Formal Methods in System Design*, 8(2):105–122, March 1996.

[Jon99] C. B. Jones. Scientific decisions which characterize VDM. In *FM'99 – Formal Methods*, volume 1708 of *Lecture Notes in Computer Science*, pages 28–47. Springer-Verlag, 1999.

[Jon00] C. B. Jones. Thinking tools for the future of computing science. In *Informatics — 10 Years Back, 10 Years Forward*, volume 2000 of *Lecture Notes in Computer Science*, pages 112–130. Springer-Verlag, 2000.

[JPZ91] W. Janssen, M. Poel, and J. Zwiers. Action systems and action refinement in the development of parallel systems. In *[BG91]*, pages 298–316, 1991.

[MPW92] R. Milner, J. Parrow, and D. Walker. A calculus of mobile processes. *Information and Computation*, 100:1–77, 1992.

[OG76] S. S. Owicki and D. Gries. An axiomatic proof technique for parallel programs I. *Acta Informatica*, 6:319–340, 1976.

[Owi75] S. Owicki. *Axiomatic Proof Techniques for Parallel Programs*. PhD Thesis, Department of Computer Science, Cornell University, 1975. 75-251.

[PW98] Anna Philippou and David Walker. On transformations of concurrent-object programs. *Theoretical Computer Science*, 195:259–289, 1998.

[San99] Davide Sangiorgi. Typed π-calculus at work: a correctness proof of Jones's parallelisation transformation on concurrent objects. *Theory and Practice of Object Systems*, 5(1):25–34, 1999.

[Sti86] C. Stirling. A compositional reformulation of Owicki-Gries' partial correctness logic for a concurrent while language. In *ICALP '86*. Springer-Verlag, 1986. LNCS 226.

[Sti88] C. Stirling. A generalisation of Owicki-Gries's Hoare logic for a concurrent while language. *TCS*, 58:347–359, 1988.

[Stø90] K. Stølen. *Development of Parallel Programs on Shared Data-Structures*. PhD Thesis, Manchester University, 1990. available as UMCS-91-1-1.

[Xu92] Qiwen Xu. *A Theory of State-based Parallel Programming*. PhD Thesis, Oxford University, 1992.

2
Enforcing behavior with contracts

Ralph-Johan Back and Joakim von Wright

Abstract

Contracts have been introduced earlier as a way of modeling a collection of agents that work within the limits set by the contract. We have analyzed the question of when an agent or a coalition of agents can reach a stated goal, despite potentially hostile behavior by the other agents. In this paper, we extend the model so that we can also study whether a coalition of agents can enforce a certain temporal behavior when executing a contract. We show how to reduce this question to the question of whether a given goal can be achieved. We introduce a generalization of the action system notation that allows both angelic and demonic scheduling of actions. This allows us to model concurrent systems and interactive systems in the same framework, and show that one can be seen as the dual of the other. We analyze enforcement of temporal behavior in the case of action systems, and show that these provide for simpler proof obligations than what we get in the general case. Finally, we give three illustrative examples of how to model and analyze interactive and concurrent systems with this approach.

2.1 Introduction

A computation can generally be seen as involving a number of agents (programs, modules, systems, users, etc.) who carry out actions according to a document (specification, program) that has been laid out in advance. When reasoning about a computation, we can view this document as a contract between the agents. We have earlier described a general notation for contracts, and have given these a formal meaning using an operational semantics [6]. Given a contract, we can analyze what goals a specific agent or coalition of agents can achieve with the contract. This will essentially amount to checking whether an agent or a coalition of agents have a winning strategy to reach the given goal.

In this paper, we consider the question of whether an agent or a coalition of agents can *enforce* a certain temporal behavior on the execution of the contract.

This means that there is a way for these agents to co-ordinate their decisions, so that the temporal property will hold for the whole execution of the contract. We show how to model temporal properties with an operational semantics for contracts, and then study how to prove that a certain temporal property can be enforced. We show that enforcement of a temporal property can be reduced to the question of achieving a goal, which in turn can be established with standard techniques that we have developed in earlier work.

We then introduce a generalization of the *action system* notation which unifies the notion of a concurrent and an interactive system. Both kinds of systems are essentially initialized loops, but the difference comes from whether the scheduling of the loop is demonic (in concurrent systems) or angelic (in interactive systems). We show how to analyze temporal properties of the special kinds of contract that action systems provide. It turns out that we get considerable simplification in the proof obligations by using action systems rather than general contracts.

Finally, we illustrate the approach by considering three examples. The first example is the game of Nim, which illustrates the interaction of two agents in a game-playing situation. The second example is the familiar puzzle of the wolf, the goat and the cabbages, which have to be transported across a river. The last example illustrates how to apply the approach described here to a resource allocation situation, here exemplified by an imaginary Chinese Dim Sun restaurant.

Our notion of contracts is based on the refinement calculus [3, 6, 18]. We have earlier extended the original notion of contracts to consider coalitions of agents [8]. Here we combine contracts and the idea of considering a system as a game between two players [1, 20, 5, 21] with the idea of temporal properties in a predicate transformer setting [14, 19].

The paper first introduces the notion of contracts, both informally and with a precise operational semantics, in Section 2. *Action systems* are described as a special kind of contract, and we give three examples of action systems, which we will analyze in more detail later on. Section 3 shows how to analyze what kind of goals can be *achieved* with contracts, introducing a weakest precondition semantics for contracts for this purpose. In Section 4 we develop the main theme of this paper: how to show that temporal properties can be *enforced* during execution of a contract. Section 5 looks at enforcement in the special case when the contracts are action systems, showing that we can get simplified proof conditions in this case. Section 6 looks at the practice of verifying enforcement properties, and illustrates the basic proof methods by showing specific enforcement properties for the example action systems introduced earlier. We conclude with some general remarks in Section 7.

We use *simply typed higher-order logic* as the logical framework in the paper. The type of functions from a type Σ to a type Γ is denoted by $\Sigma \to \Gamma$. Functions can be described using λ-abstraction and we write $f.x$ for the application of function f to argument x.

2.2 Contracts

In this section we give an overview of contracts and their operational semantics, following [7] (with some notational changes) and introduce action systems as a special kind of contract.

2.2.1 States and state changes

We assume that the world that contracts talk about is described as a *state* σ. The *state space* Σ is the set (type) of all possible states. An agent changes the state by applying a function f to the present state, yielding a new state $f.\sigma$. We think of the state as having a number of *attributes* $x_1, \ldots, x_n$, each of which can be observed and changed independently of the others. Such attributes are usually called *program variables*. An attribute x of type Γ is really a pair of two functions, the *value function* $val_x : \Sigma \to \Gamma$ and the *update function* $set_x : \Gamma \to \Sigma \to \Sigma$. The function val_x returns the value of the attribute x in a given state, while the function set_x returns a new state where x has a specific value, with the values of all other attributes left unchanged. Given a state σ, $val_x.\sigma$ is thus the value of x in this state, while $\sigma' = set_x.\gamma.\sigma$ is the new state that we get by setting the value of x to γ.

An *expression* like $x + y$ is a function on states, described by $(x + y).\sigma = val_x.\sigma + val_y.\sigma$. We use expressions to observe properties of the state. They are also used in *assignments* like $x := x+y$. This assignment denotes a state-changing function that updates the value of x to the value of the expression $x + y$. Thus

$$(x := x + y).\sigma = set_x.(val_x.\sigma + val_y.\sigma).\sigma$$

A function $f : \Sigma \to \Sigma$ that maps states to states is called a *state transformer*. We also make use of predicates and relations over states. A *state predicate* is a boolean function $p : \Sigma \to \text{Bool}$ on the state (in set notation we write $\sigma \in p$ for $p.\sigma$). Predicates are ordered by inclusion, which is the pointwise extension of implication on the booleans.

A *boolean expression* is an expression that ranges over truth values. It gives us a convenient way of describing predicates. For instance, $x \leq y$ is a boolean expression that has value $val_x.\sigma \leq val_y.\sigma$ in a given state σ.

A *state relation* $R : \Sigma \to \Sigma \to \text{Bool}$ relates a state σ to a state σ' whenever $R.\sigma.\sigma'$ holds. Relations are ordered by pointwise extension from predicates. Thus, $R \subseteq R'$ holds iff $R.\sigma \subseteq R'.\sigma$ for all states σ.

We permit a generalized assignment notation for relations. For example,

$$(x := x' \mid x' > x + y)$$

relates state σ to state σ' if the value of x in σ' is greater than the sum of the values of x and y in σ and all other attributes are unchanged. More precisely, we have that

$$(x := x' \mid x' > x + y).\sigma.\sigma' \equiv$$

$$(\exists x' \bullet \sigma' = set_x.x'.\sigma \wedge x' > val_x.\sigma + val_y.\sigma)$$

This notation generalizes the ordinary assignment; we have that $\sigma' = (x := e).\sigma$ iff $(x := x' \mid x' = e).\sigma.\sigma'$.

2.2.2 Contracts

Consider a collection of *agents*, each with the capability to change the state by choosing between different *actions*. The behavior of agents is regulated by *contracts*.

Assume that there is a fixed collection Ω of agents, which are considered to be atomic (we assume that we can test for equality between agents). We let A range over sets of agents and a, b, c over individual agents.

We describe contracts using a notation for *contract statements*. The syntax for these is as follows:

$$S ::= \langle f \rangle \mid \text{if } p \text{ then } S_1 \text{ else } S_2 \text{ fi} \mid S_1 ; S_2 \mid \langle R \rangle_a \mid S_1 \;[]_a\; S_2 \mid (\text{rec}_a\; X \bullet S) \mid X$$

Here a stands for an agent while f stands for a state transformer, p for a state predicate, and R for a state relation, all expressed using higher-order logic. X is a variable that ranges over (the meaning of) contracts.

Intuitively, a contract statement is carried out ("executed") as follows. The *functional update* $\langle f \rangle$ changes the state according to the state transformer f, i.e., if the initial state is σ_0 then the final state is $f.\sigma_0$. An *assignment statement* is a special kind of update where the state transformer is expressed as an assignment. For example, the assignment statement $\langle x := x + y \rangle$ (or just $x := x + y$ — for simplicity, we may drop the angle brackets from assignment statements) requires the agent to set the value of attribute x to the sum of the values of attributes x and y. We use the name **skip** for the identity update $\langle \text{id} \rangle$, where $\text{id}.\sigma = \sigma$ for all states σ.

In the *conditional composition* if p then S_1 else S_2 fi, S_1 is carried out if p holds in the initial state, and S_2 otherwise.

Relational update and choice introduce nondeterminism into the language of contracts. Both are indexed by an agent which is responsible for deciding how the nondeterminism is resolved.

The *relational update* $\langle R \rangle_a$ requires the agent a to choose a final state σ' so that $R.\sigma.\sigma'$ is satisfied, where σ is the initial state. In practice, the relation is expressed as a relational assignment. For example, $\langle x := x' \mid x' < x \rangle_a$ expresses that the agent a is required to decrease the value of the program variable x without changing the values of the other program variables. If it is impossible for the agent to satisfy this, then the agent has *breached* the contract. In this example, agent a must breach the contract if x ranges over the natural numbers and its initial value is 0.

An important special case of relational update occurs when the relation R is of the form $(\lambda \sigma\; \sigma' \bullet \sigma' = \sigma \wedge p.\sigma)$ for some state predicate p. In this case, $\langle R \rangle_a$ is called an *assertion* and we write it simply as $\langle p \rangle_a$. For example, $\langle x + y = 0 \rangle_a$ expresses that the sum of (the values of) x and y in the state must be zero. If the assertion holds at the indicated place when the agent a carries out the contract, then the state is unchanged, and the rest of the contract is carried out. If, on the other hand, the assertion does not hold, then the agent has breached the contract. The assertion $\langle \text{true} \rangle_a$ is always satisfied, so adding this assertion anywhere in a contract has no effect. Dually, $\langle \text{false} \rangle_a$ is an impossible assertion; it is never satisfied and always results in the agent breaching the contract.

A *choice* $S_1 \;[]_a\; S_2$ allows agent a to choose which is to be carried out, S_1 or S_2. To simplify notation, we assume that sequential composition binds stronger than choice in contracts.

In the *sequential composition* $S_1 ; S_2$, contract S_1 is first carried out, followed by S_2, provided that there is no breach of contract when executing S_1. We also permit *recursive contract statements*. A recursive contract is essentially an equation of the form

$$X =_a S$$

where S may contain occurrences of the contract variable X. With this definition, the contract X is intuitively interpreted as the contract statement S, but with each occurrence of statement variable X in S treated as a recursive invocation of the whole contract S. For simplicity, we use the syntax $(\text{rec}_a\, X \bullet S)$ for the contract X defined by the equation $X = S$.

The index a for the recursion construct indicates that agent a is responsible for termination of the recursion. If the recursion does not terminate, then a will be considered as having breached the contract. In general, agents have two roles in contracts: (i) they choose between different alternatives that are offered to them, and (ii) they take the blame when things go wrong. These two roles are interlinked, in the sense that things go wrong when an agent has to make a choice, and there is no acceptable choice available.

An important special case of recursion is the *while-loop* which is defined in the usual way:

$$\text{while}_a\, p \,\text{do}\, S \,\text{od} \;\triangleq\; (\text{rec}_a\, X \bullet \text{if}\, p \,\text{then}\, S\,;\, X \,\text{else}\, \text{skip}\, \text{fi})$$

Note the occurrence of agent a in the loop syntax; this agent is responsible for termination (so nontermination of the loop is not necessarily a bad thing).

2.2.3 Operational semantics

We give a formal meaning to contract statements in the form of a structured operational semantics. This semantics describes step-by-step how a contract is carried out, starting from a given initial state.

The rules of the operational semantics are given in terms of a transition relation between configurations. A *configuration* is a pair (S, σ), where

- S is either an ordinary contract statement or the empty statement symbol Λ, and

- σ is either an ordinary state, or the symbol $\perp_a$ (indicating that agent a has breached the contract).

The transition relation $\rightarrow$ (which shows what moves are permitted) is inductively defined by a collection of axioms and inference rules. It is the smallest relation which satisfies the following (where we assume that σ stands for a proper state while γ stands for either a state or the symbol $\perp_x$ for some agent x):

- *Functional update*

$$\overline{(\langle f \rangle, \sigma) \rightarrow (\Lambda, f.\sigma)} \quad \overline{(\langle f \rangle, \perp_a) \rightarrow (\Lambda, \perp_a)}$$

- *Conditional composition*

$$\frac{p.\sigma}{(\text{if } p \text{ then } S_1 \text{ else } S_2 \text{ fi}, \sigma) \rightarrow (S_1, \sigma)} \quad \frac{\neg p.\sigma}{(\text{if } p \text{ then } S_1 \text{ else } S_2 \text{ fi}, \sigma) \rightarrow (S_2, \sigma)}$$

$$\overline{(\text{if } p \text{ then } S_1 \text{ else } S_2 \text{ fi}, \perp_a) \rightarrow (\Lambda, \perp_a)}$$

- *Sequential composition*

$$\frac{(S_1, \gamma) \rightarrow (S_1', \gamma'), \quad S_1' \neq \Lambda}{(S_1 \,;\, S_2, \gamma) \rightarrow (S_1' \,;\, S_2, \gamma')} \quad \frac{(S_1, \gamma) \rightarrow (\Lambda, \gamma')}{(S_1 \,;\, S_2, \gamma) \rightarrow (S_2, \gamma')}$$

- *Relational update*

$$\frac{R.\sigma.\sigma'}{(\langle R \rangle_a, \sigma) \rightarrow (\Lambda, \sigma')} \quad \frac{R.\sigma = \emptyset}{(\langle R \rangle_a, \sigma) \rightarrow (\Lambda, \perp_a)} \quad \overline{(\langle R \rangle_a, \perp_b) \rightarrow (\Lambda, \perp_b)}$$

- *Choice*

$$\overline{(S_1 \,[]_a\, S_2, \gamma) \rightarrow (S_1, \gamma)} \quad \overline{(S_1 \,[]_a\, S_2, \gamma) \rightarrow (S_2, \gamma)}$$

- *Recursion*

$$\overline{((\text{rec}_a\, X \bullet S), \gamma) \rightarrow (S[X := (\text{rec}_a\, X \bullet S)], \gamma)}$$

A *scenario* for the contract S in initial state σ is a sequence of configurations

$$C_0 \rightarrow C_1 \rightarrow C_2 \rightarrow \cdots$$

where

1. $C_0 = (S, \sigma)$,

2. each transition $C_i \rightarrow C_{i+1}$ is permitted by the axiomatization above, and

3. if the sequence is finite with last configuration C_n, then $C_n = (\Lambda, \gamma)$, for some γ.

Intuitively, a scenario shows us, step by step, what choices the different agents have made and how the state is changed when the contract is being carried out. A finite scenario cannot be extended, since no transitions are possible from an empty configuration.

2.2.4 Examples of contracts

Programs can be seen as special cases of contracts, where two agents are involved, the *user* and the *computer*. In simple batch-oriented programs, choices are only made by the computer, which resolves any internal choices (nondeterminism) in a manner that is unknown to the user. Our notation for contracts already includes assignment statements and sequential composition. The *abort* statement of Dijkstra's guarded commands language [11] can be expressed as abort = $\{false\}_{user}$. If executed, it signifies that there has been a breach of contract by the user. This will release the computer from any obligations to carry out the rest of the contract, i.e., the computer is free to do whatever it wants. The abort statement thus signifies misuse of the computer by the user.

A batch-oriented program does not allow for any user interaction during execution. Once started, execution proceeds to the end if possible, or it fails because the contract is breached (allowing the computer system to do anything, including going into an infinite loop).

An interactive program allows the user to make choices during the execution. The user chooses between alternatives in order to steer the computation in a desired direction. The computer system can also make choices during execution, based on some internal decision mechanism that is unknown the user, so that she cannot predict the outcome.

As an example, consider the contract

$$S = S_1 \,;\, S_2, \text{ where}$$
$$S_1 = (x := x + 1 \; []_a \; x := x + 2)$$
$$S_2 = (x := x - 1 \; []_b \; x := x - 2)$$

Computing the operational semantics for S results in the tree shown in Fig. 2.1. After initialization, the user a chooses to increase the value of x by either one or two. After this, the computer b decides to decrease x by either one or two. The choice of the user depends on what she wants to achieve. If, e.g., she is determined that x should not become negative, she should choose the second alternative. If, again, she is determined that x should not become positive, she should choose the first alternative. We can imagine this user interaction as a *menu choice* that is presented to the user after the initialization, where the user is requested to choose one of the two alternatives.

We could also consider b to be the user and a to be the computer. In this case, the system starts by either setting x to one or to two. The user can then inspect the new value of x and choose to reduce it by either 1 or 0, depending on what she tries to achieve.

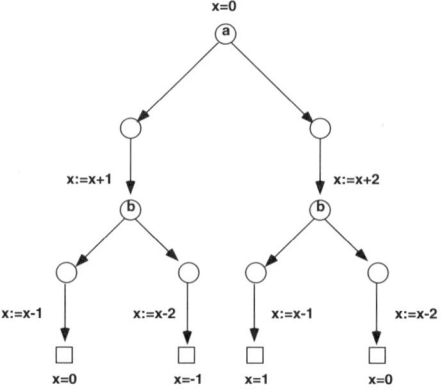

Figure 2.1. Executing contract S

A more general way for the user to influence the computation is to give input to the program during its execution. This can be achieved by a relational assignment. The following contract describes a typical interaction:

$$\langle x, e := x', e' \mid x' \geq 0 \wedge e > 0 \rangle_a \,;$$
$$\langle x := x' \mid -e < x'^2 - x < e \rangle_b$$

The user a gives as input a value x whose square root is to be computed, as well as the precision e with which the computer is to compute this square root. The computer b then computes an approximation to the square root with precision e. The computer may choose any new value for x that satisfies the required precision.

This simple contract thus *specifies* the interaction between the user and the computer. The first statement specifies the user's responsibility (to give an input value that satisfies the given conditions) and the second statement specifies the computer's responsibility (to compute a new value for x that satisfies the given condition).

The use of contracts allows user and computer choices to be intermixed in any way. In particular, the user choices can depend on previous choices by the computer and vice versa, and the choices can be made repeatedly within a loop, as we will show later.

Of course, there is nothing in this formalism that requires one of the agents to be a computer and the other to be a user. Both agents could be humans, and both agents could be computers. There may also be any number of agents involved in a contract, and it is also possible to have contracts with no agents.

2.2.5 Action systems

An *action system* is a contract of the form

$$\mathcal{A} = (\text{rec}_c \, X \bullet S \,;\, X \,[]_a \, \langle g \rangle_a)$$

The contract S inside $\mathcal{A}$ is iterated as long as agent a wants. Termination is normal if the *exit condition* g holds when a decides to stop the iteration, otherwise a will fail, i.e. breach the contract (however, we assume that an agent a will never make choices that lead to a breaching a contract, if she can avoid it; for a justification of this assumption we refer to [8]). Agent c gets the blame if the execution does not terminate.

In general, we also allow an action system to have an *initialization (begin)* statement B and a *finalization (end)* statement E, in addition to the *action* statement S. The initialization statement would typically introduce some local variables for the action system, and initialize these. The finalization statement would usually remove these local variables. The action statement S can in turn be a choice statement,

$$S = S_1 \,[]_b\, S_2 \,[]_b\, \ldots \,[]_b\, S_n$$

We refer to each S_i here as an *action* of the system. As a notational convenience, we write

$$g_1 \to S_1 \,[]_b\, \ldots \,[]_b\, g_m \to S_m$$

for

$$\langle g_1 \rangle_b \,;\, S_1 \,[]_b\, \ldots \,[]_b\, \langle g_m \rangle_b \,;\, S_m$$

Thus, an action system is in general of the form

$$\mathcal{A}(a,b,c) = B \,;\, (\text{rec}_c\, X \bullet (S_1 \,[]_b\, S_2 \,[]_b\, \ldots \,[]_b\, S_n) \,;\, X \,[]_a\, \langle g \rangle_a) \,;\, E$$

2.2.6 Examples of action systems

We present here three examples of action systems. The first example, Nim, illustrates a game, where the question to be decided is whether and when a player has a winning strategy. The second example is a classical puzzle, the Wolf, Goat and Cabbages, and illustrates a purely interactive system. The last example illustrates an imaginary Chinese Dim Sun restaurant.

The game of Nim

In the game of Nim, two players take turns removing sticks from a pile. A player can remove one or two sticks at a time, and the player who removes the last stick loses the game.

We model the players as two agents a and b. Agent c is the scheduler, who decides which player makes the first move and agent z is responsible for termination. The game is then described by the following contract:

$$\begin{aligned}
Nim &= (f := \mathsf{T} \,[]_c\, f := \mathsf{F}) \,;\, Play \\
Play &=_z\, f \wedge x > 0 \to \langle x := x' \mid x' < x \leq x' + 2 \rangle_a \,;\, f := \neg f \,;\, Play \\
&\quad []_c\, \neg f \wedge x > 0 \to \langle x := x' \mid x' < x \leq x' + 2 \rangle_b \,;\, f := \neg f \,;\, Play \\
&\quad []_c\, x = 0 \to \mathsf{skip}
\end{aligned}$$

Note that this only describes the moves and the scheduling. Notions like winning and losing are modeled using properties to be established and are part of the analysis of the system. Also note that the initial number of sticks is left unspecified (x is not initialized).

The wolf, the goat and the cabbages

The classical puzzle of the wolf, the goat and the cabbages goes as follows: A man comes to a river with a wolf, a goat and a sack of cabbages. He wants to get to the other side, using a boat that can only fit one of the three items (in addition to the man himself). He cannot leave the wolf and the goat on the same side (because the wolf eats the goat) and similarly, he cannot leave the goat and the cabbages on the same side. The question is: can the man get the wolf, the goat, and the cabbages safely to the other side?.

We model the situation with one boolean variable for each participant, indicating whether they are on the right side of the river or not: m for the man, w for the wolf, g for the goat, and c for the cabbages. The boat does not need a separate variable, because it is always on the same side as the man. There is only one agent involved (the scheduler a, who is in practice the man). The contract that describes the situation is the following:

$$\begin{aligned}
CrossRiver &= m, w, g, c := \mathsf{F}, \mathsf{F}, \mathsf{F}, \mathsf{F} \,;\, Transport \\
Transport =_a\ & m = w \rightarrow m, w := \neg m, \neg w \,;\, Transport \\
&[]_a\ m = g \rightarrow m, g := \neg m, \neg g \,;\, Transport \\
&[]_a\ m = c \rightarrow m, c := \neg m, \neg c \,;\, Transport \\
&[]_a\ m := \neg m \,;\, Transport \\
&[]_a\ \mathsf{skip}
\end{aligned}$$

The initialization says that all four are on the wrong side, and each action corresponds to the man moving from one side of the river to the other, either alone or together with an item that was on the same side.

Let us have a quick look at what the man is trying to achieve. He wants to reach a situation where all four items are on the right side of the river, i.e., we want $m \wedge w \wedge g \wedge c$ to be true at some point in the execution. Furthermore, if the wolf and the goat are on the same side of the river, then the man must also be on that side. Thus, he wants the property

$$(w = g \Rightarrow m = w) \wedge (g = c \Rightarrow m = g)$$

to be true at every intermediate point of the execution.

Note that termination is nondeterministic; the man can decide to stop at any time. The fact that we want to achieve a situation where $m \wedge w \wedge g \wedge c$ holds will be part of an analysis of the system, rather than the description.

The Dim Sun restaurant

In a Dim Sun restaurant, a waiter continuously offers customers items from a tray. We assume that there are three customers a, b, and c, and that x_0, x_1 and x_2 is the number of items that they have taken, respectively (initially set to 0). The waiter d decides in what order to offer customers items, but he may not offer items to the same customer twice in a row (we let f indicate who got the last offer). The remaining number of items is r. The manager e can decide to close the restaurant at any time (he must close it when there are no items left). This gives us the following system:

$$\begin{aligned}
\textit{Dim Sun} = {} & x_0, x_1, x_2, f := 0, 0, 0, 3 \,;\, \textit{Serve} \\
\textit{Serve} =_z {} & \langle r > 0 \rangle_e \,;\, \\
& (\quad \langle f \neq 0 \rangle_d \,;\, (\langle x_0, r := x_0 + 1, r - 1 \rangle []_a \textsf{skip}) \,;\, \langle f := 0 \rangle \,;\, \textit{Serve} \\
& []_d\ \langle f \neq 1 \rangle_d \,;\, (\langle x_1, r := x_1 + 1, r - 1 \rangle []_b \textsf{skip}) \,;\, \langle f := 1 \rangle \,;\, \textit{Serve} \\
& []_d\ \langle f \neq 2 \rangle_d \,;\, (\langle x_2, r := x_2 + 1, r - 1 \rangle []_c \textsf{skip}) \,;\, \langle f := 2 \rangle \,;\, \textit{Serve}\ ) \\
& []_e\ \textsf{skip}
\end{aligned}$$

2.3 Achieving goals with contracts

The operational semantics describes all possible ways of carrying out a contract. By looking at the state component of final configurations we can see what outcomes (final states) are possible, if all agents cooperate. However, in reality the different agents are unlikely to have the same goals, and the way one agent makes its choices need not be suitable for another agent. From the point of view of a specific agent or a group of agents, it is therefore interesting to know what outcomes are possible regardless of how the other agents resolve their choices.

Consider the situation where the initial state σ is given and a group of agents A agree that their common goal is to use contract S to reach a final state in some set q of desired final states. It is also acceptable that the coalition is released from the contract, because some other agent breaches the contract. This means that the agents should strive to make their choices in such a way that the scenario starting from (S, σ) ends in a configuration (Λ, γ) where γ is either an element in q, or $\perp_b$ for some $b \notin A$ (the latter indicating that some other agent has breached the contract). A third possibility is to prevent the execution from terminating, if an agent that does not belong to A is responsible for termination.

For the purpose of analysis we can think of the agents in A as being one single agent and dually, the remaining agents as also being one single agent that tries to prevent the former from reaching its goal. In [7, 8] we show how an execution of the contract can then be viewed as a two-person game and how this intuition can be formalized by interpreting contracts with two agents as predicate transformers. This section gives an overview of how this is done.

2.3.1 Weakest preconditions

A *predicate transformer* is a function that maps predicates to predicates. We order predicate transformers by pointwise extension of the ordering on predicates, so $F \sqsubseteq F'$ for predicate transformers holds if and only if $F.q \subseteq F'.q$ for all predicates q. The predicate transformers form a complete lattice with this ordering.

Assume that S is a contract statement and A a *coalition*, i.e., a set of agents. We want the predicate transformer wp. $S.A$ to map postcondition q to the set of all initial states σ from which the agents in A have a winning strategy to reach the goal q if they co-operate. Thus, wp. $S.A.q$ is the *weakest precondition* that guarantees that the agents in A can cooperate to achieve postcondition q.

The intuitive description of contract statements can be used to justify the following definition of the weakest precondition semantics:

$$\text{wp.} \langle f \rangle. A. q = (\lambda \sigma \bullet q.(f.\sigma))$$
$$\text{wp.} (\text{if } p \text{ then } S_1 \text{ else } S_2 \text{ fi}). A. q = (p \cap \text{wp.} S_1.A.q) \cup (\neg p \cap \text{wp.} S_2.A.q)$$
$$\text{wp.} (S_1 \,;\, S_2). A. q = \text{wp.} S_1.A.(\text{wp.} S_2.A.q)$$
$$\text{wp.} \langle R \rangle_a. A. q = \begin{cases} (\lambda \sigma \bullet \exists \sigma' \bullet R.\sigma.\sigma' \wedge q.\sigma') & \text{if } a \in A \\ (\lambda \sigma \bullet \forall \sigma' \bullet R.\sigma.\sigma' \Rightarrow q.\sigma') & \text{if } a \notin A \end{cases}$$
$$\text{wp.} (S_1 \,[]_a\, S_2). A. q = \begin{cases} \text{wp.} S_1.A.q \cup \text{wp.} S_2.A.q & \text{if } a \in A \\ \text{wp.} S_1.A.q \cap \text{wp.} S_2.A.q & \text{if } a \notin A \end{cases}$$

These definitions are consistent with Dijkstra's original semantics for the language of guarded commands [11] and with later extensions to it, corresponding to nondeterministic assignments, choices, and miracles [3, 4, 17].

The semantics of a recursive contract is given in a standard way, using fixpoints. Assume that a recursive contract statement $(\text{rec}_a X \bullet S)$ and a coalition A are given. Since S is built using the syntax of contract statements, we can define a function that maps any predicate transformer X to the result of replacing every construct except X in S by its weakest precondition predicate transformer semantics (for the coalition A). Let us call this function $f_{S,A}$. Then $f_{S,A}$ can be shown to be a monotonic function on the complete lattice of predicate transformers, and by the well-known Knaster-Tarski fixpoint theorem it has a complete lattice of fixpoints. We then define

$$\text{wp.} (\text{rec}_a X \bullet S). A = \begin{cases} \mu. f_{S,A} & \text{if } a \in A \\ \nu. f_{S,A} & \text{if } a \notin A \end{cases}$$

We take the least fixed point μ when non-termination is considered bad (from the point of view of the coalition A), as is the case when agent $a \in A$ is responsible for termination. Dually, we take the greatest fixpoint ν when termination is considered good, i.e., when an agent not in A is responsible for termination. A more careful and detailed treatment of recursion is found in [6].

The fixpoint definition of the semantics of recursion makes use of the fact that for all coalitions A and all contracts S the predicate transformer wp. $S.A$ is *monotonic*, i.e.,

$$p \subseteq q \Rightarrow \text{wp}.S.A.q \subseteq \text{wp}.S.A.q$$

holds for all predicates p and q. This is in fact the only one of Dijkstra's original four "healthiness" properties [11] that are satisfied by all contracts.

As the predicate transformers form a complete lattice, we can define standard lattice operations on them:

$$\text{abort} = (\lambda q \bullet \text{false})$$
$$\text{magic} = (\lambda q \bullet \text{true})$$
$$(F_1 \sqcup F_2).q = F_1.q \cap F_2.q$$
$$(F_1 \sqcap F_2).q = F_1.q \cup F_2.q$$

Here abort is the bottom of the lattice, and magic is the top of the lattice, while the two binary operations are lattice meet and lattice join for predicate transformers.

In addition to these operations, we define standard composition operators for predicate transformers:

$$(F_1 \, ; F_2).q = F_1.(F_2.q)$$
$$\text{if } p \text{ then } F_1 \text{ else } F_2 \text{ fi}.q = (p \cap F_1.q) \cup (\neg p \cap F_2.q)$$

Finally, let us define the following constant predicate transformers:

$$\langle f \rangle.q.\sigma \equiv q.(f.\sigma)$$
$$\{R\}.q.\sigma \equiv R.\sigma \cap q \neq \emptyset$$
$$[R].q.\sigma \equiv R.\sigma \subseteq q$$

With these definitions, we can give simpler definitions of the predicate transformers for contracts, that more clearly show the homomorphic connection between the operations on contracts and the operations on predicate transformers:

$$\text{wp}.\langle f \rangle.A = \langle f \rangle$$
$$\text{wp}.(\text{if } p \text{ then } S_1 \text{ else } S_2 \text{ fi}).A = \text{if } p \text{ then wp}.S_1 \text{ else wp}.S_2 \text{ fi}$$
$$\text{wp}.(S_1 \, ; S_2).A = \text{wp}.S_1.A \, ; \text{wp}.S_2.A$$
$$\text{wp}.\langle R \rangle_a.A = \begin{cases} \{R\} & \text{if } a \in A \\ [R] & \text{if } a \notin A \end{cases}$$
$$\text{wp}.(S_1 \, []_a \, S_2).A = \begin{cases} \text{wp}.S_1.A \sqcup \text{wp}.S_2.A & \text{if } a \in A \\ \text{wp}.S_1.A \sqcap \text{wp}.S_2.A & \text{if } a \notin A \end{cases}$$
$$\text{wp}.(\text{rec}_a \, X \bullet S).A = \begin{cases} (\mu X \bullet \text{wp}.S.A) & \text{if } a \in A \\ (\nu X \bullet \text{wp}.S.A) & \text{if } a \notin A \end{cases}$$

In the last definition, we assume that $\text{wp}.X.A = X$, so that the fixpoint is taken over a predicate transformer.

We finally make a slight extension to the contract formalism that allows us to also have implicit agents. We postulate that the set Ω of agents always contains two distinguished agents, *angel* and *demon*. Any coalition of agents A from Ω must be such that $angel \in A$ and $demon \notin A$. With this definition, we can introduce the following abbreviations for contracts:

$$\{R\} = \langle R \rangle_{angel}$$
$$[R] = \langle R \rangle_{demon}$$
$$\sqcup = []_{angel}$$
$$\sqcap = []_{demon}$$
$$\mu = \text{rec}_{angel}$$
$$\nu = \text{rec}_{demon}$$

This convention means that we can use predicate transformer notation directly in contracts. We will find this convention quite useful below, when we analyze the temporal properties of contracts.

2.3.2 *Correctness and winning strategies*

We say that *agents A can use contract S in initial state σ to establish postcondition q* (written $\sigma \, \{\!| \, S \, |\!\}_A \, q$) if there is a *winning strategy* for the agents in A which guarantees that initial configuration (S, σ) will lead to one of the following two alternatives:

(a) termination in such a way that the final configuration is some (Λ, γ) where γ is either a final state in q or $\perp_b$ for some $b \notin A$:

$$(S, \sigma) \to \cdots \to (\Lambda, \gamma) \quad \text{where } \gamma \in q \cup \{\perp_b \mid b \notin A\}$$

(b) an infinite execution caused by a recursion for which some agent $b \notin A$ is responsible.

Thus $\sigma \, \{\!| \, S \, |\!\}_A \, q$ means that, no matter what the other agents do, the agents in A can (by making suitable choices) achieve postcondition q, or make sure that some agent outside A either breaches the contract or causes nontermination.[1]

This is easily generalized to a general notion of *correctness*; we define *correctness of contract S for agents A, precondition p and postcondition q* as follows:

$$p \, \{\!| \, S \, |\!\}_A \, q \; \triangleq \; (\forall \sigma \in p \bullet \sigma \, \{\!| \, S \, |\!\}_A \, q)$$

The winning strategy theorem of [6] can now easily be generalized to take into account collections of agents, to give the following:

---

[1] If nested or mutual recursion is involved, then it may not be clear who is to blame for infinite executions. This problem is similar to the problem of how to decide who wins an infinite game. We will simply avoid nested or mutual recursion here (alternatively, we could consider Theorem 2.3.1 below to define how such situations should be interpreted).

2. Enforcing behavior with contracts

Theorem 2.3.1 *Assume that contract statement S, coalition A, precondition p and postcondition q are given. Then $p \{| S |\}_A q$ if and only if $p \subseteq \text{wp}.S.A.q$.*

Let us as an example show how to determine when agent a has a winning strategy for reaching the goal $x \geq 0$ in our example contract above. Let us as before define

$$S = S_1 ; S_2$$
$$S_1 = x := x + 1 \;[]_a\; x := x + 2$$
$$S_2 = x := x - 1 \;[]_b\; x := x - 2$$

Let $A = \{a\}$. By the rules for calculating weakest preconditions, we have that

$$\text{wp}.S.A.(x \geq 0) = \text{wp}.S_1.A.(\text{wp}.S_2.A.(x \geq 0))$$

$$\begin{aligned}
\text{wp}.S_2.A.(x \geq 0) &= \langle x := x - 1 \rangle.(x \geq 0) \cap \langle x := x - 2 \rangle.(x \geq 0) \\
&= (x - 1 \geq 0) \cap (x - 2 \geq 0) \\
&= (x \geq 1) \cap (x \geq 2) \\
&= x \geq 1 \wedge x \geq 2 \\
&= x \geq 2
\end{aligned}$$

$$\begin{aligned}
\text{wp}.S_1.A.(x \geq 2) &= \langle x := x + 1 \rangle.(x \geq 2) \cup \langle x := x + 2 \rangle.(x \geq 2) \\
&= (x + 1 \geq 2) \cup (x + 2 \geq 2) \\
&= (x \geq 1) \cup (x \geq 0) \\
&= x \geq 1 \vee x \geq 0 \\
&= x \geq 0
\end{aligned}$$

Thus, we have shown that

$$\text{wp}.S.A.(x \geq 0) = x \geq 0$$

In other words, the agent a can achieve the postcondition $x \geq 0$ whenever the initial state satisfies $x \geq 0$. Thus we have shown the correctness property

$$x \geq 0 \;\{|\; S \;|\}_{\{a\}}\; x \geq 0$$

From the wp-semantics and Theorem 2.3.1 it is straightforward to derive rules for proving correctness assertions, in the style of Hoare logic:

- *Functional update*

$$\frac{(\forall \sigma \in p \bullet q.(f.\sigma))}{p \;\{|\; \langle f \rangle \;|\}_A\; q}$$

- *Conditional composition*

$$\frac{p \cap b \;\{|\; S_1 \;|\}_A\; q \quad p \cap \neg b \;\{|\; S_2 \;|\}_A\; q}{p \;\{|\; \text{if } b \text{ then } S_1 \text{ else } S_2 \text{ fi} \;|\}_A\; q}$$

- *Sequential update*

$$\frac{p \:\{|\: S_1 \:|\}_A\: r \qquad r \:\{|\: S_2 \:|\}_A\: q}{p \:\{|\: S_1 \:;\: S_2 \:|\}_A\: q}$$

- *Relational update*

$$\frac{(\forall \sigma \in p \bullet \exists \sigma' \bullet R.\sigma.\sigma' \land q.\sigma')}{p \:\{|\: \langle R \rangle_a \:|\}_A\: q} \: a \in A \qquad \frac{(\forall \sigma \in p \bullet \forall \sigma' \bullet R.\sigma.\sigma' \Rightarrow q.\sigma')}{p \:\{|\: \langle R \rangle_a \:|\}_A\: q} \: a \notin A$$

- *Choice*

$$\frac{p \:\{|\: S_1 \:|\}_A\: q}{p \:\{|\: S_1 []_a S_2 \:|\}_A\: q} \: a \in A \qquad \frac{p \:\{|\: S_2 \:|\}_A\: q}{p \:\{|\: S_1 []_a S_2 \:|\}_A\: q} \: a \in A$$

$$\frac{p \:\{|\: S_1 \:|\}_A\: q \qquad p \:\{|\: S_1 \:|\}_A\: q}{p \:\{|\: S_1 []_a S_2 \:|\}_A\: q} \: a \notin A$$

- *Loop*

$$\frac{p \cap b \cap t = w \:\{|\: S \:|\}_A\: p \cap t < w}{p \:\{|\: \text{while}\:_a b \text{ do } S \text{ od } \:|\}_A\: p \cap \neg b} \: a \in A$$

$$\frac{p \cap b \:\{|\: S \:|\}_A\: p}{p \:\{|\: \text{while}\:_a b \text{ do } S \text{ od } \:|\}_A\: p \cap \neg b} \: a \notin A$$

- *Consequence*

$$\frac{p' \subseteq p \qquad p \:\{|\: S \:|\}_A\: q \qquad q \subseteq q'}{p' \:\{|\: S \:|\}_A\: q'}$$

In the rules for the while-loop, t (the termination argument for the loop) is assumed to range over some well-founded set W, and w is a fresh variable also ranging over W.

These are close to the traditional Hoare Logic rules for total correctness. We include a rule for the while-loop rather than for recursion, for simplicity. The existential quantifier in the first rule for relational update and the existence of two alternative rules for choice (when $a \in A$) indicate that we can show the existence of a general winning strategy by providing a witness during the correctness proof. In fact, the proof encodes a winning strategy, in the sense that if we provide an existential witness (for a relational update) then we describe how the agent in question should make its choice in order to contribute to establishing the postcondition. Similarly, the selection of the appropriate rule for a choice encodes a description of how an agent should make the choice during an execution.

2.3.3 Refinement of contracts

The predicate transformer semantics is based on total correctness. Traditionally, a notion of *refinement* is derived from a corresponding notion of correctness, so that a refinement $S \sqsubseteq S'$ holds iff S' satisfies all correctness properties that S satisfies.

Since we define correctness for a collection of agents (whose ability to guarantee a certain outcome we are investigating), refinement will also be relativised similarly. We say that *contract S is refined by contract S' for coalition A* (written $S \sqsubseteq_A S'$), if S' preserves all correctness properties of S, for A. By Theorem 2.3.1, we have

$$S \sqsubseteq_A S' \equiv (\forall q \bullet \text{wp}.S.A.q \subseteq \text{wp}.S'.A.q)$$

The traditional notion of refinement [3] is here recovered in the case when the coalition A is empty; i.e., if all the nondeterminism involved is demonic. Furthermore, the generalization of refinement to include both angelic and demonic nondeterminism [4, 6] is recovered by identifying the agents in A with as the angel and the agents outside A as the demon.

Given a contract, we can use the predicate transformer formulation of refinement to derive rules that allow us to improve a contract from the point of view of a specific coalition A, in the sense that any goals achievable with the original contract are still achievable with the new contract. These refinement rules can be used for *stepwise refinement* of contracts, where we start from an initial high level specification with the aim of deriving a more efficient (and usually lower level) implementation of the specification. In this paper we do not consider refinement, as the focus is on establishing temporal properties. The refinement relation $\sqsubseteq_A$ is investigated in more detail in [8].

2.4 Enforcing behavioral properties

The previous section has concentrated on what goals an agent can achieve while following a contract. Here we will instead look at what kind of behavior an agent can enforce by following a contract.

2.4.1 Analyzing behavior

Consider again the example contract of the previous section, but now assuming that we have just an angel and a demon involved in the contract:

$$S = (x := x+1 \sqcap x := x+2);$$
$$(x := x-1 \sqcup x := x-2)$$

A behavior property would, e.g., be that the angel can force the condition $0 \leq x \leq 2$ to hold in each state when executing the contract, if $x = 0$ initially. Using temporal logic notation, we can express this as

$$x = 0 \ \{\!| \ S \ |\!\} \ \Box(0 \leq x \leq 2)$$

Here $\Box(0 \leq x \leq 2)$ says that $0 \leq x \leq 2$ is *always* true. Note that this property need not hold for every possible execution, it is sufficient that there is a way for the angel to *enforce* the property by making suitable choices during the execution.

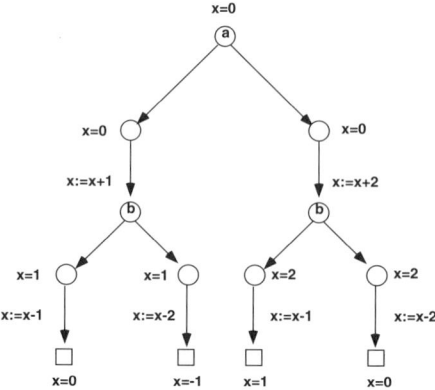

Figure 2.2. Behavior of contract

Using the operational semantics of S, we can determine all the possible execution sequences of this contract. Fig. 2.2 shows these, also indicating the value of x at each intermediate state (a is the demon, b is the angel). From this we see that the angel can indeed enforce the condition $0 \leq x \leq 2$, irrespectively of which alternative the demon chooses. If the demon chooses the left branch, then the angel should also choose the left branch, and if the demon chooses the right branch, then it does not matter which branch the angel chooses. The condition $1 \leq x \leq 2$ is, on the other hand, an example of a property that cannot be enforced by the angel.

In a similar way, we can show that the angel can also enforce that the condition $x = 1$ is *eventually* true when the initial state satisfies $x = 0$. This is expressed using temporal logic notation as

$$x = 0 \,\{\!|\ S\ |\!\}\, \Diamond (x = 1)$$

From Fig. 2.2 we see that this condition is true after two steps if the demon chooses the left alternative. If the demon chooses the right alternative, then the angel can enforce the condition upon termination by choosing the left alternative.

2.4.2 Constructing an interpreter

Let us consider more carefully how to check whether a temporal property can be enforced when carrying out a contract. Consider a contract statement S that operates on a state space Σ, and includes agents Ω. Let us check whether the temporal property $\Box p$ can be enforced by a coalition of agents $A \subseteq \Omega$.

For any predicate $p \subseteq \Sigma$, we define the the contract Always. p, called a *tester for* $\Box p$, by

$$\text{Always.} p = (\nu X \bullet \{p\} \,;\, [s \neq \Lambda] \,;\, step \,;\, X)$$
$$step = \langle s, \sigma := s', \sigma' \mid (s, \sigma) \rightarrow (s', \sigma') \rangle_{ch.\,s}$$

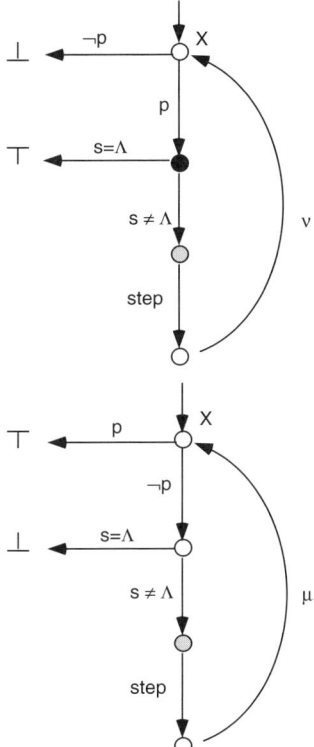

Figure 2.3. (a) A property holds always. (b) A property holds eventually

This contract operates on states τ with two components s and σ. We define $p.\tau = p.(\sigma.\tau)$. The function $ch.s$ gives the agent that makes the choice in the statement s, if there is one, otherwise there is no agent index. In other words, the tester is an *interpreter* for contract statements, which executes them with the purpose of determining whether a specific temporal property is valid.

We illustrate the behavior of the tester with the diagram in Fig. 2.3. The diagram shows the angelic choices as hollow circles, and the demonic choices as filled circles. A grey circle indicates that we do not know whether the choice is angelic or demonic. The X labels the node at which the iteration starts. The arrow labeled ν indicates that we have ν-iteration, i.e., the arrow can be traversed any number of times, without a breach of contract. An arrow labeled μ indicates μ-iteration, where the arrow can be traversed only a finite number of times during each iteration.

We now have the following general result, which we give without proof. (In a separate paper [9] we give formal definitions of behaviours and temporal properties, together with proofs of verification and refinement rules).

Lemma 2.4.1 *Let S, p, and C be as above. Let A be a coalition of agents in Ω. Then*

$$\sigma_0 \{| S |\}_A \Box p \equiv \text{wp.} (\text{Always}.p). A. \text{false}. \tau$$

where $\sigma.\tau = \sigma_0$ *and* $s.\tau = S$

This same result is expressed somewhat more clearly as a correctness property:

$$\sigma_0 \{| S |\}_A \Box p \equiv \tau \{| \text{Always}.p |\}_A \text{false}$$

Lemma 2.4.1 shows that we can reduce the question of whether a temporal property can be enforced for a contract to the question of whether a certain goal can be achieved. In this case, the goal **false** cannot really be established, so success can only be achieved by miraculous termination, or by nontermination caused by an agent that does not belong to A.

The tester contract does not, in fact, constitute a fundamental extension to the notion of contracts; it can be modeled with existing contract constructs (although it requires an infinite choice construct, if the number of agents is infinite).

In a similar way, we can define a tester Eventually.p for the property $\Diamond p$, by

$$\text{Eventually}.p = (\mu X \bullet [\neg p] ; \{s \neq \Lambda\} ; step ; X)$$

This tester is described in Fig. 2.3. We have the following result for this tester:

Lemma 2.4.2

$$\sigma_0 \{| S |\}_A \Diamond p \equiv \tau \{| \text{Eventually}.p |\}_A \text{false}$$

where $\sigma.\tau = \sigma_0$ *and* $s.\tau = S$.

Again, this shows how the question whether a temporal property can be enforced is reduced to a question about whether a goal can be achieved. In this case, the eventually-property does not hold if execution continues forever without ever encountering a state where p holds.

2.4.3 Other temporal properties

A more complicated behavior is illustrated by the *until* operator. We say that a property p holds until property q, denoted $p \,\mathcal{U}\, q$, if q will hold eventually, and until then p holds. We have that

$$\sigma_0 \{| S |\}_A p \,\mathcal{U}\, q \equiv \tau \{| \text{Until}.p.q) |\}_A \text{false}$$

where $\sigma.\tau = \sigma_0$ and $s.\tau = S$ and the tester for until is defined by

$$\text{Until}.p.q = (\mu X \bullet [\neg q] ; \{p\} ; \{s \neq \Lambda\} ; step ; X)$$

This tester is illustrated by the diagram in Fig. 2.4.

The *weak until*, denoted $p \,\mathcal{W}\, q$, can be defined in a similar matter. It differs from the previous operator in that it is also satisfied if q is never satisfied, provided p is always satisfied. We have that

$$\sigma_0 \{| S |\} p\mathcal{W}q \equiv \tau \{| \text{Wuntil}.p.q |\}_A \text{false}$$

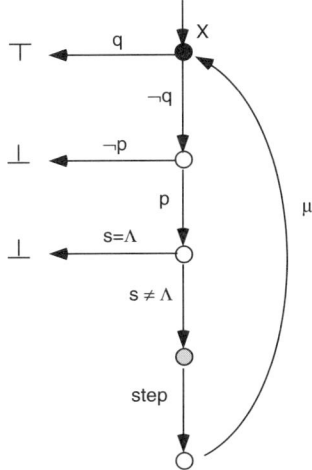

Figure 2.4. A property p holds until q

where $\sigma.\tau = \sigma_0$ and $s.\tau = S$ and

$$\text{Wuntil}.p.q = (\nu X \bullet [\neg q] ; \{p\} ; \{s \neq \Lambda\} ; \text{step} ; X)$$

The always and eventually operators arise as special cases of the until operators: $\Box p = p \, \mathcal{W} \, \text{false}$ and $\Diamond p = \text{true} \, \mathcal{U} \, p$.

Another interesting property is p *leads to* q, denoted $p \leadsto q$. We have that the tester for leads-to is

$$\text{Leadsto}.p.q = [p] ; (\mu X \bullet [\neg q] ; \{s \neq \Lambda\} ; \text{step} ; X)$$

and it holds if and only if

$$\sigma_0 \, \{\!| \, S \, |\!\}_A \, p \leadsto q \equiv \tau \, \{\!| \, \text{Leadsto}.p.q \, |\!\}_A \, \text{false}$$

where $\sigma.\tau = \sigma_0$ and $s.\tau = S$. The behavior of this tester is illustrated by the diagram in Fig. 2.5.

An even more useful property is to say that property p *always leads to* property q, denoted by $\Box(p \leadsto q)$. This requires that we use two loops, a ν- loop and a μ-loop. We have that

$$\sigma_0 \, \{\!| \, S \, |\!\}_A \, \Box(p \leadsto q) \equiv \tau \, \{\!| \, \text{Aleadsto}.p.q \, |\!\}_A \, \text{false}$$

where $\sigma.\tau = \sigma_0$ and $s.\tau = S$ and

$$\text{Aleadsto}.p.q = (\nu Y \bullet [\neg p] ; [s \neq \Lambda] ; \text{step} ; Y$$
$$\sqcap [p] ; (\mu X \bullet [\neg q] ; \{s \neq \Lambda\} ; \text{step} ; X \sqcap [q]) ; [s \neq \Lambda] ; \text{step} ; Y)$$

This is illustrated in Fig. 2.6.

The above mentioned behavioral properties all have one thing in common, they are *insensitive to finite stuttering*. This means that if a step of the computation does not change the state, then the effect is the same as if that step had been omitted.

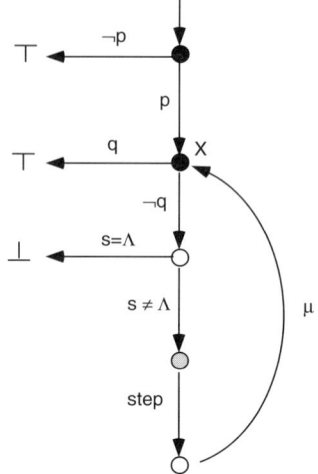

Figure 2.5. A property p leads to q

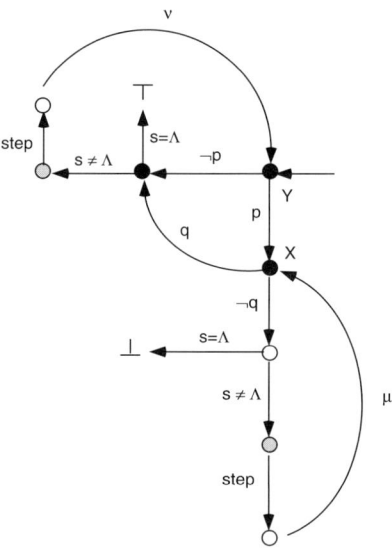

Figure 2.6. A property p always leads to q

In the diagram, this means that a stuttering step will lead back to the same state in the diagram. Being insensitive to stuttering means that the number of steps that are taken is not important for the behavioral property, only the sequence of properties that arise during the execution. Note that a computation should not be insensitive to infinite stuttering, as this is amounts to a form of nontermination (internal divergence).

2.5 Analyzing behavior of action systems

Let us now look at how to enforce temporal properties for action systems. As action systems are just contracts, we can use the techniques developed above for this. However, we will show that the simple format for action systems allows us to simplify the characterizations and proof obligations considerably.

2.5.1 Classification of action systems

In Section 2.2.5 we noted that an action system in general is of the form

$$\mathcal{A}(a,b,c) = B\,;\,(\text{rec}_c\,X \bullet (S_1\;[]_b\;S_2\;[]_b\;\ldots\;[]_b\;S_n)\,;\,X\;[]_a\;\langle g\rangle_a)\,;\,E$$

Given a coalition A that is trying to achieve some goal, there are eight different possibilities to consider: whether $a, b \in A$, or $a \in A, b \notin A$, or $a \notin A, b \in A$, or $a \notin A, b \notin A$, and, in each case, whether $c \in A$ or $c \notin A$. We will briefly characterize the intuition behind each of these cases, assuming that agent a is the user (the environment) and that agent b is the computer (the system). In each case, $c \in A$ means that the computation must terminate eventually if the goal is to be achieved, while $c \notin A$ means that the goal can be achieved even if the iteration goes on forever.

- *Angelic iteration* ($a, b \in A$): At each step, the user decides whether to quit (which is possible if g holds) or whether to continue one more iteration. In the latter case, the user decides which alternative S_i to choose for the next iteration. Angelic iteration models an *event loop*, where the user can choose what action or event to execute next, and also may choose to exit the loop whenever this is allowed by the exit constraint.

- *Angelic iteration with demonic exit* ($a \notin A, b \in A$): This case is similar to the previous one, except that the choice whether to terminate or not is made by the computer and not by the user. In other words, it is like an event loop, where termination may happen at any time when termination is enabled, the choice of when to terminate being outside the control of the user.

- *Demonic iteration* ($a \notin A, b \notin A$): The computer decides whether to stop or to continue the iteration, and in the latter case, which of the alternative actions to continue with, in a way that cannot be controlled by the user. This form of iteration models a *concurrent system*, where the nondeterminism in the choice of the next iteration action expresses the arbitrary interleaving of enabled actions.

- *Demonic iteration with angelic exit* ($a \in A, b \notin A$): Here we have a similar situation as the previous, a concurrent system, where, however, termination is decided by the user. At each step, the user can decide whether to terminate or continue (provided the exit condition is satisfied), but the user cannot influence the choice of the next action, if she decides to continue.

We get more traditional systems as special cases of these very general forms of iteration. Dijkstra's guarded iteration statement is a special kind of demonic iteration, where some action is enabled if and only if the exit condition does not hold. A traditional temporal logic model is essentially a demonic iteration where the exit condition is always false, i.e., the system never terminates, and no abortions are permitted.

Our formalization introduces three main extensions to the traditional temporal logic model: the possibility that an execution may terminate, the possibility of angelic choice during the execution, and the possibility of a failed or miraculously successful execution.

Action systems can be used to model both interactive systems, where the choice of actions is under the control of the user, and concurrent systems, where the choice of actions is outside the control of the user. In fact, the action contract formalism is much more expressive than either one of these two formalisms, because the actions themselves may also be either angelic or demonic. In a concurrent as well as in an interactive system, we may have angelic choices made inside an action. This roughly corresponds to an input statement in the action. We can also have demonic choice inside an action, which roughly corresponds to a specification statement, where only partial information about the result is known.

2.5.2 Analyzing behavior

In the action system $\mathcal{A} = (\text{rec}_c \, X \bullet S[]_a \langle g \rangle_a)$ we assume that the execution of S is atomic, in the sense that the state can not be observed inside the execution of S. Hence, to determine whether a property like $\Box p$ or $\Diamond p$ holds, we only observe the state at the beginning, immediately before each iteration, and at the end. This means that a state may violate the property p inside the execution of S, without violating the property $\Box p$ and it may satisfy the property p inside the execution of S, without satisfying the property $\Diamond p$. The justification for this is that we consider S as a *specification* of what kind of state change is taking place, rather than an actual implementation. If the internal working of S needs to be taken into account, then each internal step has to be modeled as a separate action.

Let us now consider how to determine whether an agent can enforce a temporal property like $\Box p$ during the execution of an action system. Action systems introduce a notion of atomicity that we have not modeled before, so we need to extend our operational semantics first.

We augment the syntax and operational semantics of contracts with a feature to indicates that a sequence of execution steps are internal, thus resulting in unobservable internal states. To do this, we introduce two additional statements into contracts: **hide** and **unhide**. We update the operational semantics for contracts by assuming that the state component is of the form (σ, o), where o is a boolean value, indicating whether the state is observable or not. This component is not changed by the previously introduced contract constructs. Thus, we have, e.g.,

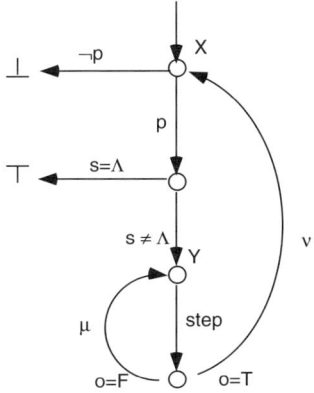

Figure 2.7. Modified tester for $\Box p$

that
$$\frac{p.\sigma}{(\text{if } p \text{ then } S_1 \text{ else } S_2 \text{ fi}, (\sigma, o)) \to (S_1, (\sigma, o))}$$

and similarly for the other contract constructs. For the hiding and unhiding operations, we introduce two new axioms:

$$\overline{(\text{hide}, (\sigma, o)) \to (\Lambda, (\sigma, \mathsf{F}))} \qquad \overline{(\text{unhide}, (\sigma, o)) \to (\Lambda, (\sigma, \mathsf{T}))}$$

The hide and unhide operations will thus just toggle the flag o, indicating whether the state is considered observable or not (we assume that there are no nested hidings). A contract statement whose internal computation is hidden is denoted $\langle S \rangle$, defined by

$$\langle S \rangle = \text{hide} \,;\, S \,;\, \text{unhide}$$

We assume as a syntactic restriction that there are no unmatched hide or unhide operations in a contract. We also do not allow nested hiding and unhiding in actions.

We also need to modify the tester, to take the hidden states into account. The modified tester for the property $\Box p$ is as follows:

$$\text{Always}.\, p = (\nu X \bullet \{p\} \,;\, [s \neq \Lambda] \,;\, (\mu\, Y \bullet \mathit{step} \,;\, \text{if } o \text{ then } X \text{ else } Y \text{ fi}))$$

The behavior of this interpreter is shown in Fig. 2.7. We have to take a position here on whether nonterminating unobservable computations (internal divergence) are good or bad. We choose here to consider them bad, although it might also be possible to argue for the opposite interpretation. Thus, internal divergence is equivalent to abortion (i.e., the designated angel breaching the contract), hence the μ label on the arrow in the inner loop.

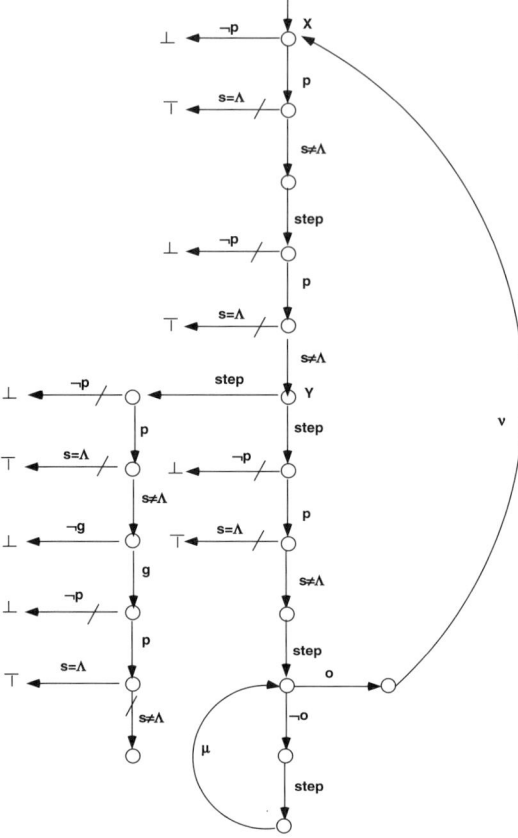

Figure 2.8. Action system tester for $\Box p$

Let us next show how we can compute the precondition for agents A to enforce the property $\Box p$ in the action system

$$\mathcal{A} = (\text{rec}_c\ X \bullet \langle S \rangle\ ;\ X[]_a\langle g \rangle_a)$$

in the case when $a \in A$. We have that

$$\sigma\ \{|\ \mathcal{A}\ |\}_A\ \Box p \equiv (\nu X \bullet \{p\}\ ;\ [\neg g]\ ;\ \text{wp}.\,S.\,A\ ;\ X).\,\text{false}.\,\sigma$$

We can show that this is indeed the case, by considering how the coalition A would execute the contract Always. p from initial state $(\mathcal{A}, (\sigma, T))$. This is done by unfolding the iteration appropriately, as shown in Fig. 2.8. We have crossed out all those branches in the figure that cannot be taken, because the condition is known to be false. By eliminating these branches, as well as branches that the coalition would avoid because they would lead to certain failure, we derive the simpler diagram shown in Fig. 2.9. This proves that our characterization of the always tester for the action system $\mathcal{A}$ given above is correct.

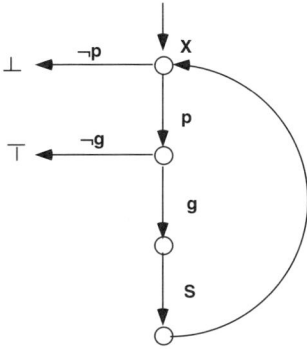

Figure 2.9. Simple action system tester for $\Box p$

The above gave the basic result that we need in order to reason about the temporal behavior of action systems. The main advantage here is that we can argue directly about the weakest preconditions of the actions, without having to go the indirect route of an interpreter for the system.

2.6 Verifying enforcement

We have shown above how to characterize enforcement of temporal properties for action systems using weakest preconditions. In this section, we will look in more detail at how one should prove enforcement in practice.

2.6.1 Predicate-level conditions for correctness

When reasoning about systems in practice, we want to talk about enforcement (correctness) with respect to a precondition rather than a specific initial state. The obvious generalization is

$$p \, \{\!\mid \mathcal{A} \mid\!\}_A \, \Box p \equiv (\forall \sigma \in p \bullet \sigma \, \{\!\mid \mathcal{A} \mid\!\}_A \, \Box p)$$

and similarly for other temporal properties. Furthermore, it is more practical to reason about fixpoints on the predicate level rather than on the predicate transformer level. A straightforward argument shows that from the rule shown in Section 2.5.2 we get the following rule:

$$p \, \{\!\mid \mathcal{A} \mid\!\}_A \, \Box q \equiv p \subseteq (\nu x \bullet q \cap (g \cup \text{wp.} S. A. x))$$

for the case when $a \in A$. In a similar way, we can derive predicate-level characterizations of correctness for the different temporal properties and for the different cases of which agents belong to the coalition that we are interested in. The following lemmas collect those cases that we will use in the examples in Section 2.6.4.

Lemma 2.6.1 *Assume that action system* $\mathcal{A} = (\text{rec}_c X \bullet \langle S \rangle \; ; \; X[]_a \langle g \rangle_a)$ *and coalition A are given. Then*

$$p \; \{| \; \mathcal{A} \; |\}_A \; \Box q \equiv \begin{cases} p \subseteq (\nu x \bullet q \cap (g \cup \text{wp}. S. A. x)) & \text{if } a \in A \\ p \subseteq (\nu x \bullet q \cap \text{wp}. S. A. x) & \text{if } a \notin A \end{cases}$$

$$p \; \{| \; \mathcal{A} \; |\}_A \; \Diamond q \equiv \begin{cases} p \subseteq (\mu x \bullet q \cup \text{wp}. S. A. x) & \text{if } a \in A \\ p \subseteq (\mu x \bullet q \cup (\neg g \cap \text{wp}. S. A. x)) & \text{if } a \notin A \end{cases}$$

$$p \; \{| \; \mathcal{A} \; |\}_A \; q \, \mathcal{U} \, r \equiv \begin{cases} p \subseteq (\mu x \bullet r \cup (q \cap \text{wp}. S. A. x)) & \text{if } a \in A \\ p \subseteq (\mu x \bullet r \cup (\neg g \cap q \cap \text{wp}. S. A. x)) & \text{if } a \notin A \end{cases}$$

In Section 2.3 we considered achieving goals (postconditions) with contracts. Since our generalized notion of temporal properties also includes finite scenarios (aborting, termination or miraculous), we can consider achieving a postcondition q as enforcing a special temporal property $\triangle q$ *(finally q)*.

We can also give the characterization for a finally-property in the same way as for other temporal properties. For simplicity we assume that $c \notin A$. We have that

Lemma 2.6.2 *Assume that action system* $\mathcal{A} = (\text{rec}_c X \bullet \langle S \rangle \; ; \; X[]_a \langle g \rangle_a)$ *and coalition A are given. If $c \in A$, then*

$$p \; \{| \; \mathcal{A} \; |\}_A \; \triangle q \equiv \begin{cases} p \subseteq (\mu x \bullet (g \cap q) \cup \text{wp}. S. A. x) & \text{if } a \in A \\ p \subseteq (\mu x \bullet (\text{wp}. S. A. \text{false} \cap q) \cup (\neg g \cap \text{wp}. S. A. x)) & \text{if } a \notin A \end{cases}$$

On the other hand, if $c \notin A$, then

$$p \; \{| \; \mathcal{A} \; |\}_A \; \triangle q \equiv \begin{cases} p \subseteq (\nu x \bullet (g \cap q) \cup \text{wp}. S. A. x) & \text{if } a \in A \\ p \subseteq (\nu x \bullet (\text{wp}. S. A. \text{false} \cap q) \cup (\neg g \cap \text{wp}. S. A. x)) & \text{if } a \notin A \end{cases}$$

Here the intuition is that if $a \in A$, then the termination is (angelically) chosen whenever g and q both hold. If $a \notin A$, then continuation is (demonically) chosen whenever q holds, if possible (i.e., if $\neg\text{wp}. S. A. \text{false}$ holds).

Note that this is the first temporal property where the agent c comes into play. In our generalizations of classical temporal operators, the notion of who is responsible for infinite executions does not matter. However, it does matter (as was the original intention) when considering establishing a postcondition.

The conditions for the case $a \notin A$ in Lemma 2.6.2 contain the odd-looking predicate wp. $S. A.$ false, but in the case when termination is deterministic we get a simplification, because then wp. $S. A.$ false $= g$).

2.6.2 Invariant-based methods

Lemma 2.6.1 shows how proving enforcement of temporal properties is reduced to proving properties of the form $p \subseteq e$ where e is a μ- or ν-expression. From fixpoint theory we know that such properties can be proved using an invariant (ν) or an invariant and a termination function (μ):

Lemma 2.6.3 *Assume that action system* $\mathcal{A} = (\text{rec}_c X \bullet \langle S \rangle \; ; \; X[]_a \langle g \rangle_a)$ *is given, together with a coalition A. Then*

2. Enforcing behavior with contracts   45

(a) *Always-properties can be proved using invariants, as follows:*

$$\frac{p \subseteq I \quad \neg g \cap I \{\!| \ S \ |\!\}_A \ I \quad I \subseteq q}{p \{\!| \ \mathcal{A} \ |\!\}_A \ \Box q} \ a \in A$$

$$\frac{p \subseteq I \quad I \{\!| \ S \ |\!\}_A \ I \quad I \subseteq q}{p \{\!| \ \mathcal{A} \ |\!\}_A \ \Box q} \ a \notin A$$

(b) *Eventually-properties can be proved using invariants and termination arguments, as follows:*

$$\frac{p \subseteq q \cup I \quad \neg q \cap I \cap t = w \ \{\!| \ S \ |\!\}_A \ q \cup (I \cap t < w)}{p \{\!| \ \mathcal{A} \ |\!\}_A \ \Diamond q} \ a \in A$$

$$\frac{p \subseteq q \cup (\neg g \cap I)}{\neg q \cap \neg g \cap I \cap t = w \ \{\!| \ S \ |\!\}_A \ q \cup (\neg g \cap I \cap t < w)} \ a \notin A$$
$$p \{\!| \ \mathcal{A} \ |\!\}_A \ \Diamond q$$

where the state function t ranges over some well-founded set.

(c) *Until-properties can be proved as follows:*

$$\frac{p \subseteq r \cup I \quad \neg r \cap I \cap t = w \ \{\!| \ S \ |\!\}_A \ r \cup (I \cap t < w) \quad I \subseteq q}{p \{\!| \ \mathcal{A} \ |\!\}_A \ q \ \mathcal{U} \ r} \ a \in A$$

$$\frac{p \subseteq r \cup (\neg g \cap I)}{\neg g \cap \neg r \cap I \cap t = w \ \{\!| \ S \ |\!\}_A \ r \cup (\neg g \cap I \cap t < w)}$$
$$\frac{I \subseteq q}{p \{\!| \ \mathcal{A} \ |\!\}_A \ q \ \mathcal{U} \ r} \ a \notin A$$

where the state function t again ranges over some well-founded set.

Enforcing finally-properties is essentially proving correctness for loops, with different combinations of angelic and demonic nondeterminism:

Lemma 2.6.4 *Finally-properties can be proved as follows, in the case when* $c \in A$:

$$\frac{p \subseteq (g \cap q) \cup I \quad \neg(g \cap q) \cap I \cap t = w \ \{\!| \ S \ |\!\}_A \ (g \cap q) \cup (I \cap t < w)}{p \{\!| \ \mathcal{A} \ |\!\}_A \ \triangle q} \ a \in A$$

$$\frac{p \subseteq I \quad \neg wp.S.A.\text{false} \cap I \cap t = w \ \{\!| \ S \ |\!\}_A \ I \cap t < w \quad g \cap I \subseteq q}{p \{\!| \ \mathcal{A} \ |\!\}_A \ \triangle q} \ a \notin A$$

where the state function t again ranges over some well-founded set. In the case when $c \notin A$ *the rules are similar, but without termination function t.*

2.6.3 Demonstrative methods

In some cases, temporal properties can be proved by demonstrating a specific sequence of correctness steps. This idea will be used in examples in Section 2.6.4. We now show how such methods can be derived from the general characterizations of temporal properties.

An eventually-property $\Diamond q$ can be proved by showing that a specific number of steps will lead to the condition q holding:

Lemma 2.6.5 *Assume that action system $\mathcal{A}$ is given as before. Then*

$$\frac{p \:\{\!|\: S^n \:|\!\}_{\mathcal{A}}\: q}{p \:\{\!|\: \mathcal{A} \:|\!\}_{\mathcal{A}}\: \Diamond q}\, a \in A \qquad \frac{p \:\{\!|\: (\{\neg g\}\,;\,S)^n \:|\!\}_{\mathcal{A}}\: q}{p \:\{\!|\: \mathcal{A} \:|\!\}_{\mathcal{A}}\: \Diamond q}\, a \notin A$$

where S^n means n-fold sequential composition $S\,;\,S\,;\,\cdots\,;\,S$ (and $S^0 = \mathsf{skip}$).

Proof. We prove that this rule is valid, for the case $a \in A$. Assume $p \:\{\!|\: S^n \:|\!\}_{\mathcal{A}}\: q$. We first note that it is straightforward to show (by induction on n) that $T^n.q \subseteq (\mu x \bullet q \cup T.x)$, for arbitrary predicate transformer T and predicate q. Thus, we have

$\quad p \:\{\!|\: \mathcal{A} \:|\!\}_{\mathcal{A}}\: \Diamond q$
$\equiv \{\text{original rule for correctness}\}$
$\quad p \subseteq (\mu x \bullet q \cup \mathsf{wp}.S.A.x)$
$\Leftarrow \{\text{comment above}\}$
$\quad p \subseteq (\mathsf{wp}.S.A)^n.q$
$\equiv \{\text{homomorphism (Section 2.3.1)}\}$
$\quad p \subseteq (\mathsf{wp}.S^n.A).q$
$\equiv \{\text{definition of correctness}\}$
$\quad p \:\{\!|\: S^n \:|\!\}_{\mathcal{A}}\: q$

$\square$

Until-properties can be proved by exhibiting a suitable correctness sequence.

Lemma 2.6.6 *Assume that action system $\mathcal{A}$ is given as before. Then*

$$\frac{q_i \subseteq q\ (i = 0..n-1) \quad q_i \:\{\!|\: S \:|\!\}_{\mathcal{A}}\: q_{i+1}\ (i = 0..n-1)}{p \:\{\!|\: \mathcal{A} \:|\!\}_{\mathcal{A}}\: q\,\mathcal{U}\,r}\, a \in A$$

and

$$\frac{q_i \subseteq q\ (i = 0..n-1) \quad q_i \:\{\!|\: \{\neg g\}\,;\,S \:|\!\}_{\mathcal{A}}\: q_{i+1}\ (i = 0..n-1)}{p \:\{\!|\: \mathcal{A} \:|\!\}_{\mathcal{A}}\: q\,\mathcal{U}\,r}\, a \notin A$$

where $p = q_0$ and $q_n = r$.

Proof. We prove that this rule is valid, for the case $a \in A$. Assume $q_i \subseteq q$ and $q_i \:\{\!|\: S \:|\!\}_{\mathcal{A}}\: q_{i+1}$ for $i = 0..n-1$. We show that $q_i \subseteq (\mu x \bullet r \cup (q \cap \mathsf{wp}.S.A.x)))$ for

$i = 0..n$, by induction down from n. As a base case we have (where $T = \text{wp}.S.A$)

$$q_n$$
$$\subseteq \{\text{assumptions}\}$$
$$q \cap T.r$$
$$\subseteq \{\text{monotonicity}\}$$
$$r \cup (q \cap T.(\mu x \bullet r \cup (q \cap T.x)))$$
$$= \{\text{fold fixpoint}\}$$
$$(\mu x \bullet r \cup (q \cap T.x)))$$

and the step case is (for $0 < i \leq n$)

$$q_{i-1}$$
$$\subseteq \{\text{assumptions}\}$$
$$q \cap T.q_i$$
$$\subseteq \{\text{monotonicity, induction assumption}\}$$
$$r \cup (q \cap T.(\mu x \bullet r \cup (q \cap T.x)))$$
$$= \{\text{fold fixpoint}\}$$
$$(\mu x \bullet r \cup (q \cap T.x))$$

which by induction gives us $q_0 \subseteq (\mu x \bullet r \cup (q \cap T.x))$ from which $p \{\!|\ \mathcal{A}\ |\!\}_A\ q\,\mathcal{U}\,r$ follows by Lemma 2.6.1, since $p = q_0$. □

2.6.4 Enforcement in example systems

Let us now apply these techniques to analyzing enforcement of temporal properties in the three example action systems that we described earlier.

The game of Nim

The game of Nim is described as the following action system:

$$Nim = (f := \mathsf{T}\ []_c\, f := \mathsf{F})\ ;\ Play$$
$$Play =_z\ f \wedge x > 0 \rightarrow \langle x := x' \mid x' < x \leq x' + 2 \rangle_a\ ; f := \neg f\ ;\ Play$$
$$[]_c\ \neg f \wedge x > 0 \rightarrow \langle x := x' \mid x' < x \leq x' + 2 \rangle_b\ ; f := \neg f\ ;\ Play$$
$$[]_c\ x = 0 \rightarrow \text{skip}$$

Before considering questions about winning or losing, we consider the general question "Will the game always terminate"? In order to answer this question in the most general way, we take the point of view of an empty coalition (so all agents are demonic, i.e., trying to prevent termination). The property that we want to enforce is $\triangle \mathsf{true}$. We use Lemma 2.6.3 (d), according to which answering this question is equivalent to proving termination of the traditional loop program

$$\text{while } x > 0 \text{ do if } f \text{ then } [x := x' \mid x' < x \leq x' + 2]\ ;\ \langle f := \neg f \rangle$$

$$\text{else } [x := x' \mid x' < x \leq x' + 2] \, ; \, \langle f := \neg f \rangle$$
$$\text{fi}$$
$$\text{od}$$

This is straightforward, with invariant true and termination argument x. Since termination is guaranteed regardless of whether the agent z (who is responsible for termination) is part of the coalition we consider or not, we can considered z to be a dummy and leave it out of the discussion when analyzing other properties.

The most obvious question that we can ask about this system is "Under what initial conditions can agent a (or b) win the game"? The desired postcondition from the point of view of agent a is $f \wedge x = 0$, while from the point of view of agent b it is $\neg f \wedge x = 0$.

We first show that in *Play*, agent a can win under the precondition

$$p = (f \wedge x \bmod 3 \neq 1) \vee (\neg f \wedge x \bmod 3 = 1)$$

regardless of how the scheduler works. We use Lemma 2.6.3 (d) again, with coalition $A = \{a\}$ and with invariant $(f \wedge x \bmod 3 \neq 1) \vee (\neg f \wedge x \bmod 3 = 1)$, i.e., the same as the precondition. The idea is that a can always make the state change from a situation where $x \bmod 3 \neq 1$ to a situation where $x \bmod 3 = 1$ while b must then re-establish $x \bmod 3 \neq 1$. The result is the same in the case $A = \{a, c\}$, since the scheduler is essentially deterministic inside *Play*.

Now it is easy to show that the initialization always establishes the precondition p if the scheduler is angelic ($c \in A$) but never if the scheduler is demonic ($c \notin A$). The conclusion of this is that in the original game, we can always win if we are allowed to decide who should start (after we know how many sticks are in the pile).

Wolf, goat and cabbage

The action system that describes the wolf, goat and cabbage problem is as follows:

$$\begin{aligned}
CrossRiver & = m, w, g, c := \mathsf{F}, \mathsf{F}, \mathsf{F}, \mathsf{F} \, ; \, Transport \\
Transport & =_a \ m = w \to m, w := \neg m, \neg w \, ; \, Transport \\
& \ []_a \ m = g \to m, g := \neg m, \neg g \, ; \, Transport \\
& \ []_a \ m = c \to m, c := \neg m, \neg c \, ; \, Transport \\
& \ []_a \ m := \neg m \, ; \, Transport \\
& \ []_a \ \mathsf{skip}
\end{aligned}$$

We want to prove that the agent (the man) can enforce the following temporal property using the contract:

$$(w = g \Rightarrow m = w) \wedge (g = c \Rightarrow m = g) \ \mathcal{U} \ m \wedge w \wedge g \wedge c$$

The simplest way to show this is to verify the following sequence of correctness steps:

$$\text{true}$$

2. Enforcing behavior with contracts

$$\{\!|\ m,w,g,c := \mathsf{F},\mathsf{F},\mathsf{F},\mathsf{F}\ |\!\}$$
$$\neg m \wedge \neg w \wedge \neg g \wedge \neg c$$
$$\{\!|\ S\ |\!\}$$
$$m \wedge \neg w \wedge g \wedge \neg c$$
$$\{\!|\ S\ |\!\}$$
$$\neg m \wedge \neg w \wedge g \wedge \neg c$$
$$\{\!|\ S\ |\!\}$$
$$m \wedge w \wedge g \wedge \neg c$$
$$\{\!|\ S\ |\!\}$$
$$\neg m \wedge w \wedge \neg g \wedge \neg c$$
$$\{\!|\ S\ |\!\}$$
$$m \wedge w \wedge \neg g \wedge c$$
$$\{\!|\ S\ |\!\}$$
$$\neg m \wedge w \wedge \neg g \wedge c$$
$$\{\!|\ S\ |\!\}$$
$$m \wedge w \wedge g \wedge c$$

where S stands for the action of the system, i.e.,

$$\{m = w\}\ ;\ m,w := \neg m, \neg w$$
$$\sqcup\ \{m = g\}\ ;\ m,g := \neg m, \neg g$$
$$\sqcup\ \{m = c\}\ ;\ m,c := \neg m, \neg c$$
$$\sqcup\ m := \neg m$$

By Lemma 2.6.5 this is sufficient, since each of the intermediate conditions implies $(w = g \Rightarrow m = w) \wedge (g = c \Rightarrow m = g)$.

The Dim Sun restaurant

The Dim Sun restaurant was described as follows:

$Dim\ Sun = x_0, x_1, x_2, f := 0, 0, 0, 3\ ;\ Serve$
$Serve =_z\ \langle r > 0 \rangle_e\ ;\ (\ \langle f \neq 0 \rangle_d\ ;\ (\langle x_0, r := x_0 + 1, r - 1 \rangle []_a \mathsf{skip})\ ;\ \langle f := 0 \rangle\ ;\ Serve$
$[]_d\ \langle f \neq 1 \rangle_d\ ;\ (\langle x_1, r := x_1 + 1, r - 1 \rangle []_b \mathsf{skip})\ ;\ \langle f := 1 \rangle\ ;\ Serve$
$[]_d\ \langle f \neq 2 \rangle_d\ ;\ (\langle x_2, r := x_2 + 1, r - 1 \rangle []_c \mathsf{skip})\ ;\ \langle f := 2 \rangle\ ;\ Serve\ )$
$[]_e\ \mathsf{skip}$

With this setup we can prove that with the help of the servant, a customer can get at least half of the items that have been taken:

$$x_0 = 0 \wedge x_1 = 0 \wedge x_2 = 0 \wedge f = 3\ \{\!|\ \mathcal{A}\ |\!\}_{\{a,d\}}\ \Box(x_0 \geq x_1 + x_2)$$

The proof uses Lemma 2.6.3 with invariant $(f = 0 \wedge x_0 > x_1 + x_2) \vee (f \neq 0 \wedge x_0 \geq x_1 + x_2)$.

Similarly, we can prove that two cooperating customers can get almost half of the items, provided that the manager helps by not closing too early:

$$x_0 = 0 \land x_1 = 0 \land x_2 = 0 \land f = 3 \ \{\!| \ \mathcal{A} \ |\!\}_{\{a,b,e\}} \ \triangle (r = 0 \land x_0 + x_1 \geq x_2 - 1)$$

In this case, the invariant is $x_0 + x_1 \geq x_2 - 1$ and the termination argument is, e.g., $3r + 3 - f$.

2.7 Conclusions and related work

The main purpose of this paper has been to show how to model enforcement of temporal properties during execution of contracts. Our results generalize the results that we have presented earlier, in particular in [6], where only achievement of specific goals with a contract was considered. At the same time, the results provide a generalization of the standard temporal logic analysis framework, where only one kind of nondeterminism is allowed (demonic). Another contribution here is the generalization of action systems. The traditional notion of action systems only allows demonic choice, and is mainly used to model concurrent systems. In [6] and [10], we generalized this to action systems with angelic choice, to model interactive systems. Here we carry this one step further, and give a general contract model for action systems that allows any number of agents to participate in the execution of the action system, getting concurrent and interactive systems as special cases. A noteworthy feature of this generalization is that now also termination in action systems is nondeterministic. Action systems turn out to be quite good for describing systems, as they allow simplified characterizations and proof obligations for enforcement of temporal properties. At the same time, action systems introduce a notion of atomicity that is not directly modeled in contracts. The examples have been chosen to illustrate the new kinds of applications that now can be handled in our approach. More traditional examples of concurrent and interactive systems have been described elsewhere.

Temporal properties have been defined and used before in a predicate transformer framework with only demonic nondeterminism in order to generalize traditional reasoning systems for sequential and parallel programs [19, 13, 15]. In our more general predicate transformer framework (with angelic nondeterminism) verification of temporal properties of contracts is reduced to traditional correctness properties of special fixpoint contracts. These fixpoint contracts are built much in the same way as corresponding specifications of temporal properties using μ/ν-calculus, as is common, e.g., in connection with model checking [12]. However, in our framework these correctness properties can be verified using traditional invariant methods, with rules similar to those in traditional temporal reasoning systems [16]. Our generalization to include agents, coalitions, and angelic nondeterminism is similar to independent recent work by Alur, Henzinger, and Kupferman [2] on *alternating-time temporal logic*. They have a more elaborate model of games and interaction, but their view of computations is more traditional, without abortion, termination, or miracles.

References

[1] M. Abadi, L. Lamport, and P. Wolper. Realizable and unrealizable specifications of reactive systems. In G. A. et al., editor, *Proc. 16th ICALP*, pages 1–17, Stresa, Italy, 1989. Springer-Verlag.

[2] R. Alur, T. Henzinger, and O. Kupferman. Alternating-time temporal logic. In *Proc. 38th Symposium on Foundations of Computer Science (FOCS)*, pages 100–109. IEEE, 1997.

[3] R .J. R. Back. *Correctness Preserving Program Refinements: Proof Theory and Applications*, volume 131 of *Mathematical Centre Tracts*. Mathematical Centre, Amsterdam, 1980.

[4] R. J. R. Back and J. von Wright. Duality in specification languages: a lattice-theoretical approach. *Acta Informatica*, 27:583–625, 1990.

[5] R. J. R. Back and J. von Wright. Games and winning strategies. *Information Processing Letters*, 53(3):165–172, February 1995.

[6] R. J. R. Back and J. von Wright. *Refinement Calculus: A Systematic Introduction*. Springer-Verlag, 1998.

[7] R. J. R. Back and J. von Wright. Contracts, games and refinement. *Information and Computation*, 156:25–45, 2000.

[8] R. J. R. Back and J. von Wright. Contracts as mathematical entities in programming logic. In *Proc. Workshop on Abstraction and Refinement*, Osaka, September 1999. Also available as TUCS Tech. Rpt. 372.

[9] R. J. R. Back and J. von Wright. Verification and refinement of action contracts. Tech. Rpt. 374, Turku Centre for Computer Science, November 2000.

[10] R. J. R. Back, A. Mikhajlova, and J. von Wright. Reasoning about interactive systems. In J. M. Wing, J. Woodcock, and J. Davies, editors, *Proceedings of the World Congress on Formal Methods (FM'99)*, volume 1709 of *LNCS*, pages 1460–1476. Springer-Verlag, September 1999.

[11] E. Dijkstra. *A Discipline of Programming*. Prentice-Hall International, 1976.

[12] E. Emerson. Automated temporal reasoning about reactive systems. In F. Moller and G. Bortwistle, editors, *Logics for Concurrency: Structure versus Automata*, volume 1043 of *Lecture Notes in Computer Science*. Springer–Verlag, 1996.

[13] W. Hesselink. *Programs, Recursion and Unbounded Choice*. Cambridge University Press, 1992.

[14] E. Knapp. A predicate transformer for progress. *Information Processing Letters*, 33:323–330, 1989.

[15] J. Lukkien. Operational semantics and generalised weakest preconditions. *Science of Computer Programming*, 22:137–155, 1994.

[16] Z. Manna and A. Pnueli. Completing the temporal picture. *Theoretical Computer Science*, 83:97–130, 1991.

[17] C. Morgan. Data refinement by miracles. *Information Processing Letters*, 26:243–246, January 1988.

[18] C. Morgan. *Programming from Specifications*. Prentice-Hall, 1990.

[19] J. Morris. Temporal predicate transformers and fair termination. *Acta Informatica*, 27:287–313, 1990.

[20] Y. Moschovakis. A model of concurrency with fair merge and full recursion. *Information and Computation*, pages 114–171, 1991.

[21] W. Thomas. On the synthesis of strategies in infinite games. In *12th Annual Symposium on Theoretical Aspects of Computer Science (STACS)*, volume 900 of *Lecture Notes in Computer Science*, pages 1–13, 1995.

Section B

Logical approaches to asynchrony

3   Asynchronous progress   57
Ernie Cohen

Concurrent programming is generally considered to be difficult: innocent-looking programs can exhibit strange behaviour under extreme timing scenarios. Painful experience has shown that reliable reasoning about such programs requires systematic consideration of all possible executions.

The standard way to reason about all possible executions is to prescribe the set of reachable states with invariants. Invariants enjoy a number of advantages over direct operational reasoning; in particular, safety properties of a large system can usually be captured with a conjunction of small, local invariants. Moreover, invariants are robust with respect to many typical program refinements (for example common procedure- or data-refinements), in the sense that such a transformation is reflected by a simple change to the invariants.

Unfortunately invariants are not always robust with respect to transformations that relax the ordering of independent operations. For example, consider a program consisting of two copies of the same deterministic program running in lock-step. This program satisfies the obvious invariant that the two component states are identical; let us call such a state synchronised. Suppose now that we allow the two components to proceed independently. The only useful invariants of the resulting system are that (1) each state is reachable by running just one component from a synchronised state, and (2) a synchronised state can be reached by running just one of the components. Working with such invariants is hardly an improvement over direct operational reasoning.

The fragility of invariants (and other linear-time properties such as "leads-to") has motivated a significant body of work on how to cope more effectively with asynchrony. Most of this work has focused on providing proof rules for specific program architectures, which can often be specified equationally. Such architectures include situations where processes can communicate asynchronously, where operations are pipelined, or where components access resources using a two-phased locking discipline.

However this approach to asynchrony has some shortcomings. First, many concurrent programming tasks are specified not with specific properties but instead with an ideal program implementing the desired behaviour (atomic memory is a typical example). Second, these theorems, while strong enough to handle many toy examples, have not improved the development of more difficult programs (for example wait-free atomic-register constructions). Finally, it is not clear how to turn such rules into a coherent methodology.

There exists an alternative approach to this methodological challenge: rather than seek robustness using available tools, robustness can be built into the method. This essay demonstrates the idea by showing how the ordinary linear-time operator "leads-to" can be made more robust with respect to asynchrony by weakening it to a branching-time operator, while preserving its logical character.

4 A reduction theorem for concurrent object-oriented programs   69
Jayadev Misra

One trend in programming-language design is towards languages that 'make it easy to do things', in the sense of automating the details that one could, in principle, do at a lower level if necessary. (A prime example of that is FORTRAN, one of the earliest high-level languages, which automated the coding of complicated arithmetical formulae.) An up-to-date, though mixed, example is Java, which makes it easy to set up and use abstractions (classes and instances) that relate to the problem description.

Another trend however is towards language designs that 'make it easy to understand what you have done'; and those tend to polarise the public. Some find the elegance of such languages beautiful and compelling; others deride them because of their 'lack of facilities', their failure to appreciate 'what real programmers actually need'. (Think of Algol-W, the guarded-command language (of Dijkstra), and occam.)

The second trend is very important, of course, and in practice one finds traces of it within the first — though perhaps some decades later. The first trend stimulates researchers to consider the topic of language design to start with. One could say that the first establishes 'that a thing should be done at all' and the second strives to determine 'how it can be done properly'.

In this article the driving force is the design of a language for concurrency. Concurrency appeared first in computing for reasons of efficiency, to allow operating systems to run users' programs independently of slow peripherals; and, ever since, programmers have been wrestling with the complexity that concurrency introduces.

The author's proposed language design has classes and objects, like Java but much simplified, and makes it possible — with some help from the programmer — to reason about interleaved parallel executions as if they were serialised. That goal has been pursued by very many researchers (e.g. also Cohen in this collection), and is perhaps one of the most important aspects in the struggle to control concurrency.

3
Asynchronous progress

Ernie Cohen

Abstract

We propose weakening the definition of progress to a branching-time operator, making it more amenable to compositional proof and simplifying the predicates needed to reason about highly asynchronous programs. The new progress operator ("achieves") coincides with the "leads-to" operator on all "observable" progress properties (those where the target predicate is stable) and satisfies the same composition properties as leads-to, including the PSP theorem. The advantage of achievement lies in its compositionality: a program inherits all achievement properties of its "decoupled components". (For example, a dataflow network inherits achievement properties from each of its processes.) The compositionality of achievement captures, in a UNITY-like logic, the well-known operational trick of reasoning about an asynchronous program by considering only certain well-behaved executions.

3.1 Introduction

It is well known that progress properties (such as leads-to [1]) are not preserved under parallel composition. That is, it is not generally possible to obtain a useful progress property of a system from a progress property of one of its components. Instead, it is usually necessary to work globally with atomic progress steps (obtained by combining local liveness properties with global safety properties). This often results in unreasonably complicated proofs.

For example, consider the following trivial producer-consumer system. The producer repeatedly chooses a function, applies it to his local value, and sends the function along a FIFO channel to the consumer; the consumer, on receiving a function, applies it to his local variable. Initially, the two variables are equal and the channel is empty; we call such a state *clean*. We would like to prove that, if the producer eventually stops, the system terminates in a clean state.

Assertional proofs of this program are rather painful; they generally require either the introduction of an auxiliary inductive definition that captures the behavior of one of the processes (e.g., in order to formulate an invariant like "the system is in a state reachable by running the producer from a clean state") or introducing history variables on the channel (which amounts to reasoning about a static execution object instead of a dynamic program). In either case, the programming logic fails to provide substantial reasoning leverage.

A more attractive, though informal, operational argument might go as follows: starting from a clean state, the producer is guaranteed to execute first. At this point, the producer cannot interfere with the consumer's first step, so we can pretend that the consumer executes next, bringing the system back to a clean state. This is repeated for every message sent by the producer, so when the system halts, the state is again clean.

A number of theorems try to systematize this sort of reasoning, typically using commutativity to turn arbitrary executions into well-behaved ones. However, theorems that yield linear-time properties have to talk about states actually arising in a computation, making them difficult to compose. For example, applying such a theorem to the producer-consumer example would yield only properties of the initial and final states (since they are the only ones guaranteed to be clean); we would prefer a program property capturing the effect of production and subsequent consumption of a single message.

We propose a new progress operator $\leadsto$ ("achieves"), that supports this kind of reasoning within the UNITY programming logic. Achievement has a number of attractive features:

- It supports the key reasoning rules of the UNITY leads-to operator; in particular, it is transitive, disjunctive, and satisfies the PSP theorem.

- It coincides with leads-to on those properties that are "observable" (i.e., those whose target predicates are stable). Thus, it is as expressive as leads-to for all practical purposes.

- Unlike leads-to, it supports a form of compositional reasoning: a program inherits achievement properties from each of its "decoupled components" (e.g., the processes of a dataflow network). Decoupling can itself be established compositionally, usually through simple structural analysis.

- Most techniques for reasoning about concurrency control (such as reduction[10, 4] or serializability [6]) are based on pretending that certain operations execute "atomically". Decoupled components, on the other hand, effectively execute "immediately". This makes them easier to compose and allows them to serve as asynchronous maintainers as invariants (section 3.6).

- Achievement and decoupling are defined semantically (i.e., in terms of the properties of a program, not its transitions). They are thus independent of program presentation, unlike related theories like communication-closed layers or stubborn sets [15], which are defined at the level of transitions.

- Unlike techniques for compositional temporal logic reasoning, our theory allows multiple processes to write to the same variable. This allows us to reason about FIFO channels without having to resort to history variables.

- Unlike interleaving set temporal logic [9], which requires reasoning about entire executions, achievement obtains the same effect using simpler UNITY-like program reasoning.

In this paper, we show the key concepts and theorems, and some simple examples. Proofs of all results can be found in [2], which also contains a number of examples, including the sliding window protocol and the tree protocol for database concurrency control.

3.2 Programs

Our programs are countable, unconditionally fair, nondeterministic transition systems. As a starting point, we describe them using operators from UNITY [1].

Let S be a fixed set of states. As usual, we describe subsets of S using state predicates (notation: p, q, r, s), and identify elements of S with their characteristic predicates. An *action* (notation: f, g) is a binary relation on S; we identify actions with (universally disjunctive) predicate transformers giving their strongest postconditions. We will make use of the following actions (given in order of decreasing binding power):

$$1.p = p$$
$$0.p = \mathit{false}$$
$$(f; g).p = g.(f.p)$$
$$(\wedge q).p = p \wedge q$$
$$(f \vee g).p = f.p \vee g.p$$
$$(f \Rightarrow g).p = f.p \Rightarrow g.p$$
$$(\exists x).p = (\exists x : p)$$
$$x := e = (\exists x'); (\wedge(x' = e)); (\exists x); (\wedge(x = x')); (\exists x')$$
$$\text{where } x' \text{ is a fresh variable}$$
$$(f \text{ if } p) = ((\wedge p); f \vee (\wedge \neg p))$$

The everywhere operator of [5] is extended to predicate transformers by

$$[h] \equiv [(\forall p : h.p)]$$

A *program* (notation: $A, B, \ldots$) is a countable set of actions. A program is executed by repeatedly stuttering or executing one of its actions, subject to the restriction that each action is chosen infinitely often; formally, an execution e is an infinite sequence of states e_i such that

$$(\forall i \geq 0 : (\exists a \in A|\{1\} : [e_{i+1} \Rightarrow a.e_i]))$$
$$\wedge (\forall i \geq 0, a \in A : (\exists j \geq i : [e_{j+1} \Rightarrow a.e_j]))$$

Under this semantics, union of programs corresponds to fair parallel composition, so we use the symbol | as a synonym for set union when composing programs.

The motivating problem of this paper is the desire to prove properties of the form $(p \mapsto q \text{ in } A)$ ("p leads-to q in A"), which says that every execution of A that starts with a p-state contains a q-state:

$$(p \mapsto q \text{ in } A) \equiv (\forall e : e \text{ an execution of } A : [e_0 \Rightarrow p] \Rightarrow (\exists i : [e_i \Rightarrow q]))$$

The standard way to prove $\mapsto$ properties is with the operators **U** and **E**, defined by

$$(p \text{ U } q \text{ in } A) \equiv (\forall a \in A : (\wedge(p \wedge \neg q)); a; (\wedge(\neg p \wedge \neg q)) = 0)$$
$$(p \text{ E } q \text{ in } A) \equiv (p \text{ U } q \text{ in } A) \wedge (\exists a \in A : (\wedge(p \wedge \neg q)); a; (\wedge \neg q) = 0)$$

$(p \text{ U } q \text{ in } A)$ ("p unless q in A") means that no A transition falsifies p without truthifying q (unless q is true already); this also means that in any execution of A, p, once true, remains true up to the first moment (if any) when q holds. $(p \text{ E } q \text{ in } A)$ ("p ensures q in A") means that, in addition, some transition of A is guaranteed to yield a q state when executed from a $p \wedge \neg q$ state. **U** properties are are used to specify safety, while **E** properties specify "atomic" progress.

Given **U** and **E**, we have the following (complete set of) rules for deriving $\mapsto$ properties:

$$(p \text{ E } q) \Rightarrow (p \mapsto q) \qquad (3.1)$$
$$(p \mapsto q) \wedge (q \mapsto r) \Rightarrow (p \mapsto r)$$
$$(\forall i : p_i \mapsto q_i) \Rightarrow (\exists i : p_i) \mapsto (\exists i : q_i)$$
$$(p \mapsto q) \wedge (r \text{ U } s) \Rightarrow ((p \wedge r) \mapsto (q \wedge r) \vee s)$$

the last rule known in UNITY lingo as "progress-safety-progress" (PSP).

The main reason for introducing **E** (instead of just working with $\mapsto$ and **U**) is that, unlike $\mapsto$, **E** properties can be composed, using the union rule:

$$(p \text{ E } q \text{ in } A) \wedge (p \text{ U } q \text{ in } B) \Rightarrow (p \text{ E } q \text{ in } A|B)$$

The main purpose of this paper is to define a replacement for $\mapsto$ that has a similar union rule (under suitable semantic constraints on A and B), while preserving the composition rules of (3.1).

It is not hard to see that, for the purpose of showing progress properties of programs under union, the **U** and **E** properties of a program are a fully abstract semantics. Therefore, we define $\sim$ (congruence) and $\triangleleft$ (containment) of programs in the obvious way (**op** : ranges over $\{\text{U}, \text{E}\}$):

$$A \sim B \equiv (\forall p, q, \textbf{op} : (p \textbf{ op } q \text{ in } A) \Leftrightarrow (p \textbf{ op } q \text{ in } B))$$
$$A \triangleleft B \equiv (A|B \sim B)$$

An example of the advantage of using semantic notions (as opposed to equality and subset) can be seen when we extend guarding to programs

$$(A \text{ if } p) \equiv \{(a \text{ if } p) \text{ s.t. } a \in A\}$$

; we then have $(A \text{ if } p) \triangleleft A$.

We will make frequent use of the following two properties derived from **U**:

$$(p \text{ stable in } A) \equiv (p \text{ U } \textit{false} \text{ in } A)$$
$$\langle A \rangle . p \equiv (\forall q : [p \Rightarrow q] \wedge (q \text{ stable in } A) : q)$$

(p **stable in** A) holds if no transition of A can falsify p. $\langle A \rangle . p$ is the strongest predicate that both contains p and is stable in A; i.e. it describes the set of all states reachable from p-states via a (possibly empty) sequence of A transitions.

3.2.1 Continuity

Some of our results make use of the following semantic property of finite programs. Let ch range over totally ordered sets of predicates, and define

$$(A \text{ cont}) \equiv (\forall ch : (\forall p \in Ch : (p \text{ E } q \text{ in } A)) \Rightarrow ((\exists p \in Ch : p) \text{ E } q \text{ in } A))$$

Intuitively, (A **cont**) means that whenever A guarantees atomic progress to (i.e., ensurity of) a goal from each of a weakening sequence of starting points, it can achieve atomic progress from their disjunction.

Although not all programs are continuous, most programs of interest can be shown to be continuous using the following theorems:

$$(\{f\} \text{ cont}) \quad (3.2)$$
$$(A \text{ cont}) \wedge (B \text{ cont}) \Rightarrow (A|B \text{ cont}) \quad (3.3)$$
$$(\forall i,j : (A_i \text{ cont}) \wedge [p_i \wedge p_j \Rightarrow i = j]) \Rightarrow ((|i : (A_i \text{ if } p_i)) \text{ cont}) \quad (3.4)$$

These rules say that any singleton program is continuous, and that continuity is preserved by finite union or arbitrary disjoint union.

3.3 Achievement

We would like to define a replacement for $\mapsto$, $\leadsto$ ("achieves"), such that an achievement property of the consumer is an achievement property of the whole producer-consumer system. The reason that this doesn't work with $\mapsto$ is that the producer might send another message before the consumer gets a chance to execute. For example, the consumer might be guaranteed to eventually make the channel empty when running in isolation, but not when run in parallel with the producer.

An obvious way to overcome this problem is to define $(p \leadsto q \text{ in } A)$ so that it holds if, from a p state, A is guaranteed to reach some state reachable from a q

state (i.e., an $\langle A \rangle.q$ state). To make sure that $\leadsto$ is transitive, we similarly weaken the antecedent p, yielding the proposed definition

$$? \; (p \leadsto q \text{ in } A) \equiv (\langle A \rangle.p \mapsto \langle A \rangle.q \text{ in } A)$$

However, this definition is too lenient – because it allows progress "backward in time", it is incompatible with the PSP theorem. For example, if A is the program $\{x := \mathit{true}\}$, we would have $(x \leadsto \neg x \text{ in } A)$ and $(x \, \mathbf{U} \, \mathit{false} \text{ in } A)$; the PSP theorem then yields $(x \leadsto \mathit{false} \text{ in } A)$, which is not what we want.

The remedy is to build into the definition of $\leadsto$ a quantification over all possible $\mathbf{U}$ properties with which it might be combined (using PSP). This leads to the definition

$$\begin{aligned} (p \leadsto q \text{ in } A) \equiv \\ (\forall r, s : (r \, \mathbf{U} \, s \text{ in } A) \Rightarrow (\langle A \rangle.(s \vee (r \wedge p)) \mapsto \langle A \rangle.(s \vee (r \wedge q)) \text{ in } A)) \end{aligned}$$

(the antecedent has again been weakened to recover transitivity.) To a good approximation, $(p \leadsto q \text{ in } A)$ means that, for any p-state $s0$,

$$\langle A \rangle.s0 \mapsto \langle A \rangle.(q \wedge \langle A \rangle.s0)$$

that is, from any state reachable from $s0$ (via A), A is guaranteed to reach a state that is reachable from $s0$ via a path that contains a q-state.

The definition of $\leadsto$ is obviously much too complex to use directly. Thankfully, we don't need to, because we can reason about $\leadsto$ pretty much as we reason about $\mapsto$. In particular, it satisfies the analogues of (3.1):

$$(p \mapsto q) \Rightarrow (p \leadsto q) \tag{3.5}$$
$$(p \leadsto q) \wedge (q \leadsto r) \Rightarrow (p \leadsto r) \tag{3.6}$$
$$(\forall i : p_i \leadsto q_i) \Rightarrow ((\exists i : p_i) \leadsto (\exists i : q_i)) \tag{3.7}$$
$$(p \leadsto q) \wedge (r \mathbf{U} s) \Rightarrow ((p \wedge r) \leadsto (q \wedge r) \vee s)) \tag{3.8}$$

We also need a way to get from $\leadsto$ back to $\mapsto$:

$$(p \leadsto q) \wedge (q \; \mathbf{stable}) \Rightarrow (p \mapsto q) \tag{3.9}$$

That is, any achievement property whose target is stable is also a leads-to property. We argue that these are the only leads-to properties that really matter, since progress to a predicate that is not stable might never be witnessed by an asynchronous observer. If one accepts this argument, then $\leadsto$ would appear to be at least as good as $\mapsto$.

The main advantage of achievement is the following powerful composition property: define $(A \text{ dec } B)$ ("A is decoupled from B") and $(A \trianglelefteq B)$ ("A is a decoupled component of B") as follows (where **op** ranges over the operators $\mathbf{E}, \mathbf{U}$):

$$(A \text{ dec } B) \equiv (\forall p, q, \mathbf{op} : (p \text{ op } q \text{ in } A) \Rightarrow (\langle B \rangle.p \text{ op } \langle B \rangle.q \text{ in } A))$$
$$(A \trianglelefteq B) \equiv (A \triangleleft B) \wedge (A \text{ dec } B) \quad ;$$

then we have

$$(p \leadsto q \text{ in } A) \wedge (A \trianglelefteq B) \Rightarrow (p \leadsto q \text{ in } B) \qquad (3.10)$$

In other words, if A is a decoupled component of B, then every achievement property of A is also an achievement property of B. Put differently, working with achievement, we can choose which decoupled component is the next one to execute. Clearly, this does not hold for leads-to.

3.4 Decoupling

Like $\leadsto$, the definition of **dec** is too complicated to use directly. Fortunately, decoupling can be established using the following (incomplete) set of rules:

$$(A|B \text{ dec } A) \qquad (3.11)$$
$$(\forall i : (A_i \text{ dec } B)) \Rightarrow ((|i : A_i) \text{ dec } B) \qquad (3.12)$$
$$(\forall i : (A \text{ dec } B_i)) \wedge (A \text{ cont}) \Rightarrow (A \text{ dec } (|i : B_i)) \qquad (3.13)$$
$$(A \text{ dec } B) \wedge (p, \neg p \text{ stable in } B) \Rightarrow ((A \text{ if } p) \text{ dec } B) \qquad (3.14)$$
$$(\forall i : (A \text{ dec } (B \text{ if } p_i))) \wedge [(\exists i : p_i)] \Rightarrow (A \text{ dec } B) \qquad (3.15)$$
$$(\neg p \text{ stable in } B) \Rightarrow ((A \text{ if } p) \text{ dec } (B \text{ if } \neg p)) \qquad (3.16)$$

It turns out to be useful to consider explicitly the property $(A \text{ dec } A|B)$, which we abbreviate $(A \text{ wdec } B)$ ("A is weakly decoupled from B"). (Note that $A \triangleleft B \wedge (A \text{ wdec } B) \Rightarrow (A \trianglelefteq B)$.) As a rule of thumb, two programs whose interactions are free of race conditions are weakly decoupled from each other, while $(A \text{ dec } B)$ means that, in addition, B cannot send information directly to A. Some useful rules for establishing weak decoupling are the following:

$$(A \text{ dec } B) \Rightarrow (A \text{ wdec } B) \qquad (3.17)$$
$$(\forall i,j : (A_i \text{ wdec } B) \wedge (A_i \text{ wdec } A_j)) \Rightarrow ((|i : A_i) \text{ wdec } B) \qquad (3.18)$$
$$(\forall i : (A \text{ wdec } B_i)) \wedge (A \text{ cont}) \Rightarrow (A \text{ wdec } (|i : B_i)) \qquad (3.19)$$
$$(A \text{ wdec } B) \wedge (p \text{ stable in } B) \Rightarrow ((A \text{ if } p) \text{ wdec } B) \qquad (3.20)$$
$$(\forall i : (A \text{ wdec } (B \text{ if } p_i))) \wedge [(\exists i : p_i)] \Rightarrow (A \text{ wdec } B) \qquad (3.21)$$
$$((A \text{ if } p) \text{ wdec } (B \text{ if } \neg p)) \qquad (3.22)$$

As these rules show, decoupling has a better left-union rule ((3.12) vs. (3.18)), which is why we work with decoupling whenever possible. For example, in a producer-consumer system, producers are decoupled from consumers, while consumers are only weakly decoupled from producers. This means that we can allow race conditions in the producer, while keeping it a decoupled component of the system, but not in the consumer (except under unusual circumstances).

For singleton programs, decoupling can be established with the following theorems:

$$(\exists p, q : [p \vee q] \wedge [p; g; f \Rightarrow f; g] \wedge [q; g \Rightarrow 1]) \Rightarrow (\{f\} \text{ dec } \{g\}) \quad (3.23)$$
$$(\exists p, q, r : [p \vee q \vee r] \wedge [r \Rightarrow f] \wedge [p; g; f \Rightarrow f; g] \wedge [q; g \Rightarrow 1]) \quad (3.24)$$
$$\Rightarrow (\{f\} \text{ wdec } \{g\})$$

The hypothesis of (3.23) says that g right-commutes with f from every state from which g can possibly change the state; the hypothesis of (3.24) says that g right-commutes with f from every state from which g can possibly change the state and f necessarily changes the state. For example, if f and g interact only through a FIFO channel on which f sends and g receives (both asynchronously), then ($\{f\}$ **dec** $\{g\}$) and ($\{g\}$ **wdec** $\{f\}$). Related forms of commutativity are studied in [14].

3.5 Example — Loosely-coupled programs

A *loosely-coupled* program [11] is one in which (1) every transition is total and deterministic, and (2) from any state from which two transitions can change the state, the transitions commute. (Dataflow networks [8] are the most familiar example.) In such a program, every transition is weakly decoupled from every other (by (3.24)); since singletons are continuous (by (3.2)), each transition is weakly decoupled from the rest of the system (by (3.19)). Grouping transitions arbitrarily into processes, each process is a decoupled component (by (3.18)). Thus, in reasoning about a system, we can choose, at each state, any enabled process to be the next one to execute. Proofs based on this are usually simpler than using the fixed point characterization of [8], since we can often reason about simple (first-order) predicates, instead of having to deal with message sequences.

As a concrete example of this kind of reasoning, consider the following loosely-coupled version of the producer-consumer system described in the introduction. Let ch be a FIFO channel, n a natural counter, let $ch!m$ (resp. $ch?m$) be the actions that send (resp. receive) the message m along the channel ch, and define

$$P = \{(n := n - 1; (\exists f : x := f.x; ch!f) \text{ if } n > 0)\}$$
$$C = \{((\exists f : ch?f; y := f.y) \text{ if } ch \neq <>)\}$$
$$clean \equiv x = y \wedge ch = <>$$
$$mid \equiv (\exists f : x = f.y \wedge ch = \langle f \rangle)$$

We can prove $(clean \mapsto clean \land n = 0 \text{ in } P|C)$ as follows:

1) $clean \land n = N > 0 \mapsto mid \land n < N$ in P def P
2) $clean \land n = N > 0 \leadsto mid \land n < N$ in P 1, (3.5)
3) $(P \trianglelefteq P|C)$ (3.24)
4) $clean \land n = N > 0 \leadsto mid \land n < N$ in $P|C$ 2, 3, (3.10)
)
5) $mid \land n < N$ $\mapsto clean \land n < N$ in C def C
6) $mid \land n < N$ $\leadsto clean \land n < N$ in C 5, (3.5)
7) $(C \trianglelefteq P|C)$ (3.24)
8) $mid \land n < N$ $\leadsto clean \land n < N$ in $P|C$ 6, 7, (3.10)
)
9) $clean \land n = N > 0 \leadsto clean \land n < N$ in $P|C$ 4, 8, (3.6)
10) $clean \land n = N$ $\leadsto clean \land n = 0$ in $P|C$ 9, (3.6), induction
11) $clean$ $\leadsto clean \land n = 0$ in $P|C$ 10, (3.7)
12) $((clean \land n = 0)$ stable in $P|C)$ def P, C
13) $clean$ $\mapsto clean \land n = 0$ in $P|C$ 11, 12, (3.9)

3.6 Asynchronous safety

Invariants (or, more generally, stable predicates) play a key role in program development. However, asynchrony can make invariants unreasonably complicated. Instead of working with real invariants, we can work with predicates that are reestablished by decoupled components. Because decoupled components can be assumed to execute immediately, these predicates are almost as good as real invariants. The component that reestablishes the invariant is called a "sweeper", because it cleans up after other components.

Sweepers are defined as follows:

$$(A \text{ sw } B \text{ to } p) \equiv (A \trianglelefteq B) \land (\langle B \rangle.p \leadsto p \text{ in } A)$$

Note that sweeping generalizes stability, that is,

$$(p \text{ stable in } A) \Leftrightarrow (1 \text{ sw } A \text{ to } p)$$

A key property of stability is that a predicate is stable in a union of components if it is stable in each component. Sweeping enjoys similar compositionality:

$$(A \text{ cont}) \land (\forall i : (A \text{ sw } B_i \text{ to } p)) \Rightarrow ((|i : A) \text{ sw } (|i : B_i) \text{ to } p) \quad (3.25)$$

The other key property of stability is that it can be combined with progress (or achievement) using a special case of the PSP rule. The corresponding property for sweepers is

$$(A \text{ sw } B \text{ to } p) \land (q \leadsto r \text{ in } B) \Rightarrow (p \land q \leadsto p \land \langle A \rangle.r \text{ in } B) \quad (3.26)$$

In most situations, workers can run far ahead of sweepers, and we don't want to have to prove $(\langle B \rangle.p \leadsto p \text{ in } A)$ directly, because $\langle B \rangle.p$ may be complicated;

we would rather sweep up after a single transition of B. In general, if (A **wdec** B) is established using the the rules of section 3.4, then

$$(p \;\mathbf{U}\; q \;\mathbf{in}\; B) \wedge (A \trianglelefteq B) \wedge (q \leadsto p \;\mathbf{in}\; A) \Rightarrow (A \;\mathbf{sw}\; B \;\mathbf{to}\; p)$$

3.6.1 Example

We modify the producer-consumer example slightly so that termination is caused by a separate component (instead of using a counter in the producer):

$$P0 = \{((\exists f : x := f.x;\; ch!f) \;\mathbf{if}\; \neg stop)\}$$
$$P1 = \{stop := true\}$$
$$P = P0|P1$$
$$C = \{((\exists f : ch?f;\; y := f.y) \;\mathbf{if}\; ch \neq <>)\}$$
$$clean \equiv (x = y \wedge ch = <>)$$
$$mid \equiv (\exists f : x = f.y \wedge ch = \langle f \rangle)$$

The proof from section 3.5 does not work here, because there is no state variable n to record progress. However, we can instead use a sweeper proof:

1) (C **wdec** P0, P1)			(3.24)
2) clean	**U** mid	**in** P0	def P0
3) mid	$\mapsto$ clean	**in** C	def C
4) mid	$\leadsto$ clean	**in** C	(3.5)
5) C **sw** P0 **to** clean			1, 2, 4
6) clean	**U** false	**in** P1	def P1
7) false	$\leadsto$ clean	**in** C	(3.5)
8) C **sw** P1 **to** clean			1, 6, 7
9) C **sw** P **to** clean			5, 8, (3.25)
10) true	$\mapsto$ stop	**in** P|C	def P0
11) true	$\leadsto$ stop	**in** P|C	10, (3.5)
12) clean	$\leadsto$ clean $\wedge \langle C \rangle$.stop	**in** P|C	9, 11, (3.26)
13) (stop **stable in** C)			def C
14) clean	$\leadsto$ clean $\wedge$ stop	**in** P|C	12, 13
15) (clean $\wedge$ stop **stable in** P|C)			def P, C
16) clean	$\mapsto$ clean $\wedge$ stop	**in** P|C	14, 15, (3.9)

3.7 Caveats

While achievement has few disadvantages with respect to leads-to in the context of UNITY-like program development, it does have one disadvantage worth mentioning: unlike linear-time properties, achievement is not preserved by program refinement[1], so to use a refinement step, it is first necessary to convert achievement properties back to leads-to. This is hardly surprising; related properties like serializability suffer from the same problem.

A minor annoyance in the theory is the continuity requirement. The definition of $(A \text{ dec } B)$ is of the form "if A has this property, it also has that property"; when the property is an **E** property, there is no way in the logic to make sure that the "that" property is being guaranteed by the same transition that guarantees the "this" property (even though it is in most practical cases). This is a minor price to pay for a theory that works entirely at the level of properties, instead of transitions.

A more serious limitation of the theory is shown in the following example. Suppose we have two producer-consumer systems, A producing for B, and C producing for D. Suppose also that these systems multiplex their communications on a shared channel. Sweeper compositionality lets us prove

$$(B \text{ sw } A|B \text{ to } p) \wedge (D \text{ sw } C|D \text{ to } p) \Rightarrow (B|D \text{ sw } A|B|C|D \text{ to } p)$$

(assuming we've correctly labelled multiplexed messages so that B and D don't try to receive the same messages) so things are fine from the sweeper standpoint. However, we would like to prove something stronger, namely $(A|B|D \text{ dec } C|D)$, which would, in effect, allow us to pretend that the communication is not multiplexed; we do not know how to strengthen the theory to make this possible. (This problem arose in trying (with Rajeev Joshi) to use sweepers to prove the correspondence of loose and tight executions in Seuss[12]; Joshi eventually resorted to reasoning about actions instead of properties [7].)

Finally, beacause it is fundamentally about progress, the theory is highly asymmetric with respect to time. Decoupled components work as weak "left-movers"; we can always pretend they happen earlier. They can be composed precisely because all of them are moving in the same direction. Reduction theorems such as [4], on the other hand, allow both left- and right-movers, so message transmissions can be moved later (instead of just moving receptions earlier).

3.8 Conclusions

We have argued that achievement has some desirable properties that make it technically superior to leads-to, particularly when reasoning about asynchronous programs. More generally, we have shown that it is possible to weaken linear-time operators to branching-time operators so as to make them more robust to asynchrony, without changing the essential structure of the logic.

---

[1] For example, $(true \leadsto x \text{ in } \{\})(x := false)$, $(x := any)$, but $\neg(true \leadsto x \text{ in } \{\})(x := false)$.

3.9 Acknowledgements

This work was originally inspired by Jay Misra's paper [11]; it has benefitted from insightful discussions with Jay Misra, J. R. Rao, and Rajeev Joshi, and from the insightful comments of the anonymous referee.

References

[1] K. M. Chandy and J. Misra. *Parallel Program Design: A Foundation*. Addison-Wesley, Reading, MA, 1988

[2] E. Cohen. *Modular Progress Proofs of Asynchronous Programs*. PhD. Thesis, University of Texas at Austin, 1993. Available from ftp://ftp.research.telcordia.com/pub/ernie/research/diss.ps.gz .

[3] Ernie Cohen. Separation and reduction. In *Mathematics of Program Construction, 5th International Conference, Portugal, July 2000. Science of Computer Programming*, pages 45–59. Springer-Verlag, 2000.

[4] E. Cohen, L. Lamport. *Reduction in TLA*. In CONCUR98 Springer-Verlag, 1998.

[5] E. Dijkstra and C. Scholten. *Predicate transformers and Program Semantics*. Springer-Verlag.

[6] K. P. Eswaran, J. N. Gray, R. A. Lorie, I. L. Traiger. *The notions of consistency and predicate locks in a database system*. CACM, 19(11):624-633, 1976.

[7] R. Joshi. *Immediacy: a technique for reasoning about asynchrony*. PhD. Thesis, University of Texas at Austin, 1999.

[8] G. Kahn. *The semantics of a simple language for parallel programming*. In *Proceedings of IFIP Congress '74* North-Holland, 1974.

[9] S. Katz, D. Peled. *Verification of Distributed Programs using Representative Interleaving Sequences*. Distributed Computing, 6:107-120, Springer-Verlag, 1992.

[10] R. J. Lipton. *Reduction: A Method of Proving Properties of Parallel Programs*. CACM 18(12):717-721, 1975.

[11] J. Misra. *Loosely Coupled Programs*. In *Parallel Architectures and Languages Europe*, pages 1—26, June 1991.

[12] J. Misra. *A discipline of multiprogramming — programming theory for distributed applications*. Springer-Verlag, 2001.

[13] J. Pachl. *A simple proof of a completeness result for leads-to in the UNITY logic*. IPL, January 1992.

[14] J. R. Rao. *Extensions of the UNITY Methodology, Compositionality, Fairness and Probability in Parallelism*. Springer LNCS #908, 1995.

[15] A. Valmari. *Stubborn Sets for Reduced State Space Generation*. 10th International Confeence on Application and Theory of petri Nets, Bonn (2) pp 1-22, 1989.

4

A reduction theorem for concurrent object-oriented programs

Jayadev Misra[1]

Abstract

A typical execution of a concurrent program is an interleaving of the threads of its components. It is well known that the net effect of a concurrent execution may be quite different from the serial executions of its components. In this paper we introduce a programming notation for concurrent object-oriented programs, called **Seuss**, and show that concurrent executions of its programs are, under certain conditions, equivalent to serial executions. This allows us to reason about a Seuss program as if its components will be executed serially whereas an implementation may execute its components concurrently, for performance reasons.

4.1 Introduction

A typical execution of a concurrent program is an interleaving of the threads of its component programs. For instance, consider a concurrent program that has α and β as component programs, where the structures of α, β are as follows:

$\alpha :: \alpha_1; \alpha_2; \alpha_3$, and

$\beta :: \beta_1; \beta_2; \beta_3$.

The concurrent execution $\alpha_1\ \beta_1\ \alpha_2\ \beta_2\ \alpha_3\ \beta_3$ interleaves the two sequential executions. It is well known that the net effect of a concurrent execution may be quite different from the serial executions of the components. In this example, suppose α_1, β_1 are "read the value of variable x", α_2, β_2 are "increment the value read" and α_3, β_3 are "store the incremented value in x". Then, the given interleaved execution increases the value of x by 1 whereas an execution in which the threads are not interleaved increases x by 2.

---

[1]This material is based in part upon work supported by the National Science Foundation Award CCR–9803842.

The method of reduction was proposed by Lipton[3] to simplify reasoning about concurrent executions. Lipton develops certain conditions under which the steps of a component program may be considered indivisible (i.e., occurring sequentially) in a concurrent execution. A step f in a component is a *right mover* if for any step h of another component whenever fh is defined then so is hf and they yield the same result (i.e., their executions result in the same final state). Similarly, g is a *left mover* if for any h of another component hg is defined implies gh is defined, and $hg = gh$. Lipton shows that a sequence of steps of a component, $r_0\ r_1\ \ldots\ r_n\ c\ l_0\ l_1\ \ldots\ l_m$, may be considered indivisible for proof of termination of a concurrent program if each r_i is a right mover, l_j a left mover and c is unconstrained. This result has been extended to proofs of more general properties by Lamport and Schneider [2], Misra [4], and, more recently, by Cohen and Lamport [1].

In section 4.2, we introduce a programming notation for concurrent object-oriented programming, called **Seuss**. Briefly, a seuss program consists of **boxes**; a box is similar to an object instance. A box has local variables whose values define the state of the box. A box has **actions** and **methods**, both of which will be referred to as **procedures**. Actions are executed autonomously; a method is executed by being called by an action or a method of another box. In section 4.2.2, we introduce two different execution styles for programs, *tight and loose*. In a tight execution an action is completed before another action is started. In a loose execution the actions may be executed concurrently provided they satisfy certain *compatibility* requirements. A tight execution, being a single thread of control, may be understood more easily than a loose execution. Loose execution, on the other hand, is the norm where the computing platform consists of a large number of processors.

In this paper we develop a reduction theorem that establishes that for every loose execution there is a corresponding tight execution: if a loose execution of some finite set of actions starting in state s terminates in state t then there is a tight execution of those actions that can also end in state t starting in state s. This result is demonstrated by prescribing how to transform a loose execution into a tight execution in the above sense. This correspondence allows a programmer to understand a program in terms of its tight executions – a single thread of control – whereas an implementation may exploit the available concurrency through a loose execution.

The proof of the reduction theorem is considerably more difficult in our case because (1) procedure calls introduce interleavings of "execution trees" rather than execution sequences, and (2) executions of any pair of actions may be interleaved provided the actions are compatible. The notion of compatibility is central to our theory. Roughly, two procedures are compatible if their interleaved execution may be simulated by executing them one after the other in some order. We give an exact definition and show how compatibility of procedures may be proven.

Compatibility information can not be deduced automatically. Yet it is unrealistic to expect the user to provide this information for all pairs of procedures; in most cases, different boxes will be coded by different users, and no user may even know which other procedures will be executing. Therefore, we have developed a theory whereby compatibility of procedures belonging to different boxes may be deduced automatically from the compatibility information about procedures belonging to the same box. Users simply specify which procedures in a box are compatible and an algorithm then determines which pairs of actions are compatible, and may be executed concurrently.

Plan of the paper

In the next section, a brief introduction to Seuss is given; the reader may consult [5] for a detailed treatment. An abstract model of Seuss is given in section 4.3. In section 4.2.1 we state certain restrictions on programs which we elaborate in section 4.4. The definition of compatibility appears in section 4.5. A statement of the reduction theorem and its proof are given in section 4.6. Concluding remarks appear in section 4.7.

4.2 The Seuss programming notation

The central construct in Seuss is **box**; it plays the role of an object. A program consists of a set of boxes. Typically, a user defines generic boxes, called **cat**s (*cat* is short for *category*), and creates several boxes from each cat through instantiation. A cat is similar to a class; a box is similar to a class instance.

The state of a box is given by the values of its variables. The variables are local to the box. Therefore, their values can be changed only by the steps taken within the box. To enable other boxes to change the state of a box, each box includes a set of **procedures** that may be called from outside. Procedure call is the only mechanism for interaction among boxes.

A procedure is either an **action** or a **method**. A method is called by a procedure of another box. An action is not called like a traditional procedure; it is executed from time to time under the following fairness rule: each action is executed eventually. Both actions and methods can change the state (values of the variables) of their own box, and, possibly, of other boxes by calling their methods. A method may have parameters; an action does not have any parameter.

A method may *accept* or *reject* a call made upon it. If the state of the box does not permit a method to execute – for instance, a *get* method on a channel can not execute if the channel is empty – then the call is rejected. Otherwise, the call is accepted. Some methods accept every call; such methods are called **total** methods. A method that may reject a call is called a **partial** method. Similarly, we have total and partial actions.

4.2.1 Seuss syntax

In this section, we introduce a notation for writing programs. The notation is intended for implementation on top of a variety of host languages. Therefore, no commitment has been made to the syntax of any particular language (there are different implementations with C++ and Java as host languages) and syntactic aspects that are unrelated to the model are left unspecified in the notation.

Notational Conventions

The notation is described using BNF. All non-terminal identifiers are in Roman and all terminal identifiers are in boldface type. The traditional meta symbols of BNF – ::= { } [ ] ( ) – are used, along with ∨ to stand for alternation (the usual symbol for alternation, "|", is a terminal symbol in our notation). The special symbols used as terminals are | |/ ; : :: in the syntax given below. A syntactic unit enclosed within "{" and "}" in a production may be instantiated zero or more times, and a unit within "[" and "]" may be instantiated zero or one time. In the right-hand side of a production, $(p \vee q)$ denotes that a choice is to be made between the syntactic units p and q in instantiating this production; we omit the parentheses, "(" and ")", when no confusion can arise. Text enclosed within " { " and " } " in a program is to be treated as a comment.

Program

> program ::= **program** program-name {cat ∨ box} **end**
> cat ::= **cat** cat-name [parameters]: {variable} {procedure} **end**
> box ::= **box** box-name [parameters]: cat-name

A program consists of a set of cats and boxes in any order. The declaration of a cat or box includes its name and, possibly, parameters. The names of programs, cats and boxes are identifiers. The parameters of a cat or box could be ordinary variables, cats or boxes. A cat consists of (zero or more) variable declarations followed by procedure declarations. A box is an instance of a cat. Variables are declared and initialized in a cat as in traditional programming languages.

Example

We use a single running example to illustrate the syntax of Seuss. A ubiquitous concept in multiprogramming is the *Semaphore*. The skeletal program given below includes a definition of *Semaphore* as a cat and two instances of *Semaphore*, s and t. Cat *user* describes a group of users that execute their critical sections only if they hold both semaphores, s, t; there are three instances of *user*.

4. A reduction theorem for concurrent object-oriented programs

---

program *MutualExclusion*
  cat *Semaphore*
    var *n*: nat **init** 1 {initially, the semaphore value is 1}
    {The procedures of *Semaphore* are to be included here}
  end {*Semaphore*}

  box *s, t* : *Semaphore*

  cat *user*
    var *hs, ht*: boolean **init** *false*
    {*hs* is *true* when *user* holds *s*. Similarly, *ht*.}
    {The procedures of *user* are to be included here}
  end {*user*}

  box *u, v, w* : *user*
end {*MutualExclusion*}

---

procedure

  procedure ::= partial-procedure ∨ total-procedure
  partial-procedure ::= **partial** partial-method ∨ partial-action
  total-procedure ::= **total** total-method ∨ total-action
  partial-method ::= **method** head :: partial-body
  partial-action ::= **action** [label] :: partial-body
  total-method ::= **method** head :: total-body
  total-action ::= **action** [label] :: total-body

A procedure is either **partial** or **total**; also, a procedure is either a **method** or an **action**. Thus, there are four possible headings identifying each procedure. Each method has a head and a body. The head is similar to the form used in typical imperative languages; it has a procedure name followed by a list of formal parameters and their types. The labels are optional for actions; they have no effect on program execution.

Example (contd.)

We add the procedure names to the previous skeletal program.

---

program *MutualExclusion*
  cat *Semaphore*
    var *n*: nat **init** 1 {initially, the semaphore value is 1}
    partial method *P*:: { Body of *P* goes here}
    total method *V*:: { Body of *V* goes here}
  end {*Semaphore*}

box s, t : *Semaphore*

cat *user*
  var hs, ht: boolean **init** *false*
  partial action *s.acquire*:: {acquire s and set hs *true*.}
  partial action *t.acquire*:: {acquire s and set hs *true*.}
  partial action *execute*::
    {Execute this body if both hs, ht are *true*. Then, set hs, ht *false*.}
  end {*user*}

box u, v, w : *user*
end {*MutualExclusion*}

---

procedure body

A procedure body has different forms for partial and total procedures. For this manuscript, we take a total-body to be any sequential program. The partial-body is defined by:

partial-body ::= alternative {(| alternative) ∨ (|/alternative)}
alternative ::= precondition [; preprocedure] → total-body
precondition ::= predicate
preprocedure ::= partial-method-call

  The body of a partial procedure consists of one or more alternatives. Each alternative has a precondition, an optional preprocedure and a total-body. A precondition is a predicate on the state of the box to which this procedure belongs (i.e., it is constrained to name only the local variables of the box in which the procedure appears). A preprocedure is a call upon a partial method (in some other box).

Example (contd.)

Below, we include code for each procedure body. The partial actions *s.acquire* and *t.acquire* in *user* include calls upon the partial methods *s.P* and *t.P* as preprocedures. The partial action *execute* in *user* calls the total methods *s.V* and *t.V* in its body. The partial action *P* in *Semaphore* has no preprocedure.

---

program *MutualExclusion*
  cat *Semaphore*
    var n: nat **init** 1 {initially, the semaphore value is 1}
    partial method P:: $n > 0 \rightarrow n := n - 1$
    total method V:: $n := n + 1$
  end {*Semaphore*}

box s, t : *Semaphore*

  cat *user*
    var hs, ht: boolean **init** *false*
    partial action *s.acquire*:: $\neg hs$; $s.P \rightarrow hs := true$
    partial action *t.acquire*:: $\neg ht$; $t.P \rightarrow ht := true$
    partial action *execute*::
      $hs \wedge ht \rightarrow$ *critical section*; $s.V$; $t.V$; $hs := false$; $ht := false$
  end {*user*}

  box u, v, w : *user*
end {*MutualExclusion*}

The operational semantics of Seuss programs is described in section 4.2.2. The program, given above, may become deadlocked, that is, it may not allow any user to enter its critical section because one may have acquired s and another t. This problem may be avoided by acquiring s, t in order (that is, by changing the precondition of $t.acquire$ to $hs \wedge \neg ht$).

Multiple alternatives

Each alternative in a partial procedure is *positive* or *negative*: the first alternative is always positive; an alternative preceded by | is positive and one preceded by |/is negative. For each partial procedure at most one of its alternatives holds in any state; that is, the preconditions in the alternatives of a partial procedure are pairwise disjoint. The distinction between positive and negative alternatives is explained under the operational semantics of Seuss in section 4.2.2.

Restrictions on programs

Procedure Call

A total-body can include a call only to a total method; a partial method cannot be called by a total body. A partial method can only appear as a preprocedure in an alternative of a partial procedure. The syntax specifies that an alternative can have at most one preprocedure. In the example in page 74, partial action *s.acquire* calls $s.P$ as a preprocedure, and *execute* calls the total methods $s.V, t.V$ in its total body (i.e., in the code following $\rightarrow$).

Partial Order on Boxes

See section 4.4.1.

Termination Condition

Execution of each total body (the body part of any action, total or partial) must terminate; this is a proof obligation that has to be discharged by the programmer.

The termination condition can be proven by induction on the "level" of a procedure. First, show that any procedure that calls no other procedure terminates whenever it accepts a call. Next, show that execution of any procedure p terminates assuming that executions of all procedures that p calls terminate.

4.2.2 Seuss semantics (operational)

At run time, a program consists of a set of boxes; their states are initialized at the beginning of the run. There are two different execution styles for a program. In a *tight execution* one action is executed at a time. There is no notion of concurrent execution; each action completes before the next action is started. In a *loose execution* actions may be executed concurrently.

The programmer understands a program by reasoning about its tight executions only. We have developed a logic for this reasoning. An implementation may choose a loose execution for a program in order to maximize resource utilization. Loose execution is described in Sec. 4.6.1.

Tight execution

A tight execution consists of an infinite number of steps; in each step, an action of a box is chosen and executed as described below (in section 4.2.2). The choice of action to execute in a step is arbitrary except for the following fairness constraint: each action of each box is chosen eventually.

Observe that methods are executed only when they are called from other methods or actions, though actions execute autonomously (and eventually).

Procedure execution

A method is executed when it is called. To simplify description, we imagine that an action is called by a *scheduler*. Then the distinction between a method and an action vanishes; each procedure is executed when called.

A procedure *accepts* or *rejects* a call. A total procedure always *accepts* calls; its body is executed whenever it is called. Termination condition (see section 4.2.1) ensures that execution of each total procedure terminates. A partial procedure may *accept* or *reject* a call. Consider a partial procedure g that consists of a single (positive) alternative; then, g is of the following form:

partial method $g(x, y) :: p; \ h(u, v) \to S$

Execution of g can be described by the following rules.

---

if $\neg p$ then *reject*
else $\{p \text{ holds}\}$ call h with parameters (u, v);
   if h *rejects* then *reject*
   else $\{h \text{ accepts}\}$

          execute S using parameters, if any, returned by h;
          return parameters, if any, to the caller of g and *accept*
     endif
endif

As stated earlier, the programmer must ensure that execution of each total procedure terminates. It can be then be shown that the execution of any partial procedure g terminates, by using induction on the partial order induced by $\geq_g$ (see section 4.2.1).

The caller is oblivious to rejection, because then its body is not executed and its state remains unchanged. If all alternatives in a program are positive, then the effect of execution of an action is either rejection – then the state does not change for any box – or acceptance – some box state may change then. This is because, if any procedure rejects during the execution of an action then the entire action rejects. If any procedure accepts – the lowest procedure, that has no preprocedure, accepts first, followed by acceptances by its callers in the reverse order of calls – then the entire action accepts. This execution strategy meets the *commit* requirement in databases where a transaction either executes to completion or does not execute at all.

We have described the execution of a partial procedure that has a single (positive) alternative. In case a procedure has several alternatives, positive and negative, the following execution strategy is adopted. Recall that preconditions of the alternatives are disjoint.

---

if preconditions of all alternatives are *false* then *reject*
else {precondition of exactly one alternative, f, holds}
   if f is a positive alternative then execute as described previously
   else {f is a negative alternative}
      execute f as a positive alternative except on completion of f:
         reject the call and do not return parameter values
   endif
endif

The execution of a negative alternative always results in rejection. The caller is still oblivious to rejection, because its body is not executed and its state remains unchanged. However, a called method may change the state of its own box even when it rejects a call, by executing a negative alternative.

For a partial action the effect of execution is identical for positive and negative alternatives because the scheduler does not discriminate between acceptance and rejection of an action. Therefore, partial actions, generally, have no negative alternatives.

4.3 A model of Seuss programs

In this section, we formalize the notion of box, procedure and executions of procedures (program execution is treated in section 4.6). The *cats* of Seuss are not modeled because they have no relevance at run time. Also, we do not distinguish between action and method because this distinction is unnecessary for the proof of the theorem. Negative alternatives are not considered in the rest of this paper.

- A *box* is a pair (S, P) where
  S is a set of *states* and
  P is a set of *procedures*.
  Each procedure has a unique name and is designated either *partial* or *total*.

- A *procedure* is a tuple (T, N, E) where
  T is a set of *terminal* symbols; each is a binary relation over the states of its box.
  N is a set of *non-terminal* symbols; each is the name of a procedure of another box.
  E is a non-empty set of *executions*, where each execution is a finite string over $T \cup N$.
  An execution of a total procedure is a sequence where each element of the sequence is either a terminal or a total procedure of another box. An execution of a partial procedure is of the form: $b\ h\ e$, where b is a terminal, h – which is optional – is a non-terminal that names a partial procedure of another box, and e is a sequence in which each element is either a terminal or a total procedure of another box.

- A *program* is a finite set of boxes. Program state is given by the box states. (Therefore, each terminal symbol is a binary relation over the program states.)

Convention and Notation:

(1) Terminal symbols of different procedures are distinct.
(2) Each execution of procedure p begins with a $begin_p$ symbol and ends with an end_p symbol. Both of these are terminal symbols of procedure p.
(3) For terminal s, $s.box$ is the box of which s is a symbol. Similarly, $p.box$ is defined for a procedure p.

Justification for the Model

A terminal symbol of a procedure – an element of T – denotes a local step within the procedure. The local step can affect only the state of the corresponding box, and we allow a step to have non-deterministic outcome. Hence, each terminal is modeled as a binary relation over box states.

In the formal model, procedures are parameter-less. Although this would be an absurd assumption in practice, it simplifies mathematical modeling considerably.

4. A reduction theorem for concurrent object-oriented programs

We justify this assumption as follows. First, we can remove a value parameter from a procedure by creating a set of procedures, one for each possible value of the parameter, and the caller can decide which procedure to call based on the parameter value. Thus, all value parameters may be removed at the expense of increasing the set of procedures. Next, consider a procedure with result parameters; to be specific, let *read(w)* return a boolean value in *w*. The caller of *read* cannot decide a priori what the returned value will be. However, we can remove parameter *w*, as follows. First, model *read* by two different procedures, *readt* and *readf*, which return the values *true* and *false*, respectively. Now, we have two different execution fragments modeling the call upon *read(w)*:

readt; *w* := *true*, and
readf; *w* := *false*.

An execution that calls *read(w)* will be represented by two executions in our model, one for each possible value returned by *read* for *w*. Thus, we can remove all parameters from procedures.

Next, we justify our model of procedure execution. An execution is a sequence of steps taken by a procedure and the procedures it calls. To motivate further discussion, consider a procedure P that calls *read(w)*, described above, twice in succession. The terminal symbols of P are α, β where

α denotes *w* := *true*, and β denotes *w* := *false*.

The non-terminals of P are *readt* and *readf*, as described above.

An execution of P does the following steps twice: call *read* and then assign the value returned in the parameter to *w*. If P is executed alone then the possible executions are

begin$_P$ readt α readt α end$_P$, and
begin$_P$ readf β readf β end$_P$.

These are the *tight* executions of P. If, however, other procedures execute concurrently with P then the value of the boolean could change in between the two read operations (by other concurrently executing procedures) and the loose executions of P are:

begin$_P$ readt α readt α end$_P$,
begin$_P$ readf β readf β end$_P$,
begin$_P$ readt α readf β end$_P$, and
begin$_P$ readf β readt α end$_P$.

In particular, the execution *begin$_P$ readt α readf β end$_P$* denotes that the boolean value is changed from *true* to *false* by another procedure during the two calls to *read* by P. Our goal is to model concurrent executions; therefore, we admit all four executions, shown above, as possible executions of P.

We have not specified the initial states of the boxes, because we do not need the initial states to prove the main theorem.

4.4 Restrictions on programs

We impose two restrictions on programs.

- (Partial Order on Boxes) For each procedure, there is a partial order over the boxes of the program such that during execution of that procedure, one procedure may call another only if the former belongs to a higher box than the latter; see section 4.4.1. Different procedures may impose different partial orders on the boxes. A static partial order – i.e., one that is the same for all procedures – is inadequate in practice.
  A consequence of the requirement of partial order is that if some procedure of a box is executing then no procedure of that box is called; therefore, at most one procedure from any box is executing at any moment.

- (Box Condition) For any box, at most one of its procedures may execute at any time; see section 4.4.3. This restriction disallows concurrency within a box.

4.4.1 Partial order on boxes

Definition:

For procedures p, q, we write p *calls* q to mean that p has q as a non-terminal. Let *calls*$^+$ be the transitive closure of *calls*, and *calls** the reflexive transitive closure of *calls*. Define a relation *calls*$_p$ over procedures where
$$(x \; calls_p \; y) \equiv (p \; calls^* \; x) \wedge (x \; calls \; y).$$

In operational terms, $x \; calls_p \; y$ means procedure x may call procedure y in some execution of procedure p. Each program is required to satisfy the following condition.

Partial Order on Boxes:

For every procedure p, there is a partial order $\geq_p$ over the boxes such that
$$x \; calls_p \; y \Rightarrow x.box >_p y.box.$$

Note: $b >_p c$ is a shorthand for $b \geq_p c \wedge b \neq c$. Relation $\geq_p$ is reflexive and $>_p$ is irreflexive.

Observation 1:

$p \; calls^* \; x \Rightarrow p.box \geq_p x.box$, and
$p \; calls^+ \; x \Rightarrow p.box >_p x.box$.

Proof: Define $calls^i$, for $i \geq 0$, as follows.

$p \; calls^0 \; p$, and
$p \; calls^{i+1} \; q \equiv (\exists r :: p \; calls^i \; r \wedge r \; calls \; q).$

Using induction over i we can show that

$p\ calls^i\ x \Rightarrow p.box \geq_p x.box$, for all $i, i \geq 0$
$p\ calls^i\ x \Rightarrow p.box >_p x.box$, for all $i, i > 0$.

The desired results follow by noting that

$p\ calls^*\ x \equiv (\exists i : i \geq 0 : p\ calls^i\ x)$, and
$p\ calls^+\ x \equiv (\exists i : i > 0 : p\ calls^i\ x)$. □

Note that $p\ calls^+\ q \Rightarrow$ {by Observation 1} $(p.box >_p q.box) \Rightarrow p, q$ are in different boxes. It follows that no call is ever made upon a box when one of its procedures has started but not completed its execution.

Observation 2:

$calls^+$ is an acyclic (i.e., irreflexive, asymmetric and transitive) relation over the procedures.
Proof: From its definition $calls^+$ is transitive. Also, $p\ calls^+\ p \Rightarrow$ {from Observation 1} $p.box >_p p.box$, a contradiction. Therefore, $calls^+$ is irreflexive. Asymmetry of $calls^+$ follows similarly.

Definition:

The *height* of a procedure is a natural number. The height is 0 if the procedure has no non-terminal. Otherwise, $p\ calls\ q \Rightarrow p.height > q.height$. This definition of height is well-grounded because $calls^+$ induces an acyclic relation on the procedures.

Definition:

An *execution tree* of procedure p is an ordered tree where (1) the root is labeled p, (2) every non-leaf node is labeled with a non-terminal symbol, and (3) the sequence of labels of the children of a non-leaf node q is an execution of q. A *full execution tree* is an execution tree in which each leaf node is labeled with a terminal symbol.

Any execution tree of procedure p is finite. This is because if procedure q is an ancestor of procedure r in this tree then $q\ calls_p\ r$; hence, $q.box >_p r.box$. Since the program has a finite number of boxes, each path in the tree is finite; also, the degree of each node is finite because each execution is finite in length. From Koenig's lemma, the tree is finite.

Definition:

The *frontier* of an execution tree is the ordered sequence of symbols in the leaf nodes of the tree. An *expanded execution* of procedure p is the frontier of some full execution tree of p. Hence, an expanded execution consists of terminals only.

4.4.2 Procedures as relations

With each terminal symbol we have associated a binary relation over program states. Next, we associate such a relation with each procedure and each execution of a procedure; to simplify notation we use the same symbol for an execution (or a procedure) and its associated relation. For execution e, $(u, v) \in e$ means that if e is started in state u then it is possible for it to end in state v. For a procedure p, $(u, v) \in p$ means that there is an execution e of p such that $(u, v) \in e$. Formally,

- The relation for a procedure is the union of relations of all its executions.
- The relation for an execution $x_0, \cdots, x_n$ is the relational product of the sequence of relations corresponding to the x_i's.

Observe that a symbol x_i in an execution may be a terminal for which the relation has already been defined, or a non-terminal for which the relation has to be computed using this definition. We show in the following lemma that the rules given above define unique relations for each execution and procedure; the key to the proof is the acyclicity of $calls^+$.

Lemma 1:

There is a unique relation for each procedure and each execution.

Proof: We prove the result by induction on n, the height of a procedure.

For $n = 0$: The procedure has only terminals in all its executions. The relation associated with any execution of the procedure is the relational product of its terminals. The relation associated with the procedure is the union of all its executions, and, hence, is uniquely determined.

For $n > 0$: Each execution of the procedure has terminals (for which the relations are given) or non-terminals (whose heights are at most n, and, hence, they have unique relations associated with them). Therefore, the relation for an execution –which is the relational product of the sequence of relations of its terminals and non-terminals– is uniquely determined. So, the relation for the procedure is also uniquely determined. □

Note that an execution may have the empty relation associated with it, denoting that the steps of the execution will never appear contiguously in a program execution. Such is the case with the execution *read α read β* in the example of section 4.3, where two successive reads of the same variable yield different values. Such an execution may appear as a non-contiguous subsequence in a program execution where steps of another procedure's execution could alter the value of the variable in between the two read operations.

Henceforth, each symbol – terminal or non-terminal – has an associated binary relation over program states. Concatenation of symbols corresponds to their relational product. For strings x, y, we write $x \subseteq y$ to denote that the relation corresponding to x is a subset of the relation corresponding to y.

Observation 3:

For terminal symbols s, t of different boxes, $st = ts$ (i.e., the relations st and ts are identical).

4.4.3 Box condition

The execution strategy for a program ensures that at most one procedure from a box executes at any time. This strategy can be encoded in our model by making it impossible for procedure q to start if procedure p of the same box has started and not yet completed. This is formalized below.

Definition:

Let σ and τ be sequences of symbols (terminals and non-terminals). Procedure p is *incomplete* after σ (before τ in $\sigma\tau$) if σ contains fewer end_p's than $begin_p$'s.

Box Condition

Let p, q be procedures of the same box, and p be incomplete after σ. Then, $\sigma\, begin_q = \epsilon$, where ϵ denotes the empty relation.

The following lemma shows that under certain conditions a terminal symbol can be transposed with a non-terminal symbol adjacent to it.

Lemma 2:

Let p, q be procedures, t a terminal of p, and σ any sequence of symbols.
1. If p is incomplete after σ then $\sigma\, q\, t \subseteq \sigma\, t\, q$.
2. If p is incomplete after $\sigma\, t$ then $\sigma\, t\, q \subseteq \sigma\, q\, t$.
Proof: We prove the first part. The other part is left to the reader.

$$
\begin{aligned}
&\sigma\, q\, t \\
={}& \{q \text{ is the union of all its expanded executions, } g\} \\
&(\cup_g (\sigma\, g\, t)) \\
={}& \{\text{partition } g \text{ into } e, f;\ e \text{ has a terminal from } p.box, \text{ and } f \text{ does not}\} \\
&(\cup_e (\sigma\, e\, t)) \cup (\cup_f (\sigma\, f\, t)) \\
={}& \{e \text{ is of the form } \sigma' begin_r\, \sigma'', \text{ where:} \\
&\quad \sigma' \text{ has no terminal from } p.box;\ r \text{ is some procedure from } p.box\} \\
&(\cup (\sigma\sigma'\, begin_r\, \sigma''\, t)) \cup (\cup_f (\sigma\, f\, t)) \\
={}& \{\sigma\sigma'\, begin_r = \epsilon, \text{ because from Box Condition:} \\
&\quad p \text{ is incomplete after } \sigma, \text{ and hence, after } \sigma\sigma', \text{ and } r.box = p.box\} \\
&(\cup_f (\sigma\, f\, t)) \\
={}& \{f \text{ has no terminal from } p.box,\ t \text{ is a terminal of } p.box;\ \text{Observation 3}\} \\
&(\cup_f (\sigma\, t\, f)) \\
\subseteq{}& \{f \text{ is a subset of the (expanded) executions of } q\} \\
&\sigma\, t\, q
\end{aligned}
$$

4.5 Compatibility

A loose execution of a program allows only compatible actions to be executed concurrently. We give a definition of compatibility in this section. We expect the user to specify the compatibility relation for procedures within each box; then the compatibility relation among all procedures (in different boxes) can be computed automatically in linear time from the definition given below.

Procedures p, q are *compatible*, denoted by $p \sim q$, if all of the following conditions hold. Observe that $\sim$ is a symmetric relation.

C0. p calls $p' \Rightarrow p' \sim q$, and q calls $q' \Rightarrow p \sim q'$.

C1. If p, q are in the same box,
$\quad\quad$ (p is total $\Rightarrow qp \subseteq pq$), and
$\quad\quad$ (q is total $\Rightarrow pq \subseteq qp$).

C2. If p, q are in different boxes, the transitive closure of the relation $(\geq_p \cup \geq_q)$ is a partial order over the boxes.

Condition C0 requires that procedures that are called by compatible procedures be compatible. Condition C1 says that for p, q in the same box, the effect of executing a partial procedure and then a total procedure can be simulated by executing them in the reverse order. Condition C2 says that compatible procedures impose similar (i.e., non-conflicting) partial orders on boxes.

Notes:

(1) If partial procedures p, q of the same box call no other procedure then they are compatible.
(2) Total procedures p, q of the same box are compatible only if $pq = qp$.
(3) The condition (C0) is well-grounded because if p calls p' then the height of p exceeds that of p'.
(4) In a Seuss program compatibility of procedures with parameters has to be established by checking the compatibility with all possible values of parameters; see the example of channels in section 4.5.1

4.5.1 Examples of compatibility

Semaphore

Consider the *Semaphore* box of page 74. We show that $V \sim V$ and $P \sim V$, i.e.,

$VV = VV$, and
$PV \subseteq VP$

The first identity is trivial. For the second identity, we compute the relations corresponding to P and V, as follows:

$\quad\quad\quad P$
$= \{\text{from the program text}\}$
$\quad\quad (n > 0) \times (n := n - 1)$
$= \{\text{definitions of predicate and assignment}\}$

$$\{(x,x) \mid x > 0\} \times \{(x, x-1) \mid x > 0\}$$
$$= \{\text{simplifying}\}$$
$$\{(x, x-1) \mid x > 0\}$$

Similarly, $V = \{(x, x+1) \mid x \geq 0\}$. Taking relational product, $PV = \{(x,x) \mid x > 0\}$, and $VP = \{(x,x) \mid x \geq 0\}$. Therefore, $PV \subseteq VP$.

Channels

Consider the unbounded FIFO channel of section that $get \sim put$, i.e., for any x, y,

$$get(x)\, put(y) \subseteq put(y)\, get(x)$$

That is, any state reachable by executing $get(x)\, put(y)$ is also reachable by executing $put(y)\, get(x)$ starting from the same initial state.

Let $(u, v) \in get(x)\, put(y)$. We show that $(u, v) \in put(y)\, get(x)$. Given $(u, v) \in get(x)\, put(y)$, we conclude from the definition of relational composition, that there is a state w such that $(u, w) \in get(x)$ and $(w, v) \in put(y)$. Since $(u, w) \in get(x)$, from the implementation of get, u represents a state where the channel is non-empty; i.e., the channel state s is of the form $a \dplus S$, for some item a and a sequence of items S. Then we have

$$\{s = a \dplus S\}\, put(y)\, \{s = a \dplus S \dplus y\}\, get(x)\, \{x \dplus s = a \dplus S \dplus y\}$$
$$\{s = a \dplus S\}\, get(x)\, \{x \dplus s = a \dplus S\}\, put(y)\, \{x \dplus s = a \dplus S \dplus y\}$$

The final states, given by the values of x and s, are identical. This completes the proof.

The preceding argument shows that two procedures from different boxes that call put and get (i.e., a sender and a receiver) may execute concurrently. Further, since $get \sim get$ by definition, multiple receivers may also execute concurrently. However, it is not the case that $put \sim put$ for arbitrary x, y, that is,

$$put(x)\, put(y) \neq put(y)\, put(x)$$

because a FIFO channel is a sequence, and appending a pair of items in different orders results in different sequences. Therefore, multiple senders may not execute concurrently.

Next, consider concurrent executions of multiple senders and receivers, as is the case in a client-server type interaction. As we have noted in the last paragraph, multiple senders may not execute concurrently on a FIFO channel. Therefore, we use an unordered channel, of section for communication in this case. We show that $put \sim put$ and $put \sim get$ for unordered channel, i.e., for all x, y

$$put(x)\, put(y) = put(y)\, put(x)\, , \text{ and}$$
$$get(x)\, put(y) \subseteq put(y)\, get(x)$$

The proof of the first identity is trivial because put is implemented as a bag union. The proof of the second result is similar to that for the FIFO channel. We need consider the initial states where the bag b is non-empty. In the following, $x \cup b$ is an abbreviation for $\{x\} \cup b$.

$\{b = B, B \neq empty\} \; get(x) \; \{x \cup b = B\} \; put(y) \; \{x \in B, \; x \cup b = B \cup y\}$
$\{b = B, B \neq empty\} \; put(y) \; \{b = B \cup y\} \; get(x) \; \{x \in (B \cup y), \; x \cup b = B \cup y\}$

The postcondition of (1) implies the postcondition of (2) because $x \in B \Rightarrow x \in (B \cup y)$. Hence, any final state of $get(x) \; put(y)$ is also a final state of $put(y) \; get(x)$.

4.5.2 Semi-commutativity of compatible procedures

In Lemma 3, below, we prove a result for compatible procedures analogous to condition C1 of page 84. This result applies to any pair of compatible procedures, not necessarily those in the same box.

Lemma 3:

Let $p \sim q$ where p is total (p, q need not belong to the same box). Then $qp \subseteq pq$.

Proof: We apply induction on n, the sum of the heights of p and q, to prove the result. The result holds from the definition of $\sim$ if p, q are in the same box. Assume, therefore, that p, q are in different boxes.

For $n = 0$: Both p, q are at height 0; hence, p, q have only terminals in all their executions. Since, p, q are from different boxes, the result follows by repeated application of Observation 3.

For $n > 0$: From (C2), the transitive closure of $(\geq_p \cup \geq_q)$ is a partial order over the boxes; we abbreviate this relation by $\geq$. We prove the result for the case where $\neg(q.box > p.box)$. A similar argument applies for the remaining case, $\neg(p.box > q.box)$. Consider an execution, e, of p. Let x be any symbol in that execution. We show that $qx \subseteq xq$.

- x is a terminal: Consider any expanded execution of q. A terminal t in this expanded execution is a symbol of procedure r where $q \; calls^* \; r$.

    $\quad x.box = t.box$
    $\Rightarrow \quad \{x, t \text{ are terminals of } p, r, \text{ respectively}\}$
    $\quad\quad x.box = t.box \; \wedge \; x.box = p.box \; \wedge \; t.box = r.box$
    $\Rightarrow \quad \{\text{logic}\}$
    $\quad\quad p.box = r.box$
    $\Rightarrow \quad \{q \; calls^* \; r; \text{ Observation 1}\}$
    $\quad\quad p.box = r.box \; \wedge \; q.box \geq_q r.box$
    $\Rightarrow \quad \{\text{logic}\}$
    $\quad\quad q.box \geq_q p.box$
    $\Rightarrow \quad \{\geq \text{ is the transitive closure of } (\geq_p \cup \geq_q)\}$
    $\quad\quad q.box \geq p.box$
    $\Rightarrow \quad \{p, q \text{ are from different boxes}\}$
    $\quad\quad q.box > p.box$
    $\Rightarrow \quad \{\text{assumption: } \neg(q.box > p.box)\}$
    $\quad\quad false$

Thus, x, t belong to different boxes, and from Observation 3, $xt = tx$. Applying this argument for all terminals t in the expanded execution of q, we have $qx = xq$.

- x is a non-terminal: From (C0), $x \sim q$. The combined heights of x and q is less than n. Also, x is total, since it is a non-terminal of p, and p is total. From the induction hypothesis, $qx \subseteq xq$.

Next we show that for any execution e of p, $qe \subseteq eq$. Proof is by induction on the length of e. If the length of e is 1 then the result follows from $qx \subseteq xq$. For e of the form fx:

$$qfx$$
$\subseteq$ {Induction: $qf \subseteq fq$; monotonicity of relational product}
$$fqx$$
$\subseteq$ {$qx \subseteq xq$; monotonicity of relational product}
$$fxq$$

Next, we show $qp \subseteq pq$.

$$qp$$
$=$ {definition of p}
$$q(\cup_{e \in p} e)$$
$=$ {distributivity of relational product over union}
$$(\cup_{e \in p} qe)$$
$\subseteq$ {$qe \subseteq eq$ from the above proof}
$$(\cup_{e \in p} eq)$$
$=$ {distributivity of relational product over union}
$$(\cup_{e \in p} e)q$$
$=$ {definition of p}
$$pq$$
□

Lemma 4:

$(p \sim q \wedge p\ calls^*\ p' \wedge q\ calls^*\ q') \Rightarrow (p' \sim q')$.

Proof: The result follows from

$(p \sim q \wedge p\ calls^i\ p' \wedge q\ calls^j\ q') \Rightarrow (p' \sim q')$

which is proved by induction on $i + j$, $i, j \geq 0$.

4.6 Proof of the reduction theorem

A finite *loose execution* of a program is a finite sequence of steps taken by some of the procedures of the program. The executions of the procedures could be interleaved. A loose execution satisfies: (1) the steps taken by each procedure is an expanded execution of that procedure, and (2) executions of two procedures are interleaved only if they are both part of the execution of the same procedure, or if they are compatible.

In this section, we formally define loose execution of a program and show a scheme to convert a loose execution into a tight execution. The reduction scheme establishes the following theorem.

Reduction Theorem:

Let E be a finite loose execution of a program. There exists a tight execution F of the program such that $E \subseteq F$.

4.6.1 Loose execution

A loose execution is given by: (1) a finite set of full execution trees (of some of the procedures), and (2) a finite sequence of terminals called a *run*. the relation corresponding to a loose execution is the relational product of the terminals in the run. Each execution tree (henceforth called a tree) depicts the steps of one action in this loose execution, and the run specifies the interleaving of the executed steps. The trees and the run satisfy the conditions M0 and M1, given below.

Condition M0 states that each symbol of the run can be uniquely identified with a leaf node of some tree, and conversely, and that the loose execution contains the procedure executions (the frontiers of the corresponding trees) as subsequences. Since each symbol of the run belongs to a tree we write $x.root$ for the root of the tree that symbol x belongs to.

Condition M1 states that if two procedures are incomplete at any point in the run then they either belong to the same tree (i.e., they are part of the same execution) or they are compatible.

- **(M0)** There is a 1-1 correspondence between the symbols in the run and the leaf nodes of the trees. The subsequence of the run corresponding to symbols from a tree T is the frontier of T.

- **(M1)** Suppose procedure p is incomplete before symbol s in the run. Then, either $p.root = s.root$ or $p.root \sim s.root$.

4.6.2 Reduction scheme

Suppose R is the run of some loose execution. We transform run R and the execution trees in stages; let R' denote the transformed run. The transformed run may consist of terminals as well as non-terminals, and its execution trees need not be full (i.e., leaf nodes may have non-terminal labels). We show how to transform the execution trees and the run so that the following invariants are maintained. Note the similarity of N0, N1 with M0, M1.

- **(N0)** There is a 1-1 correspondence between the symbols in the run and the leaf nodes of the trees. The subsequence of the run corresponding to symbols from a tree T is the frontier of T.

- **(N1)** Suppose procedure p is incomplete before symbol s in the run. Then, either $p.root = s.root$ or $p.root \sim s.root$.

- **(N2)** $R \subseteq R'$.

The conditions (N0, N1, N2) are initially satisfied by the given run and the execution trees: N0, N1 follow respectively from M0, M1, and N2 holds because $R = R'$.

The reduction process terminates when there are no *end* symbols in the run; then all symbols are the roots of the trees. This run corresponds to a tight execution, and according to N2, it establishes the reduction theorem. The resulting tight execution can simulate the original loose execution: if the original execution starting in a state u can lead to a final state v then so does the final tight execution.

For a run that contains an *end* symbol, we apply either a *replacement* step or a *transposition* step. Let the first *end* symbol appearing in the run belong to procedure q.

Replacement Step:

If a contiguous subsequence of the run corresponds to the frontier of a subtree rooted at q (then the subsequence is an execution of q) replace the subsequence by the symbol q, and delete the subtree rooted at q (retaining q as a leaf node).

This step preserves N0. N1 also holds because for any symbol x in the execution that is replaced by q, $p.root \sim x.root$ prior to replacement, and $x.root = q.root$. Hence, $p.root \sim q.root$ after the replacement. The relation for a procedure is weaker than for any of its executions; therefore, the replacement step preserves N2.

Transposition step:

If a run has an *end* symbol, and a replacement step is not applicable then execution of some procedure q is non-contiguous. We then apply a transposition step to transpose two adjacent symbols in the run (leaving the execution trees unchanged) that makes the symbols of q more contiguous. Continued transpositions make it possible to apply a replacement step eventually.

Suppose q is a partial procedure (similar arguments apply to partial procedures that have no preprocedures and to total procedures). An execution of procedure q is of the form $(begin_q\ b\ h\ \cdots\ x\ \cdots\ end_q)$ where h is the preprocedure of q and x is either a terminal symbol or a non-terminal, designating a total procedure, of q. All procedures that complete before q have already been replaced by non-terminals, because the first *end* symbol appearing in the run belongs to q. Note that h is a procedure that completes before q.

Suppose x is preceded by y which is not part of the execution of q. We show how to bring x closer to h. Transposing x, y preserves N0, N1. We show below that transposition preserves N2, as well.

- Case 0 (Both x, y are terminals): Let y be a terminal of procedures p. Procedure q is incomplete before y because its end_q symbol comes later. If p, q are in the same box then the relation corresponding to prefix σ of the run up to y is ϵ, from the Box condition. Hence, $\sigma\ y\ x = \sigma\ x\ y$. If p, q belong to different boxes, from Observation 3, the symbols x, y can be transposed.

- Case 1 (Both x, y are non-terminals): Symbol x is part of q's execution; therefore, $q.root\ calls^*\ x$. Symbol y is not a part of q's execution, nor can it be a part of the execution of any procedure that calls q because q is incomplete before y; therefore, $q.root \neq y.root$.

  q is incomplete just before y
  $\Rightarrow \{(N1)\}$
  $\quad q.root = y.root \lor q.root \sim y.root$
  $\Rightarrow \{q.root \neq y.root \text{ (see above)}\}$
  $\quad q.root \sim y.root$
  $\Rightarrow \{q.root\ calls^*\ x \land y.root\ calls^*\ y; \text{ Lemma 4}\}$
  $\quad x \sim y$
  $\Rightarrow \{x \text{ is total; Lemma 3}\}$
  $\quad yx \subseteq xy$

- Case 2 (x is a terminal, y a non-terminal): q is incomplete just before y. Applying Lemma 2 (part 1), x, y may be transposed.

- Case 3 (x is a non-terminal, y is a terminal): Let Y be the procedure of which y is a symbol. Since the first end symbol in the run belongs to q, end_Y comes after x. Therefore, Y is incomplete before x. Applying Lemma 2 (part 2) with Y as the incomplete procedure, x, y may be transposed.

Thus, x, y may be transposed in all cases, preserving N3. Hence, all symbols in the execution of q to the right of h can be brought next to h.

Next, we bring the $begin_q$ symbol and the predicate b next to h, using an argument similar to Case 3, above. Thus, all of q's symbols to the left and right of h can be made contiguous around h, and a replacement step can then be applied.

For a total procedure q the reduction is done similarly; $begin_q$ serves the role of h in the above argument. For a procedure q that has no preprocedure, the reduction process is similar with b serving the role of h.

Proof of Termination of the Reduction Scheme

We show that only a finite number of replacement and transposition steps can be applied to any loose execution. For a given run, consider the procedure q whose end symbol, end_q, is the first end symbol in the run. Define two parameters of the run, n, c, as follows.

n = number of end symbols in the run,
$c = \Sigma c_j$,

where c_j is the number of symbols not belonging to q between the preprocedure h of q and the jth symbol of q, and the sum is over all symbols of q. c has an arbitrary value if the run has no *end* symbol.

The pair (n, c) decreases lexicographically with each transposition and replacement step. This is because a replacement step removes one end symbol from the run, thus decreasing n. A transposition step decreases c while keeping n unchanged. Ultimately, therefore, n will become 0; then the run has no *end* symbol, and, from (N0), the symbols are the roots of the execution trees.

4.7 Concluding remarks

The following variation of the Reduction theorem may be useful for applications on the world-wide web. Consider a Seuss program in which every procedure calls at most one other procedure. Define all pairs of procedures to be compatible. The reduction theorem then holds: any loose execution may be simulated by some tight execution.

The proof of this result is similar to the proof already given. As before, we reduce procedure q, whose end symbol, end_q, is the first end symbol in the run. If this procedure calls no other procedure then all its symbols are terminals and, by applying Case (0) and Case (2) of the transposition step, we can bring all its symbols together next to its first symbol. If the procedure calls another procedure then, according to the reduction procedure, the called procedure has already been reduced and we bring all the symbols next to the called procedure symbol in a similar fashion.

The major simplification in the reduction scheme for this special case is due to the fact that it is never necessary to transpose two non-terminals. Therefore, Case (1) of the transposition step never arises. Consequently, the condition for compatibility of two procedures (page 84) is irrelevant in this case.

Acknowledgments

This paper owes a great deal to discussions with Rajeev Joshi and Will Adams. I am grateful to Carroll Morgan who gave me useful comments on an earlier draft. Ernie Cohen has taught me a great deal about reduction theorems, in general.

References

[1] Ernie Cohen and Leslie Lamport. Reduction in TLA. In David Sangiorgi and Robert de Simone, editors, *CONCUR'98 Concurrency Theory*, volume 1466 of *Lecture Notes*

in Computer Science, pages 317–331. Springer-Verlag, 1998. Compaq SRC Research Note 1998-005.

[2] L. Lamport and Fred B. Schneider. Pretending atomicity. Technical Report 44, DEC Systems Research Center, May 1989.

[3] Richard J. Lipton. Reduction: A method of proving properties of parallel programs. *Communications of the ACM*, 18(12):717–721, December 1975.

[4] Jayadev Misra. Loosely coupled processes. *Future Generation Computer Systems*, 8:269–286, 1992. North-Holland.

[5] Jayadev Misra. *A Discipline of Multiprogramming*. Monographs in Computer Science. Springer-Verlag, New York, 2001. The first chapter is available at http://www.cs.utexas.edu/users/psp/discipline.ps.gz

Section C

Systems and real time

5 Abstractions from time   **95**
Manfred Broy

Verification of computer systems is based on the ideas of specification, refinement and implementation. Whereas implementations are intricate, often complicated by details of optimisation and timing, specifications are abstractions and summarise the system's basic logical characteristics.

Indeed the role of abstraction is generally understood to be as a tool for tackling logical correctness of systems, and generally it has nothing to say about 'operational' issues such as time. Adopting this attitude has the advantage of simplifying the theory, but in reality the correctness of most of today's concurrent applications is acutely sensitive to timing properties — thus insisting on such a 'purist' approach is not as tenable as it used to be. In fact it now seems vital that time should become an integral part of the specification and development process for those applications.

This paper argues for a development paradigm in which some timing information is specified at the 'high level'. The feasibility of such an approach, in particular its impact on refinement, is demonstrated within the stream-based model of programming.

6 A predicative semantics for real-time refinement   **109**
Ian Hayes

Real-time programs are those which have to be not only functionally correct, but timely: for those programs, an answer that's correct but too late might as well be wrong.

A core principle of mastering complexity is the *separation of concerns*, the treatment of independent aspects of a problem each on its own, because the cost of dealing with them together is much more than additive. Two such concerns are functional behaviour (is correct) and timing (is not too late). In this paper they are treated together. Why?

Separation of concerns led initially to researchers' considering small 'toy' programs and programming languages: sequential, untimed, short and simple.

Because of that simplicity however, the notions of programming-language semantics, programming logic, specifications, implementations and refinement could be isolated and developed separately, and seen in their purest forms.

One very pure view that emerged is that specifications and programs are essentially the same — each is a description of behaviour, and they differ only in their language and degree of abstraction — and that refinement is just (reverse) implication. That view is nowadays known as 'predicative programming', and it is a good test of any approach to program development that it can, at least in principle, be reduced to such descriptions and reverse implication.

In fact it turned out to be such a useful view that it seems worth trying to move beyond the short and simple, to see 'now that we know what we are doing' whether it is after all possible to treat several concerns uniformly and simultaneously in the same style — for example functional correctness and timing. That is what is attempted in in this paper.

The novelty of this work is that it places the two concerns directly in the predicative framework, and so for example it derives its notion of refinement (as it should) directly from reverse implication. A conspicuous feature, however, is that the timing constraints — although carried along throughout the refinements — are extracted at the end for later checking against hardware performance specifications, and are until that point machine-independent. So perhaps separation of concerns is achieved after all.

5
Abstractions from time

Manfred Broy

Abstract
Mathematical models of the timed behaviour of system components form a hierarchy of timing concepts. This is demonstrated for systems that communicate via input and output streams. We distinguish *non-timed streams*, *discrete streams* with *discrete* and with *continuous time*, and *dense streams with continuous time*. We demonstrate how exchanges of the timing models during the system-development process are captured as classical abstraction steps.

5.1 Introduction

Although the timing of events is an important issue for many information processing systems, all the first attempts to provide logical, algebraic, or mathematical foundations for programming and for system development tried to abstract entirely from timing issues. This is of course fine as long as we are only interested in sequential, non-reactive algorithms. However, looking at interactive systems, especially at reactive embedded systems, timing issues immediately become crucial. In fact, many application systems of today have to react within timed bounds to time events. However, at a logical level of system specification and design the main issue is not the reaction within time bounds, but rather the reaction to abstract events. Only if there is no sensor to record such events, and if by physical theories time bounds on the events are available, can quantitative time replace the observation of events.

We are interested in the following in the description of components that react interactively to input by output. Operationally, input and output take place within a global time frame. It is one of the goals of this paper to show what consequences the abstraction from time within a semantic model actually has. In fact, the semantics becomes less robust since the flow of time leads to a quite explicit modelling of causality and thus to more realistic, simpler models of computation. As a consequence, fixpoint theory becomes more straightforward as well, and does not need more sophisticated theoretical concepts such as least fixpoints, complete partially-ordered sets or metric spaces (see [17] and [18]). This simplicity is lost, however, if we abstract from timing information partially or completely. Exemplars for these problems are models of computations based on the idea of full synchrony (see [5]). Here the lack of explicit information about causality leads into semantic pathologies such as *causal loops*.

In the following, we introduce a semantic model of system behaviour that includes discrete and dense streams with discrete and continuous time. In the first section, we introduce our mathematical basis. Then we show how to describe the syntactic interfaces and the dynamic behaviours of interactive systems. We introduce concepts for systematic and schematic abstractions of time. In particular, we show how the different time models can be related by refinement relations.

5.2 Streams

Streams are helpful models for many aspects of information processing systems. A stream describes the communication history of a channel, the flow of values assumed by a variable of a system, or the sequence of actions executed.

5.2.1 Mathematical foundation: streams

By $\mathbb{N}$ we denote the set of natural numbers $\{0, 1, \ldots\}$; by $\mathbb{N}^+$ we denote $\mathbb{N}\backslash\{0\}$. By $\{i, \ldots, j\}$ we denote for $i, j \in \mathbb{N}$ the set $\{n \in \mathbb{N} : i \leq n \leq j\}$. By $\mathbb{R}$ we denote the set of real numbers and by $\mathbb{R}^+$ the set $\{r \in \mathbb{R} : 0 < r\}$. By $[r : s]$ we denote for $r, s \in \mathbb{R}$ the set $\{x \in \mathbb{R} : r \leq x \leq s\}$, by $[r : s[$ we denote for $r, s \in \mathbb{R}$ the set $\{x \in \mathbb{R} : r \leq x < s\}$ and by $]r : s]$ we denote for $r, s \in \mathbb{R}$ the set $\{x \in \mathbb{R} : r < x \leq s\}$. By M^* we denote the set of finite sequences over the set M.

A time domain is a linearly ordered set of elements representing time points. A stream is a mapping

$$s : T \to S(M)$$

where T is a time domain and $S(M)$ is the stream domain. Typically, the stream domain $S(M)$ is identical to M or M^*.

An example of a time domain is the set $\mathbb{R}^+$ of the positive reals. *Continuous infinite streams* of sort M are mappings from the positive reals into the set M. Hence a continuous infinite stream s is a mapping

$$s : \mathbb{R}^+ \to M$$

A finite continuous stream is a mapping

$$s :]0 : r] \to M$$

where $r \in \mathbb{R}$. We call r the length of the stream s and denote it by $\#s$. Also concatenation easily extends from discrete to continuous streams.

Next we study four different classes of streams in connection with the modelling of time: *non-timed streams*, *discrete streams* with *discrete* and *continuous* time, and finally *dense streams* with *continuous time*.

5.2.2 Modelling time

Streams represent communication histories for sequential channels. Given a set M of messages, a non-timed history for a sequential channel is given by a discrete stream of sort M. Such a stream reflects the order in which the messages are communicated. It does not contain any quantitative aspects of the timing of its messages. Hence we speak of a *non-timed* stream.

If additional quantitative time information is contained, we speak of a timed stream. In the following, we are interested in separating aspects of data and message flow of a channel from timing aspects.

Typical time models that we find in the literature are the natural numbers $\mathbb{N}$ and the positive real numbers $\mathbb{R}^+$. We might also work with the rational numbers, however: as long as we do not study limits and infinitely small differences, there is not a significant difference between the real numbers and the rational numbers when modelling time. These numbers are all models of *linear* time. Linear time is most appropriate for system models with a *global* time.

A timed communication history for a channel carrying messages from a given set M is represented by a timed stream. A timed stream with discrete time is a finite or infinite sequence of messages with additional timing information from a discrete time space. We work with the following models of streams with notions of quantitative time.

	time domain	stream domain
non-timed streams	$T = \mathbb{N} \vee \exists n \in \mathbb{N} : T = \{0, \ldots, n\}$	M
discrete streams/ discrete time	$T \subseteq \mathbb{N}$	M^*
discrete streams/ continuous time	$T \subseteq \mathbb{R}^+$ where T is finite or countable	M
dense streams/ continuous time	$T = \mathbb{R}^+ \vee \exists r \in \mathbb{R}^+ : T = [0 : r[$	M

Note that we use M^* as the stream domain in the case of discrete streams with discrete time to allow for several messages in one time slot.

$s{\downarrow}i$ denotes the communication history of the stream s till time i. We extend this notation, of truncating streams at time points, to sets W of streams pointwise, as follows

$$W{\downarrow}t = \{s{\downarrow}t : s \in W\}$$

Let s be a discrete stream with discrete time and with stream domain M^*; then $s : \mathbb{N} \to M^*$. By $(M^*)^\mathbb{N}$ we denote the set of discrete streams. By $\bar{s}$ we denote the finite or infinite discrete stream in $\mathbb{N} \to M$ that is the result of replacing its time domain by that of non-timed streams while retaining the sequence of data elements. Consider as an example the stream $s : \mathbb{N} \to \{a,b,c\}^*$ where $s.n = \langle abc \rangle$. Then we get $\bar{s}.n = a$ if $n \bmod 3 = 0$, $\bar{s}.n = b$ if $n \bmod 3 = 1$ and $\bar{s}.n = c$ if $n \bmod 3 = 2$. Seen as sequences we have:

$$s = \langle \langle abc \rangle \langle abc \rangle \langle abc \rangle \langle abc \rangle \ldots \rangle$$
$$\bar{s} = \langle abcabcabcabc \ldots \rangle$$

This corresponds to a time abstraction in which we forget all the timing information in the stream s and only keep the sequence of its elements.

Each discrete stream s contains a finite or infinite number $\#s$ of messages. For each discrete stream s we define a mapping

$$s\dagger : \{n \in \mathbb{N} : n < \#\bar{s}\} \to \mathbb{R}^+$$

that associates its time point with the i-th message in the discrete stream s.

Working with real numbers to represent time, the time points can be chosen more freely. Actually, we require strict monotonicity for the timing function of the time stamps since continuous time is the finest time granularity we can choose. The set of discrete streams over the message set M with continuous time is represented by the set

$$M^{\mathcal{R}}$$

Using real numbers for modelling time, we have to cope with Zeno's paradox. Given a stream s, we speak of Zeno's paradox if we have

$$\forall i \in \mathbf{dom}[s] : s\dagger i < t$$

for some time $t \in \mathbb{R}^+$, although $\#\bar{s} = \infty$. A simple example of a stream that exhibits Zeno's paradox is given in the following. Define the infinite stream s by the equations

$$s.i = i$$
$$s\dagger i = 1/2^i$$

Then the time function is strictly monotonic, and the stream is infinite, but its time points are bounded. In many applications such a behaviour is not of interest and should be excluded. We therefore require for any infinite stream s the proposition

$$\forall k \in \mathbb{N} : \exists i \in \mathbb{N} : s\dagger i > k$$

to avoid Zeno's paradox. A simple way to achieve this is to assume a minimal time distance $\delta \in \mathbb{R}$, $\delta > 0$, for all the messages in the timed stream s such that

$$s\dagger(i+1) - s\dagger i > \delta \quad \text{for all } i \text{ with } i, i+1 \in \mathbf{dom}[s].$$

The notation for streams with discrete time can easily be extended to streams with continuous time. For a stream s we denote for $t \in \mathbb{R}^+$ by

$$s \downarrow t$$

the stream of messages till time point t.

The crucial difference between discrete and continuous time is as follows. In the case of continuous time we have in contrast to discrete time:

- separability: we can always find a time point in between two given distinct time points; and
- limits: we can make our time intervals infinitely small leading to limit points.

Separability is certainly helpful since it supports the flexibility of the timing. Limits lead to Zeno's paradox and are better ruled out whenever possible.

A discrete stream is a sequence of messages such that we can speak about the first, second, third, and so on, message in a stream. Using continuous time a stream may contain uncountably many message elements. We speak of a *dense stream* in that case: a dense stream is represented by a function

$$s : \mathbb{R}^+ \to M$$

For every time $t \in \mathbb{R}^+$ we obtain a message $s(t) \in M$. By

$$M^{\mathbb{R}}$$

we denote the set of dense streams. We easily extend the notation $s\downarrow t$ to dense streams for $t \in \mathbb{R}$. $s\downarrow t$ is a finite stream obtained from s by restricting it to the time domain $]0 : t]$.

5.3 Components as functions on streams

In this section we introduce the general concept of a component as a function on timed streams. We consider the most general case of dense streams. (Since all other streams can be seen as special cases or abstractions of dense streams, these are included automatically.)

5.3.1 Behaviours of components

We work with channels as identifiers for streams. By C we denote the set of channels. Given a set of sorts T and a function

$$\text{sort} : C \to T$$

we speak of sorted channels. Given a set C of sorted channels we denote by

$$\vec{C}$$

the set of channel valuations

$$x : C \to M^{\mathbb{R}}$$

where $x.c$ is a timed stream of the appropriate sort $\text{sort}(c)$ of channel $c \in C$.

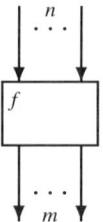

Figure 5.1. Graphical representation of a component as a dataflow node with n input and m output channels

A function

$$F : \vec{I} \to \mathbb{P}(\vec{O})$$

is called a *component behaviour*. F is called

- *timed* or *weakly causal*, if for all $t \in \mathbb{R}$ we have for all $x, z \in \vec{I}$:

$$x\downarrow t = z\downarrow t \Rightarrow F(x)\downarrow t = F(z)\downarrow t$$

- *time guarded by a finite delay* $\delta \in \mathbb{R}^+$, $\delta > 0$, or *causal*, if for all $t \in \mathbb{R}$ we have for all $x, z \in \vec{I}$:

$$x\downarrow t = z\downarrow t \Rightarrow F(x)\downarrow(t+\delta) = F(z)\downarrow(t+\delta)$$

A timed function has a proper time flow. That is, the choice of the output at the time point t does not depend on input that comes only after time t. Time guardedness models some delay in the reaction of a system, which introduces a fundamental notion of causality.

We use time-guarded stream-processing functions F to model the behaviour of a component. A graphical representation of the function F as a nondeterministic dataflow node is given in Fig. 5.1.

A behaviour F on discrete streams with discrete time is called *time-unbiased*, if for discrete input histories x and z we have

$$F.x = \{y : \exists x' \in \vec{I}, y' \in \vec{O} : y' \in F.x' \wedge \overline{y} = \overline{y'} \wedge \overline{x} = \overline{x'}\}$$

For time unbiased behaviours the timing of the messages in the input streams does not influence the messages in the output streams, but it may influence their timing.

5.4 Time abstraction

Refinement is the basic concept for the stepwise development of components. We describe only one form of refinement: *interaction refinement*. It is the basis of abstraction.

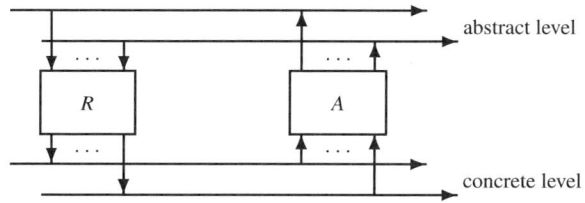

Figure 5.2. Communication History Refinement

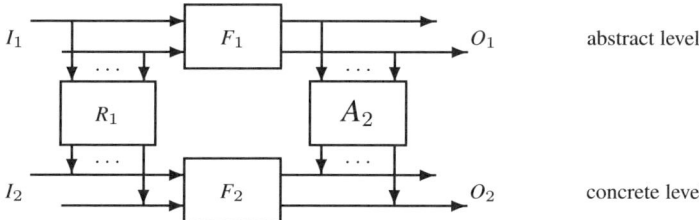

Figure 5.3. Commuting Diagram of Interaction Refinement (*U-simulation*)

5.4.1 General concepts of abstraction

By abstractions the syntactic interface of a component is changed. We work with pairs of abstraction and representation functions.

By interaction refinement we can change the number of input and output channels of a system, as well as the type and granularity of their messages, but still relate the behaviours in a formal way. A *communication-history refinement* requires timed functions

$$A : \vec{I} \to \mathbb{P}(\vec{O}) \qquad R : \vec{O} \to \mathbb{P}(\vec{I})$$

where

$$R \circ A = \text{Id}$$

Here $R \circ A$ denotes the functial composition of R and A, defined by

$$(R \circ A).x = \{z \in A.y : y \in R.x\}$$

and Id denotes the identity relation

$$\text{Id}.x = \{x\}$$

Fig. 5.2 shows the "commuting diagram" of history refinement.

Note that the requirement $R \circ A \subseteq \text{Id}$ instead of $R \circ A = \text{Id}$ is too weak, since this way we would allow abstract streams not to be represented at all.

Based on the idea of a history refinement we introduce the idea of an interaction refinement for components.

Given two communication history refinements

$$A_1 : \vec{I}_2 \to \mathbb{P}(\vec{I}_1) \qquad R_1 : \vec{I}_1 \to \mathbb{P}(\vec{I}_2)$$
$$A_2 : \vec{O}_2 \to \mathbb{P}(\vec{O}_1) \qquad R_2 : \vec{O}_1 \to \mathbb{P}(\vec{O}_2)$$

we call the behaviour

$$F_1 : \vec{I}_1 \to \mathbb{P}(\vec{O}_1)$$

an *interaction abstraction* of the behaviour

$$F_2 : \vec{I}_2 \to \mathbb{P}(\vec{O}_2)$$

if one of the following four propositions holds:

$R_1 \circ F_2 \circ A_2 \subseteq F_1$ *U-simulation*
$R_1 \circ F_2 \subseteq F_1 \circ R_2$ *downward simulation*
$F_2 \circ A_2 \subseteq A_1 \circ F_1$ *upward simulation*
$F_2 \subseteq A_1 \circ F_1 \circ R_2$ U^{-1}*-simulation*

Note that U^{-1}-simulation is the strongest condition, from which all others follow by straightforward algebraic manipulation.

5.4.2 Abstractions from time

In this section we study interaction abstractions that support abstractions from dense streams to streams with continuous time and further on to streams with discrete time and finally to non-timed streams.

From discrete timed to non-timed streams

A non-timed stream can be seen as the abstraction from all discrete timed streams with the same message set but arbitrary timing. The specification of the abstraction function A is simple:

$$A.y = \{\bar{y}\}$$

The specification of the representation function R is also simple:

$$R.x = \{y : \bar{y} = x\}\,.$$

Although the abstraction is so simple to specify, forgetting about time has serious consequences for functions that describe the behaviour of components. Time guardedness is lost and, as a consequence, we also lose the uniqueness of fixpoints — which has crucial impacts on the compositionality of the semantic models (for an extensive discussion, see [8]).

From continuous- to discrete Time

For relating discrete streams with discrete time to discrete streams with continuous time we work with an abstraction function

$$\alpha : M^{\mathcal{R}} \to (M^*)^{\mathbb{N}}$$

5. Abstractions from time

It is specified by the following equations (let $r \in M^{\mathcal{R}}$)

$$(\alpha.r).j = r.j$$
$$(\alpha.r)\dagger j = \min\{n \in \mathbb{N} : r\dagger j \leq n\}$$

We define the abstraction relation

$$A : M^{\mathcal{R}} \to \mathbb{P}(M^*)^{\mathbb{N}}$$

as

$$A.r = \{\alpha.r\}$$

and the representation specification

$$R : (M^*)^{\mathbb{N}} \to \mathbb{P}(M^{\mathcal{R}})$$

by the equation

$$R.s = \{r : s = \alpha.r\}$$

The step from discrete to continuous time (or back) is rather simple and does not have many consequences for the semantic techniques, as long as the time granularity chosen is fine enough to maintain time-guardedness.

From dense streams to discrete streams

To abstract a dense stream into a discrete stream we can use the following two techniques:

- sampling; and
- event discretisation.

In sampling, we select a countable number of time points as samples. We define the abstraction specification

$$A : M^{\mathbb{R}} \to \mathbb{P}(M^{\mathcal{R}})$$

that maps dense to discrete streams by

$$A.r = \{\alpha.r\}$$

where (choosing a simple variant of sampling in which we select the natural numbers as the sample time points)

$$(\alpha.r).j = r.j$$
$$(\alpha.r)\dagger j = j$$

A representation specification for *sampling* in continuous time is obtained by the function

$$R : M^{\mathcal{R}} \to \mathbb{P}(M^{\mathbb{R}})$$

defined by (we ignore for simplicity the possibility of successive identical messages in a stream)

$$R.s = \{r : s = \alpha.r\}$$

By sampling, continuous streams are related to discrete streams of events.

5.5 Conclusions

Modelling information processing systems appropriately is a matter of choosing the adequate abstractions in terms of the corresponding mathematical models. This applies for the models of time, in particular.

5.5.1 Time models in the literature

Time issues were always of great practical relevance for a number of applications of software systems such as embedded software and telecommunications. Nevertheless, in the scientific literature of mathematical models for software, time issues were considered only in the late seventies and then only in a few publications (see, for instance [20]). In the theoretical foundations of interactive systems, timing aspects were ignored in the beginning. It seems that the researchers tried hard to abstract from time, which was considered an operational notion. Early logical approaches were given in [12] and [6]. An early denotational model is found in [7].

Since then the interest in real time and its modelling has considerably increased in scientific research. In most of the approaches one particular time model is selected, without arguing much about the rationale of the particular choice. Often the time model is implicit (such as in statecharts, see [9], in SDL, see [19], or in Esterel [4]). This caused a lot of discussion about the right time model for such modelling languages. Other approaches such as the duration calculus (see [21]), where continuous time and dense message streams are essential, are explicitly directed towards time and a specific model of time.

Only a few publications discuss and compare different time models. One example is [10] which discusses the relation between the task of the specification and verification of real time programs and representations of time. Another example is [11] by Kopetz who compares what he calls dense time with what he calls sparse time. In sparse time events can only occur at "some sections of the time line". So sparse time seems to be what we call discrete time. A careful discussion of time models for hardware is found in [15], chapter 6. However, so far there is no approach that defines a formal relationship between systems working with different time models as we do with the concept of interaction abstraction.

Operational models of timing issues are found in [1], [2], [3], and [13, 14]. A specific issue is system models that incorporate aspects of continuous time and discrete events (see [2], [16]). In [17] and [18] the introduction of "hiatons", which are very similar to time ticks, are used to avoid problems with fixpoint theory.

5.5.2 Concluding remarks

Giving straightforward operational models that contain all the technical computational details of interactive nondeterministic computations is relatively simple. However, for systems-engineering purposes operational models are not very helpful. Finding appropriate abstractions for operational models of distributed systems is a difficult but nevertheless important task. Good abstract non-operational models are the basis for tractable system specifications and of a discipline of systems development.

Abstraction means forgetting information. Of course, we may forget only information that is not needed. Which information is needed does not only depend upon the explicit concept of observation, but also upon the considered forms of the composition of systems from subsystems.

As shown above, there are many ways to obtain time abstractions. Typical examples are

- from dense streams to discrete streams with continuous time,
- from discrete streams with continuous time to discrete time,
- from a finer discrete time to a coarser discrete time,
- from timed to non-timed streams.

In fact, all four abstraction steps mean that we use a coarser, more abstract time model. This way we lose some information about the timing of messages. As a consequence, messages at different time points may be represented by identical time points. This means we lose the principle of causality for certain input and output. This leads to intricate problems as we find them in the approaches that work with the assumption of so-called *perfect synchrony* (cf. [5]). The specification of interactive systems has to be done in a time/space frame. A specification should indicate which events (communication actions) can take place where, and when, and how they are causally related. Time information can be treated as any other information except, however, that the time flow follows certain laws. This is expressed by the timing requirements such as time guardedness. Such specification techniques are an important prerequisite for the development of safety-critical systems.

Acknowledgement

I am grateful to Ketil Stølen for a number of discussions that were helpful to clarify the basic concepts. It is a pleasure to thank my colleagues Olaf Müller and Jan Philipps for many useful remarks on a draft version of this paper.

References

[1] R. Alur, D. Dill. A theory of timed automata. *Theoretical Computer Science* 126, 1994, 183–235

[2] R. Alur, C. Courcoubetis, N. Halbwachs, T.A. Henzinger, P.-H. Ho, X. Nicollin, A. Olivero, J. Sifakis, S. Yovine. Algorithmic analysis of hybrid systems. *Theoretical Computer Science* 138, 1995, 3–34

[3] J.C.M. Baeten, J.A. Bergstra. Real Time Process Algebra. *Formal Aspects of Computing* 3, 1991, 142–188

[4] G. Berry, G. Gonthier. The ESTEREL Synchronous Programming Language: Design, Semantics, Implementation. INRIA, Research Report 842, 1988

[5] G. Berry. Preemption in Concurrent Systems. In: *Proceedings of the FSTTCS '93*, Lecture Notes in Computer Science 761, Springer Verlag 1993, 72–93

[6] A. Bernstein, P.K. Harter. Proving Real Time Properties of Programs with Temporal Logic. In: *Proceedings of the 8th Annual ACM Symposium on Operating Systems*, 1981, 1–11

[7] M. Broy. Applicative real time programming. In: *Information Processing 83, IFIP World Congress*, Paris 1983, North Holland 1983, 259–264

[8] M. Broy. Functional Specification of Time Sensitive Communicating Systems. *ACM Transactions on Software Engineering and Methodology* 2:1, January 1993, 1–46

[9] D. Harel. Statecharts: A Visual Formalism for Complex Systems. *Science of Computer Programming* 8, 1987, 231–274

[10] M. Joseph. Problems, promises and performance: Some questions for real-time system specification. In: *Real Time: Theory in Practice, REX workshop*. Lecture Notes in Computer Science 600, 1991, 315–324

[11] H. Kopetz. Sparse Time versus Dense Time in Distributed Real-Time Systems. In: *Proceedings of the 12th International Conference on Distributed Computing Systems*. IEEE Computer Society Press 1992, 460–467,

[12] L. Lamport. TIMESETS: a new method for temporal reasoning about programs. In: D. Kozen (ed.): *Logics of Programs*. Lecture Notes in Computer Science 131, 1981, 177–196

[13] N. Lynch, F. Vaandrager. Action Transducers and Time Automata. *Formal Aspects of Computing* 8, 1996, 499–538

[14] N. Lynch, F. Vaandrager. Forward and Backward Simulations, Part II: Timing-Based Systems. *Information and Computation* 128:1, 1996

[15] T. Melham. *Higher Order Logic and Hardware Verification*. Cambridge University Press. 1993

[16] O. Müller, P. Scholz. Functional Specification of Real-Time and Hybrid Systems. In: *HART'97, Proc. of the 1st Int. Workshop on Hybrid and Real-Time Systems*, Lecture Notes in Computer Science 1201, 1997, 273–286

[17] D. Park. On the Semantics of Fair Parallelism. In: D. Bjørner (ed.): *Abstract Software Specification*. Lecture Notes in Computer Science 86, Springer 1980, 504–526

[18] D. Park. The "Fairness" Problem and Nondeterministic Computing Networks. *Proc. 4th Foundations of Computer Science*, Mathematical Centre Tracts 159, Mathematisch Centrum Amsterdam, (1983) 133–161

[19] Specification and Description Language (SDL), Recommendation Z.100. Technical Report, CCITT, 1988
[20] N. Wirth. Towards a Discipline of Real Time Programming. *Communications of the ACM* 20:8, 1977, 577–583
[21] Zhou Chaochen, C.A.R. Hoare, A.P. Ravn. A Calculus of Durations. *Information Processing Letters* 40:5, 1991, 269–276

6

A predicative semantics for real-time refinement

Ian Hayes

Abstract

Real-time systems play an important role in many safety-critical systems. Hence it is essential to have a formal basis for the development of real-time software. In this chapter we present a predicative semantics for a real-time, wide-spectrum language. The semantics includes a special variable representing the current time, and uses timed traces to represent the values of external input and outputs over time so that reactive control systems can be handled. Because a real-time control system may be a nonterminating process, we allow the specification of nonterminating programs and the development of nonterminating repetitions. We present a set of refinement laws covering the constructs in the language. The laws make use of a relational style similar to that of Cliff Jones, although they have been generalised to handle nonterminating constructs.

6.1 Background

The sequential refinement calculus for non-real-time programs is a mature theory for the development of sequential programs [1, 2, 19, 20]. Our goal is to develop an equivalent theory for real-time programs. Work by Mahony modelled real-time systems by representing the observable variables as timed traces: functions from time (real numbers) to their type [17, 18]. That work concentrated on modeling system components over all time, and on decomposing systems into parallel combinations of such components, and had a semantics based on predicate transformers [16]. Mark Utting and Colin Fidge used a related approach to develop a sequential real-time refinement calculus that was also based on timed traces and predicate transformers [22, 23]. In that work, in common with a number of other approaches to real-time [21, 13], an execution time is associated with each component of a command. This leads to complex timing conditions as well as overly restricted timing constraints on the execution of individual commands and their components.

A breakthrough came with the introduction of the *deadline* command [9, 3]. The deadline command has a simple semantics: it takes no time to execute and guarantees to complete by a given time. For example, the following code reads the value of the input d_1 into the local variable x, calculates $f(x)$ and assigns it to y, writes y to the output d_2. The special variable τ stands for the current time. The starting time of the commands is captured in the auxiliary variable m, and the final command is a deadline of $m + U$; this ensures that the commands complete within U time units of their beginning.

$$
\begin{aligned}
&m := \tau; \quad \text{-- } \tau \text{ is the current time variable} \\
&x : \mathbf{read}(d_1); \\
&y := f(x); \\
&d_2 : \mathbf{write}(y); \\
&\mathbf{deadline}\, m + U
\end{aligned}
\tag{1}
$$

In isolation a deadline command cannot be implemented, but if it can be shown that all execution paths leading to a deadline command reach it before its deadline, then it can be removed. The deadline command allows *machine-independent* real-time programs to be expressed. It also allows one to separate out timing constraints to leave components that are purely calculations [5]; these components can then be developed as in the non-real-time calculus.

The semantics used in the earlier work was based on that of Utting and Fidge [22, 23]. The current time variable, τ, was treated in the same manner as in the standard refinement calculus with a before and after value for each command, but all other variables were treated as functions of time (real numbers), which were constrained by the execution of a command [10].

As real-time systems often use processes which are potentially nonterminating, we desired to extend the approach to handle these. At the specification level this was quite easy: the current time variable, τ, was allowed to take on the value infinity to indicate nontermination. However, the earlier semantics was based on weakest-precondition predicate transformers and hence dealt only with terminating commands and only allowed the development of terminating repetitions. As in the standard refinement calculus, nonterminating repetitions were identified with abort. Hence that semantics was unsuitable.

For the new semantics, the primary influences are the work of Hehner [11], and Hoare and He [12] using predicative semantics for program development. These were first used to tackle the semantics of nonterminating repetitions [7]. Hooman's work on real-time Hoare logic [13] also allows nonterminating repetitions and was influential in the approach taken to the laws for introducing nonterminating repetitions. Auxiliary variables and procedure parameters were also added to facilitate the expression of timing constraints [6].

The final influence on this paper is the work of Jones [15] on a relational approach to proof rules for sequential programs. This paper brings together the above pieces of work to give a relational, predicative semantics for a sequential real-time refinement calculus that supports nonterminating processes and auxiliary variables.

6.1.1 Related work

Hooman and Van Roosmalen [14] have developed a platform-independent approach to real-time software development similar to ours. Their approach makes use of timing annotations that are associated with commands. The annotations allow the capture in auxiliary timing variables of the time of occurrence of significant events that occur with the associated command, and the expression of timing deadlines on the command relative to such timing variables. They give an example similar to (1) above, using their notation:

$in(d_1, x)[m?];$
$y := f(x);$
$out(d_2, y)[< m + U]$

The constructs in square brackets are timing annotations [14, Sect. 2]. On the input the annotation '$m?$' indicates that the time at which the input occurs should be assigned to timing variable m, and on the output the annotation '$< m + U$' requires the output to take effect before $m + U$, i.e. within U time units of the input time. Hooman and Van Roosmalen keep timing annotations separate from the rest of the program. They give Hoare-like rules for reasoning about programs in their notation, but there is no semantics against which to justify the rules. The approach to real-time semantics given in this paper could be used to justify their Hoare axioms.

Section 6.2 introduces the machine-independent, wide-spectrum language and gives its semantics, along with suitable refinement rules. Section 6.3 presents an example refinement that makes use of the refinement laws, Section 6.4 discusses repetitions, and Section 6.5 discusses timing constraint analysis.

6.2 Language and semantics

We model time by nonnegative real numbers:

$Time \,\widehat{=}\, \{r : \mathbf{real}_\infty \mid 0 \leq r < \infty\}.$

where $\mathbf{real}_\infty$ stands for the real numbers extended with plus and minus infinity, and real operators such as '$<$' are extended to work with infinite arguments. The real-time refinement calculus makes use of a special real-valued variable, τ, for the current time. To allow for nonterminating programs, we allow τ to take on the value infinity (∞):

$Time_\infty \,\widehat{=}\, Time \cup \{\infty\}.$

We refer to the set of variables in scope as the environment, and use the name ρ for the environment. In real-time programs we distinguish four kinds of variables:

- inputs, $p.in$, which are under external control;
- outputs, $p.out$, which are under the control of the program;
- local variables, $p.local$, which are under the control of the program, but unlike outputs are not externally visible; and
- auxiliary variables, $p.aux$, which are similar to local variables, but are restricted to appear only in assumptions, specifications, deadline commands and assignments to auxiliary variables.

To simplify the presentation in this paper, we only treat the types of variables informally.

Inputs and outputs are modelled as timed traces: functions from *Time* to the declared type of the variable. This allows one to model both continuous and discrete inputs within the same framework. As a running example, we use the simple real-time task of closing a railway gate when a train is detected as being near, and reopening the gate when the train is out of the danger region. The example is treated in more detail in Sec. 6.3. The controller reads from the external inputs *near* and *out*, and writes to the output *gate*.

> **input** *near, out* : *boolean*;
> **output** *gate* : $\{open, close\}$;

The inputs *near* and *out* are modelled as functions from *Time* to boolean, and the output *gate* is modelled as a function from *Time* to $\{open, close\}$. For t in *Time* (which does not include infinity), the expression $near(t)$ gives the value of *near* at time t.

The primitive commands in our language only constrain an output over the execution interval of the command, which is the left-open, right-closed interval from the start time, τ_0, to the finish time of the command, τ, which we write as $(\tau_0 \ldots \tau]$. The initial value of the output at τ_0 is determined by the previous command, and then the command determines the values up to and including τ. Any programs composed of these commands using the standard structures like sequential composition, selection and repetition also satisfy this property.

In earlier work [22, 10] all variables, except τ, were modelled as functions of time (timed traces). With the addition of auxiliary variables [6] this is not possible, because assignments to auxiliary variables take no time and a timed trace only allows a variable to have a single value at any one time. Hence to represent the effect of a command on an auxiliary variable, z, we use a relation between its initial value (represented in predicates by z_0) and its final value (represented in predicates by z). Having introduced this model for auxiliary variables, we decided to use the same model for local variables. Either model could be used for local variables, but choosing a similar model for auxiliary and local variables makes the semantics a little simpler. In addition, this model is more abstract because it does not consider intermediate values of local variables during the execution of a command. We refer to the combination of local and auxiliary variables as the *state*, and use the abbreviation $\rho.v$ to stand for the state variables, and decorations of $\rho.v$, such as $\rho.v_0$, to stand for the decorated state variables.

For the railway crossing example, we declare a local boolean variable, *sens*, and an auxiliary time-valued variable, *before*, as follows.

var *sens* : *boolean*;
aux *before* : *Time*;

We represent the semantics of a command by a predicate in a form similar to that of Hehner [11], and Hoare and He [12]. The predicate is in terms of the input and output traces over time, the initial and final values of the state variables, and the initial and final values of the current time, τ_0 and τ. The meaning function, $\mathcal{M}$, takes the variables in scope, ρ, and a command C and returns the corresponding predicate, $\mathcal{M}_\rho(C)$. Refinement of commands (in an environment, ρ) is defined as reverse entailment:

$$C \sqsubseteq_\rho D \mathrel{\hat{=}} (\mathcal{M}_\rho(C) \Leftarrow \mathcal{M}_\rho(D)) \;,$$

where '$P \Leftarrow Q$' holds if for all values of the variables, whenever Q holds, P holds. We use the relation '$\sqsubseteq_\rho$' for refinement equivalence, i.e. refinement in both directions. When the environment is clear from the context the subscript ρ may be omitted.

6.2.1 Real-time specification command

We introduce a possibly nonterminating real-time *specification command*,

$$\infty\,\vec{x}\!: [P,\;Q] \;,$$

where $\vec{x}$ is a vector of variables (called the *frame*) that may be modified by the command, the predicate P is the assumption made by the specification, and the predicate Q is its effect. The '∞' at the beginning is just part of the syntax; it reminds us that the command might not terminate. The assumption P is assumed to hold at the start time of the command. It is a *single-state predicate*. That is, it may reference any of the variables in the environment plus τ, but it may not reference τ_0 or initial state (zero-subscripted) variables. The effect predicate Q describes a relation between before and after state variables in the environment, and τ_0 and τ, as well as a constraint on the values of the outputs. To simplify the presentation in this paper, we refer to such predicates as *relations*. We also assume that all predicates and relations are well formed with respect to the relevant environment in the context in which they are used.

We define a *terminating* specification command similarly. The only difference is the additional requirement that the effect should achieve $\tau < \infty$.

$$\vec{x}\!: [P,\;Q] \mathrel{\hat{=}} \infty\,\vec{x}\!: [P,\;Q \wedge \tau < \infty]$$

This is the real-time equivalent of the Morgan specification command, which is guaranteed to terminate [19]. Below we state laws for the more general, possibly nonterminating, specification command, but special cases for a terminating specification command are easily derived, and we make use of those in the examples.

For example, in the following specification the frame consists of the local variable, *sens*, and the time-valued, auxiliary variable, *before*. The notation *near* $\uparrow 0$ stands for the time at which the input *near* makes its first transition from *false* to *true*, or it is infinity if there is no such transition. If *near* does make a transition, then the following specification terminates at some time after that transition. However, if *near* never makes a transition, the specification never terminates.

$$\infty \, sens, before: \left[S, \; near \uparrow 0 \leq \tau < \infty \lor near \uparrow 0 = \tau = \infty \right]$$

The assumption S (which is needed for the refinement of this specification) will be explained further below.

The frame of a specification command lists those variables that may be modified by the command. The frame may not include inputs. The current time variable, τ, is implicitly in the frame. All outputs not in the frame are defined to be stable for the duration of the command, provided the assumption holds initially. We define the predicate *stable* by

$$stable(z, TS) \mathrel{\widehat=} TS \neq \{\} \Rightarrow (\exists x \bullet z(\!| TS |\!) = \{x\})$$

where $z(\!| TS |\!)$ is the image of the set (of times) TS through the function z (representing an external variable). We allow the first argument of *stable* to be a set (or vector) of variables, in which case all variables in the set are stable. To specify the closed interval of times from s until t, we use the notation $[s \ldots t]$. The open interval is specified by $(s \ldots t)$.

Any state variable, y, not in the frame is unchanged. Hence for these variables we require that $y_0 = y$, except that in the case of a nonterminating command there is no final state and hence the equality is not required if the final time is infinity. For a vector of outputs, $\vec{out}$, a vector of state variables, $\vec{z}$, and times t_0 and t, we introduce the following notation.

$$eq(\vec{out}, t_0, t, \vec{z_0}, \vec{z}) \mathrel{\widehat=} stable(\vec{out}, [t_0 \ldots t]) \land (t < \infty \Rightarrow \vec{z_0} = \vec{z})$$

Definition 6.2.1 (real-time specification) *Given an environment, ρ, a specification command, $\infty \vec{x} \colon [P, \; Q]$, is well-formed provided its frame, $\vec{x}$, is contained in $\rho.local \cup \rho.aux \cup \rho.out$, P is a single-state predicate, and Q is a relation. The meaning of a possibly nonterminating real-time specification command is defined by the following,*

$$\mathcal{M}_\rho \left(\infty \vec{x} \colon [P, \; Q] \right) \mathrel{\widehat=} \tau_0 \leq \tau \land$$
$$(\tau_0 < \infty \land P \left[\tfrac{\rho.v_0, \tau_0}{\rho.v, \tau} \right] \Rightarrow (Q \land eq(\rho.out \setminus \vec{x}, \tau_0, \tau, \rho.v_0 \setminus \vec{x_0}, \rho.v \setminus \vec{x})))$$

where the operator '$\setminus$' is set difference. □

As abbreviations, if P is omitted, then it is taken to be *true*, and if the frame is empty the ':' is omitted. Note that if P does not hold initially the command still guarantees that time does not go backwards.

6. A predicative semantics for real-time refinement

Because τ may take on the value infinity, the above specification command allows nontermination. If the command does not terminate then the final values of the state variables have no counterpart in reality. Hence it does not make sense to write specifications that require, for example, the final value of a local variable y to be zero and the command to not terminate: $y = 0 \land \tau = \infty$. There is no program code that can implement such a specification, so they are of little use. The following property states the condition under which an effect relation (a predicate) is independent of the final values of the state variables if the command does not terminate.

Definition 6.2.2 (nontermination state independent) *Given a relation, Q, that is well-formed in an environment, ρ, Q is nontermination state independent provided*

$$\tau = \infty \Rightarrow (Q \Leftrightarrow (\exists \rho.v \bullet Q)) \quad \Box$$

A command, C, is nontermination state independent if its meaning predicate, $\mathcal{M}_\rho(C)$, is nontermination state independent. In the definition of the specification command the equality within eq between the initial and final values of state variables that are not in the frame does not apply if the command does not terminate. All the primitive real-time commands defined in Sec. 6.2.2 satisfy this property, and compound commands preserve it. Hence the only commands that may not satisfy it are specification commands, because the effect Q constrains the final values of the state variables at time infinity. We require all specifications to satisfy this healthiness property.

The law for weakening an assumption is similar to that for the standard refinement calculus.

Law 6.2.3 (weaken assumption) *Provided $P \Rightarrow P'$,*

$$\infty \vec{x} \colon [P, \ Q] \sqsubseteq \infty \vec{x} \colon [P', \ Q] \quad \Box$$

A common refinement step is to strengthen the effect of a specification command. In the real-time case one can take into account the following: time cannot go backwards; if the start time of the command is infinity (i.e., the finishing time of the previous command was infinity) it is never executed so its effect is irrelevant; the assumption holds for the initial state of the variables; any outputs not in the frame are stable; and any state variables not in the frame are unchanged.

Law 6.2.4 (strengthen effect) *Provided*

$$\tau_0 \leq \tau \land \tau_0 < \infty \land P\left[\tfrac{\rho.v_0, \tau_0}{\rho.v, \tau}\right] \land$$
$$eq(\rho.out \setminus \vec{x}, \tau_0, \tau, \rho.v_0 \setminus \vec{x}_0, \rho.v \setminus \vec{x}) \land Q'$$
$$\Rightarrow Q$$

then $\infty \vec{x} \colon [P, \ Q] \sqsubseteq \infty \vec{x} \colon [P, \ Q']. \quad \Box$

For a time interval I, and a predicate P, that contains unindexed occurrences of external inputs and outputs, the notation P **on** I stands for $(\forall t : I \bullet P @ t)$

where $P @ t$ stands for the predicate P with all occurrences of each external input or output, e, replaced by $e(t)$. For example, the notation

$$(gate = open) \text{ on } [\tau_0 \ldots near \uparrow 0]$$

stands for

$$(\forall t : [\tau_0 \ldots near \uparrow 0] \bullet gate(t) = open) \ .$$

The following is an example of strengthening the effect of a specification. The predicate *SENS* will be explained later.

$$gate : \begin{bmatrix} gate(\tau) = open \land \\ \tau \leq near \uparrow 0 \land \\ SENS \end{bmatrix}, \begin{bmatrix} (gate = open) \text{ on } [\tau_0 \ldots near \uparrow 0] \land \\ near \uparrow 0 \leq \tau \land SENS \end{bmatrix} \quad (2)$$

$\sqsubseteq$ Law 6.2.4 (strengthen effect); Law 6.2.3 (weaken assumption)

$$gate : \begin{bmatrix} \tau \leq near \uparrow 0 \land SENS, & stable(gate, [\tau_0 \ldots \tau]) \land \\ & near \uparrow 0 \leq \tau \end{bmatrix} \quad (3)$$

The strengthening of the effect is valid provided the following condition holds. The occurrences of the conjunct $\tau < \infty$ come from the fact that the specifications are terminating.

$$\tau_0 \leq \tau \land \tau_0 < \infty \land$$
$$gate(\tau_0) = open \land \tau_0 \leq near \uparrow 0 \land SENS\left[\frac{\tau_0}{\tau}\right] \land$$
$$stable(gate, [\tau_0 \ldots \tau]) \land near \uparrow 0 \leq \tau \land \tau < \infty$$
$$\Rightarrow (gate = open) \text{ on } [\tau_0 \ldots near \uparrow 0] \land near \uparrow 0 \leq \tau \land SENS \land \tau < \infty$$

Ignoring the occurrences of *SENS* (which is defined later) the remainder holds because the gate is initially open at time τ_0 and stable until time τ, which is after time $near \uparrow 0$.

A state variable can always be removed from the frame. This effectively strengthens the post-condition to ensure that the variable is unchanged.

Law 6.2.5 (contract frame) *For a state variable z, not in $\vec{x}$,*

$$\infty z, \vec{x} : [P, \ Q] \sqsubseteq \infty \vec{x} : [P, \ Q] \quad \square$$

If an output is to be stable for the whole of the execution time of a command, it can be removed from the frame.

Law 6.2.6 (output stable) *For an output o, not in $\vec{x}$,*

$$\infty o, \vec{x} : [P, \ Q \land stable(o, [\tau_0 \ldots \tau])] \sqsupseteq \infty \vec{x} : [P, \ Q] \quad \square$$

For example, the following holds the *gate* open by keeping it stable (i.e., not changing it) over the required interval.

$$gate : \begin{bmatrix} \tau \leq near \uparrow 0 \land SENS, & stable(gate, [\tau_0 \ldots \tau]) \land \\ & near \uparrow 0 \leq \tau \end{bmatrix} \quad (3)$$

$\sqsubseteq$ Law 6.2.6 (output stable) for *gate*

$$[\tau \leq near \uparrow 0 \land SENS, \ near \uparrow 0 \leq \tau] \quad (4)$$

Let $\vec{x}$ be a vector of variables, not including any inputs; $\vec{E}$ be a vector of idle-stable expressions of the same length as $\vec{x}$ and assignment compatible with $\vec{x}$; D be a time-valued expression; z be a local variable; i be an input that is assignment compatible with z; o be an output; and E be an idle-stable expression that is assignment compatible with o.

$$\mathbf{skip} \;\widehat{=}\; [\tau_0 = \tau] \tag{5}$$

$$\mathbf{idle} \;\widehat{=}\; [\tau_0 \leq \tau] \tag{6}$$

$$\vec{x} := \vec{E} \;\widehat{=}\; \vec{x}\colon \left[\vec{x} = (\vec{E}\,[\tfrac{\vec{x}_0}{\vec{x}}]) \,@\, \tau_0\right], \;\; \text{-- } \vec{x} \text{ only locals} \tag{7}$$

$$\vec{x} := \vec{E} \;\widehat{=}\; \vec{x}\colon \begin{bmatrix} \tau_0 = \tau \,\wedge \\ \vec{x} = (\vec{E}\,[\tfrac{\vec{x}_0}{\vec{x}}]) \,@\, \tau_0 \end{bmatrix}, \;\; \text{-- } \vec{x} \text{ only auxiliaries} \tag{8}$$

$$\mathbf{deadline}\, D \;\widehat{=}\; [\tau_0 = \tau \leq D \,@\, \tau] \tag{9}$$

$$z : \mathbf{read}(i) \;\widehat{=}\; z\colon [z \in i(\!(\tau_0 \ldots \tau)\!)] \tag{10}$$

$$o : \mathbf{write}(E) \;\widehat{=}\; o\colon [o(\tau) = E \,@\, \tau_0] \tag{11}$$

Figure 6.1. Definition of primitive real-time commands

All our commands insist that time does not go backwards.

Law 6.2.7 (time progresses) *For any command, C, that is well-formed in an environment, ρ, the following holds:* $\mathcal{M}_\rho(C) \Rightarrow \tau_0 \leq \tau$. □

6.2.2 Primitive real-time commands

The primitive real-time commands can be defined in terms of equivalent specification commands. In Fig. 6.1 we define: the null command, **skip**, that does nothing and takes no time; a command, **idle**, that does nothing but may take time; multiple assignment commands for both local and auxiliary variables; the deadline command; a command, **read**, to sample a value from an external input; and a command, **write**, to output a value to an external output, o.

We allow expressions used in programs, e.g. in assignments and guards, to refer to external variables without explicit time indices. When these expressions are used within predicates within the equivalent specification commands, all references to external variables need to be explicitly indexed. Hence we use the notation $E \,@\, t$ to refer to the expression E with all occurrences of any external variable e replaced by $e(t)$, and all occurrences of τ replaced by t.

Because an expression takes time to evaluate, we require that its value does not change over the interval during which it is being evaluated. We refer to such expressions as being *idle-stable*, that is, their value does not change over time provided all the variables under the control of the program are stable. In practice this means that such expressions cannot refer to τ or to the value of external inputs.

Definition 6.2.8 (idle-stable) *Given an environment ρ, an expression E is* idle-stable *provided,*

$$\tau_0 \leq \tau < \infty \land stable(\rho.out, [\tau_0 \ldots \tau]) \Rightarrow E@\tau_0 = E@\tau \quad \square$$

The deadline command guarantees to meet its deadline, even if the deadline time has already passed. If the deadline has already passed, the effect of the deadline command is false, which means that the command is miraculous and cannot possibly be implemented.

6.2.3 Sequential composition

Because we allow nonterminating commands, we need to be careful with our definition of sequential composition. If the first command of the sequential composition does not terminate, then we want the effect of the sequential composition on the values of the outputs over time to be the same as the effect of the first command. This is achieved by ensuring that for any command in our language, if it is 'executed' at $\tau_0 = \infty$, it has no effect.

Law 6.2.9 (nontermination preserved) *For any command, C, that is well-formed in an environment, ρ, the following holds:* $\tau_0 = \infty \Rightarrow (\mathcal{M}_\rho(C) \Leftrightarrow \tau = \infty)$. $\quad \square$

For the specification command this is achieved by the assumption $\tau_0 < \infty$ in Def. 6.2.1 (real-time specification).

The definition of sequential composition combines the effects of the two commands via a hidden intermediate state ($\rho.v'$ in the definition below). First we introduce a forward relational composition operator, '$\mathbin{\raise.5ex\hbox{$\scriptscriptstyle\circ$}}$'.

Definition 6.2.10 (relational composition) *Given an environment ρ and two relations R_1 and R_2 the (forward) relational composition of R_1 and R_2 is defined as follows,*

$$R_1 \mathbin{\raise.5ex\hbox{$\scriptscriptstyle\circ$}} R_2 \triangleq \exists \tau' : Time_\infty; \rho.v' : T_v \bullet R_1 \left[\frac{\tau', \rho.v'}{\tau, \rho.v} \right] \land R_2 \left[\frac{\tau', \rho.v'}{\tau_0, \rho.v_0} \right] .$$

where T_v is the type of $\rho.v'$. $\quad \square$

Definition 6.2.11 (sequential composition) *Given an environment ρ, and real-time commands C and D, their sequential composition is defined as the relational composition of their meaning predicates.*

$$\mathcal{M}_\rho(C; D) \triangleq \mathcal{M}_\rho(C) \mathbin{\raise.5ex\hbox{$\scriptscriptstyle\circ$}} \mathcal{M}_\rho(D) . \quad \square$$

Because both C and D guarantee $\tau_0 \leq \tau$, their sequential composition does also. Note that even if the assumption of the second command does not hold, the sequential composition still guarantees the effect of the first command for the external variables. It also guarantees that the finish time is greater than or equal to the finish time of the first command.

6. A predicative semantics for real-time refinement   119

The following law is a generalisation of the standard law for refining a specification to a sequential composition of specifications. For the termination case both commands must terminate. The first establishes the intermediate single-state predicate P_1 as well as the relation R_1 between the start and finish states of the first command. The second command assumes P_1 initially and establishes the single-state predicate P_2 as well as the relation R_2 between its initial and final states. Hence the sequential composition establishes P_2 as well as the relational composition of R_1 and R_2 between its initial and final states.

For the nontermination case either the first command does not terminate and establishes Q_1, or the first command terminates establishing P_1 and R_1 and the second command does not terminate and establishes Q_2. The overall effect is thus either Q_1 or the composition of R_1 and Q_2.

Law 6.2.12 (sequential composition) *Given single-state predicates P_0, P_1 and P_2, and relations R_1, R_2, Q_1 and Q_2,*

$$\infty \vec{x} \colon \big[P_0, \; (\tau < \infty \wedge P_2 \wedge (R_1 \mathbin{\raisebox{0.5pt}{\textit{\scriptsize 9}}} R_2)) \vee (\tau = \infty \wedge (Q_1 \vee (R_1 \mathbin{\raisebox{0.5pt}{\textit{\scriptsize 9}}} Q_2)))\big]$$
$$\sqsubseteq$$
$$\infty \vec{x} \colon \big[P_0, \; (\tau < \infty \wedge P_1 \wedge R_1) \vee (\tau = \infty \wedge Q_1)\big] \; ;$$
$$\infty \vec{x} \colon \big[P_1, \; (\tau < \infty \wedge P_2 \wedge R_2) \vee (\tau = \infty \wedge Q_2)\big] \qquad \square$$

Taking Q_1 and Q_2 as *false* reduces the law back to the standard law of Jones [15] for terminating commands:

$$\vec{x} \colon \big[P_0, \; P_2 \wedge (R_1 \mathbin{\raisebox{0.5pt}{\textit{\scriptsize 9}}} R_2)\big] \sqsubseteq \vec{x} \colon \big[P_0, \; P_1 \wedge R_1\big] \; ; \; \vec{x} \colon \big[P_1, \; P_2 \wedge R_2\big] \; .$$

For example, if we instantiate the above law with P_0 the predicate S, P_1 the predicate *true*, P_2 the predicate $\tau \leq near \uparrow 0 + err$, R_1 the relation $\tau_0 = \tau = before$, R_2 the relation $sens \in near(\![\tau_0 \dots near \uparrow 0 + err]\!)$, and Q_1 and Q_2 both *false*, then because $R_1 \mathbin{\raisebox{0.5pt}{\textit{\scriptsize 9}}} R_2$ is the following

$$(\exists \tau' : Time; \; sens' : boolean; \; before' : Time \bullet \tau_0 = \tau' = before \wedge$$
$$sens \in near(\![\tau' \dots near \uparrow 0 + err]\!))$$
$$\equiv \tau_0 = before \wedge sens \in near(\![\tau_0 \dots near \uparrow 0 + err]\!)$$

we can derive the following refinement.

$$sens, before \colon \left[S, \; \begin{array}{l} before = \tau_0 \wedge \tau \leq near \uparrow 0 + err \wedge \\ sens \in near(\![\tau_0 \dots near \uparrow 0 + err]\!) \end{array}\right] \qquad (12)$$

$\sqsubseteq$ Law 6.2.12 (sequential composition)

$$sens, before \colon \big[S, \; \tau_0 = \tau = before\big] \; ; \qquad (13)$$

$$sens, before \colon \left[true, \; \begin{array}{l} \tau \leq near \uparrow 0 + err \wedge \\ sens \in near(\![\tau_0 \dots near \uparrow 0 + err]\!) \end{array}\right] \qquad (14)$$

Specification (13) can be refined as follows.

(13) $\sqsubseteq$ Law 6.2.5 (contract frame) by *sens*; Law 6.2.3 (weaken assumption)

$$before \colon \big[before = \tau \wedge \tau = \tau_0\big]$$

□ Def. 8 (auxiliary assignment)

before := τ

A deadline command can be used to ensure that a command completes by a given time. The following law can be proved using Law 6.2.12 (sequential composition), with the deadline command given in its specification command equivalent (9).

Law 6.2.13 (separate deadline) *Provided D does not refer to initial variables,*

$$\vec{x}\colon [P,\ Q \wedge \tau \leq D] \sqsubseteq \vec{x}\colon [P,\ Q]\ ;\ \textbf{deadline}\, D \quad \square$$

For example, the specification (14) can be refined as follows.

(14) $\sqsubseteq$ Law 6.2.5 (contract frame) by *before*; Law 6.2.4 (strengthen effect)

$sens\colon \big[sens \in near(\![\tau_0\ ...\ \tau]\!)\, \wedge \tau \leq near \uparrow 0 + err\big]$

$\sqsubseteq$ Law 6.2.13 (separate deadline)

$sens\colon \big[sens \in near(\![\tau_0\ ...\ \tau]\!)\big]\ ;$ \hfill (15)

$\textbf{deadline}\ near \uparrow 0 + err$

The specification (15) is equivalent to *sens* : **read**(*near*).

Commonly a specification is refined to a sequence of more than two specifications. The following law follows by multiple application of Law 6.2.12 (sequential composition) for the terminating case. A more complex version for nonterminating commands can also be devised.

Law 6.2.14 (multiple sequential compositions) *Given single-state predicates* $P_0, P_1, \ldots, P_n$, *and relations* $R_1, R_2, \ldots, R_n$, *where* $n \geq 1$, *then*

$$\vec{x}\colon [P_0,\ P_n \wedge (R_1 \mathbin{\raisebox{0.5ex}{\scriptsize$\circ$}\hspace{-0.5ex}\raisebox{-0.3ex}{\scriptsize$\circ$}} R_2 \mathbin{\raisebox{0.5ex}{\scriptsize$\circ$}\hspace{-0.5ex}\raisebox{-0.3ex}{\scriptsize$\circ$}} \cdots \mathbin{\raisebox{0.5ex}{\scriptsize$\circ$}\hspace{-0.5ex}\raisebox{-0.3ex}{\scriptsize$\circ$}} R_n)]$$

$\sqsubseteq$

$\vec{x}\colon [P_0,\ P_1 \wedge R_1]\ ;$
$\vec{x}\colon [P_1,\ P_2 \wedge R_2]\ ;$
$\vdots$
$\vec{x}\colon [P_{n-1},\ P_n \wedge R_n] \quad \square$

6.2.4 Nondeterministic choice, guards and selection

The selection (**if**) command is defined in terms of sequential composition and (nondeterministic) choice. We first define choice ($[\!]$).

Definition 6.2.15 (choice) *Given an environment,* ρ, *and real-time commands, C and C'*, *the nondeterministic choice between C and C' is defined by the following.*

$$\mathcal{M}_\rho(C \mathbin{[\!]} C') \mathrel{\widehat{=}} \mathcal{M}_\rho(C) \vee \mathcal{M}_\rho(C') \quad \square$$

Nondeterministic choice is symmetric, associative and idempotent.

For a selection command we model evaluation of a guard B by $[B @ \tau]$, i.e., a specification command with an empty frame. The guard may take time to evaluate (note that τ is implicitly in the frame of any specification command, including guards). A guard is only feasible if the guard B evaluates to true when the command is reached. A selection assumes that one of its guards holds, and hence that one of the guards is feasible. The guard expressions are required to be idle-stable so that their values do not change while they are being evaluated. The final **idle** command allows for the time taken to exit the selection.

Definition 6.2.16 (selection) *Given a set of real-time commands, $C_1, \ldots, C_n$, and idle-stable, boolean-valued expressions, $B_1, \ldots, B_n$, a* selection *command is defined as follows.*

$$\text{if } B_1 \rightarrow C_1 \;[\!]\; \cdots \;[\!]\; B_n \rightarrow C_n \text{ fi} \;\widehat{=}\;$$
$$([BB,\; B_1 @ \tau]\,;\, C_1 \;[\!]\; \cdots \;[\!]\; [BB,\; B_n @ \tau]\,;\, C_n);\, \textbf{idle}$$

where $BB \;\widehat{=}\; B_1 @ \tau \vee \cdots \vee B_n @ \tau$. □

The definition of a selection puts no bounds on the time to evaluate the guards or the time to exit the selection. It is expected that deadline commands, either within branches of the selection or following the selection, will indirectly introduce time bounds on these activities. Evaluation of the guards of a selection command takes time. Hence if some assumption P holds before guard evaluation, P may no longer hold after guard evaluation. Even though none of the variables under the control of the program are modified during guard evaluation, P may refer to the current time τ or to external inputs, both of which may change during the time taken for guard evaluation. To avoid this problem we restrict our attention to assumptions that are invariant over the execution of an **idle** command. Such assumptions are referred to as being *idle-invariant*.

Definition 6.2.17 (idle-invariant) *A single-state predicate P is* idle-invariant *provided,*

$$\tau_0 \leq \tau < \infty \wedge stable(\rho.out, [\tau_0 \ldots \tau]) \wedge P\!\left[\tfrac{\tau_0}{\tau}\right] \Rightarrow P. \quad \Box$$

Note that predicates of the form $\tau \leq D$ (where D is idle-stable) are not idle-invariant, but predicates of the form $D \leq \tau$ are. If the only references to τ in P are as indices of outputs, then P is idle-invariant.

Similarly, the effect of a specification command being refined to a selection is required to be impervious to the time taken to evaluate the guards and to exit the selection. We refer to it as being both *pre-idle-invariant* and *post-idle-invariant*. A relation R is pre-idle-invariant if prefixing it with an idle period has no effect. That is, whenever it holds over an interval from τ_0 to τ, then for any u less than or equal to τ_0 it holds over the interval from u to τ, provided the variables under the control of the program are not modified over the interval from u to τ_0.

Definition 6.2.18 (pre-idle-invariant) A relation R is pre-idle-invariant provided,

$$\tau_0 < \infty \wedge u \leq \tau_0 \leq \tau \wedge stable(\rho.out, [u \ldots \tau_0]) \wedge R \Rightarrow R\left[\tfrac{u}{\tau_0}\right] \quad \square$$

The interval from u to τ_0 corresponds to the idle period before executing the command with effect R.

A predicate R is post-idle-invariant if adding a postfix idle period has no effect. That is, for any u greater than or equal to τ, whenever R holds over an interval from τ_0 to τ, it also holds over the interval from τ_0 to u, provided the variables under the control of the program are not modified between τ and u.

Definition 6.2.19 (post-idle-invariant) A relation R is post-idle-invariant provided,

$$\tau_0 \leq \tau \leq u < \infty \wedge stable(\rho.out, [\tau \ldots u]) \wedge R \Rightarrow R\left[\tfrac{u}{\tau}\right] \quad \square$$

The interval from τ to u corresponds to the idle period after executing the command with effect R. Note that we rule out τ and u being infinity; if τ is infinity the command does not terminate and nothing can follow it. If the only references to τ_0 and τ in R are as indices of outputs, then R is both pre- and post-idle-invariant.

Law 6.2.20 (selection) Given an idle-invariant, single-state predicate P, a pre- and post-idle-invariant relation R, and idle-stable boolean-valued expressions $B_1, \ldots, B_n$, provided $P \Rightarrow (B_1 \@ \tau \vee \cdots \vee B_n \@ \tau)$,

$$\infty \vec{x} \colon [P, R]$$
$$\sqsubseteq \text{if } B_1 \to \infty \vec{x} \colon [P \wedge B_1 \@ \tau, R] \, [\!] \ldots [\!] \, B_n \to \infty \vec{x} \colon [P \wedge B_n \@ \tau, R] \text{ fi}$$

$\square$

For example,

$$gate \colon \left[true, \begin{array}{l}(gate(\tau_0) = close \Rightarrow (gate = close) \text{ on } [\tau_0 \ldots \tau]) \wedge \\ gate(\tau) = close\end{array}\right]$$

$\sqsubseteq$ **if** $gate = close \to$

$$gate \colon \left[gate(\tau) = close, \begin{array}{c}(gate(\tau_0) = close \Rightarrow \\ (gate = close) \text{ on } [\tau_0 \ldots \tau]) \wedge \\ gate(\tau) = close\end{array}\right] \quad (16)$$

$[\!]$ $gate = open \to$

$$gate \colon \left[gate(\tau) = open, \begin{array}{c}(gate(\tau_0) = close \Rightarrow \\ (gate = close) \text{ on } [\tau_0 \ldots \tau]) \wedge \\ gate(\tau) = close\end{array}\right] \quad (17)$$

fi

The first branch (16) can be refined via Law 6.2.6 (output stable) to **skip**, and the second branch (17) to $gate : \textbf{write}(close)$.

6.2.5 Local and auxiliary variables

A variable block introduces a new local or auxiliary variable. The allocation and deallocation of a local variable may take time. This is allowed for in the definition by the use of **idle** commands. Auxiliary variables require no allocation or deallocation time. In the definition of a local or auxiliary variable block we need to allow for the fact that a variable of the same name may be declared at an outer scope, i.e. that it is already in ρ. Hence we introduce a fresh variable name, not in ρ, that we use in the definition via appropriate renamings. If the variable name is itself fresh, it may be used instead and the renaming avoided.

Definition 6.2.21 (block) *Given an environment, ρ, a command, C, a nonempty type T, and a fresh variable, w, not in ρ,*

$$\mathcal{M}_\rho(\|[\,\mathbf{var}\,y:T;\,C\,]\|) \triangleq (\exists w_0, w:T \bullet \mathcal{M}_{\rho'}\left(\mathbf{idle};\,C\left[\tfrac{w_0,w}{y_0,y}\right];\,\mathbf{idle}\right))$$

where ρ' is ρ updated with the local variable w, and

$$\mathcal{M}_\rho(\|[\,\mathbf{aux}\,y:T;\,C\,]\|) \triangleq (\exists w_0, w:T \bullet \mathcal{M}_{\rho''}\left(C\left[\tfrac{w_0,w}{y_0,y}\right]\right))$$

where ρ'' is ρ updated with the auxiliary variable w. □

For the law to refine a specification to a local variable block, we require that the assumption of a specification be impervious to the time taken to allocate the local variable, and the effect be impervious to both the time taken to allocate and deallocate the local variable.

Law 6.2.22 (local variable) *Provided P is an idle-invariant, single-state predicate, R is a pre- and post-idle-invariant relation, T is a nonempty type, and y does not occur free in $\vec{x}$, P and R,*

$$\vec{x}:[P,\,R] \sqsubseteq \|[\,\mathbf{var}\,y:T;\,y,\vec{x}:[P,\,R]\,]\| \quad \square$$

Because no time is required to allocate and deallocate auxiliary variables, the law for them is the same as above but without all the idle-invariant requirements. We abbreviate multiple declarations with distinct names by merging them into a single block, e.g., $\|[\,\mathbf{var}\,y;\,\mathbf{aux}\,x;\,C\,]\| = \|[\,\mathbf{var}\,y;\,\|[\,\mathbf{aux}\,x;\,C\,]\|\,]\|$. For example,

$$\infty\,[S,\ near \uparrow 0 \leq \tau < \infty \vee near \uparrow 0 = \tau = \infty] \quad (18)$$
$\sqsubseteq$ Law 6.2.22 (local variable)
$\|[\,\mathbf{var}\,sens:boolean;\,\mathbf{aux}\,before:Time;$

$$\infty\,sens, before:[S,\ near \uparrow 0 \leq \tau < \infty \vee near \uparrow 0 = \tau = \infty] \quad (19)$$

$]\|$

provided the assumption, S, is idle-invariant (see below), and the effect is pre-idle-invariant, that is, provided $\tau_0 < \infty$ and $u \leq \tau_0 \leq \tau$ the following holds,

$$stable(gate,\,[u\,...\,\tau_0\,]) \wedge (near \uparrow 0 \leq \tau < \infty \vee near \uparrow 0 = \tau = \infty)$$
$$\Rightarrow near \uparrow 0 \leq \tau < \infty \vee near \uparrow 0 = \tau = \infty$$

and post-idle-invariant, that is, provided $\tau_0 \leq \tau \leq u < \infty$ the following holds,

$$stable(gate, [\tau \ldots u]) \land (near \uparrow 0 \leq \tau < \infty \lor near \uparrow 0 = \tau = \infty)$$
$$\Rightarrow near \uparrow 0 \leq u < \infty \lor near \uparrow 0 = u = \infty$$

which holds because $\tau \leq u < \infty$.

6.3 An example

The example we consider is that of a railway crossing. There are sensors that detect when a train arrives *near* to the crossing and when it has passed *out* of the region of the crossing.

input *near, out* : *boolean*;

The gate at the crossing is controlled by an output *gate*, which has values either *open* or *close*.

output *gate* : {*open, close*}

We use the notation *near* $\uparrow$ 0 to refer to the time at which the train reaches the *near* sensor and it rises (from *false* to *true*) for the first time, and *out* $\uparrow$ 0 for the time it reaches the *out* sensor. The sensors remain true for a minimum period when a train passes. The *near* sensor is placed so that there is a period of at least 300 seconds between a train arriving at the sensor and its arriving at the crossing. From the time the *gate* is set to *close* it takes at most 100 seconds for the gate to actually reach the closed position, and a similar time for it to rise. The gate should start reopening within 5 seconds of the train passing the *out* sensor.

const $err = 1\,\mathsf{s}$; -- minimum time the sensors are true
const $train\_to\_crossing = 300\,\mathsf{s}$;
const $time\_to\_close\_gate = 100\,\mathsf{s}$;
const $out\_lim = 5\,\mathsf{s}$;

The *out* sensor is placed to ensure that the train has left the crossing before it reaches the *out* sensor. The controller may assume the following holds initially.

$$SENS \triangleq \begin{array}{l} (near = false) \text{ on } (\tau \ldots near \uparrow 0) \land \\ (near = true) \text{ on } (near \uparrow 0 \ldots near \uparrow 0 + err) \land \\ (out = false) \text{ on } (\tau \ldots out \uparrow 0) \land \\ (out = true) \text{ on } (out \uparrow 0 \ldots out \uparrow 0 + err) \land \\ near \uparrow 0 + train\_to\_crossing < out \uparrow 0 \end{array} \quad (20)$$

Because the above predicate is idle-invariant and no variables appearing within it are in the frame, it may be assumed throughout the development. Note that $(\tau \ldots near \uparrow 0)$ may be empty, but the predicate is still idle-invariant.

The specification of the gate controller is as follows, in which the constant 200 s is derived from *train_to_crossing* minus *time_to_close_gate*. The final conjunct in the effect, $gate(\tau) = open$, is required because the interval in the second last conjunct may be empty.

$$gate: \begin{bmatrix} gate(\tau) = open \\ \wedge\, \tau \leq near \uparrow 0, \\ \wedge\, SENS \end{bmatrix} \begin{matrix} (gate = open)\ \text{on}\ \dashv\tau_0 \ldots near \uparrow 0\vdash \wedge \\ (gate = close)\ \text{on} \\ \dashv near \uparrow 0 + 200\,\text{s} \ldots out \uparrow 0\vdash \wedge \\ (gate = open)\ \text{on}\ \dashv out \uparrow 0 + out\_lim \ldots \tau \vdash \wedge \\ gate(\tau) = open \end{matrix} \end{bmatrix}$$

$\sqsubseteq$ Law 6.2.14 (multiple sequential compositions)

$$gate: \begin{bmatrix} gate(\tau) = open \\ \wedge\, \tau \leq near \uparrow 0, \\ \wedge\, SENS \end{bmatrix} \begin{matrix} (gate = open)\ \text{on}\ \dashv\tau_0 \ldots near \uparrow 0\vdash \\ \wedge\, near \uparrow 0 \leq \tau \wedge SENS \end{matrix} \end{bmatrix};\quad (2)$$

$$gate: \begin{bmatrix} near \uparrow 0 \leq \tau \\ \wedge\, SENS \end{bmatrix}, \begin{matrix} (gate = close)\ \text{on} \\ \dashv near \uparrow 0 + 200\,\text{s} \ldots out \uparrow 0\vdash \\ \wedge\, out \uparrow 0 \leq \tau \wedge SENS \end{matrix} \end{bmatrix};\quad (21)$$

$$gate: \begin{bmatrix} out \uparrow 0 \leq \tau \\ \wedge\, SENS \end{bmatrix}, \begin{matrix} (gate = open)\ \text{on}\ \dashv out \uparrow 0 + out\_lim \ldots \tau \vdash \\ \wedge\, gate(\tau) = open \end{matrix} \end{bmatrix} \quad (22)$$

The specification (2) is refined earlier. Specification (21) is refined as follows.

(21) $\sqsubseteq$ Law 6.2.12 (sequential composition)

$$gate: \begin{bmatrix} near \uparrow 0 \leq \tau \\ \wedge\, SENS \end{bmatrix}, \begin{matrix} gate(\tau) = close \wedge \tau \leq near \uparrow 0 + 200\,\text{s} \\ \wedge\, SENS \end{matrix} \end{bmatrix};\quad (23)$$

$$gate: \begin{bmatrix} gate(\tau) = close\ \wedge \\ \tau \leq near \uparrow 0 + 200\,\text{s}, \\ \wedge\, SENS \end{bmatrix} \begin{matrix} (gate = close)\ \text{on} \\ \dashv near \uparrow 0 + 200\,\text{s} \ldots out \uparrow 0\vdash \\ \wedge\, out \uparrow 0 \leq \tau \wedge SENS \end{matrix} \end{bmatrix} \quad (24)$$

The specification (23) may be refined by setting $gate$ to $close$ by the deadline.

(23) $\sqsubseteq$ Law 6.2.13 (separate deadline); Law 6.2.4 (strengthen effect)

$gate: [near \uparrow 0 \leq \tau \wedge SENS,\ gate(\tau) = close]$; (25)

deadline $near \uparrow 0 + 200\,\text{s}$

Specification (25) can be implemented by $gate : \textbf{write}(close)$. Specification (24) can be refined in a manner similar to (2) to give the following specification.

$$[SENS,\ out \uparrow 0 \leq \tau] \quad (26)$$

Specification (22) can be refined to the following (similar to (23)).

$gate : \textbf{write}(open);\ \textbf{deadline}\ out \uparrow 0 + out\_lim$

The program so far is shown in Fig. 6.2. The initial assumption, $\tau \leq near \uparrow 0$, has been factored out of the specification (4). The remaining unrefined components, B and D, require a repetition for their implementation.

$A :: \{\tau \leq near \uparrow 0\}$;
$B :: [SENS, \ near \uparrow 0 \leq \tau]$;
  $gate : \mathbf{write}(close)$;
$C :: \mathbf{deadline} \ near \uparrow 0 + 200\,\mathrm{s}$;
$D :: [SENS, \ out \uparrow 0 \leq \tau]$;
  $gate : \mathbf{write}(open)$;
$E :: \mathbf{deadline} \ out \uparrow 0 + out\_lim$

Figure 6.2. Collected program without repetitions

6.4 Repetitions

The specification $[SENS, \ near \uparrow 0 \leq \tau]$ can be implemented by repeatedly testing the near sensor until it becomes true. The specification $[SENS, \ out \uparrow 0 \leq \tau]$ can be implemented in a similar manner. Hence we only consider the former here. To provide an example of refinement to a possibly nonterminating repetition, we generalise the specification to

$$\infty \ [S, \ near \uparrow 0 \leq \tau < \infty \ \lor \ near \uparrow 0 = \tau = \infty] \tag{18}$$

although in this particular example we know $near \uparrow 0 < \infty$. From the assumption $SENS$ we may assume the near sensor is false until time $near \uparrow 0$ and then true for a minimum period of err. We need to sample the sensor frequently enough to ensure its high transition is not missed.

$$S \triangleq \begin{array}{l}(near = false) \ \mathbf{on} \ \{\tau \ldots near \uparrow 0\} \ \land \\ (near = true) \ \mathbf{on} \ \{near \uparrow 0 \ldots near \uparrow 0 + err\}\end{array} \tag{27}$$

The predicate (27) is idle-invariant because

$\tau_0 \leq \tau < \infty \land stable(out, [\tau_0 \ldots \tau]) \land$
$(near = false) \ \mathbf{on} \ \{\tau_0 \ldots near \uparrow 0\} \land$
$(near = true) \ \mathbf{on} \ \{near \uparrow 0 \ldots near \uparrow 0 + err\}$
$\Rightarrow (near = false) \ \mathbf{on} \ \{\tau \ldots near \uparrow 0\} \land$
$(near = true) \ \mathbf{on} \ \{near \uparrow 0 \ldots near \uparrow 0 + err\}$

We introduce a local variable $sens$, which is used for sampling the sensor, and an auxiliary variable $before$, which is used to record the time immediately before the sensor is sampled. Specification (18) has been refined in Sect. 6.2.5 to such a block with body (19).

$$\infty \, sens, before : [S, \ near \uparrow 0 \leq \tau < \infty \ \lor \ near \uparrow 0 = \tau = \infty] \tag{19}$$

Specification (19) can be refined by a repetition. We do not attempt to give a complete definition of repetitions; more complete details can be found elsewhere

[7, 8]. A repetition,

$$R \mathrel{\widehat{=}} \textbf{repeat}\ C\ \textbf{until}\ B,$$

can (as a first approximation) be characterised by the following recurrence.

$$R = \textbf{idle};\ C;\ \bigl(\bigl[B\ @\ \tau\bigr] \mathbin{[\!]} \bigl(\bigl[\neg B\ @\ \tau\bigr];\ R\bigr)\bigr)$$

Before the body of the repetition is executed there is an **idle** to allow for any overheads at the start of an iteration. After executing the body C, there is a (deterministic) choice between two guarded alternatives. The guard evaluation typically takes time (unless the guard is a constant, *true* or *false*). The first alternative corresponds to the guard evaluating to true and termination of the repetition. The second alternative corresponds to the guard evaluating to false and the iteration being repeated from the beginning.

Unfortunately, the above recurrence allows a single iteration of a repetition (for example of '**repeat skip until** *false*') to take zero time, or each successive iteration to take half the time of the previous (as in Zeno's paradox). To avoid this unrealistic behaviour, we define every iteration to take a minimum amount of time, d, which is strictly positive (1 attosecond will do). Hence a repetition is characterised by: there exists a strictly positive time, d, such that

$$\begin{aligned}R = \|[\ \textbf{aux}\ s;\ s := \tau;\ \textbf{idle};\ C;\\ \bigl(\bigl[B\ @\ \tau\bigr] \mathbin{[\!]} \bigl(\bigl[\neg B\ @\ \tau\bigr];\ \bigl[s + d \leq \tau\bigr];\ R\bigr)\bigr)\\ ]\|\end{aligned}$$

where s is a fresh auxiliary variable, which captures the start time of an iteration. Before the repetition is restarted from the beginning there is a delay $[s + d \leq \tau]$ to ensure the time is at least d time units later than the start time of the iteration, s. This ensures that even if the guard is the constant *false* and the body is the null command **skip**, each iteration takes at least d time units and hence Zeno-like behaviour is avoided.

We give a rule for introducing a repetition with a body that terminates on every iteration. The predicate Q' acts as an invariant that is established at the end of the body on every iteration. Q' is not required to be idle-invariant. Hence we introduce a weaker predicate Q that is idle-invariant. Only Q can be assumed after the guard evaluation. If the repetition terminates both B and Q hold. If the guard evaluates to false, then at the start of the next iteration one can assume both $\neg B$ and Q. The body is executed initially when P is known to hold, or on a repetition when the guard is false, in which case $\neg B$ and Q hold. The body of the repetition establishes Q'.

The stronger (non-idle-invariant) predicate Q' is used in the case when the repetition does not terminate. If the repetition never terminates but the body always terminates then there is an infinite sequence of ever increasing times, corresponding to the times at which the end of the body is reached, at which both Q' and $\neg B$ hold for the current time and the current values of the state variables. This is captured by the predicate Q_∞ in the following law:

Law 6.4.1 (repetition) *Given idle-invariant, single-state predicates P and Q, a single-state predicate Q' such that Q' ⇒ Q, and an idle-stable, boolean-valued expression B,*

$$\infty \, \vec{x} \colon [P, \; (B @ \tau \land Q \land \tau < \infty) \lor (Q_\infty \land \tau = \infty)]$$
$$\sqsubseteq \textbf{repeat}\, \vec{x} \colon [P \lor (\neg B @ \tau \land Q), \; Q'] \, \textbf{until}\, B$$

where $Q_\infty \,\widehat{=}\, (\forall t : \textit{Time} \bullet (\exists \tau : \textit{Time}; \, \rho.v : T_v \bullet t \leq \tau \land \neg B @ \tau \land Q'))$. □

Note that the existential quantification in Q_∞ ensures that Q_∞ satifies Def. 6.2.2 (nontermination state independent).

For the train crossing example, a repetition can be used to test for the train passing the near sensor. We have weakened the assumption of the body (28) to S.

(19) ⊑ Law 6.4.1 (repetition); Law 6.2.3 (weaken assumption)

$$\textbf{repeat}$$

$$\textit{sens}, \atop \textit{before:} \left[S, \; \begin{array}{l} (\textit{sens} \Rightarrow \textit{near} \uparrow 0 \leq \tau) \land \\ (\neg \textit{sens} \Rightarrow \textit{before} \leq \textit{near} \uparrow 0) \land \\ \tau \leq \textit{near} \uparrow 0 + \textit{err} \land S \end{array} \right] \quad (28)$$

until *sens*

The effect of the body corresponds to the loop invariant Q' of Law 6.4.1 (repetition). The conjunct $\tau \leq \textit{near} \uparrow 0 + \textit{err}$ is not idle-invariant, but the remaining conjuncts ($\textit{sens} \Rightarrow \textit{near} \uparrow 0 \leq \tau$), ($\neg \textit{sens} \Rightarrow \textit{before} \leq \textit{near} \uparrow 0$) and S are idle-invariant. Hence these form the weaker condition Q in the law. If the repetition terminates both Q and the termination guard (*sens*) hold. Together these imply $\textit{near} \uparrow 0 \leq \tau$, which along with termination ($\tau < \infty$), implies the effect of (19).

For nontermination, for any time t there exists a later time τ and corresponding values of the state variables, such that the invariant Q' and the negation of the termination guard ($\neg \textit{sens}$) hold. This implies the following.

$$(\forall t : \textit{Time} \bullet (\exists \tau : \textit{Time}; \, \textit{sens} : \textit{boolean}; \, \textit{before} : \textit{Time} \bullet$$
$$ t \leq \tau \land \neg \textit{sens} \land \textit{before} \leq \textit{near} \uparrow 0 \land \tau \leq \textit{near} \uparrow 0 + \textit{err}))$$
$$\Rightarrow (\forall t : \textit{Time} \bullet t \leq \textit{near} \uparrow 0 + \textit{err})$$
$$\Rightarrow \textit{near} \uparrow 0 = \infty$$

Along with $\tau = \infty$, this implies the effect of (19).

The refinement of the body (28) of the repetition depends on the assumption about the sensor behaviour (27). The sensor is sampled between the start time of the body of the repetition, which is captured in the time-valued auxiliary variable *before*, and time $\textit{near} \uparrow 0 + \textit{err}$. If the sampled value is false, the body must have begun execution before time $\textit{near} \uparrow 0$, and if it is true, the finish time of the body must be after $\textit{near} \uparrow 0$. Together these guarantee the effect of (28).

(28) ⊑ Law 6.2.4 (strengthen effect)

$$\textit{sens}, \textit{before:} \left[S, \; \begin{array}{l} \textit{before} = \tau_0 \land \tau \leq \textit{near} \uparrow 0 + \textit{err} \land \\ \textit{sens} \in \textit{near}(\![\bar{\epsilon}\tau_0 \ldots \textit{near} \uparrow 0 + \textit{err}\,\bar{]}\!]) \end{array} \right] \quad (12)$$

$\|[$ **var** *sens* : *boolean*; **aux** *before* : *Time*;
    repeat
        $F ::$ *before* $:= \tau$;
        sens : **read**(*near*);
        $G ::$ **deadline** *near* $\uparrow 0 + err$;
$$\left\{\begin{array}{l}(\textit{sens} \Rightarrow \textit{near} \uparrow 0 \leq \tau) \wedge \\ (\neg\, \textit{sens} \Rightarrow \textit{before} \leq \textit{near} \uparrow 0) \wedge \\ \tau \leq \textit{near} \uparrow 0 + \textit{err} \wedge S\end{array}\right\}$$
    until *sens*
$]|$

Figure 6.3. Sensor detection repetition

$A :: \{\tau \leq \textit{near} \uparrow 0\}$;
    alloc var *sens* : *boolean*; **aux** *before* : *Time*;
$F ::$ *before* $:= \tau$;
    sens : **read**(*near*);
$G ::$ **deadline** *near* $\uparrow 0 + err$

Figure 6.4. Initial path entering sensor detection repetition

---

This specification is equivalent to (12), which has been refined earlier.

The complete repetition is given in Fig. 6.3. The deadline command in the repetition ensures that the high transition of the sensor is not missed.

6.5 Timing-constraint analysis

In order for compiled machine code to implement a machine-independent program it must guarantee to meet all the deadlines. The auxiliary variables introduced above aid this analysis. There is a deadline within the sensor detection repetition (Fig. 6.3) labelled G. It is reached initially from the entry to the repetition and subsequently on each iteration. The initial entry path (shown in Fig. 6.4) starts at the assumption A in Fig. 6.2 before entering the sensor detection repetition (which refines $[SENS,\ near \uparrow 0 \leq \tau]$) in Fig. 6.3. The path allocates the local variable *sens*, extends the auxiliary variables with *before*, and follows the path into the repetition, assigning τ to *before* and reading *near* into *sens*, before reaching the deadline G. From the assumption at A, we know that the start time of the path is before $near \uparrow 0$ and the deadline on the path is $near \uparrow 0 + err$. If

$F :: before := \tau;$
  $sens : \textbf{read}(near);$
$G :: \textbf{deadline } near \uparrow 0 + err;$
$\left\{ \begin{array}{l} (sens \Rightarrow near \uparrow 0 \leq \tau) \wedge \\ (\neg sens \Rightarrow before \leq near \uparrow 0) \wedge \\ \tau \leq near \uparrow 0 + err \wedge S \end{array} \right\};$
$[\neg sens];$ -- repetition exit condition false
$F :: before := \tau;$
  $sens : \textbf{read}(near);$
$G :: \textbf{deadline } near \uparrow 0 + err$

Figure 6.5. Repetition path in sensor detection repetition

this path is guaranteed to execute in a time of less than *err* then the deadline is guaranteed to be met. Hence the timing constraint on the path is *err*.

For an iteration we consider the path (shown in Fig. 6.5) that starts at the assignment to *before* (*F*), reads the value of *near* into *sens*, passes through the deadline (*G*), branches back to the start of the repetition because *sens* is not true, performs the assignment to *before* (*F*), reads the value of *near*, and reaches the deadline (*G*). The guard evaluation is represented by $[\neg sens]$, which indicates that in order for the path to be followed, *sens* must be false. Using the loop invariant we can determine that the initial time assigned to *before*, i.e. the time at which the path begins execution, must be before $near \uparrow 0$ because the value of *sens* is false. The final deadline on the path is $near \uparrow 0 + err$. Hence, if the path is guaranteed to execute in less than time *err*, it will always meet its deadline.

If this path is guaranteed to reach its deadline then any path with this as a suffix is also guaranteed to meet the final deadline, and hence any number of repeated iterations will meet the deadline. The constraint on this path corresponds to a maximum time of *err* between successive reads of the sensor. Although the repetition is written as a busy wait, in a multi-tasking environment the repetition could be implemented by scheduling the body to execute so that the deadline is always met. For example, a common scheduling strategy is periodic scheduling in which a task is scheduled with a period of *P* seconds and has to complete within *D* seconds of the start of the period. In this case as long as $P + D$ is less than or equal to *err*, the requirements for meeting the deadline will be met.

The path shown in Fig. 6.6 starts from the deadline *G* within the body of the repetition, exits the repetition (because *sens* is true), deallocates *sens* and *before*, and sets the *gate* to *close*, before reaching the deadline at *C*. The initial deadline guarantees the start time of the path is less than or equal to $near \uparrow 0 + err$. The deadline on the path is $near \uparrow 0 + 200\,\text{s}$. Therefore a suitable constraint on the path is $near \uparrow 0 + 200\,\text{s} - (near \uparrow 0 + err) = 200\,\text{s} - err$.

G :: **deadline** *near* ↑ $0 + err$;
   [*sens*]; -- exit repetition
   dealloc var *sens* : *boolean*; **aux** *before* : *Time*;
   gate : **write**(*close*);
C :: **deadline** *near* ↑ $0 + 200$ s

Figure 6.6. Exit path from sensor detection repetition

We have considered all the paths concerned with the repetition testing the near sensor. The remainder of the program which handles the sensor for the train leaving the crossing is treated in a similar manner.

In general, timing constraint analysis is undecidable because it encompasses the halting problem for a path containing a complete repetition without any internal deadlines. However, for restricted forms of programs automating timing constraint analysis is possible [4].

6.6 Conclusions

The real-time refinement calculus presented in this paper supports the development of *machine-independent* real-time programs. This has the advantage of decoupling the program development process from the timing analysis required for a particular machine. Timing constraints within the program are represented by deadline commands.

In this paper we have developed a predicative semantics for the calculus, in a style similar to that used by Hehner, and Hoare and He. A novel feature is that external inputs and outputs are represented by timed traces, and hence the values of such variables over time, and not just their initial and final values are significant. In addition, programs may be nonterminating. Commands in the language satisfy a number of healthiness properties: time cannot go backwards; the semantics of a nonterminating command is independent of the final values of the state variables; and all commands have no effect if 'executed' at time infinity.

In the laws for reasoning about compound commands we desired that reasoning about the behaviour of commands is independent of the time taken to execute components of the commands, such as guard evaluation. This is achieved by requiring predicates to be idle invariant. As to be expected the most interesting constructs to handle are sequential composition and repetitions. For a sequential composition, in order to model the reactive nature of real-time programs, we desired that the behaviour of the sequential composition over time be composed from the behaviour of the individual commands. Care needs to be taken with the case in which the first command in the composition does not terminate, and the behaviour of the sequential composition is the same as that of the first command.

For a nonterminating repetition, the values of the outputs are extended on each iteration. The law for reasoning about such repetitions relies on the loop invariant being repeatedly re-established at an infinite sequence of ever increasing times.

Acknowledgements

This research was supported by Australian Research Council (ARC) Large Grant A49801500, *A Unified Formalism for Concurrent Real-time Software Development*. I would like to thank Yifeng Chen, Colin Fidge, Karl Lermer, and Mark Utting for fruitful discussions on the topic of this paper, and the members of IFIP Working Group 2.3 on Programming Methodology for feedback on this topic, especially Eric Hehner for his advice on how to simplify our approach, and Cliff Jones for his insights into the relational approach. I would like to acknowledge the support of the University of Queensland Special Studies Program and thank the Department of Computer Science at the University of York (UK) for their hospitality.

References

[1] J.-R. Abrial. *The B-Book: Assigning Programs to Meanings*. Cambridge University Press, 1996.

[2] R.-J. Back and J. von Wright. *Refinement Calculus: A Systematic Introduction*. Springer-Verlag, 1998.

[3] C. J. Fidge, I. J. Hayes, and G. Watson. The deadline command. *IEE Proceedings—Software*, 146(2):104–111, April 1999.

[4] S. Grundon, I. J. Hayes, and C. J. Fidge. Timing constraint analysis. In C. McDonald, editor, *Computer Science '98: Proc. 21st Australasian Computer Sci. Conf. (ACSC'98)*, Perth, 4–6 Feb., 575–586. Springer-Verlag, 1998.

[5] I. J. Hayes. Separating timing and calculation in real-time refinement. In J. Grundy, M. Schwenke, and T. Vickers, editors, *Int. Refinement Workshop and Formal Methods Pacific 1998*, 1–16. Springer-Verlag, 1998.

[6] I. J. Hayes. Real-time program refinement using auxiliary variables. In M. Joseph, editor, *Proc. Formal Techniques in Real-Time and Fault-Tolerant Systems*, volume 1926 of *Lecture Notes in Comp. Sci.*, 170–184. Springer-Verlag, 2000.

[7] I. J. Hayes. Reasoning about non-terminating loops using deadline commands. In R. Backhouse and J. N. Oliveira, editors, *Proc. Mathematics of Program Construction*, volume 1837 of *Lecture Notes in Computer Science*, 60–79. Springer-Verlag, 2000.

[8] I. J. Hayes. Reasoning about real-time repetitions: Terminating and nonterminating. Technical Report 01-04, Software Verification Research Centre, The University of Queensland, Brisbane 4072, Australia, February 2001.

[9] I. J. Hayes and M. Utting. Coercing real-time refinement: A transmitter. In D. J. Duke and A. S. Evans, editors, *BCS-FACS Northern Formal Methods Workshop (NFMW'96)*. Springer-Verlag, 1997.

[10] I. J. Hayes and M. Utting. A sequential real-time refinement calculus. *Acta Informatica*, 37(6):385–448, 2001.

[11] E. C. R. Hehner. *A Practical Theory of Programming*. Springer-Verlag, 1993.

[12] C. A. R. Hoare and He Jifeng. *Unifying Theories of Programming*. Prentice Hall, 1998.

[13] J. Hooman. Extending Hoare logic to real-time. *Formal Aspects of Computing*, 6(6A):801–825, 1994.

[14] J. Hooman and O. van Roosmalen. Formal design of real-time systems in a platform-independent way. *Parallel and Distributed Computing Practices*, 1(2):15–30, 1998.

[15] C. B. Jones. Program specification and verification in VDM. Technical Report UMCS-86-10-5, Department of Computer Science, University of Manchester, 1986.

[16] B. P. Mahony. *The Specification and Refinement of Timed Processes*. PhD thesis, Department of Computer Science, University of Queensland, 1992.

[17] B. P. Mahony and I. J. Hayes. Using continuous real functions to model timed histories. In P. A. Bailes, editor, *Proc. 6th Australian Software Engineering Conf. (ASWEC91)*, 257–270. Australian Comp. Soc., 1991.

[18] B. P. Mahony and I. J. Hayes. A case-study in timed refinement: A mine pump. *IEEE Trans. on Software Engineering*, 18(9):817–826, 1992.

[19] C. C. Morgan. *Programming from Specifications*, Second edition. Prentice Hall, 1994.

[20] J. M. Morris. A theoretical basis for stepwise refinement and the programming calculus. *Science of Computer Programming*, 9(3):287–306, 1987.

[21] A. C. Shaw. Reasoning about time in higher-level language software. *IEEE Transactions on Software Engineering*, 15(7):875–889, July 1989.

[22] M. Utting and C. J. Fidge. A real-time refinement calculus that changes only time. In He Jifeng, editor, *Proc. 7th BCS/FACS Refinement Workshop*, Electronic Workshops in Computing. Springer-Verlag, July 1996.

[23] M. Utting and C. J. Fidge. Refinement of infeasible real-time programs. In *Proc. Formal Methods Pacific '97*, 243–262, Wellington, New Zealand, July 1997. Springer-Verlag.

Section D

Specifying complex behaviour

7   Aspects of system description   137
    Michael Jackson

Getting large-scale computer systems to work from scratch involves a complicated chain of activities all devoted to turning an informal description of a particular requirement, in some problem world, into a machine that satisfies it — the machine being a computer and its peripheral devices, all controlled by software.

Thus at some stage the informalities describing the boundaries of the job or problem must be converted into the language of mathematical symbols and abstract models — a program specification — the final benchmark against which software designers for instance can (in principle) check their programs. Once the problem is formally specified, it is able to establish a life of its own which, for a while at least, is comfortably distant from the real world; and software engineers can forget about the customers waiting impatiently for the arrival of their lift, or the thousands of motorists driving straight through an intersection because their traffic light shows green.

It is at the nebulous boundary between the formal and the informal where many misunderstandings lurk, and failure to pay proper attention to the 'real world' and how computer systems interact with it have meant that completed systems sometimes fail to work when finally introduced to their ultimate real-world context. Whether they do or not depends crucially on whether the formal specifications relate realistically to the original requirement description.

Whilst this distinction between 'requirements' and ' progam specification' has long been recognised, still insufficient effort is devoted to understanding how to describe real-life problems in a way that reduces the gap between informality and formality. All too often the temptation is to blur that distinction, to forget the special operating conditions or the fact that the real world is not exact.

This article describes some of the problems associated with the development of systems in the context of the real world. It argues that explicitly admitting reality to the design process is the proper way to deal with the problems, by providing well understood techniques for 'problem description'. It clarifies the distinction between 'real world' requirements in the problem domain and abstract 'program

136   Section D. Specifying complex behaviour

specification' at the computer interface, and shows that this is the most robust way to preserve an accurate chain of associations between a customer's expectations and the end product.

8   Modelling architectures for dynamic systems   161
   Peter Henderson

Current trends in large computing systems are moving towards systems that evolve as new components are added and old ones retired. The problem addressed in this paper is the design and analysis of such systems — in particular finding the right language simple enough to facilitate rapid expression and analysis of a dynamically evolving system.

A major concern is the survival of systems that evolve, rather than on how to understand detailed patterns of communications. This paper presents a language and architecture focusing on this issue, and builds on the UML-style of specification, adapted to a more abtract setting of simpler 'relationships' which allows the consequences of evolution to be explored.

9   What is a method?   175
   Dines Bjørner

The development of software systems relies on both the specification of the product and a detailed knowledge of the context or domain in which that product will operate. This article takes a broad view of domains, putting forward the idea that a more accurate description of 'the domain' goes beyond the traditional boundary of the physical characteristics of the software problem. For example there are many other 'environmental conditions' that affect the reality of system development and its operation, ranging from the pressures associated with human activity to legal requirements and management styles. Although this paper stresses that practicalities limit the extent of the domain description, nevertheless it is still viable to identify and distil semi-formal modelling paradigms of these important issues.

7

Aspects of system description

Michael Jackson

Abstract

This paper discusses some aspects of system description that are important for software development. Because software development aims to solve problems in the world, rather than merely in the computer, these aspects include: the distinction between the hardware/software machine and the world in which the problem is located; the relationship between phenomena in the world and formal terms used in descriptions; the idea of a software model of a problem world domain; and an approach to the decomposition of problems and its consequences for the larger structure of software development descriptions.

7.1 Introduction

The business of software development is, above all, the business of making descriptions. A *program* is a description of a computation—or, perhaps, of a machine behaviour. A *specification* is a description of the input-output relation of a computation—or, perhaps, of the externally observable behaviour of a machine. A *requirement* is a description of some observable effect or condition that our customer wants the computation—or the machine— to guarantee. A *software design* is a description of the structure of the computation—or, perhaps, of a machine that will execute the computation.

In spite of its importance, we pay surprisingly little attention to the practice and technique of description. For the most part, it is treated only implicitly and indirectly, either because it is thought too trivial to engage our attention, or because we suppose that all software developers must already be fully competent practitioners. In the same way, the great universities in the eighteenth and early nineteenth century ignored the study of English literature. It was a truth universally acknowledged that anyone qualified to study Latin and Greek and mathematics in the university must already know everything worth knowing about the subject of English literature.

But the discipline of description, like the study of English literature, is neither trivial nor universally understood. Many aspects of description technique are important in software development and merit explicit discussion. The following sections discuss particular aspects, setting them in the context of some simple problems. A concluding section briefly discusses the relationship between the view presented here and a narrower view of the scope of research, teaching and practice in software development.

7.2 Symbol manipulation

It has often seemed attractive to regard software development as a branch of pure mathematics. The computer is a symbol-processing machine. Each problem to be solved is formal, drawn from a pure mathematical domain. The development methods to be used are largely formal, with the addition of the intuitive leaps that are characteristic of creative mathematical work. And the criterion of success—correctness with respect to a precise program specification—is entirely formal.

This view has underpinned some notable advances in programming. It has led to the evolution of a powerful discipline based on simultaneous development of a program and its correctness proof, and a clear demonstration that, for some programs at least, correctness is an achievable practical goal. The class of such programs is large. It includes a repertoire of well-known small examples—such as GCD and searching or sorting an array— and many substantial applications—such as compiling program texts, finding maximal strong components in a graph, model-checking, and the travelling-salesman problem.

These are all problems with a strong algorithmic aspect. Their subject matter is abstract and purely mathematical, even when the abstraction and the mathematics have clear practical application. This is what allows the emphasis in software development to be placed on symbol manipulation. As Hermann Weyl expressed it [11]:

> "We now come to the decisive step of mathematical abstraction: we forget about what the symbols stand for. ...[The mathematician] need not be idle; there are many operations he may carry out with these symbols, without ever having to look at the things they stand for."

He might have gone further. We can't look at what the symbols stand for, because they don't stand for anything outside the mathematics: they are themselves the subject matter of the computation. The task of relating the mathematics to a practical problem is not part of the software developer's concern: it is someone else's business. Although our problem may be called *the Travelling Salesman problem* we are not really interested in the real salesmen and their travels, but only in the abstraction we have made of them.

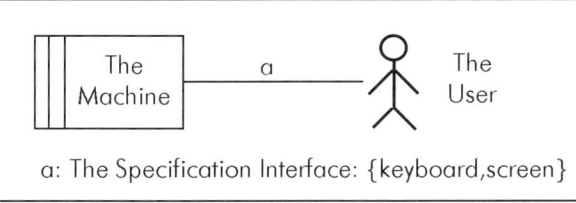

Figure 7.1. The machine and the user

7.2.1 The specification firewall

But even in the most formal problems an element of informality may intrude. A useful program must make its results visible outside the computer; most programs also accept some input. So questions of external representation and of data formats, at least, must be considered. How, for example, should we require our program's user to enter the nodes and arcs of the graph over which the salesman travels?

These less formal concerns arise outside the core computation itself, in the world of the software's users and the software developer's customers. In many cases they can relegated to a limbo beyond a *cordon sanitaire* by focusing on the *program specification*. As Dijkstra wrote [3]:

> "The choice of functional specifications—and of the notation to write them down in—may be far from obvious, but their role is clear: it is to act as a logical 'firewall' between two different concerns. The one is the 'pleasantness problem', i.e. the question of whether an engine meeting the specification is the engine we would like to have; the other one is the 'correctness problem,' ie the question of how to design an engine meeting the specification. ... the two problems are most effectively tackled by ... psychology and experimentation for the pleasantness problem and symbol manipulation for the correctness problem."

Figure 7.1 pictures the situation. The specification interface a is an interface of shared physical phenomena connecting the customer to the machine. At this interface the customer enters input data, perhaps by keyboard, and receives output data, perhaps by seeing it displayed on the screen. The shared phenomena for the input are the keystrokes: these are shared events controlled by the customer. The shared phenomena for the output are the characters or graphics visible on the screen: these are shared states, controlled by the machine.

The specification firewall is erected at this interface. It enforces a fruitful separation of the 'hard' formal concerns of the software developer and computer scientist from the 'soft' concerns of the 'systems analyst', addressing informal problems in the world outside the computer. The software developers are relieved of responsibility for the world outside the computer: they need no more discuss

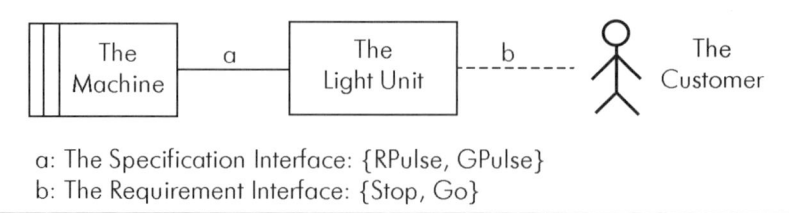

a: The Specification Interface: {RPulse, GPulse}
b: The Requirement Interface: {Stop, Go}

Figure 7.2. The machine, the world and the customer

the external data format for a graph than automobile engineers need discuss the range of paint colours for their cars' bodywork or the choice of upholstery fabric for the seats. The subject matter for serious attention and reasoning is restricted to the mathematics of the problem abstraction and of the computation that the machine will execute.

The 'soft' concerns, then, are relatively unimportant; they are relegated to a secondary place. The customer—who may well be the developer or another computer scientist with similar concerns and interests—may be slightly irritated by an inferior choice of input-output format at the specification interface, but is not expected to regard it as a crucial defect. The essential criterion, by which the work is to be judged, is the correctness and efficiency of the computation.

7.3 The Machine and the World

Not all customers will be so compliant. For most practical software development the customer's vital need is not to solve a mathematical problem, but to achieve specific observable physical effects in the world. Consider the very small problem of controlling a traffic light unit. The unit is placed at the gateway to a factory, and controls incoming traffic by allowing entry only during 15 seconds of each minute. The unit has a Stop lamp and a Go lamp. The problem is to ensure that the light shows alternately Stop for 45 seconds and Go for 15 seconds, starting with Stop. We can picture the problem as it is shown in Figure 7.2.

In addition to the machine, we now show the *problem domain*: that is, the part of the world in which the problem is located. There is no user: in this problem—as in many others—it is not clear who is the *user*, or even whether the notion of a user is useful. But there is certainly a *customer*: the person, or the group of people, who pay for the development work and will look critically at its results.

7.3.1 The specification interface

As before, the specification interface *a* is an interface of phenomena shared by the *machine domain* and the *problem domain*. Here the problem domain is the lights

7. Aspects of system description   141

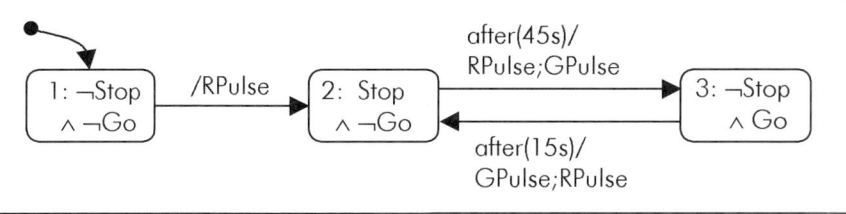

Figure 7.3. A system description

unit, and the shared phenomena are the signal pulses {*RPulse, GPulse*} by which the machine can cause it to switch on and off its Stop and Go lamps. The lights unit itself is on the other side of the specification interface.

7.3.2 The requirement interface

The customer is more remote from the machine than the user in a symbol manipulation problem. The customer's need is no longer located at the specification interface: the customer is interested in the regime of Stop and Go lamps, not in the signal pulses. So a new interface has appeared in the picture. The requirement interface *b* is a notional interface at which we can think of the customer as observing the world outside the machine. The phenomena of interest at this interface are the states of the Stop and Go lamps of the lights unit; these are, of course, quite distinct from the signal pulses at the interface with the machine.

The problem is about something physical and concrete. The externally visible behaviour of the machine, and the resulting behaviour of the lights unit, are not matters of pleasantness: they are the core of the problem.

7.3.3 A system description

Figure 7.3 is a description of the system as it might be described using a currently fashionable [10] diagrammatic notation derived from Statecharts [5]. In the transition markings the external stimulus, if any, is written before the slash ('/'), and the sequence of actions, if any, taken by the machine is written after it.

The initial state is 1, in which neither lamp is lit. Immediately the machine emits an RPulse, causing a transition to state 2, in which Stop is lit but not Go. 45 seconds after entering state 2, the machine emits an RPulse followed by a GPulse, causing a transition to state 3, in which Go is lit but not Stop. 15 seconds later the machine emits a GPulse followed by an RPulse, causing a transition back to state 2, and so on.

7.3.4 Purposeful description

It is always salutary in software development to ask why a particular description is worth making, and what particular purpose it serves in the development. In this tiny problem we can recognise three distinct roles that our system description is intended to play:

The requirement The *requirement* is a description that captures the effects our customer wants the machine to produce in the world. When we talk to the customer, we treat the description as a requirement. We ignore the actions that cause the pulses, and focus just on the timing events and the states. "To begin with," we say, "both lamps should be off; then, for 45 seconds, the Stop lamp only should be lit; then, for the next 15 seconds, the Go lamp only should be lit;" and so on. The requirement that emerges is:

```
forever {
  show only Stop for 45 seconds;
  show only Go for 15 seconds;
}
```

The machine specification The *specification* describes the behaviour of the machine in terms of the phenomena at the specification interface. It provides an interface between the problem analyst, who is concerned with the problem world, and the programmer, who is concerned only with the computer. When we talk to the programmer, we treat the description as a specification of the machine. We look only at the transitions with the timing events and the pulses. "First the machine must cause an RPulse," we tell the programmer, "then, after 45 seconds, an RPulse and a GPulse;" and so on. The Stop and Go states have no significance to the programmer, because they aren't visible to the machine; at best they are enlightening comments suggesting why the pulses are to be caused. The specification that emerges is:

```
{ RPulse;
  forever {
    wait 45 seconds; RPulse; GPulse;
    wait 15 seconds; GPulse; RPulse;
  }
}
```

The domain description The *domain description* bridges the gap between the requirement and the specification. The customer wants a certain regime of Stop and Go lamps, but the machine can directly cause only RPulses and GPulses. The gap is bridged by the properties of the problem domain. Here that means the properties of the lights unit. When we talk to the lights unit designer to check our understanding of the domain properties, we focus just on the pulses and the way they affect the states. "In the unit's initial state both lamps are off: That's right, isn't it? Then an initial RPulse turns the Stop lamp on; then an RPulse followed by a GPulse turns the Stop lamp

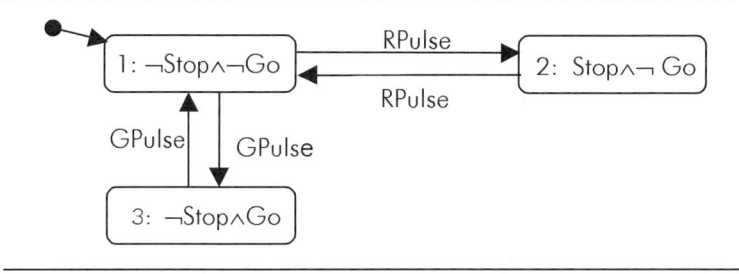

Figure 7.4. A partial domain description

off and lights the Go lamp, doesn't it?" and so on. The domain properties description that emerges[1] is shown in Figure 7.4.

7.3.5 Why separate descriptions are needed

Combining the three descriptions into one is tempting, but in a realistic problem it is very poor practice for several reasons. First, if the description were only slightly more complex it could be very hard to tease out the *projection* needed for each of the three roles.

Second, the adequacy of our development must be shown by an argument relating the three separate descriptions. Our goal is to bring about the regime of Stop and Go lamps that our customer desires. We must show that a machine programmed according to our specification will ensure this regime by virtue of the properties of the lights unit. That is:

$$\textit{specification} \land \textit{domain properties} \Rightarrow \textit{requirement}$$

In other words: if the machine meets its specification, and the problem world is as described in the domain properties, then the requirement will be satisfied[2]. The combined description does not allow this argument to be made explicitly.

Third, the single description combines descriptions of what we desire to achieve—the *optative* properties described in the requirement and specification—with a description of the known and given properties relied on—the *indicative* properties described in the domain description. It is always a bad idea to mix indicative and optative statements in the same description.

Fourth, the combined description is inadequate in an important way. Being based on a description of the machine behaviour, it can't accommodate a de-

---

[1] In fact, Figure 7.4 asserts much more than can be seen from the System Description given in Figure 7.3. For example: that it is possible to return to the dark state; that the first lamp turned on from the initial dark state may be the Go lamp; and that the RPulses affect only the Stop lamp and the GPulses only the Go lamp. Nothing in Figure 7.3 warrants these assertions.

[2] A fuller and more rigorous account of the relationship among the three descriptions is given in [4].

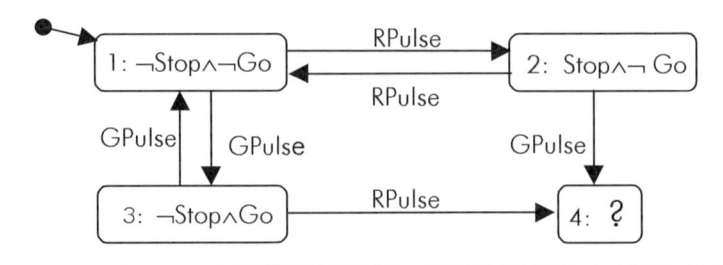

Figure 7.5. Lights-unit domain properties description

scription of what would happen if the machine were to behave differently—for example, by reversing the order of GPulse and RPulse in each pair. Figure 7.5 shows what a separate, full description of the domain properties might be.

Each lamp is toggled by pulses of the associated type: RPulse for Stop and GPulse for Go. The designer tells us that the unit can not tolerate the illumination of both lamps at the same time. We show state 4 as the *unknown state*, meaning that nothing is known about subsequent behaviour of the unit once it has entered state 4. Effectively, the unit is broken.

Fifth, the combined description isn't really re-usable. Because the embodied domain description, in particular, is merged with the requirement and the specification, it can't easily be re-used in another problem that deals differently with the same problem domain.

7.4 Describing the World

The three descriptions—requirements, domain properties and machine specification—are all concerned with event and state phenomena of the world in which the problem is located. But the first two are different from the third. The specification phenomena, shared with the machine, can properly be regarded as *formal*. Just as the machine has been carefully engineered so that there is no doubt whether a particular keystroke event has or has not occurred, so it has been carefully engineered to avoid similar doubt about whether an RPulse or a GPulse event has or has not occurred. The continuous underlying physical phenomena of magnetic fields and capacitances and voltages have been tamed to conform to sharply-defined discrete criteria.

But in general the phenomena and properties of the world have not been tamed in this way, and must be regarded as *informal*. The formalisation must be devised and imposed by the software developer. As W. Scherlis remarked [8] in his response to Dijkstra's observations [3] cited earlier:

> "One of the greatest difficulties in software development is formalization—capturing in symbolic representation a worldly computational

problem so that the statements obtained by following rules of symbolic manipulation are useful statements once translated back into the language of the world."

This task of formalization, along with appropriate techniques for its successful performance, is an integral, but regrettably much neglected, aspect of software development. Two important elements of this task are the use of *designations*, and the use and proper understanding of *formal definitions*.

7.4.1 Designations

Because the world is informal it is very hard to describe precisely. It is therefore necessary to lay a sound basis for description by saying as precisely as possible what phenomena are denoted by the formal terms in our requirements and domain properties descriptions. The appropriate tool is a set of *designations*. A designation gives a formal term, such as a predicate, and gives a—necessarily informal—rule for recognising instances of the phenomenon.

For example, in a genealogical system we may need this designation:

$Mother(x, y) \approx x$ is the mother of y

Probably this is a very poor recognition rule: it leaves us in considerable doubt about what is included. Does it encompass adoptive mothers, surrogate mothers, stepmothers, foster mothers? Egg donors? Probably we must be more exact. Perhaps what we need is:

$Mother(x, y) \approx x$ is the human genetic mother of y

Even this more conscientious attempt may be inadequate in a future world in which genetic engineering has become commonplace.

Adequate precision of the underlying designations is fundamental to the precision and intelligibility of the requirement and domain descriptions that rely on them. If it proves too hard to write a satisfactory recognition rule for phenomena of a chosen class, that chosen class should be rejected, and firmer ground should be sought elsewhere.

This harsh stipulation is less obstructive than it may seem at first. The designated terminology is intended for describing a particular part, or domain, of the problem world for a particular problem. As so often in software development, we may be tempted to multiply our difficulties a thousandfold by trying to treat the general case instead of focusing, as practical engineers, on the particular case in hand. The temptation must be resisted.

For example, in an inventory problem for the OfficeWorld Company, whose business is supplying office furniture, we may need to designate the entity class Chair. Perhaps we write this designation:

$Chair(x) \approx x$ is a single unit of furniture whose primary
            use is to provide seating for one person

Philosophers have often cited 'chair' as an example of the irreducibly uncertain meaning of words in natural language. In the general case no designation of 'chair' can be adequate. Is a bar stool a chair? A bean bag? A sofa? A park bench? A motor car seat? A chaise longue? A shooting stick? These questions are impossibly difficult to answer: there are no right answers. But we do not have to answer them. The OfficeWorld Company has quite a small catalogue. It doesn't supply bar stools or park benches or bean bags. Our recognition rule is good enough for the case in hand.

7.4.2 Using definitions

Another factor mitigating the severity of the stipulation that designations must be precise is that the number of phenomenon classes to be designated usually turns out to be surprisingly small. Many useful terms do not denote distinctly observable phenomena at all, but must be *defined* on the basis of terms that do and of previously defined terms. For example:

$Sibling(a, b) \stackrel{\text{def}}{=}$
$\quad a \neq b \land \exists\ p, q \bullet Mother(p, a) \land Mother(p, b)$
$\quad\quad\quad \land\ Father(q, a) \land Father(q, b)$

The difference between definition and designation is crucial. A designation introduces a fresh class of observations, and thus enlarges the scope of possible assertions about the world. A definition, by contrast, merely introduces more convenient terminology without increasing the expressive power at our disposal.

In an inventory problem, suppose that we have designated the event classes[3] *receive* and *issue*:

$Receive(e, q, t) \approx$ *e is an event occurring at time t*
$\quad\quad\quad\quad\quad\quad\quad$ *in which q units of stock are received*
$Issue(e, q, t) \approx$ *e is an event occurring at time t*
$\quad\quad\quad\quad\quad\quad$ *in which q units of stock are issued*

Then the definition:

$ExpectedQuantity(qty, tt) \stackrel{\text{def}}{=}$
$\quad (\Sigma\ e\ |\ ((Receive(e, q, t) \lor Issue(e, -q, t)) \land t < tt) : q) = qty$

defines the predicate *ExpectedQuantity(qty,tt)* to mean that at time *tt* the number *qty* is equal to a certain sum. This sum is the total number of units received in *receive* events, minus the total number issued in *issue* events, taken over all events *e* occurring at any time *t* that is earlier than time *tt*. Being a definition, it says nothing at all about the world. By contrast, the designation and assertion:

---

[3] For uniformity, it is convenient to designate all formal terms as predicates. For any set of individuals, such as a class of events, the formal term in the designation denotes the characteristic predicate of the set.

InStock(qty, tt) ≈ At time *tt qty* items are in the stock bin
   in the warehouse

∀ *qty, tt* • *InStock(qty, tt)* ⇔
   $(\Sigma e \mid ((\textit{Receive}(e, q, t) \lor \textit{Issue}(e, -q, t)) \land t < tt) : q) = qty$

say that initially *InStock(0,t0)* and that subsequently stock changes only by the quantities issued and received. There is no theft, no evaporation and no spontaneous creation of stock. The definition of *ExpectedQuantity* expressed only a choice of terminology; the designation of *InStock*, combined with the accompanying assertion, expresses a falsifiable claim about the physical world.

7.4.3 Distinguishing Definition From Description

Many notations commonly used for description can also be used for definition, distinguishing the two uses by certain restrictions and by suitable syntactic conventions.

For example, it is often convenient to define terms for state components by giving a finite-state machine. Since mixing definition with description—like mixing indicative with optative—is very undesirable, the state-machine description should be empty *qua* description[4]. That is, in defining states it should place no constraint on the described sequence of events. Suppose, for example, that in some domain the sequence of events is

   < *a, b, a, b, a, ...* >

and that we wish to define the state terms *After-a* and *After-b*. Figure 7.6 shows the definition: it avoids assuming that the sequence of events is as given above. *After-a* is defined to mean the state identified as state 2 in this state machine, and *After-b* is defined similarly. Of course, if the meanings are intended to include the clause "... and the given sequence of events has been followed so far", then a different definition is necessary.

7.5 Descriptions and models

An important aspect of description in software development is clarity in the distinction between a *description* and a *model*. Unfortunately, the word *model* is much overused and much misused. Its possible meanings[5] include:

- An *analytical model* of a domain: that is, a formal description from which further properties of the domain can be inferred. For example, a set of differential equations describing a country's economy, or a labelled transition diagram describing the behaviour of a vending machine.

---

[4] A term defined in a non-empty description is undefined whenever the description is false. It then becomes necessary either to use a three-valued logic or to prove at each of its occurrences that the term is well-defined.

[5] This distinction among the three kinds of model is due to Ackoff [1].

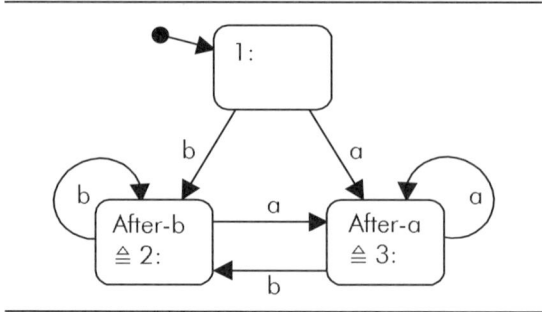

Figure 7.6. Defining states in a FSM

- An *iconic model* of a domain: that is, a representation that captures the appearance of the domain. For example, an artist's drawing of a proposed building.

- An *analogic model* of a domain: that is, another domain that can act as a surrogate for purposes of providing information. For example, a computer-driven wall display showing the layout of a rail network in the form of a graph, and the current train traffic on the network in the form of a blob for each train moving along the arcs of the graph.

Much difficulty arises from confusion between the first and third of these meanings. It is a common and necessary device in software development to introduce an analogic model, in the form of a database or other data structure, into the solution of an information problem or subproblem. Such an analogic model domain is to be regarded as an elaboration of a certain class of local variables of the machine. Descriptions of this model domain are often confused with descriptions of the domain for which it is a surrogate.

7.5.1 A model of a lift

A small hotel has an old and somewhat primitive lift. Now it is to be fitted with an information panel in the lobby, to show waiting guests where the lift is at any time and its current direction of travel, so that they will know how long they can expect to wait until it arrives.

The panel has a square lamp for each floor, to show that the lift is at the floor. In addition there are two arrow-shaped lamps to indicate the direction of travel. The panel display must be driven from a simple interface with the floor sensors of the lift. A floor sensor is on when the lift is within 6 inches of the rest position at the floor.

Figure 7.7 is the problem diagram. Here the customer manikin is replaced by the more impersonal dashed oval, representing the requirement. The requirement is that the lamp states of the lobby display (the phenomena d) should corre-

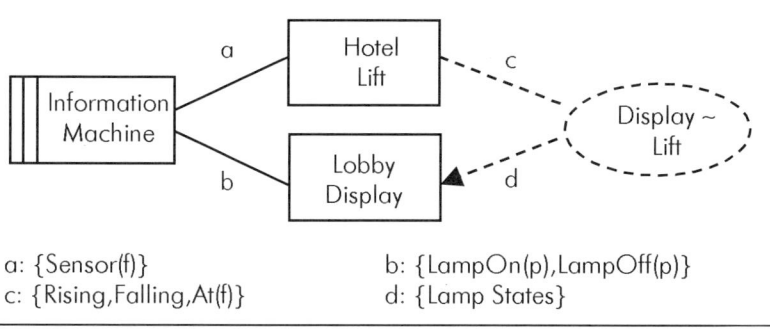

a: {Sensor(f)}
c: {Rising,Falling,At(f)}
b: {LampOn(p),LampOff(p)}
d: {Lamp States}

Figure 7.7. Lift position display problem

spond in a certain way to the states of the lift (the phenomena c). The arrow head indicates that the requirement constrains the display, but not the hotel lift itself.

This simple information problem presents a standard *concern* of problems of this class[6]. The information necessary to maintain the required correspondence is not available to the machine at the specification interface *a* at the moment when it is needed. The requirement phenomena include the current lift position and its current direction of travel; the specification phenomena include only the floor sensor states. To satisfy the requirement as well as possible, the machine must store information about the past history of the lift, and must interpret the current state and events in the light of this history.

The local phenomena of the machine in which this history is stored—perhaps in the form of program variables, or a data structure or small database—constitute an *analogic model domain*. If these local phenomena are not totally trivial it is desirable to decompose the original problem into two subproblems: one to build and maintain the model, and one to use the model in producing the lobby display. This problem decomposition is shown in Figure 7.8.

As the decomposed problem diagram shows clearly, the lift model and the hotel lift itself are disjoint domains, with no phenomena in common. In designing the lift model, the developer must devise model state phenomena f to correspond to the lift domain requirement phenomena c. These model phenomena might be called *MRising* and *MFalling*, corresponding to the lift states *Rising* and *Falling*, and *MAt(f)*, corresponding to *At(f)*.

The modelling subproblem is then to ensure that *MRising* holds in the model if and only if the lift is rising, that *MAt(f)* holds in the model if and only if the lift is at floor f, and so on. The model constructor operations—the phenomena e—will be invoked by the modelling machine when sensor state changes occur at its interface *a* with the hotel lift domain.

The display subproblem is much simpler: the display machine must ensure that the *Up* lamp is lit if and only if *MRising* holds; the floor lamp f is lit if and only if *MAt(f)* holds; and so on.

150   Jackson

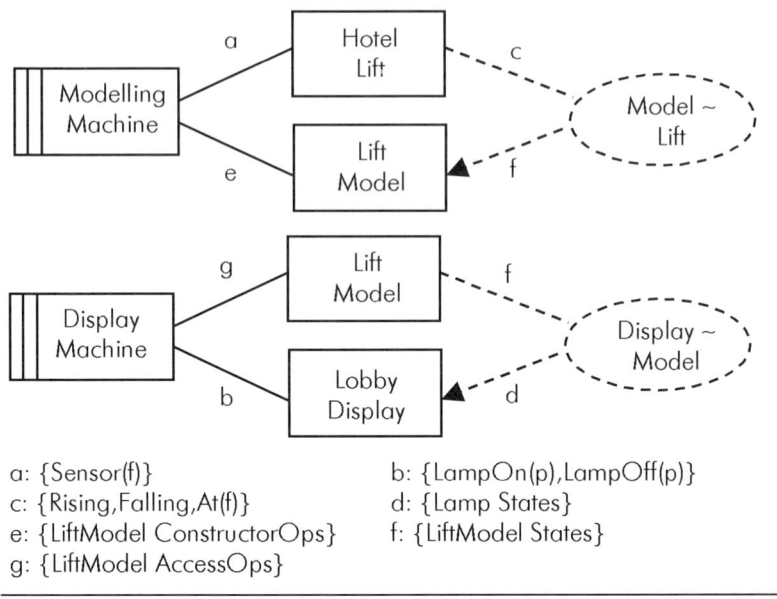

a: {Sensor(f)}
c: {Rising,Falling,At(f)}
e: {LiftModel ConstructorOps}
g: {LiftModel AccessOps}

b: {LampOn(p),LampOff(p)}
d: {Lamp States}
f: {LiftModel States}

Figure 7.8. Lift position display problem decomposition

7.5.2   The modelling relationship

The desired relationship between a model domain and the domain it models is, in principle, simple. There should be a 1–1 correspondence between phenomena of the two domains and their values. For example, the lift has state phenomena $At(f)$ for $f = 0 \ldots 8$ and the model has state phenomena $MAt(f)$ for $f = 0 \ldots 8$.[6] For any f, $MAt(f)$ should hold if and only if $At(f)$ holds.

Because of this relationship it seems clear that a description that is true of one domain must be equally true of the other, with a suitable change of interpretation. For example, the description:

"in any trace of values of $P(x)$, $0 \leq x \leq 8$ for each element of the trace,
and adjacent values of x differ by at most 1."

is true of the lift domain if we take $P(x)$ to mean $At(f)$, and must be true also of the model domain if we take $P(x)$ to mean $MAt(f)$.

It therefore seems very attractive and economical to write only one description. In a further economy, even the work of writing the two interpretations can be eliminated by using the same names for phenomena in the lift and the corresponding phenomena in the model. Unfortunately, this is usually a false economy.

---

[6]Floor 0 is the lobby. In Europe floor 1 is the first above the ground floor; in the US the floors would be numbered $1 \ldots 9$.

Although almost universally attempted, both by practitioners and by researchers, it can work well only for an ideal model in which the desired relationship to the model domain is known to hold; practical models are almost never ideal.

7.5.3 Practical models

The lift domain phenomenon *At(f)* means that the lift is closer to floor f than to any other floor. However, it is not possible to maintain a precise correspondence between *At(f)* and the model phenomenon *MAt(f)*, because the specification state phenomena *Sensor(f)* do not convey enough information. The best that can be done is, perhaps, to specify the modelling machine so that *MAt(f)* is true if and only if *Sensor(f)* is the sensor that is on or was most recently on. So the correspondence between *At(f)* and *MAt(f)* is very imperfect. When the lift travels from floor 1 to floor 2, *MAt(1)* remains true even when the lift is six inches from the floor 2 home position and the state *Sensor(2)* is just about to become true.

The *Rising* and *Falling* phenomena are even harder to deal with. Once again, the modelling machine has access only to the *Sensor(f)* phenomena, and must maintain the model phenomena *MRising* and *MFalling* from the information they provide. Initially the lift may be considered to be *Rising*, because from the Lobby it can go only upwards; subsequently, when it reaches floor 8 (or floor 0 again) it must reverse direction. But it may also reverse direction at an intermediate floor, provided that it makes a service visit there and does not simply pass it without stopping.

Investigation of the lift domain shows that on a service visit the floor sensor is on for at least 4.8 seconds, allowing time for the doors to open and close. Passing a floor takes no more than 1 second. The model phenomena *MRising* and *MFalling* will be maintained as follows:

- Initially: $MRising \land \neg MFalling$

- Whenever *MAt(n+1)* becomes true when *MAt(n)* was previously true, for $(n = 0\ldots 6)$: $MRising \land \neg MFalling$

- Whenever *MAt(8)* becomes true when *MAt(7)* was previously true: $MFalling \land \neg MRising$

- Whenever *MAt(n-1)* becomes true when *MAt(n)* was previously true for $(n = 2\ldots 8)$: $MFalling \land \neg MRising$

- Whenever *MAt(0)* becomes true when *MAt(1)* was previously true: $MRising \land \neg MFalling$

- Whenever *MAt(n)* has been true for 2 seconds[7] continuously, for $(n = 1\ldots 7)$: $\neg MFalling \land \neg MRising$

---

[7] A compromise between the limits of 1.0 and 4.8 seconds, affording an early but reasonably reliable presumption that the lift has stopped to service the floor.

These practical choices represent unavoidable departures from exact correspondence between the model and the lift domain. For example, during the first two seconds of a service visit either *MRising* or *MFalling* is true, although neither *Rising* nor *Falling* is true. Also, when the lift has reversed direction at an intermediate floor but has not yet reached another floor, either *Rising* or *Falling* is true, but neither *MRising* nor *MFalling* is true. Speaking anthropomorphically, we might say that the modelling machine is waiting to discover whether the next floor arrival will invite the inference of upwards or downwards travel.

7.5.4 Describing the model and modelled domains

Other factors that may prevent exact correspondence in a practical model include errors and delays in the interface between the modelling machine and the modelled domain, and the approximation of continuous by discrete phenomena. A further factor is the need to model the imperfection of the model itself. For example, NULL values are often used in relational databases to model the absence of information: a NULL value in a *date-of-birth* column indicates only that the date of birth is unknown. In the presence of such discrepancies it may still be possible to economise by using the same basic description for both domains and noting the discrepancies explicitly.

Another factor militating against a single description is that a model domain itself usually has additional phenomena that correspond to nothing in the modelled domain. The source of these phenomena is the underlying implementation of the model. A relational database, for example, usually has delete operations to conserve space, indexes to speed access to particular elements of the model, and ordering of tuples within relational tables to speed *select* and *join* operations. These discrepancies between the model and modelled domains can sometimes be regarded as no more than the difference between abstract and concrete views of the model. Introduction of the additional model phenomena is a refinement: the resulting implementation satisfies the model's abstract specification. This view applies easily to the introduction of tuple ordering and of indexing. It is less clear that it can apply to record deletion.

The use of only one description for the two domains fails most notably when the modelled domain has phenomena that do not and can not appear in the model. For example, the lift domain has the moving and stationary states of the lift car, and the opening and closing of the lift doors during a service visit to a floor. These phenomena can not appear in the model because there is not enough evidence of them in the shared phenomena of the specification interface. They are completely hidden from the modelling machine, and can enter into the model only in a most attenuated form—the choices based on assumptions about them. But they must still appear in any careful description of the significant domain properties.

In sum, therefore, it is essential to recognise that a modelled domain and its model are two distinct subjects for description. Confusion of the two results in importing distracting irrelevancies and restrictions into the problem domain description. For example, in UML [10] descriptions of a business domain must be based on irrelevant programming concepts, such as *attributes*, *visibility*, *interfaces* and *operations*, taken from object-oriented languages such as C++ and Smalltalk. At the same time, UML notations provide no way of describing the syntax of a lexical problem domain, other than by describing a program to parse it.

This vital distinction between the model and the modelled domain is difficult to bear in mind if the verb *model* is used where the verb *describe* would do as well or better. The claim "We are modelling the lift domain" invites the interpretation "We are describing the lift domain", when often it means in fact "We are not bothering to describe the lift domain: instead we are describing a domain that purports to be an analogical model of it."

7.6 Problem decomposition and description structures

Realistic problems must be decomposed into simpler subproblems. Almost always, the subproblems are related by having problem domains in common: that is, they are not about disjoint parts of the world. The common problem domains must, in general, be differently viewed and differently described in the different subproblems. This section gives two small illustrations of this effect of problem decomposition.

7.6.1 An auditing subproblem

A small sluice, with a rising and falling gate, is used in a simple irrigation system. A control computer is to be programmed to raise and lower the sluice gate: the gate is to be open for ten minutes in each hour, and otherwise shut.

The gate is opened and closed by rotating vertical screws. The screws are driven by a small motor, which can be controlled by *Clockwise*, *Anticlockwise*, *On* and *Off* pulses. There are sensors at the top and bottom of the gate travel; at the top the gate is fully open, at the bottom it is fully shut. The connection to the computer consists of four pulse lines for motor control and two status lines for the gate sensors.

The requirement phenomena are the gate states *Open* and *Shut*. The specification phenomena are the motor control pulses, and the states of the *Top* and *Bottom* sensors. A mechanism of this kind moves slowly and has little inertia, so a specification of the machine behaviour to satisfy the requirement is simple and easily developed. Essentially, the gate can be opened by setting the motor to run in the appropriate sense and stopping it when the *Top* sensor goes on; it can be closed similarly, stopping the motor when the *Bottom* sensor goes on.

The domain properties on which the machine must rely include:

- The behaviour of the motor unit in changing its state in response to externally caused motor control pulses;

- the behaviour of the mechanical parts of the sluice that govern how the gate moves vertically, rising and falling according to whether the motor is stopped or rotating clockwise or anticlockwise;
- the relationship between the gate's vertical position and its Open and Shut states; and
- the relationship between the gate's vertical position and the states of the Top and Bottom sensors.

To develop a specification of the control machine it is necessary to investigate and describe these domain properties explicitly.

7.6.2 Fruitful contradiction

Being physical devices, the sluice gate and its motor, on whose properties the control machine is relying, are not so reliable as we might wish. Power cables can be cut; motor windings burn out; insulation can be worn away or eaten by rodents; screws rust and corrode; pinions become loose on their shafts; branches and other debris can become jammed in the gate, preventing it from closing. The behaviour of the control computer should take account of these possibilities—at least to the extent of stopping the motor when something has clearly gone wrong.

Possible evidences of failure, detectable at the specification interface, include:

- the *Top* and *Bottom* sensors are on simultaneously;
- the motor has been set to raise the gate for more than m seconds but the *Bottom* sensor is still on;
- the motor has been set to lower the gate for more than n seconds but the *Top* sensor is still on;
- the motor has been set to raise the gate for more than p seconds but the *Top* sensor is not yet on;
- the motor has been set to lower the gate for more than q seconds but the *Bottom* sensor is not yet on.

Detecting these possible failures should be treated as a separate subproblem, of a class that we may call *Auditing problems*. The machine in this auditing subproblem runs concurrently with the machine in the basic control problem. The two subproblem machines are connected: the control machine, on detecting a failure, causes a signal in response to which the control machine turns the motor off and keeps it off thereafter.

The particular interest of this problem is that in a certain sense the domain property description of the auditing subproblem contradicts the description on which the solution of the control subproblem must rely. The indicative domain description for the control subproblem asserts that when the motor is set in such-and-such a state the gate will reach its *Open* state within p seconds; but the description for the auditing problem contradicts this assertion by explicitly showing the possibility of failure.

At a syntactic level, this conflict can be resolved by merging the two descriptions to give a single consistent description that accommodates both the correct and the failing behaviour of the gate mechanism. This merged description might then be used for the control subproblem, the auditing subproblem being embedded in the control subproblem as a collection of local behaviour variants. But this merging is not a wise strategy. It is better to solve the control subproblem in the context of explicit appropriate assumptions about the domain properties, leaving the complications of the possible failures for a separate concern and a separate subproblem.

7.6.3 An identities concern

In the lift display problem it was necessary to pay careful attention to the gap between the requirement phenomena (the *At(f), Rising and Falling* states) and the specification phenomena (the *Sensor(f)* states) of the lift domain. But we were not at all careful about another phenomenological concern in the problem. We resorted—naturally enough—to the standard mathematical practice of indexing multiple phenomena: we wrote f for the identifier of a floor, and used that identifier freely in our informal discussion and—by implication—in our descriptions.

This was too casual. The use of 'abstract indexes' in this way is sometimes an abstraction too far: it throws out an important baby along with the bathwater. Essentially, it distracts the developer from recognising an important class of development concern: an *Identities* concern [6]. The potential importance of this concern can be seen from an anecdote in Peter Neumann's book about computer risks [7]:

> "A British Midland Boeing 737-400 crashed at Kegworth in the United Kingdom, killing 47 and injuring 74 seriously. The right engine had been erroneously shut off in response to smoke and excessive vibration that was in reality due to a fan-blade failure in the left engine. The screen-based 'glass cockpit' and the procedures for crew training were questioned. Cross-wiring, which was suspected—but not definitively confirmed—was subsequently detected in the warning systems of 30 similar aircraft."

'Cross-wiring' is the hardware manifestation of an archetypal failure in treating an identities concern.

7.6.4 Patient monitoring

In the well-known Patient Monitoring problem [9] the machine is required to monitor temperature and other vital factors of intensive-care patients according to parameters specified by medical staff. The physical interface between the machine and the problem world of the intensive-care patients is essentially restricted to the shared register values of the analog-digital sensor devices attached to the patients. A significant concern in this problem is therefore to associate these shared registers correctly with the individual patients, and to describe how this association is realised in the problem domain. The complete chain of associations is this:

- each patient has a name, used by the medical staff in specifying the parameters of monitoring for the patient;
- each patient is physically attached to one or more analog-digital devices;
- each device is plugged into a port of the machine through which its internal register is shared by the machine;
- each port of the machine has a unique name.

To perform the monitoring as required, the machine must have access to a data structure representing these chains of associations. This data structure is a very specialised restricted *identities model* of the problem world of patients, devices and medical staff. It is, of course, quite distinct from any model of the patients that may be needed for managing the frequency of their monitoring and for detecting patterns in the values of their vital factors. The two models may be merged in an eventual joint implementation of the machines of the constituent subproblems, but they must be kept distinct in the earlier stages of the development process.

There is a further concern. Since neither the population of patients, nor the set of monitoring devices deemed necessary for each one, is constant, there must be an editing process in which the identities model data structure is created and changed. Concurrent access to this data structure by the monitoring and modifying processes therefore raises concerns of mutual exclusion and process scheduling. An excessively abstract view of the problem context will miss the existence of the data structure, and with it these important concerns and their impact on the Patient Monitoring system.

7.7 The scope of software development

The description concerns raised in this paper are primarily concerns about describing the problem world rather than designing the software to be executed by the machine. It's natural to ask again whether these description concerns are really the business of software developers at all. Perhaps the specification firewall does, after all, divide the business of software development from the business of the application domain expert.

Barry Boehm paints a vivid picture of software developers anxious to remain behind the firewall and not to encroach on application domain territory [2]:

> "I observed the social consequences of this approach in several aerospace system-architecture-definition meetings ("Integrating

Software Engineering and System Engineering", Journal of IN-COSE, pages 61-67, January 1994). While the hardware and systems engineers sat around the table discussing their previous system architectures, the software engineers sat on the side, waiting for someone to give them a precise specification they could turn into code."

It's clearly true that software developers can not and should not try to be experts in all application domains. For example, in a problem to control road traffic at a very complex intersection it must be the traffic engineer's responsibility to determine and analyse the patterns of incoming traffic, to design the traffic flows through the intersection, and to balance the conflicting needs of the different pedestrian and vehicle users. Software developers are not traffic engineers. But this is far from the whole answer.

There are several reasons why a large part of our responsibility must lie outside the computer, beyond the specification firewall. Here we will mention only two of them. First, the specification firewall usually cuts the development project along a line that makes the programming task unintelligibly arbitrary when viewed purely from the machine side: effectively, pure specifications are meaningless. And second, having created the technology that spawns huge discrete complexity in the problem domain, we have a moral obligation to contribute to mastering that complexity.

7.7.1 Meaningless specifications

In the problem of controlling traffic at a complex road intersection the pure specification is an I/O relation. Its domain is the set of possible traces of clock ticks and input signals at the computer's ports; its range is a set of corresponding traces of output signals. These trace sets may be characterised more or less elegantly, but, however described, they are strictly confined to these signals. The specification alphabet will be something like this—

{*clocktick, outsignal_X1FF, ..., insignal_X207, ...* }

— where the event classes in the alphabet are events occurring in the hardware I/O interface of the computer. Nothing is said about lights or push buttons, about the layout of the intersection, or about vehicles and pedestrians. These are all private phenomena of the problem domain, hidden from the machine because they are not shared at the specification interface.

It's clear that such a specification is unintelligible. A small improvement can be achieved by naming the signals at the specification interface to indicate the corresponding lights and buttons—

{*clocktick, outsignal_red27, ..., insignal_button8, ...* }

—but the improvement is very small. Further improvement would need additional descriptions, showing the layout of the intersection and the positions of the lights. Then the domain properties of vehicles and pedestrians, existing and desired traffic flows, and everything else necessary to justify and clarify the otherwise impenetrable machine behaviour specification.

In short, the machine behaviour specification makes sense only in the larger context of the problem; and the problem is not located at the specification interface. If we restrict our work to developing software to meet given formal specifications, most of what we do will make no sense to us. We will be deprived of the intuitive understanding of the customer's problem that is essential both as a stimulus to creativity in program design and as a sanity check on the program we write.

7.7.2 Discrete complexity

Computers frequently introduce an unprecedented behavioural complexity into problem worlds with which they interact. This behavioural complexity arises naturally from the complexity of the software itself, and from its interplay with the causal, human and lexical properties of the problem domains.

In older systems behavioural complexity was kept under control by three factors. First, the software itself—whether in the form of a computer program or an administrators' procedure manual—was usually smaller and simpler than today's software by more than one order of magnitude. Second, there was neither the possibility nor the ambition of integrating distinct systems, and so bringing about an exponential increase in their combined behavioural complexity. Third, almost every system, whether a 'data-processing' or a 'control' system, relied explicitly on human cooperation and intervention. When inconvenient and absurd results emerged, some human operator had the opportunity, the skill and the authority to intervene and overrule the computer.

In many application areas we have gradually lost all of these safeguards. The ambitions of software developers increase to keep pace with the available resources of computational power and space. Systems are becoming more integrated, or, at least, more interdependent. And it is increasingly common to find levels of automation—as in flight control systems—that preclude human intervention to correct errors in software design or specification.

A large part of the responsibility for dealing with the resulting increased behavioural complexity must lie with computer scientists and software developers, if only because no other discipline has tools to master it. We can not discharge this responsibility by mastering complexity only in software: we must play a major role in mastering the resulting complexity in the problem world outside the computer.

7.8 Acknowledgements

Many of the ideas presented here have been the subject of joint work over a period of several years with Pamela Zave. They have also been discussed at length on many occasions with Daniel Jackson. This paper has been much improved by his comments.

References

[1] R L Ackoff. *Scientific Method: Optimizing Applied Research Decisions*; Wiley, 1962.

[2] Barry W Boehm. Unifying Software Engineering and Systems Engineering; IEEE Computer Volume 33 Number 3, pages 114-116, March 2000.

[3] Edsger W Dijkstra. On the Cruelty of Really Teaching Computer Science; Communications of the ACM Volume 32 Number 12, page 1414, December 1989.

[4] Carl A Gunter, Elsa L Gunter, Michael Jackson, and Pamela Zave. A Reference Model for Requirements and Specifications; Proceedings of ICRE 2000, Chicago Ill, USA; reprinted in IEEE Software Volume 17 Number 3, pages 37-43, May/June 2000.

[5] David Harel. Statecharts: A visual formalism for complex systems; Science of Computer Programming 8, pages 231-274, 1987.

[6] Michael Jackson. *Problem Frames: Analysing and Structuring Software Development Problems*; Addison-Wesley, 2000.

[7] Peter G Neumann. Computer-Related Risks; Addison-Wesley, 1995, pages 44–45.

[8] W L Scherlis. responding to E W Dijkstra "On the Cruelty of Really Teaching Computing Science"; Communications of the ACM Volume 32 Number 12, page 1407, December 1989.

[9] W P Stevens, G J Myers, and L L Constantine; Structured Design. IBM Systems Journal Volume 13 Number 2, pages 115-139, 1974. Reprinted in Tutorial on Sofware Design Techniques; Peter Freeman and Anthony I Wasserman eds, pages 328-352, IEEE Computer Society Press, 4th edition 1983.

[10] James Rumbaugh, Ivar Jacobson and Grady Booch. *The Unified Modeling Language Reference Manual*; Addison-Wesley Longman 1999.

[11] Hermann Weyl. The Mathematical Way of Thinking; address given at the Bicentennial Conference at the University of Pennsylvania, 1940.

8

Modelling architectures for dynamic systems

Peter Henderson

Abstract

A dynamic system is one that changes its configuration as it runs. It is a system into which we can drop new components that then cooperate with the existing ones. We are concerned with formally defining architectures for such systems and with realistically validating designs for applications that run on those architectures. We describe a generic architecture based on the familiar registry services of CORBA, DCOM and Jini. We illustrate this architecture by formally describing a simple point-of-sale system built according to this architecture. We then look at the sorts of global properties that a designer of applications would wish a robust system to have and discuss variations on the architecture which make validation of applications more practical.

8.1 Introduction

The advent of ubiquitous computing, where everything is connected to everything else, has created a new challenge for Software Engineering and for Software Reuse in particular. It is now increasingly important that software components are designed for a life of constant change and frequent reuse.

With everything connected to everything else, systems are necessarily subject to dynamic change. You can't stop the whole world just to plug in a new component. Components need to be as nearly plug-and-play as possible. Flexible architectures such as Jini [35], are making the evolution of dynamic systems possible. The question is, how do you design for such architectures and how do you design components which will survive a lifetime of use and reuse even though their environment and the expectations which their users have of them, are constantly changing?

8.1.1 Dynamic systems

In [16] dynamic systems are described as being built from components and having the property that a new component could be added to a running system at any time and the system would embrace its contribution without having to stop. It is the requirement that the system can evolve by accretion, without ever having to stop, that leads us to call the system "dynamic". The consequences for component reuse are dramatic. Components will be reused in ways that were not imagined by their original designers. In [16] we addressed the issue of who would be to blame if the consequence of adding a new component was that something broke.

In this paper, we formally describe some of the issues which arise for the developer of dynamic systems, not least of all the evolution of functionality in an incremental way. We do this by introducing an elementary architecture modelling language, ARC [17], which allows for experimentation with alternative architectural designs and for the validation of these designs using state-space search. In particular, ARC models can be compiled to run on the SPIN model-checker [21]. The ARC modelling paradigm, it is conjectured, is simple enough to allow many experiments to be performed quickly with modest cost and yet powerful enough to describe a range of practical architectures and generate valuable insight into their properties.

8.1.2 The context of constant change

We are concerned with dynamic systems in the context of constant change, where the system supports a business process which is constantly needing to be changed to match the rapidly moving marketplace. We wish to explore architectures which will allow the incremental enhancement of the system without having to be stopped for upgrade. Consequently we are concerned with issues of reconfigurability, where new components can be added to the system which then embraces the new services which they offer. We are less concerned with the removal of old components in that we anticipate architectures which will allow such components to gradually become obsolete and eventually retire.

However we are concerned with issues of survival. We will articulate scenarios in which the system can survive despite the fact that some components fail. One way of looking at this issue is to characterise the interaction between a system and its environment as a two-person game [1]. The moves made by the system are to maximise the number of components which can operate. The moves of the environment are to damage key components with the intention of preventing as many components as possible from operating successfully. We show how our modelling paradigm lends itself to this metaphor.

8. Modelling architectures for dynamic systems   163

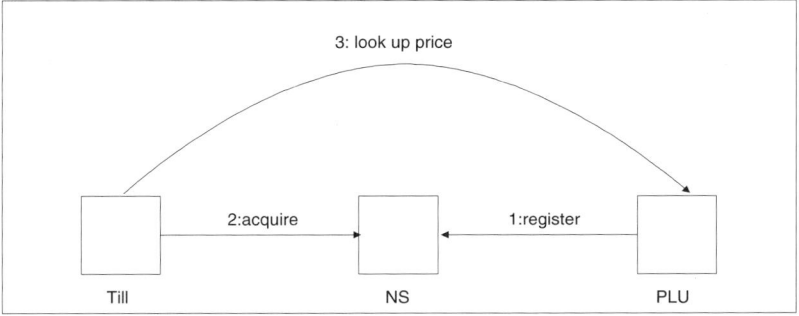

Figure 8.1. A UML Collaboration Diagram

8.2 Models of dynamic systems

In order to be able to make precise statements about alternative architectural proposals we need to use a language which has a precise meaning and which operates at a level of abstraction appropriate to the kinds of reasoning which we wish to perform. There is a choice of paradigms. Many architecture modelling languages base themselves on a message-passing, process-oriented view. Examples are Wright [2, 3, 32], Darwin [27, 28] and more recently FSP/LTSA [29]. Others, such as Rapide [24, 25, 26] take an event-based approach where events are specified by condition-action rules. This is the approach we will take in ARC. Architecture languages concern themselves with structure and behaviour [36]. We are, of course, concerned with both here. But, in a dynamic system, structure is dynamic and so structure merges into behaviour.

8.2.1 The ARC notation

Our conjecture is that our modelling language is appropriate to the design of reusable components for dynamic systems, because it operates at a level-of-abstraction that allows reasonably large systems to be modelled, but still allows a useful degree of validation of the models in a cost-effective manner.

The modelling paradigm is influenced by the collaboration diagrams of UML [9]. These diagrams are a variety of Object Interaction Diagram, where the behaviour of a (scenario) from a system is depicted. In collaboration diagrams (see Figure 8.1), objects (rather than classes) are shown along with the messages which pass between them. The objects are usually boxes and the messages are arrows. The sequencing is shown by numbering the messages. The reader can then follow a scenario by reading the messages in order. Designers use such a diagram to first convince themselves, then others, that they have a valid behaviour.

Figure 8.1 shows an example of a UML collaboration diagram and also serves to introduce the example which we will use throughout this paper both to introduce ARC and to consider alternative architectures. Figure 8.1 shows an EPOS (Electronic Point-of-Sale) system. It shows three objects: *Till* is the (hardware and

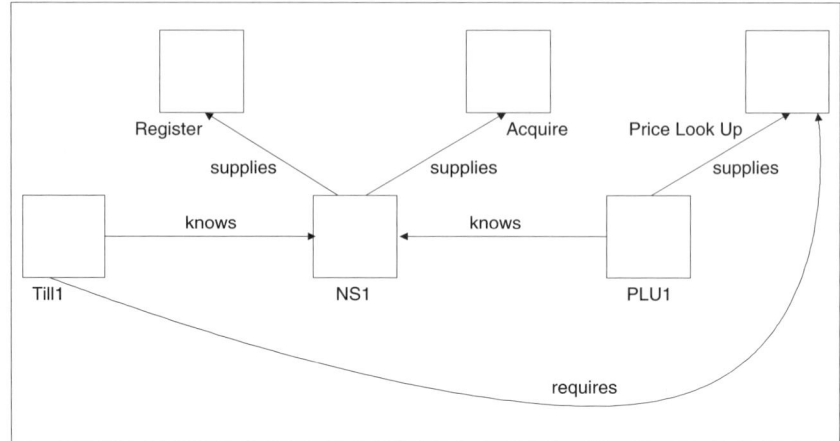

Figure 8.2. An ARC Diagram

software) component where customers' purchases are scanned and paid for; *NS* is the Name Server which (in this client-server architecture) acts as the registry for objects offering and requiring services; and *PLU* is the Price Look Up component which offers the service of supplying prices for purchased items.

The scenario depicted in the UML diagram of Figure 8.1 shows a sequence of three operations: first the *PLU* invokes a *register* operation on *NS* to register its availability as a supplier of the *PriceLookUp* service; then *Till* acquires from *NS* the name (*PLU*) of the supplier of this service; finally the *Till* invokes a look-up-price operation on the *PLU*.

Although inspired by the collaboration diagrams of UML, our paradigm uses a slightly higher level of abstraction. Rather than show messages, we show relationships or associations, between objects. The implication is that, if an appropriate relationship exists between two objects, one may have access to the services of the other. We will illustrate this in detail in what follows. The behavioural aspect of the system that we will then be able to illustrate is the configuration and reconfiguration of those relationships as, in a dynamic system, components first join and then acquire relationships with other components which they intend to use.

In ARC we use the terms component and object interchangeably. We think of objects or components as having state, behaviour and autonomy. That is, they are active, as if they were servers or clients.

Figure 8.2 shows the state of a system in ARC diagrammatic form. There are six components (*Till1*, *PLU1*, *NS1*, *Register*, *Acquire* and *PriceLookUp*) and three relationships (*knows*, *supplies* and *requires*). The diagram depicts the state in which, among other things, *Till1* requires *PriceLookUp*, *PLU1* supplies *PriceLookUp* and while *Till1* does not yet know of *PLU1*, it does know *NS1* which in turn knows *PLU1*. *NS1* is, of course, the Name Server in this distributed system. *Till1* will ask *NS1* for the name of a component which supplies *PriceLookUp*, and as a con-

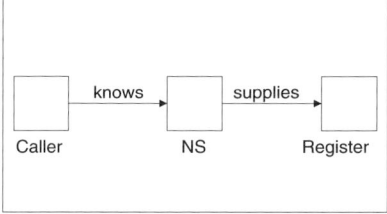 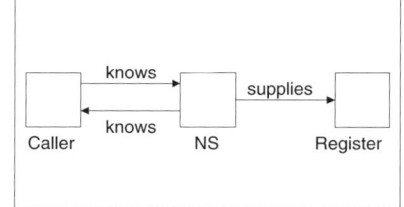

Figure 8.3. The Register Action

sequence the configuration will change dynamically to add the relationship that *Till*1 knows *PLU*1.

In practice, the ARC diagrams become too cluttered to express realistic scenarios, so we use them only to illustrate partial states. They come into their own when a group of engineers are designing a new solution on a whiteboard, because changes to the solution are quickly understood by all the participants. But for formal presentation we use a textual form to capture the full meaning of any situation. That is what we shall use here.

The ARC textual notation is based on logic, and in particular on the use of logic in Prolog strongly influenced by conceptual modelling [4]. A similar use of notation has recently been adopted in Alloy [22].

The state depicted in Figure 8.1 would be expressed by the conjunction

knows(*Till*1, *NS*1)&*knows*(*NS*1, *PLU*1)&*supplies*(*NS*1, *Register*)&
supplies(*NS*1, *Acquire*)&*supplies*(*PLU*1, *PriceLookUp*)&
requires(*Till*1, *PriceLookUp*)

This is how we describe a state, as a conjunction of (usually) binary relations. Next we describe Actions which will enable us to move from state to state. We use Condition-Action rules. Figure 8.3 shows a diagrammatic form of a rule, with the condition to be met depicted in the left-hand box and the state to be moved to depicted in the right hand box. What the Action in Figure 8.3 depicts is the act of registering with a Name Server *NS*. The *Caller* knows *NS* initially, and in the eventual state *NS* knows the *Caller*.

Putting this Action into textual form, we have

register(*Caller*, *NS*) =
knows(*Caller*, *NS*)&*supplies*(*NS*, *Register*)
→ +*knows*(*NS*, *Caller*)

Thus we define actions, which we give names to, which have a side-effect of adding and deleting relationships. Actions have parameters. The addition and deletion of relationships is denoted by + and − signs just in front of the relationship name. An example of relationship-deletion would be the reverse of the Register operation, shown in Figure 8.4.

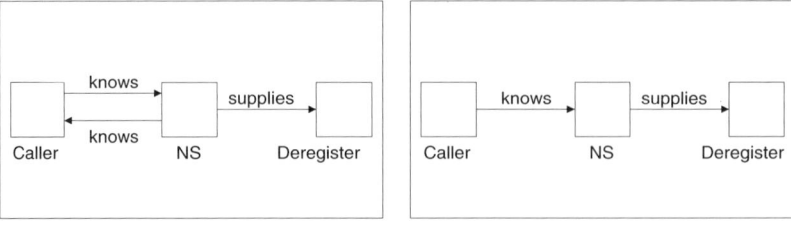

Figure 8.4. The deRegister Action

$deregister(Caller, NS) =$
$knows(Caller, NS) \& knows(NS, Caller) \& supplies(NS, Deregister)$
$\rightarrow -knows(NS, Caller)$

A more complex Action is shown in Figure 8.5. This is the Acquire action that also involves a Name Server. It is the way that components obtain knowledge of others that supply services which they require. The Action depicted in Figure 8.3 has the meaning

$acquire(Caller, NS, Service) = $ **exists** $Object.$
$knows(Caller, NS) \& knows(NS, Object) \& supplies(NS, Acquire) \&$
$supplies(Object, Service) \& requires(Caller, Service)$
$\rightarrow +knows(Caller, Object)$

You can see how this would match a state in which, for example

$knows(Till1, NS1) \& knows(NS1, PLU1)$

and *NS*1, *Till*1 and *PLU*1 are as previously described. So if this action is performed on that state, we would move to a state in which *Till*1 knows *PLU*1, an obviously desirable state of affairs.

This is mostly all there is to ARC. In the formula for *acquire*, the component *Object* has a particular status. It is not a parameter of the operation. It is a local variable, which can match any component that satisfies the relational structure in which it is involved. In logical terms, it is existentially quantified with scope the condition and action parts of the rule. In addition to the logical structures which we have exhibited here, we allow explicit negation, disjunction, implication and universal quantification. Negation could have been used in the formula for *acquire*, for example, to strengthen the condition in such a way as to ensure that the *Caller* did not acquire something which supplied a service which was already supplied by some component which it already knew (add $\neg(knows(Caller, Object1) \& supplies(Object1, Service))$ to the condition).

8.2.2 Validation of models

The models we have made are particular forms of finite state machines, with the states represented by a particular edge-coloured graph, where the nodes are Components, the edges are Relationships and the colours are the actual Relations.

8. Modelling architectures for dynamic systems   167

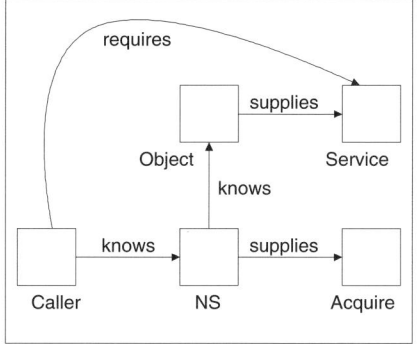 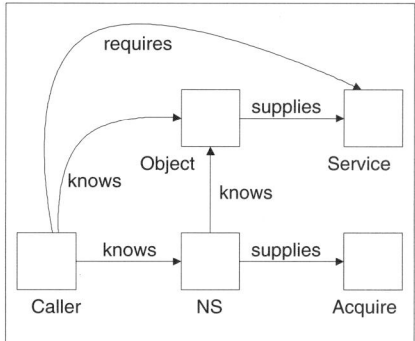

Figure 8.5. The Acquire Action

Transitions between states are accomplished by Actions, which add and remove edges from the graph.

Consequently, validation of the models can be accomplished by various finite-state-machine checking capabilities. In particular, model checking can be used [6, 13, 21, 22, 29]. It is also straightforward to build animations of the models, and this is an effective way for a group of engineers to persuade themselves that their design is complete and consistent, and to look at the consequences, for example, of component failure.

As an example of validating a model, consider the example we have used throughout this introduction to ARC. In the simplest scenario, we might begin in the state

$knows(Till1, NS1) \& knows(PLU1, NS1) \& supplies(NS1, Acquire) \&$
$supplies(NS1, Register) \& requires(Till1, PriceLookUp) \&$
$supplies(PLU1, PriceLookUp)$

Now the reader will realise that the sequence of Actions

$register(PLU1, NS1); acquire(Till1, NS1, PriceLookUp)$

will move us to a situation where, in addition to the above state, we also have the following relationships

$knows(NS1, PLU1) \& knows(Till1, PLU1)$

Figure 8.6 shows the ARC validation tool which supports various types of state space search. The model developed in this section has been presented to the tool which displays three panels each containing a list. The user chooses to instantiate a small number of objects of each type, in this case one Name Server (*NS*1), two Tills (*Till*1 and *Till*2) and two PLUs (*PLU*1 and *PLU*2). The list of Actions displays (in alphabetical order) just those which are effective in that their condition part evaluates to true and their action part will actually change the state. The State list comprises terms in the conjunction which describes part of the (graph representing the) current state in which we have expressed an interest. Selecting

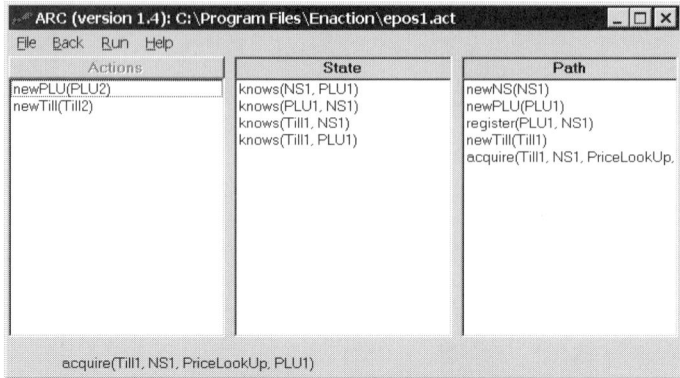

Figure 8.6. The ARC evaluation tool

an action from the Action list applies it to the current state and hence progresses to the next state. The actions which have been invoked so far are shown (this time in sequential order) in the Path list. Various methods of searching the state space are provided.

ARC models can also be translated into Promela [21] in a very straightforward way and executed on the SPIN model-checker. Every relationship of the form $rel(obj1, obj2)$ (that is, every edge potentially in the graph representing the state) is represented as a Promela (bit) variable. Adding the relationship to the state corresponds to setting this variable to true, removing the relationship to setting it to false. Experiments have shown that ARC and SPIN generate the same state machines. Translating to SPIN has the advantage that we can make use of SPIN's mature model-checking capabilities, particularly its performance and its ability to check temporal properties expessed in LTL.

8.3 Architectures for reuse

The client-server architecture which we have used to illustrate our modelling language is an example of a flexible architecture designed for reuse of (Services supplied by) Servers. We have shown that it is able to support the elementary kind of reconfiguration required by the initial marriage of clients to servers. And we can show that it is tolerant of some types of failure and incremental change.

8.3.1 Survival

Consider the following kind of attack on the client-server architecture

$break(Object) =$
all $Service.supplies(Object, Service) \rightarrow$
$-supplies(Object, Service)$

Clearly, if we execute *break(PLU1)* then this can be fixed by the system performing *acquire(Till1, NS1, PriceLookUp)* again, which will locate *PLU2*, assuming it has registered with *NS1*.

Breaking *NS1* with *break(NS1)* is a little more serious, but not immediately. The system continues to function. It runs into trouble after *break(PLU1)*, for now *Till1* cannot find *PLU2*. Unless of course *Till1* had had the foresight to prepare for this eventuality by acquiring *PLU2* even though, having *PLU1*, it didn't strictly need it. But of course, eventually the loss of *NS1* is more serious.

The semantics of creation of new objects gives a telling insight

$$newPLU(PLU) =$$
$$true \rightarrow +knows(PLU, NS1); \ +supplies(PLU, PriceLookUp)$$

The other object creating definitions are similar. In this system, every new object comes into existence knowing the name of the same single registry *NS1*. When *NS1* dies, the system can only deteriorate.

But even here, there is a solution. It has to do with where the initiative for performing actions is assigned. In the model, we have purposely not assigned the actions to the objects. But we should, because we want objects to be autonomous and active. The reason we haven't done this in the model is that we don't want to decide early either who has the initiative or what their goal is. But suppose that all objects know how to invoke *acquire* on objects which supply that service and that their objective (goal) is to acquire as many instances of the objects which supply services which they may be able to use. Then, if *NS2* is created and registers with *NS1*, all the objects which know *NS1* can now acquire *NS2* and thus increase their chances of survival.

Note that formally our architecture requires one of two changes. Either we weaken the condition on *acquire* to omit *requires(Caller, Service)* so that objects can acquire anything, whether they need it or not. Or, we strengthen the requirements of all objects to include *+requires(Object, Acquire)*.

8.3.2 Incremental change

This leads to another consideration of how systems evolve, rather than just survive. Suppose that we plan to upgrade our EPOS system with a new service. For the sake of argument let us assume it is a Loyalty scheme whereby the system identifies the customer at the point-of-sale and offers bespoke services (such as targeted coupons). We will run through one scenario which illustrates this happening.

First we have a new Loyalty Server,

$$newLS(LS) =$$
$$true \rightarrow +knows(LS, NS1); \ +supplies(LS, Loyalty)$$

Then we have a new Till

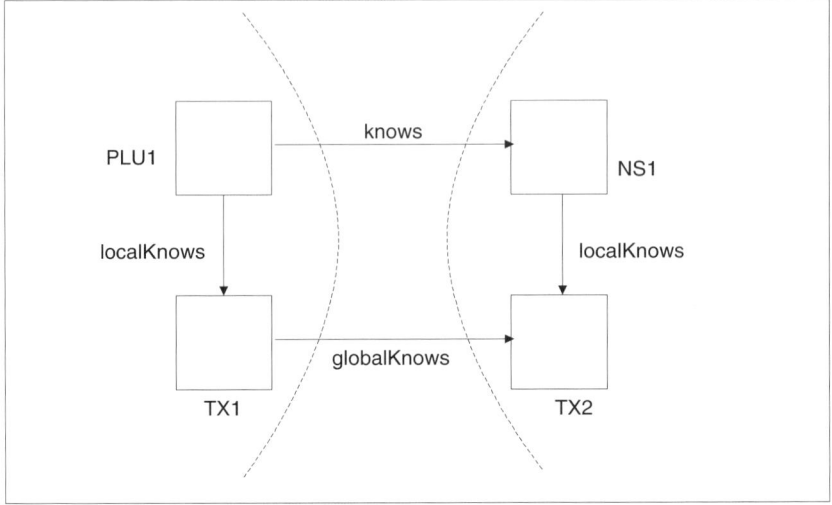

Figure 8.7. Separation of Levels

newLSTill(LSTill) =
  true → +*knows(LSTill, NS1)*;
  +*requires(LSTill, PriceLookUp)*; + *requires(LSTill, Loyalty)*

The interesting question is, if we create *newLSTill(Till1)* say, does it inherit the existing configuration of *Till1*. The formal model says it does. If that is not what we intended, then we need a tighter description.

Suppose we define

exists(Object) =
  exists *relationship.(relationship(Object, Something)* **or**
  relationship(Something, Object))

then we can strengthen the precondition on *newLSTill* to be ¬*exists(LSTill)*.

If however, what we require is to genuinely model the fact that the old *Till1* and the new *Till1* actually share something other than a name, for example that they share the same hardware, then we need to separate the objects which represent the Till application from those that represent the Till hardware. This can be done, but we will not go into it here.

Of course, in all practical cases we must realise that systems are implemented at different levels and we will need to model components at different levels of abstraction. Figure 8.7 shows how this is done. In a high level model, the relationship *knows* will be stored explicitly. In a refinement of that model, the relationship *knows* will be derived from other relationships (stored or derived). Figure 8.7 shows how the *PLU1* and the *NS1*, in separate environments (processes, name spaces, machines etc) come to know each other by a conjunction of relationships, set up presumably by more primitive actions than *acquire*.

$knows(A, B) =$
$localKnows(A, TX1)\&localKnows(B, TX2)\&$
$globalKnows(TX1, TX2)$

8.3.3 Loosely-coupled components

The architectures we are trying to describe to support reuse in the context of constant change, with its consequent need for dynamic reconfiguration, are leading us towards increasingly loosely-coupled components.

The architecture which we have used as our example, the client-server architecture, has some of this looseness of coupling. Dynamic binding is achieved through the use of registry services such as the Name Server which we have used.

As an example of something more loosely coupled consider the following architecture which is a development of the client-server. We don't have specialised Name Servers. Rather, every object is a Name Server. This is achieved by ensuring that every object supplies both *Register* and *Acquire*. Now, on creation, every object must know the name of some other object, but that doesn't have to be always the same object.

Given the initiative to seek out as many new objects as it can, a new object can increase substantially its chances of being able to survive and continue to function, notwithstanding attacks from elsewhere.

8.3.4 It's all a game

We can characterise the fight for survival of a system, or perhaps more accurately the components within the system as a 2-person game. Imagine that the two players are the System itself and the Environment. The System can make a move comprising a sequence of actions, thus moving to a desired state, whereupon it yields. The Environment can then make a move which we presume will break something. The Environment wins if the System gets into a position from which it can not recover to a position which it is required to achieve.

Restricting the Environment to a single break action is a modelling choice, but it does allow us now to specify an interesting property of a System state. The property is an integer which counts the number of moves the System is away from losing.

Consider Figure 8.8. This shows a common situation in the game of survival. Each node in the diagram represents a state of the system and the integer in the circle is the number of moves the System is away from disaster. The game starts at node A. If the System is astute enough always to move to C, whenever it is at A, then the System survives. If it ever moves to D, then there is the chance that the Environment will win by moving to B.

You can see how this metaphor reasonably captures the notation of survival for a dynamic system. We hope to show that it also reasonably captures the notion of incremental change and improvement as the System moves further away from zero. We expect that this will require a considerably more complex numbering

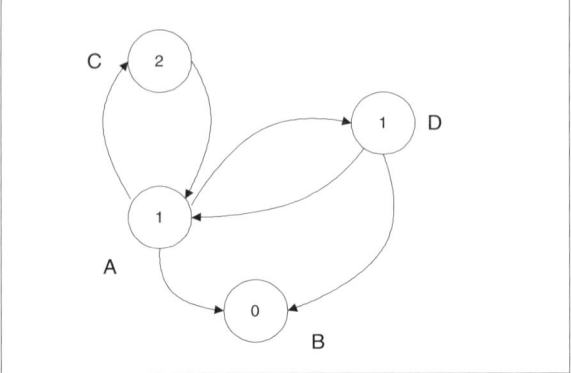

Figure 8.8. Positions in a game of Survival

scheme. We are investigating whether or not we can develop state models based on the game representation schemes devised by Conway [7].

8.4 Conclusions

We have concerned ourselves with the formalisation of dynamic systems, which we have characterised as systems of components that need to reconfigure themselves in order to respond to changes in the requirements upon them. We have shown how systems based on registry services are basically appropriate to this problem and have suggested some refinements to this architecture, specifically generalising the reasons why any component might store information about another. Another extension is to make every component (at a certain level) able to provide the capabilities of a registry.

We have introduced an architecture modelling language, ARC, which adopts the paradigm of modelling systems as objects and relations. This leads to an elementary behavioural description language which we have shown to be powerful enough to describe the systems which we wished to discuss. Validating the properties which we have proposed for solutions is possible using state-space search. We have a tool for doing this which we described briefly. More details, and the tool itself, are available on the web [17]

Further work on architecture modelling is ongoing. In particular we are building models of MQM [8], of Jini [35] and of the Ambients [5] paradigm as well as showing whether or not ARC can model most of the things that other architectural modelling languages can. Of course, theoretically it is possible to show that ARC can represent anything but we are more concerned with the practical use of the paradigm by software architects and software engineers in practice in real industrial scale tasks. We are confident that this objective will be achieved.

References

[1] Abramsky, S and G McCusker. Game Semantics, *see http://dcs.ed.ac.uk/abramsky* .

[2] R. J. Allen and D. Garlan, A Formal Basis For Architectural Connection, *ACM transactions on Software Engineering and Methodology*, July 97.

[3] R. J. Allen, Remi Douence, and David Garlan, Specifying Dynamism in Software Architectures *Workshop of Foundations of Component Based Systems*, Zurich, 1997, see http://www.cs.iastate.edu/ leavens/FoCBS/index.html

[4] M. Boman, J .A . Bubenko, P. Johannesson, and B Wangler, *Conceptual Modelling*, Prentice Hall, 1997.

[5] Luca Cardelli, Abstractions for Mobile Computation. *Microsoft Research Technical Report MSR-TR-98-34* available at research.microsoft.com.

[6] E. M. Clarke et al. Model Checking and Abstraction, *ACM Transactions on Programming Languages and Systems*, Sept. 94.

[7] J. Conway. *On Numbers and Games*, Academic Press, 1976.

[8] A. Dickman. *Designing Applications with MSMQ*, Addison Wesley, 1998.

[9] M. Fowler. *UML Distilled - Applying the standard Object Modelling language*, Addison Wesley, 1997.

[10] David Garlan et al. Architectural Mismatch, or, why it's hard to build systems out of existing parts. *ICSE*, 179–185, 1995.

[11] A. Gravell and P. Henderson. Executing formal specifications need not be harmful, *Software Engineering Journal*, vol. 11, num 2., IEE, 1996.

[12] David N. Gray et al. Modern Languages and Microsoft's Component Object Model. *Communications of the ACM*, Vol 41, No 5, 55–65, 1998.

[13] O. Grumberg and D. Long. Model Checking and Modular Verification, *ACM Transactions on Programming Languages and Systems*, 843–871, May 1994.

[14] M. Heimdahl and N. Leveson. Completeness and Consistency in hierarchical state-based requirements, *IEEE Transactions on Software Enginerring*, 22(6):363–377, 1996.

[15] P. Henderson and G. D. Pratten. POSD - A Notation for Presenting Complex Systems of Processes, *Proceedings of the First IEEE International Conference on Engineering of Complex Systems*, IEEE Computer Society Press, 1995.

[16] Peter Henderson. Laws for Dynamic Systems, *International Conference on Software Re-Use (ICSR 98)*, Victoria, Canada, June 1998, IEEE Computer Society Press.

[17] Peter Henderson. ARC: A language and a tool for system level architecture modelling, July 1999, see http://www.ecs.soton.ac.uk/ ph/arc.htm .

[18] Peter Henderson and Bob Walters. System Design Validation using Formal Models, *Proceedings 10th IEEE Conference on Rapid System Prototyping, RSP'99*, IEEE Computer Society Press, 1999.

[19] Peter Henderson and Bob Walters. Component Based systems as an aid to Design Validation, *Proceedings 14th IEEE Conference on Automated Software Engineering, ASE'99*, IEEE Computer Society Press, 1999.

[20] C. A. R. Hoare. How did Software get to be so reliable without proof? *Keynote address at the 18th International Conference on Software Engineering*. IEEE Computer Society Press, 1996. See also http://www.comlab.ox.ac.uk/oucl/users/tony.hoare/publications.html .

[21] G. J. Holtzmann. The Model Checker SPIN, *IEEE Transactions on Software Engineering*, Vol 23, No 5, 279–295, 1997.

[22] D. Jackson. Alloy: A lightweight Object Modelling Notation, available at http://sdg.lcs.mit.edu/ dnj/abstracts.html, July 1999.

[23] R. Kurki-Suoni. Component and Interface Refinement in Closed-System Specifications, *Proceedings of World Congress on Fomal Methods, Toulouse, September 1999*, LNCS 1709, 134–154.

[24] D. C. Luckham et al. Specification and Analysis of System Architecture using Rapide, *IEEE Transactions on Software Engineering*, 21(4):336–355, April 1995.

[25] D. C. Luckham and J. Vera. An event-based architecture definition language, *IEEE Transactions on Software Engineering*, 21(9):717–734, September 1995.

[26] D. C. Luckham. Rapide: A language and toolset for simulation of distributed systems by partial orderings of events, http://pavg.stanford.edu .

[27] J. Magee and J. Kramer. Dynamic Structure in Software Architecture, *Proceeedings of the ACM Conference on Foundations of Software Engineering*, Software Engineering Notes, 21(6):3–14, IEEE Computer Society Press, 1996.

[28] J. Magee, N. Dulay, S. Eisenbach, and J. Kramer. Specifying Distributed Software Architectures, *Proceedings of 5th European Software Engineering Conference (ESEC 95)*, Sitges, Spain, LNCS 989, 137–154, September 1995.

[29] J. Magee and J. Kramer. Concurrency: State Models and Java Programs, Wiley, 1999.

[30] Object Management Group. Common Object Request Broker: Architecture Specification, http://www.omg.com .

[31] M. Shaw et al. Abstractions for Software Architecture and Tools to Support Them, *IEEE Transactions on Software Engineering*, 21(4) 314–335, April 1995.

[32] M. Shaw and D. Garlan. *Software Architecture - Perspectives on an emerging discipline*. Prentice Hall, 1996.

[33] K. Sullivan J. C. Knight. Experience Assessing an Architectural Approach to Large Scale Reuse, *Proceedings of ICSE-18*, 1996 IEEE Computer Society Press.

[34] K. Sullivan, J. Socha, and M. Marchukov. Using Formal Methods to Reason about Architectural Standards, *19th International Conference on Software Engineering*, Boston, IEEE Computer Press, 1997.

[35] Sun Microsystems. Jini Software Simplifies Network Computing, available at www.sun.com/jini .

[36] D. Wile. AML: an Architecture Meta-Language, *Proceedings ASE 1999*, IEEE Computer Society Press, pp 183-190.

9

"What is a method?" — an essay on some aspects of domain engineering

Dines Bjørner

Abstract

We discuss a concept of **method** in terms of its postulated **principles, techniques** and **tools** for the realm of software engineering. Software engineering is here seen as a confluence of *domain engineering, requirements engineering* and *software design*. Our scope is the concept of *domains* and *domain engineering,* and, our span is the concept of *domain facets*. We shall briefly contrast these with *domain attributes* such as for example put forward by Michael Jackson [1]. For the *domain facet* area of software development we then identify, exemplify and investigate, the latter rather briefly, a number of *domain facet* development principles and techniques. The main contributions of this essay are believed to be the identification of the *domain facet* concept, and the collection (including identification), classification, part investigation, and "fitting into a larger whole", of *domain facet* principles and techniques, as well as the thereby substantiated claim that these principles and techniques help characterise methods.

The essay has technical examples, but they are merely sketches. Had they been more substantial, the essay would not have been an essay. More substantial examples are given elsewhere[1]

9.1 Introduction

9.1.1 Domains, Requirements and Software Design

We assume the basic dogma: Before *software* can be *designed* it must be *requirements specified*. And before *requirements* can be expressed, an understanding of the world in which these *requirements* reside, the *domain*, must be formulated.

---

[1] See the author's lecture notes: http://www.imm.dtu.dk/~db/setap/contents.ps

The *software design* describes how a computer (the hardware) is to proceed in order to achieve stated *requirements*. The *requirements* usually describe three things: (1) Which phenomena of the *domain* shall be supported by computing (the *domain requirements*); (2) which interface between the *machine* (*hardware + software*) and external phenomena — People, and other sensors and actuators — shall be provided (the *interface requirements*); and (3) what performance, dependability, maintenance, platform, and documentation measures are expected (the *machine requirements*).

Domain descriptions are **indicative**: Describe the "chosen world as it is", i.e. the *domain* — without any reference to *requirements*, let alone *software design*. Requirements prescriptions are **putative**: Prescribe what there is to be — properties, not designs, of the *machine*.

Domain descriptions must describe the chosen *domain* with its imperfections, not try to "paint a picture" of a "world as one would like it to be". In this essay we shall focus on such *domain descriptions*.

In this essay we shall not touch upon the methodological principles, techniques and tools that allow the software developer, based on formal descriptions of the domain to rigorously *project, instantiate, extend* and *initialise* a *domain description* "into" a *domain requirements definition*, and, from *domain* and *interface requirements definitions*, to similarly rigorously develop *software architecture designs*. We cover such principles, techniques and tools in other papers, e.g. [2, 3, 4, 5], and in our lecture notes.

We summarise:

- **Domains**

- **Requirements**

- **Software Design:**
    - **Software Architecture**
    - **Program Organisation**
    - **Etc. — Coding**

9.1.2 The Problem to be Addressed

In this essay we shall study some aspects of domain engineering only.

The overall problem that we are generally studying is that of **methods** for the development of large scale, typically infrastructure component software systems.

Excluded from our **software development method** concerns are therefore those related to the discovery, the invention of **algorithms & data structures**, for well-delineated problems such as sorting and searching, graph operations, fast Fourier transforms, parsing, *etc.* The borderline between **infrastructure software systems** and **algorithms and & structures** is indeed a fuzzy one — and one that we really do not wish to further investigate here. Suffice it to say that the **infrastructure software systems** we have in mind will indeed contain many examples of **algorithms & data structures** ! But as concerns the principles and techniques of methods — we only claim that we investigate some that are deemed applicable to infrastructure software systems development.

9.1.3 Aspirations

The current author's ambition is to understand — in a comprehensive manner — suitable complements of principles and techniques for software development: *Where to start, how to proceed, and when to end.*

As forcefully pointed out by Jackson [1, 6, 7, 8], no one method suffices for all software development. Compilers seems best developed using one approach [9, 10, 11, 12], while real-time embedded and safety critical systems are perhaps best developed using an altogether different approach [13, 14, 15, 16].

Many software development principles and techniques transcend, however, their use in the development of individual, (frame) specific program packages and software systems. This essay is about such development issues.

9.1.4 Structure of Essay

In Section 9.2 we put forward a characterisation of what we consider to be a **method**, with its **principles, teachniques,** and **tools,** for (efficiently) **analysing** and **synthesizing**, i.e. **constructing,** (efficient, in this case) software.

The main section, Section 9.3, has two parts:

In Section 9.3.1 we look at problems of modelling the concerns of *stake-holders:* Their *perspective* on the domain[2].

In Section 9.3.2 we then look at a number of what we term *domain facets:* We currently list five such facets: *Intrinsics, support technology, management & organisation, rules & regulations* and *human behaviour.* Singling those out for individual, or otherwise clearly identified, modelling, we claim, satisfies an overall **principle,** that of **separation of concerns,** and seems to lead to more elegant descriptions.

Section 9.3 follows up on Section 9.2 in which we delineate what we, in general, see to be **methods, methodology, principles, techniques,** and **tools.**

9.1.5 Some Typographical Conventions

The text alternates between paragraphs which either contain plain text, or `characterises`, or `defines` a concept, which are then usually followed by paragraphs which `discuss` the concept, and paragraphs which state a `principle`, a `technique`, or a `tool`. We use the ∎ delimiter to show the end of the `specialised paragraphs`.

---

[2] As these stake-holders will also, later (but not to be covered in this essay) have a perspective on requirements

We make a distinction between characterisations and definitions: The former are (oftentimes necessarily) informal, the latter sometimes formalisable.

9.2 Method and Methodology

The notions of **method** and **methodology** are being "bandied about": "Some rules for engineering conduct", "some notation", or other, is claimed to be 'a method'. Some 'methods' are claimed to be 'formal'. In this section we take a first look at what might constitute a **method**. And we make a necessary distinction between method and **methodology**.

9.2.1 Method

Characterisation: *Method.* By a **method** we understand a set of **principles** for `selecting` amongst, and `applying`, a set of designated **techniques** and **tools** such which allow *analysis* and *construction* of artefacts. ∎

Discussion: The `selections` (of *analysis* and *synthesis* **techniques** and **tools**) and some of the *deployments* (of these **techniques** and **tools**) are to be carried out by people. The **principles** are usually of such a nature as to guide the developer, not to interfere with that person's possible ingenuity and creativeness, that person's ability to discover, to reflect and be skeptic. Hence we cannot ever expect to get anywhere near a formalisation of such **principles**. Therefore the term 'formal method' is unfortunate. Better would be **formal techniques** and **formally based tools**. Even better, to paraphrase Michel Sintzoff, would be to speak of **logical** or **precise techniques** and **tools**, as informal such are very much needed, but illogical or imprecise not. ∎

9.2.2 Methodology

Characterisation: *Methodology.* By **methodology** we understand the study of and knowledge about **methods**. ∎

Discussion: The two terms 'method' and 'methodology' are often used interchangeably — especially, it seems, in the US. ∎

9.2.3 Method Constituents

Discussion: The above 'method' characterisation identifies the following concepts: **principle**, *analysis*, **construction**, **technique**, **tool**, and 'artefact'. We need characterise these concepts. In the following we focus on domain descriptions as being the artefacts of interest. ∎

Principle

Characterisation: *Principle (I).* We quote from [17]: "An accepted or professed rule of action or conduct, ..., a fundamental doctrine, right rules of conduct, ...". ∎

Discussion: The concept of 'principle' is "fluid". Usually, by a method, some people understand an orderliness. Our 'definition' makes the orderliness part of the overall principles. Also: One usually expects analysis and construction to be efficient and to result in efficient artefacts. This too we relegate to be implied by some principles, techniques and tools. ∎

Characterisation: *Principle (II).* We make here the distinction between *development principles* (δ), and principles related to *concepts* (γ) of domain other than software development. We highlight the former by the texts "The Development Principle of δ", and the latter by the texts "The Principle of Modelling the γ Domain Concept". ∎

Analysis

Characterisation: *Analysis* is performed on descriptions. There seem to be three kinds of analysis. (i–ii) Informal validation or formal verification, including proof or model checking. This kind of analysis is performed, typically on narratives[3], respectively on formal texts. Such analyses lead to statements (i.e. meta-linguistic document texts) such as *"Such-and-such description text(s) denotes such-and--such properties"* ('is correct', or 'is not correct' [relating one part of the text to another], or 'denotes an NP-complete problem', etc.). (iii) Analysis performed on rough sketches, are not formalisable, but have the aim of forming concepts. ∎

Discussion: Descriptions describe some universe of discourse. We may claim that we are analysing that universe, but really, it is the model of that universe, in the form of some description, that we analyse. ∎

Construction [or: Synthesis]

Characterisation: *Construction* (or: *Synthesis*) means: The creation of a description, and thereby of a theory: A collection of properties that can be deduced

---

[3] We take it for granted that software development (in each (*domain, requirements* or *software design*) phase, and for each refinement or other development stage within phases, and for steps within stages) aims at constructing a number of documents: (a) informative, (b) descriptive — both informal and formal — and (c) analytic. Within informal descriptions we distinguish between those that are [non–deliverable] rough sketches — where rough sketches, often contain rough formalisations, cf. Example of Section 9.3.1 — and those that are narratives and terminologies. Informative documents inform about the development. Descriptions "inform" about (i.e. describe) a universe of discourse, as here: domain. And analyses "inform" about (i.e. analyse) descriptions; they are, in that sense, meta–linguistic.

from that description. The creation involves elicitation (acquisition), writing, analysis, rewriting, analysis again, rewriting, etc. ∎

Discussion: Writing informative or analytical documents may not be considered construction. They are necessary documents, but they do not describe manifest phenomena in the domain. ∎

Technique

Characterisation: *Technique.* [17]: "Method or technical skill, ...". ∎

Discussion: Already here we see a possible conflict: Our characterisation of 'method' involves the term 'technique' which by [17] is defined in terms of the term 'method'. We shall use the term 'technique' in the sense of the, or a specific 'procedure', 'routine' or 'approach' that characterises the technical skill. ∎

Tool

Characterisation: *Tool.* [17]: "An instrument for performing mechanical operations, a person used by another for his own ends, ..., to work or shape with a tool, ...". ∎

Discussion: We shall use the term tool in a wider sense: Any language is a tool, so is paper & pencil, blackboard & chalk, and so is any software package. Indeed, with language we shape concepts. ∎

9.2.4 The Method Principles

If, as we are now claiming, one can indeed identify a set of principles, techniques and tools that apply, conditionally, in a number of development situations, then these principles, techniques and tools ought probably also be deployed. Hence:

The Development Principle of *'Methodicity'* — *being Methodical* is now that of actually deploying relevant domain [and requirements] engineering [as well as software design] principles, techniques and tools during software development. ∎

Discussion: The hedge here is, obviously, the term 'relevant'. There is thus another meta-principle buried here. ∎

The Development Principle of *'Development Choice'* is a meta-principle, a 'conditional' that is part of every principle, technique and tool characterisation — is: Apply only a principle, a technique or a tool if its pre–conditions are met. ∎

The Meta–Technique of *'Methodicity'* expresses that, in respective phases of software development, one adheres to a list of (i) general abstraction & modelling, (ii) domain attribute, perspective and facet, (iii) domain requirements projection, instantiation, extension and initialisation, (iv) interface and (v) machine requirements, (vi) software architecture, (vii) program organisation — and many other program design — principles, techniques and tools, ensuring that all due consideration is paid to these in the development. ∎

Discussion: In the current paper we shall only cover domain perspective and facet principles and techniques. In other papers and in lecture notes available over the net we cover many of the other principles and techniques mentioned above. ∎

The Meta–Technique of *'Development Choice'* expresses, relative to the previous 'methodicity' techniques, that for each of these one carefully writes down the assumptions upon which a choice of specific principle, technique or tool was deployed. ∎

Discussion: We have not, in this pape, for the sake of print space, enunciated these conditionals explicitly: They are, however, part of, and hence transpire indirectly from our coverage. ∎

9.2.5 *Discussion*

We have risked some debate as to whether the above delineations of what might constitute a method form a suitable basis.

Since 'methods' are to be deployed primarily by humans we prefer to characterise than to define. Definitions seem to have something more definite, more absolute about them. Characterisations seem more at ease.

Some may argue that the method principles, techniques and tool that we shall now endeavour to enumerate and investigate may unduly constrain the ingenuity of software developers: That having to follow these principles, to use those techniques and to deploy those tools may stifle their creativity. We believe the contrary: That the principles set the developer free, that having recognized techniques and tools allow the developer to focus on concepts, and put the mind to work on those: thinking, rather than "bureaucratic" labouring.

9.3   Domain Perspectives and Facets

We treat the subject of domain engineering in two parts. First we consider the plethora of stake-holders, that is: Individuals and institutions that are more-or-less interested in, or influenced by what goes on in the domain. Then we consider a concept of domain facets.

Thus we omit consideration of domain attributes ((i) *static* and *dynamic*, (ii) *tangible* and *intangible*, (iii) **configuration** spectra between **contexts** and **states**, (iv) **time, space** and **space–time**, (v) **discreteness, continuity** and **chaos**, (vi) **hierarchies** and **compositions**, and many others)[4] — *some of which, (i–ii), have been put forward by Michael Jackson* [1].

---

[4]This omission is due to page limitations. A proper study of 'methods', 'principles', 'techniques', and 'tools', would benefit, it is believed, from more comprehensive comparisons.

Domain attributes and domain facets are different: Attributes of different domain entities can be modelled more or less independently, i.e. "in parallel" ! In contrast, one usually tackles the description of a domain facet-by-facet. The domain attributes (tangibility, statics vs. dynamics, etc.) are not exclusively domain attributes: One may reasonably claim that during subsequent development phases (after domain engineering: Requirements engineering and software design) one may also reconsider (hence: New) deployments of attendant attribute principles and techniques.

Modelling stake-holder perspectives, domain attributes and domain facets otherwise takes place, during development, "concurrently": One alternates "to-and-from" iteratively.

There are additional description principles that we also do not cover: **Property** versus **model oriented specification, representational** and **operational abstraction, denotational** vs. **computational models**, etc. They "belong" in a class of modelling issues that we consider different from those of attributes and facets.

Our choice of the term 'facet' is just a choice. Whatever term was chosen, it had to be different from the term 'attribute'. Maybe for that other ("belong") class of modelling issues, just referred to above, we could then choose the term 'aspects' !

9.3.1 Stake–holders and Stake–holder Perspectives

Stake-holders

Characterisation: *Stake–holder.* By a stake–holder we mean a closely knit, tightly related group of either people or institutions, pressure groups — where the "fabric" that "relates" members of the group, "separates" these from other such stake-holder groups, and from non-stake-holder entities. ∎

Discussion: We shall not here try establish an ontology for the stake-holder concept. If one tried, that ontology would, on one hand, need to deal with issues of 'part of' and 'whole', as for system and component ontologies, and, on the other hand, since we are dealing mostly with human institutions, the ontology would probably have to incorporate a fuzzy membership notion. ∎

Examples: *Stake–holders* include enterprise staff: (i) owners, (ii) management (a) executive management (b) line management, and (c) "floor", i.e. operations management, and (iii) workers of all kinds, (iv) families of the above, (v) the customers of the enterprise, (vi) competitors, and the external, "2nd tier" stake–holders: (vii) resource providers (a) IT resource providers[5], (b) non–IT/non–finance [6], and (c) financial service providers, (viii) regulatory agencies

---

[5] Viz.: Computer hardware and other IT equipment, software houses, facilities management, etc.
[6] Viz.: Consumable goods, leasing agencies, etc.

who oversee enterprise operations[7], (ix) local and state authorities, (x) politicians, and the (xi) "public at large". They all have a perspective on the enterprise. . ▪

Discussion: It always makes good, commercial as well as technical, sense to incorporate the views of as many stake–holder groups as are relevant in the software development process. One need not refer to social, including so-called democratic, reasons for this inclusion. It is simply more fun to make sure that one has indeed understood as much of the domain (and, for that matter, as much of possible requirements) as is feasible, before embarking on subsequent, costly software development phases. ▪

The Principle of Modelling the *Stake–holder* **Concept** expresses that the developer and the client, when setting out on a domain description, clearly defines which stake-holders must be recognised and duly involved in the development. ▪

Technique of Modelling the *Stake–holder* **Concept**: Consider modelling each stake-holder group as a process, or a set of processes (i.e. behaviour[s]), or define suitable stake-holder specific context and/or state components and associated (observer and generator) functions. ▪

Stake-holder Perspectives

Characterisation: *Stake–holder Perspective*. By a stake–holder perspective we mean a partial description, a description which emphasises the designations, definitions and refutable assertions[8] that are particular to a given stake-holder group, or the interface between pairs, etc., of such. ▪

Discussion: Each perspective usually gives rise to a distinct view of the domain. These views share properties. A good structuring of the "totality" of perspectives can be helped by suitable, usually algebraic specification langauge constructs, such as possibly the class, scheme and object constructs of the **RAISE** [18] Specification Language **RSL** [19]. We shall not illustrate this point at present. ▪

The Principle of Modelling the *Stake–holder Perspective* **Concept** expresses that the developer and the client, when setting out on a domain description together, suitably as part of the contract, clearly defines which stake-holder perspectives must be recognised and duly included in the descriptions. ▪

Example: *Strategic, Tactical and Operations Resource Management*. We now present a rather lengthy example. It purports to illustrate the interface between a number of stake-holder perspectives. The stake-holders are here: An enterprises's top level, executive management (which plan, takes and follows up on strategic decisions), its line management (which plan, takes and follows up on tactical decisions), its operations management (which plan, takes and follows up on operational decisions), and the enterprise "workers" (who carry out decisions through

---

[7] Viz.: Environment bureaus, financial industry authorities (e.g.: The US Federal Reserve Board), food and drug administration (e.g.: The US FDA), health authorities (e.g.: The US HEW), etc., depending on the enterprise.

[8] Designations, definitions and refutable assertions are concepts defined in [1].

tasks). Strategic management here has to do with upgrading or downsizing, i.e. converting an enterprise's resources from one form to another — making sure that resources are available for tactical management. Tactical management here has to do with temporally scheduling and spatially allocating these resources, in preparation for operations management. Operations management here makes final scheduling and allocation, but now to tasks, in preparation for actual enterprise ("floor") operations.

Let R, Rn, L, T, E and A stand for resources, resource names, spatial locations, times, enterprises (with their estimates, service and/or production plans, orders on hand, etc.), respectively tasks (actions). SR, TR and OR stand for strategic, tactical and operational resource views, respectively.[9] SR expresses (temporal) schedules: Which sets of resources are either bound or free in which (pragmatically speaking: overall, i.e. "larger") time intervals. TR expresses temporal and spatial allocations of sets of resources, in certain (pragmatically speaking: mode finer "grained", i.e. "smaller") time intervals, and to certain locations. OR expresses that certain actions, A, are to be, or are being, applied to (parameter–named) resources in certain time intervals.

type R, Rn, L, T, E, A
  RS = **R-set**
  SR = (T×T) $\overrightarrow{m}$ RS,   SRS = SR-**infset**
  TR = (T×T) $\overrightarrow{m}$ RS $\overrightarrow{m}$ L,   TRS = TR-**set**
  OR = (T×T) $\overrightarrow{m}$ RS $\overrightarrow{m}$ A
  A = (Rn $\overrightarrow{m}$ RS) $\xrightarrow{\sim}$ (Rn $\overrightarrow{m}$ RS)
value
  obs_Rn: R → Rn
  srm: RS → E×E $\xrightarrow{\sim}$ E × (SRS × SR)
  trm: SR → E×E $\xrightarrow{\sim}$ E × (TRS × TR)
  orm: TR → E×E $\xrightarrow{\sim}$ E × OR
  p: RS × E → **Bool**
  ope: OR → TR → SR → (E×E×E×E) → E × RS

The partial, including loosely specified, and in cases the non-deterministic functions: srm, trm and orm stand for strategic, tactical, respectively operations resource management. p is a predicate which determines whether the enterprise can continue to operate (with its state and in its environment, e), or not. To keep our model "small", we have had to resort to a "trick": Putting all the facts knowable and needed in order for management to function adequately into E ! Besides

---

[9]In the formalisation, take for example that of OR, i.e.: OR = (T×T) $\overrightarrow{m}$ RS $\overrightarrow{m}$ A = defines OR to be the type of maps ($\overrightarrow{m}$) fro time periods (intervals (T×T)) into maps from sets of resources RS into actions (A) [to be performed on these resources during the stated time interval]. These actions are partial functions ($\xrightarrow{\sim}$) from argument (Rn) named sets of resources (RS) into similarly such named results.

9. "What is a method?" — an essay on some aspects of domain engineering

the enterprise itself, E also models its environment: That part of the world which affects the enterprise.

There are, accordingly, the following management functions:

Strategic resource management, srm(rs)(e,e''''),let us call the result (e',(srs,sr)) [see "definition" of the enterprise "function" below],proceeds on the basis of the enterprise (e) and its current resources (rs), and "ideally estimates" all possible strategic resource acquisitions (upgrading) and/or downsizings (divestmments) (srs), and selects one, desirable strategic resource schedule (sr). The "estimation" is heuristic. Too little is normally known to compute sr algorithmically. One can, however, based on careful analysis of srm's pre/post conditions, usually provide some form of computerised decision support for strategic management.

Tactical resource management, trm(sr)(e,e''''),let us call the result(e'',(trs,tr)), proceeds on the basis of the enterprise (e) and one chosen strategic resource view (sr) and "ideally calculates" all possible tactical resource possibilities (trs), and selects one, desirable tactical resource schedule & allocation (tr). Again trm can not be fully algorithmitised. But some combinations of partial answer computations and decision support can be provided.

Operations resource management, orm(tr)(e,e''''),let us call the result(e''',or), proceeds on the basis of the enterprise (e) and one chosen tactical resource view (tr) and effectively decides on one operations resource view (or). Typically orm can be algorithmitised — applying standard operations research techniques.

We refer to [20] for details on the above and below model.

Actual enterprise operation, ope, enables, but does not guarantee, some "common" view of the enterprise: ope depends on the views of the enterprise, its context, state and environment, e, as "passed down" by management; and ope applies, according to prescriptions kept in the enterprise context and state, actions, a, to named (rn:Rn) sets of resources.

The above account is, obviously, rather "idealised". But we hope it is indicative of what is going on. To give a further abstraction of the "life cycle" of the enterprise, we "idealise" it, as now shown:

value
    enterprise: RS $\xrightarrow{\sim}$ E $\xrightarrow{\sim}$ **Unit**
    enterprise(rs)(e) $\equiv$
        if p(rs)(e) **then**
            let (e',(srs,sr)) = srm(rs)(e,e''''),
                (e'',(trs,tr)) = trm(sr)(e,e''''),
                (e''',or) = orm(tr)(e,e''''),
                (e'''',rs') = ope(or)(tr)(sr)(e,e',e'',e''') **in**
            let e''''':E • p'(e'''',e''''') **in**
            enterprise(rs')(e''''') **end end**
        else stop end

    p': E × E → **Bool**

The enterprise re-invocation argument, rs′, a result of operations, is intended to reflect the use of strategially, tactically and operationally acquired, spatially and task allocated and scheduled resources, including partial consumption, "wear & tear", loss, replacements, etc.

The **let** e′′′′′:E • p′(e′′′′,e′′′′′) **in** ... shall model a changing environment.

Thus there were two forms of recursion at play here: The simple tail-recursion, and the recursive "build-up" of the enterprise state e′′′′. The latter is the interesting one. Solution, by iteration towards some acceptable, not necessarily minimal fix-point, "mimics" the way the three levels of management and the "floor" operations change that state and "pass it around, up-&-down" the management "hierarchy". The **operate** function "unifies" the views that different management levels have of the enterprise, and influences their decision making. Dependence on E also models potential interaction between enterprise management and, conceivably, all other stake-holders. ∎

Discussion: We remind the reader that — in the previous example — we are "only" modelling the domain ! That model is, obviously, sketchy. But we believe it portrays important facets of domain modelling and stake-holder perspectives. The stake–holders were, to repeat: Strategy ("executive") management (srm, p), tactical ("line") management (trm), operations ("floor") management (orm), and the workers (ope). The perpective being modelled focused on two aspects: Their individual jobs, as "modelled" by the "functions" (srm, p, trm, orm, ope), and their interactions, as "modelled" by the passing around of arguments (e, e′, e′′, e′′′, e′′′′) The **let** e′′′′′:E • p′(e′′′′,e′′′′′) **in** ... which "models" the changing environment is thus summarising the perspectives of "all other" stake–holders ! We are modelling a domain with all its imperfections: We are not specifying anything algorithmically; all functions are rather loosely, hence partially defined, in fact only their signature is given. This means that we model well-managed as well as badly, sloppily, or disastrously managed enterprises. We can, of course, define a great number of predicates on the enterprise state and its environment (e:E), and we can partially characterise intrinsics — facts that must always be true of an enterprise, no matter how.

If we "programme-specified" the enterprise then we would not be modelling the domain of enterprises, but a specifically "business process engineered" enterprise. Or we would be into requirements engineering — we claim. ∎

Technique of Modelling the *Stake–holder Perspective* Concept: Emphasize how the distinct stake-holders interact, which phenomena in the domian they generate, share, or consume. This 'technique' follows up on the 'Stake–holder' modelling technique. ∎

Discussion

The stake-holder example given above is "sketchy". It identifies, we believe, the most important entities and operations that are relevant to a small number of interacting stake-holders. We believe that "rough sketches" like the above are necessary in the iterative development of domains.

9.3.2 Domain Facets

We shall outline the following facets:

Domain intrinsics: That which is common to all facets.

Domain support technologies: That in terms of which several other facets (intrinsics, management & organisation, and rules & regulations) are implemented.

Domain management & organisation: That which primarily determines and constrains communication between enterprise stake-holders.

Domain rules & regulations: That which guides the work of enterprise stake-holders, their interaction, and the interaction with non-enterprise stake-holders.

Domain human behaviour: The way in which domain stake-holders despatch their actions and interactions with respect to enterprise: dutifully, forgetfully, sloppily — yes, even criminally.

We shall briefly characterise each of these facets. We venture to express "specification patterns" that "most closely capture" essences of the facet.

Separating the treatment of each of these (and possibly other) facets reflect a principle:

The Development Principle of *Separation of Concerns* expresses that when possible one should separate distinguishable concerns and treat them separately. ▪

Discussion: We believe that the facets we shall present can be treated separately in most developments — but not necessarily always. Separation or not is a matter also of development as well as of presentation style.

The separation, in more generality, of computing systems development into the triptych of domain engineering, requirements engineering and machine (hardware + software) design, is also a result of separation of concerns — as are the separations of domain requirements, interface requirements and machine requirements (within requirements engineering), as well as the separations of software architecture and program organisation design [3]. ▪

Intrinsics

The Concept

Characterisation: *Intrinsics:* That which is common to all facets. ▪

An Example

Example: *Rail nets and switches.* We first give a summary view of a domain model for railway nets, first informally, then formally, leaving out axioms: A railway net consists of two or more stations and one or more lines. Nets, lines and stations consists of rail units. A rail unit is either a linear unit, or a switch unit, or a crossover unit, etc. Units have connectors. A linear unit has two connectors, a switch unit has three, a crossover unit has four, etc. A line is a linear sequence of connected linear units. A station usually has all kinds of units. A line connects exactly two distinct stations. A station contains one or more tracks (say, pragmatically, for passenger platforms or for cargo sidings). A path is a pair of connectors of a unit, and pragmatically defines a way for a train to traverse that unit. A unit is at any one time in a state (σ), which we may consider a set of paths. Over a lifetime a unit may attain one or another state in that unit's state space (ω).

type
   N, L, S, U, C
value
   obs_Ls: N $\to$ L-set, obs_Ss: N $\to$ S-set,
   obs_Us: (N|L|S) $\to$ U-set, obs_Cs: U $\to$ C-set
   obs_Trs: S $\to$ Tr-set
type
   P$'$ = U $\times$ (C$\times$C), Σ = P-set, Ω = Σ-set
   P = {| p:P$'$ • **let** (u,(c,c$'$))=p **in** (c,c$'$)$\in$ obs_Σ(u) **end** |}
value
   obs_Σ: U $\to$ Σ, obs_Ω: U $\to$ Ω

From the perspective of a train passenger or a cargo customer it is not part of the intrinsics that nets have units and units have connectors. Therefore also paths, states and state–spaces are not part of the intrinsics of a net as seen from such stake–holders.

From the perspective of the train driver and of those who provide the setting of switches and signalling in general, units, paths, and states are indeed part of the intrinsics: The intrinsics of a rail switch is that it can take on a number of states. A simple switch ($^{c_|}Y^{c_/}_c$) has three connectors: $\{c, c_|, c_/\}$. c is the connector of the common rail from which one can either "go straight" $c_|$, or "fork" $c_/$.

ω_{g_s} : { {},
   $\{(c,c_|)\}, \{(c,c_|),(c_|,c)\}, \{(c_|,c)\}$,
   $\{(c,c_/)\}, \{(c,c_/),(c_/,c)\}, \{(c_/,c)\}$,
   $\{(c,c_/),(c_|,c)\}, \{(c,c_/),(c_/,c),(c_|,c)\}, \{(c_/,c),(c_|,c)\}$ }

ω_{g_s} ideally models a general switch. Any particular switch ω_{p_s} may have $\omega_{p_s} \subset \omega_{g_s}$. Nothing is said about how a state is determined: Who sets and resets it, whether determined solely by the physical position of the switch gear, or also by visible or virtual (i.e. invisible, intangible) signals up or down the rail away from the switch.

■

Methodological Consequences

The Principle of Modelling the *Intrinsics* Domain Facet expresses that in any modelling one first form and describe the intrinsic concepts. ■

Technique of Modelling the *Intrinsics* Domain Facet: The intrinsics model of a domain is a partial specification. As such it involves the use of well–nigh all description principles. Typically we resort to property oriented models, i.e. sorts and axioms. ■

Discussion

Thus the intrinsics become part of every one of the next facets. From an algebraic semantics point of view these latter are extension of the above.

Support Technologies

The Concept

Characterisation: *Support Technology* — that in terms of which several other facets (intrinsics, management & organisation, and rules & regulations) are implemented. ∎

An Example

Example: *Railway switches.* An example of different technology *stimuli:* A railway switch, "in ye olde days" of the "childhood" of railways, was *manually "thrown"*; later it could be mechanically controlled from a distance by *wires and momentum "amplification"*; again later it could be electro-mechanically controlled from a further distance by *electric signals that then activated mechanical controls*; and today switches are usually *controlled in groups that are electronically interlocked*.

An aspect of supporting technology includes the recording of state-behaviour in response to external stimuli. Figure 9.1 indicates a way of formalising this aspect of a supporting technology.

Figure 9.1. Probabilistic State Switching

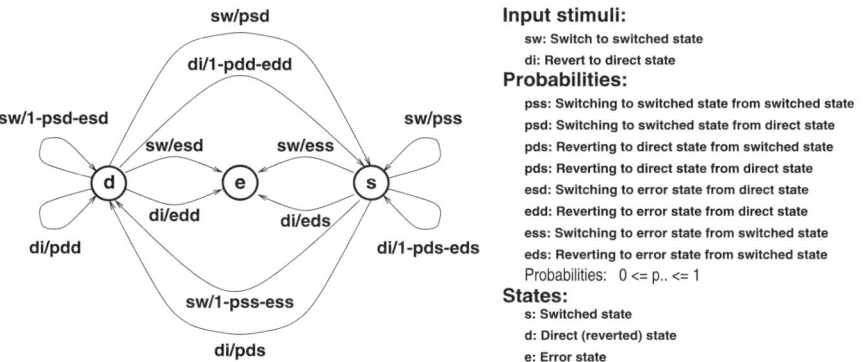

Figure 9.1 intends to model the probabilistic (erroneous and correct) behaviour of a switch when subjected to settings (to switched (s) state) and re–settings (to direct (d) state). A switch may go to the switched state from the direct state when subjected to a switch setting s with probability psd.. ∎

Another Example

Another example shows another aspect of support technology.

Example: *Air traffic radar.* Air traffic (iAT), intrinsically, is a total function over some time interval, from time (T) to monotonically positioned (P) aircraft (A).

A conventional air traffic radar "samples", at regular intervals, the intrinsic air traffic. Hence a radar is a partial function[10] from intrinsic to sampled air traffics (sAT).

type
    iAT = T → (A $\overrightarrow{m}$ P), sAT = T $\overrightarrow{m}$ (A $\overrightarrow{m}$ P)
value
    [radar] r: iAT $\overset{\sim}{\to}$ sAT, [close] c: P × P → **Bool**
axiom
    ∀ iat:iAT • **let** sat = r(iat) **in** ∀ t:T • t ∈ **dom** sat •
        t ∈ **dom** iat ∧ ∀ a:A • a ∈ **dom** iat(t) ⇒
           a ∈ **dom** sat(t) ∧ c((iat(t))(a),(sat(t))(a)) **end**

The axioms express a property that one expects to hold for a radar: That the radar-displayed aircraft positions are close to those of the aircraft in the actual world.

■

Methodological Consequences

Technique of Modelling the *Support Technology* Domain Facet: The support technologies model of a domain is a partial specification — hence all the usual abstraction and modelling principles, techniques and tools apply. More specifically: Support technologies (st:ST) "implements" intrinsic contexts and states: $\gamma_i : \Gamma_i, \sigma_i : \Sigma_i$ in terms of "actual" contexts and states: $\gamma_a : \Gamma_a, \sigma_a : \Sigma_a$

type
    Syntax,
    Γ_i, Σ_i, VAL_i, Γ_a, Σ_a, VAL_a,
    ST = Γ_i × Σ_i $\overset{\sim}{\to}$ Γ_a × Σ_a
value
    sts:ST-**set**
axiom
    ∀ st:ST • st ∈ sts ⇒ ...

Support technology is not a refinement, but an extension. Support technology typically introduces considerations of technology accuracy, failure, etc. Axioms

---

[10]This example is due to my former MSc Thesis student Kristian M. Kalsing.

characterise members of the set of support technologies sts. An example axiom was given in the air traffic radar example. ∎

The Principle of Modelling the *Support Technology* Domain Facet is a principle that is relative to all other domain facets. It expresses that one must first describe essential intrinsics. Then it expresses that support technology is any means of implementing concrete instantiations of some intrinsics, of some management & organisation, and/or of some rules & regulations. Generally the principle states that one must always be on the look-out for and inspire new support technologies. The most abstract form of the principle is: *"What is a support technology one day becomes part of the domain intrinsics a future day"*. ∎

Discussion

[14, 13] exemplify the use of the Duration Calculus [21, 22, 23, 24, 25] in describing supporting technologies that help achieve safe operation of a road level rail crossing, and of a gas burner.

The support technology facet descriptions "re–appear" in the requirements definitions: Projected, instantiated, extended and initialised [3]. In the domain description we "only" record our understanding of all aspects of support technology "failures". In the requirements definition we then follow up and make decisions as to which kinds of "breakdowns" the computing system, the machine, is to handle, and what is to be achieved by such "handlings".

Management and Organisation

The Concept

Characterisation: *Management and Organisation:* That which primarily determines and constrains communication between enterprise stake-holders. ∎

Conceptual Examples — I

Discussion: People staff enterprises, the components of infrastructures with which we are concerned, for which we develop software. The larger these enterprises, these infrastructure components, are, the more need there is for management & organisation. The rôle of management is roughly, for our purposes, twofold: Firstly, to perform strategic, tactical and operational work (cf. example of Section 9.3.1), to make strategic, tactical and operational policies — including rules & regulations, cf. Section 9.3.2 — and to see to it that they are followed. The rôle of management is, secondly, to react to adverse conditions, unforeseen situations, and decide upon their handling, i.e. conflict resolution. Policy setting should help non-management staff operate in normal situations — for which no management interference is thus needed. And management "back--stops" problems: Takes these problems off the shoulders of non-management staff.

To help management and staff know who's in charge with respect to policy setting and problem handling, a clear conception of the overall organisation is needed: Organisation defines lines of communication within management and staff and between these. Whenever management and staff has to turn to others for assistance they usually, in a reasonably well–functioning enterprise, follow the command line: The paths of organigrams — the usually hierarchical box and arrow/line diagrams.

■

Methodological Consequences — I

Techniques of Modelling the *Management & Organisational* **Domain Attributes Concepts:** The management & organisation model of a domain is a partial specification — hence all the usual abstraction and modelling principles, techniques and tools apply. More specifically: Management is a set of predicates, observer and generator functions which either parameterise others, the operations functions, (that is, determine their behaviour), or yield results that become arguments to these other functions. We have indicated, in the example of Section 9.3.1, some of the techniques. Organisation is a set of constraints on communication behaviours. "Hierarchical", rather than "linear", and "matrix" structured organisations can also be modelled as sets (of recursively invoked sets) of equations.

■

Conceptual Example — II

Examples: *Management & Organisation* To relate "classical" organigrams to formal descriptions we first show such an organigram, see Figure 9.2, and then we show schematic processes which — for a rather simple case (i.e. scenario) — model managers and managed !

Figure 9.2. Organisational Structures

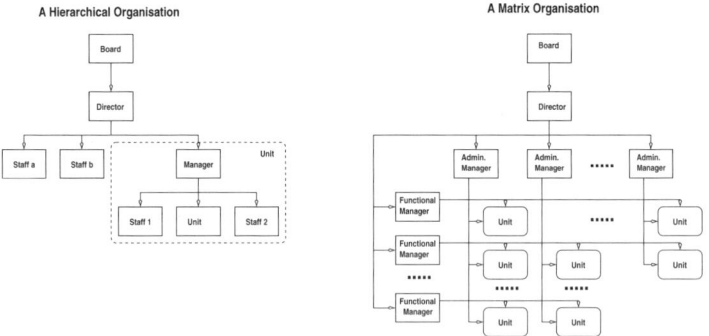

type Msg, Ψ, Σ, Sx
channel { ms[i]:Msg | i:Sx }
value
   sys: **Unit** $\to$ **Unit**

mgr: $\Psi \to$ **in,out** $\{$ ms[i] | i:Sx $\}$ **Unit**
stf: i:Sx $\to \Sigma \to$ **in,out** ms[i] **Unit**
sys() $\equiv \| \{$ stf(i)(iσ) | i:Sx $\} \|$ mgr(ψ)

value
  mgr(ψ) $\equiv$
    let $\psi' = \ldots$;
      ($\|$ $\{$ms[i]!msg;f_m(msg)(ψ)|i:Sx $\}$)
      $[]$
      ($[]$ $\{$**let** msg$'$ = ms[i]? **in** g_m(msg$'$)(ψ) **end**|i:Sx$\}$) **in**
    mgr(ψ') **end**

  stf(i)(σ) $\equiv$
    let $\sigma' = \ldots$;
      ((**let** msg = ms[i] ? **in** f_s(msg)(σ) **end**)
      $[]$
      (ms[i] ! msg$'$; g_s(msg$'$)(σ))) **in**
    stf(i)(σ') **end**

  f_m, g_m: Msg $\to \Psi \to \Psi$,
  f_s, g_s: Msg $\to \Sigma \to \Sigma$

Both manager and staff processes recurse (i.e. iterates) over possibly changing states. Management process non-deterministically, external choice, "alternates" between "broadcast"–issuing orders to staff and receiving individual messages from staff. Staff processes likewise non-deterministically, external choice, "alternates" between receiving orders from management and issuing individual messages to management. The example also illustrates modelling stake-holder behaviours as interacting (here **CSP**–like, [26, 27, 28]) processes. ∎

Methodological Consequences — II

Discussion: The *strategic, tactical and operations resource management* example of Section 9.3.1 (pages 183–186) illustrated another management & organisation description pattern. It is based on a set of, in this case, recursive equations. Any way of solving these equations, finding a suitable fixpoint, or an approximation thereof, including just choosing and imposing an arbitrary "solution", reflects some management communication. The syntactic ordering of the equations — in this case: a "linear" passing of enterprise "results" from "upper" equations onto "lower" equations — reflects some organisation. ∎

The Principle of Modelling the *Management & Organisation* Domain Facets expresses that relations between resources, and decisions to acquire and dispose resources, to de–, re– and schedule and de–, re– and allocate resources, and to de–, re– and activate resources, are the prerogatives of well-functioning management, reflect a functioning oranisation, and imply invocation of procedures that are modelled as actions that "set up" and "take-down" contexts and change states. As such these principles tell us which sub-problems of development to tackle. ▪

Techniques of Modelling the *Management & Organisation* **Domain Facet:** We have already, under techniques for modelling 'Stake–holder' and 'Stake–holder Perspectives', mentioned some of the techniques. In this section we have used these techniques. Two "extremes" were shown: In Section 9.3.1 we modelled individual management groups by their respective functions (**strm, trm, orm**), and their interaction (i.e. organisation) by "solutions" to a set of recursive equations ! In this section we modelled management & organisation, especially the latter, by communicating sequential behaviours. ▪

Discussion

The domain models of management and organisation, of this section, as well as of the earlier section 9.3.1, eventually find their way into requirements, and, hence, the software design — for the cases that the requirements are about computing support of management and its organisation.

Support to solution of the recursive equations of the example of Section 9.3.1 may be offered in the form of constraint based logic solvers which may partially handle logic characterisations of the strategic and tactical management functions, and in the form of computerised support of message passing between the various management groups of the example of Section 9.3.1, as well as of the generic example of the present section.

Rules & Regulations

The Concept

Characterisation: *Rule.* That which guides the work of enterprise stake-holders as well as their interaction and the interaction with non-enterprise stake-holders. ▪
    Characterisation: *Regulation.* That which stipulate what is to happen if a rule can be detected not to have been followed when such was deemed necessary. ▪
    Rules & regulations are set by enterprises, enterprise associations, [government] regulatory agencies, and by law.

Three Examples

Examples: *Rail and Banking.* (i) Rail: **Rule:** *In China arrival and departure of trains at, respectively from railway stations are subject to the following rule: In any three minute interval at most one train may either arrive or depart.* **Regulation:** *Disciplinary procedures.* (ii) Rail: **Rule:** *In many countries railway lines (between stations) are segmented into blocks or sectors. The purpose is to stipulate that if two or more trains are moving — obviously in the same direction — along the line, then there must be at least one free sector (i.e. without a train) between any two such trains.* **Regulation:** *Disciplinary procedures.* (iii) Banking: **Rule:** *In the United States of America personal checks issued in any one state of* the Union must be cleared by the sending and receiving banks, if within the same state, then within 24 hours, and else within 48 or 72 hours, depending on certain further stipulated relations between the states. **Regulation:** *Fines and triple damages to affected clients.* ∎

Methodological Consequences

Technique of Modelling the *Rules & Regulations* **Domain Facets:** There are usually three kinds of syntax involved with respect to (i.e. when expressing) rules & regulations (resp. when invoking actions that are subject to rules & regulations: The syntaxes (**Syntax_rul**, **Syntax_reg**) describing rules, respectively regulations; and the syntax (**Syntax_cmd**) of [always current] domain external action stimuli. A rule, denotationally, is a predicate over domain stimuli, and current and next domain configurations ($\Gamma \times \Sigma$). A regulation, denotationally, is a state changing function over domain stimuli, and current and next domain configurations ($\Gamma \times \Sigma$). We omit treatment of [current] stimuli:

type Syntax_cmd, Syntax_rul, Syntax_reg, Γ, Σ
 Rules_and_Regulations = Syntax_rul × Syntax_reg
 RUL = $(\Gamma \times \Sigma) \to (\Gamma \times \Sigma) \to$ **Bool**,
 REG = $(\Gamma \times \Sigma) \to (\Gamma \times \Sigma)$
value
 interpret: Syntax_rul $\to \Gamma \to \Sigma \to$ RUL-**set**,
 interpret: Syntax_reg $\to \Gamma \to \Sigma \to$ REG

 valid: RUL-**set** $\to (\Gamma \times \Sigma) \times (\Gamma \times \Sigma) \to$ **Bool**
 valid(ruls)$((\gamma,\sigma),(\gamma',\sigma')) \equiv$
  $\forall$ rul:RUL • rul $\in$ ruls $\Rightarrow$ rul$(\gamma,\sigma)(\gamma',\sigma')$

 valid: REG $\to (\Gamma \times \Sigma) \to (\Gamma \times \Sigma) \to$ **Bool**
 valid(reg)(γ,σ) **as** (γ',σ')
  post reg$(\gamma,\sigma) = (\gamma',\sigma')$

axiom
 $\forall$ (ruls,reg):Rules_and_Regulations • $\exists$ $(\gamma,\sigma),(\gamma',\sigma')$:$\Gamma \times \Sigma$ •
   $\exists$ γ'':Γ, σ'':Σ
    • $\sim$valid(ruls)$((\gamma,\sigma),(\gamma'',\sigma''))$
     $\Rightarrow$ valid(reg)$(\gamma'',\sigma'') = (\gamma',\sigma')$

Rules & regulations are therefore modelled by abstract or concrete syntaxes of syntactic rules etc., by abstract types of denotations, and by semantics definitions, usually in the form of axioms or denotation–ascribing functions. ∎

The Principle of Modelling the *Rules & Regulations* **Domain Facet** expresses that domains are governed by rules & regulations: By laws of nature or edicts by humans. Laws of nature can be part of intrinsics, or can be modelled as rules & regulations constraining the intrinsics. Edicts by humans usually change, but are usually considered part of an irregularly changing context, not a recurrently changing state. Modelling techniques follow these priciples. ▪

Rules & Regulation Scripts

We discuss an issue that arises with the above and which points to possible precautionary and/or remedial actions — as they would first be expressed in some reguirements:

Discussion: Domain rules & regulations are usually formulated in "almost legalese", i.e. in rather precise, albeit perhaps "stilted" subsets of the professional language of the domain in question. In cases such rules & regulation languages can be formalised, and we then call them script languages. A particular set of rules & regulations is thus a script. Such script languages can be mechanised: Making it "easy" for appropriate (rules & regulation issuing) stake-holders to script such scripts — and to have them inserted into their computing system: As predicates that detect rule violations, respectively suggest alternative actions (rather than causing a potentially violating action) or remedy an actual rule violation. ▪ The rules & regulations, that may be stipulated for a domain, can thus find their way into requirements that specify computerised support for their enforcement.

Human Behaviour

The Concept

Discussion: Some people try their best to perform actions according to expectations set by their colleagues, customers, etc. And they usually succeed in doing so. They are therefore judged reliable and trustworthy, good, punctual professionals (b_p) of their domain. Some people set lower standards for their professional conduct: Are sometimes or often sloppy (b_s), make mistakes, unknowingly or even knowingly. And yet other people are outright delinquent (b_d) in the despatch of their work: Couldn't care less about living up to expectations of their colleagues and customers. Finally some people are explicitly criminal (b_c) in the conduct of what they do: Deliberately "do the opposite" of what is expected, circumvent rules & regulations, etc. And we must abstract and model, in any given situation where a human interferes in the "workings" of a domain action, any one of the above possible behaviours. ▪

Characterisation: *Human Behaviour.* The way in which domain stake--holders despatch their actions and interactions with respect to an enterprise: professionally, sloppily, delinquently, yes even criminally. ▪

Methodological Consequences

Techniques of Modelling the *Human Behaviour (I–II)* **Domain Facet:** We often model the "arbitrariness" of human behaviour by internal non-determinism:

$$\ldots b\_p \sqcap b\_s \sqcap b\_d \sqcap b\_c \ldots$$

The exact, possibly deterministic, meaning of each of the b's can be separately described.

In addition we can model human behaviour by the arbitrary selection of elements from sets and of subsets of sets:

type
    X
value
    hb_i: X-**set** ... → ... , hb_i(xs,...) ≡ **let** x:X • x ∈ xs **in** ... **end**
    hb_j: X-**set** ... → ... , hb_j(xs,...) ≡ **let** xs':X-**set** • xs' ⊆ xs **in** ... **end**

The above shows just fragments of formal descriptions of those parts which reflect human behaviour. Similar, loose, descriptions are used when describing faulty supporting technologies, or the "uncertainties" of the intrinsic world. ∎

Technique of Modelling the *Human Behaviour (III)* **Domain Facet:** Commensurate with the above, humans interpret rules & regulations differently, and not always "consistently" in the sense of repeatedly applying the same interpretations. Our final specification pattern is therefore:

type
    RULS = RUL-**set**
    Action = $\Gamma \xrightarrow{\sim} \Sigma \xrightarrow{\sim} (\Gamma \times \Sigma)$-**infset**
value
    interpret: Syntax_rul → Γ → Σ → RULS-**infset**

    human_behaviour: Action → Syntax_rr → $\Gamma \xrightarrow{\sim} \Sigma \xrightarrow{\sim} \Gamma \times \Sigma$
    human_behaviour(α)(srr)(γ)(σ) **as** (γ',σ')
        post
            let $\gamma\sigma$s = $\alpha(\gamma)(\sigma)$ **in**
            $\exists\ (\gamma',\sigma'):(\Gamma\times\Sigma) \bullet (\gamma',\sigma') \in \gamma\sigma$s $\land$
                let rules:RULS • rules ∈ interpret(srr)(γ)(σ) **in**
                    $\forall$ rule:RUL • rule ∈ rules ⇒ rule(γ,σ)(γ',σ') **end end**

The above is, necessarily, sketchy: There is a possibly infinite variety of ways of interpreting some rule[s]. A human, in carrying out an action, interprets applicable rules and chooses a set which that person believes suits some (professional, sloppy, delinquent or criminal) intent. "Suits" means that it satisfies the intent, i.e. yields **true** on the pre/post state pair, when the action is performed — whether as intended by the ones who issued the rules & regulations or not. ∎

Discussion: Please observe the difference between the version of **interpret** as indicated in Section 9.3.2 and the present version: The former reflected the semantics as intended by the stake–holder who issued the rules & regulations. The latter reflects the professional, or the sloppy, or the delinquent, or the criminal semantics as intended by the similarly "qualified" staff which carries out the rule abiding rule violating actions. Please also observe that we do not here exemplify any regulations.

The Principle of Modelling the *Human Behaviour* Domain Facet expresses what has now been mentioned several times, namely that some people are perfect: Follow rules & regulations as per intentions; other people are sloppy: fail to follow the prescriptions; and yet other people are derelict or even criminal in the pursuit of their job: Deliberately flaunt rules & regulations. And the principle concludes that one must be prepared for the "worst". That is: Model it all.

Discussion

The results of informal as well as formal domain descriptions of human shortcomings find their way into those requirements which define computerised support for taking precautionary actions should human errors be detected.

Discussion

We have covered a number of domain facets: *Intrinsics* ('the very basics'), *support technologies* (implementations of some parts of other facets), *management & organisation, rules & regulations,* and *human behaviour.* One can possibly think of other facets. With each domain facet the "full force" of all abstraction and modelling principles and techniques apply, and a careful "sequencing" ("fitting-in") of the treatment of 'that' facet with respect to other facets must be considered.

For each of the facets we have shown principles of and techniques for their modelling, and we have indicated that these facet models may eventually find their way into requirements models, and hence determine software designs.

3.3 Discussion

And we have covered, on a larger scale, the domain modelling of (domain) stake-holder perspectives and domain facets. The two concepts are not orthogonal. Their individual and combined treatment again demands judicious choice.

It has, throughout, been indicated how the domain model predicates the requirements, and hence the design.

One will never be able, it is conjectured, to achieve a complete domain model. But one can do far better than is practice today — where no such models are even attempted. Most claims of domain models are really biased towards contemplated software designs, embodying requirements, and are just covering at most the domain being projected, etc.

In the validation interaction between the software developers — who are major "players" in the development of both domain descriptions and requirements definitions — and the domain stake–holders, in that validation process, we claim, many errors — that before could, and hence would, creep unconsciously into the software development — can now be avoided. When indeed errors, i.e. "holes" in the domain description, are still discovered, later, perhaps after final software delivery, then it is now easier, we claim, to pinpoint where these errors first occurred, and hence who were the perpetrators: The software, cum domain or requirements or design, developers, or the stake-holders, or both parties. On one hand it is now easier to resolve legal issues, and, as well, to repair malfunctioning software. The latter because, in its development, from domains via requirements to designs, we adhere to an unstated principle: That of homomorphic development: *If two or more algebraically independent ("orthogonal") concepts are expressed in the domain and are to be "found", somehow, also in the software, then their implementation must be likewise distinguishable.*

9.4 Conclusion

We have tried, more precisely, than what is normally experienced, to formulate a concept of method, in particular as it applies to a narrow part of domain engineering.

We have emphasised method principles and techniques, and we have proposed a number of domain perspective and facet modelling principles and related techniques.

We have only briefly referred to tools, and then only to linguistic tools such as natural language, the professional (i.e. subset natural) languages of specific universes of discourse, here almost exclusively domains, and the formal languages that "carry" formal techniques such as **RSL, Finite State Machines** and the **Duration Calculi**.

9.4.1 Discussion

Now: Have we achieved what we wished ?

To some extent, "Yes !" To some other extent, "No !".

As concerns the 'Yes', the essay speaks for itself: Presents our "Yes !".

As concerns the 'No', we discuss now some shortcomings, such as we presently see them.

Not all principles need or seem to need associated tecniques: 'Separation of Concern' appears to be a meta-principle that is then followed up by a choice between various techniques — but we cannot really say that these latter techniques are that intimately associated with the 'Separation of Concern' principle ?

Those principles, for which we have listed associated techniques, these techniques have be rather simple-mindedly expressed. We should like to see sharper characterisations — of a nature that sets them more apart, that distinguishes them more uniquely.

For some techniques we have achieved a formal characterisation, viz.: 'Support Technology', 'Rules & Regulations' and, partly, 'Human Behaviour'. We should like to see these further elaborated; and we should like to see remaining facets characterised more formally.

Then the essay, as it stands, isolated from treatments of many other software development principles and techniques, risks being too narrow in its view of methods, their principles and techniques. We refer here to the obvious lack of the mentioning of principles and techniques for such **general abstraction & modelling** issues as *property vs. model-oriented descriptions, representation & operation abstraction, denotation, computation and process abstractions, time, space and time–space* concerns, *'hierarc[h]ality' vs. compositionality, configuration, context and state* modelling, etc.; to such **domain attribute** issues as *statics and dynamics* [1], *tangibility* [1], *dimensionality* [1], *discreteness, continuity and chaos*, etc.; to such **domain requirements** issues as *projection, instantiation, extension* and *initialisation*, etcetera, etcetera !

Since we can identify very many principles and techniques, some specific to distinct phases of development (to domains, or to requirements, or to software design), some generally applicable — since this is possible — it gives, we believe, strength to the argument that we must collect all these principles and techniques, we must investigate them individually and in relation to others, structure their presentation, and come up with such structured lists of principles and techniques as were referred to in the 'Methodicity' principles and its related technique, etc.

9.4.2 Future Work

The above discussion has pointed out some weaknesses, and has indicated additional work to be done: In meta–formalising some techniques, in collating "all so far identifiable" principles and techniques across at least the spectrum from and including domain engineering via requirements engineering [2] to inital parts of software design, notably software architecture and program organisation [3].

9.4.3 Acknowledgements

Acknowledgements are gratefully extended to Michael A. Jackson for his inspiring publications [29, 30, 31, 6, 32, 1, 7, 33, 34, 8], to the WG 2.3 membership for discussions of topics presented; to Hidetaka Kondoh of Hitachi Software Development Laboratories, Tokyo, for his thoughtful views on software development; and to my many, patient students, who have "suffered" lectures along the lines of this essay, and who have tested out their import in innumerable term and MSc projects.

It was at UNU/IIST[11] that we[12] systematically studied and applied, amongst may other programming and software engineering methodological issues, also the domain facets expounded in this chapter. My warmest acknowledgements goes to my colleagues during those years at UNU/IIST, 1991–1997, and beyond.

References

[1] Michael A. Jackson. *Software Requirements & Specifications: a lexicon of practice, principles and prejudices*, Addison-Wesley, 1995.

[2] Dines Bjørner. Domains as Prerequisites for Requirements and Software &c. In M. Broy and B. Rumpe, editors, *RTSE'97: Requirements Targeted Software and Systems Engineering*, volume 1526 of *Lecture Notes in Computer Science*, pages 1–41. Springer-Verlag, Berlin Heidelberg, 1998.

[3] Dines Bjørner. Where do Software Architectures come from ? Systematic Development from Domains and Requirements. A Re–assessment of Software Engneering ? *South African Journal of Computer Science*, 22: 3–13, 1999.

[4] Dines Bjørner. Formal Software Techniques in Railway Systems. In Eckehard Schnieder, editor, *9th IFAC Symposium on Control in Transportation Systems*, pages 1–12, Technical University, Braunschweig, Germany, 13–15 June 2000. VDI/VDE-Gesellschaft Mess– und Automatisierungstechnik, VDI-Gesellschaft für Fahrzeug– und Verkehrstechnik. Invited plenum lecture.

[5] Dines Bjørner. Pinnacles of Software Engineering: 25 Years of Formal Methods. *Annals of Software Engineering*, 10:11–66, 2000. Eds. Dilip Patel and Wang Yi.

[6] Michael A. Jackson. Problems, Methods and Specialisation. *Software Engineering Journal*, pages 249–255, November 1994.

[7] Michael A. Jackson. Problems and requirements (software development). In *Second IEEE International Symposium on Requirements Engineering (Cat. No.95TH8040)*, pages 2–8. IEEE Comput. Soc. Press, 1995.

[8] Michael A. Jackson. The meaning of requirements. *Annals of Software Engineering*, 3:5–21, 1997.

[9] Dines Bjørner and O. Oest, editors. *Towards a Formal Description of Ada*, LNCS, vol. 98. Springer-Verlag, 1980.

[10] Dines Bjørner and M. Nielsen. Meta Programs and Project Graphs. In *ETW: Esprit Technical Week*, pages 479–491. Elsevier, May 1985.

[11] Dines Bjørner. Project Graphs and Meta-Programs: Towards a Theory of Software Development. In N. Habermann and U. Montanari, editors, *Proceedings Capri '86 Conference on Innovative Software Factories and Ada, Lecture Notes on Computer Science*. Springer-Verlag, 1986.

---

[11]UNU/IIST is a Research and Post-graduate & –doctoral Training Centre whose financial basis has been provided, 1992–1996, by The Republic of Portugal (US $ 5 mio), The [then] Portuguese administrated Territory of Macau (US $ 20 mio), and The People's Republic of China (US $ 5 mio).

[12]The author, as first and founding Director, Prof. Zhou Chaochen (then Principal Research Fellow, now Director), Søren Prehn, Chris W. George, Dr. Xu Qiwen, Dr. Richard C. Moore, Dr. Tomasz Janowski, and Dr. Cornelis A. Middelburg.

[12] Dines Bjørner. Software Development Graphs — A Unifying Concept for Software Development? In K.V. Nori, editor, *Vol. 241 of Lecture Notes in Computer Science: Foundations of Software Technology and Theoretical Computer Science*, pages 1–9. Springer-Verlag, Dec. 1986.

[13] A.P. Ravn and H. Rischel. Requirements capture for embedded real-time systems. In P. Borne, editor, *IMACS-IFAC Symposium MCTS, Villeneuve d'Ascq, France, May 1991*. IMACS Transaction Series, 1991.

[14] Jens U. Skakkebaek, Anders P. Ravn, Hans Rischel, and Zhou ChaoChen. Specification of Embedded, Real-time Systems. Technical report, Dept. of Computer Science, Technical University of Denmark, EuroMicro Workshop on Formal Methods for Real-time Systems, 1992 December 1991. The example: A railway road/rail crossing.

[15] Jens Ulrik Skakkebaek. Development of Provably Correct Systems. Technical report, Dept. of Computer Science, Technical University of Denmark, 30 August 1991 M.Sc. Thesis.

[16] Dines Bjørner. A ProCoS Project Description. *Published in two slightly different versions: (1) EATCS Bulletin, October 1989, (2) (Ed. Ivan Plander:) Proceedings: Intl. Conf. on AI & Robotics, Strebske Pleso, Slovakia, Nov. 5-9, 1989, North-Holland*, Dept. of Computer Science, Technical University of Denmark, October 1989.

[17] Jess Stein (Ed.). *The Random House American Everyday Dictionary*. Random House, New York, N.Y., USA, 1949, 1961.

[18] Chris George, Anne Haxthausen, Steven Hughes, Robert Milne, Søren Prehn, and Jan Storbank Pedersen. *The RAISE Method*. The BCS Practitioner Series. Prentice-Hall, 1995.

[19] Chris George, Peter Haff, Klaus Havelund, Anne Haxthausen, Robert Milne, Claus Bendix Nielsen, Søren Prehn, and Kim Ritter Wagner. *The RAISE Specification Language*. The BCS Practitioner Series. Prentice-Hall, Hemel Hampstead, England, 1992.

[20] Dines Bjørner. Domain Modelling: Resource Management Strategics, Tactics & Operations, Decision Support and Algorithmic Software. In J.C.P. Woodcock, editor, Millennial perspectives in computer science, Palgrave, 2000.

[21] Zhou Chaochen, C. A. R. Hoare, and A. P. Ravn. A Calculus of Durations. *Information Proc. Letters*, 40(5), 1992.

[22] Zhou Chaochen and Li Xiaoshan. A Mean Value Duration Calculus. Research Report 5, UNU/IIST, P.O.Box 3058, Macau, March 1993. Published as Chapter 25 in *A Classical Mind*, Festschrift for C.A.R. Hoare, Prentice-Hall International, 1994, pp 432–451.

[23] Zhou Chaochen, Anders P. Ravn, and Michael R. Hansen. An Extended Duration Calculus for Real-time Systems. Research Report 9, UNU/IIST, P.O.Box 3058, Macau, January 1993. Published in: *Hybrid Systems*, LNCS 736, 1993.

[24] Zhou Chaochen. Duration Calculi: An Overview. Research Report 10, UNU/IIST, P.O.Box 3058, Macau, June 1993. Published in: *Formal Methods in Programming and Their Applications*, Conference Proceedings, June 28 – July 2, 1993, Novosibirsk, Russia; (Eds.: D. Bjørner, M. Broy and I. Pottosin) LNCS 736, Springer-Verlag, 1993, pp 36–59.

[25] Zhou Chaochen, Zhang Jingzhong, Yang Lu, and Li Xiaoshan. Linear Duration Invariants. Research Report 11, UNU/IIST, P.O.Box 3058, Macau, July 1993. Published in: Formal Techniques in Real-Time and Fault-Tolerant systems, LNCS 863, 1994.

[26] C.A.R. Hoare. Communicating Sequential Processes. *Communications of the ACM*, 21(8), Aug. 1978.

[27] C.A.R. Hoare. *Communicating Sequential Processes*. Prentice-Hall International, 1985.

[28] A.W. Roscoe. *Theory and Practice of Concurrency*. Prentice-Hall, 1997.

[29] Michael A. Jackson. Description is Our Business. In *VDM '91: Formal Software Development Methods*, pages 1–8. Springer-Verlag, October 1991.

[30] Pamela Zave and Michael A. Jackson. Techniques for partial specification and specification of switching systems. In S. Prehn and W.J. Toetenel, editors, *VDM'91: Formal Software Development Methods*, volume 551 of *LNCS*, pages 511–525. Springer-Verlag, 1991.

[31] Michael A. Jackson. Problems, methods and specialisation. *Software Engineering Journal*, 9(6):249–255, November 1994.

[32] Michael A. Jackson. *Software Development Method*, chapter 13, pages 215–234. Prentice Hall Intl., 1994. Festschrift for C. A. R. Hoare: *A Classical Mind*, Ed. W. Roscoe.

[33] Pamela Zave and Michael A. Jackson. Where do operations come from? a multi-paradigm specification technique. *IEEE transactions on software engineering*, 22(7), July 1996.

[34] Pamela Zave and Michael A. Jackson. Four dark Corners of Requirements Engineering. *ACM Transactions on Software Engineering and Methodology*, 6(1):1–30, January 1997.

Part II

Programming techniques

Section E

Object orientation

10 Object-oriented programming and software development — a critical assessment   **211**
Manfred Broy

The object-oriented paradigm of programming heralded a radical change in language design in the 1960's. Its authors recognised that programming languages did not need to reflect the concrete structure of primitive machine operations, and instead they took the revolutionary view that languages should be based on 'high level' structuring constructs, the better to facilitate the rapid design of large software systems and reuse of code.

Whilst its progressive features have established object orientation as one of the most popular programming tools for large-scale systems, it is also true that the environment of its inception is very different from that of today. Indeed object orientation falls short of the changed and changing demands of concurrency and interoperability which form a large part of modern applications. For example the inherent sequential nature of the object-oriented paradigm reveals very compellingly how its use can place an unnecessary impediment on the development process of concurrent applications.

Program developers recognise that software must above all be adaptable over its lifetime to evolving interactive environments yet, as this paper points out, it is unfortunate that the object-oriented style (as it is currently implemented) is unable to respond to this (and other) issues. So whilst object orientation represents a significant landmark in programming language design, as always, new applications constantly demand ever more accurate tools, and they need a new generation object-oriented language to meet them.

11 A trace model for pointers and objects   **223**
    C.A.R. Hoare and He Jifeng

Object-oriented programming is a synthesis of at least three ideas, each with its own separate history: modularity (including extensibility and information hiding); independent (concurrent) execution; and pointer-based data structuring. The last of those is the subject of this paper.

Like many other ideas in computing, the *pointer* can be traced back to a feature of computing hardware, in this case the *memory address*. Just as the 'GOTO' (itself based on the machine-level branch instruction) once escaped into high-level languages, the pointer became conspicuous because of the contrast between its potentialy unbridled use (resembling spaghetti) and the otherwise well designed data structures of the language containing it. Both the GOTO and pointers were tamed in the 1970's, however: the former by E.W. Dijkstra's article "GOTO statement considered harmful" [CACM 11(3) 1968]; and the latter in the article "Recursive Data Structures" by Hoare [Int. J. Comp. Inf. Sci. 4(2) 1975], that captured and hid the use of pointers within the more abstract concept of an *abstract syntax tree*. That approach lives on in modern functional languages.

Unlike GOTO's however, still more-or-less banned twenty-five years later, pointers have escaped again; and in some of the current batch of object-oriented languages their spaghetti-like nature is not as well understood as it should be. In this article, Hoare and He once more attempt to tame pointers' complexity by abstraction, but this time using a more general trace model, rather than one based on trees. The result has the usual powerful simplicity that is characteristic of these authors. Because of that, it reveals quite starkly how complicated the reasoning about pointers will be in the general case.

12 Object models as heap invariants 247
Daniel Jackson

Some specification techniques are interesting because of their mathematical structures alone; some are remarkable for their generality; and some are useful because they are closely matched to their applications.

Abrial's Z specification method, for example, owes much of its success to its simplicity and the fact that it is so well matched to the 'state-modelling' approach of specification and design; and its being based on elementary set theory allows it a widespread use. But because it makes no attempt to deal systematically with — for example — higher-order structures, it is limited in other areas; the corresponding advantage is that it is not necessary to carry that baggage around when dealing with common every-day problems.

The technique proposed here resembles Z in that (and other) respects. It is a specification and design technique very carefully aimed at one target, object-oriented applications, and benefits from the simplicity that the careful matching brings. Along with that is, again, a carefully limited logical language which allows just enough expressivity — and not too much.

The contribution can be read not only for its specific proposals on object-model specification, but more generally as an example of designing the right tool for the job.

13 Abstraction dependencies **269**
  K. Rustan M. Leino and Greg Nelson

This paper presents *abstraction dependencies* as a key construct in specifying modular programs.

In data abstraction, one distinguishes two secrets: the abstraction function that defines the representation; and the identity of the (generally concrete but possibly abstract) variables that appear in (as arguments to) the abstraction function. The main point of the paper is that the identity of the variables should often be less closely guarded (that is, visible in more modules) than the abstraction function itself. The abstraction dependency makes it possible to achieve that.

10

Object-oriented programming and software development — a critical assessment

Manfred Broy

Abstract

In software engineering, object-oriented development is today the most popular programming, design and analysis approach. However, object orientation does not manage to address the needs of today's software construction in as radical and fundamental a way as is needed in highly distributed interoperating software applications. In the following, we argue that object orientation indeed offers interesting features, but continues to suffer from a number of severe shortcomings for the engineering of large distributed software systems. This shows that object-oriented techniques of today are not in accordance with the state of the art in scientific, well understood, programming methodology and software engineering.

10.1 Introduction

Object orientation was originally invented by Ole-Johan Dahl and Kristen Nygaard in their design of the programming language Simula 67 (see [18]). Before that, most programming languages were mainly influenced either by the commands of machine languages such as assembler languages or by the logical foundations of computability, such as the λ-calculus. Only gradually programming languages were gaining step-by-step more abstract views of data- and control structures. However, these languages were still mainly devoted to concepts of programming in the small and sequential, noninteractive programs. Typically, I/O was considered a minor issue and therefore not part of the programming language definition, for instance in ALGOL.

Simula 67 introduced radically new ideas by its concepts of coroutines and classes. Such an approach to programming and software development was badly needed to master the requirements of the development of large complex software systems, distributed over many computers connected by high-speed networks and thus operating concurrently and interacting asynchronously. These issues are addressed by the idea of object orientation, as found in Simula.

During the last three decades in software engineering, object orientation developed into the most popular programming, design and analysis approach. Object orientation, it is claimed, offers better structuring features and more flexible concepts than conventional imperative, functional, or logical programming styles — especially for development and programming in the large.

Software development techniques and methods of today have to cope with the growing complexity and size of software applications, with interoperability demands, with applications that are executed on large distributed networks, and the long-term perspective of software systems being in operation over 30 years or more in a still quickly developing technology with rapidly changing requirements. Therefore development in the large, management of change, and interoperability are key issues in software development and programming.

However, object orientation does not manage to address these needs of software construction of today in such a radical and fundamental way as is truly needed. In many respects, object orientation stays within the conventional approach to programming, mainly influenced by the sequential stand-alone machines of the early 1960's.

One might object to those claims by saying that, for instance, Java as a recent object-oriented programming language is a modern programming language that addresses all the needs of today. However, although certainly an advantage over some of the programming languages available so far, Java is in many respects a rather conventional language. Moreover, the success of Java is not only due to its object orientation. It is also due to its universal availability, its concept of portability, and code mobility guaranteed by the idea of byte code.

Over the past five decades, computer science and software engineering became a respectable scientific discipline. A lot of insights have been gained and principles have been discovered, scientifically analyzed, and are now part of the growing knowledge of programming and engineering of large software systems. In the following, we argue that object orientation indeed offers interesting features and programming constructs, yet suffers from a number of severe shortcomings that are not in accordance with the state of the art in scientifically well understood programming methodology and software engineering.

10.2 Object orientation — its claims and its limitations

Let us begin our discussion by briefly restating the main characteristics of object orientation. Object orientation is based on the following main concepts and principles:

10. Object-oriented programming and software development — a critical assessment

- classes with attributes and methods as the major units for describing and structuring programs,
- access interfaces in terms of methods in objects and their attributes described by classes,
- creating objects as instances of classes,
- encapsulation of data and state represented by programming variables called attributes in classes and objects,
- persistence, meaning the durable storage of local attribute values within objects between method invocations,
- data abstraction and implementation hiding,
- identifying and addressing objects by object identifiers, and
- inheritance and polymorphism.

One of the main claims of object orientation is that it provides the capabilities and potentials to support the following recognized design principles:

- modularity by state encapsulation,
- data abstraction,
- information hiding,
- dynamics and flexibility by object instantiation,
- architectural structuring,
- reusability by inheritance and aggregation, and
- well-specified interfaces.

Object orientation is advocated both as a programming paradigm supported by a number of object-oriented programming languages, and as a software-development method supporting the entire spectrum of program development, such as analysis, design, and implementation. In particular, in network applications such as the Internet or client/server systems, object orientation is claimed to be the better programming technique, superior to other programming styles.

In fact, object-oriented programming languages dominate these application areas. Java, for instance, provides the idea of portability and code mobility as a decisive feature in Internet applications.

In spite of the claims and the popularity of object orientation in practice, there are severe shortcomings in object orientation. These are in particular for object-oriented programming its limitation to:

- intrinsically-sequential execution models following the paradigm of sequential control flow of procedural programs,

- code inheritance as a danger of violation of the principle of information hiding and data abstraction,
- missing interface specification techniques for classes,
- the missing concept of composition of classes into composite classes,
- instantiation of objects via references, and
- the missing concept of a software component as a basis for a software architecture.

In fact, recent object-oriented programming languages offer a number of extensions to classical object orientation to overcome some of these shortcomings. For instance, the syntactic interfaces of classes provide a useful concept for interface description. However, for most object-oriented languages abstract semantic interface description concepts do not exist. They only offer syntactic notions of interfaces. In fact, experiments and experiences with object-oriented frameworks show crucially the weakness of object orientation in that respect.

Also the so-called object-oriented techniques for the analysis, design, and implementation of software such as OMT (see [15]), the methods by Jacobson (see [13]) and Booch (see [3]), and in particular the recent UML show severe drawbacks — some of them in common with object oriented programming, such as:

- lack of proper semantic foundations and semantic models,
- missing support of concurrency and asynchronous interaction,
- missing integration of the various description techniques, and
- the missing concept of a software component as a basis for a software architecture.

In fact, UML unfortunately proves to be rather a rough union of concepts (similar to PL1 for programming languages in the 60's) comprising in a rather baroque way many concepts instead of unifying these concepts into a proper analysis and design instrument.

10.3 Object-oriented programming — a critique

In this section we discuss the shortcomings of object-oriented programming. In particular, we argue that object orientation falls short of addressing some of the requirements for a programming language and technique needed for writing large distributed software systems.

10.3.1 Class specification

A class manifests the basic idea of a module in object orientation. Classes are the fundamental building blocks in object oriented programs. In some sense they are the only structuring means in object orientation.

For an interface specification we have to be able to describe the behavior of a component in an interface view. This means that we describe the observable behavior of a class. This is a description that identifies under what circumstances two different classes can be used in the same environment without any observable difference in their behavior. Such a notion is mandatory for a top-down as well as a bottom-up specification and design approach.

For classes and objects, however, a simple description of their observable behavior is, not surprisingly, complicated. The reason lies in the interaction mechanism between objects, called method invocations, which are of course nothing but procedure calls. Method invocations may change the state of the system, given by values of the attributes of objects. Method invocations may result in invocations of methods again and therefore change not only the state of the object addressed by the method invocation but in addition the state of other objects. This way, method invocations in object oriented programs have to be seen as operating on a large state space — the global program state. In contrast to the principle of state encapsulation, by object orientation only special scopes are introduced such that the access to attributes is only possible inside of the bodies of the respective classes. The effect of a method invocation including all the subinvocations of methods during the execution of the call has to be described as one state change on the global state space.

The specification of the observable behavior of classes and objects runs into all the difficulties of the description of distributed interactive systems — except issues of concurrency and action granularity (see below). In fact, object orientation introduces by its concept of a class nearly everything needed and typical for concurrent interactive program execution — but without being brave enough to carry out the step into concurrency.

10.3.2 Object instantiation

A concept considered essential in object orientation is the possibility to instantiate objects from classes. The idea of instantiation has two facets. First we generate a behavior from a description. This is rather straightforward in programming, where we in general generate behaviors from programs. A second and certainly more characteristic concept of object orientation is the creation of an object identifier with a type identified by the class name, which allows us to refer to the individual instantiations. Although considered as very essential for object orientation, this idea is very implementation oriented, strongly influenced by the old machine-oriented idea of references and pointers as well known in procedural programming.

In object orientation the dynamics of systems is modeled by generating objects via class instantiation. A class instantiation generates a new object and an object identifier for it. An object identifier is like a reference or pointer in conventional programming languages.

References or pointers are highly artificial concepts. A reference has no meaning outside of the computer. References introduce a lot of flexibility and efficiency for the price of a complex concept for the identification of objects by references. It is well known that pointer structures are very difficult to deal with. Algorithms dealing with pointer structures are very implementation-oriented and error-prone. The reason is obvious. Pointers are a low-level machine concept — reflecting the addresses of machine memory. They are for data structures what GOTO's are for control structures.

In fact, references (and similarly object identifiers) do not have a machine-independent meaning. It is very strange to introduce classes and corresponding objects such as, for instance, accounts — and then not to identify them by their account number but rather by machine-dependent anonymous references.

10.3.3 Software architectures and the component concept

The dominant concept in object orientation is that of a class. From a methodological point of view the notion of a module or a component has to fulfill certain principles in the development of large software systems such as:

- hierarchical composition/decomposition,

- interface specification, and

- appropriate scaling up.

All these three requirements are not sufficiently well addressed and satisfied by the class concept.

Class composition

In object orientation there is no explicit operator to compose several classes into another, composite class. There is no common concept of a composite class. Note that the idea of multiple inheritance may look similar to class composition but it is, in fact, a completely different concept. Consequently there is no way in object orientation to form larger subsystems structured from appropriate subunits. This is a serious flaw of object orientation since a support for a hierarchical structuring of systems is badly needed for a programming language for large scale software systems.

In fact, it is rather surprising that the concept of class composition does not exist in object orientation. It can and should be introduced into object orientation without much overhead.

Component concept

One of the severe drawbacks of object orientation is a missing notion of component complementary to that of a class. Classes are certainly a too small, too fine-grained concept. They rather are implementation units (such as modules) and therefore not appropriate for structuring large scale systems.

In fact, software component notions are a prerequisite for software architectures. Components are larger-grain units that should be composable hierarchically again.

Software architecture

For the design of large software systems the notion of a software architecture is decisive. A software architecture is the structuring of a software system into components and their principles and forms of co-operation and interaction.

For small software systems, classes may be appropriate to form the structure of the software architecture. For large systems, however, in object orientation we find thousands of classes. Then classes cannot be any longer the appropriate basis for a software architecture.

10.3.4 *Inheritance and polymorphism*

One of the major characteristics and essential concepts of object orientation is inheritance. In object oriented programming *inheritance* usually is realized by *code reuse*. If a class, a *subclass*, inherits from another class the main effect is that the subclass comprises the same attributes and the same methods, more precisely, the same program code for its methods. It may contain, of course, additional attributes and methods. It may moreover overwrite some methods. As a result, there is nothing that can be guaranteed for the behavior of a subclass with respect to the behavior of its superclass besides the syntactic property that it contains the same set of methods and attributes.

The idea of code reuse is very helpful when building software prototypes. There, a quick (and often dirty) implementation may be supported by code inheritance very well as a means of saving coding effort. For the development of large-scale software systems, however, the coding effort is not the critical factor. What counts much more is readability, changability, maintainability — all being quality attributes not improved but rather undermined by code inheritance.

In fact, the technique of code- and attribute inheritance does not follow consistently the classical idea of encapsulation and information hiding. Changing the internal data structure representation of a class affects all its subclasses. Therefore, independence of data representation does not apply for inheritance, in general. Inheritance, as it is found in today's object-oriented programming, is mainly code reuse and therefore rather a low-level technique for implementation and not good for high-level structuring.

Inheritance is seen as a very helpful technique for reuse. However, as defined today it is mainly used for code reuse. As a consequence, the principle of data abstraction and information hiding is violated. It is impossible to change the data representation in a class without changing a lot of code in its subclasses. This demonstrates that the reusing of classes by inheritance is a glass-box usage and does not follow the fundamental idea of an interface principle.

It has been suggested by several authors before that the idea of code reuse for inheritance is a much too low-level concept for structuring large systems. This idea should better be replaced by behavior inheritance. Behavior inheritance respects the principle of data abstraction and implementation hiding also for the inheritance relation.

Another criticism concerns the expressive power of inheritance. Many straightforward modifications of the behavior of a class cannot be easily expressed by inheritance, but rather by higher-order functional-programming concepts. An example is the introduction of an undo method into a class that allows the undoing the effect of the last method call. The reader might try to arrange the introduction of such a method in object orientation by inheritance. This shows that inheritance does not offer the required flexibility.

A further argument in favor of inheritance is the flexibility of code achieved by polymorphism. However polymorphism makes the code of object- oriented programs very complex to comprehend. The identification of method calls is no longer possible by static analysis.

10.3.5 Sequentiality

The object-oriented paradigm as it is found in many object-oriented programming languages is inherently sequential. The reason lies in the interaction mechanism between objects, called method invocations, which are nothing but procedure calls: we noted that because of sub-invocations, a method invocation has to be considered as a state change on the complete global state space. This concept makes the execution model inherently sequential, since all method calls have to be seen as atomic actions.

The introduction of parallelism and concurrency brings in all the classical difficulties and complexities of shared memory parallelism such as the question of which actions are indivisible, how to co-ordinate and synchronise and how to express waiting. The classical ways of introducing concurrency into state-based systems do not lead to the high-level abstract models of the real world as advocated and claimed by the basic philosophy of object orientation.

However, most applications of today run in a highly concurrent distributed environment in networks of computers. Therefore, object-oriented programs have to react and interact to many concurrent activities. Moreover, we want to model concurrent activities in object-oriented programs. This is not properly addressed in object-orientation.

10.4 Object-oriented analysis and design — a critique

In this section we tackle a number of critical issues in object-oriented analysis and design — in particular for languages like UML. A lot of what we have said critically about object-oriented programming languages applies also — in many respects even more seriously — to object-oriented modelling languages.

10.4.1 System model and semantic integration

Clearly a software- and system-development technique needs a system philosophy including a clear concept of a system model. Such a system model serves several purposes. It guides the system development. It is the basis of the semantic understanding. It serves the integration of the various description techniques and thus provides the ultimate unifying frame.

Of course, object orientation supplies a specific system philosophy and a system model. However, first of all the system model does not meet the universal claims that object orientation provides a natural model for the real world. A procedure call does not model all the forms of interaction of the real world. Moreover, concurrency is a phenomenon of the real world. However, concurrency is not addressed at all in object-oriented modelling languages such as UML (see below).

10.4.2 Software and systems architecture

One of the most significant tasks of a design language is the description of software- and systems architectures. This is perhaps the weakest point of the object-oriented modelling languages of today. For instance, in UML, there is no way to choose a concept of a component at the appropriate level of granularity. However, component concepts are at the core of software architecture descriptions.

10.4.3 Concurrency

Practically all interesting systems of today are concurrent, distributed and interactive. High-level abstract models of modern software systems need, therefore, well worked-out system models that support all kinds of concurrency and interaction.

Actually the formalism of statecharts on which the state machine diagram technique of UML is based is easily extended to a concurrent execution model. This is not exploited, however, in the popular OOA/OOD techniques of today.

10.4.4 Data modelling in UML

A good and well-understood technique for data modelling is E/R-modelling. For many applications it is much more suggestive and "natural" to work with data models where the objects (the entities) are identified by high-level key concepts and not by low-level concepts of object identifiers (see above). An account in the data model of a bank is identified much better by its account number than by an object identifier. The use of references like object identifiers at the level of abstract analysis and design is certainly a misconception. Therefore a combination of E/R-modelling techniques with object orientation could lead to much more natural and appropriate data models.

10.5 Concluding remarks

Are we able to create an approach to software system design and to programming that does not show the weaknesses of object orientation of today and nevertheless still manages to maintain most of its advantages? We think yes! There are approaches to the programming of distributed systems based on state machines (such as statecharts) that support asynchronous models of concurrent execution. An interesting approach in that direction is ROOM (see [21]) that in a very consequent way introduces the required techniques.

A generalization of this model along the lines of Focus (see [8]) and the prototype CASE tool AutoFocus (see [1]) shows many of the features described above. The introduction of the classical concepts of object orientation into this model is an interesting exercise.

References

[1] P. Braun, H. Lötzbeyer, B. Schätz, O. Slotosch Consistent Integration of Formal Methods. In: *Proc. 6th Intl. Conf on Tools and Algorithms for the Construction and Analysis of Systems (TACAS'00)*, 2000, to appear

[2] M. v.d. Beeck A Comparison of Statecharts Variants. In: H. Langmaack, W.-P. de Roever, J. Vytopil (eds): *Formal Techniques in Real Time and Fault-Tolerant Systems*. Lecture Notes in Computer Science 863, 128–148, Springer, 1994.

[3] G. Booch *Object Oriented Design with Applications*. Benjamin Cummings, Redwood City, CA, 1991

[4] M. Broy Towards a Formal Foundation of the Specification and Description Language SDL. *Formal Aspects of Computing* 3, 21-57 (1991)

[5] M. Broy Compositional Refinement of Interactive Systems. *Journal of the ACM*, Volume 44, No. 6 (Nov. 1997), 850-891. Also in: DIGITAL Systems Research Center, SRC 89, 1992.

[6] M. Broy (Inter-)Action Refinement: The Easy Way. In: Broy, M. (ed.): *Program Design Calculi*. Springer NATO ASI Series, Series F: Computer and System Sciences, Vol. 118, pp. 121-158, Berlin, Heidelberg, New York: Springer 1993

[7] M. Broy Advanced Component Interface Specification. In: Takayasu Ito, Akinori Yonezawa (Eds.). *Theory and Practice of Parallel Programming*, International Workshop TPPP'94, Sendai, Japan, November 7-9, 1994. Proceedings, Lecture Notes in Computer Science 907, Berlin: Springer 1995

[8] M. Broy Compositional Refinement of Interactive Systems Modelled by Relations. In: W.-P. de Roever, H. Langmaack, A. Pnueli (eds.): *Compositionality: The Significant Difference*. LNCS State of the Art Survey, Lecture Notes in Computer Science 1536, 1998, 130-149

[9] O. Dahl, E.W. Dijkstra, C.A.R. Hoare (eds.) *Structured Programming*. Academic Press 1971

[10] GRAPES-Referenzmanual, DOMINO, Integrierte Verfahrenstechnik. Siemens AG, Bereich Daten-und Informationstechnik 1990

[11] R. Grosu A Formal Foundation for Concurrent Object-Oriented Programming. Dissertation, Fakultt fr Informatik, Technische Universitt Mnchen, December 94

[12] D. Harel Statecharts: A Visual Formalism for Complex Systems. *Science of Computer Programming* 8, 1987, 231–274

[13] I. Jacobsen: *Object-Oriented Software Engineering*. Addison-Wesley, ACM Press 1992

[14] R. Milner, J. Parrow, D. Walker: A calculus of mobile processes. Part i + ii, *Information and Computation*, 100:1 (1992) 1-40, 41-77

[15] J. Rumbaugh *Object-Oriented Modelling and Design*. Prentice Hall, Englewood Cliffs: New Jersey 1991

[16] J. Philipps, P. Scholz Compositional Specification of Embedded Systems with Statecharts. In: *Theory and Practice of Software Development* TAPSOFT'97, Lille, Lecture Notes in Computer Science 1214, Berlin: Springer 1995

[17] Specification and Description Language (SDL), Recommendation Z.100. Technical report, CCITT, 1988

[18] O.-J. Dahl, B. Myrhaug, K. Nygaard Simula 67 — common base language. Technical Report N. S-22, Norsk Regnesentral (Norwegian Computing Center), Oslo, 1968.

[19] G. Booch, J. Rumbaugh, I. Jacobson The Unified Modeling Language for Object-Oriented Development, Version 1.0, RATIONAL Software Cooperation

[20] M. Wirsing Algebraic Specification, *Handbook of Theoretical Computer Science*, Vol. B Amsterdam: North Holland 1990, 675-788

[21] B. Selic, G. Gullekson, P.T. Ward *Real-time Object-oriented Modeling*. Wiley, New York 1994

11

A trace model for pointers and objects

C.A.R. Hoare and He Jifeng[1]

Abstract

Object-oriented programs [5, 6, 10] are notoriously prone to the following kinds of error, which could lead to increasingly severe problems in the presence of tasking:

1. Following a null pointer;
2. Deletion of an accessible object;
3. Failure to delete an inaccessible object;
4. Interference due to equality of pointers; and
5. Inhibition of optimisation due to fear of (4).

Type disciplines and object classes are a great help in avoiding these errors. Stronger protection may be obtainable with the help of assertions, particularly invariants, which are intended to be true before and after each call of a method that updates the structure of the heap. This note introduces a mathematical model and language for the formulation of assertions about objects and pointers, and suggests that a graphical calculus [4] may help in reasoning about program correctness. It deals with both garbage-collected heaps and the other kind. The theory is based on a trace model of graphs, using ideas from process algebra; and our development seeks to exploit this analogy as a unifying principle.

11.1 Introduction: the graph model

Figure 11.1.0 shows a rooted edge-labelled graph. Its **nodes** are represented by circles and its **edges** by arrows from one node to another. The letter drawn next

---

[1] This paper is reprinted from Lecture Notes in Computer Science, Volume 1628, Springer Verlag.

to each arrow is its **label**. The set of allowed labels is called the **alphabet** of the graph. A double-shafted arrow singles out a particular node as the **root** of the graph.

Figure 11.1.0 (Rooted edge-labelled graph)

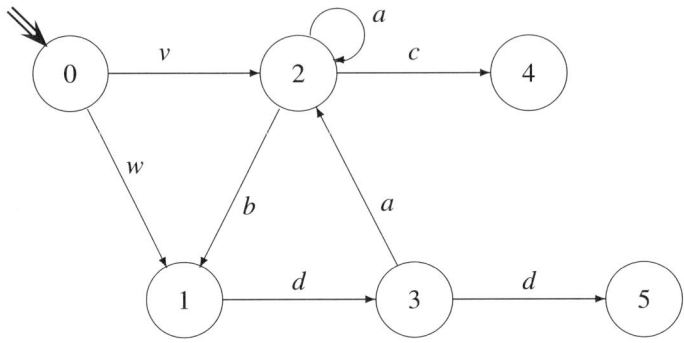

Such a graph can be defined less graphically as a tuple

$$G \;=\; (A_G, N_G, E_G, \text{root}_G),$$

where A_G is the alphabet of labels
  N_G is the set of nodes
  E_G is the set of edges with their labels,
    i.e., a subset of $N_G \times A_G \times N_G$
  root_G is the node selected as the root

We use variables G, G' to stand for graphs, l, m, n to stand for nodes, x, y, z to stand for general labels and s, t, u to stand for sequences of labels (traces). We write $l \xrightarrow{x}_G m$ to mean $(l, x, m) \in E_G$. Where only one graph is in question, we omit the subscript G. The smallest graph (called 0_A) with given alphabet A consists only of the root node, with no edges, i.e. $(A, \{\text{root}\}, \{\}, \text{root})$. Another small but interesting graph is $1_A =_{df} \{(A, \{\text{root}\}, (\{\text{root}\} \times A \times \{\text{root}\}), \text{root})$.

Example 11.1.1 (Tuple from graph) The graph of Figure 11.1.0 is coded as the mathematical structure defined by the following equations

$$
\begin{aligned}
A &= \{v, w, a, b, c, d\} \\
N &= \{0, 1, 2, 3, 4, 5\} \\
E &= \{(0, v, 2), (0, w, 1), (2, a, 2), (2, b, 1), \\
&\quad (1, d, 3), (2, c, 4), (3, a, 2), (3, d, 5)\} \\
\text{root} &= 0
\end{aligned}
$$

The awkward feature of this encoding is the arbitrary selection of the first six natural numbers to serve as the nodes. Any other six distinct values would have done just as well. We are only interested in properties of graphs that are preserved by one-one transformations (isomorphisms) of the node-set. The use of isomorphism in place of mathematical equality is an inconvenience. We aim to avoid it by constructing a canonical representation for the nodes of a graph. For this, we will have to restrict the theory to graphs satisfying certain healthiness conditions.

Rooted edge-labelled graphs are useful in the study of many branches of computing science, of which data diagrams and heap storage are relevant to object-oriented programming.

Example 11.1.2 (Automata theory) A graph defines the behaviour of an automaton. The nodes stand for states, with the root as the initial state. The labels stand for events, and the presence in E of an edge $l \xrightarrow{x} m$ means that event x happens as the automaton passes from state l to state m. □

Example 11.1.3 (Data diagrams) In a data diagram, a node stands for a set of values, e.g., a type or a class of objects. The labels stand for functions, and the presence of an edge $l \xrightarrow{x} m$ means that x maps values of type l to results of type m. The root is somewhat artificial: the labels on arrows leading from the root can be regarded as the names of the types that they point to. □

Example 11.1.4 (Control flow) In a control flow graph, the nodes represent basic blocks, i.e. sections of program code with no internal label. The edge $l \xrightarrow{x} m$ represents the presence in block l of a jump to a label x which is placed at the beginning of block m. The root is the main block of the program. The same analysis applies when the jumps are procedure calls and the nodes are procedure bodies. □

Example 11.1.5 (Heap storage) A graph can describe the instantaneous content of the entire heap at a particular point in the execution of an object-oriented program. The nodes stand for the objects, and the labels are the names for the attributes. An edge $l \xrightarrow{x} m$ means that m is the value of the x-attribute of the object l. □

When used to model objects and heaps, the labelled graph is both simple and general, in that it allows more complex concerns to be treated separately. For example,

1. Simple values (e.g., like 5, which is printable) can be treated in the usual way as sinks of the graph, i.e. as nodes from which no pointer can ever point. A method local to an object can be similarly represented as a value of one of its attributes.

2. The labels on pointers from the unique root represent the directly accessible program variables. There is no restriction on pointing from the heap into declared program workspace; such pointers are often used in legacy

code for cyclic representations of chains, even if their use is deprecated or forbidden in higher level languages.

3. Absence of a pointer from an object in which space has been allocated for it is often represented by filling the space with a **nil** value. The model allows this; another representation permitted by our model is to introduce a special **nil** object, with special properties, e.g. all arrows from it lead back to itself.

4. The model describes the statics and dynamics of object storage, and is quite independent of the class declarations and inheritance structure of the source language in which a program has been written. In fact, the relationship between the run-time heap and a data diagram is a special case of an invariant assertion, that remains true throughout the execution of the program. The invariant is elegantly formalised with the aid of graph homomorphisms, as described in Definition 11.1.10.

The main operation for updating the value of the heap is written $l \to a := m$. It causes the a-labelled arrow whose tail rests at node l to point to node m, instead of what it pointed to before. The operation changes only the edges of the graph, leaving the nodes, the alphabet, and the root unchanged.

Definition 11.1.6 (Pointer swing)

$$(l \to a := m) \ :=_{df} \ (E := (E - \{l\} \times \{a\} \times N) \cup \{(l, a, m)\}), \text{ where } l, m \in N$$

Example 11.1.7 (Pointer swing) After execution of $1 \to d := 4$, the graph of Figure 11.1.0 would appear as follows

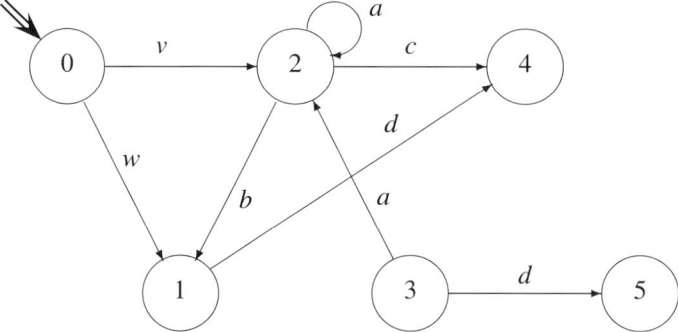

Further operations are needed for deleting an edge and for creating a new node. Node creation introduces an arbitrary new object into the node-set and swings a pointer to point to it. Deletion of a node is more problematic, and will be treated later.

Definition 11.1.8 (Edge deletion, Node creation)

$$(l \to a := \textbf{nil}) =_{df} E := E - \{l\} \times \{a\} \times N$$
$$(l \to a := \textbf{new}) =_{df} N := N + \{m\}; \; l \to a := m,$$
$$\text{where } m \; \widetilde{\in} \; N$$

There are two problems with the above definitions of operations on the heap. The first is that an object-oriented program has no means of directly naming the objects l and m. These references have to be made indirectly by quoting the sequence of labels on a path which leads from the root to the desired object. Thus the assignment in Example 11.1.7 might have been written

$$w \to d := w \to d \to a \to c$$

The second problem is that, after the assignment, two of the nodes (3 and 5) have become inaccessible: the program will never again be able to refer to those nodes by any path. In a garbage-collected heap, such nodes are subject to disappearance at any time. In a non-collected heap they could represent a storage leak. Our trace model of object-orientation will solve all these problems, with the help of a canonical representation of the graph.

When a graph is used as a data diagram it specifies the classes of object to which each variable and attribute is allowed to point. A compiler can therefore allocate to each object only just enough store to hold all its permitted attributes. The compiler will also check all the operations of a program to ensure that all the rules have been observed. As a result, at all times during execution it is possible to ascribe each object in the heap to a node in the data diagram representing the object class to which it belongs. This can be pictured by drawing a polygon around all nodes belonging to the same particular class. Each polygon is then contracted to a single node, dragging the heads and tails of the arrows with it. The result will be a data diagram, which will match the intended structure of class declarations.

Figure 11.1.9 (Object classes)

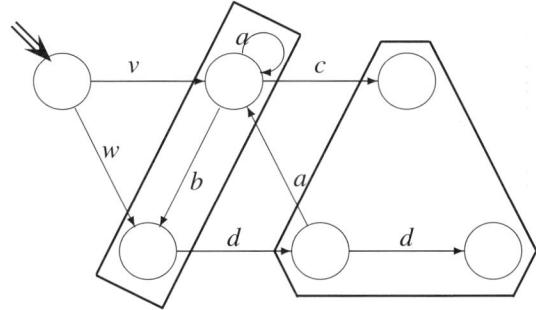

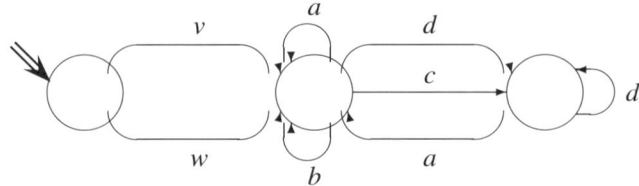

The informal description of the transformation of a heap structure to a class diagram is formalised in the mathematical definition of a homomorphism. This is a function from the nodes of one graph to the nodes of another that preserves the root and the labels on the edges.

Definition 11.1.10 (Homomorphism) Let $G = (A, N, E, \text{root})$ and $G' = (A', N', E', \text{root}')$. Let f be a total function from N to N'. The triple $f : G \to G'$ is called a homomorphism if $A \subseteq A'$, and for all x in A

1. $f(\text{root}) = \text{root}'$

2. $m \xrightarrow{x}_G n$ implies $f(m) \xrightarrow{x}_G f(n)$, for all x in A. □

Examples 11.1.11 (Homomorphisms) From every graph G with alphabet A, there is just one homomorphism to 1_A; from 0_A to G, there are as many homomorphisms as nodes in G. □

Homomorphisms can also be used to define the relationship between a subclass and its parent class in a class hierarchy [2, 3]. For this, we will later introduce a method of reducing the alphabet of labels to match that of the target of the homomorphism. Multiple inheritance is simply modelled by asserting the existence of more than one homomorphism from the heap to several different data diagrams. Different languages enforce differing conventions and rules, to ensure that the invariance of such assertions at run time is checkable by compiler. Our theory is claimed to be sufficiently expressive to describe all such checkable rules in any language. It can also formulate much more general assertions, whose truth cannot be checked at compile time, but only at run time or by proof.

Another important role for a homomorphism is to select from a large graph a smaller subgraph for detailed consideration. The shape of the subgraph is specified by the source of the homomorphism, and the target specifies which particular subgraph of that shape is selected. For example, consider the graph

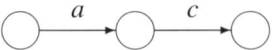

A subgraph of this shape occurs just twice in Figure 1.0; there is only one injective homomorphism from it into the figure, and one that is non-injective. This kind of

subgraph homomorphism has to be redefined to allow for absence of a root.

The remaining role of the homomorphism is to define the concept of an isomorphism of graphs, and so specify what it means for two graphs with different node sets to be essentially the same.

Definition 11.1.12 (Isomorphism) Let $f : G \to G'$ be a homomorphism. This is said to be an isomorphism if f is invertible, and $f^{-1} : G' \to G$ is also a homomorphism. G and G' are isomorphic if there is an isomorphism from one to the other.
□

This rather indirect definition represents the very simple intuitive idea of laying one graph on top of another, and ensuring that it has nodes and edges and labels in all the same places. Like congruent triangles in geometry, they are just two copies of the same graph!

11.2 The trace model

The problem of inaccessible objects is the same as that of inaccessible states in automata theory; and the solution that we adopt is the same: calculate the language of traces that are generated by the graph. A trace of an automaton is a sequence of consecutive events that can occur during its evolution. A trace can be read from the graph by starting at node l and following a path of consecutive edges leading from each node to the next, along a path of directed edges. The trace is extracted as the sequence of labels encountered on the path up to its last node m. The existence of such a trace s is denoted $l \xrightarrow{s} m$. A formal definition uses recursion on the length of the trace.

Definition 11.2.0 (Traces)

$$
\begin{aligned}
l \xrightarrow{<>} m \quad &\text{iff} \quad l = m \\
l \xrightarrow{<a>} m \quad &\text{iff} \quad (l, a, m) \in E \\
l \xrightarrow{s \frown t} m \quad &\text{iff} \quad \exists n \bullet l \xrightarrow{s} n \wedge n \xrightarrow{t} m \\
l \xrightarrow{*} m \quad &=_{df} \quad \{s \mid l \xrightarrow{s} m\} \\
\text{traces}\,(l) \quad &=_{df} \quad \text{root} \xrightarrow{*} l
\end{aligned}
$$

Example 11.2.1 (Figure 1.0) From the graph of Figure 11.1.0 the sets of traces of each of the six nodes are given by the following six regular expressions:

$$
\begin{aligned}
n_0 &= \varepsilon \\
n_1 &= w + n_2\, b \\
n_2 &= v + n_2\, a + n_3\, a \\
n_3 &= n_1 d \\
n_4 &= n_2 c \\
n_5 &= n_3 d
\end{aligned}
$$

In the canonical trace model of a graph, each node l is represented by the set $\text{traces}(l)$, containing all traces on paths to it from the root. The set of nodes is therefore a family N of sets of traces ($N \subseteq \mathbf{P}A^*$). The labelled edges and the root of the graph can be defined in terms of this family.

Definition 11.2.2 (Canonical representation)

$$
\begin{aligned}
\text{Let}\quad G &= (A, N, E, r) \\
\widehat{N} &=_{df} \{\text{traces}(n) \mid n \in N\} \\
\widehat{E} &=_{df} \{l \xrightarrow{x} m \mid l, m \in \widehat{N} \wedge l\widehat{\ }<x> \subseteq m\} \\
\widehat{r} &=_{df} \text{the unique } n \text{ in } \widehat{N} \text{ containing } <>. \\
\widehat{G} &=_{df} (A, \widehat{N}, \widehat{E}, \widehat{r})
\end{aligned}
$$

Theorem 2.3

For all $l, m, n \in \widehat{N}$ and $X \subseteq A^*$

(1) $(l\widehat{\ }X) \subseteq m$ **iff** $X \subseteq (l \xrightarrow[\widehat{G}]{*} m)$

(2) $(l \xrightarrow[\widehat{G}]{*} m)\widehat{\ }(m \xrightarrow[\widehat{G}]{*} n) \subseteq (l \xrightarrow[\widehat{G}]{*} n)$

(3) $(\widehat{r} \xrightarrow[\widehat{G}]{*} m) = m$

Proof: (1) From the fact that for all $s \in A^*$

$$(l\widehat{\ }s) \subseteq m \ \text{ iff }\ l \xrightarrow[\widehat{G}]{s} m$$

(2) From the associativity of the catenation operator and the Galois connection (1)

(3)
$$\begin{aligned}
&\equiv \{(1)\} \\
&\Rightarrow \{<> \in \hat{r}\} \\
&\equiv \{\text{let } m = \text{traces}(n)\} \\
&\Rightarrow \{\forall t \in \hat{r} \bullet (\text{root} \xrightarrow[G]{t} \text{root})\} \\
&\equiv \{\text{def of traces}\} \\
&\equiv \{(1)\}
\end{aligned}$$

$$\begin{aligned}
&X \subseteq \text{LHS} \\
&\hat{r} \hat{} X \subseteq m \\
&X \subseteq \text{RHS} \\
&\forall s \in X \bullet (\text{root} \xrightarrow[G]{s} n) \\
&\forall t \in \hat{r}, s \in X \bullet (\text{root} \xrightarrow[G]{t s} n) \\
&(\hat{r} \hat{} X) \subseteq \text{traces}(n) = m \\
&X \subseteq \text{LHS}
\end{aligned}$$

In the theory of deterministic automata, the language generated by the automaton is just the union of the set of traces of all its states

$$\text{language}(G) = \bigcup \{\text{traces}(l) \mid l \in N_G\}$$

The great advantage of this is that an inaccessible state has no traces at all, and so makes no contribution to the language. Two automata are therefore decreed to be identical if they have the same language.

Example 11.2.4 (Identical automata)

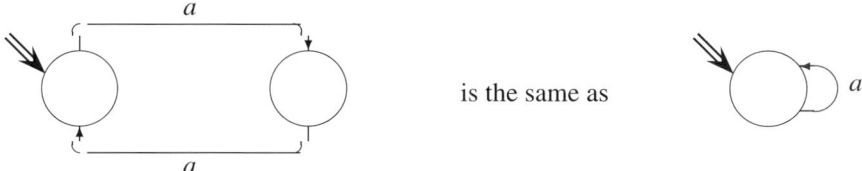

because in both cases the language is $\{a\}^*$ □

For automata, the purpose of this identification is to allow automatic minimisation of the number of states needed to generate or recognise a specified language. But in object-oriented programming, such identification of objects would be wholly inappropriate. The reason is that the pointer swinging operation (not considered by automata theory) distinguishes graphs which automata theory says should be the same.

Example 11.2.5 (after swing) After the assignment $a \to a := \mathbf{nil}$, the two graphs of example 11.2.4 now look like

and

Even in automata theory, these two graphs are distinct. For this reason, we cannot model a heap simply as a set of traces, and we have to go up one level in complexity to model it as a **set** of sets of traces, as shown in the definition of $\widehat{N}$.

Nevertheless, there are many interesting analogies between our trace model and the process algebra of non-deterministic automata. For example, as in CSP [7], the entire set of valid traces is prefix-closed.

Theorem 11.2.6 (Prefix closure) $\bigcup \widehat{N}$ is non-empty; and if it contains $s\frown t$, it also contains s. □

An important property of the $\frown$ operator, transforming a graph to its canonical representation, is that it leaves unchanged an argument that is already canonical.

Theorem 11.2.7 (Idempotence)

$$\widehat{\widehat{G}} = \widehat{G}$$

Proof $\quad$ traces(traces(n))

$= \{\text{def of traces}\}$

$\quad$ traces(root) $\xrightarrow{*}_{\widehat{G}}$ (traces(n))

$= \{\text{Theorem 2.3(3)}\}$

$\quad$ traces(n)

Note that this is an equality, not just an isomorphism. But the claim that the result is canonical for all graphs is not justified: there are G such that $\widehat{G}$ is not even isomorphic to G.

Counter-examples 11.2.8 (Disappearing nodes)

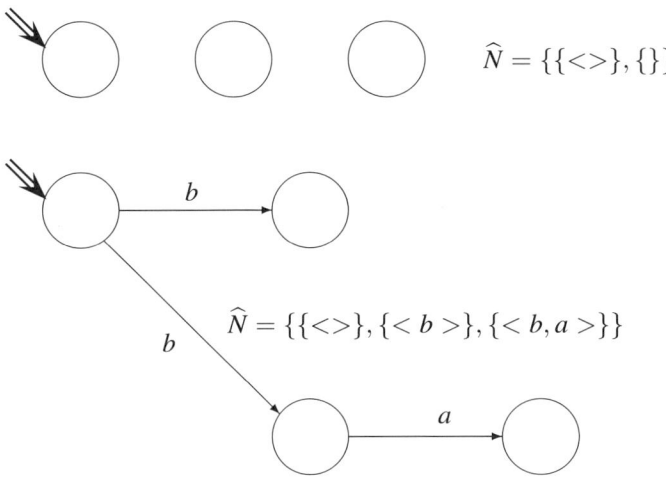

$\widehat{N} = \{\{<>\}, \{\}\}$

$\widehat{N} = \{\{<>\}, \{<b>\}, \{<b,a>\}\}$

In choosing to study the canonical representation, we exclude such counter-examples from consideration. The remainder of this section will define and justify the exclusion.

An important property in object-oriented programming is that each name should uniquely denote a single object. This is assured if the graph is deterministic.

Definition 11.2.9 (Determinism) A graph is deterministic if for each l and x there is at most one m such that $l \xrightarrow{x} m$. This is necessary for determinism of the corresponding automaton. In a data diagram, determinism permits automatic resolution of the polymorphic use of the same label to denote different functions on different data types. In object-oriented programming, it states the obvious fact that each attribute of each object can have only one value. □

If the original graph is deterministic, its canonical node-set $\widehat{N}$ satisfies an additional property familiar from process algebra — it is a bisimulation [11].

Definition 11.2.10 (Bisimulation) A family N of sets of traces is a bisimulation if it is a partial equivalence which is respected by trace extension. More formally, for all p, q in N

$$p = q \;\;\lor\;\; p \cap q = \{\}$$
$$s, t \in p \;\;\land\;\; t\widehat{\;}u \in q \;\Rightarrow\; s\widehat{\;}u \in q$$

Determinism ensures that any two distinct objects will have distinct trace sets, except in the extreme case that both have empty trace sets. Such objects can never be accessed by a program, so they might as well not exist.

Definition 11.2.11 (Accessibility) A node n is accessible if traces(n) is nonempty. A graph is accessible if all its nodes are, i.e. $\{\} \; \widetilde{\in} \; \widehat{N}$. For automata, inaccessible nodes represent unreachable states, which can and should be ignored in any comparison between them. In a heap, they represent unusable storage, which can and should be garbage-collected (or otherwise explicitly deleted). □

At last we can show that we can model all the graphs that we are interested in by simply considering canonical graphs; furthermore, we can assume that N is always a prefix-closed bisimulation.

Theorem 11.2.12 (Representability) If G is deterministic and accessible, it is isomorphic to $\widehat{G}$

Proof Let $f(n) =_{df}$ traces(n) for all $n \in N$. Because G is deterministic

$$(n \neq m) \Rightarrow (\text{traces}(n) \neq \text{traces}(m))$$

Futhermore we have

$$f(n) \xrightarrow[\widehat{G}]{x} f(m)$$
$$\equiv \{\text{def of } \widehat{E}\}$$
$$\text{traces}(n)\widehat{\;} <x> \subseteq \text{traces}(m)$$
$$\equiv \{\text{traces}(n) \neq \{\} \text{ and } G \text{ is deterministic}\}$$
$$n \xrightarrow[G]{x} m$$

We can now solve the problems of graph representation left open in the previous section: objects will be named by traces, and inaccessible objects will disappear. We will assume that the heap G is at all times held in its canonical representation; and redefine each operation of object-oriented programming as an operation on the trace sets N.

Edge deletion $t \to x := \mathbf{nil}$ now has to remove not only the single edge x, but also all traces that include this edge. Every such trace must begin with a trace of the object t itself, i.e. a trace which is equivalent to t by the equivalence N. The trace to be removed must of course contain an occurrence of $<x>$, the edge to be removed. It ends with a trace leading to some other node n in N. The traces removed from n are therefore exactly defined by the set

$$[t]\,\hat{}\,<x>\,\hat{}\,(t\,\hat{}\,<x>\xrightarrow{*} n)$$

We use the usual square bracket notation $[t]_N$ that contains t to denote the equivalence class (or more simply just $[t]$). Of course, x may occur more than once in the trace, either before or after the occurrence shown explicitly above. In the following definition, the removal of the edge is followed by removal of any set that becomes empty – a simple mathematical implementation of garbage-collection.

Re-definition 11.2.13 (Edge deletion, Node creation)

$$(t \to x := \textbf{nil}) \quad =_{df} \quad N := \{n - [t]\,\hat{}\,<x>\,\hat{}\,(t\,\hat{}\,<x>\xrightarrow{*} n) \mid n \in N\} - \{\{\}\}$$

$$(t \to x := \textbf{new}) \quad =_{df} \quad t \to x := \textbf{nil}; \ N := N + \{[t]\,\hat{}\,<x>\}$$

Unfortunately, pointer swing is even more complicated than this. We consider first the effect of $t\,\hat{}\,<y>:= s$, in the case where y is a **new** label, occurring nowhere else in the graph. The question now is, what are all the new traces introduced as a result of insertion of this new and freshly labelled edge? As before, every such trace must start with a trace from $[t]$, followed by the first occurrence of y. But now we must consider explicitly the possibility that the new edge occurs many times in a loop. The trace that completes the loop from the head of y back to its tail must be a path leading from s to t in the original graph, i.e. a member of $(s \xrightarrow{*} t)$. After any number of repetitions of $((s \xrightarrow{*} t)\,\hat{}\,<y>)$, the new trace concludes with a path from s to some node n. The traces added to an arbitrary equivalence class n are exactly defined by the set

$$[t]\,\hat{}\,<y>\,\hat{}\,((s \xrightarrow{*} t)\,\hat{}\,<y>)^{*}\,\hat{}\,(s \xrightarrow{*} n)$$

Note that in many cases $(s \xrightarrow{*} n)$ will be empty, because there is no path from s to n. Then by definition of $\hat{}\,$ between sets, the whole of the set described above is empty, and no new traces are added to n.

After inserting these new traces, it is permissible and necessary to remove the original edge x from the original graph and from the newly added traces too. Finally, the freshly named new edge y can be safely renamed as x.

Re-definition 11.2.14 (Pointer swing)

$$(t \to x := s) \quad =_{df} \quad \text{let } y \text{ be a fresh label in}$$
$$N := \{n + [t]\,\hat{}\,<y>\,\hat{}\,((s \xrightarrow{*} t)\,\hat{}\,<y>)^{*}\,\hat{}\,(s \xrightarrow{*} n) \mid n \in N\};$$
$$t \to x := \textbf{nil}; \quad \text{rename } y \text{ to } x \qquad \square$$

Note that it is **not** permissible to delete the edge x before adding the new edge: this could make inaccessible some of the objects that need to be retained because they are accessible through s. The problem is clearly revealed in the simplest case:

$t \to x := t \to x$. The necessary complexity of the pointer swing is a serious, perhaps a crippling disadvantage of the trace model of pointers and objects.

11.3 Applications

The purpose of our investigations is not just to contribute towards a fully abstract denotational semantics for an object-oriented programming language. We also wish to provide assistance in reasoning about the correctness of such programs, and to clarify the conditions under which they can be validly optimised. Both objectives can be met with the aid of assertions, which describe useful properties of the values of variables at appropriate times in the execution of the program. To formulate clear assertions (unclear ones do not help), we need an expressive language; and to prove the resulting verification conditions, we need a toolkit of powerful theorems. This section makes a start on satisfying both these needs.

Two important properties of an individual node are defined as follows. It is acyclic if the only path leading from itself to itself is the empty path.

$$n \text{ is acyclic } =_{df} (n \xrightarrow{*} n) = \{<>\}$$

A graph is acyclic if all its nodes are. A node is a sink if there is no node accessible from it except itself

$$n \text{ is a sink } =_{df} \forall m \bullet n \xrightarrow{*} m \subseteq \{<>\}$$

These definitions can be qualified by a subset B of the alphabet, e.g.

$$n \text{ is a } B\text{-sink } =_{df} \forall m \bullet (n \xrightarrow{*} m) \cap B^* \subseteq \{<>\}$$

Two important relationships between nodes are connection and dominance. Connection is defined by the existence of a path between the nodes; and this path may be required to use only labels from B

$$m \xRightarrow{B} n =_{df} (n \xrightarrow{*} m) \cap B^* \neq \{\}$$

$\xRightarrow{B}$ is clearly a pre-order, i.e., transitive, and reflexive, but it is antisymmetric only in acyclic graphs. The root is the bottom of any accessible graph. The superscript B is omitted when it is the whole alphabet of the graph under discussion. The relation of dominance between objects is stronger than connection. One object l in a graph dominates an object m if every path to m leads through l

$$l \sqsubseteq m =_{df} l \widehat{\ } (l \xrightarrow{*} m) = m$$

Deletion of a dominating object makes a dominated object inaccessible. So this relationship is very important in proving that a graph remains accessible and/or acyclic after a pointer swing. Its properties are similar to those of the prefix ordering over simple traces.

Theorem 11.3.0 (Dominance ordering) $\sqsubseteq$ is a partial order with the root as a bottom and the empty set as its top. The dominators of any node are totally ordered, i.e.

$$\text{if } l \sqsubseteq n \text{ and } m \sqsubseteq n \text{ then } l \sqsubseteq m \text{ or } m \sqsubseteq l$$

Proof see appendix. □

For non-empty nodes, dominance implies connection. If a node has only one trace, then every node that connects to it will dominate it. If all nodes have this property, the graph is called a divergent tree — divergent because all its pointers point away from the root and towards its sinks (i.e. the leaves).

In a language without garbage-collection, there is a grave danger that a pointer swing will leave an object that has no other pointer pointing to it. Such an object can never again be accessed by the program, and the storage space that it occupies will never be reused. This phenomenon is known as a space leak. In order to prevent it, the programmer must accept the obligation to ensure that a certain precondition is satisfied before each pointer swing $s \to x := t$. The relevant precondition is expressed as non-dominance

$$\neg s \sqsubseteq s\hat{\ }<x>$$

In a language without garbage-collection, the only way in which heap storage can be recovered for reuse is by an explicit command in the program, declaring that a particular object will never be accessed again. We will treat the simplest form of atomic deletion, as for example the delete command in PASCAL. This command must be given at the same time that the last pointer to the object is deleted by $s \to x := \textbf{nil}$. The precondition of such a deletion is the opposite of that for an assignment

$$s \sqsubseteq s\hat{\ }<x>$$

In fact, a stronger precondition is necessary. All the objects accessible through $s\ \hat{\ }<x>$ must be accessible through some other object as well (otherwise their space would leak anyway). The full precondition for deletion is

$$\forall y \bullet (s\hat{\ }<x> \sqsubseteq s\hat{\ }<x>\hat{\ }y \textbf{ iff } y =<>).$$

The complexity of these preconditions may explain why control of space leaks is a difficult problem in practice.

A heap as represented in the store of a computer must be described as a single variable, even though its value is of great size and complexity. Any pointer in the heap can at any time be swung to point to any other object whatsoever. To control this complexity, a programmer usually constrains the use of a heap in a highly disciplined way. The heap is understood to be split into a number of component subgraphs, satisfying invariant properties that limit the connections within and between the components. A component of a graph can readily be selected in two ways: by restricting the alphabet, or by concentration on a single branch.

Definition 11.3.1 (Subgraphs)

$$N \upharpoonright B =_{df} \{n \cap B^* \mid n \in N\} - \{\{\}\}$$

$N \upharpoonright B$ is a canonical graph with alphabet B, containing just those objects nameable by chains of labels drawn wholly from B.

$$N/n = \{n \xrightarrow{*} m \mid m \in N\} - \{\{\}\}, \text{ where } n \in N$$

N/n is a canonical graph, isomorphic to the subgraph of all nodes accessible from n. It consists of just that part of the heap that is seen by a method local to n. □

These subgraph operations obey laws identical to those found in process algebra:

$$
\begin{aligned}
N \upharpoonright A &= N, \text{ if } A \text{ is the alphabet of the graph} \\
(N \upharpoonright B) \upharpoonright C &= N \upharpoonright (B \cap C) \\
N \upharpoonright \{\} &= 0_{\{\}} \\
N/<> &= N \\
(N/s)/t &= N/(s\widehat{\,}t)
\end{aligned}
$$

The purpose of this paper has been to provide a conceptual framework for formalisation of invariant assertions about data structures represented as objects in a heap. Class and type declarations serve the same purpose; they are also carefully designed to enjoy the additional advantage that their validity can be checked by compiler. Assertions have more expressive power, but they can be tested only at run time, and they can be validated only by proof. In the remainder of this section we explore the power of the trace model in the formulation of assertions, and suggest that a diagram may be helpful in visualising them.

Definition 11.3.2 (Chain) Consider a pair of labels $B = \{base, next\}$. This defines a chain if $C = (N/base) \upharpoonright \{next\}$ is invariantly acyclic.

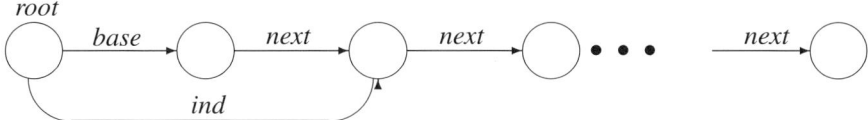

A variable *ind* is an index into this chain if invariantly $base \stackrel{next}{\Longrightarrow} ind$. A last-pointer is an index that always points to a *next*-sink. A final segment of the chain, chopped off at a given index, is C/ind. □

A chain is often used to scan a set of objects of interest. A good example is a convergent tree — convergent because the pointers point away from the leaves towards the root (a sink). Without a chain through them, the leaves (and indeed the whole tree) would be inaccessible.

Figure 11.3.3 (Convergent tree)

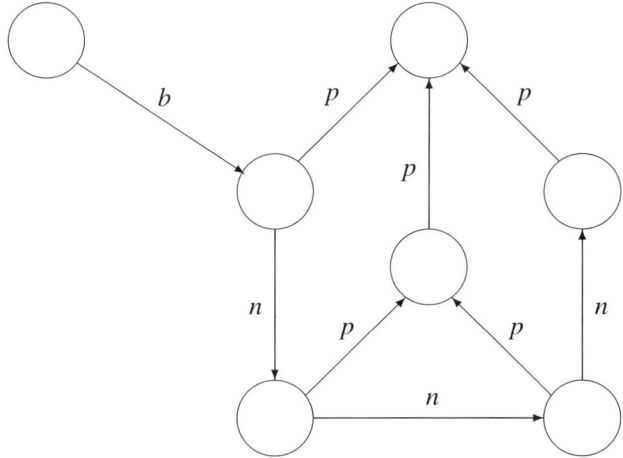

The attribute p points from an offspring to its parent in the tree; the attribute n constructs the leaf chain starting at a declared base variable b. □

We wish to formalise the properties shared by all such trees, without restriction on size or shape, and without defining which other attributes besides p and n may be pointing to or from the nodes. Let us first confine attention to the subgraph T of interest

$$T =_{df} (N/b) \upharpoonright \{p, n\}$$

The aim is to formulate the desired invariant properties of T as a conjunction of simple conditions that can be checked separately, and reused in different combinations for different purposes. The first condition has already been given a formal definition

1. T is acyclic

2. Every object on the chain has a parent: if $j \xrightarrow{n} k$ then $(\exists l \bullet k \xrightarrow{p} l) \wedge (\exists l \bullet j \xrightarrow{p} l)$

3. No parent is an object on the chain: if $l \xrightarrow{p} m$ then $(\neg k \xrightarrow{n} m) \wedge (\neg m \xrightarrow{n} k)$

4. Any two nodes on the tree share a common ancestor: $\forall j, k \; \exists l \bullet j \xRightarrow{p} l \wedge k \xRightarrow{p} l$

There is one more property that is usually desired of a leaf-chain: it should visit the leaves in some reasonable order, for example, close relatives should appear close in the chain. In particular, the following picture should **not** appear in the graph.

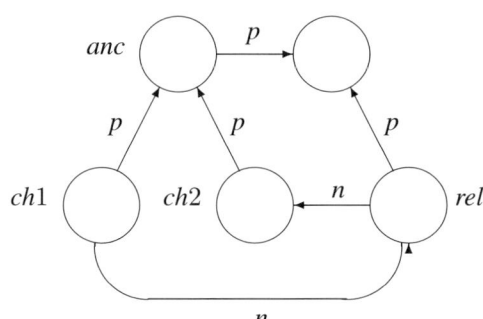

Note that $ch1$ and $ch2$ are more closely related to each other than to rel, which therefore should not separate them in the chain. The requirement is formalised

5. If $ch1 \xRightarrow{p} anc \wedge ch2 \xRightarrow{p} anc \wedge ch1 \xRightarrow{n} rel \wedge rel \xRightarrow{n} ch2$ then $rel \xRightarrow{p} anc$.

These invariants are expressed in the predicate calculus, using variables that have either implicit quantification over all traces in $\bigcup T$, or explicit existential quantification. The invariants can also be conveniently represented pictorially in the graphical calculus [4]. The simpler invariants directly prohibit occurrence in the heap of any subgraph of a certain shape. For example, condition (2) prohibits any occurrence of the two shapes

11. A trace model for pointers and objects   241

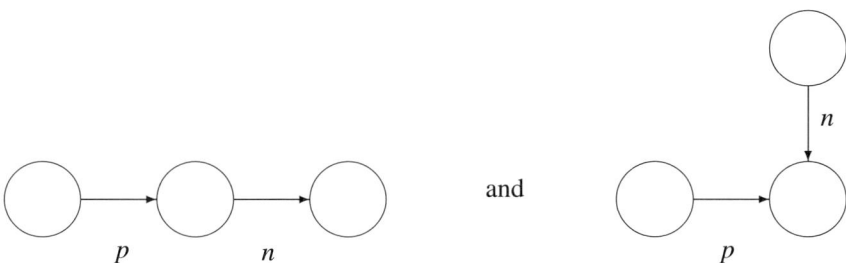

More formally, there is no homomorphism from either of these graphs into the heap. The acyclic condition (1) can be pictured by using a single arrow to represent a complete (non-empty) trace drawn from the specified alphabet; the following is prohibited

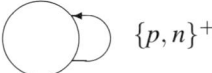

The more complicated invariants take the form of an implication, whose consequent has existentially quantified variables. These are drawn as dotted lines rather than the solid lines that represent variables universally quantified over the whole formula. So the condition (2) would be drawn

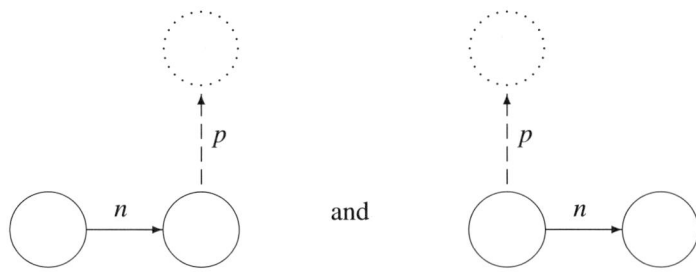

The condition (4) combines this convention with the path convention

The fifth condition is the most elaborate

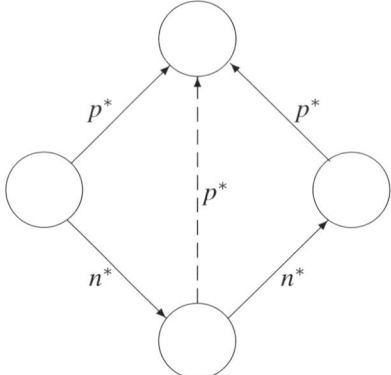

The meaning of the dotted line convention illustrated above can be formalised, again in terms of graph homomorphisms. The picture states that every homomorphism from the graph drawn as solid lines and nodes can be extended to a homomorphism from the whole picture, including dotted lines and nodes. The extension must not change the mapping of any of the solid components. Even more formally, the diagram defines an obvious injective homomorphism $j : solid \to diagram$ from its solid components to the whole diagram. It states that for all $h : solid \to T$ there exists an $h' : diag \to T$ such that $h = j; h'$ (h factors through j). In plainer words, perhaps the programmer's instinct to draw pictures when manipulating pointers can be justified by appeal to higher mathematics.

11.4 Conclusion

The ideas reported in this paper have not been pursued to any conclusion. Perhaps, in view of the difficulties described at the end of section 2, they never will be. Their interest is mainly as an example of the construction of a generic mathematical model to help in formalisation of assertions about interesting and useful data structures. Such assertions can be helpful in designing and maintaining complicated class libraries, and in testing the results of changes, even if they are never used for explicit program proof.

Other published approaches to reasoning about pointer structures have been much better worked out. An early definition of a tree-structured machine with an equivalence relation for sharing was given in [9]. The closest in spirit to the trace model is described in [14] and applied to the proof of an ingenious graph marking algorithm. A similar approach using nice algebraic laws was taken in [15]. Another promising approach [12] exploits the proof obligation as a driver for the design of the algorithm in a functional style. It models each label as a function from addresses to values or other addresses contained in the addressed location.

Other authors too have been deterred by the complexity of sharing structures introduced by pointer swing [16].

Acknowledgements For useful comments on earlier drafts we thank Frances Page, Bernhard Möller, Manfred Broy, Jay Misra, Paul Rudin, Ralph Steinbrüggen, Zhou Yu Qian.

References

[1] M. Abadi and L. Cardelli. *A theory of objects.* Springer (1998).

[2] L. Cardelli. A semantics of multiple inheritance. *Information and Computation* 76: 138–164 (1988).

[3] W. Cook and J. Palsberg. A denotational semantics of inheritance and its correctness. *Information and Computation* 114(2), 329–350 (1994).

[4] S. Curtis and G. Lowe, A graphical calculus. In B. Möller (ed) *Mathematics of Program Construction*, LNCS 947 Springer (1995).

[5] O. Dahl and K. Nygaard. Simula, an Algol-based simulation language. *Communications of the ACM* 9(9) 671–678 (1966).

[6] A. Goldberg and D. Robson. *Smalltalk-80. The language and its implementation.* Addison-Wesley (1983).

[7] C.A.R. Hoare, *Communicating Sequential Processes.* Prentice-Hall (1985).

[8] S.N. Kamin and U.S. Reddy. Two semantic models of object-oriented languages. In C.A. Gunter and J.C. Mitchell (eds): *Theoretical Aspects of Object-Oriented Programming*, 463–495, MIT Press, (1994).

[9] P.J. Landin, A correspondence between ALGOL 60 and Church's lambda-notation Part 1. *Communications ACM* 8(2) 89–101 (1965).

[10] B. Meyer. *Object-oriented Software Construction*, Prentice-Hall second edition (1997).

[11] R. Milner. *Communication and Concurrency*, Prentice Hall (1987)

[12] B. Möller, Towards pointer algebra. *Science of Computer Programming* 21 (1993), 57-90.

[13] B. Möller, Calculating with pointer structures. *Proceedings of Mathematics for Software Construction, Chapman and Hall* (1997), 24-48.

[14] J.M.Morris, A general axiom of assignment, Assignment and linked data structure, A proof of the Schorr-Waite algorithm. In M Broy and G. Schmidt (eds.) *Theoretical Foundations of Programming Methodology*, 25-51, Reidel 1982 (Proceedings of the 1981 Marktoberdorf Summer School).

[15] G. Nelson, Verifying reachability invariants of linked structures. *Proceedings of POPL* (1983), ACM Press, 38–47.

[16] N. Suzuki, Analysis of pointer rotation. *Communications ACM* 25(5) 330–335 (1982).

Appendix

Proof of Theorem 11.3.0

First we are going to show that dominance is a partial order.

(reflexive)
$$l$$
$$= \{s\widehat{\ }<> = s\}$$
$$l\widehat{\ }\{<>\}$$
$$\subseteq \{<> \in (l \xrightarrow{*} l)\}$$
$$l\widehat{\ }(l \xrightarrow{*} l)$$
$$\subseteq \{\text{Theorem 2.3.(1)}\}$$
$$l$$

(antisymmetric) Assume that $l \sqsubseteq m$ and $m \sqsubseteq l$. If $l = \{\}$ then
$$m = l\widehat{\ }(l \xrightarrow{*} m) = \{\}\widehat{\ }(l \xrightarrow{*} m) = \{\} = l$$

Assume that $l \neq \{\}$. From the fact that
$$l = l\widehat{\ }(l \xrightarrow{*} m)\widehat{\ }(m \xrightarrow{*} l)$$

and $l \neq \{\}$ we conclude that
$$<> \in (l \xrightarrow{*} m)\widehat{\ }(m \xrightarrow{*} l)$$
$$\equiv \{s\widehat{\ }t = <> \text{ iff } s = t = <>\}$$
$$<> \in (l \xrightarrow{*} m) \cap (m \xrightarrow{*} l)$$
$$\Rightarrow \{l = m\widehat{\ }(m \xrightarrow{*} l) \text{ and } m = l\widehat{\ }(l \xrightarrow{*} m)\}$$
$$(l \sqsubseteq m) \wedge (m \sqsubseteq l)$$
$$\equiv l = m$$

(transitive) Assume that $l \sqsubseteq m$ and $m \sqsubseteq n$.
$$n$$
$$\supseteq \{\text{Theorem 2.3(1)}\}$$
$$l\widehat{\ }(l \xrightarrow{*} n)$$
$$\supseteq \{\text{Theorem 2.3(2)}\}$$
$$l\widehat{\ }(l \xrightarrow{*} m)\widehat{\ }(m \xrightarrow{*} n)$$
$$= \{l \sqsubseteq m \text{ and } m \sqsubseteq n\}$$
$$n$$

Let n be a non-empty node. Assume that
$$l \sqsubseteq n \text{ and } m \sqsubseteq n$$

For any subset X of A^* we define $sht(X)$ as the set of shortest traces of X

$$sht(X) =_{df} \{s \in X \mid \forall t \in X \bullet t \leq s \Rightarrow t = s\}$$

From the fact that $n \neq \{\}$ we conclude that neither $sht(l)$ nor $sht(m)$ is empty. Consider the following cases:

(1) $sht(l) \cap sht(m) \neq \{\}$: From the determinacy it follows that

$$l = m$$

(2) $sht(l) \cap sht(m) = \{\}$: From the assumption that $l \sqsubseteq n$ and $m \sqsubseteq n$ it follows that

$$\forall u \in sht(l) \, \exists v \in sht(m) \bullet (u \leq v \lor v \leq u)$$

and

$$\forall v \in sht(m) \, \exists u \in sht(l) \bullet (u \leq v \lor v \leq u)$$

(2a) $\forall u \in sht(l) \, \exists v \in sht(m) \bullet v \leq u$: From the bisimulation property it follows that

$$m \sqsubseteq l$$

(2b) $\forall v \in sht(m) \, \exists u \in sht(l) \bullet u \leq v$: In this case we have

$$l \sqsubseteq m$$

(2c) There exist $u, \hat{u} \in sht(l)$ and $v, \hat{v} \in sht(m)$ such that

$$u < v \text{ and } \hat{v} < \hat{u}$$

Let

$$j =_{df} min\{length(s) \mid s \in sht(l \stackrel{*}{\rightarrow} n)\}$$

$$k =_{df} min\{length(t) \mid t \in sht(m \stackrel{*}{\rightarrow} n)\}$$

From $u \leq v$ we conclude that $j > k$, and from $\hat{v} < \hat{u}$ we have $j < k$, which leads to contradiction.

From the above case analysis we conclude that

$$l \sqsubseteq m \text{ or } m \sqsubseteq l \qquad \square$$

12

Object models as heap invariants

Daniel Jackson

Abstract

Object models are widely used for describing structural properties of object-oriented programs, but they suffer from two problems. First, their semantics is usually unclear. Second, the textual constraints that are often used to annotate diagrams are not integrated with the diagrammatic notation itself. In this paper, we show how to interpret an object model as a heap invariant by translation to a small relational logic. With a few additional shorthands, this logic can be used for textual constraints, so that annotation is just conjunction. Our semantics is simpler than those proposed by others, and accounts for features of the object model that have not been addressed in treatments that focus on more abstract models.

Introduction

Semantic data models, developed originally for databases [1, 5, 13, 26, 29], are called 'object models' in the context of object-oriented programs, and are widely used for describing both problem and implementation structure. An object model is a better starting point for a development than a description that treats objects as interacting entities with local state, because it highlights fundamental structural properties of the problem domain, and postpones decisions about the allocation of state and function to objects. For this reason, object models lie at the core of many object-oriented methods, such as OMT [24], Fusion [3], Syntropy [4], and Catalysis [7].

Object models are good for describing implementations also, since their relational structure is a close match to the class/field structure of object-oriented programming languages such as Java. An object model, unlike a traditional specification, emphasizes sharing of objects and interactions, an aspect of design that is becoming more important because of the popularity of design patterns [9], which encourage a style of design in which programs are assembled from tightly coupled configurations of collaborating objects.

Object models are simple but surprisingly powerful. The ability to represent basic aspects of the model diagramatically is also an important attraction for many developers. Despite their popularity, however, object models are not well understood, and are often used in a way that barely exploits their power. In many cases, a purported object model is just a class diagram—a graphical representation of the class hierarchy and field declarations of a program. As we shall see, an object model is an invariant and can express properties of the program state that are not immediately evident from the syntax of the program. An object model is also not bound by the syntactic restrictions of the programming language; it is legitimate, for example, to associate fields with Java interfaces.

Most work [2, 8, 11, 12, 18, 21] has given meaning to object models by translation to a formal specification language such as Larch [10] or Z [28]. In our opinion, this loses the key benefit of object models. An object model is a lightweight formal specification; converting it to a full-fledged formal specification language obscures its simplicity, and eliminates opportunities for analysis that take advantage of its limited expressiveness.

Instead, we have developed a tiny logic that is sufficient to express object model properties, but which is still amenable to fully automatic semantic analysis [17]. Object model diagrams are translated rather directly into the logic. Moreover, a version of the logic extended with some simple shorthands gives a textual annotation language that is compatible with the diagrammatic form. This language, which with the addition of structuring mechanisms not described here is called Alloy [16], offers the 'navigation expressions' made popular by Syntropy [4], but with a more uniform structure and simpler semantics than in other languages.

In our previous work [16], we have focused on object models that describe problem structure. In this paper, we focus on the issues that arise when object models are used to describe implementations. In this context, an object model is a heap invariant, and describes a set of legal program states. Giving meaning to such an object model obviously requires interpreting the abstract mathematical notions (of sets and relations) in terms of code notions (of classes and fields). But it also seems to require giving a slightly different semantics. It seems necessary to drop the disjointness constraints that are implicit in problem models, and to introduce a notion of 'qualified sets' that allows distinctions to be made between different usages of polymorphic classes.

This paper represents work in progress, and is more a collection of observations than a coherent theory. Nevertheless, we believe that it demonstrates that a much simpler notion of object modelling is possible than has previously been assumed. Recently, the Object Management Group ratified as a standard the Unified Modeling Language [25], whose object modelling notation is of unprecedented complexity. A simpler semantics may not only clarify the meaning of basic object modelling constructs, but may point the way to an object modelling language that is simpler, more expressive, and easier to use.

12.1 Snapshots and object models

The heap of an object-oriented program can be represented by a graph, with nodes for objects and edges for field references. Such a graph is called a *snapshot*, since it represents the state of the program at a particular point in time. A snapshot is usually partial, showing only the objects of certain types.

For example, a program that includes the class

>   class ZipCity {
>   String zip;
>   String city;
>   }

may have the following snapshot:

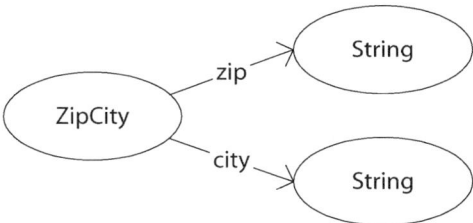

The *ZipCity* class will be used later as part of a datatype that provides a mapping from zipcodes to city names. For now, however, we are concerned only with the existence of objects and fields, and not their interpretations. In a snapshot, a node labelled C represents an object of class C; additional labels can be used to show that the object conforms to particular interfaces. An edge labelled f from m to n says that the field f of the object m holds a reference to object n. Null-valued fields are represented simply omitting the edge. (We are ignoring namespace issues, such as whether the field is accessible from outside the class, although we do discuss abstraction below.)

A program typically has infinitely many snapshots. A more useful kind of diagram, the *object model*, describes an invariant: that is, a set of snapshots that are regarded as well-formed. Sometimes, the object model is merely a class diagram, showing only those properties that follow directly from the syntactic structure of the program. But it can incorporate properties that are not easily inferred from the program text, especially when textual annotations are admitted.

The following object model, for example, expresses the property that no two *ZipCity* objects have *zip* fields with the same value:

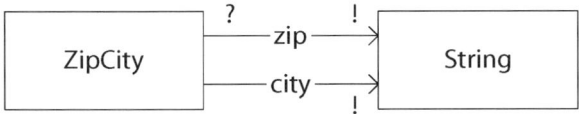

Each box in the object model represents a set of objects; arrows between boxes represent fields. The markings on the ends of the arrows indicate relative multiplicities. The exclamation mark on the head of the *zip* arrow says that each *ZipCity* object is mapped by the *zip* field to exactly one string. In other words, the *zip* field is never null. The question mark on the tail of the arrow says that each *String* object is mapped to by the *zip* field of at most one *ZipCity* object. In other words, *ZipCity* objects do not share *zip* strings. Omission of a marking implies no constraint, so the lack of a marking on the tail of the city arrow, for example, allows *ZipCity* objects to share *city* strings. The object model thus admits the snapshot on the left but not the one on the right:

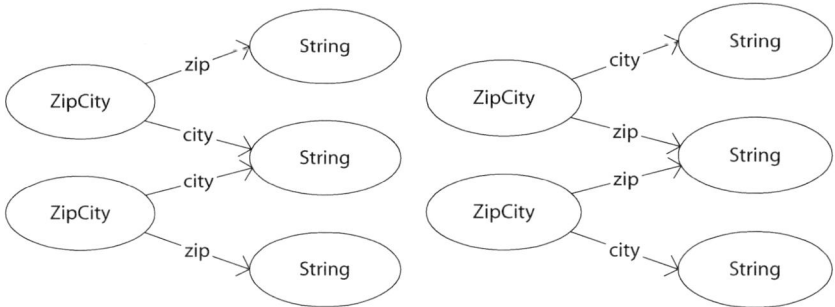

Like any invariant, an object model is a constraint with a scope limited to the fields and classes mentioned. There is no closed world assumption: the heap may contain objects of other classes, and objects may have additional fields not shown in the object model. This is important because it admits partial models that can be developed incrementally and composed with one another.

12.2 Object-model examples

We now illustrate some additional features of object models with a series of small examples: classification of sets, shown with a linked list; instantiation of a polymorphic type, shown by using the list as the representation of a mapping from zipcodes to city names; indexed fields, shown in an array representation of the mapping; and abstract fields, shown in two more abstract views of the array representation.

12.2.1 Linked list

Linked lists can be represented with an abstract class and two concrete subclasses for empty and non-empty lists:

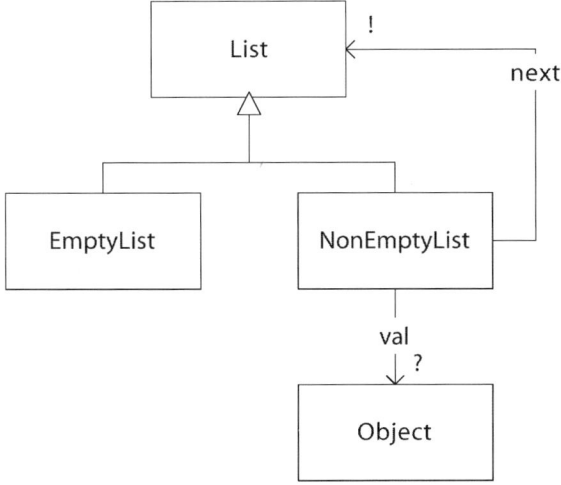

This model illustrates classification of objects. The arrow with the closed head denotes subset: each element of the set *EmptyList* is also an element of the set *List*. The sharing of the arrowhead indicates disjointness: that no object is both an *EmptyList* and a *NonEmptyList*. The multiplicity marking on the *next* field (!, meaning *exactly one*) indicates that a *NonEmptyList* always points to a *List*; the marking on the *val* field (?, meaning *zero* or *one*) allows *Lists* to contain null references as well as objects.

12.2.2 List of records

A mapping from zipcodes to city names may be implemented as a linked list of *ZipCity* objects:

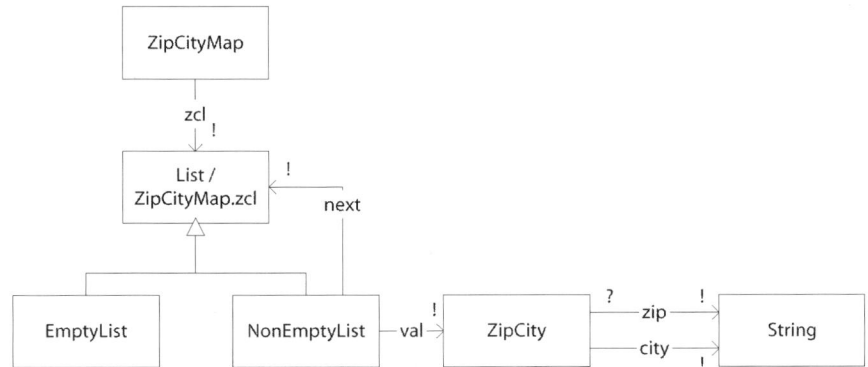

The expression that qualifies the name *List* indicates that the box does not denote all *List* objects, but only those occupying the *zcl* field of *ZipCityMap* objects.

This allows the object model to show that the *val* field of a *NonEmptyList* is non-null, and holds a reference to a *ZipCity* record, not an arbitrary object. The notation permits arbitrary expressions to be used to qualify sets.

12.2.3 Array of records

The mapping may alternatively be implemented as an array of *ZipCity* objects. The array is an object in its own right, with a field *elt[i]* for each index *i* mapping the array to the *i*th element. The edge labelled *elt[Index]* represents a collection of fields, each corresponding to one value of *Index*.

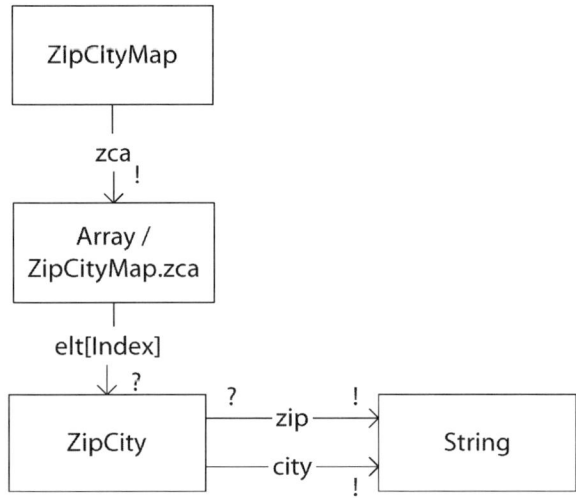

Again, the qualifier makes the *Array* box denote only those objects of class *Array* that are referenced by *ZipCityMap* objects.

12.2.4 Set of records

Abstracting away the array, we can show a direct association between *ZipCityMap* and its records:

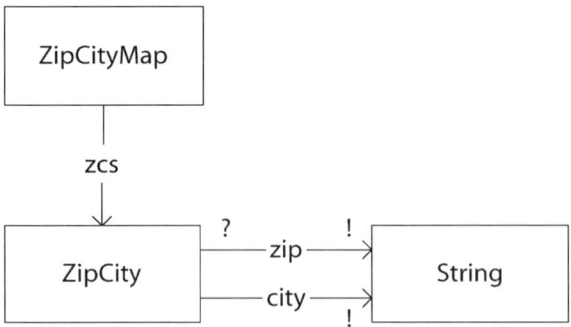

In this case, the field *zcs* is an *abstract field*, and does not correspond to a field of a class. Instead, it represents part of the state of a *ZipCityMap* object that can be observed by calling its methods. The lack of a multiplicity marking on its head says that each *ZipCityMap* may be associated with any number of *ZipCity* records. The lack of a marking on the tail says that each record may belong to any number of *ZipCityMaps*.

12.2.5 Mapping

Abstracting further, we can hide the *ZipCity* record itself, using an indexed field:

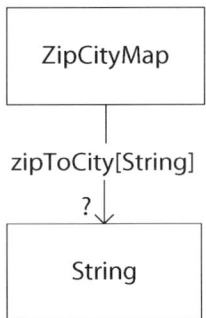

The edge *zipToCity* represents a collection of fields, one for each string. For a given zipcode string, it associates a *ZipCityMap* object with at most one city name string. If zipcodes and city names were instead represented as user-defined classes *Zip* and *City* say, the object model would show an edge labelled *zipToCity*[*Zip*] to *City*, making it more apparent that the index is the zipcode and that the target of the relation is the city name.

12.3 A relational logic

To give meaning to object models, we define a logic into which diagrams are translated, and then interpret the free variables of logical formulas in terms of programming notions.

We assume there is a universe of objects, *Object*, each of which is an uninterpreted atom. A special atom, *unit*, not in *Object*, is used to encode sets as relations, with $\{(unit,x), (unit, y), \ldots\}$ for the set $\{x, y, \ldots\}$. Scalars are represented as singleton sets; below, we use the abbreviation $set(x)$ for $\{(unit,x)\}$. Every variable in a formula therefore has a value that is a relation consisting of pairs whose first elements are drawn from the set $Object \cup \{unit\}$ and whose second elements are drawn from the set $Object$:

$$Val = \mathcal{P}\ (Object \cup \{unit\} \times Object)$$

Expressions and formulas are interpreted in an environment that assigns values to variables:

$$Env = Var \rightarrow Val$$

We shall write $\varepsilon[x/v]$ for the environment that is like ε but which binds the value x to the variable v.

To define the meaning of an expression or formula, we use two semantic functions

$$[\![\#]\!]\#: Expr, Env \rightarrow Val$$

which assigns a relational value to an expression in a given environment and

$$[\![\#]\!]\#: Formula, Env \rightarrow Bool$$

which assigns a boolean value to a formula in a given environment.

Here are the expression forms and their meanings, where p and q are arbitrary expressions, v and w are variables, and f is a formula:

$[\![p + q]\!]\varepsilon = [\![p]\!]\varepsilon \cup [\![q]\!]\varepsilon$ *union*
$[\![p - q]\!]\varepsilon = [\![p]\!]\varepsilon \setminus [\![q]\!]\varepsilon$ *difference*
$[\![p \,\&\, q]\!]\varepsilon = [\![p]\!]\varepsilon \cap [\![q]\!]\varepsilon$ *intersection*
$[\![\sim p]\!]\varepsilon = \{(y,x) \mid (x,y) \in [\![p]\!]\varepsilon\}$ *transpose*
$[\![+p]\!]\varepsilon = [\![p]\!]\varepsilon \cup [\![p.p]\!]\varepsilon \cup [\![p.p.p]\!]\varepsilon \ldots$ *closure*
$[\![p.q]\!]\varepsilon = \{(a,c) \mid \exists b.(a,b) \in [\![p]\!]\varepsilon \wedge (b,c) \in [\![q]\!]\varepsilon\}$ *composition*
$[\![\{v,w \mid f\}]\!]\varepsilon = \{(a,b) \mid [\![f]\!]\varepsilon[set(a)/v, set(b)/w]\}$ *relation comprehension*
$[\![\{v \mid f\}]\!]\varepsilon = \{(unit, a) \mid [\![f]\!]\varepsilon[set(a)/v]\}$ *set comprehension*
$[\![v]\!]\varepsilon = \varepsilon(v)$ *variable*

The composition operator has its standard definition, but due to the encoding of sets as relations it plays several roles. When the expressions s and r represent a set and a relation respectively, the expression $s.r$ denotes the image of s under the relation r. When s and t are both sets, $\sim s.t$ is the cross-product of s and t; when these sets are scalars, $\sim s.t$ represents the pair (s, t). In practice of course, one does not write expressions in this form, but uses shorthands instead (see below).

Here are the formulas, where f and g are formulas, p and q are arbitrary expressions, and v is a variable:

$[\![p \text{ in } q]\!]\varepsilon = [\![p]\!]\varepsilon \subseteq [\![q]\!]\varepsilon$ *subset*
$[\![f \&\& g]\!]\varepsilon = [\![f]\!]\varepsilon \wedge [\![g]\!]\varepsilon$ *conjunction*
$[\![!f]\!]\varepsilon = \neg\, [\![f]\!]\varepsilon$ *negation*
$[\![all\ v \mid f]\!]\varepsilon = \wedge\{\,[\![f]\!]\varepsilon[set(a)/v] \mid a \in Object\}$ *universal quantification*

There is only one elementary formula p in q, written equivalently $p : q$, which is true when the relation denoted by p is a subset of the relation denoted by q

(viewed as a set of pairs). Due to the encoding of scalars as sets, when x is a scalar and s is a set, x in s holds when x is a member of the set s.

12.3.1 Shorthands

To make this logic practical, it must be extended with a collection of shorthands. The following are taken from our Alloy language [16]. Obviously we define the other logical operators (such as disjunction and implication), relational operators (such as * for reflexive transitive closure), and an equality operator on expressions. We let $s \to t$ be short for $\sim s.t$, so that

$$p : s \to t$$

is a formula asserting that p is a relation from the set s to the set t.

Several useful quantifiers are defined: *some* (existential quantification), the dual of *all*; *no*, the negation of *all*; and *sole* and *one* for asserting that there is at most one value, and exactly one value satisfying the formula:

$$\text{sole } v \mid f \equiv \text{some } w \mid \{v \mid f\} \text{ in } w$$
$$\text{one } v \mid f \equiv \text{some } w \mid \{v \mid f\} = w$$

We use the standard shorthands for quantifier bounds, such as

$$\text{all } v \colon e \mid f \equiv \text{all } v \mid (v \text{ in } e) \text{ implies } f$$

Rather than defining the empty relation as a constant, we let Qe, where Q is any quantifier, be short for

$$Q v \mid v \text{ in } e$$

so that *no e*, *sole e*, *some e*, *one e* mean that e contains no elements, at most one element, some element and exactly one element respectively.

12.4 Diagrams to logic

The meaning of an object-model diagram is given by translation to a formula in the logic. Features of the diagram generate constraints, which are then conjoined to give a single formula. The formula is then interpreted in terms of programming notions by binding free set variables to class names and free relation variables to field names.

12.4.1 Translating fields and classification

For each open-headed (relation) arrow labelled f from box A to box B, we introduce variables A, B and f, and assert

$$f : A \to B$$

A constraint is obtained from each multiplicity marking. If f has a marking of ! on its head for example, we generate

all a: A | one a.f

For each closed-headed (subset) arrow from box A to box B, we assert

A in B

and whenever two boxes A and B share such an arrowhead, we add the disjointness constraint

no A & B

12.4.2 Qualified sets

Qualifications cause definitions to be generated. For each box labelled S/e, where S is the set name and e is some expression, we generate a fresh name, S_i say, with the constraint

$S_i = S \ \& \ e$

Additionally, each box that appears as a subset (direct or indirect) of S/e is given a fresh name and its own definition in the same way. For example, the diagram of Section 12.2.2 may give

$List_1$ = List & ZipCityMap.zcl
$EmptyList_1$ = EmptyList & ZipCityMap.zcl
$NonEmptyList_1$ = NonEmptyList & ZipCityMap.zcl

12.4.3 Interpreting concrete-object models

The formula obtained by conjoining all the constraints obtained from field arrows, classification arrows and defined subsets is then interpreted as follows. Each set variable denotes the set of all objects in the heap that belong to the class or interface with that name; each relational variable denotes the field of that name on the relevant class. A given object in the heap is considered to be a member of the set S if its type is S, or a type that *implements* or *extends* S (in Java terminology). The pair (x, y) is considered to be a member of a relation f when the f field of the object x holds a reference to object y. The heap as a whole satisfies the object model when the formula obtained from the model is true when interpreted in this fashion.

12.4.4 Combining object models

Note that there are no implicit constraints that assert disjointness of the top-level sets. We cannot infer, for example, from the object models of Section 12.2 that the sets *String* and *ZipCityMap* are disjoint. This constraint would instead be obtained from the object model that captures the standard class hierarchy (and need not be drawn), which includes these two sets as disjoint subsets of *Object*. Each object model is an invariant in its own right; the meaning of a collection of object models is simply the conjunction of their corresponding formulas.

12.4.5 Abstract fields

Abstract fields cannot be directly interpreted. Instead, each abstract field must be defined in terms of concrete fields (as illustrated below in Section 12.5.3). The formula obtained from the object model is conjoined with these definitions to give a composite formula with which to evaluate a heap.

12.4.6 Indexed fields

Indexed fields are encoded as binary relations. Suppose we have an arrow with label $f[I]$ that connects a box labelled A to a box labelled B. We introduce a set variable $Edge_f$ whose elements correspond to edges in snapshots that are instances of the field f, and relations

$$f : I \rightarrow Edge_f$$
$$\pi_a : Edge_f \rightarrow A$$
$$\pi_b : Edge_f \rightarrow B$$

We constrain the projections π_a and π_b to be total functions

    all e: $Edge_f$ | one $e.\pi_a$ && one $e.\pi_b$

The field corresponding to an index i, written $f[i]$, is now defined by

$$f[i] = \{v, w \mid (some\ e: i.f \mid v = e.\pi_a\ \&\&\ w = e.\pi_b)\}$$

This definition allows i to be an arbitrary (set-valued) expression, in which case $f[i]$ is the union of the individual relations.

Domain and range constraints are translated as if for a simple field, but quantifying over all values of the index:

    all i | $f[i] : A \rightarrow B$

Multiplicity markings induce similarly quantified constraints. For example, if the head of the arrow carries an exclamation point, we would generate

    all i | all v: A | one $a.f[i]$

In terms of a concrete heap, we interpret the field $f[i]$ on an array object a as the *i*th element of a. All other indexed fields are abstract and must be defined explicitly.

12.5 Textual annotations

An object-model diagram has limited expressiveness. Constraints that involve objects that are not directly related must usually be expressed textually. Three kinds of constraint are most common: representation invariants, which describe the allowed configurations of objects that form the representation of an abstract type; global invariants, which describe how objects of different abstract types may be configured with respect to one another; and abstract field definitions, which define abstract fields in terms of concrete ones.

12.5.1 Representation invariants

The representation of *ZipCityMap* as a linked list of *ZipCity* records (Section 12.2.2) would likely be required to satisfy the following invariants:

> // no cycles in the list
> all *m*: *ZipCityMap* | no *p*: *m.zcl.*next* | *p* in *p.+next*
>
> // every list cell has a non-null val field
> all *m*: *ZipCityMap* | all *p*: *m.zcl.*next* & *NonEmptyList* | some *p.val*
>
> // each ZipCity record appears at most once in the list
> all *m*: *ZipCityMap* |
>   all *zc*: *m.zcl.*next.val* | sole *p*: *m.zcl.*next* | *p.val* = *zc*
>
> // each zipcode appears in at most one ZipCity record in the list
> all *m*: *ZipCityMap* |
>   all *z*: *m.zcl.*next.val.zip* | sole *zc*: *m.zcl.*next.val* | *zc.zip* = *z*

Note how the dot operator allows sets of objects to be defined by navigations through the object graph. An expression such as *m.zcl.*next*, for example, which denotes the list cells of the map *m*, can be read 'start at *m*, then follow the *zcl* field once, and the *next* field zero or more times'.

The form of these constraints identifies them as representation invariants. Their scope is a single instance of the class *ZipCityMap*, and objects reachable from that instance, evidenced by the omission of references to other sets, and the fact that the transpose operator does not appear. These conditions are sufficient but not necessary; the third constraint

> all *m*: *ZipCityMap* |
>   all *zc*: *m.zcl.*next.val* | sole *p*: *m.zcl.*next* | *p.val* = *zc*

might have been written equivalently

> all *m*: *ZipCityMap* | all *zc*: *ZipCity* | sole *zc.~val* & *m.zcl.*next*

for example.

In fact, these structural conditions are only part of the story. Whether a constraint is a representation invariant depends on whether the implementations of the methods of the abstract type, in this case *ZipCityMap*, rely on it. The objects whose fields are referred to in the representation invariant will generally also be those that are elided when concrete fields are replaced by abstract fields. But the drawing of a boundary around the representation of a type is fraught with difficulties. It is not clear, for example, whether the String objects that hold the city name and zipcode should be regarded as part of the *ZipCityMap* abstraction. If *ZipCityMap* interns strings, they must be; if a client uses reference equality to compare strings passed into and out of the abstraction, they must not be.

12.5.2 Global invariants

Global invariants reflect decisions about the program as a whole rather than particular abstract types. Some examples for a program that uses the list representation of *ZipCityMap*:

> // list cells are not shared amongst ZipCityMap objects
> all p: List | sole p.~zcl
>
> // ZipCity records are not shared amongst lists
> all zc: ZipCity | sole zc.~val
>
> // no String is both a zipcode and a city name
> no (ZipCity.zip & ZipCity.city)

and perhaps

> // there is only one ZipCityMap
> one ZipCityMap

Although sharing constraints are not representation invariants, their violation can cause *representation exposure*, and prevent a representation invariant from being established locally. They can often be enforced by the code of an abstract data type, using a combination of access control mechanisms, strong typing and programmer discipline. To ensure that *ZipCity* records are not shared, for example, the *ZipCityMap* abstraction would likely provide no methods with arguments or results of type *ZipCity* or *List*, and would declare the *zcl* field to be private.

Global invariants are becoming increasingly important due to the popularity of a style of design encouraged by the design patterns literature [9] in which objects are tightly coupled to one another, often linked with mutual references, and interacting by elaborate protocols. The *Observer* pattern, for example, has the following object model:

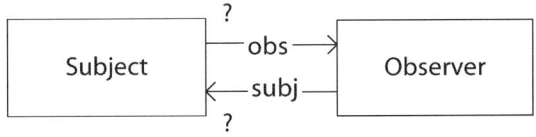

(assuming the common restriction that an observer may observe at most one subject) and depends on global invariants such as

// each observer points to a subject for which it is an observer
all o: Observer | o in o.subj.obs

// no observer observes itself, directly or indirectly
no o: Observer | o in o.+obs

Note the field *subj* emanating from *Observer*; this is legitimate even if *Observer* is an interface since the object model describes abstract heap structure and is not constrained by the syntactic rules of Java (which do not allow fields to be declared in interfaces). This is a fundamental difference between an object model and a class diagram, which is instead a graphical representation of the program text.

12.5.3   Abstract-field Definitions

Abstract fields can be defined in terms of concrete fields. The view of *ZipCityMap* as a set of records (in section 12.2.4), for example, can be obtained from the list and array representations:

// define abstract field zcs in terms of list structure
all m: ZipCityMap | m.zcs = m.zcl.*next.val

// define abstract field zcs in terms of array structure
all m: ZipCityMap | m.zcs = m.zca[Index]

Likewise, the view of *ZipCityMap* as a mapping from zipcodes to cities is given by

// define abstract indexed field zipToCity in terms of list structure
all m: ZipCityMap | all z: String | m.zipToCity[z] =
  {c: String | some zc: m.zcl.*next.val | zc.zip = z && zc.city = c}

// define abstract indexed field zipToCity in terms of array structure
all m: ZipCityMap | all z: String | m.zipToCity[z] =
  {c: String | some zc: m.zca[Index] | zc.zip = z && zc.city = c}

12.6   Discussion

In our discussion below, we compare our approach to object model semantics to previous approaches (12.6.1); compare our annotation language to others (12.6.2); summarize the differences between the interpretations of object models of problems and object models of code (12.6.3); point out some advantages of object models over more conventional specifications (12.6.4, 12.6.5); and finally comment on some deficiencies of our approach (12.6.6, 12.6.7, 12.6.8).

12.6.1 Related approaches

The most common approach to giving meaning to object models has been translation to a existing formal specification language.

Algebraic languages, especially the Larch Shared Language [10], are the most popular. Such translations [2, 12] benefit from the purity of algebraic specifications, but tend to be rather elaborate, because algebraic operators are total functions, whereas object models are based on relations. Partiality is encoded with special error values; relations are treated differently from functions; navigation expressions call for explicit lifting of functions or relations from scalar to set application; and classification requires the explicit construction of a simulation.

Z [28] is a more natural target, because it is based, like object models, on sets and relations. Rather than using the basic notions of sets and relations, translations into Z exploit its schema calculus. Some encode classification with schema extension, so that the subbox is mapped to a schema containing the components of the superbox and some additional ones [21]; others use an encoding more like an implementation of subclassing, in which the subbox schema has a component whose type is the schema of the superbox [27]. Like the algebraic approach, both of these assign different types to subboxes and superboxes. Consequently, given a relation r from a box A with a subbox B, and objects a and b of those boxes, the meaning of the expressions $a.r$ and $b.r$ must be obtain differently, since in the latter case some kind of conversion must first be applied. It seems better to treat subbox and superbox objects as belonging to the same type [8].

The Object Constraint Language (OCL) [30] has been used as a target also to give meaning to a subset of its own constraints [18]. OCL is much more complicated than Z or Larch, so the semantics is more of an exercise to demonstrate OCL's expressiveness than to explain its meaning.

Richters and Gogolla give a semantics for OCL [22] that addresses several of its complexities, such as n-ary associations and the operational *iterate* construct. To resolve problems with OCL's flattening rules, they chose to interpret a one-to-many association as a function from an object to a set of objects, and to have navigation result in nested collections that are then implicitly flattened. This introduces a higher-order aspect into the language, which we have been reluctant to do.

12.6.2 Related languages

The object-modelling language of choice for many developers will be the Unified Modeling Language (UML) [25]. UML's constraint language, OCL [30], is more complicated than languages such as Z and Alloy. Navigation expressions are less uniform than ours, and the type system forces one to apply explicit coercions when following relations on a subbox. For example, consider writing a textual constraint saying that, for any *ZipCityMap* object m, the first cell of the list $m.zcl$ (if any) holds a *ZipCity* object:

ZipCityMap.zcl.val in ZipCity

In OCL, we would have to write something like

ZipCityMap
zcl.oclIsKindOf(NonEmptyList) implies
zcl.oclAsType(NonEmptyList).val.oclIsKindOf(ZipCity)

because applying the *val* relation to an *EmptyList* is a type error (where in our approach it would just give the empty set). The assertion that all reachable cells hold *ZipCity* objects

ZipCityMap.zcl.*next.val in ZipCity

cannot be expressed declaratively at all in OCL, because there is no transitive closure. Instead, one must write an operational definition of a navigation, and then invoke it.

Z can be used, of course, not only to give meaning to object models, but as an object-modelling language in its own right. But because Alloy has been tailored to object models, it is a bit more concise and direct than Z in this application, primarily in allowing sets to appear in declarations, and in the syntax of navigation expressions.

Hoare and He [15] give a theory of object models in which each object is characterized by the set of traces of field labels that reach it. In our formalism, objects have identities, so two heaps that have identical structure—and are thus observationally equivalent—may be distinguished. Their theory, in contrast, is fully abstract. Their constraint notation is based on regular expressions, and thus bears a striking similarity to our notation. The trace view does not permit arbitrary relations, however, since, in a snapshot, an object may only have one outgoing field edge with a given label. Representing abstract fields may therefore be a problem.

12.6.3 Code vs. problem-object models

Previous work on giving meaning to object models [2, 8, 11, 18, 22], including our own [16], has focused on object models that are used to describe problems or abstract systems rather than heap invariants. This paper was motivated by our discovery that object models that describe implementations require a slightly different interpretation.

- In a problem-object model, one typically assumes that all top-level sets or *domains* are disjoint. The presence of interfaces and the root class *Object* makes this assumption infeasible. Instead of using a typed relational logic in which each domain has a basic type associated with it, we treated each class as a subset of the set *Object*; disjointness amongst classes was provided by conjoining the interpretation of the standard class hierarchy.

- In a problem-object model, a set may appear at most once in a diagram. We introduced the notion of qualified sets to allow us to instantiate polymorphic containers.

- In a problem-object model, all fields are in a sense abstract. It is common to include redundant relations that are defined in terms of other relations and sets, but unlike abstract fields, these do not replace existing relations.

12.6.4 Abstract fields vs. abstract objects

Abstract fields, also called 'specification fields' by some authors, offer several advantages over an approach in which an abstraction function is defined that maps concrete objects to abstract mathematical objects [14, 20].

- Many abstract types have a tuple structure anyway, so it is cleaner to define a collection of fields than a function that maps the concrete object to a tuple, and then a collection of projection functions to deconstruct it.

- Abstract fields can be used to define more fine-grained frame conditions than abstract objects; the JML specification language [19] and the annotation language for the Extended Static Checker [6], for example, both allow *modifies* clauses to indicate which abstract fields of an object may change.

- The abstract object approach still requires explicit mention of the abstraction function in specifications. To specify insertion of an element e into a set s, for example, one has to write something like

$$s_{post} = s \cup \{e\}$$

where the *post* suffix indicates dereferencing and application of the abstraction function in the post-state, and other names are implicitly dereferenced and abstracted in the pre-state. Unfortunately, this is not correct: the second mention of s must indeed be dereferenced and abstracted thus, but the mention of e must be treated differently. The abstract mathematical set object contains *references* to objects, so e must not be dereferenced. In the abstract field approach, the set insertion would be specified like this:

$$s.elems' = s.elems + e$$

which makes clear the dereferencing of s but not e.

The abstract object approach seems to work well in a traditional data abstraction setting in which objects are immutable and can be viewed in terms of pure mathematical values, but is less useful in object-oriented programs where mutation and sharing are common.

12.6.5 Fields as relations

In an object model, every field is treated as a relation. In contrast, more expressive specification approaches allow fields to map object references to arbitrary mathematical objects. JML, for example, allows fields to take on values defined by an algebraic specification. An abstract field may map an object to a priority queue, for example. In the object-model approach, one would either have to make do with a partial specification (ignoring the ordering of objects in the queue entirely, for example), or model the queue using indexed fields, or perhaps even by introducing objects purely for specification purposes, in the style of model-oriented languages.

The object-model approach has a few important advantages. It is simpler, is closer to the true structure of the heap, and more easily represented graphically. Navigation expressions allow reachability relationships to be described uniformly and simply; with arbitrary types as the values of fields, images of sets can no longer be taken in the obvious way, and fields cannot be navigated backwards. Object models also have a strong similarity to the kinds of shape graph computed by static analyses, suggesting the possibility of checking conformance of code to object models fully automatically.

12.6.6 Qualified sets

The ability to split sets into subsets, and use the same label for two different boxes in the object model is crucial. It allows representation details to be shown, since one can distinguish an array used in the representation of one class from an array used in another, for example. Without splitting, no generic structure can be instantiated. A program that used the *Observer* pattern, for example, would not be able to distinguish observers of different subject classes.

Splitting might also be useful for primitive classes. For example, if we represented the images of the *zipcode* and *city* fields as defined subsets of *String*, we would draw an object model that incorporates graphically the constraint

> // no String is both a zipcode and a city name
> no (ZipCity.zip & ZipCity.city)

of section 12.5.2:

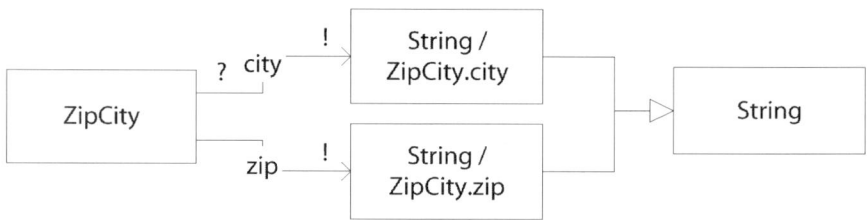

We considered viewing splitting as instantiation of type parameters: regarding two boxes labelled *Vector* as representing *Vector[S]* and *Vector[T]* for distinct types *S* and *T*, for example. But this does not sit well with Java's lack of parametric polymorphism, and is more complicated than the scheme based on defined subsets presented here. One can always qualify a set according to its contents: *Vector / S.~elts*, for example, for *Vector[S]*.

Our scheme is an instance of a more general scheme developed by Rinard and Kuncak [23], in which arbitrary sets can be defined over the actual heap state. They allow a set representing a class to be partitioned, for example, into subsets according to the value of a particular field. Their aim is to bridge the gap between shape graphs that can be extracted by static analysis and abstract object models that capture essential design constraints.

A deficiency of our approach is that there is no easy way to indicate that the subset used in one context is not used elsewhere. One cannot say, for example, that the set of *List* objects used in the representation of *ZipCityMap* is disjoint from other sets of *List* objects; such constraints would have to be added explicitly for each other such set (eg, by including both qualified *List* sets as disjoint subsets of *List* in a single diagram).

12.6.7 Indexed fields

The encoding of indexed fields described in Section 12.4.6 is clumsy. Alloy in fact offers indexed relations as a built-in feature, and they are supported by our analysis tool. But indexed relations are also problematic, and in a future version of the language we expect to support relations of arbitrary arity: 1 for sets and scalars, 2 for binary relations, 3 for relations with one index, and so on. This will allow the dot operator to be used uniformly, so that $e.f[i]$ will be equivalent to $e.(i.f)$. A similar view is taken by Richters and Gogolla in their semantics for OCL, in which fields are modelled as hyperarcs [22].

We have been a bit cavalier in introducing index sets, such as *Index* in Section 12.2.3. An index set may correspond to a class of objects, or, as in the case of *Index*, it may be a specification artifact (in the style of model-based specification).

12.6.8 Extensional equality

In some invariants, we want an extensional notion of equality that equates two (possibly distinct) objects when their fields have the same values. In Java, for example, two distinct strings may contain the same sequence of characters. Instead of the representation invariant of section 12.5.1

> // each zipcode appears in at most one ZipCity record in the list
> all m:ZipCityMap |
>   all z: m.zcl.*next.val.zip | sole zc: m.zcl.*next.val | zc.zip = z

we might want to say that no *ZipCity* records in the list contain strings with the same sequence of characters. One might define an equivalence relation *eq* as an abstract field, so that x in $y.eq$ is true when x and y are equivalent. The invariant would then become

> all m: ZipCityMap | all z: m.zcl.*next.val.zip |
>   sole zc: m.zcl.*next.val | z in zc.zip.eq

Acknowledgments

This work grew out of an attempt to use object models in an undergraduate software engineering course at MIT, as a pervasive framework for explaining the Java heap model, rep invariants, abstraction functions, and global invariants. It has benefited from the criticisms of my co-lecturer, Michael Ernst, and of our teaching assistants, especially Felix Klock and Allison Waingold. I am very grateful also to Alan Fekete, Michael Jackson and Annabelle McIver who read an early draft, spotted mistakes and suggested many improvements, and to Ed Wang who converted the paper from FrameMaker to LaTeX.

Martin Rinard and Viktor Kuncak contributed essential ideas. Martin had developed the idea of 'content-based classification', in which objects would be classified according to the values of their fields. Viktor suggested that an object model be viewed in the context of the class hierarchy, so that the standard relationships between a class and *Object* can be omitted.

This research was funded by an Information Technology Research grant (#0086154) from the National Science Foundation, by a grant from NASA, and by an endowment from Douglas and Pat Ross.

References

[1] Serge Abiteboul and Richard Hull. IFO: A Formal Semantic Database Model. *ACM Transactions on Database Systems*, Vol. 12, No. 4, December 1987, pp. 525–565.

[2] Robert H. Bourdeau and Betty H.C. Cheng. A Formal Semantics for Object Model Diagrams. *IEEE Transactions on Software Engineering*, October 1995.

[3] Derek Coleman, Patrick Arnold, Stephanie Bodoff, Chris Dollin, Helena Gilchrist, Fiona Hayes and Paul Jeremaes. *Object-Oriented Development: The Fusion Method.* Prentice Hall, 1994.

[4] Steve Cook and John Daniels. *Designing Object Systems: Object-Oriented Modelling with Syntropy.* Prentice Hall, 1994.

[5] Peter P. Chen. The Entity-Relationship Model-Toward a Unified View of Data. *ACM Transactions on Database Systems*, Vol. 1, No. 1, (1976), pp. 9–36.

[6] David L. Detlefs, K. Rustan M. Leino, Greg Nelson, and James B. Saxe. *Extended Static Checking.* Research Report 159, Compaq Systems Research Center, December, 1998.

[7] Desmond F. D'Souza and Alan Cameron Wills. *Objects, Components and Frameworks With UML. The Catalysis Approach.* Addison-Wesley, 1998.

[8] Robert B. France, Jean-Michel Bruel, Maria M. Larrondo-Petrie, and Malcolm Shroff. Exploring the Semantics of UML Type Structures with Z. *Proceedings of the Formal Methods for Open Object-based Distributed Systems* (FMOODS'97), Canterbury, England, July 1997. Chapman & Hall, 1997.

[9] Erich Gamma, Richard Helm, Ralph Johnson, and John Vlissides. *Design Patterns: Elements of Reusable Object-Oriented Software.* Addison Wesley, October 1994.

[10] John V. Guttag, James J. Horning, and Andres Modet. *Report on the Larch Shared Language: Version 2.3*. Technical Report 58, Compaq Systems Research Center, Palo Alto, CA, 1990.

[11] Ali Hamie, John Howse and Stuart Kent. Interpreting the Object Constraint Language. *Proceedings of Asia Pacific Conference in Software Engineering*, IEEE Press, 1998.

[12] Ali Hamie, John Howse and Stuart Kent. Navigation expressions in object-oriented modelling. *Proceedings Fundamental Approaches to Software Engineering* (FASE'98), *European Joint Conferences on the Theory and Practice of Software* (ETAPS'98), Lisbon, Portugal, March 1998. LNCS 1382, Springer-Verlag, 1998.

[13] Michael Hammer and Dennis McLeod. Database description with SDM: a semantic database model. *ACM Transactions on Database Systems*, Vol. 6, No. 2, June 1981, pp. 351–386.

[14] C.A.R. Hoare. Proof of correctness of data representations. *Acta Informatica*, 1(4), pp. 271–281, 1972.

[15] C.A.R. Hoare and Jifeng He. A trace model for pointers and objects. *Proc. 13th European Conference on Object-Oriented Programming*, Lisbon, Portugal, June 14-18, 1999. LNCS 1628, Springer-Verlag, 1999. Reprinted in this volume.

[16] Daniel Jackson. *Alloy: A Lightweight Object Modelling Notation*. Technical Report 797, MIT Laboratory for Computer Science, Cambridge, MA, February 2000. Latest version available at: http://sdg.lcs.mit.edu/~dnj/publications. To appear, *ACM Transactions on Software Engineering*.

[17] Daniel Jackson. Automating first-order relational logic. *Proc. ACM SIGSOFT Conf. Foundations of Software Engineering*. San Diego, November 2000.

[18] Stuart Kent, Stephen Gaito, Niall Ross. A meta-model semantics for structural constraints in UML. In H. Kilov, B. Rumpe, and I. Simmonds, editors, *Behavioral specifications for businesses and systems*, chapter 9, pages 123–141. Kluwer Academic Publishers, Norwell, MA, September 1999.

[19] Gary T. Leavens, Albert L. Baker, and Clyde Ruby. *Preliminary design of JML: a behavioral interface specification language for Java*. Department of Computer Science, Iowa State University, TR #98-06j, June 1998, revised May 2000. Available at http://www.cs.iastate.edu/~leavens.

[20] Barbara Liskov with John Guttag. *Program Development in Java*. Addison-Wesley, 2001.

[21] E.-R. Olderog and A.P. Ravn. Documenting design refinement. *Proc. ACM SIGSOFT Workshop on Formal Methods in Software Practice*, Portland, Oregon, August 2000, pp. 89–100.

[22] Mark Richters and Martin Gogolla. On Formalizing the UML Object Constraint Language OCL, *Proc. 17th Int. Conf. Conceptual Modeling* (ER'98), 1998, LNCS 1507, pp. 449–464, Springer-Verlag.

[23] Martin Rinard and Viktor Kuncak. *Object Models, Heaps and Interpretations*. Technical Report 816, MIT Laboratory for Computer Science, Cambridge, Massachusetts, January 2001.

[24] James Rumbaugh, Michael Blaha, William Prémerlani, Frederick Eddy and William Lorensen. *Object-Oriented Modeling and Design*. Prentice Hall, 1991.

[25] James Rumbaugh, Ivar Jacobson and Grady Booch. *The Unified Modeling Language Reference Manual*. Addison-Wesley, 1999.

[26] David W. Shipman. The Functional Data Model and the Data Language DAPLEX. *ACM Transactions on Database Systems*, Vol. 6, No. 1, March 1981, pp. 140–173.

[27] Malcolm Shroff and Robert B. France. Towards a formalization of UML class structures in Z. *Proceedings of Twenty-First Annual International Computer Software and Applications Conference* (COMPSAC'97), pages 646–651. IEEE Computer Society Press, 1997.

[28] J. Michael Spivey. *The Z Notation: A Reference Manual*. Second edition, Prentice Hall, 1992.

[29] Toby J. Teorey, DongQing Yang and James P. Fry. A logical design methodology for relational databases using the extended entity-relationship model. *ACM Computing Surveys*, 18(2), June 1986, pp. 197–222.

[30] Jos Warmer and Anneke Kleppe. *The Object Constraint Language: Precise Modeling with UML*. Addison Wesley, 1999.

13
Abstraction dependencies

K. Rustan M. Leino and Greg Nelson

Abstract

Modern computer programs use patterns of data abstraction that are richer than those considered previously in the literature for specifying and reasoning about programs. This paper presents *abstraction dependencies* as a key construct in specifying modular programs. The paper motivates abstraction dependencies through an extended example and outlines how they solve the immediate problems of previous techniques.

13.1 Introduction

This paper contains an extended example that illustrates an approach for verifying programs in the presence of data abstraction, object types, and information hiding. The principal novelty of the approach is a new specification construct: the abstraction dependency. The genesis of this work was the Extended Static Checking project (ESC) [5], which applies program verification technology to systems programs written in Modula-3. The aim of ESC is not to prove full functional correctness, but to prove the absence of common errors such as array index errors, **nil** dereference errors, race conditions, deadlocks, etc.

One of the biggest problems we encountered in the ESC project is that the verification technology we know from the literature does not seem to apply to the systems programs in the Modula-3 libraries. The problem is not that the programs use low-level tricks or unsafe code; the problem is that the programs use patterns of modularization and data abstraction that are richer than those treated in the verification literature. This is not an artifact of Modula-3, but would apply to any modern object-oriented language.

The data abstraction technology we know from the literature extends and refines the seminal paper on data abstraction by C.A.R. Hoare in 1972 [13]. In particular, Hoare and all subsequent treatments that we know impose the requirement that all of the concrete variables used to represent an abstraction must be declared in the same module. This requirement is too strict: if it were applied to the Modula-3 libraries, many small modules would have to be combined, with a loss of desirable information hiding. For example, this requirement would force the various subtypes of *readers* (buffered input streams) to be declared in one common module, as we shall see when we present the details of the reader design in the rest of the paper. Writing specifications is supposed to improve the structure of a program, so it is ironic that standard treatments of data abstraction are incompatible with good modularization. Therefore, in this paper we weaken Hoare's requirement and allow the concrete variables used to represent an abstraction to be divided among several modules.

A key technical challenge is to check modules where an abstract variable is visible, some of the concrete variables used to represent it are visible, but the representation function that connects them is not visible. To meet this challenge, we introduce a new specification construct called **depends**. This construct specifies that an abstraction connection exists between the variables, but does not specify the actual representation function, which can be confined to a more private scope. There are different types of dependencies, and these types produce a useful taxonomy of the patterns of abstraction in modular software.

The **depends** construct gives the programmer considerable freedom in arranging the declarations of abstract variables, concrete variables, abstraction representation functions, and dependencies among the modules of a program. Too much freedom: without further restrictions, we would lose the property of modular soundness, that is, the property that the separate verifications of the individual modules of the program suffice to ensure the correctness of the composite program. We therefore impose several requirements, called *modularity requirements*. The details of the modularity requirements are beyond the scope of this paper. They and other details are in our longer paper *Data abstraction and information hiding* [23] (hereafter referred to as "the tome").

The fundamental relationship between data abstraction and information hiding was enunciated in a classic paper of Parnas [32], which we paraphrase as "every module hides a secret". To clarify the rôle of our dependencies, we distinguish two secrets involved in data abstraction: (a) the representation function and (b) the identity of the variables that are arguments to the representation function. We have found designs in which secret (b) should be less closely guarded (visible in more modules) than secret (a). The abstraction dependency makes it possible to achieve this.

13.2 On the need for data abstraction

Before we get into the details of our generalization, we set the stage by reviewing the rôle of data abstraction in modular verification.

To check that a large program does what it is supposed to do, we must study it piece by piece. Nobody's short-term memory is big enough to hold all the details of a large program. If the checking effort (formal or informal) is to be manageable, we cannot afford to re-examine the body of a procedure for every one of its calls. This is the reason for writing specifications, formal or informal. Given specifications, we check that each procedure meets its specification, assuming that the procedures it calls meet theirs.

This checking process is called modular verification, and for simple programming languages it has been understood since Hoare's work on axiomatic semantics in the 1960s. (As long as the bulk of the verification is done modularly, we do not exclude simple whole-program checks, such as the check that each procedure is implemented somewhere in the program.) The central goal of our work is to understand modular verification in the presence of two modern programming features: data abstraction and information hiding.

A procedure specification includes a precondition and a postcondition. The precondition is the part of the contract to be fulfilled by the caller of the procedure, and the postcondition is the part of the contract to be fulfilled by the procedure implementation. But precondition and postcondition are not enough: the specification also includes a "modifies list" that limits which variables the procedure is allowed to modify. Without the modifies list, the contract would allow a procedure to have arbitrary side effects on any variable not constrained by the postcondition, which would make the contract useless to the caller.

It is possible to view the modifies list as syntactic sugar for extra conjuncts in the postcondition, asserting that every variable not mentioned in the modifies list is unchanged. That is, in a program with three variables x, y, and z, the specification

requires P **modifies** x **ensures** Q

could be "desugared" into

requires P **ensures** $Q \land y = y' \land z = z'$,

in which primed variables denote post-values and unprimed variables denote pre-values. We cannot, however, use this desugaring to pretend that each procedure specification consists of a precondition and postcondition only. The reason is that, in modular verification, we never know, when verifying a procedure, what the set of all variables in the final program will be. Perhaps x, y, and z are the only variables visible where the procedure is declared, but more variables may be visible where the procedure is called. Therefore, in this paper we take the view that the modifies list is an integral part of the specification. Although we will rewrite modifies lists, the rewriting is different for different scopes.

Unfortunately, and perhaps surprisingly to those who have used verification more in principle than in practice, the methodology described so far is still inadequate. In many cases, it would be preposterous to try to list every piece of state that might be modified by a call to a procedure. For example, what would be the list for the `putchar` procedure from the C standard I/O library? What `putchar` does is simply write a character to output, but anybody who has implemented an I/O system will be aware that the list of what can be modified during the execution of a call to putchar is very long. It includes, for example, the I/O buffers, the internal state of the device drivers for the disk and network, the device registers in these drivers, and the disk and network themselves. The minor problem is that this list is long; the major problem is that the variables in the list are not visible at the point of declaration of putchar, and to make them visible would be to give up on information hiding, which would be to resign the game before it starts.

The solution to this difficulty —at least the only solution that we can imagine— is data abstraction. Abstractly, putchar modifies a single abstract variable, of a simple type (say, sequence of byte). All the internal state, from buffers to devices, must be treated as concrete state that is part of the representation of the abstract state.

Some people see data abstraction as an algorithm design methodology only, as a methodology for producing an efficient algorithm from a simple algorithm by changing the representation of the state. We have no quarrel with their use of data abstraction, but our point is that data abstraction is also an essential ingredient in any scheme for modular verification of large systems, since it seems to be the only hope for writing a useful modifies list for a procedure whose implementation changes the system state at many levels of abstraction.

Having identified the general idea of the solution to the putchar problem as data abstraction, we would add that the patterns of data abstraction that arise in verifying putchar are beyond the current state of the art of specification: we believe that no semantics or methodology presented in the literature is equal to the task. We hope the abstraction dependency will be a useful contribution in this neglected area.

13.3 Validity as an abstract variable

The generalized data abstraction illustrated in this paper is important regardless of whether verification is being used for full functional correctness or for more limited aims, such as the ESC aim of verifying the absence of certain classes of errors only. The examples in this paper will be ESC verifications. These verifications tend to have a typical form, which is described in this section.

In a typical ESC verification, we associate two abstract variables with each type, *valid* and *state*. The first of these records whether objects of the type satisfy the internal representation invariant required by the implementation, and the second represents the abstract value of variables of the type.

If we were doing full-scale verification, we would have to write many specifications about the *state* variable. But in doing extended static checking, we rarely say anything about the state. We aren't proving that the program meets its full functional specification, only that it doesn't crash. The only purpose of the *state* variable is to account for the side effects in the implementations of the methods, which otherwise would lead to spurious errors reported by the verifier. Indeed, in most ESC verifications, we don't bother to provide the concrete representation for *state*.

In contrast to *state*, the checking performed by ESC depends critically on *valid*. Most operations on an object o will have $valid[o]$ as a precondition. The checker uses the concrete representation for *valid* to translate $valid[o]$ into a concrete precondition, which it then uses in proving that the implementation of the operation does not cause an error.

In Hoare's original paper, the notion of a validity invariant was built into the methodology. Initialization was required to establish the validity and all other operations were required to preserve it. In contrast, we consider *valid* to be an abstract variable like any other; the programmer explicitly provides *valid* as a precondition (and/or postcondition), and the implementation infers the details of validity in terms of the concrete state via the usual process of data abstraction. Our approach has several advantages over Hoare's, of which we mention one: we allow operations like closing a file, which destroy validity. Such operations are frequently essential in order to deallocate resources.

13.4 Definition of notation

This section introduces the notation and terminology that we use in the rest of the paper.

Modularity

A *program* is a collection of *declarations*. Declarations introduce names for entities (such as types, abstract and concrete variables, and methods) and/or specify properties of named entities (such as subtype relationships, representations of abstract variables, method specifications, and method implementations). The declarations of a program are partitioned into *units* (sometimes called interfaces and modules). The declarations in effect in a unit are its own declarations and the declarations in effect in units that it *imports*. If an entity E is declared in a unit M, it is known as $M.E$ in importers of M and known simply as E within M. For example:

    unit M **unit** N **import** M
       type T ... uses of $M.T$ ...
       ... uses of T ...

In this paper, we sometimes write E instead of $M.E$ when M is clear from the context.

One of the purposes —perhaps the main purpose— of module systems is to reduce the portion of a program that must be read and potentially fixed to accommodate a change, addition, or deletion of a declaration. With our very general system of units, the portion of the program sensitive to a declaration in a unit M is exactly the set of units that import M directly or indirectly.

A set of units D is called a *scope* if it is closed under imports, that is, if whenever a unit M in D imports a unit N, then N is also in D. A declaration is *visible* in a scope if it appears in one of the units in the scope.

We use units and imports in this paper since they are simple and extremely general. Restrictive patterns are common in practice. For example, Modula-3 requires that every unit be an interface unit, which can declare methods but not provide implementations, or an implementation unit, which cannot be imported (and therefore has the property that no other portion of the program can be sensitive to it). As another example, CLU imposes a correspondence between units and type declarations. We have not imposed such restrictions in this paper, because they seem orthogonal to the modularity issues that we are discussing.

Types

In this paper, we will use primitive types like **int** and **bool**, as well as object types and array types. Our objects are like those of Simula and Modula-3: they are implicitly references, and each object type has a uniquely determined direct supertype. More precisely, an *object* is either **nil** or a reference to a set of data fields and methods; a method is a procedure that will accept the object as its first parameter. Equality of objects is reference equality. An *object type* determines the names and types of a prefix of the fields and the names and signatures of a prefix of the methods of its objects.

An object type T is declared

$$\textbf{type}\, T <: S \quad ,$$

where S is an object type declared elsewhere. This introduces the name T for a new object type whose direct supertype is S, meaning that T contains all the fields and methods of S and possibly includes other fields and methods declared elsewhere. The "$<: S$" is optional; if omitted, S defaults to an anonymous object type serving as the root of the subtype hierarchy.

Every object has a *dynamic type* determined when it is allocated. Every expression has a *static type* determined at compile time. If v is the dynamic value of an expression E, v has dynamic type D, and E has static type S, then conventional static type-checking rules assure that D is a subtype of S.

We consider a data field, abstract or concrete, to be a map from objects to values. Thus, where others write

$$\textbf{class}\, T = \{\, \ldots f\colon \textbf{int} \, \ldots \} \quad ,$$

we write

$$\textbf{type}\, T$$
$$\textbf{var}\, f\colon T \to \textbf{int} \quad .$$

Also, we write $f[t]$ where others write $t.f$ to denote the value of the f field of object t. We refer to T and **int** as the *index type* and *range type* of f, respectively. The **class** notation forces f to be co-declared with T, whereas our notation allows them to be declared independently. This generality is not problematical; in fact, it simplifies the semantics.

If T is a type, we write

$$\mathbf{array}[T]$$

to denote the type of (references to) arrays with element type T. If a is of type $\mathbf{array}[T]$ and is non-**nil**, then $\mathbf{number}(a)$ denotes the number of elements in a, and $a[i]$ denotes element i of a for $0 \leq i < \mathbf{number}(a)$. To properly model the fact that arrays are references, we introduce the predeclared map variable *elems*: the expression *elems*$[a]$ denotes the sequence of elements referred to by an array a. For example, $a = b$ means that a and b reference the same sequence, while *elems*$[a] = $ *elems*$[b]$ means that the sequences referenced have the same elements. In fact, $a[i]$ is shorthand for *elems*$[a][i]$.

If T is an object type, $\mathbf{new}(T)$ allocates and returns a new object of dynamic type T. For any type T, $\mathbf{new}(T, n)$ allocates and returns a new array of dynamic type $\mathbf{array}[T]$ and of length n.

A method m for type T is declared and specified as follows:

    proc $m(t: T, \ldots \text{args} \ldots): R$
        requires P
        modifies w
        ensures Q ,

where in the *signature* "$(t: T, \ldots \text{args} \ldots): R$", T is an object type, t is the self parameter, *args* lists the names and types of any additional parameters, and R is the result type. In this paper, all parameters are in-parameters. In addition to declaring the name and signature of the method, the declaration associates with it the precondition P, postcondition Q, and modifies list w. A program can contain at most one declaration for a given method for a given type; for example, we don't allow strengthening a method specification in a subtype (this is a simplification that does not actually limit expressiveness, see p. 348 of [22]). In the postcondition, **result** denotes the result value, primed variables denote values in the post-state, and unprimed variables denote values in the pre-state. If the precondition or postcondition is omitted, it defaults to *true*; if the modifies list is omitted, it defaults to the empty list.

A method m for type T can be implemented differently for each subtype of T. A method implementation of m for some subtype U of T is declared by

    impl $m(u: U, \ldots \text{args} \ldots): R$ **is** S **end** ,

where S is an executable statement, and the implementation signature

$$(u: U, \ldots \text{args} \ldots): R$$

coincides with the declared signature except (possibly) for the type of the first parameter. Statement S must satisfy (that is, the verifier checks that it satisfies) the specification associated with the m method for T. The ideas in this paper don't depend on the particular executable statements allowed. The examples in this paper use Algol-like executable statements, whose meaning we hope will be clear to the reader.

A method is called by

$$t.m(\ldots args \ldots) \quad ,$$

where t is an object (the actual self parameter), m is a method name, and *args* is a list of any additional actual parameters. The static type of t is used in determining the declaration and specification of m. The declaration is used to type-check the actual parameters and determine the static type of the result, the specification is used to reason about the semantics of the call. The dynamic type of t is used at run-time to determine which implementation of m to invoke. Since all method implementations are proved to meet their specifications, and since the dynamic type of t is a subtype of the static type of t, it is sound to reason about the semantics of the dynamic dispatch in this way.

Abstraction

A data field can be declared to be *abstract* by preceding its declaration with **spec**. For example:

spec var *valid*: $T \to$ **bool** .

An abstract field occupies no memory at run-time; it is a fictitious field whose value (or *representation*) is defined as a function of other fields. The representation is declared by a syntax like

$$\textbf{rep } valid[t\colon T] \;\equiv\; f[t] \neq 0 \quad , \tag{13.1}$$

which means that for any object t of type T, the abstract value of $valid[t]$ is *true* if and only if $f[t] \neq 0$.

The representation of an abstract variable can be different for different subtypes. As an example, consider the object type *Rat* representing rational numbers, and two of its subtypes, *Ratio*, which represents each rational as a ratio, and *CFrac*, which represents each rational as a continued fraction (which is a representation of a rational as a sequence of integers).

$$\begin{aligned}
&\textbf{type } Rat \\
&\textbf{spec var } valid\colon Rat \to \textbf{bool} \\
&\textbf{type } Ratio <\colon Rat \\
&\textbf{var } num, den\colon Ratio \to \textbf{int} \\
&\textbf{rep } valid[r\colon Ratio] \;\equiv\; den[r] > 0 \\
&\textbf{type } CFrac <\colon Rat \\
&\textbf{var } pq\colon CFrac \to \textbf{array}[\textbf{int}] \\
&\textbf{rep } valid[cf\colon CFrac] \;\equiv\; \\
&\quad pq[cf] \neq \textbf{nil } \wedge \\
&\quad (\forall\, i \;::\; 1 \leq i < \textbf{number}(pq[cf]) \;\Rightarrow\; pq[cf][i] > 0\,)
\end{aligned} \tag{13.2}$$

These declarations specify that the concrete representation of $valid[q]$ varies depending on the dynamic type of q: for rationals represented as ratios, validity means that the denominator is positive, whereas for continued fractions, validity means that each partial quotient is positive, except possibly the first.

A **rep** declaration given for a type T applies to all non-**nil** objects of type T, including those whose dynamic type is a subtype of T. One might think that it would be possible to override a **rep** declaration for T with another **rep** declaration for some subtype of T, but this is not allowed. This rule is enforced at link-time.

The variables appearing in the right-hand side of the **rep** declaration for an abstract variable are called *dependencies* of the abstract variable. The dependencies can themselves be either concrete or abstract. Our notion of dependencies is not to be confused with use-def dependencies [1].

A major novelty of our approach is to require that dependencies be declared explicitly. For example, the representation (13.1) would cause an "undeclared dependency" error unless $f[t]$ were declared as a dependency of $valid[t]$, which is done by a declaration of the form

$$\textbf{depends}\ valid[t\colon T]\ \textbf{on}\ f[t] \quad .$$

The **depends** declaration can be subtype-specific, just like the **rep** declaration. For example, the representations (13.2) might be accompanied by

$$\textbf{depends}\ valid[r\colon Ratio]\ \textbf{on}\ den[r]$$
$$\textbf{depends}\ valid[cf\colon CFrac]\ \textbf{on}\ pq[cf], elems[pq[cf]] \quad .$$

The validity of the continued fraction cf depends both on the array $pq[cf]$ and on the contents of the array. These are different dependencies and both must be declared, as shown above. The validity of the ratio r depends only on $den[r]$.

We distinguish two forms of dependencies, static and dynamic. A *static* dependency has the form

$$\textbf{depends}\ a[t\colon T]\ \textbf{on}\ c[t] \quad . \tag{13.3}$$

A *dynamic* dependency has the form

$$\textbf{depends}\ a[t\colon T]\ \textbf{on}\ c[b[t]] \quad . \tag{13.4}$$

In each case, a is an abstract variable and c is either an abstract or a concrete variable. In the case of the dynamic dependency, b is concrete. A dependency on the contents of an array counts as a dynamic dependency, with *elems* playing the rôle of c. Other forms of dependencies are discussed in the tome [23], but static and dynamic dependencies are more common and fundamental.

A major goal of this work is to design a discipline for the placement of dependency declarations in a multi-module program. The argument is long, but the main conclusion is short: the static dependency (13.3) must be visible wherever c is, and the dynamic dependency (13.4) must be visible wherever b is. The two rules are simple examples of *modularity requirements*.

Dependencies affect the verification process in several ways. One way is *modifies list desugaring*. For example, in a scope where

$$\textbf{depends}\ a[t\colon T]\ \textbf{on}\ c[t]$$

is visible, the modifies list

   modifies $a[t]$

is desugared into

   modifies $a[t], c[t]$.

This reflects the common-sense view that the license to modify an abstract variable implies the license to modify its representation. The precise details of modifies list desugaring are described in the tome [23].

13.5 Example: Readers

From our experience with ESC, we have found that dependencies are not just a detail but a key ingredient of the specification language that we used constantly. However, since dependencies are a tool for programming in the large, no small example does them full justice. This section presents the smallest example we know that motivates the essential points: a simplified version of *readers*, which are the object-oriented buffered input streams used in the standard I/O library of Modula-3. A key point that the example will illustrate is that modern information hiding together with subtyping creates situations where both an abstract variable and one or more of its dependencies are visible, but the associated representation is not visible. In these situations, sound modular verification would be impossible, but dependencies save the day.

Readers (and their output counterparts, *writers*) were invented by Stoy and Strachey for the OS6 operating system [33]. Although Stoy and Strachey never used the word "object" or "class" in describing them, they are in fact one of the most compelling examples of the engineering utility of object-oriented programming. Each reader is an object with a buffer and a method for refilling the buffer. Different subtypes of readers override the refill method with code appropriate to that type of reader; for example, a disk reader fills the buffer from the disk, a network reader from the network.

As part of the ESC project, we have mechanically verified the absence of errors from most of the Modula-3 standard I/O library, including all the standard reader subtypes. In this paper we want to focus on generalized data abstraction, and many of the complexities of the actual I/O system would distract us from this focus, so we will simplify the reader interface rather drastically. (The actual code and specifications that we have used as input to the Extended Static Checker can be found on the Web [8].)

Our simplified interface *Rd* declares the type *T* representing a reader, and specifies the two methods *getChar* and *close*:

> **unit** *Rd*
> **type** *T*
> **spec var** *valid*: *T* → **bool**
> **spec var** *state*: *T* → **any**
> **proc** *getChar*(*rd*: *T*): **int**
>   **requires** *valid*[*rd*]
>   **modifies** *state*[*rd*]
>   **ensures** $-1 \leq$ **result** < 256
> **proc** *close*(*rd*: *T*)
>   **requires** *valid*[*rd*]
>   **modifies** *valid*[*rd*], *state*[*rd*]   .

Since our examples show ESC verifications only, we specify the range type of *state* as **any**, and we ignore the effects on *state* in the **ensures** clauses. We use the convention that *rd*.*getChar*() returns -1 when *rd* is exhausted, and otherwise returns the next byte of input. The specification of *close* reflects the design decision that a reader can be closed only once (a second call to *close* requires validity, which may have been destroyed by the first call).

We call attention to the absence of *valid*[*rd*] from the modifies list of *getChar*. In our system, this specifies that calls to *getChar* preserve validity. This specification is enforced even if *state* and *valid* are represented in terms of the same data fields.

Next we describe the unit that defines the generic buffer structure (by generic, we mean common to all readers, as opposed to subtype-specific), see Figure 13.1. The integer *cur*[*rd*] is the index in the abstract stream *rd* of the next byte to be returned by *getChar*. The integers *lo*[*rd*] and *hi*[*rd*] delimit the range of bytes in the abstract stream that are contained in the buffer *buff*[*rd*] (see Figure 13.2).

Interface *RdRep* declares and specifies the *refill* method, but leaves its implementation to various subtypes. The convention used by *refill* is that the call *rd*.*refill*() must make at least one new byte available (that is, it must establish *cur*[*rd*] $<$ *hi*[*rd*]), unless *rd* is exhausted, in which case it must establish *cur*[*rd*] $=$ *hi*[*rd*].

The postconditions of *getChar* and *refill* don't reflect the conventions for signaling that the reader is exhausted (nor does the variable *state* describe the condition that the reader is exhausted), because our example is an ESC verification, not a verification of full functional correctness.

The **rep** declaration reveals the representation of the abstract variable *valid* in terms of the concrete variables *lo*, *cur*, *hi*, and *buff*. In addition, because subtypes may have their own validity invariants, the interface declares the abstract variable *svalid*, and adds the conjunct *svalid*[*rd*] to the representation of *valid*[*rd*]. The intended meaning of *svalid*[*rd*] is that *rd* satisfies the validity invariant of its dynamic type. Each subtype of *Rd*.*T* will include a **rep** declaration specifying the representation of *svalid* for readers of that subtype. For example, a reader for

unit *RdRep* **import** *Rd*
 var *lo, cur, hi*: *Rd.T* → **int**
 var *buff*: *Rd.T* → **array**[**byte**]
 spec var *svalid*: *Rd.T* → **bool**
 rep *valid*[*rd*: *Rd.T*] ≡
  rd ≠ **nil** ∧
  $0 \leq lo[rd] \leq cur[rd] \leq hi[rd]$ ∧
  buff[*rd*] ≠ **nil** ∧ $hi[rd] - lo[rd] \leq$ **number**(*buff*[*rd*]) ∧
  svalid[*rd*]
 proc *refill*(*rd*: *Rd.T*)
  requires *valid*[*rd*]
  modifies *state*[*rd*]
  ensures $cur[rd] = cur'[rd]$
 depends *valid*[*rd*: *Rd.T*] **on** *lo*[*rd*], *cur*[*rd*], *hi*[*rd*], *buff*[*rd*],
        svalid[*rd*]
 depends *state*[*rd*: *Rd.T*] **on** *lo*[*rd*], *cur*[*rd*], *hi*[*rd*], *buff*[*rd*],
        elems[*buff*[*rd*]]
 depends *svalid*[*rd*: *Rd.T*] **on** *lo*[*rd*], *hi*[*rd*], *buff*[*rd*]

Figure 13.1. The interface *RdRep*, which defines the buffer structure common to all objects of type *Rd.T*.

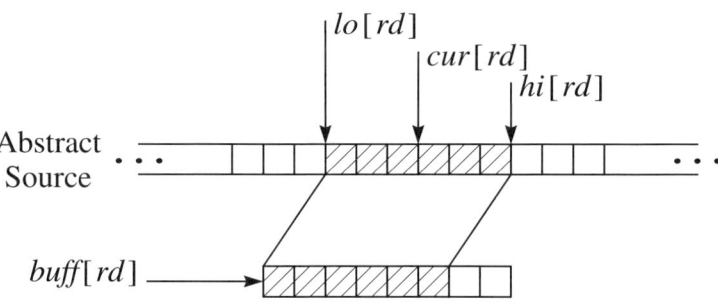

Figure 13.2. Buffer representation of readers.

a disk file would include a file handle as one of its fields, and its *svalid* would include the validity of the file handle.

The **depends** declaration for *valid* is explained by our requirement that dependencies be explicit—without it, the checker would complain that the **rep** declaration for *valid* contains undeclared dependencies. The **depends** declarations for *state* and *svalid* are more subtle and will be explained later.

Next we present the generic implementation:

    unit *RdImpl* **import** *Rd*, *RdRep*
      impl *getChar*(*rd*: *Rd.T*): **int is**
        if $cur[rd] = hi[rd]$ **then** *rd.refill*() **end** ;
        if $cur[rd] = hi[rd]$ **then**
          result $:= -1$
        else
          result $:= buff[rd][cur[rd] - lo[rd]]$;
          $cur[rd] := cur[rd] + 1$
        end
      end .

To give the flavor of an ESC verification, consider checking that $cur[rd] - lo[rd]$ is a valid index into $buff[rd]$ in the implementation of *getChar*. Since $valid[rd]$ is a precondition of *getChar*, and is specified to be preserved by *rd.refill*(), we conclude that $valid[rd]$ holds at the first semicolon. Thus, the validity of the index boils down to showing that

$$0 \leq cur[rd] - lo[rd] \;\wedge\; cur[rd] - lo[rd] < \mathbf{number}(buff[rd]) \qquad (13.5)$$

follows from

$$valid[rd] \;\wedge\; cur[rd] \neq hi[rd] \qquad . \qquad (13.6)$$

Since *RdImpl* imports *RdRep*, the representation of $valid[rd]$ is visible. Since this representation contains the conjunct $lo[rd] \leq cur[rd]$, the first conjunct of (13.5) follows immediately. The proof of the second conjunct is:

      $cur[rd] - lo[rd]$
$<$ { $cur[rd] \leq hi[rd] \;\wedge\; cur[rd] \neq hi[rd]$ (from (13.6)) }
      $hi[rd] - lo[rd]$
$\leq$ { $valid[rd]$ }
      $\mathbf{number}(buff[rd])$.

Returning to general comments about *rd.getChar*(), notice that the implementation modifies $cur[rd]$, but the **modifies** clause in the specification of *getChar* does not mention $cur[rd]$. Why does the checker not complain? Because of modifies list desugaring, as mentioned in the previous section. Modifies list desugaring gives *getChar* the license to modify $cur[rd]$, because *getChar* is specified to modify $state[rd]$, which is declared in *RdRep* to depend on $cur[rd]$. This explains why $cur[rd]$ was declared a dependency of $state[rd]$.

Having written *RdRep* and *RdImpl*, we have specified a design for the input streams, but please note that our implementation has barely begun, since we have not yet implemented a single *refill* method. The design allows the rest of the implementation to be structured as a collection of subtypes of *Rd.T*, each of which implements its own *refill* (and *close*) method. The design also allows the private declarations of these subtypes to be hidden in separate units. To illustrate the

    unit *BlankRdImpl* **import** *Rd*, *RdRep*, *BlankRd*
        var *num*: *BlankRd.T* → **int**
        rep *svalid*[*brd*: *BlankRd.T*] ≡ *hi*[*brd*] ≤ *num*[*brd*]
        impl *init*(*brd*: *BlankRd.T*, *n*: **int**): *BlankRd.T* **is**
            num[*brd*] := *n* ;
            buff[*brd*] := **new**(**byte**, **min**(8192, *n*)) ;
            lo[*brd*] := 0 ; *cur*[*brd*] := 0 ;
            hi[*brd*] := **number**(*buff*[*brd*]) ;
            for *i* := 0 **to** *hi*[*brd*] − 1 **do**
                buff[*brd*][*i*] := 32
            end ;
            result := *brd*
        end
        impl *refill*(*brd*: *BlankRd.T*) **is**
            lo[*brd*] := *cur*[*brd*] ;
            hi[*brd*] := **min**(*lo*[*brd*] + **number**(*buff*[*brd*]), *num*[*brd*])
        end
        depends *state*[*brd*: *BlankRd.T*] **on** *num*[*brd*]
        depends *svalid*[*brd*: *BlankRd.T*] **on** *num*[*brd*]

Figure 13.3. The blank reader implementation unit *BlankRdImpl*.

modularity issues that arise when a subtype is defined, we now give the interface and implementation of a trivial type of reader, a *blank reader*, which delivers a sequence of blanks whose length is determined at initialization time. More precisely, the expression **new**(*BlankRd.T*).*init*(*n*) allocates, initializes, and returns a reader that delivers a stream of exactly *n* blanks.

   unit *BlankRd* **import** *Rd*
      type *T* <: *Rd.T*
      proc *init*(*brd*: *T*, *n*: **int**): *T*
         requires $0 \leq n$
         modifies *valid*[*brd*], *state*[*brd*]
         ensures *valid'*[*brd*] ∧ **result** = *brd*

The conjunction "**result** = *brd*" in the postcondition specifies that the *init* method returns the object that it initializes, a convention we have found useful. The implementation is shown in Figure 13.3. The method *init* stores the argument *n* in the field *num*[*brd*] for later use by the method *refill*. The method also initializes the *lo*, *cur*, and *hi* fields in the obvious way, allocates a buffer of size up to 8192 (that is, up to 8 kilobytes), and fills the buffer with blanks (code 32).

As we shall see later, it is critical to the verification of the module that each blank reader *brd* satisfy the invariant *hi*[*brd*] ≤ *num*[*brd*]. Therefore, the *BlankRdImpl* unit provides a subtype-specific representation for *svalid*, effectively strengthening the general reader validity invariant as needed for the particular subtype *BlankRd.T*.

Recall that the *refill* method is specified to preserve validity. Each *refill* implementation must therefore be proved to maintain validity, so we must prove that $brd.refill()$ does not change $valid[brd]$. Sometimes proof obligations of this form can be discharged simply by observing that no operation in the method body has any effect on the variable that must be preserved. But in the present case, this simple approach doesn't suffice, since the *refill* implementation modifies the representation of *valid*. Instead we must use the **rep** declaration and prove the conjuncts of $valid[brd]$ one by one. Among them is that at exit,

$$cur'[brd] \leq hi'[brd] \quad .$$

Since the body of *refill* does not change $cur[brd]$ and makes $hi'[brd]$ equal to

$$\min(cur[brd] + \mathbf{number}(buff[brd]), num[brd]) \quad ,$$

proving this postcondition boils down to showing that each argument to **min** is at least $cur[brd]$. For the first argument, this follows from the fact that the **number** of any array is non-negative. The proof for the second argument is:

$$\begin{aligned}
& valid[brd] \\
\Rightarrow \quad & \{ \ \mathbf{rep} \text{ for } valid \ \} \\
& cur[brd] \leq hi[brd] \ \wedge \ svalid[brd] \\
= \quad & \{ \ brd \text{ is of type } BlankRd.T, \mathbf{rep} \text{ for } svalid \text{ for this type } \} \\
& cur[brd] \leq hi[brd] \ \wedge \ hi[brd] \leq num[brd] \\
\Rightarrow \quad & \{ \ \text{transitivity} \ \} \\
& cur[brd] \leq num[brd] \quad .
\end{aligned}$$

We present this calculation in detail to illustrate that the verification of the *refill* method of even the trivial *BlankRd.T* requires the subtype-specific validity conjunct. (The need for the *svalid* conjunct is more conspicuous in more interesting reader subtypes.)

Read-only by specification

The calculation that $cur[brd] \leq num[brd]$ follows from $valid[brd]$ would be in vain if the generic code could modify $hi[brd]$. If, for example, the generic implementation of $rd.getChar()$ would sometimes increment $hi[rd]$, then it could destroy $svalid[rd]$, which could cause all kinds of errors. To prevent this, the Modula-3 interface from which we translated *RdRep* contains the following English comment:

> The generic code modifies $cur[rd]$, but not $lo[rd]$, $hi[rd]$, or $buff[rd]$. (13.7)

This guarantee is essential to subtypes, since between calls to their *refill* methods, they may need to know that *lo*, *hi*, and *buff* have not been changed by the generic code.

How do we translate the sentence (13.7) into a formal specification? The Modula-3 language does not have any kind of **readonly** qualifier for field declarations. Java and C++ have qualifiers like `private` and `protected`, but these declarations don't help with the current problem. Both of them allow the implementation to read and write the fields, while limiting the access from subtypes (and from other clients). What we need here is almost the opposite: a declaration that will forbid the generic implementation from writing the fields, while allowing subtypes to write them. We can hardly expect a programming language to have a declaration qualifier that enforces this highly particular access policy, but modular verification will not be sound unless the access policy is formally stated and enforced.

We wrestled with the problem for some time before realizing happily that **depends** provides a neat solution. In fact, the third dependency declaration in *RdRep*, which states that $svalid[rd]$ depends on $lo[rd]$, $hi[rd]$, and $buff[rd]$, is the desired formalization of (13.7). For if the generic code were to modify any of these fields, the presence of the dependency would alert the checker to the possibility that *svalid*, and therefore *valid*, might be changed. In other words, in a scope where $lo[rd]$, $hi[rd]$, and $buff[rd]$ are known to be part of the representation of $svalid[rd]$, but the explicit representation is unknown, the only hope for maintaining the invariance of $svalid[rd]$ is to avoid modifying $lo[rd]$, $hi[rd]$, and $buff[rd]$. We call this technique "read-only by specification".

Summary

To repeat our main conclusion from this example, we see that modular verification with subtyping creates situations where both an abstract variable and one or more of its dependencies are visible, but where the associated representation is not visible. We have seen two instances of this:

- The dependencies of *state* are specified in *RdRep*, but no representation for *state* is specified. The dependencies must be visible so that the implementations of operations that modify the state (for example, *getChar*) will have the license to modify the concrete variables that represent the state. The representation declaration cannot be visible, for two reasons. First, because we are doing extended static checking only, we never give a representation for the state. Second, even if we were doing full-scale verification, the representation would be subtype-specific, but the dependencies must be visible in the generic scope.

- The dependencies of *svalid* are specified in *RdRep*, but no representation for *svalid* is given there. The dependencies are necessary to prevent generic operations from modifying the variables that are reserved for the use of subtypes. But it is clearly impossible to present a representation declaration for *svalid* in the *RdRep* scope, since the whole point of *svalid* is to allow subtypes to include their own invariants as part of validity: these invariants can't be known in the generic scope.

Explicit dependencies may seem verbose, and it would be nice to be able to infer them automatically. But this will not always be possible. For example, of the three **depends** declarations in *RdRep*, we can imagine inferring the first (from the **rep** declaration for *valid*), but the second and third could not be automatically inferred since they are used to specify non-trivial design decisions (namely, which fields can be modified by generic code, and which can be modified by subtypes only).

This concludes our example of the rôle of dependencies in modular verification.

13.6 Related work

Most work on data abstraction seems to be directed at one of two goals: algorithm design or structuring large systems.

When data abstraction is used for algorithm design, the representation is "inlined" into the site of use as the refinement step of the design [3, 11, 17, 15, 28, 12, 9]. Consequently, the work on this kind of data abstraction is largely unconnected with the large system structuring problems that we are concerned with in this paper. This is not to deny that the underlying mathematics of data abstraction applies to both enterprises. Indeed, our first verification condition generator for ESC did not use explicit functionalization of abstract variables (described in the tome [23]) but instead used the "change of coordinates" approach common in algorithm refinement. However, we found that the result was that our theorem-prover was constantly forced to apply the "one-point rule" and that for our purposes, explicit functionalization is preferred.

Turning to data abstraction for the purpose of structuring large systems, the earliest treatments were in contexts where there was no independent information-hiding mechanism (like our units) and therefore the problems addressed in the present paper did not arise, or were ignored in the semi-formal treatments in the literature. These treatments include Milner's definition of simulation [26], Hoare's classic treatment of abstraction functions [13], and the influential work of Liskov and Guttag and the rest of the CLU community [25].

The first programming language to support information hiding in the way our units do was Mesa [27], with its definition modules and implementation modules. The Mesa designers appear to have been influenced by Parnas's classic paper on decomposing systems into modules [32]. Mesa in turn influenced Modula [35], Modula-2 [36], Modula-3 [31], Oberon-2 [29], and Ada [2]. Ernst, Hookway, and Ogden have studied the problem of specifying Modula-2 programs where the objects of a module may share some global state [7]. These authors share our concern for modular verification, but the possible scopes they consider are not rich enough to allow subtypes or the *RdRep* interface of our example.

Another, rather different, approach of hiding information is to classify declarations as public or private. This approach is used in Oberon [34], C++ [6], and Java [10]. In the course of the ESC/Java project [8], we used the modularity requirements of the units approach to guide our design for visibility of invariants in the public/private approach [24].

Abstraction dependencies were introduced in Leino's PhD thesis [20] in 1995. Between that time and this, they have been applied in a number of contexts: they played a central rôle in ESC/Modula-3 [5], and they were incorporated in the specification languages Larch/C++ [18] and JML [19] and in the programming logic of Müller and Poetzsch-Heffter [30]. Another application (or reformulation) of dependency declarations is Leino's technique of Data Groups [21]. We have also found that our framework of modular soundness and dynamic dependencies provides a more precise way of approaching the problem of rep exposure [4] than previous approaches in the literature have.

A few other researchers have employed declarations similar to our abstraction dependencies. Daniel Jackson's Aspect system features dependencies much like ours, but his motivation seems to be to avoid the need for reasoning about the details of the actual representation, whereas we have argued that dependency declarations are necessary even in the presence of full representation declarations [14]. The COLD specification language of Jonkers includes abstract variables (called functions) and dependency declarations between them, but COLD seems not to allow an abstract variable to appear in a modifies list, so it doesn't address many of the problems we have wrestled with [16].

13.7 Conclusions

We have applied precise formal methods to systems programs that are typical examples of the programming techniques used by careful and experienced contemporary programmers. We found that the formal methods described in the verification literature are inadequate to deal with the patterns of data abstraction and modularization in these programs. We have developed new formal methods to address these shortcomings.

Central to the new methods is the concept of a *dependency*. A dependency is an abstraction of an abstraction function, in the same sense that an opaque type is an abstraction of a concrete type. A dependency specifies one or more of the variables that occur in an abstraction function, but hides the detailed definition of the function. Just as an opaque type may be widely visible in a multi-module program, while the corresponding concrete type may be visible only narrowly, we discovered that it is often useful to make a dependency more widely visible than the abstraction function itself.

Different kinds of dependencies occur in different styles of design. Top-down programming leads to static dependencies, where an abstract field of an object is represented in terms of other fields of that same object. Bottom-up programming with reusable libraries leads to dynamic dependencies, where an abstract field of an object is represented in terms of fields of other objects, reachable indirectly from the first object.

In our experience with static checking of contemporary program libraries, we have found that we use dependencies constantly in our annotations. We have also found that dependencies provide a new perspective on old problems like the problem of encapsulation and rep exposure.

Acknowledgments

Implementing our ideas in a realistic program checker was critical to many of our discoveries. And Dave Detlefs was critical: he wrote the majority of the code, and he was often the first to see the methodological implications of practical issues.

We also thank Raymie Stata and Jim Saxe, who shared their methodological wisdom in many helpful discussions.

Finally, we thank our colleagues who commented on earlier drafts of this paper: Dave Detlefs, Cynthia Hibbard, Mark Lillibridge, Annabelle McIver, Carroll Morgan, Raymie Stata, and Mark Vandevoorde.

References

[1] Alfred V. Aho, Ravi Sethi, and Jeffrey D. Ullman. *Compilers: Principles, Techniques, and Tools*. Addison-Wesley, 1986.

[2] American National Standards Institute, Inc. *The Programming Language Ada Reference Manual*, volume 155 of *Lecture Notes in Computer Science*. Springer-Verlag, Berlin, 1983. ANSI/MIL-STD-1815A-1983.

[3] R. J. R. Back. *Correctness Preserving Program Refinements: Proof Theory and Applications*, volume 131 of *Mathematical Centre Tracts*. Mathematical Centre, Amsterdam, 1980.

[4] David L. Detlefs, K. Rustan M. Leino, and Greg Nelson. Wrestling with rep exposure. Research Report 156, Digital Equipment Corporation Systems Research Center, July 1998.

[5] David L. Detlefs, K. Rustan M. Leino, Greg Nelson, and James B. Saxe. Extended static checking. Research Report 159, Compaq Systems Research Center, December 1998.

[6] Margaret A. Ellis and Bjarne Stroustrup. *The Annotated C++ Reference Manual*. Addison-Wesley, 1990.

[7] George W. Ernst, Raymond J. Hookway, and William F. Ogden. Modular verification of data abstractions with shared realizations. *IEEE Transactions on Software Engineering*, 20(4):288–307, April 1994.

[8] Extended Static Checking home page, Compaq Systems Research Center. On the web at research.compaq.com/SRC/esc/.

[9] P. H. B. Gardiner and Carroll Morgan. A single complete rule for data refinement. *Formal Aspects of Computing*, 5(4):367–382, 1993.

[10] James Gosling, Bill Joy, and Guy Steele. *The Java™ Language Specification*. Addison-Wesley, 1996.

[11] David Gries and Jan Prins. A new notion of encapsulation. In *Proceedings of the ACM SIGPLAN 85 Symposium on Language Issues in Programming Environments*, volume 20, number 7 in *SIGPLAN Notices*, pages 131–139. ACM, July 1985.

[12] David Gries and Dennis Volpano. The transform — a new language construct. *Structured Programming*, 11(1):1–10, 1990.

[13] C. A. R. Hoare. Proof of correctness of data representations. *Acta Informatica*, 1(4):271–81, 1972.

[14] Daniel Jackson. Aspect: Detecting bugs with abstract dependences. *ACM Transactions on Software Engineering and Methodology*, 4(2):109–145, April 1995.

[15] Cliff B. Jones. *Systematic Software Development using VDM*. International Series in Computer Science. Prentice-Hall, 1986.

[16] H. B. M. Jonkers. Upgrading the pre- and postcondition technique. In S. Prehn and W. J. Toetenel, editors, *VDM '91 Formal Software Development Methods: 4th International Symposium of VDM Europe. Volume 1: Conference Contributions*, volume 551 of *Lecture Notes in Computer Science*, pages 428–456. Springer-Verlag, October 1991.

[17] Leslie Lamport and Fred B. Schneider. Constraints: A uniform approach to aliasing and typing. In *Conference Record of the Twelfth Annual ACM Symposium on Principles of Programming Languages*, pages 205–216, January 1985.

[18] Gary T. Leavens. An overview of Larch/C++: Behavioral specifications for C++ modules. In Haim Kilov and William Harvey, editors, *Specification of Behavioral Semantics in Object-Oriented Information Modeling*, pages 121–142. Kluwer Academic Publishers, 1996.

[19] Gary T. Leavens, Albert L. Baker, and Clyde Ruby. Preliminary design of JML: A behavioral interface specification language for Java. Technical Report 98-06f, Iowa State University, Department of Computer Science, July 1999. Available at ftp://ftp.cs.iastate.edu/pub/techreports/TR98-06/.

[20] K. Rustan M. Leino. *Toward Reliable Modular Programs*. PhD thesis, California Institute of Technology, 1995. Available as Technical Report Caltech-CS-TR-95-03.

[21] K. Rustan M. Leino. Data groups: Specifying the modification of extended state. In *Proceedings of the 1998 ACM SIGPLAN Conference on Object-Oriented Programming, Systems, Languages, and Applications (OOPSLA '98)*, volume 33, number 10 in *SIGPLAN Notices*, pages 144–153. ACM Press, October 1998.

[22] K. Rustan M. Leino. Recursive object types in a logic of object-oriented programs. *Nordic Journal of Computing*, 5(4):330–360, Winter 1998.

[23] K. Rustan M. Leino and Greg Nelson. Data abstraction and information hiding. Research Report 160, Compaq Systems Research Center, November 2000.

[24] K. Rustan M. Leino and Raymie Stata. Checking object invariants. Technical Note 1997-007, Digital Equipment Corporation Systems Research Center, Palo Alto, CA, January 1997. Available at research.compaq.com/SRC/publications/.

[25] Barbara Liskov and John Guttag. *Abstraction and Specification in Program Development*. MIT Electrical Engineering and Computer Science Series. MIT Press, 1986.

[26] Robin Milner. An algebraic definition of simulation between programs. Technical Report Stanford Artificial Intelligence Project Memo AIM-142, Computer Science Department Report No. CS-205, Stanford University, February 1971.

[27] James G. Mitchell, William Maybury, and Richard Sweet. The Mesa language manual, version 5.0. Technical Report CSL-79-3, Xerox PARC, Palo Alto, CA, April 1979.

[28] Joseph M. Morris. Laws of data refinement. *Acta Informatica*, 26(4):287–308, February 1989.

[29] H. Mössenböck and N. Wirth. The programming language Oberon-2. *Structured Programming*, 12(4):179–195, 1991.

[30] Peter Müller and Arnd Poetzsch-Heffter. Modular specification and verification techniques for object-oriented software components. In Gary T. Leavens and Murali Sitaraman, editors, *Foundations of Component-Based Systems*, pages 137–159. Cambridge University Press, 2000.

[31] Greg Nelson, editor. *Systems Programming with Modula-3*. Series in Innovative Technology. Prentice-Hall, 1991.

[32] D. L. Parnas. On the criteria to be used in decomposing systems into modules. *Communications of the ACM*, 15(12):1053–1058, December 1972. Reprinted as www.acm.org/classics/may96/.

[33] J. E. Stoy and C. Strachey. OS6—an experimental operating system for a small computer. Part II: Input/output and filing system. *The Computer Journal*, 15(3):195–203, 1972.

[34] N. Wirth. The programming language Oberon. *Software—Practice & Experience*, 18(7):671–690, July 1988.

[35] N. Wirth. Modula: a language for modular multiprogramming. *Software—Practice & Experience*, 7(1):3–35, January–March 1977.

[36] Niklaus Wirth. *Programming in Modula-2*. Springer-Verlag, 1982.

Section F

Type theory

14 Type systems   293
Benjamin C. Pierce

Type systems in computing can be seen as yet another remarkable example of a theoretical tool which owes its existence to basic research in science and mathematics, yet is critical to many techniques currently at the forefront of technology.

Type theory was invented at the turn of last century as the theoretical idea that was to rescue 'foundational mathematics'. This was by no means a humble beginning, but it wasn't until much later — in the 1940's — that its structuring ability was exploited more widely to solve the practical problems that arose in the creation of programming languages and compilers. Nowadays it plays a central role in the construction of 'advanced debugging tools', an almost universal feature in many of today's programming environments.

This article outlines this and many other uses to which type systems are now put in modern computer science.

15 What do types mean? — from intrinsic to extrinsic semantics   309
John C. Reynolds

Type systems, which appeared in rudimentary form in early programming languages, have become key elements in many modern approaches to checking and reasoning about programs. There are, however, two distinct ways to understand typed languages. In 'intrinsic' semantics, types denote sets of abstract values or meanings, such as complex numbers, personnel records, or automobiles; and the way in which such values are represented is hidden. In contrast, in 'extrinsic' semantics each value is equated with its set of representations, so that a complex number might be understood as the set of pair of numbers that represent it in polar coordinates.

Given the importance of types in computer science, and in mathematics and the exact sciences in general, this question naturally arises: How are the two views of types related? That is the topic of this paper.

14

Type systems

Benjamin C. Pierce

Abstract

The study of *type systems* has emerged as one of the most active areas of research in programming languages, with applications in software engineering, language design, high-performance compiler implementation, and security. This chapter discusses the motivations and history of type systems and their role in programming language design.

14.1 Type systems in computer science

Current approaches to the challenges of software development include a broad range of *formal methods* for helping ensure that a software system behaves correctly with respect to some specification, implicit or explicit, of its desired behavior. On one end of this spectrum are powerful frameworks such as Hoare logic, algebraic specification languages, modal logics, and denotational semantics; these can be used to express very general correctness properties, but are often cumbersome to use and demand a good deal of sophistication on the part of programmers. At the other end are techniques of much more modest power—modest enough that they can be built into compilers, linkers, or program analyzers and thus applied even by programmers unfamiliar with the underlying theories. Such "lightweight formal methods" often take the form of *type systems*.

As with many terms shared by large communities, it is difficult to define "type system" in a way that covers its informal usage by programming language designers and implementors, but that is still specific enough to have any bite. One plausible definition is:

> *A type system is a syntactic method for automatically proving the absence of certain program behaviors by classifying phrases according to the kinds of values they compute.*

This chapter is based on the introductory chapter of [65].

A number of points here deserve comment. First, this definition identifies type systems as tools for reasoning about *programs*. This choice of words reflects the orientation of this chapter toward the type systems found in programming languages. The term "type systems" (or, more commonly, "type theory") is also applied in more abstract areas of computer science where the focus is on connections between pure "typed lambda-calculi" and varieties of logic, via the so-called *Curry-Howard isomorphism*. Similar concepts, notations, and techniques are used, but with some important differences in orientation. For example, research on typed lambda-calculi is typically concerned with systems in which every well-typed computation is guaranteed to terminate, whereas most programming languages sacrifice this property by including features like recursive function definitions.

Another important element in the above definition is its emphasis on *classification* of terms—syntactic phrases—according to the properties of the values that they will compute when executed. A type system can be regarded as calculating a kind of *static* approximation to the run-time behaviors of the terms in a program. (Moreover, the types assigned to terms are generally calculated *compositionally*, with the type of an expression depending only on the types of its sub-expressions.)

The word "static" is sometimes added explicitly—we speak of a "statically typed programming language," for example—to distinguish the sorts of compile-time analyses we are considering here from the *dynamic* or *latent type systems* found in languages such as Scheme [73, 43, 29], where run-time *type tags* are used to distinguish different kinds of structures in the heap. Terms like "dynamically typed" are arguably misnomers and should perhaps be replaced by something like "dynamically checked," but the usage is standard.

Being static, type systems are necessarily also *conservative*: they can be used to categorically prove the *absence* of some bad program behaviors, but they cannot prove their presence, and hence they must also sometimes reject programs that actually behave well at run time. For example, a program of the form

```
if <complex test> then 5 else <type error>
```

will be rejected as ill-typed, even if it happens that the `<complex test>` will always evaluate to `true`, because a static analysis cannot determine that this is the case. The tension between conservativity and expressiveness is a fundamental fact of life in the design of type systems. The desire to allow more programs to be typed—by assigning more accurate types to their parts—is the main force driving research in the field.

A related point is that the relatively straightforward analyses embodied in most type systems are not capable of preventing arbitrary undesired program behaviors; they can only guarantee that well-typed programs are free from *certain* kinds of misbehaviors. For example, most type systems can check statically that the arguments to primitive arithmetic operations are always numbers, that the receiver object in a method invocation always provides the requested method, etc., but not that the second argument to the division operation is non-zero or that array accesses are always within bounds.

The bad behaviors that can be eliminated by the type system in a given language are often called *run-time type errors*. It is important to keep in mind that this set of behaviors is a per-language choice: although there is, of course, substantial overlap between the behaviors considered to be run-time type errors in different languages, in principle each type system comes with a definition of the behaviors it aims to prevent. The *safety* (or *soundness*) of each type system must be judged with respect to its own set of run-time errors.

The sorts of bad behaviors detected by type analysis are not restricted to low-level faults like invoking non-existent methods: type systems are also used to enforce higher-level *modularity* properties and to protect the integrity of user-defined *abstractions*. Violations of information hiding, such as directly accessing the fields of a data value whose representation is supposed to be abstract, are run-time type errors in exactly the same way as, for example, treating an integer as a pointer and using it to crash the machine.

Typechecking algorithms are typically built into compilers. This implies that they must be able to do their job *automatically*, with no manual intervention or interaction with the programmer. However, there is still plenty of room for requiring guidance from the programmer, in the form of explicit *type annotations* in programs. Usually, these annotations are kept fairly light, to make programs easier to write and read. But, in principle, a full proof that the program meets some arbitrary specification could be encoded in type annotations; in this case, the typechecker would effectively become a *proof* checker. Technologies like Extended Static Checking [28] are working to settle this territory between type systems and full-scale program verification methods, implementing fully automatic checks for some broad classes of correctness properties that rely only on "reasonably light" program annotations to guide their work.

By the same token, we are most interested in methods that are not just automatable in principle, but that actually come with *efficient* algorithms for checking types. However, exactly what counts as efficient is a matter of debate. Even widely used type systems like ML's [26] may exhibit huge typechecking times in pathological cases [40]. There are even languages with typechecking or type reconstruction problems that are undecidable, but for which algorithms are available that halt quickly "in most cases of practical interest" [66, 58, 64].

14.2 What are type systems good for?

14.2.1 Error detection

The most obvious benefit of static typechecking is that it allows early detection of some programming errors. Errors that are detected early can be fixed immediately, rather than lurking in the code to be discovered much later, when the programmer is in the middle of something else or even after the program has been deployed. Moreover, errors can often be pinpointed more accurately during typechecking than at run time, when their effects may not become visible until some time after the actual moment when things begin to go wrong.

In practice, static typechecking exposes a surprisingly broad range of errors. Programmers working in richly typed languages often remark that their programs tend to "just work" once they pass the typechecker, much more often than they feel they have a right to expect. The likely explanation for this is that not only trivial mental slips (e.g., forgetting to convert a string to a number before taking its square root), but also deeper conceptual errors (e.g., neglecting a boundary case in a complex case analysis), will often tend to manifest as inconsistencies at the level of types. The strength of this effect depends, of course, on the expressiveness of the type system and on the programming task in question: programs that manipulate a variety of data structures (e.g., symbol processing applications such as compilers) offer more purchase for the typechecker than programs involving just a few simple types, such as numerical calculations in scientific applications (though, even here, refined type systems supporting *dimension analysis* [44] can be quite useful).

Obtaining maximum benefit from the type system generally involves some attention on the part of the programmer, as well as a willingness to make good use of the facilities provided by the language; for example, a complex program that encodes all its data structures as lists will not get as much help from the compiler as one that defines a different datatype or abstract type for each. Expressive type systems offer numerous "tricks" for encoding information about program structure in terms of types.

For some sorts of programs, a typechecker can also be an invaluable *maintenance* tool. For example, a programmer who needs to change the definition of a complex data structure need not search by hand to find all the places in a large program where code involving this structure needs to be fixed. Once the declaration of the datatype has been changed, all of these sites become type-inconsistent, and they can be enumerated simply by running the compiler and jumping to the points where typechecking fails.

14.2.2 Abstraction

Another important way in which type systems support the programming process is by enforcing disciplined programming. In particular, in the context of large-scale software composition, type systems form the backbone of the *module languages* used to package and tie together the components of large systems. Types show up in the interfaces of modules (and related structures such as objects); indeed, an interface itself can be viewed as "the type of a module," providing a summary of the facilities provided by the module—a kind of partial contract between implementors and users.

Structuring large systems in terms of modules with clear interfaces leads to a more abstract style of design, where interfaces are designed and discussed independently from their eventual implementations. More abstract thinking about interfaces, in turn, generally leads to better design.

14.2.3 Documentation

Types are also useful when *reading* programs. The type declarations in procedure headers and module interfaces constitute a form of documentation, giving useful hints about behavior. Moreover, unlike descriptions embedded in comments, this form of documentation cannot become outdated as the program evolves, since it is checked during every run of the compiler.

The role of types as documentation is particularly important at the level of module signatures.

14.2.4 Language design

It is not usually easy to retrofit type systems onto languages that were not designed with typechecking in mind; rather, language design should go hand in hand with type system design.

One reason for this is that languages without type systems—even safe, dynamically checked languages—tend to offer features or encourage programming idioms that make typechecking difficult or infeasible. Indeed, in typed languages the type system itself is often taken as the foundation of the design and the organizing principle in light of which every other aspect of the design is considered.

Another point is that the concrete syntax of typed languages tends to be more complicated than that of untyped languages, since type annotations must be taken into account. It is easier to do a good job of designing a clean and comprehensible syntax when all the issues can be addressed together.

The fact that types should be an integral part of a programming language is separate from the question of where the programmer must physically write down type annotations and where they can instead be inferred by the compiler. A well-designed statically typed language will never require huge amounts of type information to be explicitly and tediously maintained by the programmer. (There is some disagreement, of course, about how much explicit type information is too much. The designers of languages in the ML family have worked hard to keep annotations to a bare minimum, using type inference methods to recover the necessary information. Languages in the C family, including Java, have chosen a somewhat more verbose style.)

14.2.5 Language safety

The role of type systems in language design is closely connected to the issue of *language safety*.

The term "safe language" is, unfortunately, even more contentious than "type system." Although people generally feel they know it when they see it, their notions of exactly what constitutes language safety are strongly influenced by the language community to which they belong. Informally, though, safe languages can be defined as ones that make it impossible to shoot yourself in the foot while programming.

Refining this intuition a little, we could say that *a safe language is one that protects its own abstractions*. Every high-level language provides *abstractions* of machine services. Safety refers to the language's ability to guarantee the integrity of these abstractions (and of higher-level abstractions introduced by the programmer using the definitional facilities of the language). For example, a language may provide arrays, with access and update operations, as an abstraction of the underlying memory. A programmer using this language then expects that an array can only be changed by using the update operation on it explicitly—and not, for example, by writing past the end of some other data structure. Similarly, one expects that lexically scoped variables can only be accessed from within their scopes, that the call stack truly behaves like a stack, etc. In a safe language, such abstractions can be used *abstractly*; in an unsafe language, they cannot: in order to completely understand how a program may behave, it is necessary to keep in mind all sorts of low-level details such as the layout of data structures in memory and the order in which they will be allocated by the compiler. In the limit, programs in unsafe languages may disrupt not only their own data structures but even those of the run-time system; the results in this case can be completely arbitrary.

Language safety is seldom absolute. Safe languages often offer programmers "escape hatches" such as foreign function calls to code written in other, possibly unsafe, languages. Indeed, such escape hatches are often provided within the language itself—Obj.magic in OCaml [46], Unsafe.cast in the New Jersey implementation of Standard ML, etc. Modula-3 [12, 63] and C$^\sharp$ [80] go yet further, offering an "unsafe sublanguage" with a whole collection of features intended for implementing low-level run-time facilities such as garbage collectors within the language itself. These features may only be used in special modules explicitly marked as unsafe.

Language safety is not the same thing as static type safety. Language safety can be *achieved* by static checking, but also by run-time checks that trap nonsensical operations just at the moment when they are attempted and stop the program or raise an exception. For example, Scheme is a safe language, even though it has no static type system at all. (Conversely, unsafe languages often provide "best effort" static type checkers that help programmers eliminate at least the most obvious sorts of slips, but such languages do not qualify as type-safe either, according to our definition, since they are generally not capable of offering any sort of guarantees about absence of undesired behaviors.)

	Statically checked	Dynamically checked
Safe	ML, Haskell, Java, etc.	Lisp, Scheme, Perl, Postscript, etc.
Unsafe	C, C++, etc.	

Run-time safety is not normally achievable by static typing alone. For example, all of the languages listed as safe above actually perform array-bounds checking dynamically.

Conversely, some kinds of safety properties—in particular, the enforcement of non-primitive, programmer-defined abstractions and interfaces—can *only* be achieved through static checking.

14.2.6 Efficiency

The first type systems in computer science, beginning in the 1950s in languages such as Fortran [5], were introduced to improve the efficiency of numerical calculations by distinguishing between integer-valued arithmetic expressions and real-valued ones, allowing the compiler to use different representations and generate appropriate machine instructions for primitive operations. In safe languages, further efficiency improvements are gained by eliminating many of the dynamic checks that would be needed to guarantee safety (by proving statically that they will always be satisfied). Today, most high-performance compilers rely heavily on information gathered by the typechecker during optimization and code-generation phases. Even compilers for languages without type systems *per se* work hard to recover approximations to this typing information.

Efficiency improvements relying on type information can come from some surprising places. For example it has recently been shown that not only code generation decisions but also data representation in parallel scientific programs can be improved using the information generated by type analysis. The Titanium language [83] uses type inference techniques to analyze the scopes of pointers, and is able to make measurably better decisions on this basis than programmers explicitly hand-tuning their programs.

14.2.7 Further applications

Beyond their traditional uses in programming and language design, type systems are now being applied in many more specific ways in computer science and related disciplines. We sketch just a few here.

An increasingly important application area for type systems is computer and network security. Static typing lies at the core of the security model of Java and of the JINI "plug and play" architecture for network devices [4], for example, and is the main enabling technology for Proof-Carrying Code [62, 60, 61]. At the same time, many fundamental ideas developed in the security community are being re-explored in the context of programming languages, where they often appear as type analyses [2, 1, 47].

Typechecking and type inference algorithms are appearing in many sorts of program analysis tools other than compilers. For example, AnnoDomini, a Y2K-conversion utility for Cobol programs, is based on an ML-style type inference engine [30].

In automated theorem proving, type systems (usually very powerful ones involving dependent types) are used as a notation for representing logical propositions and proofs. Several popular proof assistants, including Lego [49, 67], Coq [7], and Alf [51], are based directly on type theory.

Interest in type systems is also on the increase in the database community, with the introduction of numerous forms of "web metadata" such Document Type Definitions (DTDs) [81] and XML-Schema [82].

A quite different application of type systems appears in the field of linguistics, where typed lambda-calculi form the basis for formalisms such as *categorial grammar* [77, 76, etc.].

14.3 History

Type theories in mathematics were invented in the early 1900s as ways of getting around the paradoxes that had shaken the foundations of mathematics (such as the famous Russell Paradox). Over time, they gradually came to be regarded as standard tools in logic, especially in proof theory. (See [32] and [41].)

In computer science, the earliest type systems were used to make very simple distinctions between integer and floating point representations of numbers (e.g., in Fortran). In the late 1950s and early 1960s, this classification was extended to structured data (arrays of records, etc.) and higher-order functions. In the 1970s, a number of even richer concepts (parametric polymorphism, abstract data types, module systems, and subtyping) were introduced, and type systems emerged as a field in its own right.

The following table presents a rough chronology of some important high points in the history of type systems in computer science. Related developments in logic are also included, in italics, to give a sense of the importance of this field's contributions.

1870s	
origins of formal logic	[31]
1900s	
formalization of mathematics	[79]
1930s	
untyped lambda-calculus	[18]
1940s	
simply typed lambda-calculus	[17], [25]
1950s	
Fortran	[5]
Algol	[59]

1960s	
Automath project	[27]
Simula	[8]
Curry-Howard isomorphism	[42]
1970s	
Martin-Löf type theory	[52], [53]
System F, F^ω	[34]
polymorphic lambda-calculus	[70]
CLU	[48]
polymorphic type inference	[54], [26]
ML	[37]
intersection types	[20][21], [68]
1980s	
NuPRL project	[19]
subtyping	[71][9], [55]
ADTs as existential types	[56]
calculus of constructions	[22][23]
linear logic	[35], [36]
bounded quantification	[16][24], [14]
Edinburgh Logical Framework	[38]
Forsythe	[72]
pure type systems	[6]
dependent types and modularity	[50]
Quest	[11]
Effect systems	[33][74]
row variables; extensible records	[78], [69][15]
1990s	
higher-order subtyping	[10], [13]
typed intermediate languages	[75]
Object Calculus	[3]
translucent types and modularity	[39][45]
typed assembly language	[57]

References

[1] Martín Abadi. Secrecy by typing in security protocols. *Journal of the ACM*, 46(5):749–786, September 1999. Summary in the *Proceedings of TACS '97*, LNCS 1281, Springer.

[2] Martín Abadi, Anindya Banerjee, Nevin Heintze, and Jon G. Riecke. A core calculus of dependency. In ACM, editor, *POPL '99. Proceedings of the 26th ACM SIGPLAN-SIGACT on Principles of programming languages, January 20–22, 1999, San Antonio, TX*, ACM SIGPLAN Notices, pages 147–160, New York, NY, USA, 1999. ACM Press.

[3] Martín Abadi and Luca Cardelli. *A Theory of Objects*. Springer-Verlag, 1996.

[4] Ken Arnold, Ann Wollrath, Bryan O'Sullivan, Robert Scheifler, and Jim Waldo. *The Jini specification*. Addison-Wesley, 1999.

[5] John Backus. The history of Fortran I, II, and III. In R. L. Wexelblat, editor, *History of Programming Languages*, pages 25–45. Academic Press, 1981.

[6] Henk Barendregt. Introduction to generalized type systems. *Journal of Functional Programming*, 1992.

[7] Bruno Barras, Samuel Boutin, Cristina Cornes, Judicael Courant, Jean-Christophe Filliatre, Eduardo Gimenez, Hugo Herbelin, Gerard Huet, Cesar Munoz, Chetan Murthy, Catherine Parent, Christine Paulin-Mohring, Amokrane Saibi, and Benjamin Werner. The coq proof assistant reference manual : Version 6.1. Technical Report RT-0203, Inria (Institut National de Recherche en Informatique et en Automatique), France, 1997.

[8] Graham M. Birtwistle, Ole-Johan Dahl, Bjorn Myhrhaug, and Kristen Nygaard. *Simula Begin*. Studentlitteratur (Lund, Sweden), Bratt Institut fuer neues Lernen (Goch, FRG), Chartwell-Bratt Ltd, 1979.

[9] Luca Cardelli. A semantics of multiple inheritance. In G. Kahn, D. MacQueen, and G. Plotkin, editors, *Semantics of Data Types*, volume 173 of *Lecture Notes in Computer Science*, pages 51–67. Springer-Verlag, 1984. Full version in *Information and Computation* 76(2/3):138–164, 1988.

[10] Luca Cardelli. Notes about $F^\omega_{\leq:}$. Unpublished manuscript, October 1990.

[11] Luca Cardelli. Typeful programming. In E. J. Neuhold and M. Paul, editors, *Formal Description of Programming Concepts*. Springer-Verlag, 1991. An earlier version appeared as DEC Systems Research Center Research Report #45, February 1989.

[12] Luca Cardelli, James Donahue, Lucille Glassman, Mick Jordan, Bill Kalsow, and Greg Nelson. Modula-3 report (revised). Research report 52, DEC Systems Research Center, November 1989.

[13] Luca Cardelli and Giuseppe Longo. A semantic basis for Quest. *Journal of Functional Programming*, 1(4):417–458, October 1991. Preliminary version in ACM Conference on Lisp and Functional Programming, June 1990. Also available as DEC SRC Research Report 55, Feb. 1990.

[14] Luca Cardelli, Simone Martini, John C. Mitchell, and Andre Scedrov. An extension of system F with subtyping. *Information and Computation*, 109(1–2):4–56, 1994. Preliminary version in TACS '91, Sendai, Japan, pp. 750–770.

[15] Luca Cardelli and John Mitchell. Operations on records. *Mathematical Structures in Computer Science*, 1:3–48, 1991. Also in Carl A. Gunter and John C. Mitchell, editors, *Theoretical Aspects of Object-Oriented Programming: Types, Semantics, and Language Design* (MIT Press, 1994); available as DEC Systems Research Center Research Report #48, August, 1989, and in the proceedings of MFPS '89, LNCS 442, Springer.

[16] Luca Cardelli and Peter Wegner. On understanding types, data abstraction, and polymorphism. *Computing Surveys*, 17(4):471–522, December 1985.

[17] Alonzo Church. A formulation of the simple theory of types. *Journal of Symbolic Logic*, 5:56–68, 1940.

[18] Alonzo Church. *The Calculi of Lambda Conversion*. Princeton University Press, 1941.

[19] Robert L. Constable et al. *Implementing Mathematics with the NuPRL Proof Development System.* Prentice–Hall, 1986.

[20] M. Coppo and M. Dezani-Ciancaglini. A new type-assignment for λ-terms. *Archiv Math. Logik*, 19:139–156, 1978.

[21] M. Coppo, M. Dezani-Ciancaglini, and P. Salle. Functional characterization of some semantic equalities inside λ-calculus. In Hermann A. Maurer, editor, *Proceedings of the 6th Colloquium on Automata, Languages and Programming*, LNCS 71, 133–146, Graz, Austria, July 1979. Springer.

[22] Thierry Coquand. *Une Théorie des Constructions.* PhD thesis, University Paris VII, January 1985.

[23] Thierry Coquand and Gérard Huet. The Calculus of Constructions. *Information and Computation*, 76(2/3):95–120, February/March 1988.

[24] Pierre-Louis Curien and Giorgio Ghelli. Coherence of subsumption: Minimum typing and type-checking in $F_\leq$. *Mathematical Structures in Computer Science*, 2:55–91, 1992. Also in Carl A. Gunter and John C. Mitchell, editors, *Theoretical Aspects of Object-Oriented Programming: Types, Semantics, and Language Design* (MIT Press, 1994).

[25] H. B. Curry and R. Feys. *Combinatory Logic*, volume 1. North Holland, 1958. (Second edition, 1968).

[26] Luis Damas and Robin Milner. Principal type schemes for functional programs. In *Proceedings of the 9th ACM Symposium on Principles of Programming Languages*, pages 207–212, 1982.

[27] Nicolas G. de Bruijn. A survey of the project AUTOMATH. In J. P. Seldin and J. R. Hindley, editors, *To H. B. Curry: Essays in Combinatory Logic, Lambda Calculus, and Formalism*, pages 589–606. Academic Press, 1980.

[28] David L. Detlefs, K. Rustan M. Leino, Greg Nelson, and James B. Saxe. Extended static checking. Technical Report 159, Compaq Systems Research Center (SRC), 1998. Also see http://research.compaq.com/SRC/esc/overview.html.

[29] R. Kent Dybvig. *The Scheme Programming Language.* Prentice-Hall, 1987.

[30] Peter Eidorff, Fritz Henglein, Christian Mossin, Henning Niss, Morten Heine B. Sørensen, and Mads Tofte. Annodomini in practice: A type-theoretic approach to the year 2000 problem. In Jean-Yves Girard, editor, *Proc. Symposium on Typed Lambda Calculus and Applications (TLCA)*, volume 1581 of *Lecture Notes in Computer Science*, pages 6–13, L'Aquila, Italy, April 1999. Springer-Verlag.

[31] Gottlob Frege. *Begriffschrift, eine der arithmetischen nachgebildete Formelsprache des reinen Denkens.* Halle: L. Nebert, 1879.

[32] R. O. Gandy. The simple theory of types. In *Logic Colloquium 76*, volume 87 of *Studies in Logic and the Foundations of Mathematics*, pages 173–181. North Holland, 1976.

[33] D. Gifford, P. Jouvelot, J. Lucassen, and M. Sheldon. FX-87 REFERENCE MANUAL. Technical Report MIT-LCS//MIT/LCS/TR-407, Massachusetts Institute of Technology, Laboratory for Computer Science, September 1987.

[34] Jean-Yves Girard. *Interprétation fonctionelle et élimination des coupures de l'arithmétique d'ordre supérieur.* PhD thesis, Université Paris VII, 1972. A summary

appeared in the Proceedings of the Second Scandinavian Logic Symposium (J.E. Fenstad, editor), North-Holland, 1971 (pp. 63–92).

[35] Jean-Yves Girard. Linear logic. *Theoretical Computer Science*, 50:1–102, 1987.

[36] Jean-Yves Girard, Yves Lafont, and Paul Taylor. *Proofs and Types*, volume 7 of *Cambridge Tracts in Theoretical Computer Science*. Cambridge University Press, 1989.

[37] Michael J. Gordon, Robin Milner, and Christopher P. Wadsworth. *Edinburgh LCF*. LNCS 78, Springer-Verlag, 1979.

[38] Robert Harper, Furio Honsell, and Gordon Plotkin. A framework for defining logics. *Journal of the ACM*, 40(1):143–184, 1992. Preliminary version in LICS'87.

[39] Robert Harper and Mark Lillibridge. A type-theoretic approach to higher-order modules with sharing. In *Proceedings of the Twenty-First ACM Symposium on Principles of Programming Languages (POPL), Portland, Oregon*, pages 123–137, Portland, Oregon, January 1994.

[40] Fritz Henglein and Harry G. Mairson. The complexity of type inference for higher-order typed lambda-calculi. In *Proceedings of the Eighteenth ACM Symposium on Principles of Programming Languages*, pages 119–130, Orlando, FL, January 1991.

[41] J. Roger Hindley. *Basic Simple Type Theory*, volume 42 of *Cambridge Tracts in Theoretical Computer Science*. Cambridge University Press, 1997.

[42] W. A. Howard. The formulas-as-types notion of construction. In J. P. Seldin and J. R. Hindley, editors, *To H. B. Curry: Essays on Combinatory Logic, Lambda Calculus, and Formalism*, pages 479–490. Academic Press, 1980. Reprint of 1969 article.

[43] Richard Kelsey, William Clinger, and Jonathan Rees. Revised report on the algorithmic language Scheme. *ACM SIGPLAN Notices*, 33(9):26–76, September 1998. With H. Abelson, N. I. Adams, IV, D. H. Bartley, G. Brooks, R. K. Dybvig, D. P. Friedman, R. Halstead, C. Hanson, C. T. Haynes, E. Kohlbecker, D. Oxley, K. M. Pitman, G. J. Rozas, G. L. Steele, Jr., G. J. Sussman, and M. Wand.

[44] Andrew Kennedy. Dimension types. In Donald Sannella, editor, *Programming Languages and Systems—ESOP'94, 5th European Symposium on Programming*, volume 788 of *Lecture Notes in Computer Science*, pages 348–362, Edinburgh, U.K., 11–13 April 1994. Springer.

[45] Xavier Leroy. Manifest types, modules and separate compilation. In *Conference record of POPL '94: 21st ACM SIGPLAN-SIGACT Symposium on Principles of Programming Languages*, pages 109–122, Portland, Oregon, January 1994.

[46] Xavier Leroy. The objective caml system: Documentation and user's manual, 2000. With Damien Doligez, Jacques Garrigue, Didier Rémy, and Jrôme Vouillon. Available from http://caml.inria.fr.

[47] Xavier Leroy and François Rouaix. Security properties of typed applets. In *Conference Record of POPL 98: The 25TH ACM SIGPLAN-SIGACT Symposium on Principles of Programming Languages, San Diego, California*, pages 391–403, ACM, 1998.

[48] B. Liskov, R. Atkinson, T. Bloom, E. Moss, J.C. Schaffert, R. Scheifler, and A. Snyder. *CLU Reference Manual*. Springer-Verlag, 1981.

[49] Zhaohui Luo and Robert Pollack. The LEGO proof development system: A user's manual. Technical Report ECS-LFCS-92-211, University of Edinburgh, May 1992.

[50] David MacQueen. Using dependent types to express modular structure. In *13th Annual ACM Symposium on Principles of Programming languages*, pages 277–286, St. Petersburg Beach, Florida, January 1986.

[51] Lena Magnusson and Bengt Nordström. The ALF proof editor and its proof engine. In Henk Barendregt and Tobias Nipkow, editors, *Types for Proofs and Programs*, pages 213–237. LNCS 806, Springer-Verlag, 1994.

[52] Per Martin-Löf. An intuitionistic theory of types: predicative part. In H. E. Rose and J. C. Shepherdson, editors, *Logic Colloquium, '73*, pages 73–118, Amsterdam, 1973. North Holland.

[53] Per Martin-Löf. Constructive mathematics and computer programming. In *Logic, Methodology and Philosophy of Science, VI*. North Holland, Amsterdam, 1982.

[54] Robin Milner. A theory of type polymorphism in programming. *Journal of Computer and System Sciences*, 17:348–375, August 1978.

[55] John C. Mitchell. Coercion and type inference (summary). In *Proc. 11th ACM Symp. on Principles of Programming Languages*, pages 175–185, January 1984.

[56] John C. Mitchell and Gordon D. Plotkin. Abstract types have existential types. *ACM Trans. on Programming Languages and Systems*, 10(3):470–502, 1988. Preliminary version appeared in *Proc. 12th ACM Symp. on Principles of Programming Languages*, 1985.

[57] Greg Morrisett, David Walker, Karl Crary, and Neal Glew. From System F to Typed Assembly Language. In *Twenty-fifth ACM Symposium on Principles of Programming Languages*, pages 85–97, San Diego, January 1998.

[58] Gopalan Nadathur and Dale Miller. An overview of λProlog. In Robert A. Kowalski and Kenneth A. Bowen, editors, *Logic Programming: Proceedings of the Fifth International Conference and Symposium, Volume 1*, pages 810–827, Cambridge, Massachusetts, August 1988. MIT Press.

[59] P. Naur et al. Revised report on the algorithmic language Algol 60. *Communications of the ACM*, 6:1–17, January 1963.

[60] G. C. Necula and P. Lee. Safe, untrusted agents using proof-carrying code. In G. Vigna, editor, *Mobile Agents and Security*, LNCS 1419 pages 61–91. Springer-Verlag, 1998.

[61] George C. Necula. Proof-carrying code. In *Conference Record of POPL '97: The 24th ACM SIGPLAN-SIGACT Symposium on Principles of Programming Languages*, pages 106–119, Paris, France, 15–17 January 1997.

[62] George C. Necula and Peter Lee. Safe kernel extensions without run-time checking. In *2nd Symposium on Operating Systems Design and Implementation (OSDI '96)*, October 28–31, 1996, Seattle, WA, pages 229–243, Berkeley, California, USA, October 1996. USENIX Press.

[63] Greg Nelson, editor. *Systems Programming with Modula-3*. Prentice Hall, 1991.

[64] Frank Pfenning. Elf: A meta-language for deductive systems. In A. Bundy, editor, *Proceedings of the 12th International Conference on Automated Deduction*, pages 811–815, Nancy, France, June 1994. LNAI 814, Springer-Verlag.

[65] Benjamin C. Pierce. *Type Systems and Programming Languages*. MIT Press. To appear, 2002.

[66] Benjamin C. Pierce and David N. Turner. Pict: A programming language based on the pi-calculus. Technical Report CSCI 476, Computer Science Department, Indiana University, 1997. In *Proof, Language and Interaction: Essays in Honour of Robin Milner*, Gordon Plotkin, Colin Stirling, and Mads Tofte, editors, MIT Press, 2000.

[67] Robert Pollack. *The Theory of LEGO: A Proof Checker for the Extended Calculus of Constructions*. PhD thesis, University of Edinburgh, 1994.

[68] Garrell Pottinger. A type assignment for the strongly normalizable λ-terms. In *To H. B. Curry: Essays on Combinatory Logic, Lambda Calculus, and Formalism*, pages 561–577. Academic Press, 1980.

[69] Didier Rémy. Typechecking records and variants in a natural extension of ML. In *Proceedings of the Sixteenth Annual ACM Symposium on Principles of Programming Languages, Austin*, pages 242–249. ACM, January 1989. Also in Carl A. Gunter and John C. Mitchell, editors, *Theoretical Aspects of Object-Oriented Programming: Types, Semantics, and Language Design*, MIT Press, 1994.

[70] John Reynolds. Towards a theory of type structure. In *Proc. Colloque sur la Programmation*, pages 408–425, New York, 1974. LNCS 19, Springer-Verlag.

[71] John Reynolds. Using category theory to design implicit conversions and generic operators. In N. D. Jones, editor, *Proceedings of the Aarhus Workshop on Semantics-Directed Compiler Generation*, LNCS 94, Springer-Verlag, January 1980. Also in Carl A. Gunter and John C. Mitchell, editors, *Theoretical Aspects of Object-Oriented Programming: Types, Semantics, and Language Design*, MIT Press, 1994.

[72] John C. Reynolds. Preliminary design of the programming language Forsythe. Technical Report CMU-CS-88-159, Carnegie Mellon University, June 1988.

[73] Gerald Jay Sussman and Jr. Steele, Guy Lewis. Scheme: an interpreter for extended lambda calculus. MIT AI Memo 349, Massachusetts Institute of Technology, Cambridge, Mass., December 1975.

[74] J.-P. Talpin and P. Jouvelot. The type and effects discipline. In *Proc. IEEE Symp. on Logic in Computer Science*, pages 162–173, 1992.

[75] D. Tarditi, G. Morrisett, P. Cheng, C. Stone, R. Harper, and P. Lee. TIL : A type-directed optimizing compiler for ML. In *Proceedings of the ACM SIGPLAN Conference on Programming Language Design and Implemantation*, pages 181–192, New York, May 21–24 1996. ACM Press.

[76] J. F. A. K. van Benthem and Alice Ter Meulen, editors. *Handbook of Logic and Language*. MIT Press, 1997.

[77] Johan van Benthem. *Language in Action: Categories, Lambdas, and Dynamic Logic*. MIT Press, 1995.

[78] Mitchell Wand. Complete type inference for simple objects. In *Proceedings of the IEEE Symposium on Logic in Computer Science*, Ithaca, NY, June 1987.

[79] Alfred North Whitehead and Bertrand Russell. *Principia Mathematica*. Cambridge University Press, 1910. Three volumes (1910; 1912; 1913).

[80] Christoph Wille. *Presenting C#*. SAMS, 2000.

[81] Extensible markup language (XML[TM]). http://www.w3.org/XML/.

[82] XML Schema Part 0: Primer, W3C Working Draft. http://www.w3.org/TR/xmlschema-0/, 2000.

[83] Kathy Yelick, Luigi Semenzato, Geoff Pike, Carleton Miyamoto, Ben Liblit, Arvind Krishnamurthy, Paul Hilfinger, Susan Graham, David Gay, Phil Colella, and Alex Aiken. Titanium: a high-performance Java dialect. *Concurrency: Practice and Experience*, 10(11–13):825–836, September 1998. Special Issue: Java for High-performance Network Computing.

15

What do types mean? — From intrinsic to extrinsic semantics

John C. Reynolds

Abstract

A definition of a typed language is said to be "intrinsic" if it assigns meanings to typings rather than arbitrary phrases, so that ill-typed phrases are meaningless. In contrast, a definition is said to be "extrinsic" if all phrases have meanings that are independent of their typings, while typings represent properties of these meanings.

For a simply typed lambda calculus, extended with integers, recursion, and conditional expressions, we give an intrinsic denotational semantics and a denotational semantics of the underlying untyped language. We then establish a logical relations theorem between these two semantics, and show that the logical relations can be "bracketed" by retractions between the domains of the two semantics. From these results, we derive an extrinsic semantics that uses partial equivalence relations.

There are two very different ways of giving denotational semantics to a programming language (or other formal language) with a nontrivial type system. In an *intrinsic* semantics, only phrases that satisfy typing judgements have meanings. Indeed, meanings are assigned to the typing judgements, rather than to the phrases themselves, so that a phrase that satisfies several judgements will have several meanings.

For example, consider $\lambda x.\, x$ (in a simply typed functional language). Corresponding to the typing judgement $\vdash \lambda x.\, x\, :\, \mathbf{int} \to \mathbf{int}$, its intrinsic meaning is the identity function on the integers, while corresponding to the judgement $\vdash \lambda x.\, x\, :\, \mathbf{bool} \to \mathbf{bool}$, its intrinsic meaning is the identity function on truth values. On the other hand, $\lambda x.\, x\, x$, which does not satisfy any typing judgement, does not have any intrinsic meaning.

In contrast, in an *extrinsic* semantics, the meaning of each phrase is the same as it would be in a untyped language, regardless of its typing properties. In this view, a typing judgement is an assertion that the meaning of a phrase possesses some property.

For example, the extrinsic meaning of $\lambda x.\, x$ is the identity function on the universe of all values that can occur in a computation. In the simple case where integers and booleans can be regarded as members of this universe, the judgement $\vdash \lambda x.\, x : \mathbf{int} \to \mathbf{int}$ asserts that this function maps each integer into an integer, and the judgement $\vdash \lambda x.\, x : \mathbf{bool} \to \mathbf{bool}$ asserts that the same function maps each truth value into a truth value.

The terms "intrinsic" and "extrinsic" are recent coinages by the author [1, Chapter 15], but the concepts are much older. The intrinsic view is associated with Alonzo Church, and has been called "ontological" by Leivant [2]. The extrinsic view is associated with Haskell Curry, and has been called "semantical" by Leivant.

In this paper, we will consider the denotational semantics of a very simple typed call-by-name language with integers as a primitive type, functions, conditional expressions, and recursion definitions of values (but not of types). First, we will give an intrinsic semantics and an untyped semantics, which we will relate by a logical relations theorem. Then we will define embedding-retraction pairs between the domain specified for each type in the intrinsic semantics and the universal domain used in the untyped semantics, and we will show that these pairs "bracket" the logical relations. Finally, we will use this result to derive an extrinsic semantics in which each type denotes a partial equivalence relation on the universal domain.

In the course of this paper, we will use a variety of notations for functions. When f is a function, we write $\mathrm{dom}\, f$ for its domain. When $\iota_1, \ldots, \iota_n$ are distinct, we write $[\, f \mid \iota_1{:}x_1 \mid \ldots \mid \iota_n{:}x_n \,]$ for the function with domain $\mathrm{dom}\, f \cup \{\iota_1, \ldots, \iota_n\}$ that maps each ι_k into x_k and all other arguments ι' into $f\, \iota'$; in the special case where f is the empty function, we write $[\, \iota_1{:}x_1 \mid \ldots \mid \iota_n{:}x_n \,]$.

We write $f\, ;\, g$ for the composition of functions f and g in diagrammatic order, and I_D for the identity function on the domain D. We assume that function application is left-associative, e.g., that $f\, x\, y$ abbreviates $(f\, x)y$.

15.1 Syntax and typing rules

In defining the syntax and type system of our illustrative language, we will use the following metavariables, sometimes with decorations, to range over denumerably infinite sets of syntactic entities:

ι: variables (sometimes called identifiers)

p: phrases

θ: types

π: type assignments.

We write I to denote the set of all variables.

Since our language is an extension of the lambda calculus, a phrase may be a *variable*, an *abstraction*, or an *application*:

$$p ::= \iota \mid \lambda \iota.\, p' \mid p'\, p''$$

In addition, there will be a *fixed-point* expression for defining a value by recursion, and a *conditional* expression that branches on whether a number is positive to choose between evaluating different subexpressions:

$$p ::= \mathbf{Y}\, p' \mid \mathbf{if}\ p' > 0\ \mathbf{then}\ p''\ \mathbf{else}\ p'''$$

Finally, as primitives, we will have typical constants and operations for integers:

$$p ::= 0 \mid 1 \mid 2 \mid \cdots \mid p' + p''$$

(Additional integer operators would be treated the same way as +.)

Types and type assignments can also be defined by an abstract grammar:

$$\theta ::= \mathbf{int} \mid \theta_1 \to \theta_2$$
$$\pi ::= \iota_1\!:\!\theta_1, \ldots, \iota_n\!:\!\theta_n$$

Here, $\iota_1\!:\!\theta_1, \ldots, \iota_n\!:\!\theta_n$ is a concrete representation of a type assignment that, abstractly, is the function on the set $\{\iota_1, \ldots, \iota_n\}$ that maps each variable ι_k into the type θ_k. This implies that $\iota_1, \ldots, \iota_n$ must be distinct, and that permuting the pairs $\iota_k\!:\!\theta_k$ will not change the type assignment.

Informally, the primitive type **int** denotes the set of integers, while $\theta_1 \to \theta_2$ denotes the set of functions that map values of type θ_1 into values of type θ_2.

If π is a type assignment, p is a phrase, and θ is a type, then the formula $\pi \vdash p : \theta$ is a *typing judgement*, or more briefly a *typing*, which is read "p has type θ under π". The valid typing judgements are defined by inference rules. (In the first two rules, we rely on the fact that type assignments are functions on variables.)

$$\frac{}{\pi \vdash \iota : \pi \iota} \quad \text{when } \iota \in \operatorname{dom} \pi$$

$$\frac{[\pi \mid \iota\!:\!\theta_1] \vdash p' : \theta_2}{\pi \vdash \lambda \iota.\, p' : \theta_1 \to \theta_2} \qquad \frac{\pi \vdash p' : \theta_1 \to \theta_2 \quad \pi \vdash p'' : \theta_1}{\pi \vdash p'\, p'' : \theta_2}$$

$$\frac{\pi \vdash p' : \theta \to \theta}{\pi \vdash \mathbf{Y}\, p' : \theta}$$

$$\frac{\pi \vdash p' : \mathbf{int} \quad \pi \vdash p'' : \theta \quad \pi \vdash p''' : \theta}{\pi \vdash \mathbf{if}\ p' > 0\ \mathbf{then}\ p''\ \mathbf{else}\ p''' : \theta}$$

$$\frac{}{\pi \vdash n : \mathbf{int}} \quad \text{when } n \text{ is a numeral} \qquad \frac{\pi \vdash p' : \mathbf{int} \quad \pi \vdash p'' : \mathbf{int}}{\pi \vdash p' + p'' : \mathbf{int}.}$$

15.2 An intrinsic semantics

To give an intrinsic denotational semantics to our illustrative language, we must define the meanings of types, type assignments, and typing judgements. Specifically, we must give:

- for each type θ, a domain $[\![\theta]\!]$ of *values* appropriate to θ,
- for each type assignment π, a domain $[\![\pi]\!]^*$ of *environments* appropriate to π,
- for each valid typing judgement $\pi \vdash p : \theta$, a continuous function $[\![\pi \vdash p : \theta]\!]$ from $[\![\pi]\!]^*$ to $[\![\theta]\!]$, called the *meaning of p with respect to π and θ*.

We define a *predomain* to be a poset with least upper bounds of all increasing chains, and a *domain* to be a predomain with a least element, which we will denote by $\bot$. (In fact, all of the domains we will use are Scott domains, i.e., nonempty partially ordered sets that are directed complete, bounded complete, algebraic, and countably based, but we will not make use of this fact.) A *continuous* function is one that preserves least upper bounds of all increasing chains; it is *strict* if it also preserves least elements.

In what follows, we will write $\mathbf{Z}$ for the sets of integers and $\mathbf{Z}_\bot$ for the flat domain obtained by discretely ordering the integers and then adding a least element $\bot$ below them. When P is a predomain and D is a domain, we write $P \Rightarrow D$ for the pointwise-ordered domain of continuous functions from P to D.

The meanings of types and type assignments are defined by induction on their structure:

Definition 15.2.1 *For types θ and type assignments π, the domains $[\![\theta]\!]$ and $[\![\pi]\!]^*$ are such that*

$$[\![\mathbf{int}]\!] = \mathbf{Z}_\bot$$

$$[\![\theta_1 \to \theta_2]\!] = [\![\theta_1]\!] \Rightarrow [\![\theta_2]\!]$$

$$[\![\iota_1{:}\theta_1, \ldots, \iota_n{:}\theta_n]\!]^* = \{\, [\iota_1{:}x_1 \mid \ldots \mid \iota_n{:}x_n] \mid x_1 \in [\![\theta_1]\!], \ldots, x_n \in [\![\theta_n]\!] \,\}.$$

(The set on the right of the final equation is a Cartesian product, indexed by the variables $\iota_1, \ldots, \iota_n$, that becomes a domain when ordered componentwise.)

On the other hand, the meanings of typing judgements are defined by induction on the structure of proofs of these judgements. Specifically, for each inference rule, we give a semantic equation that expresses the meaning of a proof in which the final inference is an instance of that rule, in terms of the meanings of its immediate subproofs.

To write such equations succinctly, we write $\mathcal{P}(J)$ to denote a proof of the judgement J. For example, corresponding to the inference rule for function application,

$$\frac{\pi \vdash p' : \theta_1 \to \theta_2 \qquad \pi \vdash p'' : \theta_1}{\pi \vdash p'p'' : \theta_2,}$$

15. What do types mean? — From intrinsic to extrinsic semantics 313

we have the semantic equation

$$\left[\!\!\left[\frac{\mathcal{P}(\pi \vdash p' : \theta_1 \to \theta_2) \quad \mathcal{P}(\pi \vdash p'' : \theta_1)}{\pi \vdash p' p'' : \theta_2}\right]\!\!\right]\eta$$

$$= [\![\mathcal{P}(\pi \vdash p' : \theta_1 \to \theta_2)]\!]\eta\big([\![\mathcal{P}(\pi \vdash p'' : \theta_1)]\!]\eta\big),$$

which asserts that the meaning of a proof of $\pi \vdash p' p'' : \theta_2$ in which the final inference is an instance of the function-appplication rule, is a function that, when applied to an environment η, gives $(m'\,\eta)(m''\,\eta)$, where m' and m'' are the meanings of the immediate subproofs of the proof of $\pi \vdash p' p'' : \theta_2$.

Before proceeding further, we must warn the reader of a subtle complication in this way of defining semantics. For a sufficiently rich language, there may be many different proofs of the same typing judgement, and there is no a priori guarantee that these proofs will have the same meaning. If our intrinsic semantics is to make sense, so that we can take the meaning $[\![\mathcal{P}(J)]\!]$ of any proof of a judgement J to be the meaning of J itself, then we must have the property of coherence:

Definition 15.2.2 *An intrinsic semantics is said to be* coherent *if all proofs of the same judgement have the same meaning.*

In fact, as we will see in Section 15.5, our intrinsic semantics is coherent.

The following are the semantic equations for the intrinsic semantics of our illustrative language:

$$\left[\!\!\left[\overline{\pi \vdash \iota : \pi\iota}\right]\!\!\right]\eta = \eta\iota$$

$$\left[\!\!\left[\frac{\mathcal{P}([\pi \mid \iota:\theta_1] \vdash p' : \theta_2)}{\pi \vdash \lambda\iota.\,p' : \theta_1 \to \theta_2}\right]\!\!\right]\eta = \lambda x \in [\![\theta_1]\!].\ [\![\mathcal{P}([\pi \mid \iota:\theta_1] \vdash p' : \theta_2)]\!][\eta \mid \iota:x]$$

$$\left[\!\!\left[\frac{\mathcal{P}(\pi \vdash p' : \theta_1 \to \theta_2) \quad \mathcal{P}(\pi \vdash p'' : \theta_1)}{\pi \vdash p' p'' : \theta_2}\right]\!\!\right]\eta$$

$$= [\![\mathcal{P}(\pi \vdash p' : \theta_1 \to \theta_2)]\!]\eta\big([\![\mathcal{P}(\pi \vdash p'' : \theta_1)]\!]\eta\big)$$

$$\left[\!\!\left[\frac{\mathcal{P}(\pi \vdash p' : \theta \to \theta)}{\pi \vdash \mathbf{Y}\,p' : \theta}\right]\!\!\right]\eta = \bigsqcup_{n=0}^{\infty}\big([\![\mathcal{P}(\pi \vdash p' : \theta \to \theta)]\!]\eta\big)^n \bot$$

$$\left[\!\left[\frac{\mathcal{P}(\pi \vdash p' : \mathbf{int}) \quad \mathcal{P}(\pi \vdash p'' : \theta) \quad \mathcal{P}(\pi \vdash p''' : \theta)}{\pi \vdash \mathbf{if}\ p' > 0\ \mathbf{then}\ p''\ \mathbf{else}\ p''' : \theta} \right]\!\right]\eta$$

$$= \begin{cases} \bot & \text{when } [\![\mathcal{P}(\pi \vdash p' : \mathbf{int})]\!]\eta = \bot \\ [\![\mathcal{P}(\pi \vdash p'' : \theta)]\!]\eta & \text{when } [\![\mathcal{P}(\pi \vdash p' : \mathbf{int})]\!]\eta > 0 \\ [\![\mathcal{P}(\pi \vdash p''' : \theta)]\!]\eta & \text{when } [\![\mathcal{P}(\pi \vdash p' : \mathbf{int})]\!]\eta \leq 0 \end{cases}$$

$$\left[\!\left[\overline{\pi \vdash n : \mathbf{int}} \right]\!\right]\eta = n$$

$$\left[\!\left[\frac{\mathcal{P}(\pi \vdash p' : \mathbf{int}) \quad \mathcal{P}(\pi \vdash p'' : \mathbf{int})}{\pi \vdash p' + p'' : \mathbf{int}} \right]\!\right]\eta$$

$$= [\![\mathcal{P}(\pi \vdash p' : \mathbf{int})]\!]\eta + [\![\mathcal{P}(\pi \vdash p'' : \mathbf{int})]\!]\eta.$$

15.3 An untyped semantics

Next, we consider the untyped semantics of our illustrative language. Here, independently of the type system, each phrase p possesses a unique meaning that is a mapping from environments to values, where environments map variables into values, and values range over a "universal" domain U:

$$[\![p]\!] \in E \Rightarrow U \qquad \text{where } E = (I \Rightarrow U).$$

It is vital that this untyped semantics be call-by-name, and that U be rich enough to contain "representations" of all the typed values used in the intrinsic semantics of the previous section. These conditions, however, do not fully determine the untyped semantics. To be general, therefore, rather than specify a particular universal domain, we simply state properties of U that will be sufficient for our development. (In fact, these properties hold for a variety of untyped call-by-name models of our illustrative language.)

Specifically, we require the domains $\mathbf{Z}_\bot$ of integers (viewed as primitive values) and $U \Rightarrow U$ of continuous functions (viewed as functional values) to be embeddable in U by pairs of continuous functions:

$$\mathbf{Z}_\bot \underset{\Psi_p}{\overset{\Phi_p}{\rightleftarrows}} U \qquad U \Rightarrow U \underset{\Psi_f}{\overset{\Phi_f}{\rightleftarrows}} U,$$

where each Φ_i, Ψ_i is an *embedding-retraction* pair, i.e., each composition $\Phi_i\,;\,\Psi_i$ is an identity function on the embedded domain.

Using these embedding-retraction pairs, it is straightforward to give semantic equations defining the untyped semantics of our language:

$$[\![\iota]\!]\varepsilon = \varepsilon\, \iota$$

$$[\![\lambda\, \iota.\, p']\!]\varepsilon = \Phi_f(\lambda\, y \in U.\ [\![p']\!][\varepsilon \mid \iota : y])$$

$$[\![p'\, p'']\!]\varepsilon = \Psi_f([\![p']\!]\varepsilon)([\![p'']\!]\varepsilon)$$

$$[\![\mathbf{Y}\, p']\!]\varepsilon = \bigsqcup_{n=0}^{\infty} \bigl(\Psi_f([\![p']\!]\varepsilon)\bigr)^n \bot$$

$$[\![\text{if } p' > 0 \text{ then } p'' \text{ else } p''']\!]\varepsilon = \begin{cases} \bot & \text{when } \Psi_p([\![p']\!]\varepsilon) = \bot \\ [\![p'']\!]\varepsilon & \text{when } \Psi_p([\![p']\!]\varepsilon) > 0 \\ [\![p''']\!]\varepsilon & \text{when } \Psi_p([\![p']\!]\varepsilon) \leq 0 \end{cases}$$

$$[\![n]\!]\varepsilon = \Phi_p\, n$$

$$[\![p' + p'']\!]\varepsilon = \Phi_p(\Psi_p([\![p']\!]\varepsilon) + \Psi_p([\![p'']\!]\varepsilon)).$$

15.4 Logical relations

Our next task is to connect the intrinsic and untyped semantics by means of a type-indexed family ρ of relations such that

$$\rho[\theta] \subseteq [\![\theta]\!] \times U.$$

The members $\rho[\theta]$ of this family are called *logical relations*. Informally, $\langle x, y \rangle \in \rho[\theta]$ means that the value x of type θ is represented by the untyped value y.

(Logical relations [3] are most often used to connect two intrinsic typed semantics, but the idea works just as well to connect an intrinsic and an untyped semantics.)

The logical relations are defined by induction on the structure of types:

Definition 15.4.1 *For types θ, the logical relations $\rho[\theta] \subseteq [\![\theta]\!] \times U$ are such that:*

$$\langle x, y \rangle \in \rho[\mathbf{int}] \ \textit{iff}\ x = \Psi_p y$$

$$\langle f, g \rangle \in \rho[\theta_1 \to \theta_2] \ \textit{iff}\ \forall \langle x, y \rangle \in \rho[\theta_1].\ \langle f\, x,\, \Psi_f\, g\, y \rangle \in \rho[\theta_2].$$

To explicate the logical relations, we begin with two domain-theoretic properties that will be necessary to deal with recursion:

Definition 15.4.2 *A relation r between domains is*

- strict *iff* $\langle \bot, \bot \rangle \in r$,

- chain-complete *iff*, whenever $x_0 \sqsubseteq x_1 \sqsubseteq \cdots$ and $y_0 \sqsubseteq y_1 \sqsubseteq \cdots$ are increasing sequences such that each $\langle x_i, y_i \rangle \in r$,

$$\langle \bigsqcup_{i=0}^{\infty} x_i, \bigsqcup_{i=0}^{\infty} y_i \rangle \in r.$$

Lemma 15.4.3 *For all types θ, the logical relations $\rho[\theta]$ are strict and chain-complete.*

Proof. We first note that, if Φ, Ψ is any embedding-retraction pair, then $\bot \sqsubseteq \Phi \bot$, and since Ψ is monotone (since it is continuous) and $\Phi \,;\, \Psi$ is an identity, $\Psi \bot \sqsubseteq \Psi(\Phi \bot) = \bot$. Then since $\bot \sqsubseteq \Psi \bot$, we have $\Psi \bot = \bot$, i.e., Ψ is a strict function.

The main proof is by induction on the structure of θ.

- Suppose θ is **int**. Since Ψ_p is strict, we have $\bot = \Psi_p \bot$, so that $\langle \bot, \bot \rangle \in \rho[\text{int}]$.

  Now suppose that x_i and y_i are increasing sequences, in $\mathbf{Z}_\bot$ and U respectively, such that $\langle x_i, y_i \rangle \in \rho[\text{int}]$. Then $x_i = \Psi_p y_i$ for $i \geq 0$, so that $\bigsqcup_{i=0}^{\infty} x_i = \bigsqcup_{i=0}^{\infty} \Psi_p y_i$, and since Ψ_p is continuous, $\bigsqcup_{i=0}^{\infty} x_i = \Psi_p(\bigsqcup_{i=0}^{\infty} y_i)$. Thus $\langle \bigsqcup_{i=0}^{\infty} x_i, \bigsqcup_{i=0}^{\infty} y_i \rangle \in \rho[\text{int}]$.

- Suppose θ is $\theta_1 \to \theta_2$. Let $f = \bot$ and $g = \bot$, so that $\Psi_f g = \bot$, since Ψ_f is strict. Then, for any $\langle x, y \rangle \in \rho[\theta_1]$, since the least element of a domain of functions is the constant function yielding $\bot$, $f x = \bot$ and $\Psi_f g y = \bot$. By the induction hypothesis for θ_2, $\langle f x, \Psi_f g y \rangle = \langle \bot, \bot \rangle \in \rho[\theta_2]$, and since this holds for all $\langle x, y \rangle \in \rho[\theta_1]$, we have $\langle f, g \rangle = \langle \bot, \bot \rangle \in \rho[\theta_1 \to \theta_2]$.

  Now suppose that f_i and g_i are increasing sequences, in $[\![\theta_1 \to \theta_2]\!]$ and U respectively, such that $\langle f_i, g_i \rangle \in \rho[\theta_1 \to \theta_2]$. Let $\langle x, y \rangle \in \rho[\theta_1]$. Then $\langle f_i x, \Psi_f g_i y \rangle \in \rho[\theta_2]$ for $i \geq 0$, and since function application and Ψ_f are monotone, $f_i x$ and $\Psi_f g_i y$ are increasing sequences. Then, since Ψ_f is continuous, and a least upper bound of functions distributes through application, the induction hypothesis for θ_2 gives

$$\langle (\bigsqcup_{i=0}^{\infty} f_i) x, \Psi_f(\bigsqcup_{i=0}^{\infty} g_i) y \rangle = \langle \bigsqcup_{i=0}^{\infty} f_i x, \bigsqcup_{i=0}^{\infty} \Psi_f g_i y \rangle \in \rho[\theta_2],$$

and since this holds for all $\langle x, y \rangle \in \rho[\theta_1]$, we have $\langle \bigsqcup_{i=0}^{\infty} f_i, \bigsqcup_{i=0}^{\infty} g_i \rangle \in \rho[\theta_1 \to \theta_2]$.

END OF PROOF

Now we can establish our central result. Essentially, it asserts that, in related environments, the typed and untyped meanings of the same expression give related values, where the type-dependent notion of "related" is given by the logical relations:

15. What do types mean? — From intrinsic to extrinsic semantics   317

Theorem 15.4.4 (The Logical Relations Theorem) *Suppose $\mathcal{P}(\pi \vdash p : \theta)$ is a proof of the typing judgement $\pi \vdash p : \theta$, and*

$$\forall \iota \in \mathrm{dom}\,\pi.\ \eta\,\iota \in [\![\pi\,\iota]\!]$$

$$\varepsilon \in I \Rightarrow U \qquad (A)$$

$$\forall \iota \in \mathrm{dom}\,\pi.\ \langle \eta\,\iota, \varepsilon\,\iota \rangle \in \rho[\pi\,\iota],$$

Then

$$\langle [\![\mathcal{P}(\pi \vdash p : \theta)]\!]\eta,\ [\![p]\!]\varepsilon \rangle \in \rho[\theta]. \qquad (B)$$

Proof. By induction on the structure of the proof $\mathcal{P}(\pi \vdash p : \theta)$. More precisely, we prove by induction on n that, for all π, η, ε, p, θ, and $\mathcal{P}(\pi \vdash p : \theta)$, if the depth of $\mathcal{P}(\pi \vdash p : \theta)$ is at most n, and the assumptions (A) hold, then (B) holds. However, in all of the following cases except that for abstractions (i.e., $\lambda\,\iota.\,p$), the induction hypotheses are only applied for the same values of π, η, and ε as in the theorem being proved. (Abstractions are the only exception because they are the only binding construction in our language.)

- Suppose $\mathcal{P}(\pi \vdash p : \theta)$ is

$$\overline{\pi \vdash \iota : \pi\,\iota,}$$

so that

$$[\![\mathcal{P}(\pi \vdash p : \theta)]\!]\eta = \eta\,\iota$$

$$[\![p]\!]\varepsilon = \varepsilon\,\iota.$$

Assume (A). Then

$$\langle [\![\mathcal{P}(\pi \vdash p : \theta)]\!]\eta,\ [\![p]\!]\varepsilon \rangle = \langle \eta\,\iota, \varepsilon\,\iota \rangle \in \rho[\pi\,\iota] = \rho[\theta].$$

- Suppose $\mathcal{P}(\pi \vdash p : \theta)$ is

$$\frac{\mathcal{P}([\,\pi\mid\iota{:}\theta_1\,] \vdash p' : \theta_2)}{\pi \vdash \lambda\,\iota.\,p' : \theta_1 \to \theta_2,}$$

so that

$$[\![\mathcal{P}(\pi \vdash p : \theta)]\!]\eta = \lambda x \in [\![\theta_1]\!].\ [\![\mathcal{P}([\,\pi\mid\iota{:}\theta_1\,] \vdash p' : \theta_2)]\!][\,\eta\mid\iota{:}x\,]$$

$$[\![p]\!]\varepsilon = \Phi_{\mathrm{f}}(\lambda\,y \in U.\ [\![p']\!][\,\varepsilon\mid\iota{:}y\,]).$$

Assume (A), and suppose $\langle x, y \rangle \in \rho[\theta_1]$. Then

$$\forall \iota' \in \mathrm{dom}[\,\pi\mid\iota{:}\theta_1\,].\ [\,\eta\mid\iota{:}x\,]\,\iota' \in [\![\,[\,\pi\mid\iota{:}\theta_1\,]\,\iota'\,]\!]$$

$$[\,\varepsilon\mid\iota{:}y\,] \in I \Rightarrow U \qquad (A')$$

$$\forall \iota' \in \mathrm{dom}[\,\pi\mid\iota{:}\theta_1\,].\ \langle [\,\eta\mid\iota{:}x\,]\,\iota',\ [\,\varepsilon\mid\iota{:}y\,]\,\iota' \rangle \in \rho[[\,\pi\mid\iota{:}\theta_1\,]\,\iota'],$$

so that

$$\langle [\![\mathcal{P}(\pi \vdash p : \theta)]\!] \eta\, x, \Psi_f([\![p]\!]\varepsilon)\, y \rangle$$
$$= \langle [\![\mathcal{P}([\,\pi \mid \iota{:}\theta_1\,] \vdash p' : \theta_2)]\!] [\,\eta \mid \iota{:}x\,], \Psi_f(\Phi_f(\lambda\, y.\, [\![p']\!][\,\varepsilon \mid \iota{:}y\,]))y \rangle$$
$$= \langle [\![\mathcal{P}([\,\pi \mid \iota{:}\theta_1\,] \vdash p' : \theta_2)]\!] [\,\eta \mid \iota{:}x\,], [\![p']\!][\,\varepsilon \mid \iota{:}y\,] \rangle$$
$$\in \rho[\theta_2],$$

where the last step follows from the induction hypothesis for $\mathcal{P}([\,\pi \mid \iota{:}\theta_1\,] \vdash p' : \theta_2)$, taking (A) to be (A'). Then, since this holds for all $\langle x, y \rangle \in \rho[\theta_1]$, the definition (15.4.1) of $\rho[\theta_1 \to \theta_2]$ gives

$$\langle [\![\mathcal{P}(\pi \vdash p : \theta)]\!] \eta, [\![p]\!]\varepsilon \rangle \in \rho[\theta_1 \to \theta_2].$$

- Suppose $\mathcal{P}(\pi \vdash p : \theta)$ is

$$\frac{\mathcal{P}(\pi \vdash p' : \theta_1 \to \theta_2) \qquad \mathcal{P}(\pi \vdash p'' : \theta_1)}{\pi \vdash p'\, p'' : \theta_2,}$$

so that

$$[\![\mathcal{P}(\pi \vdash p : \theta)]\!]\eta = [\![\mathcal{P}(\pi \vdash p' : \theta_1 \to \theta_2)]\!]\eta\bigl([\![\mathcal{P}(\pi \vdash p'' : \theta_1)]\!]\eta\bigr)$$

$$[\![p]\!]\varepsilon = \Psi_f([\![p']\!]\varepsilon)([\![p'']\!]\varepsilon).$$

Assume (A). Then the induction hypothesis for $\mathcal{P}(\pi \vdash p' : \theta_1 \to \theta_2)$ gives

$$\langle [\![\mathcal{P}(\pi \vdash p' : \theta_1 \to \theta_2)]\!]\eta, [\![p']\!]\varepsilon \rangle \in \rho[\theta_1 \to \theta_2],$$

and the induction hypothesis for $\mathcal{P}(\pi \vdash p'' : \theta_1)$ gives

$$\langle [\![\mathcal{P}(\pi \vdash p'' : \theta_1)]\!]\eta, [\![p'']\!]\varepsilon \rangle \in \rho[\theta_1],$$

so that

$$\langle [\![\mathcal{P}(\pi \vdash p : \theta)]\!]\eta, [\![p]\!]\varepsilon \rangle$$
$$= \langle [\![\mathcal{P}(\pi \vdash p' : \theta_1 \to \theta_2)]\!]\eta([\![\mathcal{P}(\pi \vdash p'' : \theta_1)]\!]\eta), \Psi_f([\![p']\!]\varepsilon)([\![p'']\!]\varepsilon) \rangle$$
$$\in \rho[\theta_2],$$

by the definition (15.4.1) of $\rho[\theta_1 \to \theta_2]$.

- Suppose $\mathcal{P}(\pi \vdash p : \theta)$ is

$$\frac{\mathcal{P}(\pi \vdash p' : \theta \to \theta)}{\pi \vdash \mathbf{Y}\, p' : \theta,}$$

so that

$$[\![\mathcal{P}(\pi \vdash p : \theta)]\!]\eta = \bigsqcup_{n=0}^{\infty} \bigl([\![\mathcal{P}(\pi \vdash p' : \theta \to \theta)]\!]\eta\bigr)^n \bot$$

$$[\![p]\!]\varepsilon = \bigsqcup_{n=0}^{\infty} \bigl(\Psi_f([\![p']\!]\varepsilon)\bigr)^n \bot.$$

Assume (A). By the induction hypothesis, we have
$$\langle [\![\mathcal{P}(\pi \vdash p' : \theta \to \theta)]\!]\eta, [\![p']\!]\varepsilon \rangle \in \rho[\theta \to \theta].$$
Next we can show, by induction on n, that
$$\left\langle \left([\![\mathcal{P}(\pi \vdash p' : \theta \to \theta)]\!]\eta\right)^n \bot, \left(\Psi_{\mathrm{f}}([\![p']\!]\varepsilon)\right)^n \bot \right\rangle \in \rho[\theta].$$
The case for $n = 0$ follows since, by Lemma 15.4.3, $\rho[\theta]$ is strict. For the induction step, we have
$$\left\langle \left([\![\mathcal{P}(\pi \vdash p' : \theta \to \theta)]\!]\eta\right)^{n+1} \bot, \left(\Psi_{\mathrm{f}}([\![p']\!]\varepsilon)\right)^{n+1} \bot \right\rangle$$
$$= \left\langle [\![\mathcal{P}(\pi \vdash p' : \theta \to \theta)]\!]\eta \left(\left([\![\mathcal{P}(\pi \vdash p' : \theta \to \theta)]\!]\eta\right)^n \bot\right), \right.$$
$$\left. \Psi_{\mathrm{f}}([\![p']\!]\varepsilon)\left(\left(\Psi_{\mathrm{f}}([\![p']\!]\varepsilon)\right)^n \bot\right) \right\rangle$$
$$\in \rho[\theta],$$
by the induction hypothesis for n and the definition (15.4.1) of $\rho[\theta \to \theta]$. Finally,
$$\langle [\![\mathcal{P}(\pi \vdash p : \theta)]\!]\eta, [\![p]\!]\varepsilon \rangle$$
$$= \left\langle \bigsqcup_{n=0}^{\infty} \left([\![\mathcal{P}(\pi \vdash p' : \theta \to \theta)]\!]\eta\right)^n \bot, \bigsqcup_{n=0}^{\infty} \left(\Psi_{\mathrm{f}}([\![p']\!]\varepsilon)\right)^n \bot \right\rangle$$
$$\in \rho[\theta],$$
since $\rho[\theta]$ is chain-complete by Lemma 15.4.3.

- Suppose $\mathcal{P}(\pi \vdash p : \theta)$ is
$$\frac{\mathcal{P}(\pi \vdash p' : \mathbf{int}) \quad \mathcal{P}(\pi \vdash p'' : \theta) \quad \mathcal{P}(\pi \vdash p''' : \theta)}{\pi \vdash \mathbf{if}\ p' > 0\ \mathbf{then}\ p''\ \mathbf{else}\ p''' : \theta,}$$
so that
$$[\![\mathcal{P}(\pi \vdash p : \theta)]\!]\eta = \begin{cases} \bot & \text{when } [\![\mathcal{P}(\pi \vdash p' : \mathbf{int})]\!]\eta = \bot \\ [\![\mathcal{P}(\pi \vdash p'' : \theta)]\!]\eta & \text{when } [\![\mathcal{P}(\pi \vdash p' : \mathbf{int})]\!]\eta > 0 \\ [\![\mathcal{P}(\pi \vdash p''' : \theta)]\!]\eta & \text{when } [\![\mathcal{P}(\pi \vdash p' : \mathbf{int})]\!]\eta \leq 0 \end{cases}$$

$$[\![p]\!]\varepsilon = \begin{cases} \bot & \text{when } \Psi_{\mathrm{p}}([\![p']\!]\varepsilon) = \bot \\ [\![p'']\!]\varepsilon & \text{when } \Psi_{\mathrm{p}}([\![p']\!]\varepsilon) > 0 \\ [\![p''']\!]\varepsilon & \text{when } \Psi_{\mathrm{p}}([\![p']\!]\varepsilon) \leq 0. \end{cases}$$

Assume (A). By the induction hypothesis for $\mathcal{P}(\pi \vdash p' : \mathbf{int})$,
$$\langle [\![\mathcal{P}(\pi \vdash p' : \mathbf{int})]\!]\eta, [\![p']\!]\varepsilon \rangle \in \rho[\mathbf{int}],$$
so that $[\![\mathcal{P}(\pi \vdash p' : \mathbf{int})]\!]\eta = \Psi_{\mathrm{p}}([\![p']\!]\varepsilon)$. There are three cases:

- If $\Psi_{\mathrm{p}}[\![p']\!]\varepsilon = \bot$, then
$$\langle [\![\mathcal{P}(\pi \vdash p\colon\theta)]\!]\eta, [\![p]\!]\varepsilon\rangle = \langle \bot, \bot\rangle,$$
which belongs to $\rho[\theta]$ since $\rho[\theta]$ is strict.
- If $\Psi_{\mathrm{p}}[\![p']\!]\varepsilon > 0$, then
$$\langle [\![\mathcal{P}(\pi \vdash p\colon\theta)]\!]\eta, [\![p]\!]\varepsilon\rangle = \langle [\![\mathcal{P}(\pi \vdash p''\colon\theta)]\!]\eta, [\![p'']\!]\varepsilon\rangle,$$
which belongs to $\rho[\theta]$ by the induction hypothesis for $\mathcal{P}(\pi \vdash p''\colon\theta)$.
- If $\Psi_{\mathrm{p}}[\![p']\!]\varepsilon \leq 0$, then
$$\langle [\![\mathcal{P}(\pi \vdash p\colon\theta)]\!]\eta, [\![p]\!]\varepsilon\rangle = \langle [\![\mathcal{P}(\pi \vdash p'''\colon\theta)]\!]\eta, [\![p''']\!]\varepsilon\rangle,$$
which belongs to $\rho[\theta]$ by the induction hypothesis for $\mathcal{P}(\pi \vdash p'''\colon\theta)$.

- Suppose $\mathcal{P}(\pi \vdash p : \theta)$ is
$$\frac{}{\pi \vdash n : \mathbf{int},}$$
so that
$$[\![\mathcal{P}(\pi \vdash p : \theta)]\!]\eta = n$$
$$[\![p]\!]\varepsilon = \Phi_{\mathrm{p}}\, n.$$
Then, since $\Phi_{\mathrm{p}} \,;\, \Psi_{\mathrm{p}}$ is an identity, $[\![\mathcal{P}(\pi \vdash p : \theta)]\!]\eta = \Psi_{\mathrm{p}}(\Phi_{\mathrm{p}}\, n) = \Psi_{\mathrm{p}}([\![p]\!]\varepsilon)$, so that
$$\langle [\![\mathcal{P}(\pi \vdash p : \theta)]\!]\eta, [\![p]\!]\varepsilon\rangle \in \rho[\mathbf{int}].$$

- Suppose $\mathcal{P}(\pi \vdash p : \theta)$ is
$$\frac{\mathcal{P}(\pi \vdash p' : \mathbf{int}) \quad \mathcal{P}(\pi \vdash p'' : \mathbf{int})}{\pi \vdash p' + p'' : \mathbf{int},}$$
so that
$$[\![\mathcal{P}(\pi \vdash p : \theta)]\!]\eta = [\![\mathcal{P}(\pi \vdash p' : \mathbf{int})]\!]\eta + [\![\mathcal{P}(\pi \vdash p'' : \mathbf{int})]\!]\eta$$
$$[\![p]\!]\varepsilon = \Phi_{\mathrm{p}}(\Psi_{\mathrm{p}}([\![p']\!]\varepsilon) + \Psi_{\mathrm{p}}([\![p'']\!]\varepsilon)).$$
Assume (A). By the induction hypothesis for $\mathcal{P}(\pi \vdash p' : \mathbf{int})$, we have
$$[\![\mathcal{P}(\pi \vdash p' : \mathbf{int})]\!]\eta = \Psi_{\mathrm{p}}([\![p']\!]\varepsilon),$$
and a similar argument holds for p''. Then
$$[\![\mathcal{P}(\pi \vdash p : \theta)]\!]\eta = \Psi_{\mathrm{p}}([\![p']\!]\varepsilon) + \Psi_{\mathrm{p}}([\![p'']\!]\varepsilon)$$
$$= \Psi_{\mathrm{p}}(\Phi_{\mathrm{p}}(\Psi_{\mathrm{p}}([\![p']\!]\varepsilon) + \Psi_{\mathrm{p}}([\![p'']\!]\varepsilon)))$$
$$= \Psi_{\mathrm{p}}([\![p]\!]\varepsilon),$$
since $\Phi_{\mathrm{p}} \,;\, \Psi_{\mathrm{p}}$ is an identity. Thus
$$\langle [\![\mathcal{P}(\pi \vdash p : \theta)]\!]\eta, [\![p]\!]\varepsilon\rangle \in \rho[\mathbf{int}].$$

END OF PROOF

15.5 Bracketing

Next, we show that the domains $[\![\theta]\!]$ that are the meanings of types can be embedded in the universal domain U by a type-indexed family of function pairs:

$$[\![\theta]\!] \underset{\psi[\theta]}{\overset{\phi[\theta]}{\longleftrightarrow}} U.$$

We will show that these are embedding-retraction pairs, and that they are closely related to the logical relations defined in the previous section. (The idea that types denote retractions on a universal domain is due to Scott [4].)

Definition 15.5.1 *For types θ, the functions $\phi[\theta] \in [\![\theta]\!] \to U$ and $\psi[\theta] \in U \to [\![\theta]\!]$ are such that*

$$\phi[\mathbf{int}]x = \Phi_{\mathrm{p}} x$$

$$\psi[\mathbf{int}]y = \Psi_{\mathrm{p}} y$$

$$\phi[\theta_1 \to \theta_2]f = \Phi_{\mathrm{f}}(\psi[\theta_1]\,;\,f\,;\,\phi[\theta_2])$$

$$\psi[\theta_1 \to \theta_2]y = \phi[\theta_1]\,;\,\Psi_{\mathrm{f}} y\,;\,\psi[\theta_2].$$

These function pairs are related to the logical relations $\rho[\theta]$ by the following theorem:

Theorem 15.5.2 (The Bracketing Theorem) *For each type θ:*

1. *For all $x \in [\![\theta]\!]$, $\langle x, \phi[\theta]x \rangle \in \rho[\theta]$.*

2. *For all $\langle x, y \rangle \in \rho[\theta]$, $x = \psi[\theta]y$.*

Proof. The proof is by induction on the structure of θ:

- Suppose θ is **int** and $x \in [\![\mathbf{int}]\!]$. From the fact that $\Phi_{\mathrm{p}}\,;\,\Psi_{\mathrm{p}}$ is an identity, and the definition (15.5.1) of $\phi[\mathbf{int}]$, we have $x = \Psi_{\mathrm{p}}(\Phi_{\mathrm{p}} x) = \Psi_{\mathrm{p}}(\phi[\mathbf{int}]x)$. Then the definition (15.4.1) of $\rho[\mathbf{int}]$ gives $\langle x, \phi[\mathbf{int}]x \rangle \in \rho[\mathbf{int}]$.

  Now suppose $\langle x, y \rangle \in \rho[\mathbf{int}]$. Then the definitions (15.4.1) of $\rho[\mathbf{int}]$ and (15.5.1) of $\psi[\mathbf{int}]$ give $x = \Psi_{\mathrm{p}} y = \psi[\mathbf{int}]y$.

- Suppose θ is $\theta_1 \to \theta_2$, and $f \in [\![\theta_1 \to \theta_2]\!]$. Let $\langle x, y \rangle \in \rho[\theta_1]$. By the second part of the induction hypothesis for θ_1, $x = \psi[\theta_1]y$. Then

$$\phi[\theta_2](f\,x) = \phi[\theta_2](f(\psi[\theta_1]y))$$
$$= (\psi[\theta_1]\,;\,f\,;\,\phi[\theta_2])y$$
$$= \Psi_{\mathrm{f}}(\Phi_{\mathrm{f}}(\psi[\theta_1]\,;\,f\,;\,\phi[\theta_2]))y$$
$$= \Psi_{\mathrm{f}}(\phi[\theta_1 \to \theta_2]f)y,$$

from the fact that Φ_f; Ψ_f is an identity, and the definition (15.5.1) of $\phi[\theta_1 \to \theta_2]$. Then by the first part of the induction hypothesis for θ_2,

$$\langle f\,x, \Psi_f(\phi[\theta_1 \to \theta_2]f)y\rangle \in \rho[\theta_2],$$

and since this holds for all $\langle x, y\rangle \in \rho[\theta_1]$, the definition (15.4.1) of $\rho[\theta_1 \to \theta_2]$ gives

$$\langle f, \phi[\theta_1 \to \theta_2]f\rangle \in \rho[\theta_1 \to \theta_2].$$

Now suppose $\langle f, g\rangle \in \rho[\theta_1 \to \theta_2]$, and let $x \in [\![\theta_1]\!]$. By the first part of the induction hypothesis for θ_1, $\langle x, \phi[\theta_1]x\rangle \in \rho[\theta_1]$, so by the definition (15.4.1) of $\rho[\theta_1 \to \theta_2]$, $\langle f\,x, \Psi_f g(\phi[\theta_1]x)\rangle \in \rho[\theta_2]$. Then by the second part of the induction hypothesis for θ_2, $f\,x = \psi[\theta_2](\Psi_f g(\phi[\theta_1]x))$.

Since this holds for all $x \in [\![\theta_1]\!]$, we have $f = \phi[\theta_1]\,;\,\Psi_f g\,;\,\psi[\theta_2]$, and by the definition (15.5.1) of $\psi[\theta_1 \to \theta_2]$, $f = \psi[\theta_1 \to \theta_2]g$.

END OF PROOF

An immediate consequence of the bracketing theorem is that

Corollary 15.5.3 *The $\phi[\theta], \psi[\theta]$ are embedding-retraction pairs.*

Proof. Suppose $x \in [\![\theta]\!]$. By the first part of the bracketing theorem, $\langle x, \phi[\theta]x\rangle \in \rho[\theta]$; then by the second part, $x = \psi[\theta](\phi[\theta]x)$. Since this holds for all $x \in [\![\theta]\!]$, we have $\phi[\theta]\,;\,\psi[\theta] = I_{[\![\theta]\!]}$.
END OF PROOF

The name "bracketing theorem" alludes to a more succinct formulation of the theorem as a subset relationship between graphs of functions and relations. Writing † for the reflection of a graph, we can restate the bracketing theorem as:

For each type θ, $\phi[\theta] \subseteq \rho[\theta] \subseteq (\psi[\theta])^\dagger$.

The essence of the bracketing theorem is that it connects the notion of representation provided by the logical relations with the different notion provided by the embedding-retraction pairs. For each typed value $x \in [\![\theta]\!]$, one can regard

- the set $\{y \mid x = \psi[\theta]y\}$ (i.e., the preimage of x under $\psi[\theta]$) as the set of untyped values that "weakly" represent x,

- the subset $\{y \mid \langle x, y\rangle \in \rho[\theta]\} \subseteq \{y \mid x = \psi[\theta]y\}$ as the set of untyped values that represent x,

- the member $\phi[\theta]x \in \{y \mid \langle x, y\rangle \in \rho[\theta]\}$ as the "best" or "canonical" representation of x.

An essential difference between representation and weak representation is that, since $\psi[\theta]$ is a total function, every untyped value "weakly" represents some typed value.

By combining the bracketing theorem with the logical relations theorem, one can express the intrinsic typed semantics of a phrase in terms of its untyped semantics:

Theorem 15.5.4 *Suppose $\pi \vdash p : \theta$ and $\eta \in [\![\pi]\!]^*$. Then*

$$[\![\mathcal{P}(\pi \vdash p : \theta)]\!]\eta = \psi[\theta]([\![p]\!](\lambda\iota. \text{ if } \iota \in \text{dom } \pi \text{ then } \phi[\pi\,\iota](\eta\,\iota) \text{ else } \bot)).$$

Proof. Let $\varepsilon = \lambda\iota.$ if $\iota \in \text{dom } \pi$ then $\phi[\pi\,\iota](\eta\,\iota)$ else $\bot$. For each $\iota \in \text{dom } \pi$, by this definition of ε and the first part of the bracketing theorem,

$$\langle \eta\,\iota, \varepsilon\,\iota \rangle = \langle \eta\,\iota, \phi[\pi\,\iota](\eta\,\iota) \rangle \in \rho[\pi\,\iota].$$

Then the logical relations theorem gives

$$\langle [\![\mathcal{P}(\pi \vdash p : \theta)]\!]\eta, [\![p]\!]\varepsilon \rangle \in \rho[\theta],$$

and the second part of the bracketing theorem gives

$$[\![\mathcal{P}(\pi \vdash p : \theta)]\!]\eta = \psi[\theta]([\![p]\!]\varepsilon).$$

END OF PROOF

Theorem 15.5.4 expresses the meaning of a proof of the typing judgement $\pi \vdash p : \theta$ in terms of the untyped meaning of p and the retraction-embedding pairs associated with θ and the components of π — all of which are determined by the judgement itself rather than its proof. Thus every proof of the same judgement must have the same intrinsic semantics:

Corollary 15.5.5 *The intrinsic semantics is coherent.*

In fact, the coherence of the simple kind of language we have been considering here has long been known, but we believe this is an unusually elegant proof.

It should also be noted that the above theorem expresses a particular intrinsic semantics in terms of any of a variety of untyped semantics, i.e., all of the untyped semantics meeting the constraints in Section 15.3, where we permitted variations in the universal domain U and the way in which integers and functions are embedded within it.

For example, one might take the untyped semantics to be one in which η-reduction does or does not preserve meaning [1, Section 10.5], or one in which the fixed-point combinator $\lambda f.\,(\lambda x.\,f(x\,x))(\lambda x.\,f(x\,x))$ is or is not a *least* fixed-point operator [5].

15.6 An extrinsic PER semantics

Suppose we define a type-indexed family of relations between untyped values:

Definition 15.6.1 *For types θ, the relations $\sigma[\theta] \subseteq U \times U$ are such that*

$$\langle y, y' \rangle \in \sigma[\theta] \text{ iff } \exists x \in [\![\theta]\!].\ \langle x, y \rangle, \langle x, y' \rangle \in \rho[\theta].$$

(More abstractly, using relational composition, $\sigma[\theta] \stackrel{\text{def}}{=} (\rho[\theta])^\dagger\,;\,\rho[\theta]$.)

Obviously, the $\sigma[\theta]$ are symmetric. Moreover, these relations are transitive:

Theorem 15.6.2 *If $\langle y, y' \rangle, \langle y', y'' \rangle \in \sigma[\theta]$, then $\langle y, y'' \rangle \in \sigma[\theta]$.*

Proof. If $\langle y,y'\rangle, \langle y',y''\rangle \in \sigma[\theta]$, then there are $x, x' \in [\![\theta]\!]$ such that $\langle x,y\rangle$, $\langle x,y'\rangle, \langle x',y'\rangle, \langle x',y''\rangle \in \rho[\theta]$. Then by the second part of the bracketing theorem, $x = \psi[\theta]y'$ and $x' = \psi[\theta]y'$, so that $x = x'$. Then $\langle x,y\rangle, \langle x,y''\rangle \in \rho[\theta]$, so that $\langle y,y''\rangle \in \sigma[\theta]$. END OF PROOF

Thus, the $\sigma[\theta]$ are partial equivalence relations (PER's). Although we have chosen to define them in terms of the logical relations, they can also be described directly by induction on the structure of θ:

Theorem 15.6.3

$$\langle y,y'\rangle \in \sigma[\text{int}] \quad \textit{iff} \quad \Psi_\text{p} y = \Psi_\text{p} y'$$

$$\langle g,g'\rangle \in \sigma[\theta_1 \to \theta_2] \quad \textit{iff} \quad \forall \langle y,y'\rangle \in \sigma[\theta_1].\ \langle \Psi_\text{f}\, g\, y, \Psi_\text{f}\, g'\, y'\rangle \in \sigma[\theta_2].$$

Proof. Using the definitions (15.6.1) of σ, and (15.4.1) of $\rho[\text{int}]$, we have $\langle y,y'\rangle \in \sigma[\text{int}]$ iff there is an $x \in [\![\text{int}]\!]$ such that $\langle x,y\rangle, \langle x,y'\rangle \in \rho[\text{int}]$, iff there is an $x \in [\![\text{int}]\!]$ such that $x = \Psi_\text{p} y$ and $x = \Psi_\text{p} y'$, iff $\Psi_\text{p} y = \Psi_\text{p} y'$.

Suppose $\langle g,g'\rangle \in \sigma[\theta_1 \to \theta_2]$ and $\langle y,y'\rangle \in \sigma[\theta_1]$. From the definition (15.6.1) of σ, there is an $f \in [\![\theta_1 \to \theta_2]\!]$ such that $\langle f,g\rangle, \langle f,g'\rangle \in \rho[\theta_1 \to \theta_2]$ and there is an $x \in [\![\theta_1]\!]$ such that $\langle x,y\rangle, \langle x,y'\rangle \in \rho[\theta_1]$. Then, from the definition (15.4.1) of $\rho[\theta_1 \to \theta_2]$, we have $\langle f\,x, \Psi_\text{f}\, g\, y\rangle \in \rho[\theta_2]$ and $\langle f\,x, \Psi_\text{f}\, g'\, y'\rangle \in \rho[\theta_2]$, and from the definition (15.6.1) of σ, we have $\langle \Psi_\text{f}\, g\, y, \Psi_\text{f}\, g'\, y'\rangle \in \sigma[\theta_2]$.

On the other hand, suppose

$$\forall \langle y,y'\rangle \in \sigma[\theta_1].\ \langle \Psi_\text{f}\, g\, y, \Psi_\text{f}\, g'\, y'\rangle \in \sigma[\theta_2],$$

and let $\langle x,y\rangle \in \rho[\theta_1]$. We have $\langle y,y\rangle \in \sigma[\theta_1]$ by the definition (15.6.1) of σ. Moreover, since the first half of the bracketing theorem gives $\langle x, \phi[\theta_1]x\rangle \in \rho[\theta_1]$, we also have $\langle \phi[\theta_1]x, y\rangle \in \sigma[\theta_1]$ by the definition (15.6.1) of σ. Then, by the supposition displayed above, we have both $\langle \Psi_\text{f}\, g\, y, \Psi_\text{f}\, g'\, y\rangle \in \sigma[\theta_2]$ and $\langle \Psi_\text{f}\, g(\phi[\theta_1]x), \Psi_\text{f}\, g'\, y\rangle \in \sigma[\theta_2]$, and since $\sigma[\theta_2]$ is symmetric and transitive, $\langle \Psi_\text{f}\, g(\phi[\theta_1]x), \Psi_\text{f}\, g\, y\rangle \in \sigma[\theta_2]$.

Thus we have $\langle \Psi_\text{f}\, g(\phi[\theta_1]x), \Psi_\text{f}\, \hat{g}\, y\rangle \in \sigma[\theta_2]$, where $\hat{g}$ is either g or g'. By the definition (15.6.1) of σ, there is a $w \in [\![\theta_2]\!]$ such that $\langle w, \Psi_\text{f}\, g(\phi[\theta_1]x)\rangle \in \rho[\theta_2]$ and $\langle w, \Psi_\text{f}\, \hat{g}\, y\rangle \in \rho[\theta_2]$. From the first of these inclusions, the second part of the bracketing theorem gives $w = \psi[\theta_2](\Psi_\text{f}\, g(\phi[\theta_1]x))$, or $w = f\,x$, where f is the function $\phi[\theta_1]\,;\,\Psi_\text{f}\, g\,;\,\psi[\theta_2]$. Thus the second inclusion can be written as $\langle f\,x, \Psi_\text{f}\, \hat{g}\, y\rangle \in \rho[\theta_2]$. Since this holds for all $\langle x,y\rangle \in \rho[\theta_1]$, the definition (15.4.1) of $\rho[\theta_1 \to \theta_2]$ gives $\langle f, \hat{g}\rangle \in \rho[\theta_1 \to \theta_2]$, and since this holds when $\hat{g}$ is either g or g', the definition (15.6.1) of σ gives $\langle g,g'\rangle \in \sigma[\theta_1 \to \theta_2]$. END OF PROOF

In terms of the notion of representation captured by the logical relations:

- $\langle y,y\rangle \in \sigma[\theta]$ means that y is a representation of some value of type θ.

- $\langle y,y'\rangle \in \sigma[\theta]$ means that y and y' are representations of the same value of type θ.

Thus, for each θ, the PER $\sigma[\theta]$ defines both the set $\{ y \mid \langle y,y \rangle \in \sigma[\theta] \}$ of "representations" and also, when restricted to this set, an equivalence relation of "representing the same thing".

In early extrinsic denotational semantics, such as the Sethi-MacQueen model [7, 8], types played only the first of these roles; the insight that they denote PER's (rather than subsets) on a universal domain of untyped values is due to Scott [4, Section 7], [9, Section 5], [10].

In fact, the basic idea that types represent equivalence relations on subsets of some universe of "realizers" is much older. Two examples are described by Troelstra: the "hereditarily effective operations" (HEO) [11, Section 2.4.11], [12, Section 3.3], where the realizers are natural numbers (used as Gödel numbers), and the "extensional model of hereditarily continuous functionals" (ECF) [11, Section 2.6.5], [12, Section 3.9], where the realizers are functions from natural numbers to natural numbers. Troelstra attributes HEO to Kreisel [13, Section 4.2], and ECF to both Kreisel [13] and, independently, Kleene [14].

The common thread behind all these systems is that, to be continuous (or computable) a typed value must be represented by some realizer. An overview of realizability is given by Amadio and Curien [15, Chapter 15].

The combination of our untyped semantics with the PER's $\sigma[\theta]$ gives what we have called an *extrinsic* semantics. The essential connection between these entities is that, when a phrase satisfies a typing judgement, its untyped meaning respects the type-dependent notion of representation described by the $\sigma[\theta]$. More precisely,

Theorem 15.6.4 *Suppose $\pi \vdash p : \theta$, and $\varepsilon, \varepsilon' \in I \Rightarrow U$ satisfy*

$$\forall \iota \in \mathrm{dom}\,\pi.\ \langle \varepsilon\,\iota, \varepsilon'\,\iota \rangle \in \sigma[\pi\,\iota].$$

Then

$$\langle [\![p]\!]\varepsilon, [\![p]\!]\varepsilon' \rangle \in \sigma[\theta].$$

Proof. If ε and ε' are related as supposed, then for each $\iota \in \mathrm{dom}\,\pi$, there must be an $x \in [\![\pi\,\iota]\!]$ such that $\langle x, \varepsilon\,\iota \rangle, \langle x, \varepsilon'\,\iota \rangle \in \rho[\pi\,\iota]$. Thus there must be an environment $\eta \in [\![\pi]\!]^*$ such that

$$\forall \iota \in \mathrm{dom}\,\pi.\ \langle \eta\,\iota, \varepsilon\,\iota \rangle, \langle \eta\,\iota, \varepsilon'\,\iota \rangle \in \rho[\pi\,\iota].$$

Then by two applications of the logical relations theorem,

$$\langle [\![\mathcal{P}(\pi \vdash p : \theta)]\!]\eta, [\![p]\!]\varepsilon \rangle, \langle [\![\mathcal{P}(\pi \vdash p : \theta)]\!]\eta, [\![p]\!]\varepsilon' \rangle \in \rho[\theta],$$

so that

$$\langle [\![p]\!]\varepsilon, [\![p]\!]\varepsilon' \rangle \in \sigma[\theta].$$

END OF PROOF

15.7 Further work and future directions

The development we have presented here extends in a straightforward manner to a richer programming language that includes several primitive types, subtyping, and named products (with field-forgetting implicit conversions) [16]. (Some additional properties of $\rho[\theta]$ and $\sigma[\theta]$ are also proved in this reference.)

Obviously, we would like to treat still richer type systems, such as intersection or polymorphic types. During the last year, we made a strenuous attempt to conquer intersection types, but we were unable to find a semantics for which we could prove the bracketing theorem. (This work was described in a talk at the Workshop on Intersection Types and Related Systems [17].)

It is also of interest to try to move in the opposite direction, from extrinsic to intrinsic semantics. In a sense this is straightforward: Given $\sigma[\theta]$, one simply takes $[\![\theta]\!]$ to be the set of equivalence classes of $\sigma[\theta]$. (More precisely, one takes the semantic category to be a category of PER's [15, Chapter 15].) In general, however, there may be no sensible way to order the set of equivalence classes to make $[\![\theta]\!]$ into a domain.

15.8 Acknowledgements

This research was supported in part by National Science Foundation Grant CCR-9804014. Much of the research was carried out during two delightful and productive visits to BRICS[1] in Aarhus, Denmark, September to November 1999 and May to June 2000.

References

[1] John C. Reynolds. *Theories of Programming Languages*. Cambridge University Press, Cambridge, England, 1998.

[2] Daniel Leivant. Typing and computational properties of lambda expressions. *Theoretical Computer Science*, 44(1):51–68, 1986.

[3] Gordon D. Plotkin. Lambda-definability and logical relations. Memorandum SAI–RM–4, University of Edinburgh, Edinburgh, Scotland, October 1973.

[4] Dana S. Scott. Data types as lattices. *SIAM Journal on Computing*, 5(3):522–587, September 1976.

[5] David M. R. Park. The Y-combinator in Scott's lambda-calculus models. Symposium on Theory of Programming, University of Warwick, unpublished; cited in [6], 1970.

---

[1] Basic Research in Computer Science (http://www.brics.dk/), Centre of the Danish National Research Foundation.

[6] Christopher P. Wadsworth. The relation between computational and denotational properties for Scott's D_∞-models of the lambda-calculus. *SIAM Journal on Computing*, 5(3):488–521, September 1976.

[7] David B. MacQueen and Ravi Sethi. A semantic model of types for applicative languages. In *Conference Record of the 1982 ACM Symposium on LISP and Functional Programming*, pages 243–252, New York, 1982. ACM.

[8] David B. MacQueen, Gordon D. Plotkin, and Ravi Sethi. An ideal model for recursive polymorphic types. *Information and Control*, 71(1–2):95–130, October–November 1986.

[9] Dana S. Scott. Lambda calculus: Some models, some philosophy. In Jon Barwise, H. Jerome Keisler, and Kenneth Kunen, editors, *The Kleene Symposium*, volume 101 of *Studies in Logic and the Foundations of Mathematics*, pages 223–265, Amsterdam, 1980. North-Holland.

[10] Andrej Bauer, Lars Birkedal, and Dana S. Scott. Equilogical spaces. To appear in Theoretical Computer Science, 2002.

[11] Anne Sjerp Troelstra, editor. *Metamathematical Investigation of Intuitionistic Arithmetic and Analysis*, volume 344 of *Lecture Notes in Mathematics*. Springer-Verlag, Berlin, 1973.

[12] Anne Sjerp Troelstra. Realizability. In Samuel R. Buss, editor, *Handbook of Proof Theory*, volume 137 of *Studies in Logic and the Foundations of Mathematics*, pages 407–473. Elsevier, Amsterdam, 1998.

[13] Georg Kreisel. Interpretation of analysis by means of constructive functionals of finite types. In Arend Heyting, editor, *Constructivity in Mathematics*, pages 101–128. North-Holland, Amsterdam, 1959.

[14] S. C. Kleene. Countable functionals. In Arend Heyting, editor, *Constructivity in Mathematics*, pages 81–100. North-Holland, Amsterdam, 1959.

[15] Roberto M. Amadio and Pierre-Louis Curien. *Domains and Lambda-Calculi*, volume 46 of *Cambridge Tracts in Theoretical Computer Science*. Cambridge University Press, Cambridge, England, 1998.

[16] John C. Reynolds. The meaning of types — from intrinsic to extrinsic semantics. Research Series RS–00–32, BRICS, DAIMI, Department of Computer Science, University of Aarhus, December 2000.

[17] John C. Reynolds. An intrinsic semantics of intersection types (abstract of invited lecture). In *Proceedings of the Workshop on Intersection Types and Related Systems*, 2000.
The slides for this lecture are available at ftp://ftp.cs.cmu.edu/user/jcr/intertype.ps.gz.

Part III

Applications and automated theories

Section G

Putting theories into practice by automation

16 Automated verification using deduction, exploration, and abstraction   333
Natarajan Shankar

In practice the formal verification of programs is at best time-consuming and at worst detailed and error-prone. Nevertheless it is a crucial component in the development of correct programs, a major concern particularly in security and safety-critical systems. Automated verification, which can save both time and verifier-introduced inaccuracies, is thus a highly attractive tool.

There are essentially two ways to use automation — either in deduction (theorem proving) or in exploration (model checking) — but both methods have inherent weaknesses when used separately. Theorem proving, for example verifies by induction, but sometimes 'inductive' properties of programs can be hard for the prover to find. Model checking works by searching state spaces — it is therefore only able to verify finite, rather than general (usually infinite) properties.

This paper describes how these individual drawbacks can be overcome by using the efficient search strategies of the model checking paradigm to find the inductive properties required by the theorem proving system. The key idea in making the techniques complementary is that of 'property-preserving abstractions' which can turn a property that looks infinite into one that is not.

17 An experiment in feature engineering   353
Pamela Zave

Like many other large, complex, long-lived systems, telecommunications systems are developed incrementally, by adding 'features'. Feature-oriented specification techniques allow each feature to be specified as a separate module. This makes it easy to understand each new feature in isolation, at the cost of making the inevitable interactions among features implicit and somewhat mysterious.

This paper addresses the problem of finding a paradigm, for construction of specifications of telecommunication services, that allows both feature modularity and easy analysis of feature composition.

The solution is based on the modular DFC architecture, which is discussed briefly. Feature 'precedence' (a partial order on features) is the major mechanism used to control the effects of feature composition.

Within the framework of this architecture, certain feature interactions are defined so that potential occurrences are easy to detect. Human judgment, as illustrated by a case study, must determine which potential interactions are good and bad. In the case study, simple manipulation of precedence turns out to be sufficient to allow all the good interactions and prevent all the bad ones.

16

Automated verification using deduction, exploration, and abstraction

Natarajan Shankar[1]

Abstract

Computer programs are formal texts that are composed by programmers and executed by machines. Formal methods are used to predict the execution-time behavior of a program text through formal, symbolic calculation. Automation in the form of computer programs can be used to execute formal calculations so that they are reproducible and checkable. Deduction and exploration are two basic frameworks for the formal calculation of program properties. Both deduction and exploration have their limitations. We argue that these limitations can be overcome through a methodology for automated verification that uses property-preserving abstractions to bridge the gap between deduction and exploration. We introduce models, logics, and verification methods for transition systems, and outline a methodology based on the combined use of deduction, exploration, and abstraction.

Computer programs are formal texts composed by programmers and executed by computers. The behavior of the program when executed on a computer can be observed by its users, which can include, for example, other programs. The programmer attempts to design the program so that its behavior conforms to that expected by the user. Any discrepancy between actual and expected program behavior could be because the programmer misconstrued the user's requirements, the user misunderstood the program's specification, the programmer designed a flawed program, or because the computer executed the program incorrectly. If program composition is to be understood in scientific terms, the formal text of the program must have a semantics that is independent of its execution on a computer.

---

[1] Affiliation: SRI International Computer Science Laboratory, Menlo Park CA 94025. This research was supported by NSF Grant CCR-0082560, DARPA/AFRL Contract F33615-00-C-3043, and NASA Contract NAS1-00079.

The computer must be designed to conform to this semantics, and the programmer can then use the semantics as a means for predicting program behavior. A well-tempered program is one where calculation at the semantic level has been employed to predict properties of program behavior from the program text.

As in science and mathematics, calculation refutes conjectures more often than it affirms them. Putative properties of program behavior are conjectures and calculational tools are used to quickly identify failure. As with arithmetic calculation, computers can also be used to automate the formal, logical calculations needed to establish program properties. Automated verification makes such calculations precise, feasible, checkable, reproducible, and easily revisable. Even with automation, formal methods can be computationally expensive and unwieldy. A well-calibrated verification methodology is one that minimizes the computational and human effort while maximizing the value of the formal, symbolic analysis of a program.

Deduction and exploration are the two dominant approaches to automated verification. In the deductive approach, a property of a program is verified by constructing a formal proof. The deductive method is often required to establish properties by induction. Frequently, such properties are not verifiable by means of proof unless they are suitably strengthened through a careful manual analysis of failed proof attempts. In the explorative approach, the states of all possible computations of a program are exhaustively examined for any violation of a program property. With exploration, properties can be directly verified or refuted without the kind of strengthening that is needed with the deductive approach. Since exploration requires the computation space to be exhaustively analyzable in a finite (and often, bounded) number of steps, it is less general than deduction. We outline a methodology that exploits the synergy between deduction and exploration. The methodology is based on the idea that specific properties or classes of properties can be inferred by examining an *abstraction* of the program using exploration. The construction of a valid abstract program from a concrete program uses deduction, and the analysis of the abstract program uses exploration. The use of abstraction makes it possible to verify programs on which deduction or exploration would individually fail.

State transition systems are a popular semantic framework since programs are often written to achieve a specified and observable sequence of states. Such sequences can be finite or infinite, but we can take them to be infinite without loss of generality. A transition system is specified by means of the *state type*, rules for obtaining an *initial* state for the system, and rules for the *transitions* of the system starting from the initial state.

An *assertion* is a predicate on system states. Typical properties of a transition system include

1. Invariance properties: An invariant is an assertion that holds of every reachable state, i.e., any state that is reachable from a valid initial state by zero or more system transitions.

16. Automated verification using deduction, exploration, and abstraction

2. Response properties: A computation is said to respond to assertion p with assertion q if whenever p holds of a state in the computation, it is inevitably followed by a state where q holds.

While the bulk of the properties of interest are invariance properties, these are perhaps the simplest class of properties that can be expressed within a program logic (see Section 16.2).

We argue that abstraction is a key element of a modern approach to automated verification of transition system properties that combines both deduction and exploration. In addressing the rigorous analysis of program behavior, we make precise the model of computation (Section 16.1), the characterization of properties (Section 16.2), and the analysis techniques based on proof construction and model exploration (Section 16.3). Section 16.4 describes the use of automated deduction in extracting abstract programs that can be analyzed using exploration or model checking. Section 16.5 summarizes the abstraction-based verification methodology, and Section 16.6 presents some concluding observations.

16.1 Models of computation

There is a wide variety of models of transition systems including simple imperative programs like Pascal, process calculi like CSP [Hoa85] and CCS [Mil89], and concurrent system description languages like UNITY [CM88], TLA [Lam94], and SPL [MP92].

Common to all of these models is the underlying idea that transitions can be modelled by relations between program states. A basic model of transition systems is therefore given by a triple $\langle \Sigma, I, N \rangle$, where Σ is the set of system states, I is the subset of Σ consisting of valid initial states, and N is a binary relation over Σ consisting of the valid transitions between states. This yields a *model* (usually called a Kripke model) consisting of a directed graph with the set of nodes given by Σ, and an edge between s and s' exactly when $N(s, s')$ holds. In Section 16.2, we show how the truth value of a property expressed in a program logic can be evaluated with respect to the Kripke model of a program.

The example transition system given in Figure 16.1 has a state consisting of two variables: pc which can either be even or odd, and x which ranges over the integers. Initially, pc = even and x = 0. In each transition, the value of pc is toggled and the value of x is incremented. This is shown by relating the values of these variables in the new state, namely pc′ and x′ to those in the old state, namely pc and x.

There are numerous variations on the basic transition system model, particularly the ways programs are described. The UNITY model [CM88] presents a program as consisting of an initialization predicate and a (possibly infinite) bag of guarded commands, where each command consists of a guard predicate and an assignment. A valid program behavior is one that starts in a valid initial state, i.e., one satisfying the initialization predicate, and takes a transition from

- **State:** pc : {even, odd}
  x : nat

- **Initialization:** pc = even
  x = 0

- **Transition:** pc′ = *toggle*(pc)
  x′ = x + 1
  where *toggle*(even) = odd
  toggle(odd) = even

Figure 16.1. An Example Transition System: even–odd

state s to state s' when there is an enabled guarded command, i.e., one whose guard predicate is satisfied by s, such that s' is obtained by applying the assignment of the chosen command to s. When none of the guard predicates are satisfied by s, then s' must be identical to s. Lamport's Temporal Logic of Actions (TLA) [Lam94] blurs the distinction between the system description language and the assertion language. In TLA, temporal logic formulas that are the conjunction of an initialization assertion, an action invariant, and a fairness condition, serve as system descriptions. Temporal formulas in TLA are built from assertions as well as actions (binary relations on states) using the linear-time temporal operators. Process calculi or algebras [Hoa85, Mil89] emphasize communication patterns over state transitions. Process algebra expressions describe *labelled* transition systems where the transitions are labelled with communication actions. A process algebra expression corresponds to a state in a transition system, and it is possible to convert a process algebra expression into a labelled state transition system. The I/O automata model [LT87] combines both state transitions and labelled communication in the style of process algebras.

Other variations of the basic model are possible. The transition system model can be augmented with various forms of fairness. The typical fairness conditions are that certain actions are weakly fair (continually executed if continuously enabled) or strongly fair (continually executed if continually enabled). Real-time considerations can be introduced into transition systems by means of a time variable that is incremented by letting time elapse [AH91]. Clocks and timers can be introduced to record the elapsed time since specific events. Timed automata [AD94] are transition systems that include time transitions (subject to constraints) and state transitions that can be guarded by time conditions. Hybrid automata [ACHH93] augment timed automata with time-varying continuous quantities such as distance, pressure, temperature, and flow rate. We will focus our attention on unlabelled state transition systems without fairness conditions, clocks, and continuous quantities, but the concepts can be easily extended to these cases.

The basic transition system model does not indicate how two systems are composed to interact concurrently. In an interleaving or asynchronous composition,

16. Automated verification using deduction, exploration, and abstraction   337

the actions of the components are interleaved to that each transition is taken by exactly a single component. In a synchronous composition, the actions of components are executed simultaneously. Labelled transition systems can be composed so that they synchronize on common action labels but are interleaved, otherwise. A verification approach is compositional if properties of the composition of two components can be derived from the properties of the components [dRLP97]. Compositionality is an important tool in automated verification with or without the use of abstraction, but it is outside the scope of this presentation.

16.2 Logics of program behavior

The computations of the transition system in Figure 16.1 can be observed to possess some simple properties:

1. x is even when pc = even.

2. x is odd when pc = odd.

3. x is infinitely often odd and infinitely often even.

4. x eventually exceeds any bound.

We now examine how such properties could be formally stated and verified. Given a Kripke model K of the form $\langle \Sigma, I, N \rangle$, σ is a trace through K if it is an infinite sequence of the form $\sigma_0, \sigma_1, \ldots$, where $I(\sigma_0)$ and $N(\sigma_i, \sigma_{i+1})$ for each i. The temporal logic CTL* [EH83, Eme90] combines linear-time and branching-time properties into a single formalism. It consists of two kinds of formulas: *state formulas* that characterize sets of states in a Kripke model, and *path formulas* that characterize sets of traces in a Kripke model. The metavariables p and q range over assertions or their negations, B and C range over state formulas, and the metavariables L and M range over path formulas. If s ranges over states in K and σ over traces in K, then the syntax and semantics of CTL* with respect to a Kripke model K can be given as

$$[\![p]\!](\sigma) = p(\sigma_0)$$
$$[\![p]\!](s) = p(s)$$
$$[\![\mathbf{X}B]\!](\sigma) = [\![B]\!](\sigma_1)$$
$$[\![B \mathbf{U} C]\!](\sigma) = (\exists i : [\![C]\!](\sigma_i) \wedge (\forall j < i : [\![B]\!](\sigma_j)))$$
$$[\![B \mathbf{V} C]\!](\sigma) = (\forall i : [\![C]\!](\sigma_i) \vee (\exists j < i : [\![B]\!](\sigma_j)))$$
$$[\![\mathbf{A}L]\!](s) = (\forall \sigma : \sigma_0 = s \supset [\![L]\!](\sigma))$$
$$[\![\mathbf{E}L]\!](s) = (\exists \sigma : \sigma_0 = s \wedge [\![L]\!](\sigma))$$

The formula $\mathbf{F}B$ is an abbreviation for (**true U** B), and $\mathbf{G}B$ is an abbreviation for $\neg \mathbf{F} \neg B$. Invariants are expressed in CTL* by formulas of the form $\mathbf{AG}B$. CTL* also contains the usual logical connectives and quantifiers with their usual meaning. The branching-time CTL fragment of CTL* is obtained by disallowing propositional combinations of path formulas, i.e., those of the form **X**B, B **U** C, or B **V** C. The linear-time LTL fragment of CTL* is obtained by allowing only formulas of the form **A**L where L contains no path quantifiers, i.e., no subformulas of the form **A**M or **E**M. For each temporal operator or connective in CTL*, the dual operator also appears in the logic. For this reason, we assume that the formulas are placed into negation normal form so that negations are applied only to assertions. Since the negation of an assertion is also an assertion, we avoid any special treatment for negation.

For $K = \langle \Sigma, I, N \rangle$, we write $K \models B$ iff for every s such that $I(s)$, $[\![B]\!](s)$ holds. Proof rules can be given for proving validities, i.e., statements that are true for any K, in the above logic [Eme90], but our interest here is in verifying properties for a specific K given by the program of interest.

The informally stated properties of the even–odd transition system given earlier can be formalized in CTL as

1. **AG** (pc = even $\supset$ *even?*(x)).

2. **AG** (pc = odd $\supset$ *odd?*(x)).

3. **AG AF***even?*(x) $\wedge$ **AG AF***odd?*(x).

4. **AF** $x > k$, for any bound k.

16.2.1 *A fixed-point calculus for temporal properties*

The CTL* properties of a transition system can be captured by means of fixed point definitions within a calculus that extends first-order logic with fixed point operators. Such definitions unify the semantics and proof theory and serve as a basis for unifying deductive and algorithmic methods. Given a transition system $\langle \Sigma, I, N \rangle$, we can define the familiar predicate transformers

- Pre-image: $pre(N)(p)(s_1) \equiv (\exists s_2 : N(s_1, s_2) \wedge p(s_2))$.

- Pre-condition: $\widetilde{pre}(N)(p)(s_1) \equiv (\forall s_2 : N(s_1, s_2) \supset p(s_2))$.

- Post-condition: $post(N)(p)(s_2) \equiv (\exists s_1 : N(s_1, s_2) \wedge p(s_1))$.

Operators like $pre(N)$, $\widetilde{pre}(N)$, and $post(N)$ are examples of *monotone* predicate transformers, i.e., maps T on $[\Sigma \rightarrow \textbf{bool}]$ such that

$$p_1 \sqsubseteq p_2 \supset T[p_1] \sqsubseteq T[p_2],$$

where $p_1 \sqsubseteq p_2 \equiv (\forall s : p_1(s) \supset p_2(s))$.

A fixed point of a predicate transformer T is a predicate p such that $p = T[p]$. When T is a monotone predicate transformer, the Tarski-Knaster theorem [Tar55] guarantees the existence of least and greatest fixed points. The least fixed point of a monotone predicate T is written as $\mu X : T[X]$ and can be defined as the greatest lower bound of the predicates X such that $T[X] \sqsubseteq X$, i.e., $\bigcap \{X \mid T[X] \sqsubseteq X\}$. The greatest fixed point of T is written as $\nu X : T[X]$ and can be defined as the least upper bound of the predicates X such that $X \sqsubseteq T[X]$, i.e., $\bigcup \{X \mid X \sqsubseteq T[X]\}$.

16. Automated verification using deduction, exploration, and abstraction   339

The temporal connectives of CTL can be defined using the fixed point operators over suitable predicate transformers. For example, the equality

$$[\![\mathbf{A}(B \mathbf{\ U\ } C)]\!](s) = (\mu X : C \vee (B \wedge \widetilde{pre}(N)(X)))(s)$$

holds because the right-hand side is satisfied by exactly those states s that can always reach a state satisfying C along a finite computation path of states satisfying B.

The predicate characterizing the reachable states of a transition system K of the form $\langle \Sigma, I, N \rangle$ can be defined as

$$\mu X : I \vee post(N)(X).$$

The fixed point definitions of the operators of CTL with fairness conditions, LTL, and CTL* are more involved and we omit the details. The fixed point operators μ and ν are not expressible in first-order logic. Such operators were introduced by Scott and de Bakker [SdB69], but the specific extension of first-order logic with predicates defined by fixed point operators yields a *mu-calculus* due to Park [Par76]. The mu-calculus operators can be defined in a higher-order (even a second-order) logic. This forms the basis for the integration of theorem proving and model checking in PVS [RSS95, Sha97, ORSvH95].

Proof rules involving these connectives can be derived from the fixed point characterizations of the temporal operators. We will however examine the use of the fixed point definitions as the basis for a verification methodology that combines theorem proving and model checking.

16.3 Verification techniques

Verification is used to establish that a transition system satisfies a given property or that it refines another transition system. Note that the programs being verified are often incorrect in subtle ways so a large part of verification actually involves refutation.

Verification methods are either *deductive* and involve proof construction, or they are *explorative* and are carried out by a systematic search of the state space when this search can somehow be bounded.

16.3.1 Deductive methods

The earliest verification methods were based on proof construction. The program is annotated with assertions and the rules of Hoare logic [Hoa69] are used to generate verification conditions that can be verified using an automated or interactive theorem prover. Verification based on deductive methods still proceeds along similar lines but within logics that admit a richer set of temporal properties than invariance and termination. For example, it is possible to use or demonstrate fairness conditions that assert that some condition holds infinitely often.

We can apply deductive verification to the even–odd transition system from Figure 16.1. Let A_1 label the invariant: x is even when pc = even. The invariant can be verified by demonstrating that $\mu X : I \vee post(N)(X) \sqsubseteq A_1$. The fixed point induction rule can be used to reduce this goal to the subgoals:

1. $I \sqsubseteq A_1$.

2. $post(N)(A_1) \sqsubseteq A_1$, or equivalently $A_1 \sqsubseteq \widetilde{pre}(N)(A_1)$, since $\widetilde{pre}(N)(post(N)(A)) = A$, for any assertions A.

However, the proof of subgoal 2 fails even though A_1 is in fact an invariant. This is because A_1 is not *inductive* since $\widetilde{pre}(N)(A_1)$ is $toggle(\text{pc}) = \text{even} \supset even?(x+1)$ which is not implied by A_1. The invariant A_1 must be strengthened as A_2 to assert that pc − even ⇔ $even?(x)$. The subgoals corresponding to A_2 can be easily verified with quite modest levels of automation.

The crucial difficulty in proving the above invariant is not in discharging the verification subgoals but in discovering a suitable strengthening that makes the invariant inductive. A similar need for strengthening arises in proofs by induction. The search space for such inductive invariants is large even for finite-state systems. Since the problem is that of finding a valid conjecture rather than proving one, an automated theorem prover is not of much help.

16.3.2 Explorative methods

When the state space is finite, the predicates defined by fixed point operators can be explicitly calculated. The bound on the state space yields a bound on the iteration of the fixed point operations. The explicit calculation of fixed points is called model checking [CGP99]. Model checking typically works for finite state spaces but can also be extended to *infinite* state spaces where the fixed point computations can be bounded. Model checking can use *explicit* representations of sets of states or *symbolic* representations of the predicates over states [BCM+92]. Examples of symbolic model checking tools include SMV [McM93], VIS [BHSV+96], and Cospan [Kur93], and examples of explicit state model checkers include SPIN [Hol91], Murphi [Dil96], and FDR [For92]. Model checking, when applicable, does not require invariant strengthening since it can restrict its search to the reachable portion of the state space.

An explicit-state model checker for reachability of an assertion p can be implemented by means of depth-first search using a variable H to maintain the set of states already visited and a variable U that contains the set of pending states. Initially, H is empty and U contains the distinguished initial state. In each step, a state s is removed from U and examined to see if $p(s)$ holds. If it does, then indeed p is reachable. If not, s is added to H, and any successor states of s not already in H are added to the set U, and the process is repeated until U is empty. Similar algorithms can be given for other temporal operators.

A symbolic model checker for finite-state systems can be given by viewing the state as a vector of boolean variables [McM93]. This turns the predicates into

n-ary boolean functions. Such boolean functions can be represented by means of a data structure called reduced, ordered, binary decision diagrams (ROBDDs) which are decision graphs where the boolean variables are ordered according to priority [BRB90]. The boolean operations such as conjunction, disjunction, and negation are easily defined as operators on ROBDDs. The operation of applying an n-ary boolean function to n boolean functions is also easily defined. Boolean quantification ($\exists b : A$) is represented as $A[b := \textbf{true}] \vee A[b := \textbf{false}]$ and can be used to compute the image of a state set with respect to a transition relation. Since ROBDDs are canonical, the equivalence of two boolean functions in ROBDD form is decidable in constant time. This makes it convenient for fixed point computations. A least fixed point is computed iteratively by starting with the everywhere-false boolean function and computing each successive ROBDD applying the predicate transformer until two successive ROBDDs are equivalent.

The even–odd example is not amenable to either explicit or symbolic model checking since the state space is unbounded. Model checking approaches usually require systems with bounded state spaces but certain classes of infinite-state systems do admit feasible model checking. For example, timed CTL properties of timed automata are verifiable algorithmically [ACD93]. Even when the computation of fixed points is not guaranteed to terminate, one can try to calculate them in the hope that the computation might converge. The application of a Presburger arithmetic routine to the even–odd example does actually converge when applied backwards from a state violating the invariant [BGP97] even though such fixed point computations do not generally converge. Techniques from abstract interpretation [CC77] can be borrowed to achieve convergence of fixed points at the cost of accuracy. This can be done either through the use of widening and narrowing, or through the use of abstraction as a way of converting a large or infinite-state system into a finite-state one. Property-preserving abstractions are covered in the next section.

16.4 Abstractions of programs and properties

Both deductive and explorative methods have serious limitations, but they are complementary in their strengths. There are various ways of combining these methods. The most promising is a technique known as *abstraction*. In this method, the verification of a large or infinite state system is reduced to that of a small finite-state system that can be easily examined using model checking. Such techniques are based on the pioneering work by Cousot and Cousot [CC77] in the abstract interpretation of programs.

Abstraction can be used syntactically to abstract program behavior in terms of live variables in the program. Abstractions are meant to *preserve* certain classes of properties. If the goal is to verify that K satisfies property P, then a property-preserving abstraction should generate $\hat{K}$ and property $\hat{P}$ such that $K \models P$ if $\hat{K} \models \hat{P}$. If additionally $\hat{K} \models \hat{P}$ if $K \models P$, then the abstraction is said to be *strongly* property-preserving. We explain the construction of abstract transition systems and properties for two kinds of *semantic* abstraction methods: *data abstraction* and *predicate abstraction*.

16.4.1 Data abstraction

In data abstraction, a concrete data domain D is replaced by an abstract one $\overline{D}$. An abstraction map $h : [D \to \overline{D}]$ is used to show how concrete data values are mapped to abstract ones. Operations on the concrete data domain are suitably reinterpreted on the abstract domain. Examples of commonly used data abstractions include parity, integers-mod-n, signs, zero-nonzero integers, intervals, and cardinalities [CGL94].

For example, in the even–odd program of Figure 16.1, the domain of natural numbers can be abstracted to the booleans through the abstraction map *even?*. A concrete operation $f : [D \to D]$ can be reinterpreted by an abstract operation $\hat{f} : [\overline{D} \to set[\overline{D}]]$ where

$$b \notin \hat{f}(a) \Leftrightarrow \vdash a = h(x) \supset b \neq h(f(x)).$$

A predicate g over type D can be reinterpreted by a predicate $\overline{g}$ over type $\overline{D}$ where

$$\neg \overline{g}(a) \Leftrightarrow \vdash a = h(x) \supset \neg g(x)$$

so that $\overline{g}(a)$ holds whenever there is an x such that $a = h(x)$ and $g(x)$ holds. The predicate g can also be underapproximated as $\underline{g}$ where

$$\underline{g}(a) \Leftrightarrow \vdash a = h(x) \supset g(x)$$

so that $\underline{g}(a)$ holds whenever $g(x)$ holds for every x such that $x = h(a)$. For example, if we take h mapping `nat` to `bool` to be *even?*, then the abstraction $\hat{S}$ of the successor operation S is given by

$$\hat{S}(\mathbf{true}) = \{\mathbf{false}\}$$
$$\hat{S}(\mathbf{false}) = \{\mathbf{true}\}$$

Theorem proving is used to construct $\hat{f}$ from f, and $\overline{g}$ and $\underline{g}$ from g. The abstraction can introduce nondeterminism since the abstraction of an expression returns a set of abstract values rather than a single value. Such a data abstraction preserves mu-calculus properties that do not contain any existential-strength path quantifiers because the abstracted program includes all the behaviors of the concrete program but may admit additional behaviors that have no concrete analogue.

Given an abstraction map h between the concrete state type D and the abstract state type $\overline{D}$, the task is to convert a concrete correctness statement $K \models B$ into an abstract statement $\hat{K} \models \hat{B}$. When B is a statement in $\forall$CTL*, the fragment of CTL without existential-strength path quantifiers, an abstraction map h is property preserving if [CGL94]:

1. $I_K \sqsubseteq I_{\hat{K}} \circ h$

16. Automated verification using deduction, exploration, and abstraction

2. $N_K \sqsubseteq N_{\hat{K}} \circ \langle h, h \rangle$

3. $\hat{B}$ is identical to B but with each assertion p replaced by $\hat{p}$, where $\hat{p} \circ h \sqsubseteq p$.

If transition system K is specified by guarded commands, then the abstract transition system $\hat{K}$ can be constructed as follows. The initialization $I_{\hat{K}}$ is just $\overline{I_K}$ with respect to the abstraction h, and $N_{\hat{K}}$ is just $\overline{N_K}$ with respect to the abstraction $\langle h, h \rangle$. If N_K is given by n guarded commands $[\![]_{i=1}^n g_i(\vec{x}) \longrightarrow \vec{x}' := f(\vec{x})$ over the state vector of variables $\vec{x}$, then $N_{\hat{K}}$ is just $[\![]_{i=1}^n \overline{g_i}(\vec{y}) \longrightarrow \vec{y}' \in \hat{f}(\vec{y})$, where $\vec{y}$ ranges over the abstract state. Given a $\forall CTL^*$ property B, the corresponding abstract property $\hat{B}$ is obtained by replacing each assertion p by $\underline{p}$.

Theorem 16.4.1 *Given a transition system K over a state type Σ, a $\forall CTL^*$ property B, and an abstraction map h from Σ to abstract state type $\hat{\Sigma}$, if $\hat{K} \models \hat{B}$, then $K \models P$.*

In the construction of $\hat{f}$, $\overline{g}$, and $\underline{g}$, the theorem proving is conservative in that the failure to discharge a proof obligation affects only the accuracy of the abstraction and not its soundness. Since many data abstractions are quite standard, it is possible to precompute $\hat{f}$, $\overline{g}$, and $\underline{g}$ for specific f and g, as is done in Bandera [CDH+00] and Cadence SMV [MQS00]. Data abstraction when applied to the even–odd transition system returns the finite-state transition system:

- **State:** pc : {even, odd}
    x : set[bool]
- **Initialization:** pc = even
    x ∈ {**true**}
- **Transition:** pc′ = *toggle*(pc)
    x′ ∈ $\hat{S}(x)$

Figure 16.2. Abstraction of even–odd transition system

The abstracted program is faithful to the concrete program since each behavior of the abstract program has a concrete analogue, and vice-versa. The invariance property can be correspondingly abstracted as pc = even ⊃ x. A proof of this invariant would also fail on the abstracted program, but model checking does verify it quite easily. This is because the only reachable states are those where pc = even ∧ x = **true** or pc = odd ∧ x = **false**.

16.4.2 Predicate abstraction

Data abstraction has the advantage that an abstract program can be constructed from a concrete program by a mostly syntactic transformation. The abstract counterparts of concrete operations can be computed once and reused over many applications. Data abstraction does not capture relations between variables and can only abstract individual variables. Predicate abstraction [SG97, BLO98, CU98, SS99] replaces relations such as $x < y$, $x + 2y = 5z$, by corresponding boolean variables. The construction of an abstract program corresponding to a predicate abstraction is not as straightforward as it is with data abstraction.

A predicate abstraction is given as a mapping from n distinct and fresh boolean variables $b_1, \ldots, b_n$ to the corresponding concrete predicates $p_1, \ldots, p_n$ by a map γ such that $\gamma(b_i) = p_i$. The mapping between abstract boolean variables and concrete predicates can be suggested as a hint to the verifier, or could be extracted from the guards and assignments in the program and the predicates occurring in the property. The mapping γ can be used as a substitution operation so that $\gamma(F)$ replaces each abstract boolean variable b_i in F with the corresponding concrete predicate p_i.

The predicate abstraction takes a transition system over a concrete state consisting of concrete variables $x_1, \ldots, x_k; y_1, \ldots, y_m$, and returns a transition system over $x_1, \ldots, x_k; b_1, \ldots, b_n$, where $\gamma(b_i)$ is a predicate over the concrete variables. Thus the concrete variables $y_1, \ldots, y_m$ have been replaced by the abstract boolean variables $b_1, \ldots, b_n$. More generally, formulas representing transition systems and properties can be approximated through predicate abstraction.

The heart of the abstraction procedure is a method for constructing the over-approximation $[\![p]\!]_\gamma^+$ of an assertion p with respect to the abstraction map γ so that

$$\vdash p \supset \gamma([\![p]\!]_\gamma^+).$$

If p is one of the abstracted predicates p_i, then $[\![p]\!]_\gamma^+$ can be taken to just be b_i. If p does not contain any of the abstracted variables y_i, then $[\![p]\!]_\gamma^+$ can be taken to be p itself. In the general case, the formula $[\![p]\!]_\gamma^+$ is constructed in conjunctive normal form as the conjunction of disjunctions of literals b_i or $\neg b_i$, where each conjunct is an over-approximation of p with respect to γ.

As an example, we can construct $[\![x = y]\!]_\gamma^+$ of the atomic formula $x = y$ over integer variables x and y using an abstraction map γ, where $\gamma(c)$ is $x > 0$ and $\gamma(d)$ is $y > 0$.

We can enumerate the disjunctions Δ in order of increasing length, and test if $x = y \supset \gamma(\Delta)$ is provable.

Δ	$\vdash^? x = y \supset \gamma(\Delta)$
c	$\not\vdash x = y \supset x > 0$
$\neg c$	$\not\vdash x = y \supset x \not> 0$
d	$\not\vdash x = y \supset y > 0$
$\neg d$	$\not\vdash x = y \supset y \not> 0$
$c \vee d$	$\not\vdash x = y \supset x > 0 \vee y > 0$
$c \vee \neg d$	$\vdash x = y \supset x > 0 \vee y \not> 0$
$\neg c \vee d$	$\vdash x = y \supset x \not> 0 \vee y > 0$
$\neg c \vee \neg d$	$\not\vdash x = y \supset x \not> 0 \vee y \not> 0$

Since none of the disjunctions other than $c \vee \neg d$ and $\neg c \vee d$ pass the test, $[\![x = y]\!]_\gamma^+$ is taken to be the conjunction $(c \vee \neg d) \wedge (\neg c \vee d)$. By enumerating the disjunctions in order of increasing length, we can obtain some saving since not all disjunctions need be tested. If the test fails on a disjunction Δ but succeeds on the disjunction $\Delta \vee q$, then we need not examine

1. The disjunction $\Delta \vee \neg q$, since if this test succeeded, then the Δ would have also succeeded, and hence $\neg q$ can be eliminated.

2. Any disjunction extending $\Delta \vee q$, since these are weaker approximations than, and therefore subsumed by, $\Delta \vee q$.

We also need not consider any literals q where $\gamma(q)$ and p share no variables since in that case q is irrelevant and can contribute nothing to the success of the test.

The pruning in the number of tests can be illustrated using a variant of the above example where the literal to be abstracted is $x > 1$ and the same map γ is used.

Δ	$\vdash^? x > 1 \supset \gamma(\Delta)$
c	$\vdash x > 1 \supset x > 0$
$\neg c$	eliminated
d	irrelevant
$\neg d$	irrelevant
$c \vee d$	subsumed
$c \vee \neg d$	subsumed
$\neg c \vee d$	eliminated
$\neg c \vee \neg d$	eliminated

Thus, just a single test is sufficient for establishing that the over-approximation $[\![x > 1]\!]_\gamma^+$ is c.

The under-approximation $[\![p]\!]_\gamma^-$ of an assertion p with respect to γ is just the over-approximation $[\![\neg p]\!]_\gamma^+$ of the negation $\neg p$.

The remaining cases of the definition of over-approximation and under-approximation for mu-calculus formulas can be given by means of a straightforward structural recursion. In the definition below, ψ ranges over $\{+, -\}$, and $inv(+) = -$ and $inv(-) = +$. Given an assignment σ for the tuple of concrete variables $x_1, \ldots, x_k; y_1, \ldots, y_m$, and an assignment $\overline{\sigma}$ for the tuple of abstract variables $x_1, \ldots, x_k; b_1, \ldots, b_n$, we denote by $\gamma[\overline{\sigma}]$, the set of assignments σ such that $\sigma(x_i) = \overline{\sigma}(x_i)$, for $1 \leq i \leq k$, and $\gamma(b_j)(\sigma) \Leftrightarrow \overline{\sigma}(b_j)$, for $1 \leq j \leq n$. Since not all abstract states are feasible, we introduce a predicate E on $\overline{\Sigma}$ such that $E(\overline{\sigma}) \Leftrightarrow \gamma[\overline{\sigma}] \neq \emptyset$.[2] Given an abstraction map γ that maps abstract variables to

---

[2] The predicate E has to be given as an input to the abstraction process since there does not appear to be a general method for constructing the predicate through failure-tolerant theorem proving unless the abstraction predicates are all in some decidable domain. The E predicate is needed only when under-approximating an existential quantification, or dually, when over-approximating a universal quantification.

concrete predicates, the over-approximation of a mu-calculus formula F is written as $[\![F]\!]_\gamma^+$, and the corresponding under-approximation is $[\![F]\!]_\gamma^-$. The definition involves the approximation of formulas F as well as state predicates P. It is assumed that the mu-calculus formulas are *pure* in the sense that distinct bound variables are named apart from each other, and from any free variables. In concrete formulas, the fixed point operators μ and ν bind state predicate variables X over the concrete state type Σ. The corresponding predicate variable over the abstract state $\overline{\Sigma}$ is written as $\overline{X}$. The metavariable s ranges over the tuple of concrete state variables, and correspondingly $\overline{s}$ ranges over a tuple of abstract state variables. The abstraction is given as a scheme ρ that takes a pair of tuples of variables $s, \overline{s}$ and generates the mapping from the variables in $\overline{s}$ to predicates in s.

$$[\![F \wedge G]\!]_\gamma^\psi = [\![F]\!]_\gamma^\psi \wedge [\![G]\!]_\gamma^\psi$$
$$[\![F \vee G]\!]_\gamma^\psi = [\![F]\!]_\gamma^\psi \vee [\![G]\!]_\gamma^\psi$$
$$[\![P(s)]\!]_\gamma^\psi = [\![P]\!]_\gamma^\psi(\overline{s})$$
$$[\![X]\!]_\gamma^\psi = \overline{X}$$
$$[\![\lambda(s:\Sigma):F]\!]_\gamma^\psi = (\lambda(\overline{s}:\overline{\Sigma}):[\![F]\!]_{\gamma \cup \rho(s,\overline{s})}^\psi)$$
$$[\![\forall(s:\Sigma):G]\!]_\gamma^\psi = (\forall(\overline{s}:E(\overline{s})):[\![G]\!]_{\gamma \cup \rho(s,\overline{s})}^\psi)$$
$$[\![\exists(s:F):G]\!]_\gamma^\psi = (\exists(\overline{s}:E(\overline{s})):[\![G]\!]_{\gamma \cup \rho(s,\overline{s})}^\psi)$$
$$[\![\mu X:T[X]]\!]_\gamma^\psi = (\mu \overline{X}:[\![T[X]]\!]_\gamma^\psi)$$
$$[\![(\nu X:T[X])]\!]_\gamma^\psi = (\nu \overline{X}:[\![T[X]]\!]_\gamma^\psi)$$

We can now define the operation $\gamma(F)$ which transforms an abstract mu-calculus formula back into a concrete one.

$$\gamma(p) = \lambda(\vec{x},\vec{y}:\Sigma):p(\vec{x},\gamma(b_1)(\vec{x},\vec{y}),\ldots,\gamma(b_n)(\vec{x},\vec{y}))$$
$$\gamma(F \wedge G) = \gamma(F) \wedge \gamma(G)$$
$$\gamma(F \vee G) = \gamma(F) \vee \gamma(G)$$
$$\gamma(P(\overline{s})) = \gamma(P)(s)$$
$$\gamma(\overline{X}) = X$$
$$\gamma(\lambda(\overline{s}:\overline{\Sigma}):F) = (\lambda(s:\Sigma):(\gamma \cup \rho(s,\overline{s}))(F))$$
$$\gamma(\forall(\overline{s}:\overline{\Sigma}):F) = (\forall(s:\Sigma):(\gamma \cup \rho(s,\overline{s}))(F))$$
$$\gamma(\exists(\overline{s}:\overline{\Sigma}):F) = (\exists(s:\Sigma):(\gamma \cup \rho(s,\overline{s}))(F))$$
$$\gamma(\mu \overline{X}:T[\overline{X}]) = \mu X:\gamma(T[\overline{X}])$$
$$\gamma(\nu \overline{X}:T[\overline{X}]) = \nu X:\gamma(T[\overline{X}])$$

Theorem 16.4.2 *The following hold*

1. $\vdash P \sqsubseteq \gamma([\![P]\!]_\gamma^+)$
2. $\vdash \gamma([\![P]\!]_\gamma^-) \sqsubseteq P$
3. $\vdash F \supset \gamma([\![F]\!]_\gamma^+)$

4. $\vdash \gamma(\llbracket F \rrbracket_\gamma^-) \supset F$

From this, it follows that

1. If $\vdash \llbracket F \rrbracket_\gamma^-$ then $\vdash F$
2. If $\vdash F$ then $\vdash \llbracket F \rrbracket_\gamma^+$

The even–odd example can also be used as an illustration of predicate abstraction. The mapping γ can be defined to map the boolean variable c to $even?(x)$, and correspondingly c' to $even?(x')$. Then the subformula of the transition relation $x' = x+1$ is over-approximated as $(c \vee c') \wedge (\neg c \vee \neg c')$ which is propositionally equivalent to $c' = \neg c$.

There are other methods for computing predicate abstractions. The elimination technique given for computing data abstractions can be used for predicate abstraction as well. This can be expensive when the abstract state space is large since computing the abstraction of the transition relation requires a number of tests that is quadratic in the size of the abstract state space [BLO98]. One can also try to abstract the reachability set of a transition system [SG97, DDP99] by letting R_0 be $\llbracket I \rrbracket_\gamma^+$, and R_{i+1} be $\llbracket post(N)(\gamma(R_i)) \rrbracket_\gamma^+$, where $R = R_n$ for $R_n = R_{n+1}$. The set R computed in this way can be more precise than the set $\mu X : \bar{I} \wedge post(\overline{N})(X)$, where $\bar{I} = \llbracket I \rrbracket_\gamma^+$ and $\overline{N} = \llbracket N \rrbracket_{\gamma \cup \gamma'}^+$.

16.5 Verification methodology

Deductive methodologies for developing verified programs are based on the annotation of programs with assertions and the generation of verification conditions that are discharged using an automated theorem prover. This methodology is unwieldy because of the burden of supplying the annotations and strengthening them so that the verification conditions can be discharged. Explorative methodologies ignore the mathematics underlying a well-designed program and instead employ search techniques that can succeed only on a limited class of programs.

We advocate an integrated approach to verification that is based on the use of abstraction to combine deductive and explorative methods. Instead of annotations, the verification is based on abstractions. Such abstractions can also be extracted automatically from the program and the conjectured properties, or suggested as hints. Automated deduction is employed to construct abstract versions of the program and property based on the suggested abstractions. The resulting systems can be analyzed effectively using model checking in order to verify temporal properties and generate useful invariants.

Such abstractions have been applied to moderately complex examples including various distributed algorithms, network protocols, and cache consistency protocols. The abstractions capture crucial insights into the working of the algorithm so that calculation can then be used for building and analyzing reduced models. Abstraction can also be used to reduce the verification of N-process protocols to finite-state form.

The tools needed for implementing the above methodology include program analyzers, model checkers, and highly automated decision procedures and semi-decision procedures such as those in PVS. With such a suite of tools, the task of the verification is reduced to that of transforming problems into a form that can be handled by one or more of the tools.

16.6 Conclusions

We advocate a verification methodology for combining automated tools for theorem proving and model checking through the use of abstraction. This approach departs from the traditional annotation/verification condition generation approach to deductive verification in several ways:

1. The program is not required to be annotated. The purpose of the automation is to generate valid annotations.

2. Deduction is used not merely to discharge verification conditions but to reduce problems to finite-state form. The theorem proving is *failure-tolerant* in the sense that the failure to discharge a proof obligation is not precipitous since it affects only the precision of the analysis.

3. The difficulty of discovering suitably strengthened invariants is somewhat alleviated through the use of model checking. Through the construction of a reachability predicate, model checking can actually compute useful invariants, particularly those that depend on program control to render certain states unreachable.

The above methodology also strengthens model checking techniques by employing deduction to build models with reduced state spaces. Program analysis techniques can also be made more powerful and precise by combining them with automated deduction tools. The crux of the methodology is that symbolic analysis of programs is reduced to the local, transition-wise use of deduction, and the global, system-wide use of model checking. This symbolic analysis methodology is currently being implemented in an experimental framework called the Symbolic Analysis Laboratory (SAL) [BGL$^+$00].

References

[ACD93]   R. Alur, C. Courcoubetis, and D. Dill. Model-checking in dense real-time. *Information and Computation*, 104(1):2–34, May 1993.

[ACHH93]   R. Alur, C. Courcoubetis, T.A. Henzinger, and P.-H. Ho. Hybrid automata: an algorithmic approach to the specification and verification of hybrid systems. In R.L. Grossman, A. Nerode, A.P. Ravn, and H. Rischel, editors, *Hybrid Systems I*, Lecture Notes in Computer Science 736, pages 209–229. Springer-Verlag, 1993.

16. Automated verification using deduction, exploration, and abstraction 349

[AD94] R. Alur and D. L. Dill. A theory of timed automata. *Theoretical Computer Science*, 126(2):183–235, 25 April 1994. Fundamental Study.

[AH91] R. Alur and T. A. Henzinger. Logics and models of real time: A survey. In J. W. de Bakker, C. Huizing, W.P. de Roever, and G. Rozenberg, editors, *Real Time: Theory in Practice*, volume 600 of *Lecture Notes in Computer Science*, pages 74–106. Springer-Verlag, 1991.

[AH96] Rajeev Alur and Thomas A. Henzinger, editors. *Computer-Aided Verification, CAV '96*, volume 1102 of *Lecture Notes in Computer Science*, New Brunswick, NJ, July/August 1996. Springer-Verlag.

[BCM+92] J. R. Burch, E. M. Clarke, K. L. McMillan, D. L. Dill, and L. J. Hwang. Symbolic model checking: 10^{20} states and beyond. *Information and Computation*, 98(2):142–170, June 1992.

[BGL+00] Saddek Bensalem, Vijay Ganesh, Yassine Lakhnech, César Muñoz, Sam Owre, Harald Rueß, John Rushby, Vlad Rusu, Hassen Saïdi, N. Shankar, Eli Singerman, and Ashish Tiwari. An overview of SAL. In C. Michael Holloway, editor, *LFM 2000: Fifth NASA Langley Formal Methods Workshop*, pages 187–196, Hampton, VA, June 2000. NASA Langley Research Center. Proceedings available at http://shemesh.larc.nasa.gov/fm/Lfm2000/Proc/.

[BGP97] Tevfik Bultan, Richard Gerber, and William Pugh. Symbolic model checking of infinite state systems using Presburger arithmetic. In Grumberg [Gru97], pages 400–411.

[BHSV+96] R. K. Brayton, G. D. Hachtel, A. Sangiovanni-Vincentelli, F. Somenzi, A. Aziz, S.-T. Cheng, S. Edwards, S. Khatri, Y. Kukimoto, A. Pardo, S. Qadeer, R. K. Ranjan, S. Sarwary, T. R. Shiple, G. Swamy, and T. Villa. VIS: a system for verification and synthesis. In Alur and Henzinger [AH96], pages 428–432.

[BLO98] Saddek Bensalem, Yassine Lakhnech, and Sam Owre. Computing abstractions of infinite state systems compositionally and automatically. In Hu and Vardi [HV98], pages 319–331.

[BRB90] K. S. Brace, R. L. Rudell, and R. E. Bryant. Efficient implementation of a BDD package. In *Proc. of the 27th ACM/IEEE Design Automation Conference*, pages 40–45, 1990.

[CC77] P. Cousot and R. Cousot. Abstract interpretation: a unified lattice model for static analysis. In *4th ACM Symposium on Principles of Programming Languages*. ACM, January 1977.

[CDH+00] James Corbett, Matthew Dwyer, John Hatcliff, Corina Pasareanu, Robby, Shawn Laubach, and Hongjun Zheng. Bandera: Extracting finite-state models from Java source code. In *22nd International Conference on Software Engineering*, pages 439–448, Limerick, Ireland, June 2000. IEEE Computer Society.

[CGL94] E.M. Clark, O. Grumberg, and D.E. Long. Model checking and abstraction. *ACM Transactions on Programming Languages and Systems*, 16(5):1512–1542, September 1994.

[CGP99] E. M. Clarke, Orna Grumberg, and Doron Peled. *Model Checking*. MIT Press, 1999.

[CM88] K. Mani Chandy and Jayadev Misra. *Parallel Program Design: A Foundation*. Addison-Wesley, Reading, MA, 1988.

[CU98] M. A. Colón and T. E. Uribe. Generating finite-state abstractions of reactive systems using decidion procedures. In Hu and Vardi [HV98], pages 293–304.

[DDP99] Satyaki Das, David L. Dill, and Seungjoon Park. Experience with predicate abstraction. In Halbwachs and Peled [HP99], pages 160–171.

[Dil96] David L. Dill. The Murϕ verification system. In Alur and Henzinger [AH96], pages 390–393.

[dRLP97] Willem-Paul de Roever, Hans Langmaack, and Amir Pnueli, editors. *Compositionality: The Significant Difference (Revised lectures from International Symposium COMPOS'97)*, volume 1536 of *Lecture Notes in Computer Science*, Bad Malente, Germany, September 1997. Springer-Verlag.

[EH83] E. Allen Emerson and Joseph Y. Halpern. "sometimes" and "not never" revisited: On branching versus linear time. In *Conference Record of the Tenth Annual ACM Symposium on Principles of Programming Languages*, pages 127–140, Austin, Texas, January 1983.

[Eme90] E. Allen Emerson. Temporal and modal logic. In Jan van Leeuwen, editor, *Handbook of Theoretical Computer Science*, volume B: Formal Models and Semantics, chapter 16, pages 995–1072. Elsevier and MIT press, Amsterdam, The Netherlands, and Cambridge, MA, 1990.

[For92] Formal Systems (Europe) Ltd, Oxford, UK. *Failures Divergence Refinement: User Manual and Tutorial*, 1.2β edition, October 1992.

[Gru97] Orna Grumberg, editor. *Computer-Aided Verification, CAV '97*, volume 1254 of *Lecture Notes in Computer Science*, Haifa, Israel, June 1997. Springer-Verlag.

[Hoa69] C. A. R. Hoare. An axiomatic basis for computer programming. *Comm. ACM*, 12(10):576–583, 1969.

[Hoa85] C. A. R. Hoare. *Communicating Sequential Processes*. International Series in Computer Science. Prentice Hall, 1985.

[Hol91] G. J. Holzmann. *Design and Validation of Computer Protocols*. Prentice-Hall, 1991.

[HP99] Nicolas Halbwachs and Doron Peled, editors. *Computer-Aided Verification, CAV '99*, volume 1633 of *Lecture Notes in Computer Science*, Trento, Italy, July 1999. Springer-Verlag.

[HV98] Alan J. Hu and Moshe Y. Vardi, editors. *Computer-Aided Verification, CAV '98*, volume 1427 of *Lecture Notes in Computer Science*, Vancouver, Canada, June 1998. Springer-Verlag.

[Kur93] R.P. Kurshan. *Automata-Theoretic Verification of Coordinating Processes*. Princeton University Press, Princeton, NJ, 1993.

[Lam94] Leslie Lamport. The temporal logic of actions. *ACM TOPLAS*, 16(3):872–923, May 1994.

[LT87] N. A. Lynch and M. R. Tuttle. Hierarchical correctness proofs for distributed algorithms. In *Proceedings of the Sixth Annual Symposium on Principles of Distributed Computing*, pages 137–151, New York, 1987. ACM Press.

[McM93]   K.L. McMillan. *Symbolic Model Checking*. Kluwer Academic Publishers, Boston, 1993.

[Mil89]   R. Milner. *Communication and Concurrency*. International Series in Computer Science. Prentice Hall, 1989.

[MP92]   Zohar Manna and Amir Pnueli. *The Temporal Logic of Reactive and Concurrent Systems, Volume 1: Specification*. Springer-Verlag, New York, NY, 1992.

[MQS00]   K. McMillan, S. Qadeer, and J. Saxe. Induction in compositional model checking. In E. A. Emerson and A. P. Sistla, editors, *Computer-Aided Verification*, volume 1855 of *Lecture Notes in Computer Science*, pages 312–327, Chicago, IL, July 2000. Springer-Verlag.

[ORSvH95]   S. Owre, J. Rushby, N. Shankar, and F. von Henke. Formal verification for fault-tolerant architectures: Prolegomena to the design of PVS. *IEEE Transactions on Software Engineering*, 21(2):107–125, February 1995.

[Par76]   David Park. Finiteness is mu-ineffable. *Theoretical Computer Science*, 3:173–181, 1976.

[RSS95]   S. Rajan, N. Shankar, and M. Srivas. An integration of theorem proving and automated proof checking. In *Computer-Aided Verification*, number 939 in Lecture Notes in Computer Science, pages 84–97. Springer-Verlag, 1995.

[SdB69]   D. Scott and J. W. de Bakker. A theory of programs, unpublished notes. IBM Seminar, Vienna, 1969.

[SG97]   Hassen Saïdi and Susanne Graf. Construction of abstract state graphs with PVS. In Grumberg [Gru97], pages 72–83.

[Sha97]   N. Shankar. Machine-assisted verification using theorem proving and model checking. In M. Broy and Birgit Schieder, editors, *Mathematical Methods in Program Development*, volume 158 of *NATO ASI Series F: Computer and Systems Science*, pages 499–528. Springer, 1997.

[SS99]   Hassen Saïdi and N. Shankar. Abstract and model check while you prove. In Halbwachs and Peled [HP99], pages 443–454.

[Tar55]   A. Tarski. A lattice-theoretical fixpoint theorem and its applications. *Pacific J. of Math.*, 5:285–309, 1955.

17
An experiment in feature engineering

Pamela Zave

Abstract

Feature-oriented specifications must be constructed, validated, and verified differently from other specifications. This paper presents a feature-oriented specification technique and a formal method applicable to some of its specifications. The method is applied to an example specification, and the results are evaluated.

17.1 Feature-oriented specification

A *feature* of a software system is an optional or incremental unit of functionality. A *feature-oriented specification* is organized by features. It consists of a base specification and feature modules, each of which specifies a separate feature. The behavior of the system as a whole is determined by applying a feature-composition operator to these modules.

A *feature interaction* is some way in which a feature or features modify or influence another feature in defining overall system behavior. Formally this influence can take many forms, depending on the nature of the feature-specification language and composition operator. A group of logical assertions, composed by conjunction, can affect each other's meanings rather differently than a group of finite-state machines, composed by exchanging messages on buffered communication channels.

In general, features might interact by causing their composition to be incomplete, inconsistent, nondeterministic, or unimplementable in some specific sense.[1] Or the presence of a feature might simply change the meaning of another feature with which it interacts.

---

[1] For example, in TLA [1] the result of feature composition could fail to be *machine-closed*. The specification would be unimplementable because it requires the system to control the environment's choices.

Feature-oriented specification emphasizes individual features and makes them explicit. It also de-emphasizes feature interactions, and makes them implicit. Feature-oriented specification is widely popular because it makes specifications easy to change and individual features easy to understand. Feature-oriented specification is also easy to abuse by ignoring feature interactions altogether.

Although the feature-oriented style of system description presents many challenges to formal methods, it cannot be ignored because it is too attractive to the majority of people who actually describe systems. For example, it is ubiquitous in the telecommunication industry (where the usual feature-specification language is English, and the usual composition operator is concatenation). As a result of this situation, problems of unmanageable feature interactions affect all segments of the telecommunication industry, and are the primary motivation for the industry's interest in formal methods [2, 4, 5, 8, 3].

Two points about feature interactions are frequently misunderstood. Since these misunderstandings make it impossible to talk about feature interaction clearly, let alone formally, it is important to emphasize these points at the outset:

- While many feature interactions are undesirable, many others are desirable or necessary. *Not all feature interactions are bad!*

- Feature interactions are an inevitable by-product of feature modularity.

"Busy treatments" in telephony are features for handling busy situations. They exemplify these points. Suppose that we have a feature-specification language in which a busy treatment is specified by providing an action, an enabling condition, and a priority. Further suppose that a special feature-composition operator ensures that, in any busy situation, the action applied will be that of the highest-priority enabled busy treatment.

In a busy situation where two busy treatments B_1 and B_2 are both enabled, with B_2 having higher priority, these features will interact: the action of B_1 will not be applied, even though its stand-alone specification says that it should be applied. This feature interaction is intentional and desirable. It is a by-product of the feature modularity that allows us to add busy treatments to the system without changing existing busy treatments. Without the special composition operator, when B_2 is added to the system, the enabling condition E_1 of B_1 must be changed to $E_1 \land \neg E_2$.

17.2 The challenge of feature engineering

I am interested in helping people write good feature-oriented formal specifications, a process I dub *feature engineering*. Figure 17.1 is a simple picture of how feature engineering might be done. It assumes that a base specification and old features already exist, and that the goal is to add new features to this legacy.

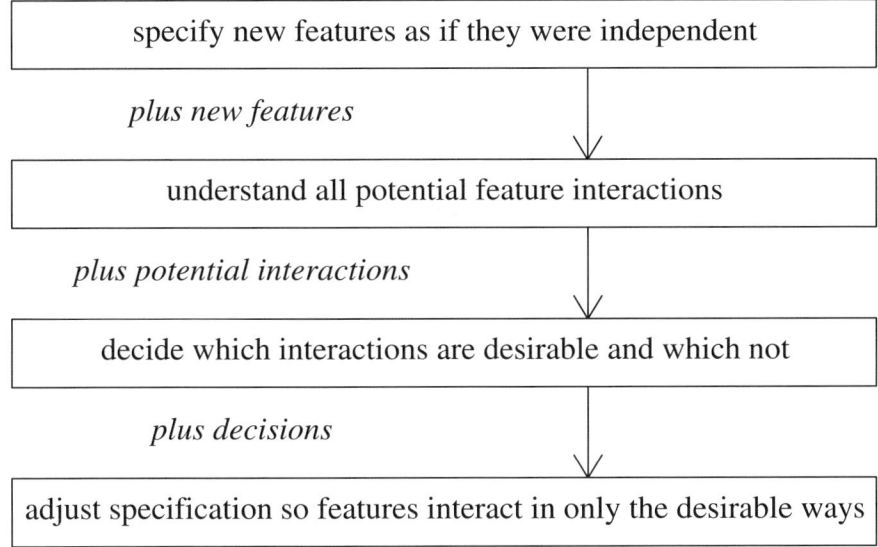

Figure 17.1. A proposed process for feature engineering.

To realize the process, we shall have to rise to many challenges. First and foremost is the need for a truly modular formalism. A modular formalism would facilitate and support the process of Figure 17.1 as follows:

- It would be possible to specify almost any increment of functionality as an independent feature.

- All diagnosed feature interactions would be meaningful. Feature composition would not generate trivial interactions.

- In most cases, the interaction choices could be implemented just by making small changes to new features, leaving old features alone.

In the domain of telecommunication services, the DFC virtual architecture has emerged as a means of specifying realistic systems with adequate modularity. DFC will be introduced in the next section, and will serve as the basis for the remainder of this paper.

The next challenge is posed by the second step of Figure 17.1. How do we detect and understand all potential feature interactions? There appear to be two major approaches. In the *correctness* approach, people write assertions stating the intended behavior of the system as a whole, and tools either help verify that the composed features satisfy the assertions, or produce counterexamples. The *structural* approach only works if the feature-specification language and composition operator constrain the ways in which features can interact. In this approach, the possible structural interactions are studied and classified. Then tools are developed to detect their presence in a feature set.

The five workshop proceedings cited above contain many examples of both approaches, used only, however, to detect undesirable feature interactions. The structural approach has the definite advantage of being easier on the user (correctness assertions for feature-oriented specifications are particularly hard to write [9]). Yet the correctness approach appears to be more comprehensive—there are examples of feature interactions that do not seem feasible to detect with a structural approach. Presumably the two approaches are complementary, and both will prove useful in the long run.

Yet another challenge is posed by the third step of Figure 17.1. Sometimes the requirements on overall system behavior are clear. More often, a specifier is confronted with a range of possible behaviors and no clear criterion for choosing among them. There has been little investigation of this problem, at least in the telecommunication domain.

This paper presents in detail a very modest, limited version of this feature-engineering process. The modest method is then applied to a case study, and the results are evaluated. One purpose is to begin the study of feature interactions in DFC. Another purpose is to check whether the new (at least to research in feature interaction) notion of desirable feature interactions makes sense in practice.

17.3 A feature-oriented specification technique

Distributed Feature Composition (DFC) is a new modular architecture for describing telecommunication services [7, 12, 13]. Hundreds of features and services have been described informally within the DFC framework, and we know of no services (including mobile and multimedia services) that cannot be fit into the architecture. The following introduction to DFC is just comprehensive enough for the case study, and is *very* incomplete.

In DFC a customer call generates and is responded to by a *usage*, which is a dynamic assembly of *boxes* and *internal calls*. A *box* is a module, and implements either a line/device interface or a feature. An *internal call* is a featureless connection between two ports on two different boxes. Figure 17.2 illustrates a simple usage at two points in time.

In Figure 17.2 a DFC internal call is shown as an arrow from the port that placed the call to the port that received the call. Each internal call begins with a *setup phase* in which the initiating port sends a setup signal to the DFC router, and the DFC router chooses a box and forwards the signal to it. The receiving box chooses an idle port for the call (if there is one) and completes the setup phase with a signal back to the initiating port. From that time until the *teardown phase*, the call exists and has a two-way signaling channel and a two-way voice channel.

Having full control of all the calls it places or receives, a feature box has the autonomy to fulfill its purpose without external assistance. When a feature box

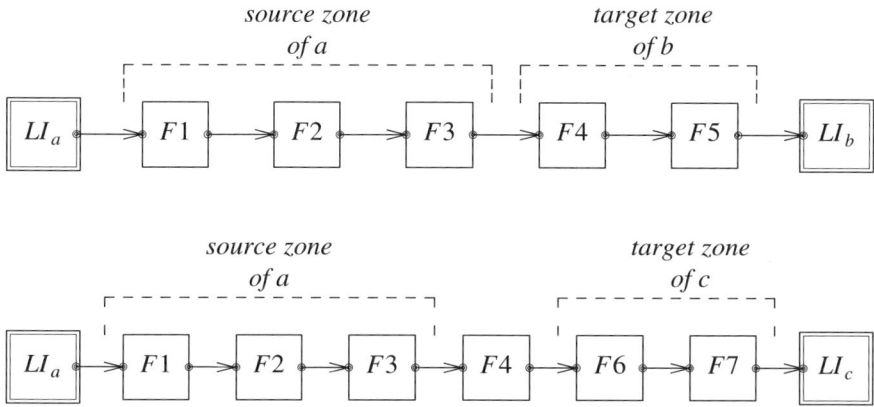

Figure 17.2. Two snapshots of a linear usage.

does not need to function, it can behave *transparently*. For a box with two ports, both of which are engaged in calls, transparent behavior is sending any signal received from one port out the other port, and connecting the voice channels in both directions. The two calls will behave as one, and the presence of the transparent box will not be observable by any other box in the usage.

When its function requires, a feature box can also behave assertively, re-routing internal calls, processing voice, and absorbing/generating signals. To give a simple example, a Call Forwarding on No Answer box (box $F4$ in Figure 17.2) first makes an outgoing internal call to address b as shown in the upper part of Figure 17.2. If CFNA receives a signal through its outgoing call that b is alerting, and then no other signal for 30 seconds, CFNA tears down its outgoing internal call and places a new outgoing internal call whose target is the forwarding address c. The resulting usage is shown in the lower part of Figure 17.2.

Most components of the DFC architecture are shown in Figure 17.3. The line-interface boxes (LI) are connected to telecommunication devices by external lines. The trunk-interface boxes (TI) are connected to other networks by external trunks. The feature boxes (F) can have any number of ports, depending on their various functions. Internal calls are provided by the port-to-port *virtual network*.

The router of the virtual network is unusual. It not only routes internal calls to the destinations associated with their target addresses, as any network router does, but it also "applies features" by routing internal calls to and from feature boxes. For this reason it needs data on feature subscriptions and feature precedences as well as normal configuration data. (All global data is shown in double rectangles in Figure 17.3.)

Figure 17.3 also shows global data called *operational data,* which is used by feature boxes. For example, the CFNA box retrieves its subscriber's forwarding address from operational data. Access to operational data is strictly partitioned by features, so its use cannot compromise feature modularity. Operational data is used mainly to provide provisioned customer information to features.

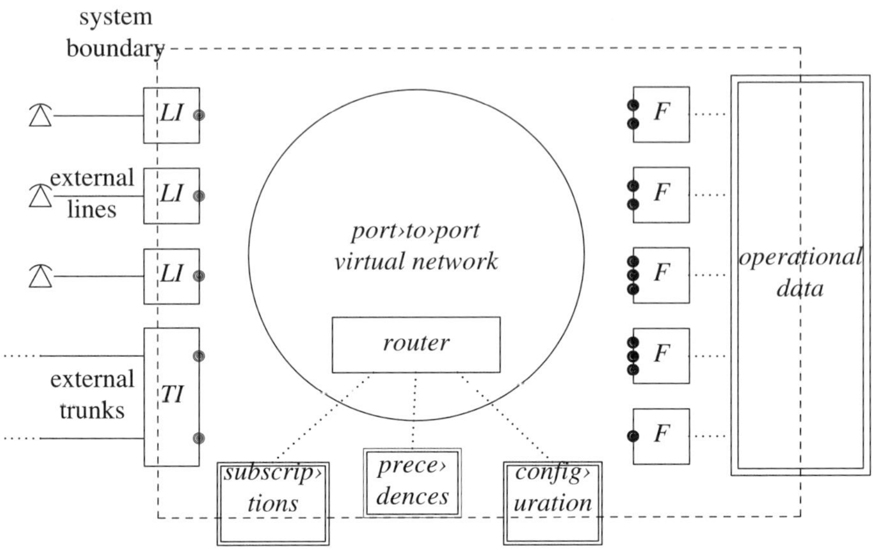

358   Zave

Figure 17.3. Components of the DFC architecture.

Each box fits into one of two large categories. A *bound box* is a unique, persistent, addressable individual. In Figure 17.2 the only bound boxes are the two line interfaces. The other boxes in Figure 17.2 are *free boxes,* meaning that each box is an anonymous, interchangeable copy of its type with no persistence outside its tenure in a usage. The value of bound feature boxes is that they make it possible to have joins in usage graphs (see Section 17.5.1).

The key to assembly of the necessary usage configurations is the DFC routing algorithm. It operates on the setup signal that initiates each internal call. The setup signal has five fields of interest to the router; in the form name : *type* they are: source : *address,* dialed : *string,* target: *address,* command: {new, continue, update}, and route : **seq** *routing_pair.* Each routing pair has a first component of type *box_type* and a second component of type *zone* = { source, target }.

We shall explain the function of the router by example, first describing how the usage in Figure 17.2 evolved. The setup signal emitted by LI_a had a source field containing a, a dialed field containing the dialed string, and a command field containing new. The other two fields were empty. Upon receiving the signal, the router first extracted the target line address b from the dialed string, and put it into the target field.

Next the router, instructed by new, computed a new route and put it into the route field. Customer a subscribes to three features F1, F2, and F3 in the source zone, so the first three pairs of the route were *(F1,*source*), (F2,*source*),* and *(F3,*source*).* The target address b subscribes to two features F4 and F5 in the target zone, so the last two pairs of the route were *(F4,*target*)* and *(F5,*target*).*

Now the router had finished manipulating the setup signal, and needed to find a box to route the internal call to. It stripped the first pair off the route, and since F1 is the type of a free box, it routed the internal call to an arbitrary fresh box of that type.

The feature boxes in the upper part of Figure 17.2 had no initial need to control the routing. So when each box prepared a setup signal for an outgoing call, it simply copied the entire setup signal from its incoming call, making sure that the command field had continue rather than new. The continue command told the router not to recompute anything in the route. The chain unfolded, one pair of the route being deleted as each free box was added to the usage. Finally, in the last internal call, the route was empty so the router routed to the bound box LI_b.

When the CFNA feature box (*F4*) made its second outgoing call, the value of target in the setup signal was the forwarding address c. To ensure correct feature application, CFNA set the command value to update(target). This caused the router to remove from the route the remnants of the target zone of b, and to replace them with a newly computed target-zone route for c. Because of this substitution the usage was routed through the target features of c before reaching LI_c, as shown in the lower part of Figure 17.2.

In constructing a route, the router uses a *precedence* relation governing the order in which features can occur in a route (precedences are the only place in a DFC system where features are related explicitly to one another). This order, of course, has important effects on how features interact. For example, a busy signal usually originates in the target interface box. So the proper coordination of busy treatments mentioned in Section 17.1 would be achieved by placing the higher-priority feature boxes later in the route, i.e., closer to the source of their triggering signal. A busy treatment absorbs and responds to a busy signal if its feature is enabled, and forwards the signal toward the earlier feature boxes if it is not enabled.

The major source of modularity in DFC is that features communicate with each other only through DFC internal calls. A feature box does not know what is on the other end of its calls, for example, whether a far port is associated with a feature or a user. So the feature box need not change when its environment changes, for example by the addition of another feature. At the same time, all the relevant signaling and media channels go through the feature box, so the feature box has the power to manipulate them in any way it finds necessary.

17.4 A modest method for feature engineering

17.4.1 *Scope of the method*

Befitting its modest nature, the scope of this method is very narrow. It applies only to voice services. It applies only to features whose sole box type is that of a free, two-port feature box subscribed to in the target zone. I call these *free target features* for short.

Furthermore, the method is only concerned with engineering interactions *among* free target features, rather than interactions between free target features and other features. This narrows the scope considerably, as there is only one feature class to analyze, both for interaction causes and interaction effects. Also, the precedence relation must cluster all free target features together, so that their interactions are not interfered with by other features.

Finally, there are some detailed restrictions on the behaviors of free target features and other features. Restrictions on other features are simply general rules for good box programming, and are presented in a more detailed report on this work [11]. Restrictions on free target features are presented along with the relevant aspects of the method.

The method uses only structural detection of feature interactions. Thus it can be applied to any set of free target features, without additional knowledge of the requirements they are intended to satisfy.

Despite all these restrictions, this modest method covers an interesting class of features, as the case study will show.

17.4.2 Semantics of features and feature composition

In a feature-oriented specification using DFC, the base module describes the DFC infrastructure (virtual network and routing algorithm) and the system's environment. The environment consists of lines, trunks, interface boxes, and configuration data.

A feature module has a number of parts. The module of a free target feature includes a program for the type of box used to realize the feature. It also includes the subscription relation for the feature, encoding which addresses subscribe to it (the *subscriptions* component in Figure 17.3 is the union of all these relations). If the feature uses any operational data, it includes the declaration and initialization of that data.

As far as free target features are concerned, the precedence relation is simply a partial order on the features. It plays the role here of a parameter to the feature-composition operator. I regard it as such because it explictly relates features to each other, and thus does not fit well into any of the specification modules.

The formal semantics of the specification is derived from a composition of Promela and Z based on the transition-axiom method [10]. Our "modest method" is so restricted in scope that the aspects of the specification dependent on Z (primarily routing and operational data) have little relevance. For present purposes, it is a reasonable approximation to say that a feature-box program is a Promela[2] program. Accesses to operational data in the full box program reduce to nondeterminism in the Promela program.

---

[2]Promela is the specification language of the model checker Spin [6].

17. An experiment in feature engineering   361

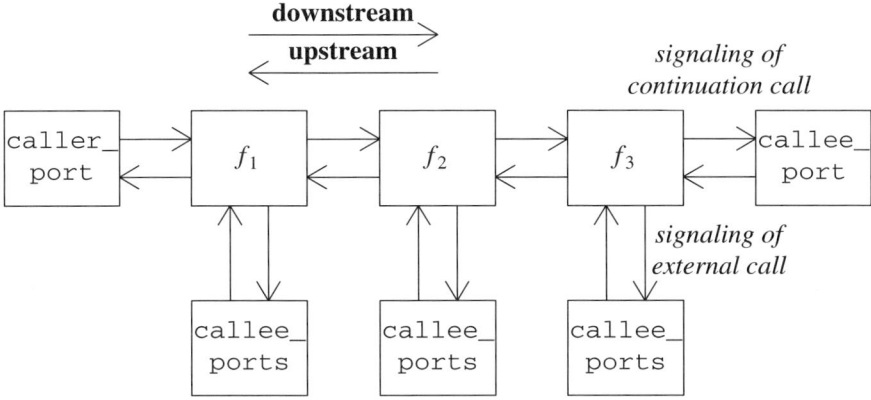

Figure 17.4. A configuration of $(\{f_1, f_2, f_3\}, P)$.

When the DFC router needs an instance of a free feature box to route an internal call to, it creates a new one. Thus an instance of a free target feature box receives exactly one incoming call in its lifetime.

The method imposes constraints on the outgoing calls made by free target features. A *continuation call* is an outgoing call that does not alter the default routing in any way—source, dialed, target, and route fields are unchanged, and command=continue. An *external call* is an outgoing call that directs the usage completely out of the target zone of the feature making the call. In the setup signal of an external call, the target field must be different from the target field of the incoming setup, and the command must be update(target). Each outgoing call of a free target feature must be a continuation call or an external call. Also, a free target feature can make at most one outgoing call.

Consider a set S of free target features to be composed under precedence relation P. A *configuration of (S,P)* is a Promela program in which there is a process for each feature in S, as shown in Figure 17.4, running its program. The processes are arranged in a pipeline, connected by Promela channels representing the two-way signaling channels of continuation calls. The order of the processes in the pipeline is consistent with P, in the sense that if $f_1 < f_2$ in P, f_1 must be upstream (left) of f_2.

At each end of the pipeline is a nondeterministic *port process* capable of all legal port behaviors. At the upstream end the port process places one call. In Promela (with data fields omitted) it is:

```
proctype caller_port(chan in,out)
{           out!setup;
            if
            :: in?upack; goto linked
            :: in?quickbusy; goto end
            fi;
```

```
linked:     do
            :: out!other
            :: out!teardown; goto unlinking
            :: in?busy
            :: in?alerting
            :: in?answered
            :: in?quiet
            :: in?other
            :: in?teardown; out!downack; goto end
            od;
unlinking:  do
            :: in?busy
            :: in?alerting
            :: in?answered
            :: in?quiet
            :: in?other
            :: in?teardown; out!downack
            :: in?downack; goto end
            od;
end:        skip
}
```

The signals setup, upack, and quickbusy are used in the setup phase of the call. The signals teardown and downack are used in the teardown phase of the call. All other signals transmitted during the call are *status signals*. The status signals busy, alerting, answered, and quiet are sent from the callee end to indicate the status of the target. Status signals in the catch-all category of other can be sent in either direction.

At the downstream end of the pipeline is a process specifying all behaviors of a port receiving one call. In Promela it is:

```
proctype callee_port(chan in,out)
{ end_begin: in?setup;
            if
            :: out!upack; goto linked
            :: out!quickbusy; goto end
            fi;
linked:     do
            :: out!busy
            :: out!alerting
            :: out!answered
            :: out!quiet
            :: out!other
            :: out!teardown; goto unlinking
            :: in?other
            :: in?teardown; out!downack; goto end
```

```
                        od;
unlinking:              do
                        :: in?other
                        :: in?teardown; out!downack
                        :: in?downack; goto end
                        od;
end:                    skip
}
```

Figure 17.4 also shows that each feature process in a configuration has a signaling connection to a `callee_ports` process. These represent the two-way signaling channels of (possibly a sequence of) external calls. A feature process cannot be using both its continuation-call channels and its external-call channels simultaneously.

The semantics of a Promela program is a trace set. If the free target features satisfy all the constraints imposed by the method, then the semantics of a set S of free target features composed under precedence relation P is the union of the trace sets of all the configurations of (S,P). There is one contributing configuration for each total order over S consistent with P.[3]

17.4.3 Syntax of features

The feature-box programs in this paper are written in a shorthand notation that expands to Promela. In the shorthand, a program is a finite-state machine with some special annotations.

Most state transitions are associated with the sending or receiving of signals. The actions of sending and receiving a signal of type v through the upstream port are denoted up!v and up?v respectively. The actions of sending and receiving a signal of type v through the downstream port are denoted down!v and down?v respectively.[4]

The general form of a transition label is *guard; action*, where the guard is a signal receive or predicate, and the action is a signal send or data update. Labels can also have the degenerate forms *guard;* or *action*. A transition is enabled when its guard is true or executable. Once a program enters a state, it must take some enabled transition as soon as there is one.

Many signals have data fields. A send action such as up!$v(t)$ uses the value of the local variable t to provide a value for the signal's data field. A receive action such as down?$v(u)$ binds the value of the signal's data field to the local variable

---

[3] This definition does not mention the subscriptions relations in feature modules, which will be considered later.

[4] In Promela code, the two signaling directions of a DFC port must be given different names such as in and out. Here the channel name identifies only the DFC port, and the symbol indicates the direction.

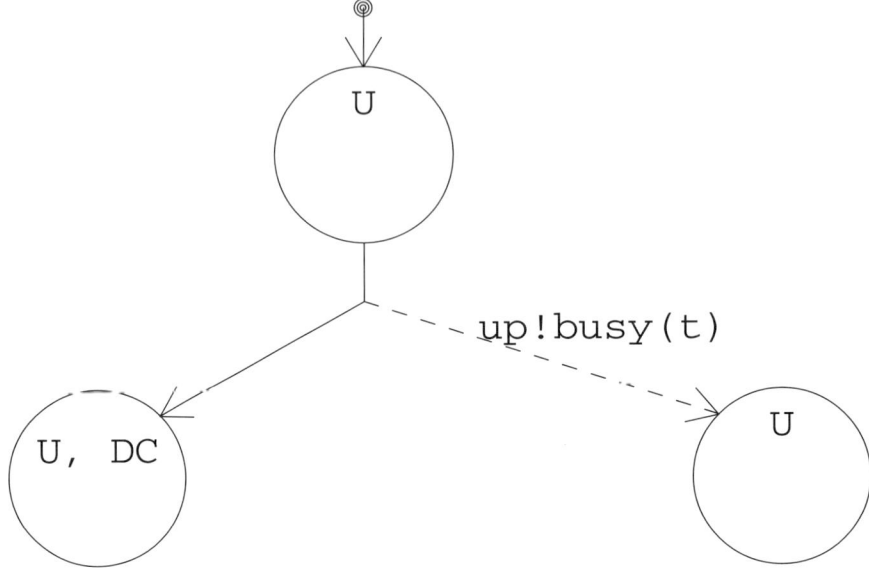

Figure 17.5. Complete program for a transparent feature box.

u. Predicates and data updates can refer to either local variables of the box or operational data of the feature.

A box program always has a single entrance transition, implicitly labeled `up?setup(s,d,t,r)` and giving the named local variables the values of the `source`, `dialed`, `target`, and `route` fields respectively. The remainder of the setup of the incoming call is implicit and atomic.

An attempt to place an outgoing call is also an atomic transition, represented by a forked arrow. The handle of the fork has an optional guard. The solid tine of the fork leads to the success destination state. If the solid tine is not labeled, as in Figure 17.5, a continuation call is being attempted. If the solid tine is labeled with `source`, `dialed` and `target` fields, then an external call is being attempted. The broken tine of the fork leads to the state arrived at if the call attempt fails; the optional label of this tine is an action to be taken in case of failure.

If a state has the annotation U, then the upstream port is engaged in a call. If a state has the annotation DC or DX, then the downstream port is engaged in a continuation or external call, respectively.

The teardown phase of a call is represented by an atomic transition on a `teardown` signal. In every state in which a port is engaged in a call, there must be a transition for the receipt of a `teardown` signal for that call. If the transition is not explicit, then it is implicit. An implicit teardown transition sends a `teardown` signal out of the other port, if it is engaged in a call, and exits from the program.

In every state in which a port is engaged in a call, there must be a transition for the receipt of every possible status signal from that call. If the transition is not explicit, then it is implicit. An implicit status transition forwards the status signal out of the other port, if the other port is engaged in a call, and returns to the state from which it originated.

In every state in which a port is engaged in a call, the feature box can do something with the voice channel of that call. Voice processing is specified using state annotations, as described in Section 17.4.7. The default (no state annotation) for a state in which only one port is busy is no voice processing at all. The default (no state annotation) for a state in which both ports are busy is to connect their voice channels in both directions.

Consistency checks are needed to ensure that this notation is used correctly; correct use is simply assumed here. The notation is designed so that no feature box can deadlock its usage. It is also designed so that transparent behavior is almost completely implicit, as can be seen from Figure 17.5.

17.4.4 Semantics of feature interactions

Intuitively the existence of a particular kind of feature interaction between features f and g under partial order P on $\{f,g\}$ means that f is capable of a particular behavior, that this behavior is potentially observable by g if the two are composed under an extension of P, and that this behavior could have a notable effect on g.

For a definition of a feature interaction to be valid, it must not be possible for a transparent feature box to play the role of either f or g. By definition, a transparent box has no feature interactions. This means, for example, that short signaling delays do not cause feature interactions.

The significance of such a feature interaction is that in the semantics of feature set S composed under Q, where $\{f,g\} \subseteq S$ and $P = \{f,g\} \triangleleft Q \triangleright \{f,g\}$ (P is Q restricted to $\{f,g\}$), there can be a trace in which f has this notable effect on g. The existence of the interaction does not guarantee the presence of the notable trace, since the context in which f and g are embedded can make a notable trace infeasible. It is clear, however, that if the interaction is not present the notable trace cannot be present.

Taking subscriptions into account does not affect the safety of this concept. If a target address does not subscribe to all the features in a feature set, then certain interactions diagnosed in the feature set might become impossible, but no additional ones can become possible.

If engineers diagnose an interaction between f and g under P and judge it to be bad, there are several things they can do. The easiest way to prevent it is to compose f and g only under partial orders inconsistent with P; this strategy is limited by the fact that it might lead to inconsistent requirements (circularities) on Q. Another strategy is to prove by other means that the interaction is a "false positive"—that the notable trace is not in fact in the semantics of the feature set being studied. Another strategy is to change f or g, which is attractive if the interaction is a result of bad feature programming, and unattractive if the interaction is inherent in the intended functions of f and g. Least attractive of all, engineers can constrain subscriptions so that no address can subscribe to both f and g.

17.4.5 *Feature interactions related to calls*

At any given time, a box's downstream port can be idle, engaged in a continuation call, or engaged in an external call. Engaging in a continuation call is the transparent behavior, so both idleness and external calls are potential sources of feature interaction. If a feature box fails to make a downstream call, or makes an external call rather than a continuation call, then the free target features that would have been downstream of this feature in the usage will never be invoked—their functions will be *cancelled*.

This is our first feature interaction. Its definition requires two new concepts. An *all-solid initial path* through a box program is a path that begins with the entrance transition and follows only solid transition arrows (it is not fair to count a broken arrow, representing a call attempt's failure, against the box). A *sink state* is a state with no transitions to other states (all its transitions are self-loops or exit transitions).

Interaction 1 (Cancels) *Feature f cancels feature g under partial order P on $\{f,g\}$ iff. $g \not< f$, and f has an all-solid initial path to a sink state with no DC annotation, and g is not transparent.*

Presumably cancellation is good if the circumstances under which f cancels obviate the need for the function of g, and bad otherwise.

The *retargeting* feature interaction concerns both calls and status signals, so it is defined in the next section.

17.4.6 *Feature interactions related to status signals*

The four *public status signals* `busy`, `alerting`, `answered`, and `quiet` are known to all feature boxes as indications of the status of the target interface box. *Private status signals* can also be introduced to provide customized communication between an interface box and the features its address subscribes to, or to send secrets between cooperating feature boxes. A status signal generated by an interface box has a data field bearing the address of that box. A status signal sent by a feature box bears the address received in a corresponding signal, or the address of the box's subscriber.

Every box program has a local variable `status: {none, busy, alerting, answered, quiet}`. The value of this variable indicates the perceived status of the downstream call (if any). It is initialized to `none`, and updated automatically according to the signals received from downstream: a successful setup phase changes it to `quiet`, receipt of a public status signal changes it to the matching value, and a teardown changes it to `none`.

This local variable can be referenced in guards. A numerical guard such as `status=alerting(30)` is not true until `status=alerting` has been true for 30 seconds. The guard `status=alerting((30))` is not true unless the box has been in the same state, and `status=alerting` has been true—both for 30 seconds.

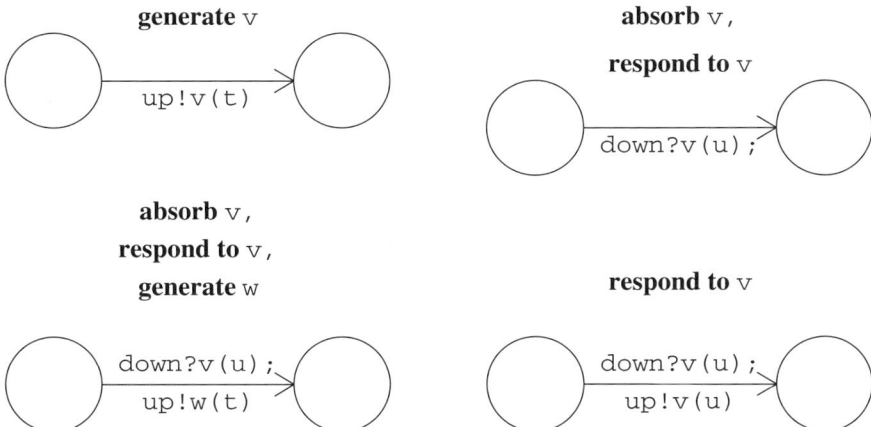

Figure 17.6. Explicit transitions that over-ride implicit transitions.

Assuming that both ports of a box are engaged in calls, the box *propagates* a signal of type v if the box receives the signal from one port, and then, as a result of having received it, sends a signal of type v out the other port. When a box handles a setup failure with `up!busy`, it is understood to be propagating a `busy` signal.

A signal of type v is *generated* by a box if the box sends it without having first received a corresponding signal of type v. If a box handles a setup failure by sending a signal other than `busy`, it is understood to be generating that signal.

A signal of type v is *absorbed* by a box if the box receives it and does not propagate it. If a box handles a setup failure by sending no signal, it is understood to be absorbing a `busy` signal.

A box *responds to* a signal of type v if v appears in a guard in its program (`up?v`, `down?v`, `status=v`, etc.). Figure 17.6 shows explicit transitions that generate, absorb, and respond to signals.

If a box makes an external call, then any box upstream of it may receive status signals that came through the external call and were propagated upstream. These signals indicate the status of some other target address rather than the address that subscribes to the upstream features.

Interaction 2 (Retargets) *Feature f retargets feature g under partial order P on $\{f,g\}$ iff. $f \not< g$, and f has an all-solid initial path to a state annotated DX, and g responds to some type of status signal.*

Presumably retargeting is bad if the function of g pertains primarily to its subscriber, and good if its function pertains primarily to the target address reached by the usage.

There are two interactions defined purely on handling of public status signals. Similar interactions can be defined concerning handling of private status signals, but they would be more complex, as private signals can travel in both directions while public signals travel upstream only.

Interaction 3 (Spoofs) *Feature f spoofs public status signal type v to feature g under partial order P on {f,g} iff. $f \not< g$, and f can generate a signal of type v, and g responds to signals of type v.*

Interaction 4 (Hides) *Feature f hides public status signal type v from feature g under partial order P on {f,g} iff. (1) $f \not< g$, and f can absorb a signal of type v, and g responds to signals of type v, OR (2) $g \not< f$, and f can generate a signal of type v, and g responds to signals of type v.*

In the second kind of hiding, f generates a signal upstream that g might like to see, but misses because g is (or might be) downstream of f. Spoofing and hiding are neutral feature interactions—good if the composed features work in the intended way, and bad otherwise. For example, the coordination of busy treatments mentioned in Sections 17.1 and 17.3 is accomplished by hiding.

17.4.7 Feature interactions related to voice

The voice-processing capabilities considered here are simplified, yet they are adequate for the case study, and also representative of the true range of voice capabilities.

If a state is annotated `playU(file)`, then the specified voice file (announcement) is played in the upstream direction during that state. The reserved guard `end;` becomes true when the playback is finished. A transition from the state with any other guard will discontinue playback if it is still in progress. The voice signal traveling downstream is transmitted transparently through the box.

If a state is annotated `recU(file)`, then while the box is in that state, the voice signal from upstream is being recorded in the specified file. The voice signals traveling in both directions are transmitted transparently through the box.

If a state is annotated `monU[x,y,...]`, then while the box is in that state, the voice signal from upstream is being monitored and analyzed for recognizable patterns. The patterns must be specified separately, but they are denoted symbolically by the vocabulary `[x,y,...]`. As soon as a pattern x is recognized, the guard `x;` becomes true, and can cause a transition out of the state. The voice signals traveling in both directions are transmitted transparently through the box.

A common combination of state annotations can be seen in the largest state of Figure 17.9. A recording is being played to ask the caller if the call is urgent and to tell the caller how to answer "yes" or "no." At the same time, the voice signal from the caller is being monitored for the "yes" (`urgent` and "no" (`normal`) patterns. If the caller is familiar with this feature, and answers the question before it has been posed, then the announcement will be aborted early.

If two different free target features are in `playU` states simultaneously, then the downstream announcement will not be heard by the caller. The downstream announcement signal will be discarded by the upstream box, which is replacing it by its own announcement. This feature interaction, called *drowning*, is always bad because the downstream box is not having the effect it is expecting to have.

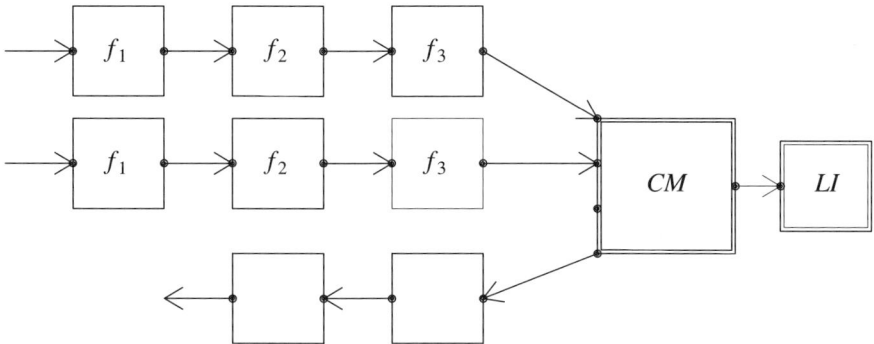

Figure 17.7. Usage with Call Multiplexing and free target features f_1, f_2, and f_3.

Interaction 5 (Drowns) *Feature f drowns feature g under partial order P on $\{f, g\}$ iff. $g \not< f$ and both f and g have states with* `playU` *annotations.*

To ensure that the caller's line interface will transmit voice to the caller, the line interface must receive `answered` before the announcement and no other public status signal during it. The S state annotation (for *seizing the voice channel* makes this easier to program. First, a box's entry into a state annotated S automatically generates an `answered` upstream. The generated signal is sent after the guard and action of the in-transition, if any, are both executed.

While the box remains in the S state, the program implicitly reads all signals arriving at the downstream port, saves them in the order received, and does not propagate any of them. The box's `status` variable continues to have the value it had just before state entrance (not `answered`).

Finally, on exit from the S state, all of the saved signals are propagated upstream in the order in which they were received. Meanwhile, this box's `status` variable is being updated to match them. If no such signals were received during the S state, then the box implementation generates an upstream status signal to match the box's `status` variable, and thus return the upstream usage to the state it was in before this box entered the S state. These signals are emitted by the box after the guard of the out-transition is executed, and before the out-transition action is executed.

In addition to ensuring proper behavior of the caller's line interface, the upstream signaling provided by S notifies other features of the use of the voice channel, and helps features coordinate to avoid drowning. Additional details will be given in Section 17.5.2.

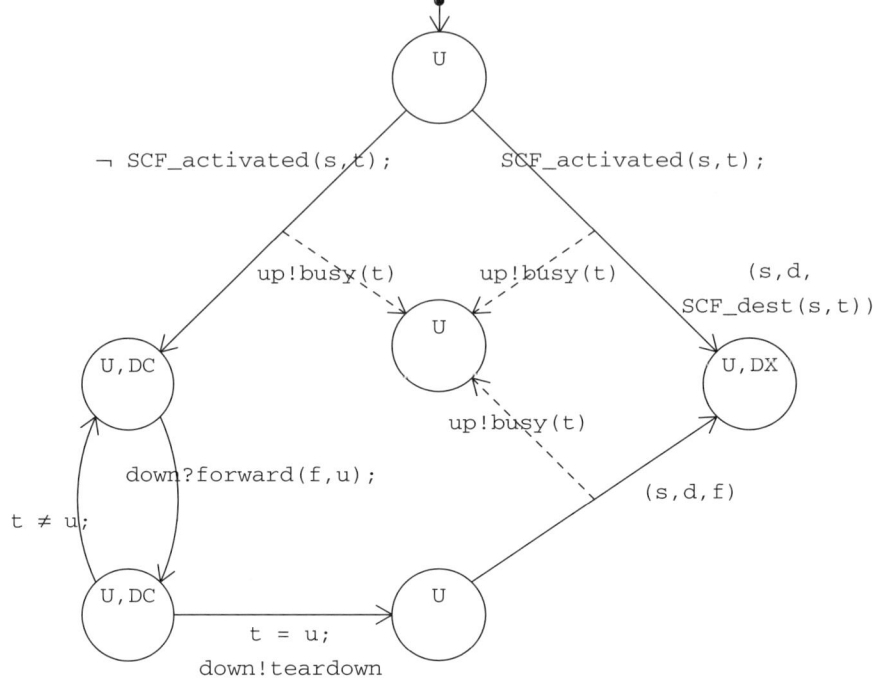

Figure 17.8. A program for Selective Call Forwarding.

17.5 An application of the method

17.5.1 Feature context

The upcoming set of free target features is designed for a customer who also subscribes to a Call Multiplexing feature allowing him to switch among a number of active customer calls simultaneously. The CM feature uses a display on the subscriber's telephone to identify the far party of each customer call, so that the subscriber can keep them straight. The CM feature joins box chains coming from or going to different customers, as shown in Figure 17.7, so it is represented by a bound box.

Two instances of free target features are shown in Figure 17.7. The purpose of the upcoming set of free target features is to provide flexible response capabilities, covering especially those situations in which the subscriber cannot answer an incoming customer call, or cannot answer it immediately. Several features are triggered by private status signals, which I assume are generated by function buttons on the subscriber's telephone, and propagated through the appropriate ports by CM.

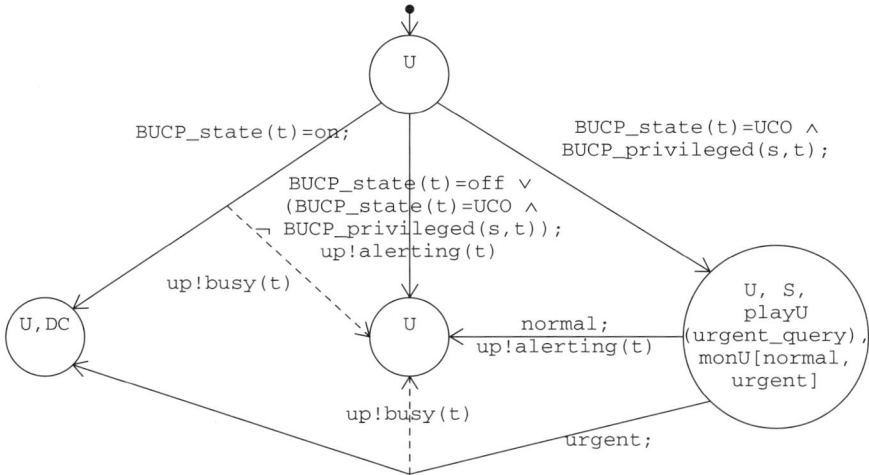

Figure 17.9. A program for Blocking with Urgent Calling Privilege.

17.5.2 A set of free target features

Selective Call Forwarding (SCF, Figure 17.8) is "selective" in the sense that only calls from certain addresses are forwarded. It has two modes of use. It can be activated ahead of time for address *a* by address *b* by establishing SCF_activated(*a,b*) in the operational data, in which case an incoming call is forwarded immediately to the forwarding address SCF_dest(*a,b*). Alternatively, any time after the target subscriber has become aware of an incoming call from *a*, he can send the private signal forward(*c,b*) and have the call forwarded to *c*.

The Blocking with Urgent Calling Privilege (BUCP, Figure 17.9) feature is most useful for mobile telephones, which may be carried into meetings, concerts, and other places where a ringing telephone is disruptive. The subscriber uses buttons on his telephone to set his BUCP_state (in the operational data for the BUCP feature) to on, off, or Urgent Calls Only (UCO). In the off state, all calls to this telephone are blocked. In the UCO state, a call is accepted only if it comes from a privileged caller and the caller designates it as urgent.

From the initial state of the feature box, the left transition leads to transparent behavior. The middle transition leads to blocking behavior; note that an alerting signal is generated and sent upstream so that the caller will not know that the call has been blocked. The right transition leads to a state in which the feature box must find out whether the caller considers the call urgent. The dialogue was described in Section 17.4.7. If the call is urgent then the behavior of the box becomes transparent; otherwise it blocks the call.

Outbound Messaging (OM, Figure 17.10) is "outbound" in the sense that the subscriber has a message for the caller. It has two modes of use. It can be activated ahead of time for address *a* by address *b* by establishing OM_ready(*a,b*) in the operational data, in which case an incoming call from *a* immediately hears the

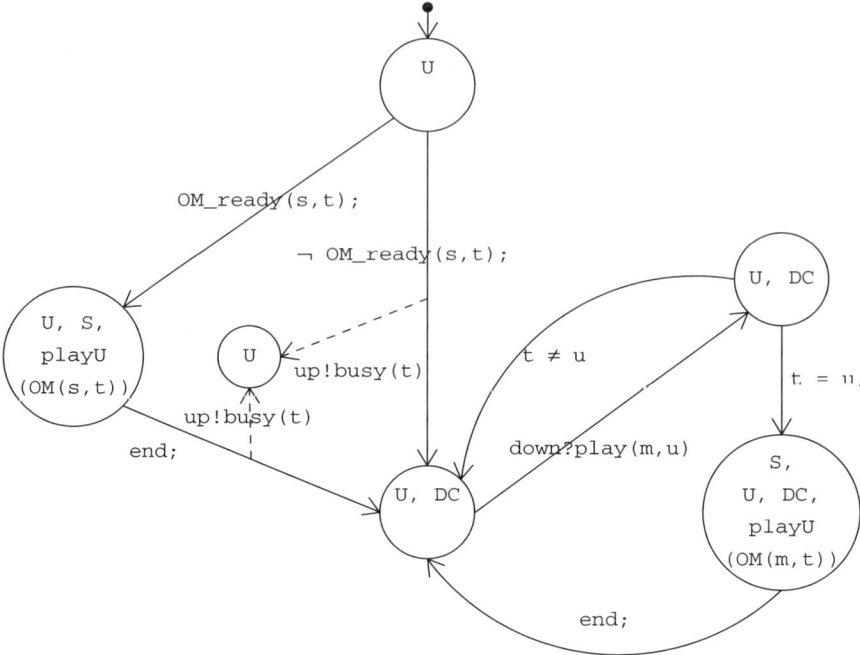

Figure 17.10. A program for Outbound Messaging.

message in voice file OM(*a,b*). Alternatively, any time after the target subscriber has become aware of an incoming call from *a*, he can send the private signal play(*m,b*) and have the voice file OM(*m,b*) played to *a*. Subscriber *b*'s message *m* has been prerecorded, and probably says something like, "I will be able to answer your call in a moment, so please don't hang up."

The final feature of the set is Inbound Messaging (IM, Figure 17.11). This feature is both a no-answer treatment and a busy treatment. It absorbs busy signals and generates alerting signals in their place, so that upstream boxes will perceive only alerting conditions. After a suitable wait, the IM feature plays an invitation to record a message, and monitors for a signal of intention from the caller. Whether the caller decides to record a message or not, he can stay on the line, and later perhaps be answered or record another message.

If the callee answers during the prompting or recording states, IM's work must be interrupted to avoid drowning or recording the person-to-person conversation. This is an explicit out-transition from an S state on a public status signal, yet the out-transition rules from Section 17.4.7 work fine.[5]

---

[5] Note also that in Figure 17.11 that there is a transition from one S state to another. With respect to the S semantics, these states are not regarded as separate. The answered signal is generated only on entrance to the S cluster, and the cleanup actions occur only on exit from the cluster.

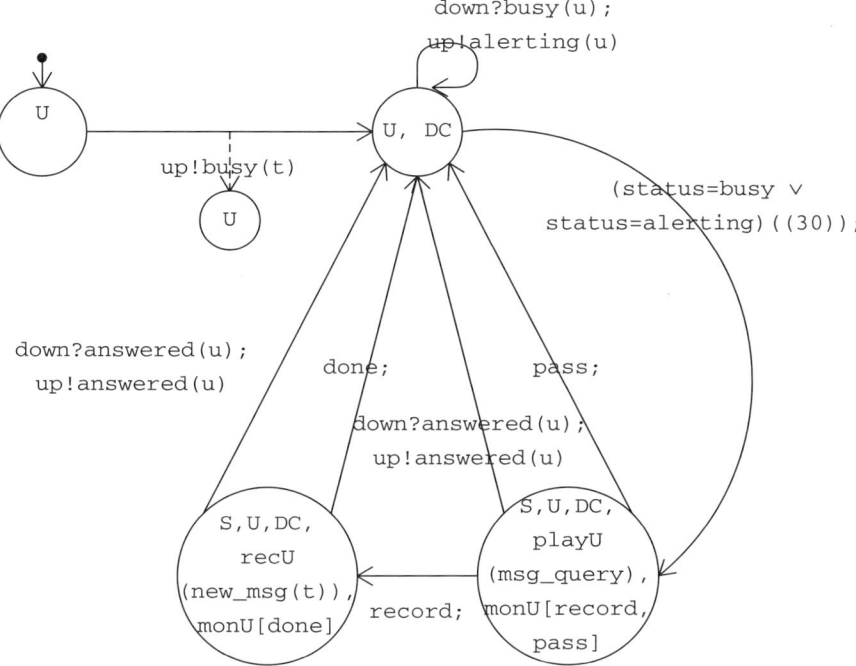

Figure 17.11. A program for Inbound Messaging.

The IM program illustrates an important point about DFC feature boxes. Within each internal call, a target line interface would send upstream exactly one of these sequences: <busy>, <alerting>, or <alerting,answered>. Yet a DFC internal call can in fact experience *any sequence whatsoever* of public status signals traveling upstream. The reason is that the sequence observable within an internal call is produced by the effects of many feature and interface boxes downstream; the richer the feature set, the more possible sequences.

For this reason, feature boxes must not be programmed to expect a rigid, fixed-length sequence of public status signals. Rather, they must be programmed cyclically, as IM is.

This also helps explain why the many implicit signals of the S annotation pass for transparent behavior, and need not be analyzed for feature interactions. S behavior produces a temporary answered state, in which other features do not act because they expect people to be talking, and then restores the state of the usage to what it would have been without the S state.

17.5.3 Analysis of the feature set

It is best to begin analysis with an empty precedence relation, and to ignore drowning (which is always bad). This will give us a complete picture of the potentially positive interactions, so that none of them will be missed. Applying the first four interaction definitions to our feature set, and assuming an empty precedence relation, we get:

Interaction			Judgment	Prevention
SCF	cancels	BUCP	+	
SCF	cancels	OM	−	OM < SCF
SCF	cancels	IM	−	IM < SCF
BUCP	cancels	SCF	−	SCF < BUCP
BUCP	cancels	OM	−	OM < BUCP
BUCP	cancels	IM	−	OM < BUCP
SCF	retargets	IM	+	
BUCP	spoofs alerting to	IM	+	
BUCP	hides alerting from	IM	−	IM < BUCP

The table also includes judgments of these feature interactions, based on the following reasoning:

- It is good for SCF to cancel BUCP, because forwarding obviates the need for BUCP.

- It is bad for SCF to cancel OM, because if there is an outbound message for the caller, he should hear it before the call is forwarded.

- It is bad for SCF to cancel IM, because IM might be useful in recording a message if the forwarded-to target does not answer.

- All cancellations by BUCP are undesirable, because a situation in which BUCP blocks an incoming call is likely to be a situation in which SCF, OM, or IM should cover the call instead.

- It is good for SCF to retarget IM, because it enables IM to cover a busy or no-answer condition even from the forwarded-to target.

- It is good for BUCP to spoof alerting to IM, and bad for BUCP to hide alerting from IM, because alerting triggers IM in situations where a call is blocked by BUCP.

The table also includes precedences by which the bad interactions can be prevented. The partial order {IM,OM} < SCF < BUCP preserves all the good ones and prevents all the bad ones. Now, applying the definition of drowning to our feature set, and using this derived precedence relation, we get:

Interaction			Judgment	Prevention
OM	drowns	IM	−	IM < OM
OM	drowns	BUCP	−	
IM	drowns	OM	−	OM < IM
IM	drowns	BUCP	−	

Additional precedence constraints can only prevent one of these interactions! However, if we choose IM < OM, then the remaining three diagnoses can be shown to be false positives—there is no trace in which both features are in a `playU` state longer than it takes for IM to respond to a signal it receives. In [11] this was proven by detailed analysis of box behavior. It could probably be established more easily by model checking, since the partial order leaves us with only two configurations to check.

We now have a derived total order on the features that allows all the good feature interactions and prevents all the bad ones. It was not necessary to change any features. *An exercise for the reader:* think of a scenario in which at least three of the features help handle the same incoming customer call.

17.6 Evaluation of the method

At least for this case study, DFC and the modest method for feature engineering are a great success. For the most part features co-exist peacefully and function independently, which is not considered to be interacting behavior. Diagnosis of interactions is very efficient, relying only on properties of individual feature programs rather than on properties of feature compositions. All the known interactions among the features can be detected automatically. The diagnosed interactions are relatively few and meaningful, and easily judged to be good or bad. The desired result is achieved without any loss of modularity.

At the same time, there are many limitations and reasons for caution. The scope of the modest method is very narrow compared to the full range of telecommunication services. Prolonged study of feature properties was required to find a successful combination of box-programming conventions and feature-interaction definitions. On the one hand, such study produces valuable domain knowledge; on the other hand, it is difficult and also susceptible to being overly biased by the particular features being studied.

Although this case study does not suffer from them, inconsistencies (cycles) in the derived precedence relation are a real problem. However, the problem has many potential solutions. For example, in the case study both SCF and OM have two modes of operation with different interaction characteristics. If a cycle had been derived, very likely it could have been broken by splitting one of these features into two features, one supporting each mode of operation.

Future work is required to extend the scope of the method in general, and to address certain weaknesses in particular. These weaknesses give rise to the following questions:

- How can completeness of detection be ensured? Could there be three-way feature interactions in linear usages?[6]

---

[6] Clearly branching usages can have three- or even many-way interactions.

- Is it worthwhile to distinguish between desirable interactions that are merely *allowed* and those that are *required* under certain circumstances? If so, how are the requirements enforced?

- How can the judgment and adjustment steps be supported by tools? How can false positives produced by the initial interaction analysis be discovered more easily?

To answer these questions, it will be necessary to understand each individual feature as a composition of multiple behavioral aspects.

17.7 Acknowledgments

Michael Jackson helped design the feature set of the case study; Manfred Broy made many helpful comments.

References

[1] Martín Abadi and Leslie Lamport. Composing specifications. *ACM Transactions on Programming Languages and Systems* XV(1):73–132, January 1993.

[2] L. G. Bouma and H. Velthuijsen, editors. *Feature Interactions in Telecommunications Systems.* IOS Press, Amsterdam, 1994.

[3] M. Calder and E. Magill, editors, *Feature Interactions in Telecommunications and Software Systems VI.*, IOS Press, Amsterdam, 2000.

[4] K. E. Cheng and T. Ohta, editors, *Feature Interactions in Telecommunications Systems III.*, IOS Press, Amsterdam, 1995.

[5] P. Dini, R. Boutaba, and L. Logrippo, editors. *Feature Interactions in Telecommunication Networks IV.* IOS Press, Amsterdam, 1997.

[6] Gerard J. Holzmann. Design and validation of protocols: A tutorial. *Computer Networks and ISDN Systems* XXV:981–1017, 1993.

[7] Michael Jackson and Pamela Zave. Distributed feature composition: A virtual architecture for telecommunications services. *IEEE Transactions on Software Engineering* XXIV(10):831-847, October 1998.

[8] K. Kimbler and L. G. Bouma, editors. *Feature Interactions in Telecommunications and Software Systems V.* IOS Press, Amsterdam, 1998.

[9] Hugo Velthuijsen. Issues of non-monotonicity in feature-interaction detection. In [4], pages 31–42.

[10] Pamela Zave. Formal description of telecommunication services in Promela and Z. In Manfred Broy and Ralf Steinbrüggen, editors, *Calculational System Design (Proceedings of the Nineteenth International NATO Summer School),* pages 395–420. IOS Press, Amsterdam, 1999.

[11] Pamela Zave. Systematic design of call-coverage features. AT&T Laboratories Technical Memorandum, November 1999.

[12] Pamela Zave and Michael Jackson. DFC modifications I (Version 2): Routing extensions. AT&T Laboratories Technical Memorandum, January 2000.

[13] Pamela Zave and Michael Jackson. DFC modifications II: Protocol extensions. AT&T Laboratories Technical Memorandum, November 1999.

Section H

Programming circuits

18 High-level circuit design   385
   Eric C. R. Hehner, Theodore S. Norvell and Richard Paige

The fundamental principle that a general-purpose computer can be customised to perform a specific task using a program lies at the heart of software design. Experience has shown that programmers work more quickly and effectively using 'high-level' languages that allow them to structure their code algorithmically without the need to deal directly with the complications of the 'machine level'. The task of converting the high level to the machine level is better and more accurately performed by automatic compilation. The result is that code is more readable and adaptable.

Despite the fact that the goals of a hardware designer are essentially the same as those of the software designer — to make a piece of circuitry compute a function — the development of customised hardware-design methods has followed a very different route. This is because, in hardware design, the machine is no longer static, but rather is built to perform a specific task; narurally the designer focusses on the connectivity of circuits rather than on the more abstract algorithmic components — the starting point for the software designer. As a result hardware-design languages tend to be very complicated and difficult to structure.

This paper sets out how the successes of high-level languages can be applied to hardware design as well. With this technique, as for software, code is generated more quickly and accurately, leaving the hardware compiler to provide the link between the code and the circuitry. Moreover the performance of the end product can be compared favourably to that of hardware designed using traditional methods.

18

High-level circuit design

Eric C.R. Hehner, Theodore S. Norvell, Richard F. Paige

Dedication
This paper is dedicated to the memory of Jan van de Snepscheut, 1953-1994.

Abstract
We present two new ways to implement ordinary programs with logic gates. One, like imperative programs, has an associated memory to store state; the other, like functional programs, passes the state from one component to the next. Application-specific circuit design can be done more effectively by using a standard programming language to describe the function that a circuit is intended to perform, rather than by describing a circuit that is intended to perform that function. The resulting circuits are produced automatically; they behave according to the programs, and have the same structure as the programs. For timing, we use local delays, rather than a global clock or local handshaking. We give a formal semantics for both programs and circuits in order to prove our circuits correct. By simulation, we also demonstrate that the circuits perform favorably compared to others.

18.1 Introduction

The design methods for digital circuits that are commonly found in current textbooks resemble the low-level machine-language programming methods of forty years ago. Manually selecting individual logic gates in a circuit is something like selecting individual machine instructions in a program. These methods may have been adequate for small circuit design when they were introduced, and they may still be adequate for large circuits that are simply repetitions of a small circuit (such as a memory), but they are not adequate for application-specific circuits that perform complicated custom algorithms.

The usual alternative to building application-specific circuits is to use a general-purpose processor, and customize it for an application by writing a program. That we can do so was a fundamental insight, due to Turing, upon which computer science is based. But for some applications, particularly where speed of execution or security is important, a custom-built circuit has some advantages over the usual processor-and-software combination. The speed is improved by the absence of the "machine-language" layer of circuitry with its "fetch-execute" cycle of interpretation, and by the ease with which we can introduce parallelism. Security is improved by the impossibility of reprogramming. In addition, unless the application requires a lengthy algorithm, there are space savings compared to the combination of software and processor.

The VHDL [8] and Verilog [14] languages are presently being used by industry. These languages allow circuit designers to describe circuits more conveniently. There are interactive synthesis tools to aid in the construction of circuits from subsets of these languages. The circuits are then "verified" by simulation.

We do not present a new language for circuit design. Instead, we advocate using a standard programming language (for example, C), not to describe circuits, but to describe algorithms. The resulting circuits are produced automatically; they behave according to the programs, and have the same structure as the programs. For timing we use local delays, rather than a global clock (synchronous) or local handshaking (asynchronous). We give a formal semantics for both programs and circuits in order to prove our circuits correct, using a theory presented in [5]. By simulation, we also demonstrate that the circuits perform favorably compared to others.

There are other high-level circuit design techniques being developed and reported in the literature. Early work includes [12], [13], and [4]. In [3, 7], a circuit is specified in a subset of CSP as a set of communicating processes, and is transformed into circuits via an intermediate mapping to production rules. A similar approach (and a similar circuit design language) is used in [1, 2], except that specifications are mapped into connections of small components for which standard transistor implementations exist. In [15] circuits are modeled as networks of finite state machines, and their formalism is used to assist in proving the correctness of their compiled circuits. The work of [6, 10] is most similar to ours, but their designs have a global clock; ours do not.

The success of high-level circuit design will probably be judged the same way high-level programming was judged: on whether the circuits produced are competitive with low-level designs, and on whether we are able to design complex circuits more easily and more reliably. The outcome will probably be the same for circuits as for programming.

This paper is intended to be self-contained, showing how circuits are built from the gate level up. Consequently we must ask for the patience of knowledgeable readers whenever we cover familiar ground. Sometimes we cover familiar ground in an unfamiliar way.

18.2 Diagrams

Circuits are often expressed as diagrams constructed from "and", "or", and "not" gates. We can give a diagram to any other operator by the expedient method of placing its symbol in a box. Here is the if then else (also called multiplexer). On the right we show an implementation using negation, conjunction, and disjunction.

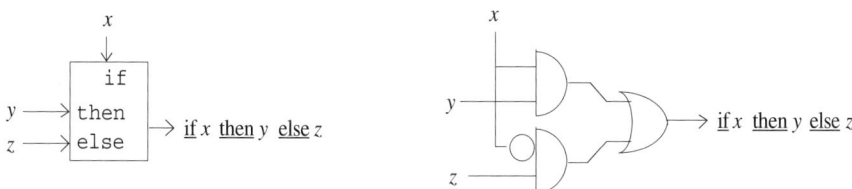

By this pair of diagrams, we do not intend to suggest that if then else is best implemented as shown, but only to show one way it can be implemented, and to show how we obtained our performance estimates by counting gate delays.

It is also convenient to define the switch (or demultiplexer), and to give it a diagram.

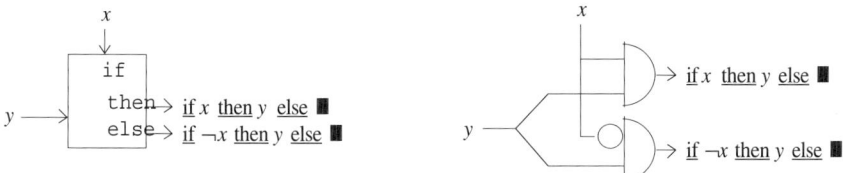

The symbol ■ is for "low voltage" or "ground" or "false". We use ■ for "high voltage" or "power" or "true".

The if then else and switch also come in a more general form in which the selection is made by an integer rather than a boolean. For a 2-bit integer selection the diagrams are

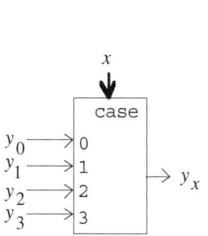
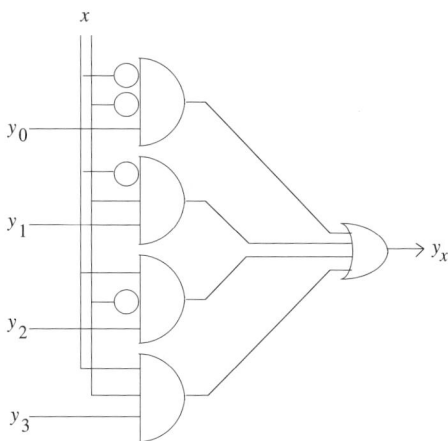

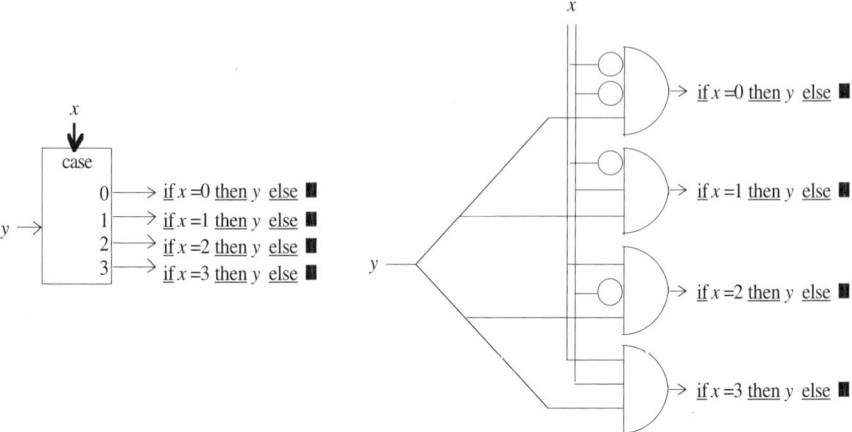

A thin line indicates a single wire, and a thick line indicates any number of wires. Crossing wires are not connected.

Circuit diagrams are helpful when planning the layout of a circuit, but for designing the logic we prefer to use algebraic notation for its ease of manipulation. We give both diagrams and algebraic descriptions, but we do not intend the diagrams to indicate layout.

18.3 Time

Ideally, we might suppose that circuit components act instantly, with no gate delays, and are represented accurately by timeless boolean expressions. Realistically, there are gate delays, and sometimes there are transient signals (glitches) while a circuit settles into a stable state. We must introduce a timing discipline to ensure that we do not require, and are not affected by, a result before it is ready. We can consider time to be continuous or discrete; nothing in this paper will depend on that choice.

To talk about time, we find it convenient to introduce the operator ■ , pronounced "delay" or "previous". It gives the value that its operand had previously, a short time ago. Its diagram looks like this:

$$■x \longleftarrow \triangleleft \longleftarrow x$$

Whenever we need to say formally what constraints a delay time must satisfy, we write it to the left of the delay operator, and inside its circuit graphic:

$$\delta\,■x \longleftarrow \triangleleft\!\delta \longleftarrow x$$

Delay time is dependent on context and technology, it is usually determined by experiment, and can be known only approximately, say with an upper and lower bound. Sometimes we want the delay to be as short as possible; when that is the case, signal propagation time through the wire and surrounding gates is sufficient, and no extra circuitry is required. When more delay is needed, it can be implemented as an even number of negations, or by a suitable choice of layout; these implementations are not subject to glitches, and so do not raise again the problem they are solving. In addition to its logical use, the delay sometimes has the electrical job of reshaping a pulse, both height and width, to compensate for degradation. But that is a level of detail below our concern in this paper.

As a formal requirement, for proof of correctness, we need to define the output of a delay to be initially ■ for the delay time, and thereafter it is the same as the input but delayed. This initial ■ is the only initialization in our circuits; we don't consider initialization circuitry in this paper.

18.4 Flip-flops

A flip-flop has inputs C (clock) and D (data), and output Q (the letter Q is like the letter O for output, but distinguishable from the digit 0). A flip-flop behaves as follows:

If the clock is ■ , then the output is the data input, otherwise the output remains as it was.

This behavior can be formalized directly as follows.

<u>if</u> C=■ <u>then</u> Q=D <u>else</u> Q=■Q

We can simplify this boolean expression in two ways. Equating to ■ is always superfluous, just as adding zero or mutiplying by one are superfluous. And we can factor out the " Q= ", obtaining

Q = <u>if</u> C <u>then</u> D <u>else</u> ■ Q

which we might well have written in the first place. We now have a definitional equation, which is the form suitable for automatic circuit fabrication. An equation is "definitional" if one side is the output. Here are the black box and implementation diagrams.

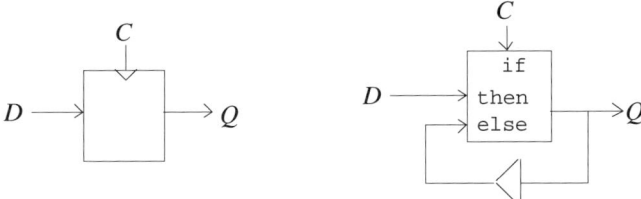

For the circuit to operate correctly, the delay must be small enough that no change to D occurs during the delay preceding the fall of the clock. For the circuit to be as fast as possible, the delay must be as small as possible. There will be a constraint on the minimum delay for electrical reasons, which we do not consider here. With no delay, this circuit is logically equivalent to a standard textbook flip-flop.

We generalize the flip-flop to allow any number of pairs of clock and data inputs. If exactly one of the clock lines is ■ , then the output is the corresponding data input; if none of the clocks are ■ , then the output remains as it was. Let the clock lines be C_0, C_1, ... and let the corresponding data lines be D_0, D_1, ... Then the formal specification is

$(\exists_1 i \cdot C_i) \Rightarrow Q = (\exists i \cdot C_i \wedge D_i)$

$(\neg \exists i \cdot C_i) \Rightarrow Q = \blacksquare Q$

Actually, the formal specification is the conjunction of the two formulas. As is customary in mathematics, we sometimes write a list of boolean expressions when we mean their conjunction. The specification is nondeterministic, or in circuit terminology, it has "don't cares", when more than one clock input is ■ (because we don't intend to make more than one clock input ■ at the same time). We can strengthen the specification if we wish (resolving nondeterminism, deciding "don't cares") because all behavior satisfying a stronger specification will also satisfy the original specification. The circuit designer's job is to find an equivalent or stronger specification in the form of a definitional equation. Here's one:

$Q = ((\exists i \cdot C_i \wedge D_i) \vee (\neg \exists i \cdot C_i) \wedge \blacksquare Q)$

We will find it convenient later to provide a clock output C that is ■ when any of the clock inputs are ■ .

$C = \exists i \cdot C_i$

Here are the more general flip-flop diagrams.

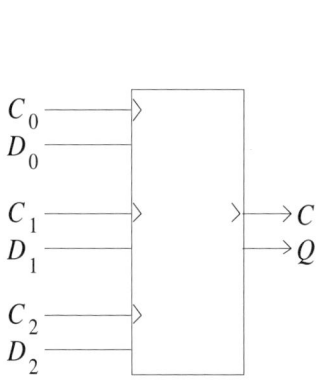
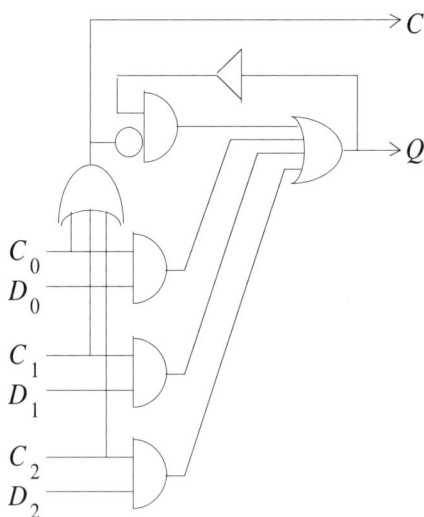

18.5 Edge-triggering

The flip-flops we have just described remain sensitive to the data input as long as the clock is ■ . Sometimes we want a flip-flop that is sensitive to its data input only at the rising or falling edge of the clock input. For example, a falling-edge-triggered flip-flop can be defined as

$Q = \text{if } \neg C \wedge \gamma \blacksquare C \text{ then } \blacksquare D \text{ else } \blacksquare Q$
$\gamma \geq$ (edge time) + (negation delay)

The expression $\neg C \wedge \blacksquare C$ says that the clock is down but was just previously up, so it is a falling edge. The C-delay γ should be just large enough to allow C to fall and to allow that falling edge to be negated. The D-delay determines what data is latched; for example, we might want the data from before the falling edge, or at its start, or at its end (this delay could be omitted). As always, the Q-delay should be as small as possible. The diagrams (note the down-arrow in the black-box diagram to indicate falling-edge-triggering):

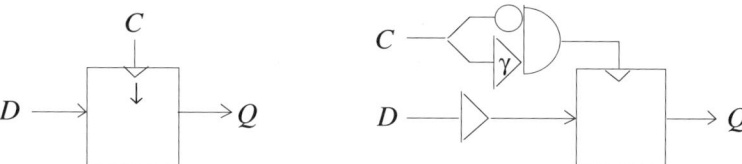

A logically equivalent, slightly larger, slightly faster circuit is obtained from

$Q = \neg C \wedge \blacksquare C \wedge \blacksquare D \vee \neg \blacksquare C \wedge \blacksquare Q \vee C \wedge \blacksquare Q$

Aside The standard way to obtain an edge-triggered flip-flop is with a master-slave pair of flip-flops. For example, we obtain a falling-edge-triggered flip-flop as follows (since we use a triangle for delay, we use just a circle for negation):

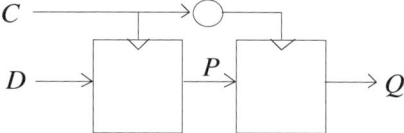

Algebraically, this is

$P = \text{if } C \text{ then } D \text{ else } \blacksquare P$
$Q = \text{if } \neg C \text{ then } P \text{ else } \blacksquare Q$

We now prove that this master-slave pair is equivalent to our single flip-flop. Apply a delay to the P equation and to the Q equation to obtain

$\blacksquare P = \text{if } \blacksquare C \text{ then } \blacksquare D \text{ else } \blacksquare \blacksquare P$
$\blacksquare Q = \text{if } \neg \blacksquare C \text{ then } \blacksquare P \text{ else } \blacksquare \blacksquare Q$

From the P, Q, and $\blacksquare P$ equations we find

$\neg C \wedge \blacksquare C \;\Rightarrow\; P = \blacksquare P \wedge Q = P \wedge \blacksquare P = \blacksquare D$

and so, by transitivity,

(*) $\neg C \wedge \blacksquare C \;\Rightarrow\; Q = \blacksquare D$

From the P, Q, and $\blacksquare Q$ equations we find

$\neg C \wedge \neg \blacksquare C \;\Rightarrow\; P = \blacksquare P \wedge Q = P \wedge \blacksquare Q = \blacksquare P$

and so, by transitivity,

$$\neg C \wedge \neg \triangleleft C \;\Rightarrow\; Q = \triangleleft Q$$
Also, from the Q equation alone,
$$C \;\Rightarrow\; Q = \triangleleft Q$$
Putting these last two implications together we find
$$\neg C \wedge \neg \triangleleft C \;\vee\; C \;\Rightarrow\; Q = \triangleleft Q$$
The antecedent can be rewritten
$$(**) \;\neg(\neg C \wedge \triangleleft C) \;\Rightarrow\; Q = \triangleleft Q$$
Putting (*) and (**) together we have
$$\underline{\text{if}}\; \neg C \wedge \triangleleft C \;\underline{\text{then}}\; Q = \triangleleft D \;\underline{\text{else}}\; Q = \triangleleft Q$$
which can be rewritten
$$Q \;=\; \underline{\text{if}}\; \neg C \wedge \triangleleft C \;\underline{\text{then}}\; \triangleleft D \;\underline{\text{else}}\; \triangleleft Q$$
So the master-slave combination is logically equivalent, but more complicated.
End of Aside

Edge-triggering is applicable to more than just flip-flops. For example, to create a switch (demultiplexer) that triggers its output on the rising edge of the y input, and then holds its output for the duration of τ on y (ignoring fluctuations on x),
$$t \;=\; \underline{\text{if}}\; y \wedge \neg \triangleleft y \;\underline{\text{then}}\; x \;\underline{\text{else}}\; \underline{\text{if}}\; y \;\underline{\text{then}}\; \triangleleft t \;\underline{\text{else}}\; \bot$$
$$e \;=\; \underline{\text{if}}\; y \wedge \neg \triangleleft y \;\underline{\text{then}}\; \neg x \;\underline{\text{else}}\; \underline{\text{if}}\; y \;\underline{\text{then}}\; \triangleleft e \;\underline{\text{else}}\; \bot$$
These equations can be simplified, and delay times can be added, to get
$$t \;=\; y \wedge \underline{\text{if}}\; \psi \triangleleft y \;\underline{\text{then}}\; \tau \triangleleft t \;\underline{\text{else}}\; x$$
$$e \;=\; y \wedge \underline{\text{if}}\; \psi \triangleleft y \;\underline{\text{then}}\; \tau \triangleleft e \;\underline{\text{else}}\; \neg x$$
$$\psi > (\text{edge time}) \;\wedge\; \tau < \psi$$
By induction over significant instants of time (induction hypothesis: it's true up to some time; induction step: it's still true after the next time that something changes), we can prove
$$t = (\neg e \wedge y) \qquad\qquad e = (\neg t \wedge y)$$
and further simplify our circuit. The diagrams (note the up-arrow in the black-box diagram to indicate rising-edge-triggering):

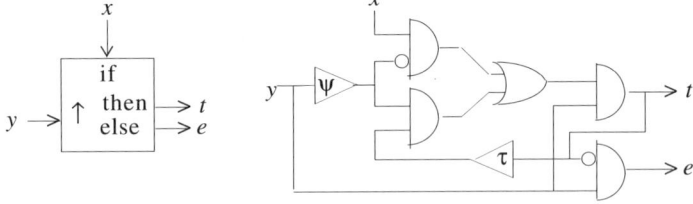

18.6 Memory

We can aggregate flip-flops into a larger amount of memory called a "word", suitable for storing an **int** or **real** value. We use the same diagram as for a flip-flop but with a thick D input and Q output to indicate many data lines.

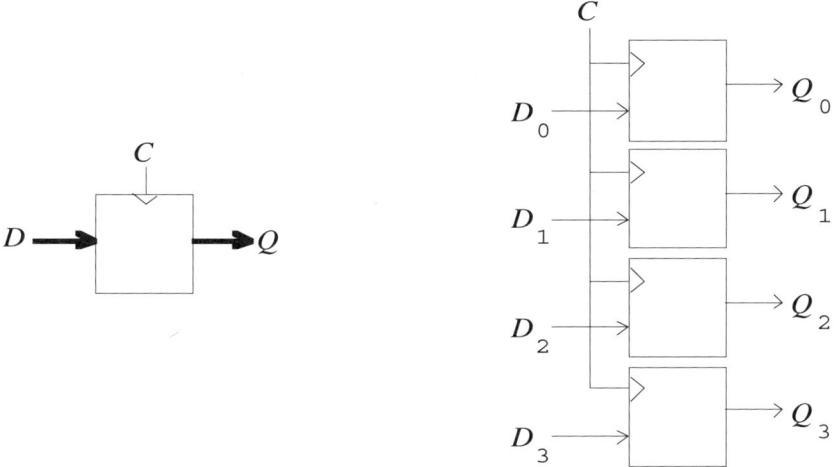

All bits in the word are written at the same time, and read at the same time. Algebraically we describe the word by

$\forall i \cdot Q_i = \text{if } C \text{ then } D_i \text{ else } \blacksquare\, Q_i$

More conveniently, we write

$Q = \text{if } C \text{ then } D \text{ else } \blacksquare\, Q$

as before, even when Q and D are several bits each.

A RAM (random access memory) is an independent way to aggregate flip-flops into a larger amount of memory. One bit is written at a time, and one bit is read at a time. A bit to be written is selected by the writing address W, and a bit to be read is selected by the reading address R.

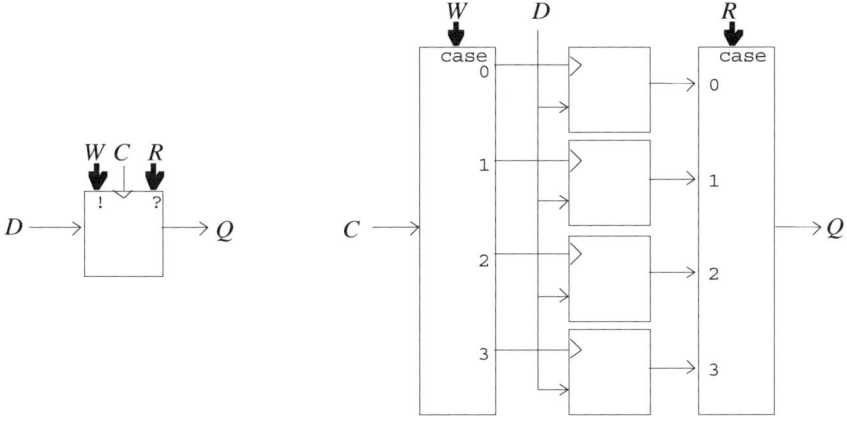

Algebraically,
$Q = M[R]$
$\forall i \cdot M[i] = \underline{\text{if }} C \wedge i{=}W \underline{\text{ then }} D \underline{\text{ else }} \blacksquare M[i]$
where $M[i]$ is bit i in the RAM.

The two ways of aggregating bits can be combined to provide a RAM of words. Here are the diagrams.

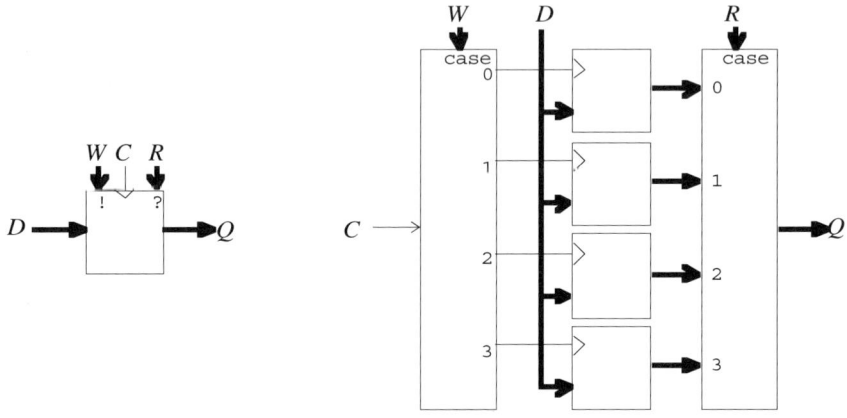

Adding an arrow in the diagram indicates that the flip-flops are edge-triggered.

18.7 Merge

A merge turns two sequences of pulses into a single sequence of pulses. (A pulse is a momentary ■). In a sense, any circuit with two inputs and one output is a kind of merge. An or-gate allows pulses on either input to pass through; an and-gate allows only simultaneous pulses to pass through.

The 1-2-merge has inputs a and b and output q. It outputs a pulse when pulses arrive on a and b in that order, or simultaneously, but not in the other order. To design a 1-2-merge, we introduce an internal wire A with the meaning "a is ■ or has been ■ ".
$A = (a \vee \alpha \blacksquare A)$
$q = (A \wedge b)$
$\alpha \leq$ (pulse time)
(Recall that ■A is initially ■ .) Unfortunately this is a one-time-only circuit; if ever there is a pulse on a, it will allow all subsequent pulses on b to pass. To obtain a circuit that resets itself on the falling edge of q ready to be used repeatedly, we introduce one more internal wire r that is ■ except at the falling edge of q. The circuit becomes

18. High-level circuit design 391

$r = (q \vee \neg\gamma\blacksquare q)$
$A = (r \wedge (a \vee \alpha\blacksquare A))$
$q = (A \wedge b)$
$\alpha \leq$ (pulse time) $\wedge$ $\alpha \leq \gamma$

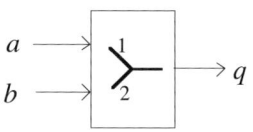
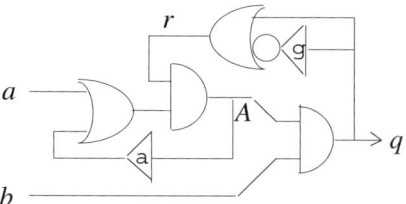

Internal wires can be left exposed, as in the above specification of 1-2-merge and the right-hand diagram, or they can be hidden as in the left-hand diagram and the following specification:

$\exists r, A \cdot \quad r = (q \vee \neg\gamma\blacksquare q)$
$\quad \wedge \quad A = (r \wedge (a \vee \alpha\blacksquare A))$
$\quad \wedge \quad q = (A \wedge b)$

If a pulse on a follows a pulse on b, there must be a delay of at least γ after the end of b before the start of a to avoid truncating the output pulse. No circuit can constrain its inputs; its context of use must constrain its inputs, so a constraint is expressed formally as an antecedent rather than a conjunct. The circuit specification is therefore

$\neg(a \wedge \neg\gamma\blacksquare a \wedge b)$
$\Rightarrow \exists r, A \cdot r = (q \vee \neg\gamma\blacksquare q) \wedge A = (r \wedge (a \vee \alpha\blacksquare A)) \wedge q = (A \wedge b)$

A merge that outputs a pulse when the second of the two input pulses arrives, regardless of their order, and resets itself for reuse, is as follows. The inputs are a and b and the output is q. Internal wire A means " a is $\blacksquare$ or has been $\blacksquare$ "; internal wire B means " b is $\blacksquare$ or has been $\blacksquare$ "; internal wire r is $\blacksquare$ except at the falling edge of q. The circuit is

$r = (q \vee \neg\gamma\blacksquare q)$
$A = (r \wedge (a \vee \alpha\blacksquare A))$
$B = (r \wedge (b \vee \beta\blacksquare B))$
$q = (A \wedge B \wedge (a \vee b))$
$\alpha \leq$ (pulse time) $\wedge$ $\alpha \leq \gamma$ $\wedge$ $\beta \leq$ (pulse time) $\wedge$ $\beta \leq \gamma$

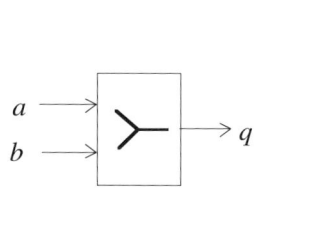
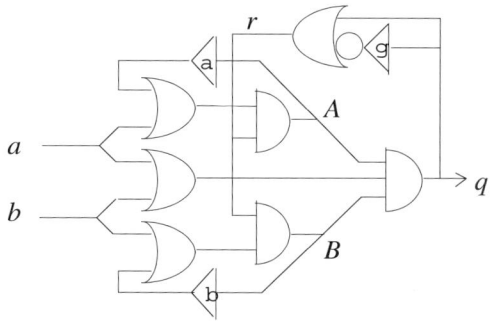

18.8 Imperative circuits

The first of our two translations from programs to circuits produces "imperative" circuits (as in "imperative programming"). An imperative circuit has two components, an imperative control I, and a memory M, connected like this.

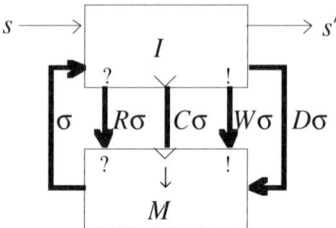

The memory consists of a word for each global variable and a RAM for each global array in the program. (We present local variables later. By making variables as local as possible, we minimize the need for the global memory.) Suppose the variables are x and y, and the arrays are A and B. Then there are four clock wires, called Cx, Cy, CA, and CB, and collectively called $C\sigma$. With one clock wire for each variable and each array, the variables and arrays can be independently and asynchronously changed. The data inputs are Dx, Dy, DA, and DB, collectively called $D\sigma$. The address wires are WA, WB, RA, and RB, collectively called $W\sigma$ and $R\sigma$. The memory outputs are x, y, $A[RA]$ and $B[RB]$, collectively called σ, the state of memory. Altogether, memory is

M = (x = (if $\neg Cx \wedge$ ■Cx then ■Dx else ■x)
$\wedge$ y = (if $\neg Cy \wedge$ ■Cy then ■Dy else ■y)
$\wedge$ ($\forall i \cdot A[i]$ = if $\neg CA \wedge$ ■$CA \wedge i=WA$ then ■DA else ■$A[i]$)
$\wedge$ ($\forall i \cdot B[i]$ = if $\neg CB \wedge$ ■$CB \wedge i=WB$ then ■DB else ■$B[i]$))

We mention again that we are depicting logic, not layout; the best place for a bit of memory may be with a part of the control that uses it.

The state is input to the control, along with an initiator wire s. A pulse on s starts the computation. As the computation progresses, the control changes the state of memory, thus providing itself with further input. To change the value of variable x in memory, the control must send a pulse on clock wire Cx and the desired new value on wire Dx. If the computation is finite, then when it is complete, the control indicates termination by a pulse on the completion wire s'. It is the responsibility of the context to ensure that the control is not restarted before it has completed an execution.

A program is sometimes composed of smaller programs. (In other terminology, a statement is sometimes composed of smaller statements; we do not distinguish between "program" and "statement".) When a program is composed of parts, the control will be composed of the controls for the parts. To make the composition easy, we require of each part that its output Dx be ■ at any instant when it is not changing variable x. Then we can disjoin the Dx wires on their way to memory. Other variables and arrays are similar. Here is the diagram:

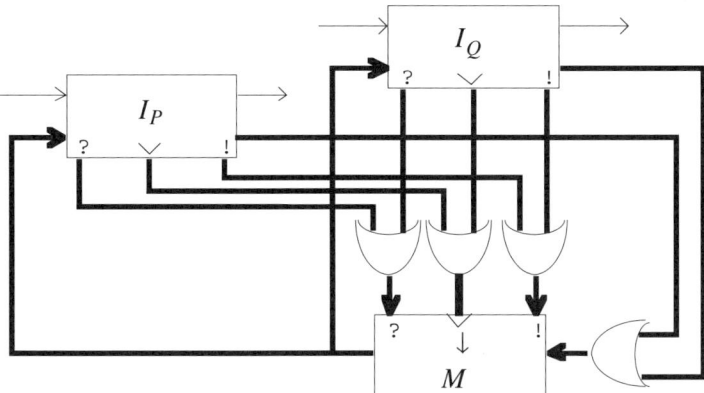

Each disjunction is really many disjunctions, one for each bit in its operands.

It is not our intention to present a new programming language for circuit design; we advocate using a standard programming language. We next describe the control for a sampling of programming constructs from typical imperative languages.

Construct: empty

We begin with the simplest program: **ok** (sometimes called **skip**). It is the "empty" program, whose execution does nothing, taking no time. Program **ok** yields the control
$$s'=s \land \neg R\sigma \land \neg C\sigma \land \neg W\sigma \land \neg D\sigma$$
Its diagram is

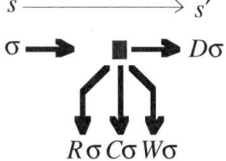

We have shown all its inputs and outputs. But since the σ input is not connected to anything, there is no point in bringing those wires from memory. And since the $R\sigma$, $C\sigma$, $W\sigma$, and $D\sigma$ outputs are ■ , there is no point in taking them into a disjunction. So the circuit reduces to nothing, which is appropriate for a circuit that does nothing.

Construct: delay

The next simplest program is **tick** , which also does nothing, but takes time δ to do it.
$$s'=\delta\blacksquare s \land \neg R\sigma \land \neg C\sigma \land \neg W\sigma \land \neg D\sigma$$

Constraints on δ must be stated with each use of **tick** . Leaving out the nonexistent wires, we have this picture:

$$s \longrightarrow \boxed{\delta} \longrightarrow s'$$

Construct: assignment

A variable assignment program $x := e$ yields the control
$s' = \tau \blacksquare \delta \blacksquare s \ \wedge \ Cx = \delta \blacksquare s \ \wedge \ Dx = (\delta \blacksquare s \wedge e$
$\neg R\sigma \ \wedge \ \neg C\rho \ \wedge \ \neg W\sigma \ \wedge \ \neg D\rho$
$\delta \geq (e \text{ time}) \ \wedge \ \tau \geq (s \text{ pulse time}) \geq (\text{memory latch time})$
where ρ is the state of memory except for x. Its diagram is

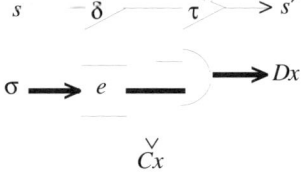

Box e evaluates the data expression in the assignment. We assume for now that adders and other circuits to perform numerical operations are available; when we have finished presenting high-level circuit design, we will have the means to design the circuits to perform integer and floating-point operations by writing programs that use only boolean variables and arrays with a restricted form of indexing. Adders and other arithmetic circuits may be duplicated at each use for maximum speed, or shared among several uses (by means of the function call circuitry which we present later), at the programmer's discretion. The input to e is shown as the entire state of memory, but in practice it is just the part of memory that e depends on.

When the expression e is a constant, there is a further simplification. For example, the assignment $x := 5$ results in the circuit

$$s \longrightarrow \boxed{\tau} \longrightarrow s'$$
$\longrightarrow$ bit 2 of Dx
$\longrightarrow$ bit 0 of Dx
$\vee$
Cx

since the binary representation of 5 , which is ...0000101 , has 1s at bit positions 0 and 2.

Expression e may depend on an array element; if so, the reading address for that array element must be output from the expression circuit, conjoined with s , and routed to memory (instead of ■ as shown in the diagram). There may be references to elements of several arrays, but for now, assume there is at most one array element reference per array in e ; later, the **result** expression will provide a way to allow an arbitrary number of array element references. We are also assuming that evaluation of expression e takes a uniform, known amount of time, and the δ delay must exceed that time; later, with the **result** expression we will remove that assumption.

An array element assignment program $A[i] := e$ yields the control
$s' = \tau \blacksquare \delta \blacksquare s$
$CA = \delta \blacksquare s \land DA = (\delta \blacksquare s \land e) \land WA = (\delta \blacksquare s \land i)$
$\neg R\sigma \land \neg C\rho \land \neg W\rho \land \neg D\rho$
$\delta \geq (e \text{ time}) \land \delta \geq (i \text{ time}) \land \tau \geq (s \text{ pulse time}) \geq (\text{memory latch time})$
where ρ is the state of memory except for A. Its diagram is

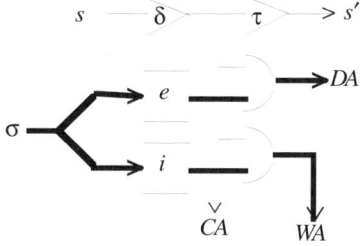

Construct: sequential composition

To implement sequential composition $P;Q$ we suppose that we already have the controls I_P and I_Q for programs P and Q. To avoid name clashes we systematically rename the inputs and outputs of I_P by adding the subscript P, and similarly for I_Q. Then the control for $P;Q$ is
$I_P \land I_Q$
$s = s_P \land s'_P = s_Q \land s'_Q = s'$
$\sigma_P = \sigma_Q = \sigma$
$R\sigma = (R\sigma_P \lor R\sigma_Q) \land C\sigma = (C\sigma_P \lor C\sigma_Q) \land W\sigma = (W\sigma_P \lor W\sigma_Q) \land D\sigma = (D\sigma_P \lor D\sigma_Q)$
Diagrammatically, ignoring the connections between the controls and memory, we have

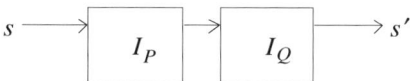

Construct: parallel composition

To implement parallel composition $P \| Q$ we need to start both programs (operands of $\|$ are often called "processes"), and then merge the completion pulses. We suppose that we already have the controls I_P and I_Q for programs P and Q. To avoid name clashes we systematically rename the inputs and outputs of I_P by adding the subscript P, and similarly for I_Q. Then the control for $P \| Q$ is
$I_P \land I_Q \land merge$
$s = s_P = s_Q \land a = s'_P \land b = s'_Q \land s' = q$
$\sigma_P = \sigma_Q = \sigma$
$R\sigma = (R\sigma_P \lor R\sigma_Q) \land C\sigma = (C\sigma_P \lor C\sigma_Q) \land W\sigma = (W\sigma_P \lor W\sigma_Q) \land D\sigma = (D\sigma_P \lor D\sigma_Q)$

Diagrammatically, ignoring the connections to memory, we have

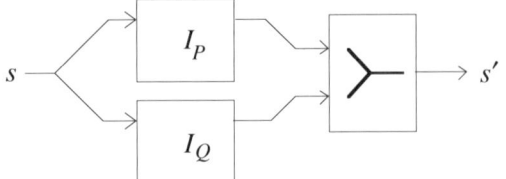

This implementation of parallel composition allows P and Q to access memory simultaneously. For the memory we have described, simultaneous access to different variables or arrays poses no problem. Even for the same variable, simultaneous reads are no problem. But simultaneously reading and writing the same variable, or two simultaneous writes to the same variable, have unpredictable results. Below we will introduce communication channels to allow programs to share information without memory contention.

Construct: conditional composition

To implement conditional composition **if** b **then** P **else** Q we suppose that we already have the controls I_P and I_Q for programs P and Q. To avoid name clashes we systematically rename the inputs and outputs of I_P by adding the subscript P, and similarly for I_Q. Then the control for **if** b **then** P **else** Q is

$I_P \wedge I_Q$
$s_P = (\delta \blacksquare s \wedge b) \wedge s_Q = (\delta \blacksquare s \wedge \neg b) \wedge s' = (s'_P \vee s'_Q)$
$\sigma_P = \sigma_Q = \sigma$
$R\sigma = (R\sigma_P \vee R\sigma_Q) \wedge C\sigma = (C\sigma_P \vee C\sigma_Q) \wedge W\sigma = (W\sigma_P \vee W\sigma_Q) \wedge D\sigma = (D\sigma_P \vee D\sigma_Q)$
$\delta \geq (b \text{ time})$

Diagrammatically, ignoring the connections between the controls and memory, we have

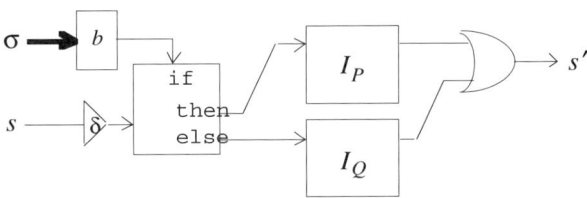

The assumptions about b are the same as those about the expression in an assignment.

A one-tailed **if** b **then** P is just **if** b **then** P **else** ok . To make a circuit for a **case** program, the **if** circuit is generalized in the obvious way.

Construct: loop

To implement **while** b **do** P we suppose that we already have the control I_P for program P. To avoid name clashes we systematically rename the inputs and outputs of I_P by adding the subscript p. The control for **while b do P** is

I_P
$s_P = (\delta \blacksquare (s \vee s'_P) \wedge b) \wedge s' = (\delta \blacksquare (s \vee s'_P) \wedge \neg b)$
$\sigma_P = \sigma \wedge R\sigma = R\sigma_P \wedge C\sigma = C\sigma_P \wedge W\sigma = W\sigma_P \wedge D\sigma = D\sigma_P$
$\delta \geq (b \text{ time})$

Diagrammatically, ignoring the connections between I_P and memory, we have

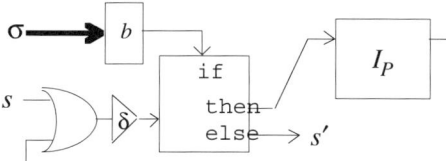

Again, the assumptions about expression b are the same as those about the expression in an assignment.

To implement **repeat P until b** we suppose that we already have the control I_P for program P. To avoid name clashes we systematically rename the inputs and outputs of I_P by adding the subscript p. Then the control for **repeat P until b** is

I_P
$s_P = (s \vee \delta \blacksquare s'_P \wedge \neg b) \wedge s' = (\delta \blacksquare s'_P \wedge b)$
$\sigma_P = \sigma \wedge R\sigma = R\sigma_P \wedge C\sigma = C\sigma_P \wedge W\sigma = W\sigma_P \wedge D\sigma = D\sigma_P$
$\delta \geq (b \text{ time})$

Diagrammatically, ignoring the connections between I_P and memory, we have

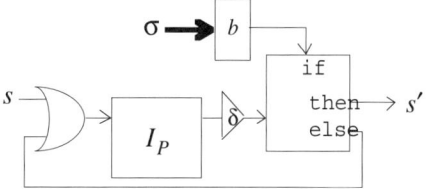

Again, the assumptions about expression b are the same as those about the expression in an assignment.

Some programming languages include a loop with intermediate exits. Unlike the previous constructs, **loop P** and **exit** cannot be implemented in isolation, but must be implemented together. Ignoring the connections between I_P and memory, the control for **loop P** is

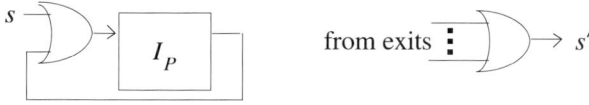

and that for an **exit** is

$s \longrightarrow$ to end of loop $\blacksquare \longrightarrow s'$

The **exit** wire to s' is shown only so that the circuit has the right inputs and outputs, but in practice it is unnecessary. To see how this works, consider the

following example.
>   **loop** $(P;$ **if** b **then exit**; $Q;$ **if** c **then exit**; $R)$

Its circuit is

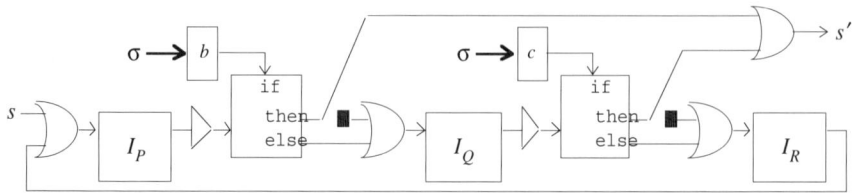

Each **exit** consists of a wire leading from a "then" to the final disjunction, and a ■ leading into a disjunction. These ■ inputs and the disjunctions they lead into can be eliminated.

Now that we have **loop** and **exit**, we could have defined **while** and **repeat** as special cases.

Construct: local variable

To declare local variable z of type T with scope P we write **var** $z: T \cdot P$. It simply adds another word of memory, which is used only within P. Formally, its control is

> $\exists z, Cz, Dz \cdot I_P$

where I_P is the control for P. Local declaration helps to locate the words of memory near the control circuitry that uses them. The diagram follows:

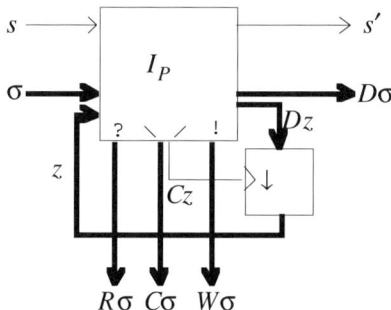

To declare local array A of size s and type T with scope P we write **var** $A[s]: T \cdot P$. The size must be a compile-time constant. It simply adds another RAM, which is used only within P. There is another way to implement array declarations that is preferable in some circumstances. We can treat the declaration of array $A[3]$ as syntactic sugar for the declaration of three variables $A0$, $A1$, $A2$. We treat the data expression $A[i]$ as sugar for **case** i **of** $A0$ | $A1$ | $A2$, and the assignment $A[i] := e$ as sugar for **case** i **of** $A0 := e$ | $A1 := e$ | $A2 := e$. This implementation allows parallel access and update of array elements.

Construct: procedure

In many programming languages, a procedure is a unit of program that can be named, so that it can be called from several places; it is a scope for local declarations; and it can have parameters. These three aspects of procedures are separable; we have already dealt with local scope, we will come to parameters in a moment, and now we consider calls and returns. We suppose that we already have the control I_P for procedure P. This circuit is started from any of the calls, and indicates its completion to all calling points.

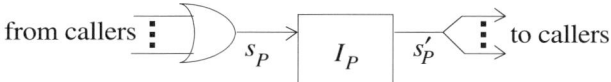

The calling points each become

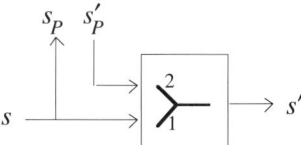

It is a programmer's responsibility (using communications to be described later) to make sure that calls from parallel programs are mutually exclusive, so that the procedure is not restarted before it completes an execution. Our implementation does not work for recursive calls in general, which are significantly harder (actually, the calls are easy but the returns are hard), but it does work for tail-recursive calls.

A parameter declaration can be treated exactly as though it were introducing a local variable instead of a parameter. Whenever a procedure P with parameter x is supplied an argument a, the resulting program $P\,a$ can be treated as though it were $(x:= a\,;\, P)$, except that x has been taken out of scope.

Construct: function

A function, in many languages, is even more of a mixture than a procedure. Its separable features are: the ability to name a data expression so that it can be used in different places; the ability to nest programs (statements) within a data expression; local scope; and parameters. The last two aspects have been dealt with, and we now consider the first two.

To associate a name with a data expression e, just put the circuit to evaluate e somewhere. Its input comes from memory, and its output goes to all uses of the name. The diagram:

Data expressions occur in various forms of program, such as assignment and **if**. We have been assuming that their evaluation time is predictable at compile-time, but to be general, we allow circuits for data expressions to have a control line (s input and s' output). The data expression P **result** e requires execution of program P in order to create the correct state for evaluation of e. Its circuit inserts the appropriate delay in the control line. The delay may depend on the initial state, varying from one evaluation to another; it is not a worst-case delay. Its diagram is

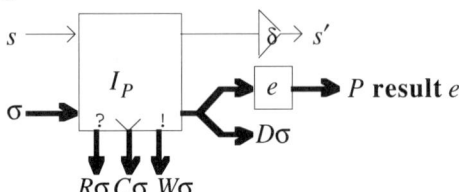

where I_P is the control for program P and $\delta \geq (e$ time). If P changes only local variables, so that there are no side-effects, then the outputs $C\sigma$, $W\sigma$, $D\sigma$ to memory are unnecessary. Expression e should be evaluated in the local scope, so the input to e should include local variables as necessary. A **result** expression is often used as the body of a function. Another use is to help us out of an earlier difficulty: we were not allowed to have references to different elements of the same array within one basic data expression. But a compiler can transform an expression like $A[i]+A[j]$ into

(**var** t: **int**· $t:= A[i]$ **result** $t+A[j]$)

and so we now lift the earlier restriction.

Construct: communication

To declare local channel c of type T with scope P we write **chan** $c: T \cdot P$. For one writing program and one reading program it is defined as follows.

(**chan** $c: T \cdot P$) = (**var** $c: T \cdot$ **var** $\sqrt{c}$: **bool**· $\sqrt{c}:=$ ■; P)

It introduces two variables, called the buffer and the probe. The buffer c (same name as the channel) holds the value being communicated, and the probe $\sqrt{c}$ (pronounced "check c") tells whether there is an unread message in the buffer. We define output of expression e and input to variable x on this channel as follows.

$c! e$ = (**while** $\sqrt{c}$ **do** tick; $c:= e$; $\sqrt{c}:=$ ■)
$c? x$ = (**while** $\neg\sqrt{c}$ **do** tick; $x:= c$; $\sqrt{c}:=$ ■)

Since we have already implemented all constructs on the right sides of these definitions, we therefore have implementations of channel declaration, input, and output. But there are two points that need attention. The **tick** delay must be longer than the control pulse (the pulse on s) so the control pulse is not lost. And the **while** must use an edge-triggered switch so the control pulse will not be truncated, split, or otherwise damaged by a change in $\sqrt{c}$ due to a parallel program. Although the buffer may also be shared by parallel programs that both read and write it, the discipline of use imposed by input and output ensures noninterference.

It may also be useful to introduce signals, which are messages without content. To declare local signal s with scope P we write **sig** $s \cdot P$. For one sending program and one receiving program it is defined as follows:

$(\mathbf{sig}\ s \cdot P)\ =\ (\mathbf{var}\ \sqrt{s}: \mathbf{bool} \cdot \sqrt{s} := \blacksquare;\ P)$

It introduces only the probe. We define sending and receiving this signal as follows.

$s!\ =\ (\mathbf{while}\ \sqrt{s}\ \mathbf{do}\ \mathbf{tick};\ \sqrt{s} := \blacksquare)$
$s?\ =\ (\mathbf{while}\ \neg\sqrt{s}\ \mathbf{do}\ \mathbf{tick};\ \sqrt{s} := \blacksquare)$

As before, the **tick** delay must be longer than the control pulse, and the **while** must use an edge-triggered switch. As examples of their use, we offer a second implementation of parallel programs. For each parallel composition $P\|Q$ we introduce a signal $endP$ and the circuit is

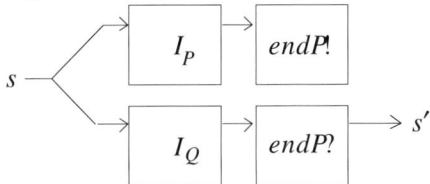

We can also use a signal to reimplement procedures. For each procedure P introduce signal $endP$ and the circuit is

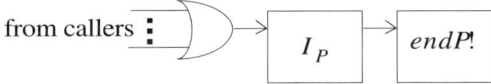

A call to P can be implemented as follows.

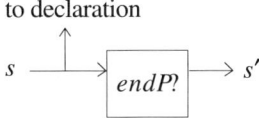

18.9 Functional circuits

The second of our two translations from programs to circuits produces "functional" circuits (as in "functional programming"). Functional circuits are not composed of a control and a memory; instead, each functional circuit computes its output σ' from its input σ without the benefit of a separate memory (although some constructs will require internal memory). There is still a start signal s to initiate the computation and a stop signal s' to indicate completion. Here's the diagram:

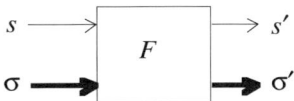

The data input σ includes all variables and array elements. To use the circuit

we must provide the desired data input σ and a pulse (momentary ■) on the start wire s , and we must hold σ constant ever after (until the circuit is restarted). The functional circuit F must provide a correct data output σ′ and a pulse on the stop wire s′ , and it must hold σ′ constant ever after (until the circuit is restarted).

Construct: empty

For program **ok** the functional circuit is trivial, as it should be.

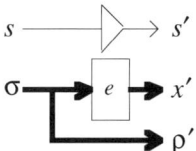

Construct: assignment

A variable assignment $x := e$ looks like this:

where ρ′ is all variables and arrays other than x' .

Array element assignment $A[i] := e$ looks like this:

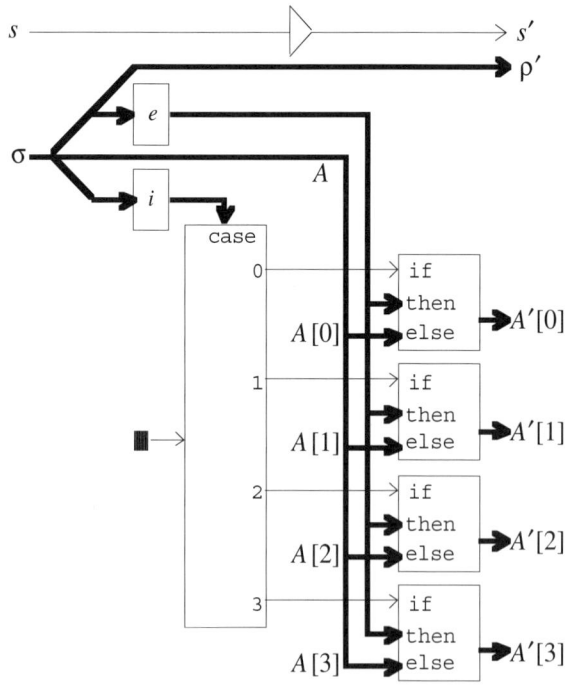

where ρ' is all variables and arrays other than A'.

Construct: sequential composition

Sequential execution is easy.

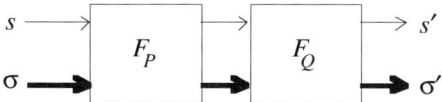

Construct: parallel composition

For parallel execution, we make the simplifying assumption that the parallel programs do not communicate via shared memory, but only via the communication constructs provided. The variables and array elements changed by one program are disjoint from those changed by a parallel program, and the changes made by one program are not seen by a parallel program.

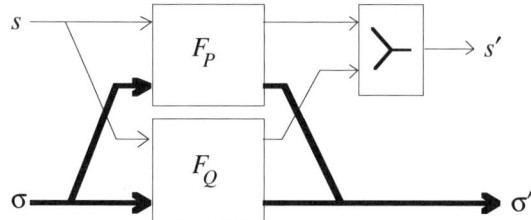

The entire input can go to both programs, but each program produces only part of the output. These outputs together form the entire output.

Construct: conditional composition

Here is the functional circuit for **if** b **then** P **else** Q.

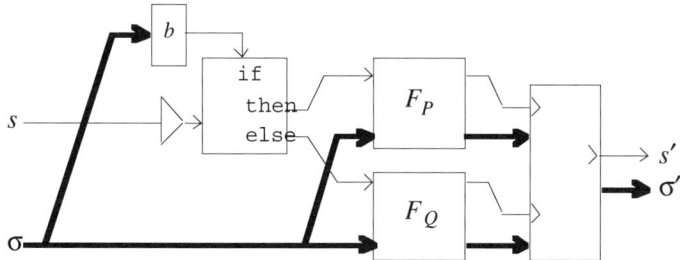

The data output could, alternatively, be selected using the b output without memory.

The **if** circuit is easily generalized to a **case** circuit.

Construct: loop

Here is the functional circuit for **loop** P with **exit**s in it:

If there is only a single exit, the exit memory is unnecessary.

Since **while** b **do** P is just **loop (if** b **then** P **else exit)** , its circuit is

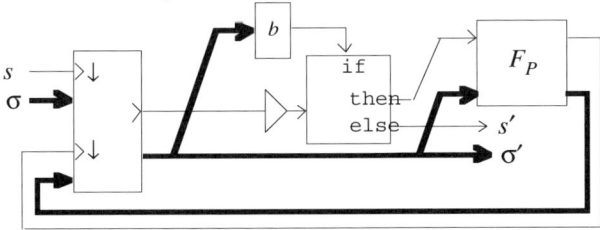

Similarly **repeat** P **until** b is just **loop** $(P;$ **if** b **then exit else ok**).

Construct: local variable

The functional circuit for local variable declaration **var** $z: T \cdot P$ is particularly easy.

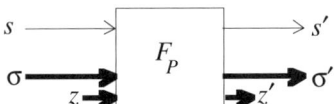

Into the functional circuit for P we must feed data lines for z, with any desired initial value. The diagram shows the final value z' coming from F_P, but it is not wanted so its wires are not needed. A local array declaration is just like a local variable declaration; there is no extra circuitry needed here for access to elements.

Construct: procedure

Program declaration and calling work the same way in functional circuits as in imperative circuits, except that the data input must also come from the calling point, and the data output must be delivered back to the calling point. Like the imperative version, our functional implementation of procedures does not work for general recursion. Because the functional parallelism is disjoint, procedures cannot be called from parallel programs. For a procedure declaration we have the circuit

18. High-level circuit design   405

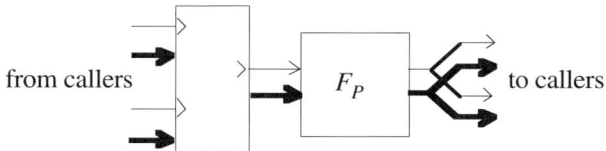

and for each call we have the circuit

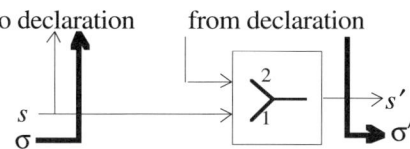

Construct: function

Function declaration is similar to procedure declaration.

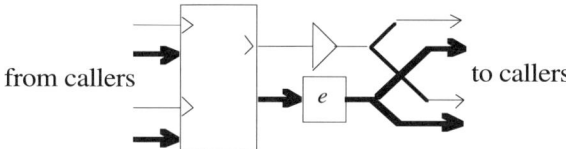

Function call and return are identical to procedure call and return. The programmer must ensure that calls from parallel programs are mutually exclusive.

The data expression *P* **result** *e* is almost identical to the imperative circuit.

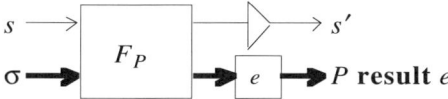

The communication constructs are not given functional implementations for lack of truly shared memory in the parallel composition. For these constructs, we use hybrid circuits, described next.

18.10 Hybrid circuits

In general, functional circuits are faster than imperative circuits, but imperative circuits occupy less space. Each approach has merit. We can obtain almost the speed of a functional circuit with almost the compactness of an imperative circuit by combining the two kinds within one hybrid circuit. For example, we might make most of a circuit imperative, but make inner loops functional.

Hybrid circuits also allow us to use our imperative implementation of communication within a larger functional circuit.

To place a functional circuit within an imperative one, we must make the functional circuit look imperative. Ignoring arrays for simplicity of presentation, here's what we do:

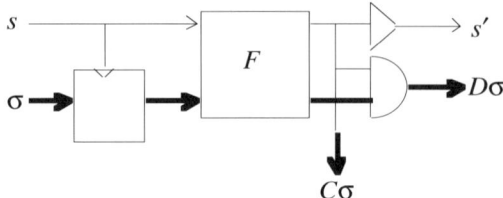

The s' output also causes memory to change state. As usual, only some of the wires to and from memory are needed. The local memory is needed only if there are parallel programs.

To place an imperative circuit within a functional one, we must make the imperative circuit look functional. Here's what we do:

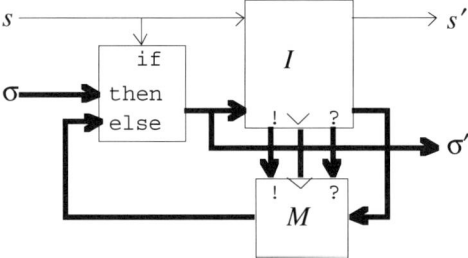

In effect, we make the memory (as much of it as necessary) local to the circuit.

18.11 Performance

Our two measures of performance are circuit size and execution time. We measured size as the number of conjunctions, disjunctions, negations, and delays. Other gates were expressed in terms of these gates; one bit of memory has size 4 (we did not count the delay). The size measure might be improved by choosing different primitives. We measured time as the number of sequential gate delays during execution. We measured circuits that were produced without any optimizations; the results might be better if we were to optimize. For example, we may find conjunctions or disjunctions with ■ or ■ , which can then be eliminated. In any case, the performance numbers are very approximate and indicate only that our circuits are competitive.

We measured our imperative circuits, our functional circuits, the circuits of Martin [3,7], the circuits of Weber et al. [15], and the circuits of Philips [1,2]. To obtain our results, we hand-compiled the circuits of Martin; for details see [11].

Our six test programs were chosen to use as many language features as

possible. They are:
  Parity: computes and verifies a parity bit for 3 bits of data
  Parallel: uses the parallelism and interprogram communication features
  Arbiter: arbitration between two parallel programs
  Counter: a 4-bit binary countdown timer and test-and-set function
  Triple: a program to compute three times its input
  Ring: mutually-exclusive execution of 7 parallel programs in a ring
              using Peterson's algorithm
A detailed description of the test programs and a similar analysis can be found in [11].
  The results are listed in the following table.

TIME	Parity	Parallel	Arbiter	Counter	Triple	Ring
imperative	16	31	165	1091	127	2321
functional	16	25	113	799	90	3792
Martin	18	23	209	1243	148	2044

SIZE	Parity	Parallel	Arbiter	Counter	Triple	Ring
imperative	73	210	52	407	400	427
functional	94	413	81	886	1240	1835
Martin	98	123	76	431	385	357
Weber et al.	259	145	95	1156	657	715
Philips	96	196	79	810	597	940

18.12 Correctness

To prove that our circuits are correct, we must have a formal semantics for our source programs and circuits. Here is the source semantics.

Let t and t' be the initial and final execution times, the times at which execution starts and ends. If the execution time is infinite, $t'=\infty$. Let the state variables x, y, ... be functions of time. The value of x at time t is $x\,t$. An expression such as $x+y$ is also a function of time; its argument is distributed to its variable operands as follows: $(x+y)t = x\,t + y\,t$. Let
  $wait\ =\ (t'{\geq}t\ \wedge\ \forall t''\colon t{\leq}t''{\leq}t'\cdot\ xt''{=}xt\ \wedge\ yt''{=}yt\ \wedge\ ...)$
so that *wait* takes an arbitrary time during which the variables are unchanging.
  The programming notations are defined as follows.
  ok $=\ (t'{=}t)$
  tick $=\ (t'{=}t{+}\delta\ \wedge\ wait)$
  $(x\colon{=}\ e)\ =\ (t'{=}t{+}\delta{+}\tau\ \wedge\ xt'{=}et\ \wedge\ wait_{y,z...})$
where $\delta \geq (e\ \text{time})\ \wedge\ \tau \geq (\text{memory time})$.
  $(P;Q)\ =\ \exists t''\cdot$ (substitute t'' for t' in P) $\wedge$ (substitute t'' for t in Q)
  $(P_\alpha\ \|\ Q_\beta)\ =\ (P_\alpha\ \wedge\ (Q;wait)_\beta\ \vee\ (P;wait)_\alpha\ \wedge\ Q_\beta)$

$$
\begin{aligned}
(\textbf{if } b \textbf{ then } P \textbf{ else } Q) &= (\underline{\textbf{if }} bt \underline{\textbf{ then }} P \underline{\textbf{ else }} Q) \\
&= (bt \wedge P \vee \neg bt \wedge Q)
\end{aligned}
$$

$(\textbf{while } b \textbf{ do } P) \Rightarrow \textbf{ if } b \textbf{ then } (P;\ \textbf{while } b \textbf{ do } P) \textbf{ else ok}$

$(\forall x, x', y, y', \dots, t, t' \cdot W \Rightarrow \textbf{ if } b \textbf{ then } (P;\ W) \textbf{ else ok})$
$\Rightarrow (\forall x, x', y, y', \dots, t, t' \cdot W \Rightarrow \textbf{ while } b \textbf{ do } P)$

$\textbf{var } z\colon T \cdot P \ =\ \exists z\colon time{\to}T \cdot P$

where $time{\to}T$ is the functions from time values (including ∞) to T values.

Here is a simple example, in variables x and y. In this example we use discrete time and take δ to be 0 and τ to be 1.

$\quad x := x+3;\ x := x+4$
$= \quad (t'=t+1 \wedge xt'=xt+3 \wedge yt'=yt);\ (t'=t+1 \wedge xt'=xt+4 \wedge yt'=yt)$
$= \quad \exists t''\cdot\ (t''=t+1 \wedge xt''=xt+3 \wedge yt''=yt) \wedge (t'=t''+1 \wedge xt'=xt''+4 \wedge yt'=yt'')$
$= \quad t'=t+2 \wedge x(t+1)=xt+3 \wedge x(t+2)=xt+7 \wedge yt=y(t+1)=y(t+2)$

In the parallel composition, α consists of those variables that appear on the left of assignments within P, and β consists of those variables that appear on the left of assignments within Q; α and β must be disjoint. The use of *wait* is just to make the faster side of the parallel composition wait until the slower side is finished. To illustrate the semantics, here is an example in variables x and y, and discrete time with $\delta=0$ and $\tau=1$. In the left-hand program, only x is assigned, so only x is treated as a state variable. In the right-hand program, only y is assigned, so only y is treated as a state variable.

$\quad (x := 2;\ x := x+y;\ x := x+y) \parallel (y := 3;\ y := x+y)$

$= \quad (t'=t+1 \wedge xt'=2;\ t'=t+1 \wedge xt'=xt+yt;\ t'=t+1 \wedge xt'=xt+yt$
$\quad \wedge (t'=t+1 \wedge yt'=3;\ t'=t+1 \wedge yt'=xt+yt;$
$\quad\quad t'\geq t \wedge \forall t''\colon t\leq t''\leq t'\cdot yt''=yt)$

$\vee \quad (t'=t+1 \wedge xt'=2;\ t'=t+1 \wedge xt'=xt+yt;\ t'=t+1 \wedge xt'=xt+yt;$
$\quad\quad t'\geq t \wedge \forall t''\colon t\leq t''\leq t'\cdot xt''=xt)$
$\quad \wedge (t'=t+1 \wedge yt'=3;\ t'=t+1 \wedge yt'=xt+yt)$

$= \quad t'=t+3 \wedge x(t+1)=2 \wedge x(t+2)=x(t+1)+y(t+1) \wedge x(t+3)=x(t+2)+y(t+2)$
$\quad \wedge t'\geq t+2 \wedge y(t+1)=3 \wedge y(t+2)=x(t+1)+y(t+1)$
$\quad \wedge \forall t''\colon t+2\leq t''\leq t'\cdot yt''=y(t+2))$

$\vee \quad t' \geq t+3 \wedge \text{(other conjuncts)}$
$\quad \wedge t' = t+2 \wedge \text{(other conjuncts)}$

$= \quad t'=t+3 \wedge x(t+1)=2 \wedge y(t+1)=3 \wedge x(t+2)=5 \wedge y(t+2)=5$
$\quad \wedge x(t+3)=10 \wedge y(t+3)=5$

The example has the appearance of lock-step parallelism, as though there were a global clock, only because, for the sake of simplicity, we used discrete time with constants $\delta=0$ and $\tau=1$ for all assignments.

The first formula concerning the **while** loop says that it refines its first unrolling. Stated differently, **while** b **do** P is a pre-fixed-point of

$\quad W \Rightarrow \textbf{ if } b \textbf{ then } (P;\ W) \textbf{ else ok}$

The second formula says that it is as weak as any pre-fixed-point, so it is the weakest pre-fixed-point.

18. High-level circuit design   409

The other programming constructs (channel declaration, input, output, signal declaration, sending, receiving, parameter declaration, argumentation) are defined in terms of the ones we have already defined, so we do not need to give them a separate semantics. And that completes the source semantics.

The imperative circuit semantics was given with each circuit. For example, the control for **ok** was
$$s'=s \land \neg R\sigma \land \neg C\sigma \land \neg W\sigma \land \neg D\sigma$$
and the control for **while b do P** was
$$I_P$$
$$s_P = (\delta\blacksquare(s \lor s'_P) \land b) \land s' = (\delta\blacksquare(s \lor s'_P) \land \neg b)$$
$$\sigma_P = \sigma \land R\sigma = R\sigma_P \land C\sigma = C\sigma_P \land W\sigma = W\sigma_P \land D\sigma = D\sigma_P$$
$$\delta \geq (b \text{ time})$$
where I_P is the control for P.

Before we can prove correctness, we need one more idea, adapted from [9]. Roughly speaking, a circuit is "busy" if it has been started and has not yet stopped. Formally, define B as
$$B = ((s \lor \delta\blacksquare B) \land \neg s')$$
$$\delta \leq (\text{pulse time})$$
The delay here must be shorter than the pulse length used on the control lines (s and s'). If time is discrete and $\delta=1$, then for any A
$$(\blacksquare A)\, 0 = \blacksquare$$
$$(\blacksquare A)\, (t+1) = At$$
and so for busy B
$$B0 = \blacksquare$$
$$B(t+1) = ((s(t+1) \lor Bt) \land \neg s'(t+1))$$
To prove that a circuit is correct, we must prove
$$I_P \land M \land st \land (\forall t''\cdot Bt'' \land \blacksquare Bt'' \Rightarrow \neg st'') \land t' = (min\ t''\cdot t'' \geq t\cdot \land s't'') \Rightarrow P$$
Suppose we have the control I_P (for program P), and we have the memory M, and we put a pulse on the start wire s at time t, and we don't try to restart the circuit while it's busy, and we give the name t' to the first time at or after t when s' becomes ■ ; then we expect the circuit to satisfy the semantics of program P. We do not have to prove correct each circuit that we design; instead, we prove that our circuit generation scheme is correct. The proof is long, and we omit it, stating only two lemmas that are useful steps on the way to the proof:
$$I \land \neg\blacksquare B \land \neg s \Rightarrow \neg s'$$
which says that a circuit does not spontaneously generate s', and
$$I \land \neg B \Rightarrow \neg R\sigma \land \neg C\sigma \land \neg W\sigma \land \neg D\sigma$$
which says that if a circuit is not busy, its $R\sigma$, $C\sigma$, $W\sigma$, and $D\sigma$ outputs are all ■ .

18.13 Synchronous and asynchronous circuits

There are two ways to control the timing in circuits. One is by using delays calculated, or experimentally determined, to be long enough to ensure that all data values have settled properly. The other way, called "delay-insensitive", is to use handshaking signals that allow a data transfer to occur just when both sender and receiver are ready. These solutions can be applied locally, or globally, or at any level in between. The word "synchronous" is usually used to describe a global delay, or clock; the word "asynchronous" is sometimes used to describe local handshaking.

The circuits resulting from the methods we have presented use local delays. But as a special case, it is possible to write a program in the form of a single loop, whose body is a parallel composition of assignments.
   loop ($x:= e_x \parallel y:= e_y \parallel z:= e_z \parallel$ ...)
This program structure forces a single, common delay for all state changes; that delay is in effect a global clock. We can thus program a synchronous circuit when we want one. When designing a circuit, there is little point in aiming for the synchronous structure, and equally little point in aiming to avoid it. One chooses a program structure that is appropriate for the task, and one gets a circuit that accomplishes that task. In principle, local delays should be faster than a single global delay. That is because a global delay must be the maximum of all the local delays. In a synchronous circuit, each state change takes as long as the slowest state change requires.

If we choose to make each assignment into a little procedure, the 1-2-merges at the calling points are an implementation of local handshaking. We can thus program local handshaking when we want it. In principle, local delays should be faster than local handshaking. That is because the handshaking takes time. A local delay is just long enough for the data to be ready, not long enough for the data to be ready and to indicate its readiness.

18.14 Conclusions

Circuit design can be done more effectively by describing the function that a circuit is intended to perform than by describing a circuit that is intended to perform that function. A programming language is more convenient for that purpose than a gate-level language. It seems quite obvious that complex circuits can be designed this way more easily and reliably than by low-level gate descriptions. And the resulting circuits seem, from a preliminary investigation, to show the promise of competing successfully with hand-crafted circuits. They should be smaller and faster than synchronous circuits due to the absence of a global clock. They should also be smaller and faster than delay-insensitive circuits due to the absence of handshaking. These gains come at a price: the language implementer must provide local delays. We do not suppose it is easy to provide local delays, but this price is paid only once; circuit designers who use the high-level language do not need to be concerned with them.

We have compiled a sampling of programming constructs that are representative of many high-level languages. Some obviously desirable constructs, such as modules, are missing only because they do not present any circuit generation problems (modules restrict the use of identifiers). For programs that we compiled and simulated, and for the text of the simulators, see [11].

We have shown two ways to implement ordinary programs with logic gates. The logic gates can, of course, be implemented with electronic transistors, resistors, and diodes. We could therefore bypass the logic gates, implementing the programs directly with transistors, resistors, and diodes. Doing so makes more optimizations and more efficient circuits possible. Ultimately, perhaps logic gates will have no remaining role in circuit design.

Acknowledgments

This paper was written in 1994 and circulated privately. We received useful feedback from IFIP WG2.3, and a lot of help from Jan van de Snepscheut.

References

[1] C.H.vanBerkel, J.Kessels, M.Roncken, R.W.J.J.Saeijs, F.Schalij. The VLSI programming language Tangram and its translation into handshake circuits. In *Proceedings of the European Design Automation Conference*, 1991.

[2] C.H.vanBerkel. *Handshake circuits – an asynchronous architecture for VLSI programming*. Cambridge University Press, 1993.

[3] S.M.Burns, A.J.Martin. Performance analysis and optimization of asynchronous circuits. In *Proceedings of the 1991 UC Santa Cruz Conference on VLSI*, MIT Press, 1991.

[4] C.DelgadoKloos. *Semantics of Digital Circuits*, Lecture Notes in Computer Science volume 285, Springer, 1987.

[5] E.C.R.Hehner. Abstractions of Time. In *A Classical Mind: Essays in Honour of C.A.R.Hoare*, A.W. Roscoe (ed.), Prentice-Hall, 1994.

[6] W.Luk, D.Ferguson, I.Page. Structured Hardware Compilation of Parallel Programs. In *More Field-Programmable Gate Arrays*, W.Moore and W.Luk (eds.), Abingdon EE&CS Books, 1994.

[7] A.J.Martin. Programming in VLSI: from communicating processes to delay-insensitive circuits. In *Developments in Concurrency and Communication*, C.A.R.Hoare (ed.), University of Texas at Austin Year of Programming Series, Addison-Wesley, 1990.

[8] S.Mazor, P.Langstraat. *a Guide to VHDL*, Kluwer, 1992.

[9] T.S.Norvell. *a Predicative Theory of Machine Languages and its Application to Compiler Correctness*. PhD thesis, University of Toronto, 1994.

[10] I.Page, W.Luk. Compiling occam into field-programmable gate arrays. In *Field-Programmable Gate Arrays*, W.Moore and W.Luk (eds.), p.271-283, Abingdon EE&CS Books, 1991.

[11] R.F.Paige. *Correctness and Performance Analysis of Imperative and Functional Circuits*. MSc thesis, University of Toronto, 1994. www.cs.yorku.ca/~paige/Writing/MSc.dvi

[12] M.Rem. *Partially Ordered Computations with Applications to VLSI Design*, Technical Report MR83/3, Eindhoven University of Technology, 1982

[13] J.L.A.van de Snepscheut. *Trace Theory and VLSI Design*, Lecture Notes in Computer Science volume 200, Springer, 1985.

[14] D.E.Thomas, P.Moorby. *the Verilog Hardware Description Language*, Kluwer, 1991.

[15] S.Weber, B.Bloom, G.Brown. Compiling Joy into Silicon. In *Advanced Research in VLSI and Parallel Systems*, T. Knight and J. Savage (eds.), MIT Press, 1992.

Section I

Security and keeping secrets

19 Power analysis: attacks and countermeasures
Suresh Chari, Charanjit S. Jutla, Josyula R. Rao and Pankaj Rohatgi

A central problem in computing today is how to build electronic systems that can keep secrets. Much research activity has been devoted to defining abstractly what it means 'to keep a secret', thus providing a benchmark to test security.

Yet such an abstraction can be difficult. Recall the puzzle of the mixed-up lightbulbs: three switches in one room are connected to three incandescent bulbs in another; can a spy determine which switch controls which bulb with only one visit to each room? No, he cannot: a simple and abstract counting argument shows that the connection pattern is 'secure'. But when the spy turns one switch on, one switch off, and the last switch on for a bit, then off, he only needs to feel for the warm bulb in the other room and the secret is out, abstraction notwithstanding. (In fact he has engaged in a primitive form of power analysis!)

The moral is that spies can cheat and step beyond the confines of a theory's assumptions and abstractions: what was 'proved' secure today may not be tomorrow, or perhaps never was.

This paper describes the situation in the context of smartcard security and how the amount of power used by smartcards as they are being operated can potentially be analysed to undermine the on-card encryption algorithms. Like the heat of the lightbulb, the extra information generated by power consumption as the encryption algorithm runs was for a long time overlooked, and was deliberately lost in the digital abstraction — partly because it was assumed that signal processing techniques were beyond the capabilities of the average spy. But the wide availability of cheap equipment has invalidated that assumption. The conclusion of the paper is that as breaches are discovered, theories must adapt and expand to keep pace with the ingenuity of technology.

20 A probabilistic approach to information hiding   441
Annabelle McIver and Carroll Morgan

Security properties in programming rely on variables' values remaining secret, or at least unknown to 'demons' or spies. A variable's value is said to be secret if a spy has no effective strategy for guessing it without actually being told what it is.

The (under-)specification of such strategies, manifest in standard programming paradigms as 'demonic behaviour' or more usually 'demonic nondeterminism', is the notion that underlies the theory of program refinement. So it might seem that all the ingredients for formulating security properties are already available, and are waiting to be so used. Such a hope is naive (as it turns out) and the recently coined 'refinement paradox' — that security properties are not robust against (standard) program refinement — is the reason. A closer look at nondeterminism tells us why, for in its standard formulation (for imperative programs) it cannot distinguish between private and global variables in the required sense. The inevitable corollary is that formulations of secrecy (and thus security properties) are impossible to achieve in a way that are preserved under program refinement, thus effectively ruling out a top-down approach to security protocols using current popular formal theories.

Suggested solutions to this paradox either avoid it (by ruling out refinement altogether) or use a different notion of nondeterminism, for which a non-standard approach to programming is essential. The success of the latter approach will depend on the simplicity of the resulting program models.

This essay explores these issues in a context of a sequential language with a probabilistic-choice operator. The advantage of probability is that it provides a very direct way to express relationships between information intended to be kept secret and a demon's strategies for adapting to security leaks.

19

Power analysis: attacks and countermeasures

Suresh Chari, Charanjit S. Jutla, Josyula R. Rao and Pankaj Rohatgi

Abstract

Side channel cryptanalytic techniques, such as the analysis of instantaneous power consumption, have been extremely effective in attacking cryptographic implementations on simple hardware platforms. The significant economic ramifications of such attacks, especially on the smart card market, have spurred a scramble for countermeasures. Unfortunately, most of the proposed countermeasures are ad hoc and ineffective. This is largely due to the absence of a sound scientific basis for understanding side channel information leakage resulting in the lack of a methodology for designing and validating proposed countermeasures.

A more scientific approach to the problem is to create a model for the power consumption characteristics of the device, and then design implementations that are *provably* secure in that model, i.e. they resist generic attacks with an *a priori* bound on the number of experiments. We propose such a model for power consumption and a generic programming technique to create provably secure implementations. We expect that this formal model will become the basis for further work in this area.

19.1 Introduction

19.1.1 Background

Traditionally, designers of secure systems have focused on justifying the correctness of the security protocols in terms of their ability to withstand adversarial attacks. The model of the adversary assumes that it can control the inputs and observe the outputs of the system but it is restricted in terms of its computational power. The implementations of such systems are further protected by the use of tamper resistance and other hardware protection mechanisms.

While this approach appears to be sound, it has been known for some time that a determined adversary can get access to much more information than is modeled traditionally. Examples of such information include timing data, system power consumption and electromagnetic radiation leakage [14, 15, 23]. In many cases, information from such *side channels* can completely undermine the security of the system. In fact, side channel cryptanalysis, i.e. cryptanalysis using information leaked during the computation of cryptographic primitives, has been successfully used to extract secret cryptographic keys from simple platforms such as chip-cards.

19.1.2 Power-analysis attacks

In this paper, we focus on a specific side channel, i.e. the leakage of information from the instantaneous power consumption of a system executing a cryptographic computation. Some researchers have claimed [15] that in chip-card like devices, *all* straightforward implementations of block ciphers (like DES) are susceptible to attack by power analysis techniques. Power traces can be easily gathered with a simple experimental setup and even a single power trace of a simple device, such as a chip card, reveals information about the sequence of instructions being executed by the device since the shape of the power signal depends on the type of instruction being executed.

A first class of attacks, termed *simple power analysis (SPA)* attacks, takes advantage of the shape of a single power signal to extract secret information. For example, if a program employs conditional statements that depend on secret information, then the instruction trace seen in the power signal can reveal the branch of the conditional that was executed and hence information about the secret.

In general, the power consumed at any point in the computation depends on the instruction executed at that point. Executing the same instruction on different data causes small variations in the power consumed. In other words, differences in the power consumed by different instructions are markedly apparent while differences due to different data are not as significant. SPA attacks take advantage of the fact that differences in the value of secret information lead to the execution of different instructions. This suggests that one can protect against SPA by ensuring that the set of instructions executed is independent of the secret information although the data manipulated by the instructions can depend on the secret information.

Even in an implementation that is protected against SPA attacks, the power signal for each instruction leaks information about the data manipulated by the instruction. This leakage is quite small, subtle and usually masked by the inherent noise in the power samples and the data collection process. Since the data being processed by these instructions depends on the secret information, it is possible to apply standard statistical techniques to multiple power samples to once again extract this information. These attacks, termed *differential and higher order differential power analysis (DPA and HODPA)* attacks, are extremely powerful and much more difficult to thwart.

The main idea of these attacks is that two very different sets of operands will induce two very different statistical distributions on the power traces for the same instruction (or set of instructions). An example of two such different sets is one in which a particular bit is 0 and the other in which the bit is 1. The adversary can then employ hypothesis testing to guess and verify the secret information. A correct guess by the adversary creates two very different sets of operands and thus two different power distributions which can be distinguished by statistical tests. An incorrect guess results in similar sets of operands and thus statistically indistinguishable power distributions.

Far from being theoretical, both these classes of attacks are fairly easy to implement and have been used successfully to attack almost all commercial chip cards. This has had a profound impact on the entire smart card industry. Just in 1998 alone, world-wide sales of smart cards plummeted when the attacks were first reported. The ensuing scramble for a solution has led to a plethora of ad hoc and half-baked countermeasures.

19.1.3 Contributions

The main contribution of this paper is to elevate the discourse on power analysis attacks and countermeasures from an ad hoc to a sound scientific basis. We begin with a process of experimentation to fully understand the sources and the implications of the attacks. We were surprised to observe that in addition to the expected and obvious leakages of information such as values of bits being accessed in registers and memory, there was unexpected leakage of other information as well. For instance, in one chip we found that the exclusive-or of the bits fetched in two successive accesses to main memory was leaking. One of the by-products of this investigation is a simple and devastating attack on the reference implementation of the Twofish symmetric block cipher [25].

Based on insights obtained by performing these experiments, we propose a power consumption model for simple CMOS devices which essentially relates the power consumed to the computations being executed. All the currently known attacks can be re-stated in terms of this model: moreover, this model can be used to design new attacks as well to validate existing and new countermeasures. We propose a generic and effective countermeasure based on secret sharing that is provably secure in this model. The countermeasure requires a source of randomness and its efficacy is enhanced by the existence of noise in the power samples. The countermeasure is generic, in the sense that it can be used to protect a family of cryptographic implementations across a variety of devices. It is effective, in the sense that with a linear increase in the complexity of the implementation, the work factor for the adversary is increased exponentially.

19.1.4 Related work

Ever since the seminal paper introducing power analysis attacks [15], a number of papers by other researchers have appeared in the literature. Most of these papers have appeared in the Workshop on Cryptographic Hardware and Embedded Systems over the past two years. The reported work ranges from different types of power analysis attacks to different types of software and hardware countermeasures.

Simple power analysis attacks are further explored in [17] where information leakage from several assembly instructions are identified. Attacks on public key systems are explored in [20] where the authors attack smart card implementations of modular exponentiation algorithms. Power analysis attacks have been extended to cryptosystems based on elliptic curves [6] and Koblitz curves [13]. In [19], the author shows how a software implementation of a data whitening routine, which is protected against first order DPA attacks is still susceptible to second order DPA attacks. A new class of power attacks, termed *inferential power analysis* (IPA) is introduced in [9].

A number of countermeasures have been proposed to protect against power analysis in the literature ([4], [11]). In [18], the author uses the masking method of [4], and an arithmetic masking method to protect the five candidate algorithms for the Advanced Encryption Standard. In [7], the authors show how one can launch DPA attacks against the schemes of [18]. One way to protect against DPA is to introduce random process interrupts. In this technique, the CPU interleaves execution of the code with that of dummy instructions so that the corresponding power samples are not aligned because of time shifts. In [5], the authors show two ways of attacking smart cards that have such countermeasures. These countermeasures do not make the attack infeasible but increase the number of power samples needed to launch the DPA attack.

In [22], the author describes a hardware countermeasure for de-correlating the external power supplied to the card from the internal power consumed by the chip. The basic idea is to use two capacitors to store charge and to alternately use one to drive the chip while the other is being charged by the external power supply. However, the practical significance of such filtering schemes is limited as such filters can be easily detected and disabled.

19.1.5 Plan of the paper

In section 19.2, we illustrate differential power analysis by showing how one can attack an implementation of Twofish. Section 19.3 describes a formalization of a general power consumption model. Section 19.3.2 restates power analysis attacks in this framework. In section 19.4, we analyze countermeasures, examine simple ad hoc solutions which are ineffective, and propose the secret sharing scheme as a general countermeasure against these attacks. We make realistic approximations on the model and rigorously prove lower bounds on the number of samples needed to mount differential power attacks against implementations with this countermeasure.

19.2 Power analysis of a Twofish implementation

In this section, we illustrate differential power analysis by showing how one can attack an implementation of Twofish. It should be noted that the same attack will work on most commonly available 6805 smart cards. Our investigations yield startling results: with power samples of only 100 independent block encryptions using the Twofish reference 6805 implementation on a ST16[1] smart card together with a 128-bit "secret" key, we were able to completely extract the secret key. With experience, the number of samples can be reduced to 50.

19.2.1 Target implementation

A publicly available implementation of the Twofish Reference code [25] for the 6805 was loaded onto the EEPROM of an ST16 smart card. The default implementation options in the code were retained. We then created an interface to invoke the Twofish implementation by inputting a 128-bit Twofish key and a 128-bit plaintext so that the card would output the corresponding ciphertext.

In practice, an implementation of Twofish would be loaded into the ST16's ROM as opposed to the EEPROM. We are confident that the behavior of such an implementation with respect to our attack would be identical since the code being in the EEPROM instead of ROM only affects the processor cycles which fetch opcodes and operand addresses and not the cycles dealing with the data and the key since these will always be in RAM. Therefore our attack against the handling of plaintext data and key will be equally effective in both situations.

19.2.2 Power-attack equipment

The power attack equipment consists of a special smart card reader with a current sensor attached to the V_{cc} contact. The output of the current sensor was sampled using a PC-based oscilloscope, a data acquisition board and software from Gage Applied Sciences Inc. This equipment is capable of acquiring and recording 12-bit power samples at a 100MHz sampling rate. A PC with a 2GB disk was enough to collect and store samples from several thousand encryptions. The smart card reader was connected to the serial port of a PC which was used to send commands to the smart card and triggering information to the data acquisition board.

19.2.3 Attacking the Twofish whitening process

In the Twofish whitening process, a 128-bit whitening key consisting of four 32-bit whitening key words K_0, K_1, K_2, K_3 are xor'ed with the input data block. The reference code for this is given below. Note that the xor4 operation which seems

---

[1] ST16 is manufactured by SGS-Thomson Micro-electronics.

to do a word whitening in the code is actually a macro which expands to do byte-wise whitening since the 6805 is an 8-bit machine.

```
jsr    computeSubkey
/* Function call to calculate K0, K1 in sk0, sk1 */
xor4 Text, sk0
/* Macro to whiten 1'st word */
xor4 Text+4,sk1
/* Macro to whiten 2'nd word */
jsr    computeSubkey
/* Function call to calculate K2, K3 in sk0, sk1 */
xor4 Text+8, sk0
/* Macro to whiten 3'rd word */
xor4 Text+12,sk1
/* Macro to whiten 4'th word */
```

On macro expansion, the actual 6805 code for the whitening process is:

```
0.  jsr computeSubkey
    /* Function call to calculate K0, K1 in sk0, sk1 */
1.  lda Text
    /* Load 1'st byte of 1'st word in accumulator */
2.  eor sk0
    /* Xor accum with contents of 1'st byte of sk0 */
3.  sta Text
    /* Store accum back as 1's byte of 1'st word */
4.  lda Text+1
    /* Load 2'nd byte of 1'st word in accum */
5.  eor sk0+1
    /* Xor accum with contents of 2'nd byte of sk0 */
6.  sta Text+1
    /* Store accum back as 2'nd byte of 1'st word */
    ...
```

As observed in [15], macro features such as a group of similar operations are clearly visible in power traces of most smart cards. This will be true for the computeSubkey subroutine which is invoked during whitening and in all rounds. Therefore, by inspection, the whitening process can be identified and the equipment can be set up to collect power samples of just the whitening process for each encryption.

Let us focus on the least significant bit (LSB) of the byte "Text" in RAM, a plaintext bit known to the attacker. Instruction 1 which brings Text and, in particular, its LSB into the accumulator accesses this bit in the whitening process. Instruction 2 xor's the whitening key with the contents of the accumulator. The following instruction stores the result back into the RAM variable Text. If the LSB of the whitening key is 1, then LSB of the Text is negated by the xor: otherwise, the LSB of the Text remains unchanged. These are the ONLY places where this bit is directly manipulated in the input whitening process. Note however that when this bit is manipulated (e.g. brought from RAM into the accumulator over the data bus), its value remains in some parts of the circuit (e.g. buses or internal lines, latches, registers, etc) until it is overwritten by activities performed in subsequent cycles. From the code, it is easy to verify that the same properties hold for all the other input and whitening key bits.

It is reasonable to assume that the power consumed depends at any point in the computation depends on the bits being manipulated at that point. This observation, also borne out by practical observations, is the basis of most power attacks. Let us focus on a bit of the input. Since the input is random, this bit is a random variable. It should also be noted that the power consumed at any point in the computation which depends on the input (and the noise in the circuit) is also a random variable. The assumption that the power consumed depends on the value of the bits being manipulated means that these two random variables will be correlated at exactly those places where the bits being manipulated are related to the value of the input bits. Thus a statistical test to quantify correlations between random variables such as covariance would be useful in identifying the points at which the input bit or its complement are being manipulated. One would be expect to see large correlations at such points in the computation.

The covariance of two random variables, X and Y, is defined by

$$\text{covariance}(X, Y) = E(XY) - E(X)E(Y)$$

where $E(X)$ refers to the expected value of the random variable X.

The DPA attack against Twofish is now easy to describe: Obtain power samples of the whitening process for several random encryptions. For each of the bits in the plaintext input to these encryptions, calculate the covariance between the bit and power samples of the runs at every sample point. For each bit i, look at the covariance plot for all the sample points. It should be flat except for a few strong peaks. Look at the first significant peak. This corresponds to the load of the plaintext. Look at the covariance at a sample point corresponding to the store of the whitened plaintext. The covariance here should also be a peak. If these peaks have the same sign then the i'th bit of the key is 0, else it is 1.[2]

19.2.4 Experimental results

We performed the above experiment using 2000 random encryptions and then repeated it with 500, 100 and 50 samples to gauge the minimim number of samples needed for the attack.

---

[2]This assumes that the ith bit's average contribution to the power in both a load from RAM and a store to RAM has the same sign, which was true in our experiment. For architectures other than the ST16, a subset of the 128 bits will have similar contributions and the rest will have dissimilar contributions. Once this subset is known, a similar attack can be mounted against that smart card. This subset can easily be learned by experimenting with load, xor and store operations with known operands.

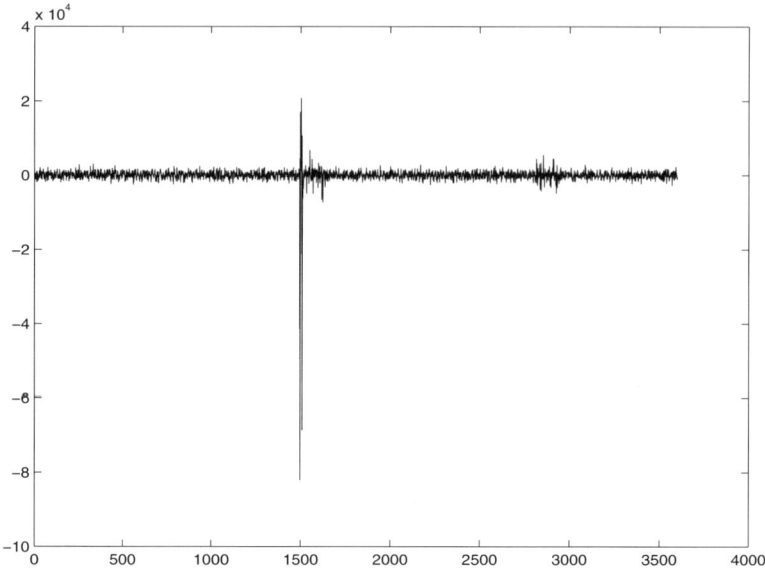

Figure 19.1. Pointwise covariance between first data bit and power consumed during whitening

Each experiment yielded 128 covariance plots, one for each plaintext/key bit. Using the above approach we were able to predict correctly all the 128 key bits when working with 2000, 500 and 100 samples. At 50 samples, there was difficulty in defining the "first significant peak", since the covariance at other points was almost comparable to the real "first peak". However, if the adversary can identify the position of the "first peak"(for instance, by looking at the shapes of the actual power signal and the code to figure out the correct cycle number), then comparing the signs of the two peaks still worked.

For example, Figure 19.1 shows the covariance plot of the whitening process for the first bit. At a higher resolution, i.e. zooming on to the region of the peaks, we see in Figure 19.2 that the first peak at position 1495 is negative and the peak corresponding to the store at 1506 is negative and hence, following the reasoning at the end of the last subsection, the key bit is 0. Note the presence of a few peaks after position 1495 and after 1506. These represent cycles where the lingering value of the directly manipulated bit in the earlier cycle is overwritten from parts of the state. Figure 19.3 which is the covariance plot of the second input bit shows that the first peak at 1495 is positive and the peak corresponding to the store at 1506 is negative which indicates that the second key bit is 1.

19.2.5 *From whitening keys to the 128-bit master key*

In this section, we describe the process of deriving the 128-bit master key from the whitening keys for the reader who is familiar with the specification of Twofish

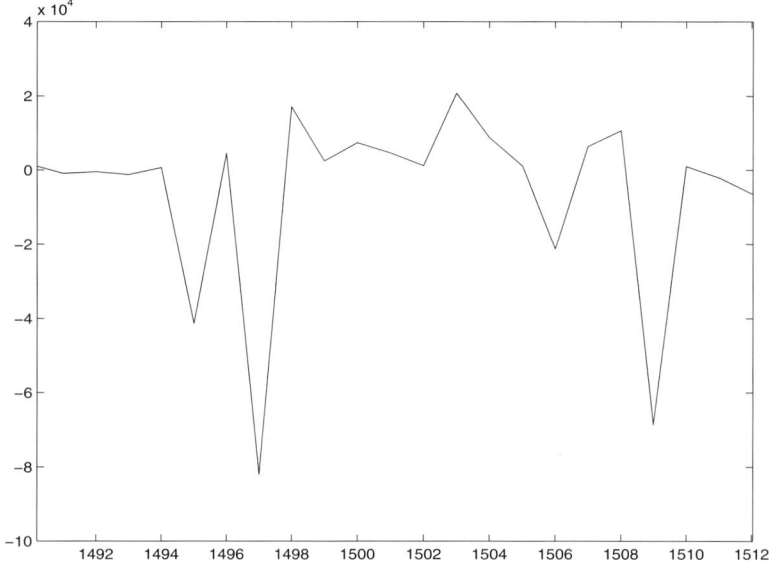

Figure 19.2. Closer look at peaks in Figure 19.1

and the notation used in [24]. From the attack described above, we can infer 32-bit whitening keys K_0, K_1, K_2, and K_3. From the Twofish specification, K_0 and K_1 are derived from the quantities A_0 and B_0 using a Pseudo-Hadamard Transform (PHT) and K_2 and K_3 are similarly derived from A_1 and B_1. By inverting the PHT we derive the quantities A_0, A_1, B_0, B_1 from the whitening keys. From the specification of A_0, A_1, B_0, B_1 we can then derive the value of the function $h(0, M_e)$, $h(\rho, M_o)$, $h(2\rho, M_e)$ and $h(3\rho, M_o)$, where if $M = (M_0, M_1, M_2, M_3)$ are the four words of the master key then $M_e = (M_0, M_2)$ and $M_o = (M_1, M_3)$;

We then use our knowledge of $h(0, M_e)$ and $h(2\rho, M_e)$ to create possible candidates for (M_0, M_2) and similarly our knowledge of $h(\rho, M_o)$ and $h(3\rho, M_o)$ to create possible candidates for (M_1, M_3). Since the process is identical we only describe how to derive (the very few) candidates for (M_0, M_2) using $h(0, M_e)$ and $h(2\rho, M_e)$.

When considering $h(0, M_e)$ and $h(2\rho, M_e)$, $L_1 = M_2$ and $L_0 = M_0$ in the specification of the h function. Consider $h(0, M_e)$. From the specification, the four-byte $h(0, M_e) = (z_3, z_2, z_1, z_0)$ is derived as

$$\begin{pmatrix} z_0 \\ z_1 \\ z_2 \\ z_3 \end{pmatrix} = \begin{pmatrix} \cdot & \cdot & \cdot & \cdot \\ \cdot & \cdot & MDS & \cdot & \cdot \\ \cdot & \cdot & \cdot & \cdot \end{pmatrix} \cdot \begin{pmatrix} y_0 \\ y_1 \\ y_2 \\ y_3 \end{pmatrix}$$

for some bytes (y_0, y_1, y_2, y_3). Since the MDS matrix is invertible, from $h(0, M_e) = (z_3, z_2, z_1, z_0)$ we derive (y_0, y_1, y_2, y_3). By definition of h,

$$y_0 = q_1[q_0[q_0[0] \oplus l_{1,0}] \oplus l_{0,0}]$$

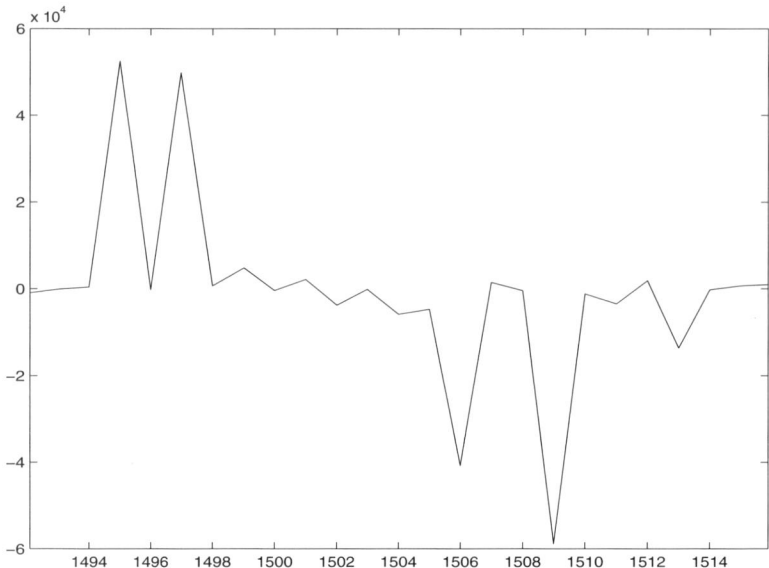

Figure 19.3. Covariance peaks for second data bit

$$y_1 = q_0[q_0[q_1[0] \oplus l_{1,1}] \oplus l_{0,1}]$$
$$y_2 = q_1[q_1[q_0[0] \oplus l_{1,2}] \oplus l_{0,2}]$$
$$y_3 = q_0[q_1[q_1[0] \oplus l_{1,3}] \oplus l_{0,3}]$$

for fixed permutations q_0 and q_1 in the Twofish specification. Now note that if we know the value of y_0 and that

$$y_0 = q_1[q_0[q_0[0] \oplus l_{1,0}] \oplus l_{0,0}]$$

then we know that for any possible value of the byte $l_{1,0}$ there can be at most one value of the byte $l_{0,0}$. We can therefore create a 256-entry dependence table T_0 between $l_{1,0}$ and $l_{0,0}$. Similarly, knowing the values of y_1, y_2, y_3 allows us to create similar dependence tables T_1 between $l_{1,1}$ and $l_{0,1}$, T_2 between $l_{1,2}$ and $l_{0,2}$ and T_3 between $l_{1,3}$ and $l_{0,3}$.

Similarly, unrolling the definition of $h(2\rho, M_e)$, we get yet another set of dependence tables G_0, G_1, G_2, G_3 for the same quantities. The actual values of the bytes $l_{1,0}$ and $l_{0,0}$ can only be those values in which T_0 and G_0 coincide. Since T_0 and G_0 are derived from different starting points in the first q_0 lookup that defines y_0, T_0 and G_0 are likely to have very few coincidences. In experiments typical coincidences have ranged from 2 to 9.

Thus from $h(0, M_e)$ and $h(2\rho, M_e)$, we get on average between 2 and 9 possibilities for each of the 4-byte pairs in M_e. A similar analysis using $h(\rho, M_o)$ and $h(3\rho, M_o)$ yields between 2 and 9 possibilities for each of the 4 byte pairs in M_o. So we are very likely to have less than 9^8 possible 128-bit master keys which are consistent with a single whitening key. This is a very small number of possibilities for the key and the right key can then be identified by encrypting known plaintext by all these possible keys to see which one yields the correct ciphertext.

If we had attacked the output whitening process and derived the output whitening keys, the attack and results would have been very similar. Had we attacked both the input and output whitening, we would have fewer candidate keys for the right key.

19.3 Power model and attacks

In this section, we propose a general, simplified model for the power consumption in simple devices, and use this to restate the basis of power analysis attacks and to analyze countermeasures.

19.3.1 Power model

CMOS devices consume power only when changes occur in logic states, while no significant power is needed to maintain a state. Examples include changes in the contents of the RAM, internal registers, bus-lines, states of gates and transistors. In simple chips almost all activity is triggered by an internal/external clock edge and all activity ceases well before the next clock edge. A few processes, such as on-chip noise generators, operate independently of the clock and consume a small, possibly random amount of power continuously. Each clock edge triggers a sequence of power consuming events within the chip, as dictated by the microcode, bringing it to the next state. This sequence depends on parts of the current state of the processor and parts of the state of other subsystems accessed in that cycle. We define *relevant* state bits as the bits of the overall state which determine the sequence of events, and hence the power, during a clock cycle. Depending on the cycle, the relevant state bits could include bits of internal registers, bits on internal and external buses, address bits and contents of memory locations being accessed.

The instantaneous power consumption of the chip shortly after a clock edge is a combination of the consumption components from each of the events that have occurred since the clock edge. Each event's timing and power consumption depends on physical and environmental factors such as the electrical properties of the chip substrate, layout, temperature and voltage, as well as coupling effects between events of close proximity. As a first approximation, we ignore coupling effects and create a linear model, i.e. we assume that the power consumption function of the chip is simply the sum of the power consumption functions of all the events that take place.

Consider a particular cycle of a particular instruction in the execution path of some fixed code. At the start of the cycle, the chip is in one of several relevant states (determined by the value of the relevant state bits) depending on the input and processing done in earlier cycles. Let $\mathcal{S}$ denote the set of possible relevant states when control reaches this cycle and let $\mathcal{E}$ be the set of all possible events that can occur in a cycle. For each $s \in \mathcal{S}$, and each $e \in \mathcal{E}$, let $occurs(e, s)$ be the binary function which is 1 if e occurs when the relevant state is s and 0 otherwise. Let $delay(e, s)$ be the time delay of the occurrence of event e in state s from the clock edge and let $f(e, t)$ denote the power consumption impulse function of event e with respect to time t ($t = 0$ when e occurs and $f(e, t) = 0$ for $t < 0$). In our linear model, $P(s, t)$, the power consumption function of the chip in that cycle with state s and time t after the clock edge can be written as

$$P(s, t) = \sum_{e \in \mathcal{E}} f(e, t - delay(e, s)) * occurs(e, s)$$

Due to the presence of noise and asynchronous power consuming components, a better model is:

$$P(s, t) = \mathcal{N}_c(t) + \sum_{e \in \mathcal{E}} (f(e, t - delay(e, s) + \mathcal{N}_d(e, s)) + \mathcal{N}(e, t)) * occurs(e, s)$$

(19.1)

where $\mathcal{N}(e, t)$ is a Gaussian noise component associated with the power consumption function of e, $\mathcal{N}_d(e, s)$ is a Gaussian noise component affecting the delay function and $\mathcal{N}_c$ is the Gaussian external noise component.

19.3.2 Statistical power attacks

Equation 19.1 shows the strong dependence between the power consumption function and the relevant state which is the basis of all statistical power attacks. Let P_1 and P_2 be two different probability distributions on the relevant state before the clock edge of a certain cycle. From equation 1, it is very likely that the distribution of the instantaneous power when the state is drawn from P_1 will be different from the distribution of the instantaneous power when the state is drawn from P_2. This difference and the distinguishability of different distributions by statistical tests on power samples, is the basis for Differential Power attacks (DPA). Simple distributions are sufficient to mount these attacks. For example, in the DPA attacks described in [15], P_1 and P_2 are very simple: P_1 is the uniform distribution on the set of all relevant states which have a particular relevant state bit 1 and P_2 is the uniform distribution on the set of all relevant states which have the same bit 0. The difference in the power distribution for these two cases represents the effect of that particular relevant state bit on the net power consumption. This can be used to extract cryptographic keys by guessing parts of keys, using this to predict a relevant state bit and defining the distributions as described above. Higher-order differential attacks are those in which the distributions P_1 and P_2 are defined over multiple internal state variables and where the adversary has access to multiple side channels.

In defining security against statistical attacks we use the strongest possible notion: using the side channel, with high probability, the adversary should not be able to predict, with even a slight advantage, any bit that he could not predict from just the knowledge of inputs, outputs and program code. In using the side channel, the adversary is limited to trying to distinguish distributions which he can affect by choice of inputs and selection based on outputs. These are limited to distributions on bits such as bits in the algorithm specification (e.g. bits of the key, bits which depend directly on the key and the input). Also, in an attack against the implementation the adversary could affect deterministic temporary variables, registers etc. We informally define the set of realizable distributions which the adversary can directly affect as follows:

Definition 19.3.1 *A distribution on state bits is* realizable *if the adversary can induce the distribution by suitable choice of inputs and selection based on outputs. In particular, this excludes distributions of state bits which result from explicit randomization introduced in the implementation outside of the specification.*

The ability to distinguish any two realizable distributions is potentially advantageous to the adversary. Using standard notations (see for example [16]) we define the distinguishing probability of an adversary as follows:

Definition 19.3.2 *Let M be a binary-valued adversary who adaptively chooses k inputs and has access to the side channel signals for the corresponding operations. Let B_1 and B_2 be any two realizable distributions on the bits of a computation, and D_1 and D_2 the distributions induced on the side channel signals, by the choice of inputs and B_1 and B_2 respectively. Let M^D denote M's output when given k input/output pairs and corresponding side-channel samples from a distribution D. The* distinguishing *probability of M when given samples from distributions D_1 and D_2 is $| \Pr(M^{D_1} = 1) - \Pr(M^{D_2} = 1) |$. M is said to distinguish B_1 from B_2 using k side-channel samples, if the distinguishing probability of M, on D_1 and D_2, is at least some constant c.*

Using this definition of adversaries, we define a secure computation. We intend to capture *extra* information that the adversary obtains from the side channel.

Definition 19.3.3 *A computation is said to be secure against N sample side channel cryptanalysis, if for all adversaries M and all realizable distributions B_1 and B_2, if M can distinguish B_1 from B_2 using fewer than N samples, then M can distinguish B_1 and B_2 without the side channel.*

The attacks described by [15] can be restated as using the side channel to distinguish distributions B_1 and B_2 which correspond to almost uniform distributions on a few relevant state bits, with a particular state bit (depending on the input and key) being 0 and 1 respectively. There the adversary bases its decision by comparing the mean of the given samples, with some known threshold.

19.4 Countermeasures to power analysis

Using these formal definitions of side channel cryptanalysis, we discuss general countermeasures against such attacks. First, we examine several ad hoc approaches to fixing this problem, which, we believe, miss the import of these attacks and can easily be rendered ineffective. We present a probabilistic encoding scheme with which we can effectively perform secure computations. Based on realistic approximations of the power model of Section 19.3 we prove lower bounds on the number of samples required to distinguish distributions.

19.4.1 Ad-hoc approaches

Due to the commercial impact, several ad hoc solutions are currently being implemented and claim to be resistant to these statistical attacks. Unfortunately, most can be defeated by signal processing in conjunction with only a moderately greater number of samples. Allowing for about 1 million possible experiments, it is reasonable to assume that the adversary can exploit every relevant state bit in any instruction to mount a statistical attack, provided he can efficiently predict that bit in a significant fraction of the runs based on the code specification, known inputs and small number of guesses for parts of the key.

Some approaches to protecting computation use simple countermeasures such as "balancing", i.e. try to negate the effects of one set of events by another "complementary" set. For example, by ensuring that all bytes used in computation have Hamming weight 4, one can try to negate the effect of each 1 bit by a corresponding 0 bit. Such approaches fail at high resolution and large number of samples, because the power consumption functions and timing of two "complementary" events will be slightly different and the adversary can maximize these differences by adjusting the operating conditions of the card. Another popular approach is to randomize the execution sequence i.e. keep operations the same, but permute the order e.g. in DES, the S-boxes are looked up in a random order. Unless this random sequencing is done extensively throughout the computation, which may be impossible since the specification forces a causal ordering, it can be undone and a canonical order re-created by signal processing. Attacks can be mounted on the re-ordered signals. Even if the entire computation cannot be canonically reordered, it is sufficient to identify "corresponding" sample points in different runs so that a significant fraction are samples from the same power function P for the same cycle. All statistical attacks that work for P are also applicable to "corresponding" points, although more samples would be needed due to "noise" introduced by unrelated samples. In the case of permuted S-boxes, if the permutation is random, in $\frac{1}{8}$ of the runs S-box 1 is looked up first, and in the remaining samples, the signal at this point, corresponding to different lookups, is essentially random. Thus, even with no reordering, we now have a signal which is attenuated by a factor of 8. Mounting the original attack with 64 times the number of samples yields the same results. Elementary reordering substantially reduces this factor. A similar countermeasure in hardware is typically achieved by making instructions take a variable number of cycles or by having the cycles be of varying length (see [8]). Once again, it is very easy to negate all these countermeasures with signal processing.

19.4.2 A general countermeasure

The aim is to ensure that the adversary cannot predict any relevant bit in any cycle. For instance, each relevant bit may be masked by a bit selected randomly for each run of the computation. This makes statistical tests involving several experiments more difficult, since the chance of the adversary making the correct assumptions for each run is extremely low. The difficulty of the statistical attack would depend on the distribution of the masking bits. While this yields secure computation, it is not clear how one can do effective computation under this requirement since no bit depending directly on the data and key can be manipulated at any cycle (since it is masked). In some cases the function being computed has algebraic properties that permits such an approach (e.g. for RSA one could use blinding [14, 2] to partially hide the actual values being manipulated). Another class of problems where this is possible is the class of random self-reducible problems [1]. Such structure is unlikely to be present in primitives such as block ciphers.

19.4.3 Encoding

The encoding we propose is to randomly split every bit of the original computation into k shares, where each share is equiprobably distributed and every proper subset of $k - 1$ shares is statistically independent of the encoded bit. Computation can then be carried securely by performing computation on only the shares, without ever reconstructing the original bit. Shares are refreshed after every operation involving them to prevent information leakage to the adversary.

For the Twofish attack described earlier, if at all points in the computation, we have two shares for all the data being manipulated (including the input plaintext and the secret key), an attack that looks at the covariance between the values of the input bits and the power would fail, because at every point the value being manipulated is independent of the bits being attacked and hence is independent of the power consumed at that point. For a successful attack, the adversary now has to focus on the two points where the shares of the input bit are being manipulated.

To fix a concrete encoding scheme, we assume that each *bit* is split into k shares using any scheme which has the required stochastic properties. For instance, bit b can be encoded as the k shares $b \oplus r_1, r_2, \ldots, r_{k-1}, r_1 \oplus \ldots \oplus r_{k-1}$, where the r_is are randomly chosen bits. Furthermore, assume that each share is placed in a separate word at a particular bit position and all other bits of the share word are chosen uniformly at random.

In practice, it would be more useful, if each word of computation is split similarly into k shares. In that case, other schemes of splitting into shares based on addition mod 2^8, subtraction mod 2^8 would also be viable. Encoding bytes of data manipulated by splitting them into shares would yield the optimal performance.

Ignoring the initial setup time, the performance penalty in performing computation using just the k shares is a factor of k. Our results which have been proved based on the bit encoding scheme would also work for this case but the bounds they yields are based only on the characteristics of the noise within the chip, and hence may not be optimal. This is discussed briefly after the analysis for the bit encoding case. The results and analysis we present here can serve as a framework in which to prove results for the byte encoding scheme.

The method to encode the bit in secret shares should be chosen based on the computation being protected. For instance, for an implementation of DES, the XOR scheme is ideal since the basic operations used are XOR, permutations, and table lookups. Table lookups can be handled by first generating a random rearrangement of the original table since a randomized index will be used to look up the table. This step increases the overhead beyond the factor of 2.

In practice, the splitting technique needs to be applied only for a sufficient number of steps into the computation until the adversary has very low probability of predicting bits, i.e. till sufficient secret key dependent operations have been carried out. Similar splitting also has to be done at end of the computation if the adversary can get access to its output. For instance, in DES, one needs to use the splitting scheme only for the first four and last four rounds.

19.4.4 Analysis

We analyze the encoding scheme described above, by making reasonable assumptions on distribution of side channel information and prove that the amount of side channel information required grows exponentially in k, the number of shares. For concreteness we fix the XOR bit encoding scheme and consider the instantaneous power consumption at some time instant in a cycle manipulating a share. The relevant state in that cycle will not only include a share of the bit, but also all the other random bits in the word. It is quite reasonable to assume that the contributions of all bits in the word will be similar in magnitude. From equation (19.1), expanding $occurs(e, s)$ as a linear form over the bits of s, the instantaneous power consumption when a particular share is being manipulated will be

$$P = b \times s_0 + P \times s_0 + R$$

where b is the contribution of just the shared bit s_0, $P \times s_0$ is the distribution of power contributions of events which require s_0 and other state bits and finally, R is the distribution of events which are independent of the bit s_0. In operations such as load, store and XOR, if s_0 is a bit in a word being manipulated, the factor P can be viewed as a small perturbation on the real value b. In simple operations there is no "interaction" between the different bits of the value being manipulated and an approximation, we will ignore the contribution of the variable P. The random variable R is typically much larger than b since it includes the sum of similar contributions from all other bits. For most operations, R is the sum of almost independent distributions which is very well approximated by the Normal Distribution. Thus, we make the realistic assumption, which has been empirically tested as shown in Appendix 1, that R has a normal distribution with mean μ and variance σ^2. The results we prove can also be shown to hold in the case that R is the sum of i.i.d's, which is the case for operations such as load, store and XOR. Further work needs to be done to analyze more complex and precise distributions which model all chip-card operations such as multiply where there is interaction between the bits being manipulated and it is unlikely that one can ignore the contribution of the variable P.

Assume that in each sample the adversary has access to the k signal values corresponding to the power consumption at instructions which access the shares $b \oplus r_1, r_2, \ldots, r_{k-1}, r_1 \oplus r_2 \ldots \oplus r_{k-1}$. Rewrite these bits as $r_1, \ldots r_k$, with $r_1 \oplus \ldots \oplus r_k = b$. Denote the distribution of the instantaneous power consumption signal at these points by random variables $Z_1, Z_2, \ldots Z_k$. Also, let $Z_i = A_i + X_i$, where A_i is the contribution due to the bit of interest and X_i is the additive factor which follows the distribution R. By the definition of the encoding, A_i takes values 0 and 1 with probability $\frac{1}{2}$ each. Any noise in the contribution due to A_i can be absorbed in R without affecting the distribution of R since R is typically much bigger than b. Thus, the power contribution due to A_i is 1 if $r_i = 1$ (and 0 if $r_i = 0$). It is important to note that the A_i's are not independent since $A_1 \oplus \ldots \oplus A_k = b$.

In defining distributions that an adversary can try to distinguish using inputs, outputs and the side channel information, note that the adversary cannot control the randomizing variables r_i's. Thus, the only realizable distributions are those with the value of the bit b being 0 and 1 i.e. distributions D_1 and D_2 where: a random variable Y sampled from D_1 is given by

$$\langle A_1 + X_1, \ldots, A_k + X_k \rangle$$

with the condition that $A_1 \oplus \ldots \oplus A_k = b$, while a random variable sampled from D_2 is given by

$$\langle A_1 + X_1, \ldots, A_k + X_k \rangle$$

with the condition that $A_1 \oplus \ldots \oplus A_k = 1 \oplus b$. This is more general than the encoding scheme specified above. It corresponds to the intuition that using $\oplus$ and k random bits there are several ways to split a bit into shares (e.g. a three-way split of a bit b can be specified as $b \oplus r_1, r_2, r_1 \oplus r_2$ or as $b \oplus r_1 \oplus r_2, r_1, r_2$.)

Let M be an adversary trying to distinguish the two distributions D_1 and D_2. It gets a sequence T of m samples, sampled from either D_1 or D_2, each element of which is a k tuple of signal values at the k points that the shares are accessed. If $S_1, \ldots, S_k$ are random variables denoting these values, let $\mathcal{S} = (S_1 - \mu) \times \cdots \times (S_k - \mu)$ where μ is the mean of the distribution R. $\mathcal{S}$ has a slightly different mean (with the difference of $\frac{1}{2^{(k-1)}}$) under distributions D_1 and D_2 and with a variance of approximately $(\sigma^2)^k$. Using standard techniques, it is easy to show that an adversary given $(2\sigma^2)^k$ samples can distinguish the two distributions using the statistic $\mathcal{S}$. Thus, approximately n^k samples are sufficient, where $n = \sigma^2$. We are interested in lower bounds on the number of samples required to distinguish the distributions. Our central result is:

Theorem 19.4.1 Let δ be a constant. Given distributions D_1 and D_2 defined above, any adversary which has access to $m < n^{\frac{k}{2}-4\delta}$ samples ($n = \sigma^2$) from one of these two distributions, has probability at most $n^{-\delta}$ of distinguishing D_1 and D_2.

Note that this not a tight lower bound and we conjecture that n^k is the tight bound. We sketch the proof for the case $k = 2$ and the general proof can be done along the same lines. We require the following basic facts from probability theory.

19.4.5 Probability-theory basics

The density function of *Normal distribution* with mean μ and variance σ^2 is

$$\eta(x) = \frac{1}{\sqrt{2\pi}\sigma} e^{-\frac{1}{2}(\frac{x-\mu}{\sigma})^2}$$

The corresponding distribution function is defined as

$$N(x) = \int_{-\infty}^{x} \eta(x) dx$$

The following inequality is useful (see for example [10]):

$$N(x) < \frac{\sigma^2}{\mu - x} \eta(x)$$

Theorem 19.4.2 *Chernoff Bound:* Let $S_n = X_1 + ... + X_n$ where the X_is are independent and are 1 and 0 with probability p and $q = 1 - p$. For $p < a < 1$, and $b = 1 - a$,

$$\Pr[S_n \geq na] \approx e^{-nK(a,p)}$$

where $K(a,p) = a \log(\frac{a}{p}) + b \log(\frac{b}{q})$.

19.4.6 Lower bound for 2-way split

In this section we outline a proof of Theorem 19.4.1 with $k = 2$. Our proof uses several techniques and ideas from Naor et. al [21]. The realizable distributions D_1 and D_2 which the adversary has to distinguish are defined on the space $\mathcal{P} = \mathcal{R} \times \mathcal{R}$, where $\mathcal{R}$ is the set of reals. If Y is the random variable sampled from one of these distributions, in D_1, $Y = \langle A+X_1, A+X_2 \rangle$ and $Y = \langle A+X_1, (1-A)+X_2 \rangle$, where X_1, X_2 are random variables with normal distribution with parameters μ, σ and A is a uniform binary-valued random variable.

Let M be an adversary trying to distinguish D_1 and D_2. By assumption, M fixes a certain precision ϵ and divides the area $\mathcal{R} \times \mathcal{R}$ into squares of length ϵ, where $\epsilon < \frac{1}{\sqrt{n}}$ without loss of generality. All inputs in a particular square are treated identically. When we refer to $\langle u, v \rangle \in \mathcal{R} \times \mathcal{R}$, we identify u and v with the boundaries of the intervals containing them and thus identify $\langle u, v \rangle$ with the the $\epsilon \times \epsilon$ square containing it.

Let $m = n^{1-4\cdot\delta}$, where δ is a constant. We show that no adversary can distinguish between sequences with at most m samples, sampled according to D_1

and D_2. In the following exposition, T is a random variable denoting a randomly drawn sequence, and s denotes a possible value of T. The outline of the proof is as follows: We first define a set of bad sequences (definition 19.4.3 below). Then we show (in Lemma 19.4.5) that under distributions D_1 and D_2 the probability that a sampled sequence T is bad, i.e. the probability of the event BAD_T is very small. Restricting ourselves to sequences which are not bad, we show that the probability that the random variable T has a particular value s is almost the same whether we are sampling according to D_1 or D_2. In particular, in Lemma 19.4.7 we show that $\mathrm{Pr}_{D_1}(T = s \mid \neg BAD_T) > \mu_n * \mathrm{Pr}_{D_2}(T = s \mid \neg BAD_T)$, where μ_n is close to 1, from above. Similarly, we show that the probability of a sequence which is not bad, when sampled according to D_2 is at least μ_n^{-1} times its probability under D_1. In other words, the occurrence probability of a sequence that is not bad, is almost the same under both distributions. Putting it all together, we then show that the adversary cannot distinguish the distributions using fewer than m samples. We begin with the definition of bad sequences.

Definition 19.4.3 *Let $f_s(x, y)$, $x, y \in R$, be the number of times that $\langle x, y \rangle$ appears in sequence s. We call a sequence s a bad sequence if either (1) $f_s(\mu - u, \mu - v) > 0$, for $u, v > n^{(0.5+\delta)}$ or (2) $f_s(\mu - u, \mu - v) > \frac{n^2}{(uv+1)} \cdot n^{-c}$, for other values, $u, v > 0$. Here $c = 1 - 3\delta$.*

In the above definition and in the rest of the proof we have ignored the cases when $u, v < 0$ and these can be treated symmetrically.

Definition 19.4.4 *Define $maxf(\mu - u, \mu - v) = 0$, for $u, v > n^{(0.5+\delta)}$ and $maxf(\mu - u, \mu - v) = \frac{n^2}{(uv+1)} \cdot n^{-c}$, for all other values $u, v \geq 0$.*

This the maximum possible number of times that $\langle u, v \rangle$ occurs in a sequence which is not bad. Denote the random sequence of m two tuples as $T = T_1 T_2 \ldots T_m$ and denote $s = s_1 s_2 \ldots s_m$.

Lemma 19.4.5 $\mathrm{Pr}_{D_1, D_2}(BAD_T) < e^{-n^\delta}$ *i.e. under either distribution, the set of bad sequences is negligible.*

Proof: We consider the two cases in the definition of a bad sequence separately. The probability that the random variable distributed according to $N(\mu, \sigma)$ takes on a particular value $\mu - x$ is given by $N(\mu - x) - N(\mu - x - \epsilon)$, which for small values of ϵ can be approximated by $\epsilon \cdot \eta(\mu - x)$. Using this approximation and taking into account the contribution of the binary-valued random variable, under either distribution D_1 or D_2 the probability that $s_i = \langle \mu - u, \mu - v \rangle$ can be approximated by probability

$$p = \frac{d\epsilon^2}{(2\pi\sigma^2)} \cdot e^{-\frac{1}{2}(\frac{u^2+v^2}{\sigma^2})} \tag{19.2}$$

where d is a small constant close to 1. Since the elements of the sequence are sampled independently, by the Chernoff bound (section 19.4.5), the probability P_{uv} that $f_s(\mu - u, \mu - v) > \frac{n^2}{(uv)} \cdot n^{-c}$ is about $e^{-m \cdot K(a,p)}$, where $a = \frac{n^{-c}}{(uv+1)}$. Since

$1 - a$ is close to 1, $K(a, p)$, a simple calculation shows that

$$P_{uv} \approx \left(\frac{p}{a}\right)^{ma} \cdot \left(\frac{1-p}{1-a}\right)^m < \left(\frac{d\epsilon^2 uvm}{2\pi\sigma^2 n^{2-c}}\right)^{\frac{n^{2-c}}{uv}} \cdot e^{n^{1-c}} < \left(\frac{\epsilon^2 e}{n^{2\delta}}\right)^{\left(\frac{n^{2-c}}{(uv+1)}\right)}$$

Since there are $\frac{\sqrt{n}^2}{\epsilon^2}$ possible values of u, v, the total probability of BAD in case (2) is at most

$$\frac{n}{\epsilon^2} \cdot \epsilon^{2\left(\frac{n^{2-c}}{(uv+1)}\right)}$$

which is exponentially small as $uv < n^{1+2\delta}$.

For case (1) of the definition of bad sequences, let s_i be the two tuple $\langle s_{i1}, s_{i2}\rangle$. For each i, using the inequality on Normal distribution in Section 19.4.5,

$$N(\mu - n^{0.5+\delta}) < \frac{\sigma^2}{n^{0.5+\delta}} e^{-\frac{1}{2}\left(\frac{n^{0.5+\delta}}{\sigma}\right)^2}$$

Thus $\Pr(s_{i1} < \mu - n^{0.5+\epsilon(n)}) < e^{-(n^{2\delta} - \log n)}$. The probability that the sequence is bad according to case (1) is at most m times this small probability. □

Thus the space of bad sequences is very small. We now argue that for sequences that are not bad, the probability of occurrence is the same under both distributions. Denote $\Pr_{D_1}(T_i = \langle \mu - u, \mu - v \rangle)$, by $X_{u,v}$. Also, let $\Pr_{D_2}(T_i = \langle \mu - u, \mu - v \rangle)$ be $X_{u,v} + \Delta_{u,v}$. The difference $\Delta_{u,v}$ is due to the contribution of the binary-valued random variable. The following lemma bounds $\Delta_{u,v}$.

Lemma 19.4.6 *For small ϵ, $\frac{\Delta_{u,v}}{X_{u,v}} \leq \frac{uv}{\sigma^4}$.*

Proof: This can be seen through the following sequence of approximations and identities. The first approximation follows from the definition of D_1 and D_2 and by choice of small ϵ.

$$\Delta_{u,v} \approx \frac{1}{2} \cdot (\eta(\mu-u)\eta(\mu-v) + \eta(\mu-u-1)\eta(\mu-v-1)$$
$$- \eta(\mu-u-1)\eta(\mu-v) - \eta(\mu-u)\eta(\mu-v-1)) \cdot \epsilon^2$$
$$= \frac{1}{2} \cdot \epsilon^2 \cdot (\eta(\mu-u) - \eta(\mu-u-1)) \cdot (\eta(\mu-v) - \eta(\mu-v-1))$$
$$= \frac{\epsilon^2}{2} \cdot \frac{1}{(\sqrt{2\pi}\sigma)^2} \cdot \left(e^{-\frac{1}{2}\left(\frac{u}{\sigma}\right)^2} - e^{-\frac{1}{2}\left(\frac{u+1}{\sigma}\right)^2}\right) \cdot \left(e^{-\frac{1}{2}\left(\frac{v}{\sigma}\right)^2} - e^{-\frac{1}{2}\left(\frac{v+1}{\sigma}\right)^2}\right)$$
$$\leq \frac{\epsilon^2}{2} \cdot \frac{1}{2\pi\sigma^2} \cdot \left(\frac{u}{\sigma^2} \cdot e^{-\frac{1}{2}\left(\frac{u}{\sigma}\right)^2}\right) \cdot \left(\frac{v}{\sigma^2} \cdot e^{-\frac{1}{2}\left(\frac{v}{\sigma}\right)^2}\right)$$
$$\leq \frac{d}{2} \cdot X_{u,v} \cdot \frac{uv}{\sigma^4}$$

The second last inequality follows from the power series expansion of e^x. The last inequality and the constant d are from (19.2). Thus the claim follows. □

Lemma 19.4.7 *The probability of occurrence of a sequence that is not bad is almost the same under both distributions. In particular, $\mu_n^{-1} * \Pr_{D_1}(T = s \mid \neg BAD_T) < \Pr_{D_2}(T = s \mid \neg BAD_T) < \mu_n * \Pr_{D_1}(T = s \mid \neg BAD_T)$, where $\mu_n = 1 + (2n)^{-\delta}$.*

Proof: We just show that

$$| Pr_{D_2}(T = s \mid \neg BAD_T) - Pr_{D_1}(T = s \mid \neg BAD_T) |$$
$$< Pr_{D_1}(T = s \mid \neg BAD_T) * n^{-c\sqrt{n}}.$$

This follows by:

$$| Pr_{D_2}(T = s \mid \neg BAD_T) - Pr_{D_1}(T = s \mid \neg BAD_T) |$$
$$= | \Pi_{u,v}(X_{u,v} + \Delta_{u,v})^{f_s(u,v)} - \Pi_{u,v}(X_{u,v})^{f_s(u,v)} |$$
$$= \Pi_{u,v} X_{u,v}^{f_s(u,v)} \cdot | (\Pi_{u,v}(1 + \Delta_{u,v}/X_{u,v})^{f_s(u,v)}) - 1 |$$
$$\leq \Pi_{u,v} X_{u,v}^{f_s(u,v)} \cdot | (\Pi_{u,v}(1 + \Delta_{u,v}/X_{u,v})^{maxf(u,v)}) - 1 |$$
$$\leq \Pi_{u,v} X_{u,v}^{f_s(u,v)} \cdot | (\Pi_{u,v}(e^{n^{-c}})) - 1 |$$
$$\leq \Pi_{u,v} X_{u,v}^{f_s(u,v)} \cdot | ((e^{n^{-c}})^m) - 1 |$$
$$\leq \Pi_{u,v} X_{u,v}^{f_s(u,v)} \cdot | (e^{n^{-\delta}}) - 1 |$$
$$\leq (\Pi_{u,v} X_{u,v}^{f_s(u,v)}) \cdot (2n)^{-\delta}$$
$$= Pr_{D_1}(T = s \mid \neg BAD_T) \cdot (2n)^{-\delta}$$

The first two equalities are by definition 19.4.3 and the fact that $(1+x)^{1/x} < e$, for $x > 0$. Although the number of u, v pairs can be about (n/ϵ^2), the third inequality is true because the number of u, v for which $f_s(u, v) > 0$ is at most m. The fifth inequality follows by the power series expansion of e^x, from which it can be shown that for $x < 1$, $e^x < 1 + 2x$. □

Proof (of Theorem 19.4.1) We put together the various pieces to show that an adversary M cannot distinguish these two distributions. Let M be a binary-valued adversary and let $M(s)$ denote the output of M on input s, a sequence of samples. Note that if C is any condition on the random variables, by definition

$$Pr(M^D = 1 \mid C) = \Sigma_s Pr_D(T = s \mid C) \cdot Pr(M(s) = 1) \text{ and } T = s) \quad (19.3)$$

By definition,

$$| Pr(M^{D_1} = 1) - Pr(M^{D_2} = 1) | =$$
$$| Pr(M^{D_1} = 1 \mid \neg BAD_T) * Pr_{D_1}(\neg BAD_T)$$
$$- Pr(M^{D_2} = 1 \mid \neg BAD_T) * Pr_{D_2}(\neg BAD_T)$$
$$+ Pr(M^{D_1} = 1 \mid BAD_T) * Pr_{D_1}(BAD_T)$$
$$- Pr(M^{D_2} = 1 \mid BAD_T) * Pr_{D_2}(BAD_T) |$$
$$\leq | Pr(M^{D_1} = 1 \mid \neg BAD_T) * (Pr_{D_1}(\neg BAD_T) - \delta_n * Pr_{D_2}(\neg BAD_T)) |$$
$$+ | Pr(M^{D_1} = 1 \mid BAD_T) * Pr_{D_1}(BAD_T)$$
$$- Pr(M^{D_2} = 1 \mid BAD_T) * Pr_{D_2}(BAD_T) |$$

where $\mu_n^{-1} \leq \delta_n \leq \mu_n$. This follows from the observation (19.3) and Lemma 19.4.7. Since μ_n is close to one, and $Pr_{D_1,D_2}(\neg BAD_T)$ is also close to one, the first summand on the right of the above inequality is close to zero. The second summand is also close to zero as $\Pr_{D_1,D_2}(BAD_T)$ is close to zero by lemma 19.4.5. Thus, the distinguishing probability is close to zero. □

Similarly we can show:

Theorem 19.4.8 *Let D_1 and D_2 be as before but with the noise being the sum of n identically and independently distributed binary variables (with $p = \frac{1}{2}$). Any adversary which has access to $n^{k/2-4\epsilon}$ samples, has probability at most $\frac{1}{n^\epsilon}$ of distinguishing D_1 and D_2.*

19.4.7 Encoding bytes

For practical computation, we would use the encoding scheme of splitting each relevant byte of the computation into k shares. It is clear from our proof techniques that if there was enough additional noise in the power signals to effectively mask the byte values, then the same proofs will go through for the byte encoding scheme. It seems unlikely to happen in limited devices. It may be possible to extend our proof techniques to account for the fact that there is uncertainty on the value of a byte being manipulated given its power signal even without any additional noise.

19.5 Conclusions

We have presented a simplified initial step into the formal analysis of computing in the presence of loss of entropy due to leaked side channel information. Our lower bounds on the amount of side channel information required are proved for reasonable approximations of the actual distributions. Substantial effort is required to find more effective and general countermeasures against such attacks. Besides proving implementations secure from power attacks, this framework could also be used to design ciphers and other primitives which readily admit a secure, efficient implementation.

19.6 Acknowledgments

The authors thank D. Coppersmith, H. Scherzer, S. Weingart, M. Witzel and E. Yashchin for fruitful discussions about several issues presented in this paper.

References

[1] M. Abadi, J. Feigenbaum, and J. Kilian. On Hiding Information from an Oracle. *Journal of Computer and System Sciences*, 39(1):21-50, Aug. 1989.

[2] D. Chaum. Blind Signatures for Untraceable Payments. In David Chaum and Ronald L. Rivest and Alan T. Sherman, editors, *Advances in Cryptology: Proceedings of Crypto 82*, pages 199-203, 23-25 August 1982. Plenum Press, New York and London, 1983.

[3] Suresh Chari, Charanjit S. Jutla, Josyula R. Rao and Pankaj Rohatgi. A Cautionary Note Regarding the Evaluation of AES Candidates on Smart Cards. *Proceedings of the Second Advanced Encryption Standard Candidate Conference*, Rome, Italy, March 1999.

[4] Suresh Chari, Charanjit S. Jutla, Josyula R. Rao and Pankaj Rohatgi. Towards Sound Countermeasures to Counteract Power-Analysis Attacks. In Michael Wiener, Editor, *Advances in Cryptology — Proceedings of Crypto '99*, Lecture Notes in Computer Science 1666, Springer-Verlag, 1999, pp 398–412.

[5] Christophe Clavier, Jean-Sebastien Coron, and Nora Dabbous. Differential Power Analysis in the Presence of Hardware Countermeasures. In C.K. Koc and C. Paar, editors, *Proceedings of the Workshop on Cryptographic Hardware and Embedded Systems 2000 — CHES 2000*, Second International Workshop, Worcester, MA, USA, August 17-18, 2000, Lecture Notes in Computer Science 1965, Springer-Verlag, pp 252–263.

[6] Jean-Sebastien Coron. Resistance against Differential Power Analysis for Elliptic Curve Cryptosystems. In C.K. Koc and C. Paar, editors, *Proceedings of the Workshop on Cryptographic Hardware and Embedded Systems 1999 — CHES 1999*, First International Workshop, Worcester, MA, USA, August 12–13, 1999, Lecture Notes in Computer Science 1717, Springer-Verlag. pp 292–302.

[7] Jean-Sebastien Coron, and Louis Goubin. On Boolean and Arithmetic Masking against Differential Power Analysis. In C.K. Koc and C. Paar, editors, *Proceedings of the Workshop on Cryptographic Hardware and Embedded Systems 2000 — CHES 2000*, Second International Workshop, Worcester, MA, USA, August 17-18, 2000, Lecture Notes in Computer Science 1965, Springer-Verlag. pp 231–237.

[8] J. Daemen and V. Rijmen. Resistance against implementation attacks: A comparative study of the AES proposals. *Proceedings of the Second AES Candidates Conference*, March 1999, Rome, Italy.

[9] P.N. Fahn and P.K. Pearson. IPA: A New Class of Power Attacks. In C.K. Koc and C. Paar, editors, *Proceedings of the Workshop on Cryptographic Hardware and Embedded Systems 1999 — CHES 1999*, First International Workshop, Worcester, MA, USA, August 12-13, 1999, Lecture Notes in Computer Science 1717, Springer-Verlag. pp 173–186.

[10] W. Feller. *An Introduction to Probability Theory and its application*, Volume 1, Wiley Mathematical Statistics Series, John Wiley and Sons, Ltd, 1968.

[11] L. Goubin and J. Patarin. DES and Differential Power Analysis. In C.K. Koc and C. Paar, editors, *Proceedings of the Workshop on Cryptographic Hardware and Embedded Systems 1999 — CHES 1999*, First International Workshop, Worcester, MA, USA, August 17-18, 1999, Lecture Notes in Computer Science 1717, Springer-Verlag. pp 158-172.

[12] H. Handschuh, P. Paillier, and J. Stern. Probing Attacks on Tamper Resistant Devices. In C.K. Koc and C. Paar, editors, *Proceedings of the Workshop on Cryptographic Hardware and Embedded Systems 1999 — CHES 1999*, First International Work-

shop, Worcester, MA, USA, August 12–13, 1999, Lecture Notes in Computer Science 1717, Springer-Verlag. pp 303–315.

[13] M.A. Hasan. Power Analysis Attacks and Algorithmic Approaches to Their Countermeasures for the Koblitz Curve Cryptosystems. In C.K. Koc and C. Paar, editors, *Proceedings of the Workshop on Cryptographic Hardware and Embedded Systems 2000 — CHES 2000*, Second International Workshop, Worcester, MA, USA, August 17-18, 2000, Lecture Notes in Computer Science 1965, Springer-Verlag. pp 93–108.

[14] P. Kocher. Timing Attacks on Implementations of Diffie-Hellman, RSA, DSS and Other Systems. In Neal Koblitz, editor, *Advances in Cryptology — Proceedings of Crypto '96*, Lecture Notes in Computer Science Vol. 1109, Springer Verlag, 1996, pp 104–113.

[15] P. Kocher, J. Jaffe and B. Jun. Differential Power Analysis: Leaking Secrets. In Michael Wiener, Editor, *Advances in Cryptology — Proceedings of Crypto '99*, Lecture Notes in Computer Science 1666, Springer-Verlag, 1999, pp 388–397.

[16] M. Luby. *Pseudorandomness and Cryptographic Applications*. Princeton University Press, Princeton, 1996.

[17] Rita Mayer-Sommer. Smartly Analyzing the Simplicity and the Power of Simple Power Analysis on Smart Cards. In C.K. Koc and C. Paar, editors, *Proceedings of the Workshop on Cryptographic Hardware and Embedded Systems 2000 — CHES 2000*, Second International Workshop, Worcester, MA, USA, August 17-18, 2000, Lecture Notes in Computer Science 1965, Springer-Verlag. pp 78–92.

[18] Thomas S. Messerges. Securing the AES Finalists Against Power Analysis Attacks. *Proceedings of the Fast Software Encryption Workshop 2000*, New York, NY, USA, April 10–12, 2000, Springer-Verlag.

[19] Thomas S. Messerges. Using Second-Order Power Analysis to Attack DPA Resistant Software. In C.K. Koc and C. Paar, editors, *Proceedings of the Workshop on Cryptographic Hardware and Embedded Systems 2000 — CHES 2000*, Second International Workshop, Worcester, MA, USA, August 17-18, 2000, Lecture Notes in Computer Science 1965, Springer-Verlag. pp 238–251.

[20] T.S. Messerges, E.A. Dabbish, and R.H. Sloan. Power Analysis Attacks of Modular Exponentiation in Smart Cards. In C.K. Koc and C. Paar, editors, *Proceedings of the Workshop on Cryptographic Hardware and Embedded Systems 1999 — CHES 1999*, First International Workshop, Worcester, MA, USA, August 17-18, 1999, Lecture Notes in Computer Science 1717, Springer-Verlag. pp 144–157.

[21] M. Naor, O. Reingold. On the construction of pseudo-random permutations: Luby-Rackoff revisited. In *Proceedings of the Twenty-Ninth Annual ACM Symposium on the Theory of Computing*, El Paso, Texas, May 4–6, 1997, pp 189–199.

[22] Adi Shamir. Protecting Smart Cards from Power Analysis with Detached Power Supplies. In C.K. Koc and C. Paar, editors, *Proceedings of the Workshop on Cryptographic Hardware and Embedded Systems 2000 — CHES 2000*, Second International Workshop, Worcester, MA, USA, August 17-18, 2000, Lecture Notes in Computer Science 1965, Springer-Verlag. pp 71–77.

[23] The complete unofficial TEMPEST web page. Available at http://www.eskimo.com/joelm/tempest.html.

[24] Available at http://www.counterpane.com/twofish.html.

[25] Twofish 6805 Reference code. Available at
`http://www.counterpane.com/download-twofish.html`.

20

A probabilistic approach to information hiding

Annabelle McIver and Carroll Morgan

Abstract

Security in a computer system must at some level be regarded as the control of information flow. Here we approach the issue 'from first principles', linking information flow in the sense of Shannon to a sequential programming model enriched with probabilities. From that we extract criteria for secure encapsulation of data, and we discuss the interaction of our criteria with refinement.

20.1 Introduction

The analysis of how computer systems keep secrets has at its basis 'information flow' as developed by Shannon [13]. Whilst the analysis of information flow is rather complicated (involving the consideration of probabilities) one expects that the analysis of program properties should be much simpler, and indeed standard semantics of programs does not address probability at all. Thus to acheive our expectation we need to find the right way to abstract from the probabilistic aspects of information flow, leaving a non-probabilistic characterisation that can be formulated simply in a standard program semantics.

In this paper we first develop a theory of information flow in a model of sequential programs that does accommodate the possibility of a probabilistic context. That supports a very general theory of information flow, similar to the classical theory of 'leaky channels', but adapted to allow for program-specific features. In particular we consider *demonic nondeterminism*, which is beyond the scope of classical information models. Our contribution is then to specialise the theory to non-probabilistic programs; and our second contribution is to abstract from the probability altogether, thus giving a characterisation of information flow in the traditional program-refinement context.

In Sec. 20.2 we set out the background of information flow, and we develop our own theory in Secs. 20.3 and 20.4. The definitions are illustrated by the small example of a secure file store, in Sec. 20.5.

We write $f.s$ for function f applied to argument s, with application associating to the left; and ":=" means "is defined to be".

20.2 Background: multi-level security and information flow

Historically, information flow is asociated with 'interference' in the context of multi-user systems [11, 3, 1] where the users have differing security clearances. The simplest scenario consists of two users *High* and *Low*, with respectively high and low security classifications, and the implication of the low classification is to prevent the access of *Low* to *High*'s activities or personal information. In a nutshell, *High*'s activities (whatever they are) should not 'interfere' with *Low*'s because, if they do, *Low* might deduce something about *High*.

Definitions of non-interference focus on *Low*'s ability to correlate behavioural phenomena with *High*'s activities, hence the introduction of the notion of users' 'views'. Roughly speaking, *Low*'s view is a description of the possible actions available to *Low*, including their outputs, during execution of the system. We say that *High*'s activities do not interfere just when *Low*'s view is independent of their presence or absence.

For example, a *history* of the system is a sequence of *High* and *Low* actions, interleaved; let tr and tr' be two histories. If they give the same subtrace when projected onto *Low*'s actions alone, then *Low*'s *view* of the system should be the same after either tr or tr' — even if the two traces' projections onto *High*'s actions differ. That is, the actions available to *Low* should be the same after either tr or tr'; and if such is the case then *High* is deemed not to interfere with *Low*.

Consideration of views forms the basis of many process-algebra style formulations of information flow, and have led to 'unwinding theorems' that express the security as local, checkable restrictions on individual actions.

However there are problems with focusing too much on sequences. In fact there are two ways that privacy is compromised in multi-user systems; and as Roscoe pointed out [10], sequence-based conditions fail to identify one of them (at (2) below):

1. *Low* can infer something about *High*'s activities, because they're not independent; and

2. *High* can act as a 'mole', leaking information to *Low* using an agreed encoding of sequences of actions.

Breach (2) can occur whenever there is some 'demonic nondeterminism' in the system, leading to the so-called "refinement paradox" which bedevilled many early characterisations of non-interference [12]. It's called a paradox because a desirable property (in this case pertaining to security) is not preserved under the relation of program refinement,[1] and as Roscoe observed [10] it would "require a a high order of sophisty to argue that a process which is allowed to behave as though it were insecure can be secure".

The impact of (2) was to suggest that definitions of non-interference be based on determinism [9], thus avoiding the paradox by default. More recently Lowe [5] has argued that another way to avoid the paradox is to adjust the program model to one that can distinguish between nondeterminism controllable by *High* and nondeterminism that cannot be so controlled (rather than banning it outright).

We discuss such a model in Sec. 20.6, and because nondeterminism is so important as a design tool, we will stress that probabilistic models provide the key to understanding the distinction between allowed and disallowed nondeterminism.

In the next section, however, we concentrate on (1), with the aim of finding a locally checkable semantic characterisation of information flow for imperative programs. To avoid the difficulties encountered with sequences, however, we do not attempt to formulate non-interference directly: instead we take classical information theory as our starting point. For that we need to consider programs in the context of probability.

20.3 Classical information theory, and program refinement

Shannon's classical theory of information [13] is founded in probability theory, and the measure of 'uncertainty' communicated by a probability distribution. We begin this section by introducing and adapting some of the standard ideas from that theory for expressing information flow.

20.3.1 Probability distributions and random variables

Let S be a finite state space and and let $\overline{S}$ be the set of probability distributions over S, so that

$$\overline{S} := \{\Delta \colon S \to [0,1] \mid \sum_{s:S} \Delta.s = 1\}.$$

As special cases, we shall frequently refer to the "uniform distribution" and "point distribution" defined as follows. For S' a subset of S, the *uniform distribution* $\overline{S'}$ over that subset is defined

$$\overline{S'}.s := \tfrac{1}{|S'|} \text{ if } s \in S' \text{ else } 0,$$

---

[1] But it is of course not a paradox; rather it is an exposure of the relative nature of the concept of refinement. For example, 'traditional' refinement does not preserve the desirable property of speedy execution either.

for s in S. And we define the *point distribution* $\overline{s}$, the case that assigns probability 1 to s and probability 0 to all other points, as

$$\overline{s} := \overline{\{s\}},$$

so that $(\overline{\cdot})$ can be seen in both cases — for both subsets and elements of S — as a canonical injection into $\overline{S}$.[2]

Subsets of S are called *events*, and if we apply a distribution Δ to an event E (rather than to a point) we mean its aggregate value over that subset; thus $\Delta.E$ is just $\sum_{s:E} \Delta.s$.

Finally, let f be a function over S, a *random variable*; then a distribution Δ on S induces a distribution on the codomain of that function: the probability that $f.s = x$ is just the value assigned by Δ to the event $f^{-1}.x$. We write $f.\Delta$ for that induced distribution $\Delta \circ f^{-1}$, on $f.S$, which is what we will mean if we refer to "the distribution of the random variable f".

20.3.2 Conditional distributions

Given a distribution Δ and event E, the *conditional distribution* Δ/E of Δ with respect to E is defined

$$(\Delta/E).s := \Delta.(E \cap \{s\})/\Delta.E,$$

with the value 1 being taken, by convention, should $\Delta.E$ happen to be 0.

The *conditional distribution of random variable f given E* is just the distribution $f.(\Delta/E)$ induced by f over Δ/E. Where Δ is understood, we will write just f/E.

20.3.3 Entropy

Entropy is a means to quantify uncertainty [13]. Given a distribution Δ, the entropy $\mathcal{H}.\Delta$ of Δ is defined

$$\mathcal{H}.\Delta := -\sum_{s:S} \Delta.s \times \lg(\Delta.s),$$

where the sum is taken only over s with $\Delta.s \neq 0$ and the logarithm "lg" is conventionally taken to the base 2. It is a measure of the uncertainty that Δ represents, and is largest when the distribution is uniform, smallest when the distribution is a point. In Fig. 20.1 we list some standard properties of the entropy of a distribution.

Given a random variable f over Δ, by the entropy of f we mean the entropy $\mathcal{H}.(f.\Delta)$ of the distribution induced by f. Again, we write just $\mathcal{H}.f$ when Δ is understood.

In our application to programs, we will use entropy as a measure of how much *Low* can know about the value of *High*'s variables.

---

[2] Whether the notation $\overline{S}$ itself denotes the whole space of distributions, or the (single) uniform distribution over that space, will be clear from context.

$\mathcal{H}.\bar{s} = 0$	Point distributions exhibit no uncertainty.
$0 \leq \mathcal{H}.\Delta \leq \lg \mid S' \mid$	The largest possible entropy of Δ over subset S', i.e. when $\Delta.S' = 1$, is $\lg \mid S' \mid$.
$\mathcal{H}.\overline{S'} = \lg \mid S' \mid$	Uniform distributions exhibit maximal uncertainty.
If random variable f is injective then $\mathcal{H}.(f.\Delta) = \mathcal{H}.\Delta$.	Entropy is independent of the domain values of Δ.

Figure 20.1. Some standard properties of entropy.

20.3.4 Conditional entropies

Given Δ and E, the *conditional entropy of* Δ *given* E is just the entropy of the conditional distribution Δ/E. The conditional entropy of random variable f with respect to E is the entropy of its induced conditional distribution $(f.\Delta)/E = f.(\Delta/E)$, which we may write $\mathcal{H}.(f/E)$ when Δ is clear.

More generally, suppose we have a second random variable g over S, and let y be an element of its codomain. The conditional entropy of f given that $g.s = y$ would be

$$\mathcal{H}.(f/\{s \mid g.s = y\}), \qquad (20.1)$$

and we would in effect be looking at the (remaining) uncertainty in our knowledge of f's value given that we know a specific value y that g has taken.

The expression (20.1) above can itself be regarded as a random variable (a function of y) over the co-domain $g.S$ of g, and as such it has an expected value over the induced distribution $g.\Delta$. That quantity is known as the *conditional entropy of* f *given* g, and is defined

$$\mathcal{H}_\Delta.(f/g) := \sum_{y:g.S} g.\Delta.y \times \mathcal{H}.(f.\Delta/\{s \mid g.s = y\}) .$$

We drop the subscripted Δ when it is understood.

We shall use conditional entropy as follows. Think of f as the projection of the state space onto the high-level variables, and g as the projection onto the low-level variables. Then $\mathcal{H}_\Delta.(f/g)$ measures the average uncertainty about *High*'s variables that still remains after the value of *Low*'s variables have been observed.

20.3.5 Information escape and channel capacity

In information theory, a channel is a model of data transmission and is described by a probabilistic function from input values to output values. The 'channel capacity' measures the additional information knowledge of the output values gives about the inputs that led to them. For our purposes we will consider the input and output spaces both to be S.

In this paper the 'channel' will be the operation of a program fragment, combined with channel-like observations of the 'before' and 'after' state via projection onto the *Low* variables: the information escape is the difference between what can be deduced about h before the program runs and what can be deduced after, the deduction being in both cases via l-observations only. Thus if l, h are respectively the projection functions from S onto the *Low*,*High* variables, then for a specific execution of the program that took initial distribution Δ to final distribution Δ', the 'net information escape' would be

$$\mathcal{H}_\Delta.(h/l) - \mathcal{H}_{\Delta'}.(h/l).$$

It is the appropriately conditioned 'uncertainty before' minus the 'uncertainty after'.

Our next task is to make that definition available for our model of programming, which admits both demonic nondeterminism and probability.

20.3.6 *Probabilistic guarded commands*

The probabilistic guarded command language [7] consists of traditional guarded commands [2] together with a binary probabilistic choice operator $_p\oplus$. The operational meaning of the expression $A \ _p\oplus B$ is that either A or B is executed with probability respectively p or $1-p$. Since there is no determined output, this behaviour is sometimes called "probabilistic nondeterminism". It is however very different from 'demonic nondeterminism', already present in standard guarded commands and which represents underspecification or demonic scheduling in distributed systems.

Indeed the two operators are modelled very differently — as usual probabilistic information is described by probability distributions, whereas demonic behaviour is is described by subsets of possibilities. Put together in probabilistic guarded commands that leads to a model in which programs are described by functions from initial state to sets of distributions over final states, with the possible multiplicity of the result set representing a degree of nondeterminism and the distributions recording the probabilistic information once that nondeterminism is resolved. We recall the following definition for the probabilistic program space $\mathcal{MS}$ [6, 7]:[3]

$$\mathcal{MS} := S \rightarrow \overline{\mathbb{P}S}.$$

We order programs using program refinement, which measures the range of nondeterminism — programs higher up the refinement order exhibit less nondeterminism than those lower down:

$$Q \sqsubseteq P \text{ iff } (\forall s: S \cdot P.s \subseteq Q.s).$$

---

[3] In our earlier work the space is $\mathcal{HS}$, but here we reserve it as the traditional notation for entropy.

(**assign** f).s	$:= \{\overline{f.s}\}$, for function f in $S \to S$
skip	$:=$ **assign** id
$(r \,_p\!\oplus r').s$	$:= r.s \,_p\!\oplus r'.s$ where $_p\!\oplus$ acts over all pairs from its arguments
$(r \sqcap r').s$	$:= (\cup p\!: [0,1] \cdot r.s \,_p\!\oplus r'.s)$
$(r;\, r').s$	$:= \{\Delta\!: r.s;\, f'\!: S \to \overline{S} \mid r' \supseteq f' \cdot \mathrm{Exp}.\Delta.f'\}$ where $\mathrm{Exp}.\Delta.f'$ is the expected value of f' over Δ

$(r \text{ if } B \text{ else } r').s := r.s \text{ if } B.s \text{ else } r'.s$

We also write $s{:}\epsilon\, S'$ for the nondeterministic assignment to s from the set S, and similarly $s{:}\epsilon\, \Delta$ for the probabilistic assignment to s according to distribution Δ. (We tell the difference by noting whether the right-hand side is a set or a distribution.) Particularly in the latter case the syntax would be rather convoluted otherwise, for we would have to write

$$x := i_0 \,_{\Delta.i_0}\!\oplus (x := i_1 \,_{\Delta.i_1/(1-\Delta.i_0)}\!\oplus \cdots).$$

Figure 20.2. Probabilistic relational semantics[4]

The full semantics is set out in Fig. 20.2.

The consequences of the refinement order are, for example, that if Q guarantees to establish a predicate ϕ with probability at least p (irrespective of the nondeterminism) then P must establish ϕ with probability at least that same p. That probabilistic properties are robust against program refinement is one way to understand the difference between probability and demonic nondeterminism.

For example a fair coin flip cannot be refined by any program except itself, hence in particular we have

$$s := 0 \,_{1/2}\!\oplus s := 1 \;\not\sqsubseteq\; s := 1 \,,$$

since the left-hand program establishes $s = 0$ with probability $1/2$, but the right-hand side establishes $s = 0$ only with probability 0. This is the sense in which probability cannot be 'refined away". Demonic nondeterminism, on the other hand, can always be refined away:

$$s := 0 \sqcap s := 1 \;\sqsubseteq\; s := 1 \,.$$

---

[4]For simplicity we do not treat non-termination, although the theory extends easily to accommodate it.

In that refinement, the left-hand side is never guaranteed to execute the assignment $s := 0$; but the right-hand side is guaranteed never to do so.

In summary, the program $A \,_p\!\oplus B$ means that A is executed predictably with probability p, whereas no such quantitative statements can be made about the program $A \sqcap B$. We shall use that property of probability to to guarantee 'refinement-proofness' in our characterisation of security, to which we now turn.

20.4 Information flow in imperative programs

Following the general scheme of *High* and *Low* users, we associate them with corresponding variables named h and l; in this framework we imagine that *Low* can read variables named l but not h. Security systems are built from a collection of procedures or operations which, when called, grant users the opportunity of updating (possibly) the values of the variables. In this setting, as for Rushby's approach [11], *Low*'s view is based on the traces of the values held on l during the use of the system, and the intention of system security can be described as follows:

> A system comprising operations Op is secure provided that if the value of *High*'s variables are not known (to *Low*) initially, then they cannot be inferred at any later time during use.

Put another way, we could say that *Low* cannot infer the value of *High*'s variables only if *Low*'s variables remain uncorrelated to those of *High*. And from Sec. 20.3.5 we can measure the degree of correlation using conditional entropy and channel capacity.

Let the projection functions from S onto its *High*- and *Low* components be called h, l; and let the corresponding types be H, L. Given a distribution Δ in $\overline{S}$, the conditional entropy of h with respect to l is, as we have seen, given by $\mathcal{H}_\Delta.(h/l)$.

To relate that to our programming model, we look for the *maximum* change in that entropy over all possible executions of a given operation; that is we maximise over all its possible initial distributions as well as all possible resolutions of demonic nondeterminism within it.

For program operation Op and distribution Δ, we write simply $Op.\Delta$ for the set of possible state distributions that could result from executing Op with Δ as the distribution of the initial state. Then, based on the notion of information escape from Sec. 20.3.5, we define the insecurity introduced by the program — with respect to flow from h to l — by considering the 'worst case' of the program's behaviour, taken over all its demonic choices and possible incoming h, l-distributions:

Definition 20.4.1 *Given an operation Op in $\mathcal{MS}$, the h-to-l channel capacity of Op is given by*

$$\mathcal{C}_l^h[\![Op]\!] \ := \ (\sqcup \Delta : \overline{S}; \ \Delta' : Op.\Delta \cdot \mathcal{H}_\Delta.(h/l) - \mathcal{H}_{\Delta'}.(h/l)) \,.$$

20. A probabilistic approach to information hiding   449

The maximising over Δ considers all possible initial distributions; and the maximising over Δ' considers all possible resolutions of nondeterminism once the initial distribution has been selected.

In the special (but common) case that S is just the Cartesian product of the spaces H and L, it can be shown that one need not consider incoming distributions over L: the initial distribution can be taken (effectively) over H alone, provided one maximises over all possible initial values of l. That is, Def. 20.4.1 implies in this case that $\mathcal{C}_l^h[\![Op]\!]$ is

$$
\begin{aligned}
&(\sqcup \lambda \in L \cdot \\
&\quad (\sqcup \Delta \colon \overline{H} \cdot \\
&\quad\quad \mathcal{H}.\Delta - \\
&\quad\quad (\sqcap \Delta' \colon (l := \lambda\,;\,h{:}\epsilon\,\Delta\,;\,Op) \cdot \\
&\quad\quad\quad \mathcal{H}_{\Delta'}.(h/l) \\
&))),
\end{aligned}
\qquad
\begin{aligned}
&\text{The maximum over all initial } l \text{ values } \lambda \text{ of} \\
&\text{the maximum over all initial } h \text{ distributions of} \\
&\text{the incoming } h\text{-entropy } \textit{minus} \\
&\text{the minimum over all outgoing}\ldots \\
&\ldots (h/l)\text{-conditional entropies.}
\end{aligned}
$$

(20.2)

where we have written $(l := \lambda\,;\,h{:}\epsilon\,\Delta\,;\,Op)$ for a the set of distributions potentially resulting from running that program fragment. As an extension of that notation, because we are minimising (acting demonically) at that point, later we will write

$$l := \lambda\,;\,h{:}\epsilon\,\Delta\,;\,Op\,;\,\mathcal{H}.(h/l)$$

for $(\sqcap \Delta' \colon (l := \lambda\,;\,h{:}\epsilon\,\Delta\,;\,Op) \cdot \mathcal{H}_{\Delta'}.(h/l))$, which has the intuitive sense of 'execute the fragment $(l := \lambda\,;\,h{:}\epsilon\,\Delta\,;\,Op)$ and take the minimum possible conditional entropy $\mathcal{H}.(h/l)$ at its end".[5]

We now consider the following program fragments in order to investigate how Def. 20.4.1 — and its equivalent (20.2) — measure up with our intuitive notions of security. The state space S is the Cartesian product $H \times L$ of the high- and low-level types, and the projection functions are the standard Cartesian projections.

1. $\mathcal{C}_l^h[\![l := h]\!] = \lg|H|$.

2. $\mathcal{C}_l^h[\![h := l]\!] = \lg|H|$.

3. $\mathcal{C}_l^h[\![h := (h+1) \bmod |H|]\!] = 0$.

4. $\mathcal{C}_l^h[\![l := h \bmod 2]\!] = 1$.

5. $\mathcal{C}_l^h[\![l{:}\epsilon\,L]\!] = \lg|H| \min \lg|L|$.

Examples (1) and (2) give channel capacities for programs that we would consider to be totally insecure — in both cases the result of execution is to establish that h and l have the same value, so that the final conditional entropy of h with respect to l is 0; the maximum possible initial conditional entropy is when h and l are independent, and is $\lg|H|$. That agrees with the quantitative assessment

---

[5] That notation is motivated by the 'expression blocks" of some Algol-like languages.

which gives maximal channel capacities — it is an extreme case of insecurity since all details of h are revealed via l.[6]

Example (3) on the other hand represents only a shuffling of the values of h and so should normally be regarded as secure — if the exact value of h is not known before execution then it cannot be known afterwards. Again we see that this agrees with the quantitative assessment, for the channel capacity of 0 signals the opposite extreme, in that there is no correlation at all between h and l.

Examples (4) and (5) lie somewhere between those extreme cases. Example (4) publishes something about h — but not everything — and the channel capacity suggests that it reveals one bit of information.

Finally, the demonic nondeterminism in (5) introduces insecurity because it can be resolved to reveal part or all of h depending on the relative ranges of h and l. When $|H| \leq |L|$, clearly all information $\lg |H|$ about h can be revealed; but one can in any case never reveal more than $\lg |L|$.

Encouraged by all this we can finally define our security property by insisting that Op is secure only if its execution releases no information at all.

Definition 20.4.2 *Using the* High *and* Low *conventions, we say that Op in $\mathcal{MS}$ is h,l-secure iff*[7]

$$\mathcal{C}_l^h[\![Op]\!] = 0.$$

In most realistic cases the calculation of exact channel capacities will of course be very difficult, and using Def. 20.4.2 directly would therefore be impractical. In the rest of this section we shall look for simpler formulations based on program refinement, and will concentrate on programs which contain no probabilistic choice at all. We call these programs standard programs, and they form a subset of $\mathcal{MS}$.[8]

20.4.1 *Information flow and program refinement*

We begin by considering properties of standard programs that imply Def. 20.4.2.
Suppose $0 \leq h < N$, and consider the program fragment

$$h := (h+1) \bmod N.$$

It is considered to be secure, since it merely permutes *High*'s variables. The program $h := 0$, on the other hand is not considered to be secure, since it guarantees to set h to 0 whatever its initial value. Nor is it a permutation (*i.e.* it does not inject H into H).

These observations are not surprising since Def. 20.4.2 is based on entropy, which we recall from Fig. 20.1 is left invariant under injections.

---

[6] Note that in some formulations [4] example (2) would be *secure* because h's initial value is not revealed. (See Sec. 20.4.2.)

[7] Because channel capacities cannot be negative, we may equate no information flow with zero channel capacities.

[8] Although standard programs contain no probabilistic choice, we must analyse them in the probabilistic model in order to use our notions of entropy and information flow.

In finite state spaces, permutations correspond to isomorphisms, and the condition "*Op* permutes the hidden part of the state space" amounts to saying that for each initial *l* value, the number of possible final *h* values after running *Op* must be exactly $|H|$. But permutations are not quite enough for security, because we need to ensure as well that the value of *h* is not communicated by the value of *l*. (Note that the program $l := h$ is the identity permutation on *H*, yet is insecure.) Those requirements are met by this definition, whose motivation follows.

Definition 20.4.3 *We say that Op in $\mathcal{MS}$ acts as a* secure permutation *if any deterministic refinement Op' of Op satisfies*

$$Op'; h{:}\epsilon\, H \;=\; h{:}\epsilon\, H;\, Op'\,.$$

Our definition of secure permutation must encapsulate two ideas involved in information flow: neither the initial nor the final high values can be deduced from the final values of *Op*. The secrecy of the initial values is preserved if the refinement

$$Op'; h{:}\epsilon\, H \;\sqsubseteq\; h{:}\epsilon\, H;\, Op'\,.$$

holds: its refinement states that one possible behaviour of Op' is as if it were run after any initialisation of *h* whatsoever (from $h{:}\epsilon\, H$ on the *rhs*). so that it cannot be communicating any information about the actual value of *h* (*lhs*). (The $h{:}\epsilon\, H$ on the left is only to allow the refinement to go through for any action on the right of *Op* on *h*.)

Similarly the secrecy of the final values can be captured by the reverse refinement. Def. 20.4.3 simply combines the two.

The next lemma shows that indeed programs that are secure permutations are secure.

Lemma 20.4.4 *If Op is a secure permuation, then Op is secure according to Def. 20.4.2.*

Proof. For any λ in *L*, it follows from Def. 20.4.3 that, for any deterministic refinement Op' of *Op*, the function $Op'.\,\lambda$, acting on *h*-values, is just a permutation. Since it is a permutation, Fig. 20.2 tells us that for any Δ' in $(l := \lambda\,;\, h{:}\epsilon\,\Delta\,;\, Op)$ we have

$$\mathcal{H}_{\Delta'}.(h/l) \;=\; \mathcal{H}.\Delta' \;=\; \mathcal{H}.\Delta\,.$$

(The first equality os from Def. 20.4.3 again: we note that it implies a single final *l*-value λ', given fixed initial λ, which makes the conditional h/l degenerate.) Hence from Def. 20.4.1 we have $\mathcal{C}_l^h[\![Op]\!] = 0$, implying Def. 20.4.2. □

In fact, as we shall see, permutations account for all the secure standard programs. To prove it we turn to refinement properties of programs that are implied by security.

One way to see how security can be described by refinement is to think of it as a problem of data abstraction in which *High*'s variables are hidden. This is reminiscent of the idea of views, in that *Low*'s view with *h* abstracted should appear as though nothing about *h* is known. Since complete ignorance of the value of h is described by the uniform distribution, that view should remain invariant on execution of P. Another way of expressing that invariance is to say that P is 'uniform preserving':

Definition 20.4.5 *We say that Op in $\mathcal{MS}$ is uniform preserving if*

$$l{:}\epsilon L;\ h{:}\epsilon \overline{H}\ \sqsubseteq\ h{:}\epsilon \overline{H};\ Op\,.$$

Def. 20.4.5 takes the form of a simulation equation typical of data abstraction, in which the program $h{:}\epsilon \overline{H}$ (that is, 'choose h from H according to the uniform distribution $\overline{H}$') is the abstraction invariant: we are saying that the operation Op 'is a data refinement under h-is-uniform" of $l{:}\epsilon L$. The effect is not to constrain Op's effect on l at all, except to maintain h's uniformity.

Lemma 20.4.6 *If Op in $\mathcal{MS}$ is secure, then it is uniform preserving.*

Proof. If Op is secure, then from Def. 20.4.2 we must have that $\mathcal{C}_l^h[\![Op]\!] = 0$ and in therefore in particular that for any λ

$$l := \lambda\,;\ h{:}\epsilon \overline{H};\ Op;\ \mathcal{H}.(h/l)\ =\ \lg |H|\,. \qquad (20.3)$$

Next from Fig. 20.1 we know that the entropy of $\overline{H}$ is maximal, and therefore (20.3) implies that the output distribution of h after executing $h{:}\epsilon \overline{H};\ Op$ must be uniform as well. Put another way, $h{:}\epsilon \overline{H};\ Op$ satisfies the refinement

$$l{:}\epsilon L;\ h{:}\epsilon \overline{H}\ \sqsubseteq\ h{:}\epsilon \overline{H};\ Op\,,$$

and the lemma follows. □

We end this section with the result that shows that uniform preserving and permutations are equivalent to security.

Theorem 20.4.7 *The following are equivalent for program Op in $\mathcal{MS}$.*

> *Op is secure (Def. 20.4.2)*
> *iff Op is uniform preserving*
> *iff Op is a secure permutation of H.*

Proof. From Lem. 20.4.6 and Lem. 20.4.4 we see that the theorem follows provided we show that "uniform preserving" implies "is a secure permutation".

We prove the contrapositive. Suppose then that Op is not a secure permutation with respect to H. That means that there is some deterministic refinement Op' of Op and some initial value λ taken by l such that Op' does not act as a permutation on H when initially $l = \lambda$. Thus it follows that the distribution of h after execution of $h{:}\epsilon \overline{H};\ Op'$ from initial state with $l = \lambda$ is not uniform over the whole of H.

That is the same as saying that

$$l{:}\epsilon L;\ h{:}\epsilon \overline{H}\ \not\sqsubseteq\ h{:}\epsilon \overline{H};\ Op'\,,$$

which shows that Op' and therefore Op is not uniform preserving. The theorem now follows. □

Unfortunately having removed probability (by focusing on secure permtations) has not yet simplified the analysis sufficiently. We end this section by considering a consequence of Thm. 20.4.7 that further reduces work in the analysis.

Thm. 20.4.7 implies that the analysis can be perfomed entirely within a model of standard (non-probabilistic) programs, and we will use the predicate transformer model since it is equivalent to relational models.

A predicate transformer over S is a function $\mathbb{P}S \to \mathbb{P}S$, monotonic with respect to the subset ordering on $\mathbb{P}S$. If Op is a standard program, then we write $wp.Op$ for the predicate transformer interpretation — that means that for any postcondition $post$, precondition $wp.Op.post$ is the weakest precondition which guarantees that Op will establish $post$.

Some standard properties of predicate transformers we use are that, for Op expressed in the non-probabilistic fragment of the programming language set out in Fig. 20.2, the transformer $wp.Op$ distributes $\wedge$; if Op is deterministic and terminating then $wp.Op$ distributes $\vee$ and $\neg$; and $wp.(x{:}\epsilon X).post = (\forall x{:}X \cdot post)$.

With those conventions we have the following corollary to Thm. 20.4.7:

Corollary 20.4.8 *If Op is secure then, for any postcondition $post$ and deterministic refinement Op' of Op,*

$$(\forall l{:}L \cdot (\exists h{:}H \cdot post)) \;\Rightarrow\; (\forall l{:}L \cdot (\exists h{:}H \cdot wp.Op'.post)) \,.$$

Proof. By Thm. 20.4.7 we know that security of P implies that it is a secure permutation and therefore by Def. 20.4.3 all deterministic refinements Op' of it satisfy

$$Op'; h{:}\epsilon H \;=\; h{:}\epsilon H; Op' \,.$$

We continue our reasoning in predicate transformers from this point: for any $post$,

$$wp.(Op'; h{:}\epsilon H).\neg post \;\equiv\; wp.(h{:}\epsilon H; Op').\neg post$$

iff $\qquad\qquad\qquad\qquad\qquad\qquad\qquad\qquad$ Op' is deterministic and terminating
$$\neg wp.Op'.(\exists h{:}H \cdot post) \;\equiv\; \neg(\exists h{:}H \cdot wp.Op'.post)$$

iff $\qquad wp.Op'.(\exists h{:}H \cdot post) \;\equiv\; (\exists h{:}H \cdot wp.Op'.post)$

implies $\quad (\forall l{:}L \cdot (\exists h{:}H \cdot post)) \;\Rightarrow\; (\exists h{:}H \cdot wp.Op'.post) \qquad\qquad$ see below

iff $\qquad\qquad\qquad\qquad\qquad\qquad\qquad\qquad\qquad\qquad$ l not free in lhs
$$(\forall l{:}L \cdot (\exists h{:}H \cdot post)) \;\Rightarrow\; (\forall l{:}L \cdot (\exists h{:}H \cdot wp.Op'.post)) \,.$$

For the deferred justification we note that for any $post'$

$$(\forall l{:}L; h{:}H \cdot post') \;\Rightarrow\; wp.Op'.post' \,,$$

and that when $post'$ is itself $(\exists h{:}H \cdot post)$, the universal $\forall h$ can be dropped. $\qquad\square$

The implication of Cor. 20.4.8 is that security can be checked by considering a reduced set of postconditions. The condition on its left-hand side, namely

$$(\forall l: L \cdot (\exists h: H \cdot post)), \qquad (20.4)$$

restricts predicates rather than programs. We say that a postcondition satisfying (20.4) is *total in l*. Thus we have the following corollary.

Corollary 20.4.9 *Op is secure provided that whenever post is total in l then so is wp.Op.post.*

Proof. Suppose for the contrapositive that for some total *post* we have non-total *wp.Op.post*. We choose deterministic refinement Op' of Op so that $wp.Op.post \equiv wp.Op'.post$, and observe from Cor. 20.4.8 that Op is therefore not secure. □

20.4.2 Comparisons with other work

Finally we end this section by considering other formulations of security in the imperative style. Typically they do not *maintain* the privacy of *High*'s variables, but rather seek to preserve secrecy of their initial values [4]. We call this property "weakly secure".

Definition 20.4.10 *We say that Op is* weakly secure *if it does not reveal any information about the initial values of h. This is equivalent to [4]*

$Op; h:\epsilon H \sqsubseteq h:\epsilon H; Op$.

As we noted earlier, this is only half of our Def. 20.4.3, which is therefore stronger.. In fact the definition we give in Sec. 20.4 is stronger than Def. 20.4.10. Intuitively, if *Op* reveals information about the initial value of *h* then it most likely reveals information about the final value as well, since that in many cases can be inferred from the text of the program. That intuition is formalised in the next lemma (whose proof is omitted).

Lemma 20.4.11 *Security of final values implies security of initial values (weak security) for standard deterministic programs.*

The difference between the two approaches is evident with program fragment $h := 0$, which is weakly secure, but not secure. That is because the initial value of *h* has been obliterated by the call, and hence cannot be known; but the current value of *h* is certainly disclosed, on the assumption that *Low* has a copy of the program specification.

In fact Rushby's formulation of non-interference would also certify that the above operation is secure, if *Low* can call it, since his view of the system is certainly unaffected, whatever *High* does.

20.5 Example: The secure file store

We illustrate our definitions on the 'secure filestore' example [10].

20. A probabilistic approach to information hiding

A filestore comprises named files, and each file is classified as having either 'high' or 'low' security status. Low-level- and high-level users operate on the two classifications separately, with the usual operations such as *create, open, read, write, close* and *delete*; and the intention is that a low-level user cannot discover anything — via those operations — about the high-level portion of the filestore.

The security breach in this example occurs when the low-level user attempts to create a file whose name happens to be the same as an extant high-level file. When the system rejects the create operation ("File name exists."), the low-level user has learned the name of a high-level file.

We treat the example at increasing levels of complexity/realism.

20.5.1 The 'bare bones'

Since the security breach occurs independently for each (potential) filename, we concentrate first on a single, arbitrary name which therefore — since it is constant — we need not model explicitly. To refer to it, however, we will call it *fileName*.

Our state space S comprises two Boolean variables h and l, each indicating whether the *fileName* exists at that level, and a third Boolean r for 'result', to indicate success or failure of operations. Invariant will be that the file cannot exist at both levels, which is in fact the source of the insecurity:

$$S := h, l, r : Boolean.$$

The create-a-low-level-file operation is then

$$CreateLow0 := \textbf{if } \neg(h \vee l) \textbf{ then } l, r := \textbf{true}, \textbf{true}$$
$$\textbf{else } r := \textbf{false}$$
$$\textbf{fi}.$$

It is the conditional that prevents the creation of a file at both levels.

Our security criterion Cor. 20.4.9 requires that total postconditions give total preconditions; and in this case our security classification gives "total" the meaning "for every l, r there must be an h". For this example we demonstrate insecurity with the (total) postcondition $h = r$; the weakest precondition through *CreateLow0* is then the partial $l \wedge \neg h$ (which has no satisfying h-value when l is false).

The intuition for choosing such postconditions is this: if there is a security leak, then from some initial value of the low-level variables (it's our choice — we are looking for leaks) there is a possible low-level result (again our choice, if demonic nondeterminism allows more than one low-level result) for which we *know* that certain high-level values are not possible. That's the knowledge that could have leaked.

In this case, when l is initially **false**, we know that after *CreateLow0* it cannot be that r and h are equal: for if the operation succeeded ($r = $ **true**) there must be no high-level file (h cannot be true); and, if it failed ($r = $ **false**), then there must be a high-level file (h cannot be false).

$CreateLow1(n: FILENAME; r: Boolean) :=$

    if $n \notin domain.s$ **then** $s[n] := (ll, emptyData); r := $ **true**
                    else $r := $ **false**
    fi ,

$ReadLow1(n: FILENAME; d: DATA; r: Boolean) :=$

    if $n \in domain.s \land s[n].level = ll$ **then** $d := s[n].data; r := $ **true**
                                      else $r := $ **false**
    fi ,

$WriteLow1(n: FILENAME; d: DATA; r: Boolean) :=$

    if $n \in domain.s \land s[n].level = ll$ **then** $s[n].data := d; r := $ **true**
                                      else $r := $ **false**
    fi ,

Figure 20.3. Selection of file-system operations

20.5.2 Adding filenames and data

The scenario of the previous section reveals the essence of the insecurity. In this section we show how the essential insecurity remains within a more realistic framework: we add filenames and data to the system.

Let a file comprise some data and an indication of its level, and let the system state be a (partial) mapping from filenames to files:

$$\begin{aligned} FILE &:= (level : \{hh, ll\}; data : DATA) \\ S &:= (s: FILENAME \rightarrow FILE) . \end{aligned} \quad (20.5)$$

Note that the invariant 'can't be both high and low' is 'built-in' to this model, since the *level* component of *FILE* can have only one value and s is a function. Rather than clutter the system state with input and output parameters, we will this time write them with the operations, that is in a more conventional way; formally, however, we continue to treat them as part of the state. A selection of the extended operations is given in Fig. 20.3.

Specifying the system as above — i.e. in a 'natural' way, without planning in advance for our security criterion — reveals a potential problem: which part of s in (20.5) is the hidden variable?

We formalise the intuition that 'it's the files with *level* set to *hh*' by imagining an alternative formulation partitioned between the two, splitting S into S_h and S_l with the obvious coupling invaraint linking s with s_h and s_l. Then by analogy with our treatment of *CreateLow0* we start off by considering postcondition ($n \in domain.s_h) \equiv (r = \mathbf{true})$. The precondition of that with respect to *CreateLow1* is

$$n \in domain.s_l, \qquad (20.6)$$

which is not total.

20.5.3 Proving security vs. demonstrating insecurity

The complementary question is of course whether the other operations — *ReadLow1* and *WriteLow1* — are secure according to our criteria. In principle we would consider all possible total postconditions, showing the corresponding precondition to be total as well; in practice however one tries to avoid quantifying over postconditions, as the resulting second-order reasoning can be unpleasant or even infeasible.

One approach is to use an equivalent algebraic formulation of the property, and then to reason within the appropriate program algebra. For example, our criterion 'total post- yields pre-' can be written algebraically as

$$l{:}\epsilon_\sqcap L; \ h{:}\epsilon_\sqcup H \ \sqsubseteq \ h{:}\epsilon_\sqcup H; \ Op,$$

where we now subscript the nondeterministic choices to indicate whether they are demonic or angelic. That, when specialised to operation *ReadLow1* in the file system, becomes

$$\begin{aligned} s_l, n, d, r \ &{:}\epsilon_\sqcap \ S_l, FILENAME, DATA, Boolean; \\ s_h{:}&\epsilon_\sqcup S_h \end{aligned}$$

$$\sqsubseteq s_h{:}\epsilon_\sqcup S_h; \ ReadLow1 \,.$$

Looking at the right-hand side, we note that the condition $n \in domain.s \wedge s[n].level{=}ll$ in *ReadLow1* can be rewritten

$$n \in domain.s_l,$$

because of the way in which s, s_h and s_l are related by the coupling invariant. Then *ReadLow1* does not refer to s_h at all; the two statements commute; and the refinement becomes trivial, as any criterion of this kind should when the high-level variables are not mentioned.

20.6 The Refinement Paradox

This so-called paradox is a modern manifestation of a (lack of) distinction between 'underspecification' and (demonic) nondeterminism. The most widely used formal models of programming — Hoare-triple, predicate-transformer, relational — rightly[9] do not distinguish these two specifications:

Prog0   'Always set l to 0, or always set l to 1'; and

Prog1   'Always set l to either 0 or 1'.

In our context the former is secure, since neither program $l := 0$ nor program $l := 1$ can reveal anything about h; yet the latter is insecure, because it can behave like (equivalently, can be refined to) the program $l := h$. Yet the two programs are identified in the usual models, and that is the 'paradox'.

The issue arises again in the interaction between any two of the three forms of nondeterminism demonic, angelic and probabilistic. Consider the two systems

$$h := 0 \;_{1/2}\oplus\; 1; \quad Prog0$$
and
$$h := 0 \;_{1/2}\oplus\; 1; \quad Prog1\,.$$

In the first case, on termination $h = l$ with probability $1/2$ exactly; but in the second case that probability can be as low as zero.

In our security context, the point is that we would like to be able to specify a modified *Prog1* that 'sets l to 0 or 1 but without looking at h', lying between the two extremes above. To do so would mean we had combined security and abstraction, thus avoiding the paradox.

20.6.1 Some algebraic difficulties

It is tempting to look for a model supporting 'nuanced' demonic choice, ranging from the 'oblivious' choice that sees nothing through an intermediate 'cannot see h' choice to the familiar 'omniscient' choice. But simple algebraic experiments show how tricky this can be.

Write $\sqcap_h$ for the choice that can't look at h: then oblivious choice is $\sqcap_{h,l}$ and our normal omniscient choice remains $\sqcap$ (because it can't look at nothing). Now consider this reasoning: we have

$$
\begin{array}{rll}
 & l := 0 \sqcap_h 1 & \\
= & l := 0; \quad l := 0 \sqcap_h 1; & \text{Principle 1, below} \\
= & (l := h; l := 0); \quad l := 0 \sqcap_h 1; & \text{Principle 2} \\
= & l := h; \quad (l := 0; l := 0 \sqcap_h 1); & \text{associativity of composition} \\
= & l := h; \quad l := 0 \sqcap_h 1; & \text{Principle 1} \\
\sqsubseteq & l := h; \quad \textbf{skip}; & \text{allowed by } \sqcap_h \\
= & l := h\,. &
\end{array}
$$

To avoid that insupportable conclusion (without giving up associativity, refinement or the meaning of **skip**), we must forgo either

Principle 1:   Demonic choice $\sqcap_h$ can be treated as simple $\sqcap$ in contexts that don't mention h, or

---

[9] ...because in everyday programming situations it does not matter.

Principle 2:   Variables h, l may be treated normally in contexts that don't mention $\sqcap_h$.

Note that we describe the principles syntactically, since their purpose is a practical one: to lay down the restrictions for a simple (syntactic) algebra. But that is not to say that they do not have operational interpretations as well: for example, Principle 1 implies that $\sqcap_h$ can 'see past program states', since otherwise the overwriting of l's value might destroy information that $\sqcap_h$ 'could have used' and the equality would not hold.[10]

20.6.2 The 'quantum' model

We explore the consequences of abandoning Principle 2, choosing that alternative for two reasons. First, any program structure that supported scoping (of h) would make it unnecessary in practice to write $\sqcap_h$, since an implied subscript h on plain $\sqcap$ could be inferred from h's not being in scope: that makes loss of Principle 1 even more problematic in practice.

Second, the statement $l := h$ at least 'crosses the encapsulation boundary', and so alerts us to our having to employ 'enhanced' reasoning about it. Indeed, the statement would probably have to be located within the module in which h was declared, a further advantage. So we abandon $(l := h;\ l := 0) = l := 0$, if h is inside a module and l outside of it: variable h will be treated differently.

The *quantum* model treats secure variables h as a distribution, separately — in fact, within — the overall distribution on the state space as a whole. Thus for example, in the ordinary (probabilistic) model the program

$$h := 0 \ _{1/2}\oplus 1; \quad l := 0 \ _{1/2}\oplus 1$$

results in a uniform distribution between four final possiblilities; we could write it (pairing as (l, h))

$$(0,0) \bullet 1/4, \quad (0,1) \bullet 1/4, \quad (1,0) \bullet 1/4, \quad (1,1) \bullet 1/4. \tag{20.7}$$

In the quantum model, instead the result is a $1/2$-$1/2$ distribution (in l) between two further $1/2$-$1/2$ distributions (in h); we would write

$$\begin{array}{ll} (0, (0 \bullet 1/2, 1 \bullet 1/2)) & \bullet\ 1/2 \\ (1, (0 \bullet 1/2, 1 \bullet 1/2)) & \bullet\ 1/2 \end{array} \tag{20.8}$$

The effect of the assignment $l := h$ is to move from state (20.8) to state (20.7), in effect 'collapsing' the hidden distribution; and a subsequent $l := 0$ does not undo the collapse.

---

[10] In fact, the standard refinement $l := 0;\ l := 0 \sqcap 1 \sqsubseteq$ **skip** suggests the same about ordinary $\sqcap$.

20.6.3 Implications for security

With the more complicated model, we are able — as we should be — to combine demonic choice and security: for example, the statement $l := 0 \sqcap_h 1$ is no longer refined by $l := h$ if h is hidden. The details of the model, however, remain complex (as do those of other similar models [5]); and it will require further work to see whether it can be made practical.

References

[1] D. Denning. *Cryptography and Data Security.* Addison-Wesley, 1983.

[2] E.W. Dijkstra. *A Discipline of Programming*. Prentice Hall International, Englewood Cliffs, N.J., 1976.

[3] J.A. Goguen and J. Meseguer. Security policies and security models. In *Proc. IEEE Symp. on Security and Privacy*, 1982.

[4] Rajeev Joshi and K. Rustan M. Leino. A semantic approach to secure information flow. *Science of Computer Programming*, 37((1-3)):113–138, May 2000.

[5] G. Lowe. Defining information flow. Technical Report 1999/3, Dept. Maths. and Comp. Sci., Univ. Leicester, 1999.

[6] Carroll Morgan and Annabelle McIver. *pGCL*: Formal reasoning for random algorithms. *South African Computer Journal*, 22, March 1999. Also available at [8].

[7] C.C. Morgan, A.K. McIver, and K. Seidel. Probabilistic predicate transformers. *ACM Transactions on Programming Languages and Systems*, 18(3):325–353, May 1996.

[8] PSG. Probabilistic Systems Group: Collected reports.
http://web.comlab.ox.ac.uk/oucl/research/areas/probs/bibliography.html.

[9] A.W. Roscoe. *The Theory and Practice of Concurrency*. Prentice-Hall.

[10] A.W. Roscoe, J.C.P. Woodcock, and L. Wulf. Non-interference through determinism. *Journal of Computer Security*, 4(1), 1996.

[11] John Rushby. Noninterference, transitivity and channel-control security policies. Technical report, SRI, 1992.

[12] P.Y.A. Ryan. A CSP formulation of interference. *Cipher*, 19-27, 1991.

[13] C.E. Shannon A mathematical theory of communication. *Bell Syst. Tech. J.* Vol 27, 379–423 and 623–656, 1948.

Index

A

Abort statement, 23
Abstract fields, 253, 257
    abstract objects versus, 263
Abstract objects, abstract fields versus, 263
Abstract variable, validity as, 272–273
Abstraction, 105, 276–278, 296–297, 335, 341–342
    data, 342–343
    general concepts of, 101–102
    predicate, 343–347
Abstraction dependencies, 269–287
Abstractions
    of programs, 341–347
    from time, 95–105
Action statement, 25
Action system notation, 18
Action systems, 18, 24–25
    analyzing behavior of, 39–43
    classification of, 39
    examples of, 25–27
Actions, 17, 20, 25, 70, 71, 165, 363
Acyclic graph, 236
Agents, 17
Algebraic languages, 261
Alternating-time temporal logic, 50
Always operator, 37
Always-property, proved, 45
Analogic model, 148
Angel, 30
Angelic iteration, 39
Angelic scheduling, 18
ARC diagram, 164
ARC evaluation tool, 168
ARC modelling paradigm, 162
ARC notation, 163–166
Architectures
    modelling, for dynamic systems, 161–172
    for reuse, 168–172
    software, *see* Software architectures
Assertion, 20–21, 334
Assumptions, 11
Asynchronous circuits, 410
Asynchronous progress, 57–67
Asynchronous safety, 65–66
Asynchrony, logical approaches to, 53–55
Atomicity, 12–13
Automata, timed, 336
Automated verification, 333–348
Auxiliary variables, 112, 123

B

Behavior(s)
    analyzing, 33–34, 40–43
    of action systems, 39–43
    complex, specifying, 135–136
    of components, 99–100
    enforcing, with contracts, 17–50
    human, 196–198
Behavior properties, 33
    enforcing, 33–38
Bisimulation, 233
Box condition, 83
Boxes, 70, 71, 356
    partial order on, 80–81
Bracketing, 321–323
Bracketing Theorem, 321–323

C

Categorial grammar, 300
Causal loops, 96
Chains, 238–239
Channel capacity, 445–446
Channels, 99
Choice, 21, 22
    nondeterministic, 120–121
Class composition, 216
Class diagram, 248
Class specification, 215
Clean state, 57–58
Coalition, 28
Code reuse, 217–218
Commitments, 11
Communication-history refinement, 101
Commutativity, 64
Compatibility, 83–87
Compatible procedures, semi-
    commutativity of, 86–87
Complexity, discrete, 158
Components, 6
    behaviors of, 99–100
    as functions on streams, 99–100
    loosely–coupled, 171
Compositionality, 5–7
Concurrency, vi, 218, 219
    compositional approach to, 5–13
    interaction and, 3–4
    interference and, 7–8
Concurrent programs, 69–70
    reduction theorem for, 69–91
    shared-variable, 8
Conditional composition, 20, 22, 396
Conditional composition declaration, 403
Conditional distributions, 444
Conditional entropy, 445
Configuration, 21
Congruence, 60
Constant change, context of, 162
Containment, 60
Continuation call, 361
Continuity, 61
Continuity requirement, 67
Continuous function, 312
Continuous infinite streams, 96
Contract statements, 20
    recursive, 21

Contracts, 17, 19–27
    achieving goals with, 27–33
    enforcing behavior with, 17–50
    examples of, 23–24
    recursive, *see* Recursive contracts
    refinement of, 32–33
    stepwise refinement of, 33
Control flow graph, 225
Convergent tree, 239
Correctness, 30, 407–409
    models and, 1–203
    predicate-level conditions for, 43–44
Curry–Howard isomorphism, 294

D

Data
    adding, 456–457
    operational, 357
Data abstraction, 342–343
    need for, 270–272
Data diagrams, 225
Dataflow networks, 64
Deadline command, 110
Decoupling, 58, 63–64
Deductive approach, 334
Deductive verification methods, 339–340
Delay operator, 384
Delay time, 384–385
Demon, 30
Demonic iteration, 39
Demonic nondeterminism, 441
Demonic scheduling, 18
Demonstrative methods, 46–47
Dense streams, 99
Descriptions, models versus, 147–153
Design process of large systems, 6
Designations, 145–146
Deterministic graph, 233
DFC (Distributed Feature Composition), 356
Differential power analysis (DPA) attacks, 416
Dim Sun restaurant, 27
    enforcement in, 49–50
Dimension analysis, 296
Discrete complexity, 158

Discrete streams
    with continuous time, 98–99
    with discrete time, 97–98
Distributed Feature Composition (DFC), 356
Domain, 175, 312
Domain descriptions, 142–143, 176
Domain engineering, 175–200
    aspects of, 176–177
Domain facets, 187–198
Domain perspectives, 181–199
Dominance ordering, 237
DPA (differential power analysis) attacks, 416
Dynamic dependency, 277
Dynamic invariants, 9–10
Dynamic systems, 162
    modelling architectures for, 161–172
    models of, 163–168
Dynamic type, 274

E

Edge-triggering, 387–388
Embedding-retraction pairs, 314–315
Encoding, 429–430
Enforcement, 18, *see also* Correctness
    in example systems, 47–50
    verifying, 43–50
Enforcing behavior with contracts, 17–50
Entropy, 444–445
    conditional, 445
Environment, 111
Equivalence transformations, 12
Error detection, 295–296
ESC (Extended Static Checking project), 269
Event loop, 39
Eventually operator, 37
Eventually-properties, proved, 45
Everywhere operator, 59
Execution trees, 70, 81
Explorative approach, 334
Explorative verification methods, 340–341
Extended Static Checking project (ESC), 269
Extensional equality, 265

External call, 361
Extrinsic PER semantics, 323–325
Extrinsic semantics, 309–310

F

Fairness conditions, 336
Falling-edge-triggering, 387
Feature composition, semantics of, 360–363
Feature engineering, 354
    application of method for, 370–375
    challenge of, 354–356
    experiment in, 353–376
    method for, 359–369
    proposed process for, 355
Feature interactions, 353
    related to calls, 366
    related to status signals, 366–368
    related to voice, 368–369
    semantics of, 365
Feature-oriented specification, 353–354
    technique, 356–359
Feature set, analysis of, 373–375
Features, 353
    semantics of, 360–363
    syntax of, 363–365
Fields as relations, 263–264
Finalization statement, 25
Finally-property, 44
Finite continuous streams, 96
Finite stuttering, 37–38
Fixed-point calculus for temporal properties, 338–339
Fixpoint theorem, Knaster-Tarski, 28
Flip-flops, 385–386
Frame, 113
Free boxes, 358
Free target features, 359–360
    set of, 371–373
Frontier, 81
Full execution tree, 81
Function declaration, 405
Functional circuits, 401–405
Functional update, 20, 22
Functions, 399–400

G

Game of Nim, *see* Nim, game of
Ghost variables, 11–12
Global invariants, 259
Global time, 97
Goals, achieving, with contracts, 27–33
Granularity, 7, 12
    assumption about, 8
Graph model, 223–229
Guarantee condition, 9–10
Guarded commands, probabilistic, 446–447
Guards, 121, 363

H

Heap storage, 225
Hereditarily effective operations (HEO), 325
Hiatons, 104
Hide operation, 40–41
Hiding, 368
High-level circuit design, 381–411
Higher order differential power analysis (HODPA) attacks, 416
Homomorphisms, 228–229
Human behavior, 196–198
Hybrid circuits, 405–406

I

I/O automata model, 336
Iconic model, 148
Identifiers, 72
Idle-invariant assumptions, 121–122
Idle-stable expressions, 117
IM (Inbound Messaging), 372–373
Imperative circuits, 392–401
Imperative programs, information flow in, 448–454
Imports, 273
Inbound Messaging (IM), 372–373
Index type, 274
Indexed fields, 257, 265
Indicative properties, 143
Infinite stream, 98
Informal phenomena, 144
Information escape, channel capacity and, 445–446
Information flow, 441
    in imperative programs, 448–454
    program refinement and, 450–454
Inheritance, 217–218
Initialization statement, 25
Interaction, concurrency and, 3–4
Interaction abstraction, 102
Interaction refinement, 100
Interactive program, 23
Interference
    concurrency and, 7–8
    reasoning about, 8–10
Interference freedom, 8
Internal calls, 356
Internal divergence, 41
Interpreters, constructing, 34–36
Intrinsic semantics, 309–310, 312–314
Intrinsics, 187–188
Invariance properties, 334
Invariant-based methods, 44–45
Invariants, 65
    dynamic, 9–10
    global, 259
    heap, object models as, 247–265
    representation, 258–259

K

Knaster–Tarski fixpoint theorem, 28
Kripke model, 335

L

Language, semantics and, 111–124
Language design, 297
Language safety, 297–299
Larch Shared Language, 261
Left movers, 67, 70
Limits, 99
Linear time, 97
Local variables, 112, 123–124, 398
Logical approaches to asynchrony, 53–55

Logical relations, 315–320
Logical Relations Theorem, 317–320
Loose execution, 70, 76, 87–88
Loosely-coupled components, 171
Loosely-coupled programs, 64–65

M

Machine domain, 140
Management, 191–194
Merge, 390–391
Mesa, 285
Method constituents, 178–180
Method invocations, 215
Method principles, 180–181
Methodological consequences, 188–189, 190–191
Methods, 70, 71, 178
Model checking, 340
Modelled domains, describing, 152–153
Modelling relationship, 150–151
Modelling time, 97–99
Models
    of computation, 335–337
    correctness and, 1–203
    describing, 152–153
    descriptions versus, 147–153
    of dynamic systems, 163–168
    of lifts, 148–153
    object, *see* Object models
    for pointers and objects, 223–245
    practical, 151–152
    of transition systems, 335–337
    validation of, 166–168
Modular verification, 271
Modularity, 273–274
Modularity requirements, 270, 277
Module languages, 296
Mu–calculus, 339
Multi–level security, 442–443

N

Negative alternatives, 75
Nim, game of, 25–26
    enforcement in, 47–48

Non-timed stream, 97
Nondeterminism, 443
Nondeterministic choice, 120–121
Normal distribution, 432

O

Object, 274
Object Constraint Language (OCL), 261, 262
Object instantiation, 215–216
Object models, 247–248
    combining, 256–257
    examples, 250–253
    as heap invariants, 247–265
    interpreting, 256
    relational logic for, 253–255
    snapshots and, 249–250
    textual annotations for, 258–260
Object orientation, 207–209, 211–212
    claims, 212–213
    limitations, 213–214
Object-oriented analysis and design, 219–220
Object-oriented programming
    software development and, 211–220
Object type, 274
Objects, models for, 223–245, *see also* Object models
OCL (Object Constraint Language), 261, 262
OM (Outbound Messaging), 371–372
Operational data, 357
Operational semantics, 21–23
Optative properties, 143
Outbound Messaging (OM), 371–372
Owicki–Gries method, 8

P

Parallel composition, 395–396
Parallel composition declaration, 403
Parallel processes, 7
Parallelism, 218
Partial equivalence relation (PER), 324
Partial order on boxes, 80–81

Path formulas, 337
PER (partial equivalence relation), 324
Perfect synchrony, 105
Performance, measures of, 406–407
Point distribution, 444
Pointer swing, 226, 235–236
Pointers, 216
    models for, 223–245
Polymorphism, 218
Port process, 361
Post-conditions, 9
Power analysis, 415–436
    countermeasures to, 428–436
    of Twofish implementation, 419–425
Power-analysis attacks, 416–417
Power-attack equipment, 419
Power attacks, statistical, 426–427
Power model, 425–426
Precedences, 359
Preconditions, 9
    weakest, 28–30
Predicate abstraction, 343–347
Predicate-level conditions for correctness, 43–44
Predicate transformer, 28
Predicates, 19
Predictive semantics for real-time refinement, 109–132
Predomain, 312
Presburger arithmetic routine, 341
Primitive real-time commands, 117–118
Primitive types, 274
Private status signals, 366
Probabilistic guarded commands, 446–447
Probability distributions, 443
Problem decomposition, 153–156
Problem domain, 140–144
Problem-object models, 262–263
Procedures, 70, 71, 399
    compatible, semi-commutativity of, 86–87
    as relations, 81–82
Process algebras, 336
Program behavior, logics of, 337–339
Program refinement, information flow and, 450–454
Programming circuits, 379
Programming techniques, 205–327

Programs, 59–61, 137, 273
    abstractions of, 341–347
    concurrent, *see* Concurrent programs
    loosely-coupled, 64–65
    restrictions on, 80–83
Progress, asynchronous, 57–67
Progress properties, 57
Progress-safety-progress (PSP), 60
Proof checker, 295
PSP (progress-safety-progress), 60
Public status signals, 366
Puzzle of wolf, goat and cabbages, *see* Wolf, goat and cabbages puzzle

Q

Qualified sets, 256, 264–265
Quantum model, 459
Quiescent points, 8

R

Railway crossing example, 124–126
Random variables, 444
Range type, 274
Read-only by specification, 283–284
Readers, 270, 278–285
Real-time commands, primitive, 117–118
Real-time refinement, predictive semantics for, 109–132
Real-time specification command, 113–117
Recursion, 22
Recursive contract statements, 21
Recursive contracts, 28
Reduced, ordered, binary decision diagrams (ROBDDs), 341
Reduction scheme, 88–91
Reduction theorem
    for concurrent programs, 69–91
    proof of, 87–91
Refinement, 32–33, 100
    real-time, predictive semantics for, 109–132
Refinement equivalence, 113
Refinement paradox, 442–443, 457–460

Regulations, 194–196
Rejection, 77
Relational logic for object models, 253–255
Relational update, 20, 22
Rely condition, 9–10
Rely/guarantee proposal, 9
Repetitions, 126–129
Replacement step, 89
Representability, 234
Representation, 276
Representation exposure, 259
Representation invariants, 258–259
Requirement, 137, 142, 176
Requirement interface, 141
Response properties, 335
Restaurant, Dim Sun, *see* Dim Sun restaurant
Retargeting, 367
Reuse
    architectures for, 168–172
    code, 217–218
Reynold's rule, 7
Right movers, 67, 70
ROBDDs (reduced, ordered, binary decision diagrams), 341
Run-time type errors, 295

S

Safe language, term, 297–299
Scenario, 22–23
SCF (Selective Call Forwarding), 370, 371
Scheduler, 76
Scope, 274
Secure filestore example, 454–457
Security, 299, 413–414, 441
    multi-level, 442–443
Selection, 121
Selective Call Forwarding (SCF), 370, 371
Semantic data models, *see* Object models
Semantics
    extrinsic, 309–310
    extrinsic PER, 323–325
    of feature interactions, 365

of features and feature composition, 360–363
    intrinsic, 309–310, 312–314
    language and, 111–124
    operational, 21–23
    predictive, for real-time refinement, 109–132
    Seuss, 76–77
    untyped, 314–315
Semaphore, 72
Semi-commutativity of compatible procedures, 86–87
Separability, 99
Sequential composition, 21, 22, 118–120, 395
Sequential composition declaration, 403
Sequentiality, 218
Set of records, 252–253
Setup phase, 356
Seuss programming notation, 71–77
Seuss programs, model of, 78–79
Seuss semantics, 76–77
Seuss syntax, 71–76
Shared-variable concurrent programs, 8
Side channels, 416
Simple power analysis (SPA) attacks, 416
Single-state predicate, 113
Sink state, 366
Snapshots, 249
    object models and, 249–250
Software architectures, 217
    component concept and, 216–217
Software design, 137, 176
Software development
    object-oriented programming and, 211–220
    scope of, 156–158
SPA (simple power analysis) attacks, 416
Specification, 40, 137, 142
Specification command, real-time, 113–117
Specification firewall, 139–140
Specification interface, 140–141
Spoofing, 368
Stability, 65
Stable variables, 114
Stake-holder perspectives, 183–186
Stake-holders, 182–183
State formulas, 337

State predicate, 19
State relation, 19
State space, 19
State transformer, 19
State type, 334
Static dependency, 277
Static type, 274
Statistical power attacks, 426–427
Status signals, 362
    feature interactions related to, 366–368
Stepwise refinement of contracts, 33
Stream domain, 96
Streams, 96–99
    components as functions on, 99–100
    dense, 99
    discrete, see Discrete streams
    mathematical foundation of, 96–97
Stuttering, finite, 37–38
Subclass, 217–218
Subgraphs, 238
Subscriptions component, 360
Support technologies, 189–190
Sweepers, 65–66
Symbol manipulation, 138–140
Synchronous circuits, 410
Syntax, 310–311
    of features, 363–365
System description, 141
    aspects of, 137–158
    purposeful, 142–143
Systems
    dynamic, see Dynamic systems
    large
        design process of, 6
        structuring, 285
    real time and, 93–94

T

Teardown phase, 356
Temporal logic, alternating-time, 50
Temporal Logic of Actions (TLA), 336
Temporal properties, 18
    fixed-point calculus for, 338–339
Terminating specification command, 113
Testers, 34–36

Textual annotations for object models, 258–260
Tight execution, 70, 76
Time
    abstractions from, 95–105
    delay, 384–385
    modelling, 97–99
Time abstraction, 100–104
Time domain, 96
Time models in the literature, 104
Time-unbiased behavior, 100
Timed automata, 336
Timed function, 100
Timed stream, 97
Timed traces, 112
Timing-constraint analysis, 129–131
Timing issues, 95
TLA (Temporal Logic of Actions), 336
Trace model, 229–236
Train crossing example, 124–126
Transition relation, 22
Transition systems, models of, 335–337
Transposition step, 89
Twofish implementation, power analysis of, 419–425
Twofish whitening process, 419–421
Type errors, run–time, 295
Type systems, 293–301
    applications of, 295–300
    in computer science, 293–295
    definition, 293
    history of, 300–301
Type tags, 294
Type theory, 291
Typechecking algorithms, 295
Typed language, 309
Types, meaning of, 309–326
Typing, 311
Typing judgement, 311
Typing rules, 310–311

U

UML (Unified Modeling Language), 248
UML collaboration diagram, 163
Unhide operation, 40–41

Unified Modeling Language, *see* UML *entries*
Uniform distribution, 443
Units, 273
UNITY model, 335
Until operator, 36
Until-properties, proved, 45
Untyped semantics, 314–315
Update function, 19

V

Validation of models, 166–168
Validity as abstract variable, 272–273
Value function, 19
Verification, automated, 333–348
Verification methodology, 347–348
Verification techniques, 339–341
Virtual network, 357
Visible declaration, 274

Voice, feature interactions related to, 368–369

W

Weak until, 36
Weakest preconditions, 28–30
Weakly causal function, 100
While-loop, 21
Winning strategy, 30
Winning strategy theorem, 30–31
Wolf, goat and cabbages puzzle, 26
  enforcement in, 48–49
Writers, 278

Z

Z notation, 261, 262
Zeno's paradox, 98